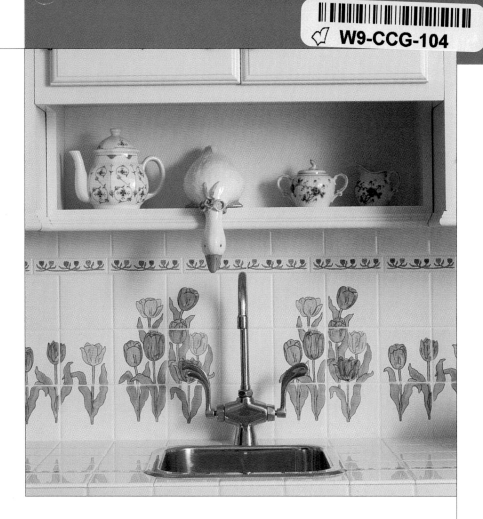

ORTHO'S HOME REPAIR PROBLEM SOLVER

Created and Designed by the Editorial Staff of Ortho Books

Writers
Robert J. Beckstrom
Jeff Beneke
Matt Phair
Naomi Wise

Project Editor
Sally W. Smith

Illustration Manager
Cyndie C. H. Wooley

Designers
Barbara Ziller and John Williams, Barbara Ziller Design

ORTHO BOOKS

Publisher
Robert B. Loperena

Editorial Director
Christine Jordan

Manufacturing Manager
Ernie Tasaki

Managing Editor
Sally W. Smith

Editor
Robert J. Beckstrom

Prepress Supervisor
Linda M. Bouchard

Editorial Assistants
Joni Christiansen
Sally J. French

Editorial Coordinator
Cass Dempsey

Copyeditor
Elizabeth von Radics

Proofreader
David Sweet

Indexer
Frances Bowles

Separations by
Color Tech Corp.

Lithographed in the USA by
Banta Company

Special Thanks to
Maja Beckstrom
Deborah Cowder
David Van Ness

Photographers
Laurie A. Black, page 3d
Saxon Holt, page 109
Kit Morris, page 3e
Ortho Library, page 5
Brent Lindstrom, front cover
Stephen Marley, page 3g
Geoffrey Nilsen, pages 11 and 79
Joyce OudkerkPool, page 3a
Kenneth Rice, pages 1, 3b, 3f, 151,
    197, and 239
Sepp Seitz/Woodfin Camp, page 3c

Art Director, Cover
Barbara Ziller

Technical Consultants
Dan Fuller
Michael Hamman
Redwood Kardon

Illustrators
Edith Allgood
William Barrett, William Barrett
    Design
Jonathan Clark, Dart
Wayne S. Clark
Deborah Cowder, Indigo Design
    & Imaging
Tim Graveson, Pandion
    Productions
Dillon Riley
Hal Lewis and Andrew Richards,
    Apple-day
Elizabeth Morales and Jim Roberts
Jenny Page and George Vrana,
    Illustrious, Inc.
Cyndie C.H. Wooley

Front Cover
A few tools, clear information, and some quick planning are all you need to solve most home repair problems.

Title Page
No matter how you try to duck them, some problems keep hanging around. In some cases they involve a major project, but most repairs require only a few tools, some replacement parts or simple materials, and a little time. This book, which features solutions to more than 1,000 home repair problems, will get you started.

Address all inquiries to:
Ortho Books
Box 5006
San Ramon, CA 94583-0906

Copyright © 1995
Monsanto Company
All rights reserved under international and Pan-American copyright conventions.

1 2 3 4 5 6 7 8 9
95 96 97 98 99 2000

ISBN 0-89721-260-6
Library of Congress Catalog Card
Number 94-69604

THE SOLARIS GROUP
2527 Camino Ramon
San Ramon, CA 94583-0906

▶ Look up the problem and read how to fix it.

The purpose of this book is to help you solve problems and get on with your life, not do major home improvements. In its seven chapters are solutions to more than 1,000 problems. Each chapter covers an easy-to-recognize area or system of the home. Each unit covers one problem (… has a crack, … won't ring, … leaks). Similar problems are grouped together. If you are not sure in which chapter and category to find your problem, consult the Index (page 314).

After you find the problem and read the solution, you may still want more information. There are four more places to look.

• Descriptions of similar problems are usually within a page or two of the problem you've looked up.

• The Appendix, beginning on page 294, has tables, lists, and other general information that is not covered under specific problems.

• Home Repair Terms, beginning on page 306, provides definitions of terms that may give you new clues about solving your problem.

• The Index, beginning on page 314, makes it easy to look up additional words or terms related to your problem.

▶ Keys to solving any home repair problem.

• Trust your common sense. This book is a useful guide, but you may figure out a better way to do something once you understand the basic principles. There is more than one way to solve most problems.

• Think of a project as a series of small steps. This makes a problem seem less overwhelming, so it's easier to get started.

• Allow plenty of time. Most repairs end up taking longer than you think they will.

• Remember how things are put together as you take them apart. Draw diagrams, make lists, or lay out disassembled parts in an orderly sequence.

• Assume that you will need to make at least one trip to the store. Therefore, don't start a repair late at night or when it will be inconvenient to make the trip.

• Find the right store. A full-range hardware store or home center will supply most needs, but if you can't find what you need there, don't give up. Many people are not aware of specialty outlets or suppliers who deal with the trades. They include appliance service centers, plumbing-supply houses, plumbing contractor showrooms, electrical-supply houses, architectural salvage yards, tile shops, paint and wallpaper dealers, stores for woodworkers and other hobbyists, and specialty lumber yards, such as a hardwood dealer.

• Take the old part to the store with you, or make a diagram of what you think you need, with accurate dimensions.

• Dress appropriately. Put on work clothes before you start, not when it's too late. Wear soft-soled shoes when working on the roof. Have safety goggles, gloves, and a dust mask handy at all times, and use them.

• Get proper permits when required. Many repairs do not require a permit, but any project that involves moving pipes or wires, installing new fixtures, altering walls, building certain outdoor structures, replacing a roof, or exceeding a certain dollar amount ($200 is typical for most communities) may require a permit. Consult the local building-inspection department before proceeding.

• Use the right tool. Some tasks that seem complicated are actually quite simple if you use the correct tool. A basic tool kit (see page 294) is sufficient for most repairs, but if you don't have the right tool, buy, rent, or borrow it. Check the hardware store for variations on common tools. All screwdrivers—or paintbrushes or putty knives or whatever—are not the same; you may think the one you have is fine, but a little investigation may reveal that one of a different size or shape will make the job much easier. See pages 294 and 295 for some ideas on building your own basic (or advanced) tool kit.

• Store your tools where you can find them. Many repairs never get done because it's too much hassle looking for the tools.

• Make time for safety. It takes very little time to secure a ladder, keep the work area clean, turn off a circuit breaker, open a window for ventilation, remove a nail, put on safety glasses, or unplug a power tool while changing blades. Don't think just about getting the job done; think about getting it done safely.

Tip   *If your home is under any kind of warranty, do not undertake any repairs without calling a professional first; your repairs may void the warranty.*

Before taking any other steps to make your home comfortable, beautiful, and problem-free, learn what to do in an emergency. In addition to the information and prevention tips presented in this chapter, you will find tips throughout the book for working safely as you make repairs around the home.

► House is on fire.

Get everyone out fast. Crawl if there is smoke. Call from a neighbor's house (or grab the cordless phone on your way out). Don't go back in; let firefighters handle rescues. Fire spreads through a home astonishingly fast. The biggest danger is smoke asphyxiation.

Evacuating the house

Phoning fire department

► Chimney has fire.

A chimney fire makes a loud, roaring sound and is incredibly hot (2,000° F or more). It is probably visible from the street. Evacuate the house. After calling fire department from neighbor's house, hose down the roof.

Some experts recommend, if you have time, closing the damper of a woodstove or smothering the fireplace fire with a fire extinguisher or huge amounts of coarse salt; never douse it with water.

Don't use the fireplace or woodstove again until you have the chimney inspected and cleaned.

► Roof is on fire.

Evacuate everyone and call the fire department.

► Smoke is emerging from around chimney area.

Extinguish the fireplace fire or close the woodstove damper. Call the fire department. The smoke may be from the fireplace, escaping through cracks in the brick chimney, or it may be from smoldering framing that could erupt into flames. Evacuate if you see flames. Do not reuse the fireplace until the chimney is inspected and repaired.

► Clothes are on fire.

Drop and roll. Do not run. If possible, smother fire with a blanket.

Dropping and rolling

Using a blanket

► House has small fire.

Get everyone out of the house. Call fire department. If you can do it safely, return and use a Class-ABC fire extinguisher, aiming toward the base of the fire. Stay between the fire and a safe exit. If you don't extinguish the fire immediately, get out.

Using a fire extinguisher

► Oven has fire.

Turn off heat. Leave it alone. Don't open the oven door until oven has cooled down. Keep watch.

Tip *With your entire family, plan escape routes ahead of time, especially from bedrooms. Establish a meeting place, usually the front of the home, and designate a person to notify neighbors and call for help.*

Tip *Chief causes of home fires: (1) cooktop flare-ups, (2) falling asleep while smoking, (3) fireplace, woodstove, or kerosene heater, (4) playing with matches, and (5) faulty electrical system or equipment.*

▶ Cooktop has grease fire.

Turn off heat. Smother fire quickly with a large lid, use Class-B fire extinguisher, or throw baking soda or salt on the fire (*never* water, flour, or sugar). Call for help if you don't extinguish the fire immediately.

Smothering a range-top fire

Oven mitt

▶ Electrical appliance or receptacle is smoking, sparking, or on fire.

If it's only sparking or smoking, unplug the appliance or turn off the circuit breaker. Have it repaired before using it again.

　　If the appliance is on fire, evacuate the house, call fire department, and use Class-C fire extinguisher. *Never* use water—it could conduct electricity to you.

Extinguishing an appliance fire

▶ Fire has damaged house.

Secure the house (board up windows, repair the roof). Remove debris. Store damaged but salvageable items in a safe place. Protect the plumbing system against freezing. Inspect the electrical system before using it. Clean up. Air out carpets and furnishings damaged by water. Take smoke-tainted clothes and fabrics to a dry cleaner with an ozone chamber. Place smoke-tainted books and valuable papers in a freezer until a time when you can have them professionally cared for. Open up walls and other covered areas where water may have caused hidden damage. It's necessary to air them out to prevent rotting. Often, more damage is done by water inside walls than from the fire itself, so make every effort to dry out the house thoroughly, including pumping the basement or crawl space.

Cleaning up after a fire

Clean walls

Plywood

Pump

Wallboard removed

Tip　*When phoning 9-1-1 or other emergency numbers, don't hang up until told to do so. You may be asked for additional critical information.*

Tip　*Do not empty ashtrays into wastebaskets. Use a metal trash can, a container of water, or other nonflammable receptacle for this purpose.*

SAFETY FIRST

Fire safety equipment.

■ *Smoke detectors: At least one for each floor. Critical areas are kitchen, rooms with fireplaces, hallway near sleeping rooms, and top of basement stairs. Combination of "hard-wired" and battery-operated types is recommended.*

■ *Extinguishers: Have several (kitchen, basement, shop, smoking areas, each floor). Locate near the room's <u>exit</u>, so you can grab it on your way back <u>into</u> the room after evacuating the house. For all-around use, keep a Class-ABC on hand. For specific uses:*

Class-A: paper, wood, cloth, rubber, dry materials

Class-B: oil, grease, gasoline, flammable liquids

Class-C: electrical

■ *Emergency lights: Place flashlights with fresh batteries by beds, in kitchen, in basement, and in other areas of house. You may also want to get lights that stay plugged into electrical receptacles and which go on only in a power failure.*

■ *Escape ladder (chain ladder that hangs from a windowsill): Locate in any upstairs bedroom that does not have two easy escape routes.*

■ *Sprinklers: Consider them if you are planning a remodeling project, especially if your household includes small children or elderly persons.*

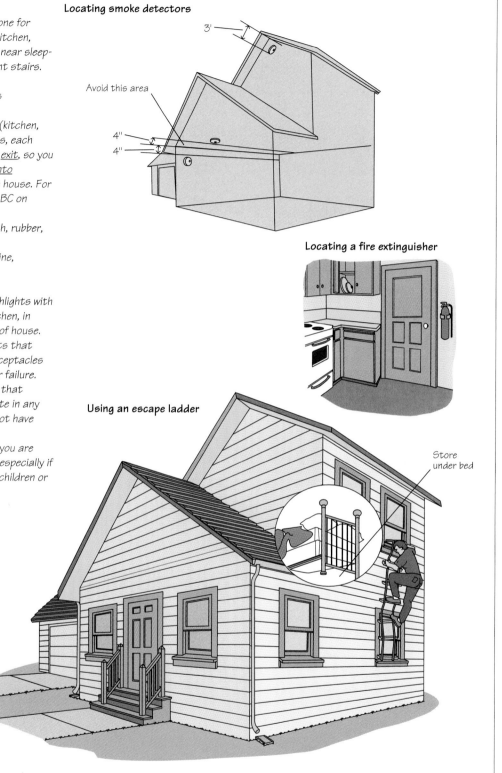

Locating smoke detectors

3'

Avoid this area

4"
4"

Locating a fire extinguisher

Using an escape ladder

Store under bed

Tip *Most fires start at night during sleeping hours. Rooms where most fires start: (1) kitchen, (2) bedrooms, and (3) heater closet or room. Rooms where most deaths occur by fire: (1) living/family room and (2) bedroom. At greatest risk are children under 10 and adults over 65.*

▶ *House has gas odor.*

Very dangerous. Evacuate house immediately, leaving doors open as you go. Call gas company or 9-1-1 from neighbor's house.

If odor is only slight, turn off gas at meter. Open windows and doors. Do not light match, use phone, switch on lights, or do anything that causes sparks or friction. Get out. Call gas company or 9-1-1 from neighbor's house.

If gas is bottled propane (LP), it is heavy and will settle to floor or basement area; things will seem normal at nose level. Do not re-enter house—and especially don't relight pilots—until you are sure the gas has dissipated. Bottled gas ignites more readily than natural gas and is much more explosive.

Turning off natural gas

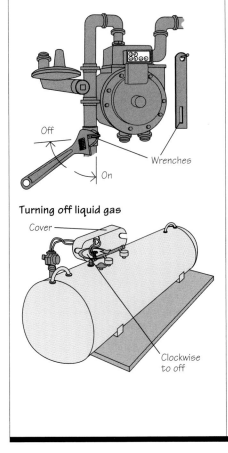

Off

Wrenches

On

Turning off liquid gas

Cover

Clockwise to off

▶ *You smell fumes.*

It's probably improper venting or backdrafting of a gas appliance (in backdrafting, flue gases are forced back down the flue because of unbalanced air pressure, a common occurrence with tightly insulated homes). Although not an immediate problem unless it is highly concentrated in a confined area, this condition is still a serious safety hazard. (The most dangerous component, carbon monoxide, is odorless.) For immediate relief, ventilate the house. Don't operate exhaust fans (such as a kitchen hood or bathroom fan) without opening a window or door first; it will only exacerbate the problem.

For a long-range solution, make sure every gas appliance has a flue to the outdoors and an adequate supply of fresh combustion air. Test by holding a smoking match or incense next to the flue intake while the appliance burner is on; the smoke should be sucked up the flue. If it isn't, have a combustion

Testing for backdrafting

Flue

Vacuum breaker

air duct installed to provide a continuous supply of fresh air, even when the house has negative air pressure. Also consider purchasing a carbon monoxide detector.

▶ *House has a sewerlike odor.*

Pinpoint the source—usually a bathroom fixture, laundry sink, or drain. Most likely the water has drained out of the trap of that fixture. Pour water into it and monitor it for several weeks to see if the smell resumes. If so, have a plumber inspect it. If you can't pinpoint the source, inspect under the house for a broken or leaking drainpipe. It could even be underground, so check along the ground above the house sewer line. If you don't know where the line runs, locate the point under the house where the main drain goes under or through the foundation and project a line from that point to the street. A cleanout plug outside the foundation may provide a clue. Dig to expose the suspected source, or call a plumber.

▶ *You smell ammonia or refrigerant.*

This sharp, strong, acrid smell is caused by gases leaking from an air-conditioning compressor, refrigerator, or freezer. It is dangerous. Evacuate the house and then call the fire department from a neighbor's house.

Tip *If you have bottled gas (LP), have the control valve inspected by a professional. Many defective valves made by various manufacturers have been recalled since 1977. If your local supplier, heating contractor, or plumbing contractor is not aware of particular recalls, contact the Consumer Products Safety Commission (look in the phone book under "U.S. Government" listings).*

▶ Electricity goes off in whole house.

Provide emergency lighting (candles, flashlights, backup lights). You need to check the main disconnect to see if it is tripped. As you approach it, examine the immediate area for loose or dangling power lines. If you see some, call the utility company. If there are no dangling wires, check the disconnect, being careful not to stand on damp ground; wear gloves. If the breaker is tripped, call an electrician. If it is a cartridge fuse or other device besides a breaker, you will need to have an electrician test it for you.

If the breaker is not tripped, see if the power for the rest of the neighborhood is also out. If so, turn on a portable radio for information. If the phone works, report the outage to the utility company. Turn off any large appliances that were on,

so there won't be a heavy demand when electricity is restored. Turn off TVs, computers, and other electronic equipment that could be damaged by a power surge. Don't open the refrigerator or freezer.

In cold weather, if power will be off for more than two or three days, drain the water system and/or put antifreeze in P-traps, appliances connected to the plumbing system (such as washing machines), and plumbing fixtures that have standing water. Steps for draining the water system: (1) turn off main valve, (2) turn off inlet valve (cold water) to water heater, (3) open faucets at the highest point of system, (4) open faucet or disconnect pipe at lowest point, and (5) drain water heater by attaching a hose to the drain valve, running it outdoors, and turning on the valve.

▶ Electricity goes off in part of house.

Blown circuit. Turn off appliances and light switches in those rooms. Reset circuit breaker (or replace fuse). If electricity goes back on, test all the fixtures and receptacles one by one until you discover the one that caused the short. (Turn off each fixture before turning on the next one.) Remove the defective appliance. If none is defective, the problem was probably too many turned on at once. Reduce the load. Eventually, you may have to add a new circuit. See page 200.

▶ Finding solutions to other emergencies.

Window glass is broken.
    See page 96.
Pipe is burst or leaking.
    See page 152.
Pipe is frozen.
    See page 154.
Faucet won't shut off.
    See page 170.
No hot water.
    See pages 165 to 168.
Hot water is scalding.
    See page 163.
Toilet is clogged.
    See page 189.
Roof leaks.
    See page 110.
Drain is clogged.
    See page 157.
Heat is off.
    See page 240.
Smoke detector goes off frequently.
    See page 231.
Floors and carpets are soaked.
    See page 35.
Carpet or upholstery is stained.
    See page 32.

Locating main disconnect

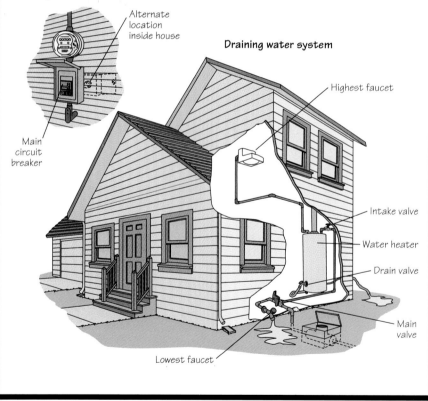

Alternate location inside house

Main circuit breaker

Draining water system

Highest faucet

Intake valve

Water heater

Drain valve

Main valve

Lowest faucet

Tip The National Fire Protection Association estimates that as many as 33 percent of all residential smoke detectors have missing or dead batteries and are therefore inoperable. Push the test button on your smoke detector to make sure the battery is working.

From basement to attic, the inside of a home contains dozens of surfaces and built-in features that are subject to daily wear or constant strain. Even minor problems become nuisances very quickly; other problems, especially those with foundations, basements, and attics, can be more serious. This chapter presents solutions to more than 245 indoor and minor structural problems.

▶ Ceiling has hairline crack.

If an otherwise flawless ceiling has one or two hairline cracks, it is worthwhile to repair them. The trick is to blend the repair into the ceiling.

If the crack is fine enough and is not likely to widen, you may be able to hide it with latex paint. Be sure the color matches the ceiling, allowing for fading or discoloration. Scrub the area along the crack with TSP or an all-purpose cleaning agent, to help the paint adhere. After the area dries, paint the crack, using a small roller. Apply a heavy coat and feather the paint away from the crack to avoid a noticeable ridge. Work enough paint into the crack so that it will stretch if the crack opens up again.

If painting doesn't solve the problem, patch the crack with flexible caulk. Choose a color that matches the ceiling or a caulk specified as "paintable." Brush or vacuum away all loose debris from the crack. Cut off the tip of the caulking tube close to the end so the nozzle emits a very fine bead of caulk; run it along the crack. Work the caulk into the crack with an old spoon (not your finger); dampen the spoon in soapy water if it sticks. Clean away excess caulk with a moist rag. Paint according to manufacturer's instructions.

▶ Plaster ceiling has narrow crack.

Fill with a nonshrinking spackling compound, and sand flush with the surrounding area. Various spackling and patching compounds, some lightweight, are especially designed for this purpose. Avoid those that shrink; they will require two layers.

Start by widening the crack with a lever-type can opener, linoleum knife, or improvised scraping tool, such as the tang end of a machinist's file or a tack puller. Widen the crack to ⅛ inch or so. Brush or vacuum out the crack and apply the filler according to manufacturer's instructions. If two layers of compound are required, scratch the first layer after applying it so it provides better adhesion for the second layer. Smooth the compound with a 3-inch taping knife (broad knife), feathering the edges. After the filler dries, sand it flush with the surrounding ceiling. If the ceiling is textured, match it by applying spackling compound with a putty knife or wet sponge (see page 19). After it dries, prime and paint the area.

Widening crack

/8" wide
— Linoleum knife

Feathering edges

Sanding

▶ Plaster ceiling has wide crack.

For cracks that seem to follow a stress joint in the house structure, apply fiberglass-mesh tape to prevent the crack from reopening. Prepare the crack, as described for a narrow crack, widening it to ¼ inch and undercutting (angling) the sides. Fill the crack with compound and let it harden overnight. Cover the crack with the self-sticking mesh tape along its entire length, making sure the tape bridges the crack. Cover the tape with a layer of compound and smooth it with a 6-inch taping knife. Let it dry, sand it, and repeat with a 10-inch knife. Then sand, texture, prime, and paint as described for a narrow crack. *Note:* Some products should not be sanded; follow manufacturer's instructions.

Embedding tape

Undercut edges
Fresh compound
6" knife
Self-sticking mesh tape
Hardened compound

Feathering compound

Feathered edge
9"–10"
Sanded previous coat
10" knife

Tip *The tape and compound applied to a crack will form a ridge over the crack. To minimize this problem, feather the compound 12 inches or more from the crack. You can eliminate the problem altogether if you scrape away enough plaster on both sides of the crack to embed the tape below the surface of the surrounding plaster, then cover it with patching compound.*

Tip *Always wear safety goggles when doing ceiling work. In addition, wear a dust mask when sanding or scraping.*

▶ *Ceiling has small hole.*

To patch a small hole (up to 3 inches), cut three or four strips of fiberglass-mesh tape and stretch them over the hole in crisscross fashion, or apply a large patch of reinforcing mesh. Apply patching compound over the mesh tape with a 6-inch taping knife. Holding the fabric taut, work the compound into the mesh so it will grip when it hardens. Spread the compound 3 or 4 inches beyond the hole, feathering it at the perimeter. After this coat dries, sand it lightly and apply a second coat, feathering it about 12 to 18 inches beyond the first layer. Let it dry, sand it smooth, texture the area as needed, prime it, and paint it.

Applying tape

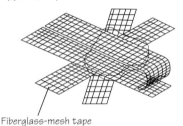

Fiberglass-mesh tape

Applying compound

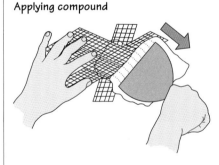

▶ *Ceiling has large hole.*

For large holes (wider than 3 inches), add backing behind the hole before applying fiberglass-mesh tape. Use a wad of newspaper or scrap of plywood or wallboard.

Secure it with paneling adhesive or with screws driven up through the ceiling. Then apply mesh tape over the hole and finish patching, as described at left.

Adding backing

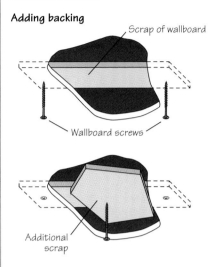

Scrap of wallboard

Wallboard screws

Additional scrap

Applying tape

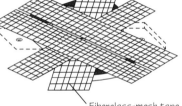

Fiberglass-mesh tape

▶ *Cracks open up between ceiling and walls.*

In newer homes that have roof trusses, cracks can occur between the ceiling and interior walls because the lumber in the trusses shrinks and causes them to rise. Thin cracks can be sealed with flexible caulk. Conceal larger cracks by installing crown molding around the room. Nail it to the ceiling, not the walls, so a new gap will not open up should the trusses (and ceiling) rise more (see page 29). Poor attic ventilation and unsealed openings between the home and

attic, although not totally responsible for this problem, contribute to it and should be taken care of. If severe gaps develop (1 inch or more), seek advice from an experienced professional.

▶ *Plaster is sagging.*

Gently probe the area where the plaster is coming loose from the lath. If it is loose, crumbly, or weak, the ceiling is a safety hazard and should be recovered with new wallboard. If the plaster remains firm and doesn't break up, you can secure it back to the lath with 1½-inch wallboard screws and plaster washers. With a power screwdriver, drive several screws, with washer attached, into the weakened area. Try to hit joists wherever possible; otherwise, wood lath. Space screws 6 to 8 inches apart. Drive them deep enough to embed the washer into the plaster slightly. Cover the washers with spackling compound. Sand, prime, and paint the patches when dry.

Reattaching plaster

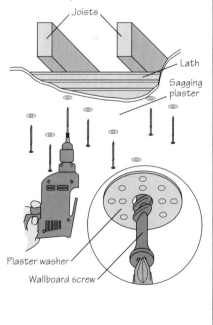

Joists

Lath

Sagging plaster

Plaster washer

Wallboard screw

Tip *Don't dump leftover plaster or patching compound into the sink or sewer—it will clog drains.*

▶ *Plaster is missing from a small area.*

Replace missing plaster with two to three coats of new plaster. First secure the old plaster around the hole with wallboard screws and washers, as described on page 13. (If the lath is also missing, screw new wood or metal lath to the studs.) Undercut the edges of the plaster around the hole, as described on page 12. Then mix enough patching compound for the first coat, according to manufacturer's instructions. Brush a coat of latex bonding agent onto the exposed edges of the old plaster and wet the lath. Trowel a layer of plaster onto the lath thick enough to fill the hole almost flush with the surrounding surface. Score hatch marks on the wet plaster with a nail. After the plaster hardens, wet it and trowel on the second layer slightly below the original plaster surface. After it hardens, add a final coat of compound and then sand, prime, and paint the area.

Brushing on bonding agent

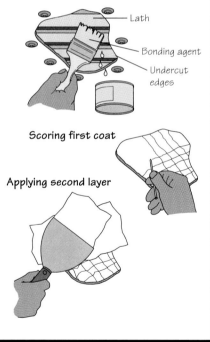

Lath

Bonding agent

Undercut edges

Scoring first coat

Applying second layer

▶ *Ceiling has extensive cracks and unevenness.*

A badly damaged plaster ceiling is not worth trying to patch. Cover it with ½-inch wallboard. First look for areas of sagging plaster. Remove the plaster or, if it's stable, secure it with wallboard screws and washers, as described on page 13. Where plaster is missing, patch the hole with ⅜- or ½-inch wallboard (no need to tape joints). Remove all molding and light fixtures from the ceiling. Add box extenders to electrical boxes. Install the wallboard with the long sides at right angles to the joists; use 12-foot sheets, if possible. If you are doing the job yourself or with only one or two helpers, rent a wallboard jack for the day. It will lift the sheets and hold them in place while you secure them with 2¼-inch wallboard screws driven into the joists, 8 to 10 inches apart.

Install, tape, texture, and paint the new wallboard as you would any new ceiling. If the ceiling is uneven, screw 1x4 furring strips (strapping) across it, at right angles to the joists and 16 inches on center, with a vapor barrier between the ceiling and the strapping. Attach the strapping with two 2½-inch screws at each joist. Bring the strapping into level alignment by inserting shims between the vapor barrier and furring strips where necessary. Then attach new ½-inch sheets of wallboard to the strapping.

Note: Check the size of joists and measure the spans before covering a ceiling with new wallboard. Consult a professional to be sure they will support the extra load (½-inch wallboard weighs 1.9 pounds per square foot, 60 pounds per 4x8 sheet).

Covering a damaged ceiling

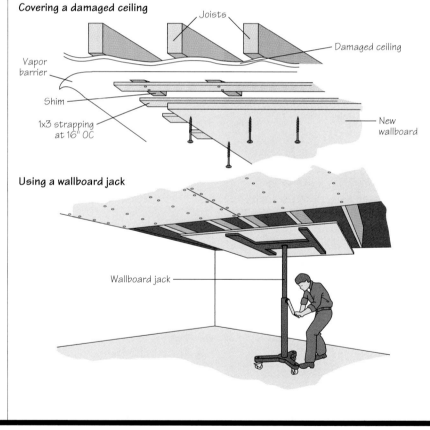

Joists

Damaged ceiling

Vapor barrier

Shim

1x3 strapping at 16" OC

New wallboard

Using a wallboard jack

Wallboard jack

Tip *Traditional plaster consisted of two coats: a "scratch coat" or "brown coat" of thick plaster applied to the lath; and a layer of white plaster, made from gauging plaster and lime, for a thin, hard, finish coat.*

Tip *To ensure a strong bond between old and new plaster, brush some latex bonding agent onto the old surface before applying new plaster.*

▶ *Ceiling wallboard sags.*

Major job. The causes might be: improper nailing; moisture in the attic; ceiling joists spaced too far apart for the thickness of wallboard used (joists must be no more than 16 inches apart, on center, to support ½-inch wallboard); the wrong type of wallboard (moisture-resistant wallboard is not intended for ceilings); or wallboard with the long sides installed in line with the joists rather than across them.

If the problem is only improper nailing, the wallboard will move upward when you push on it. You can reattach it to the joists with 1½-inch wallboard screws, spaced 6 inches apart along panel edges, 12 inches elsewhere. Use T-braces to force the sagging panels up and support them while you attach the screws. If sagging has deformed the wallboard so much that it won't flatten easily, force the panels up and hold them in place with long 1x4s screwed to the ceiling joists. After a few weeks, screw the wallboard to the joists, as explained above, and remove the 1x4s. Spackle and sand the holes and nail depressions, then touch up with primer and matching paint.

If the sagging results from any other cause, you will need to remove the existing wallboard and install the proper type (½ inch for joists 16 inches on center; ⅝ inch for wider joist spacings). First check for moisture problems and correct them (see right). If removing the old wallboard is too difficult (because of blown-in attic insulation, for instance), leave it in place and follow the procedures described on opposite page.

▶ *Ceiling has moisture.*

If the wallboard is soggy or an attic inspection reveals water stains above the ceiling, check for a leaky roof (or leaky water pipe in the attic) and fix it. If there's no leak, the moisture probably comes from condensation in the attic formed from water vapor that originates inside the house and penetrates the ceiling, a situation most prevalent in climates with freezing winters. This not only dampens the ceiling, which is a minor problem, but can lead to serious structural rot in the attic, which is a major problem. The best prevention is adequate ventilation in the attic and a vapor barrier (4 mil plastic sheeting) installed between the ceiling and ceiling joists. First try to improve attic ventilation, because installing a vapor barrier requires that you remove, or at least re-cover, the ceiling (see page 72).

Preventing moisture above ceiling

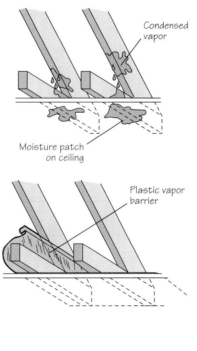

Condensed vapor

Moisture patch on ceiling

Plastic vapor barrier

▶ *Ceiling framing sags.*

Major job. The problem could be undersized ceiling joists, too much weight in the attic, or moisture problems in the attic. The solution is structural reinforcement. Consult a competent contractor, architect, or structural engineer.

▶ *Ceiling has water stains.*

Water stains seem innocuous, but are devilish to deal with. You can't just paint over them, because the stain will bleed through most paint.

First make sure the source of the stain (leaky pipe, roof leak, upstairs spill) has been fixed. Then cover the stain with an impermeable sealer such as white-pigmented shellac with a high (65 percent) titanium dioxide content. Apply the sealer in two or three light coats rather than one heavy coat. Let dry, then prime and paint.

If acoustic ceiling tiles are stained, spray a solution of 1 cup household bleach in 1 gallon water onto the stains, experimenting on a small area first. Wear protective clothing and eye protection.

▶ *"Popcorn" ceiling needs painting.*

If an acoustic texture (sometimes called a "popcorn" or "cottage cheese") ceiling was installed after 1978, there is no danger of releasing asbestos fibers, and it can safely be painted with a roller. However, test the ceiling first by lightly rolling a dry roller over it to make sure the acoustic texture won't come loose during painting. Use a roller with ½-inch or longer nap. If the texture material comes loose, or the ceiling predates 1978, use a paint sprayer to avoid disturbing the texture material.

Tip *For speedy touch-up work, you can use quick-drying primers that are ready to paint in as little as half an hour.*

Tip *Although acoustic texture applied before 1978 most likely contains asbestos fibers, patching materials currently on the market do not. If you don't disturb the existing material during the patching process, there should be no danger of releasing harmful asbestos fibers.*

▶ "Popcorn" ceiling needs patching.

Patch small areas of acoustic texture with appropriate patching materials that are widely available. Some are applied with a putty knife or trowel, some with a paint roller, and some with a disposable sprayer included with the kit. The patching materials are available in two shades of white, to match both new and older, discolored ceilings.

Patching a popcorn ceiling

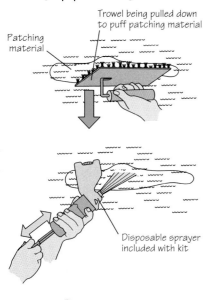

Patching material

Trowel being pulled down to puff patching material

Disposable sprayer included with kit

▶ "Popcorn" ceiling needs removing.

If the acoustic texture on the ceiling was applied before 1978, it most likely contains asbestos fibers. Consult an asbestos abatement company before deciding to remove the material. It is usually easier to leave the ceiling alone, or to cover it with wallboard, than to go through the expense and inconvenience of having the texture professionally removed.

Note: This applies only to acoustic texture, not normal wallboard texture. Acoustic texture is puffy and lumpy, like cottage cheese or popcorn.

▶ Ceiling tiles are damaged or missing.

With a utility knife score all four joints around the damaged tile and carefully pry it out of the ceiling. Remove any loose pieces, staples, glue, or other debris from the cavity. With the knife and a straightedge, cut off the tongue from one side of the replacement tile. Apply adhesive, according to manufacturer's instructions, and press the tile into place. Secure it with a long brace until the adhesive dries.

Replacing a ceiling tile

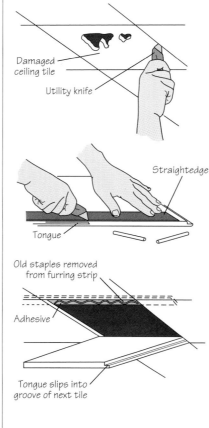

Damaged ceiling tile

Utility knife

Straightedge

Tongue

Old staples removed from furring strip

Adhesive

Tongue slips into groove of next tile

▶ Exposed beams have cracks.

It is normal for beams and timbers to crack, or check, as they age, especially those cut from the center portion of the log (so the end grain resembles a target with a bull's-eye). In severe cases the beam will also twist and warp. If it is severely deformed, it must be replaced; consult a professional. Otherwise, the cracks can be ignored. However, if their appearance is not pleasing, you can have the beams sandblasted. This accentuates the grain pattern and makes cracks seem more "at home" in the rustic beam. Another approach is to stain the beams a dark color to camouflage the cracks. Or, if only one or two cracks are objectionable, fill them with wood putty mixed with sawdust or stain pigment to match the beam color (experiment with wood scraps first).

▶ Water leaks along beams from outside.

If the ceiling beams slope upward toward the exterior wall, as is the case in homes with clerestory windows, rainwater may collect on the outdoor section of the beams and seep back toward the windows and possibly into the room. Cut a shallow groove along the bottom and both sides of each beam at a point well protected by the overhang. This drip groove stops water from traveling farther along the beam.

Cutting a drip groove

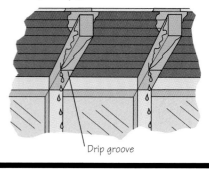

Drip groove

Tip *Finding replacement tiles may be the hardest part of repairing a ceiling with damaged tiles. If you can't find exact replacements at a local supplier, use existing tiles from a closet or back bedroom and replace them with whatever you can find at the store.*

▶ Wall studs are hard to find.

One technique for finding studs is to knock along the wall with your knuckles or a wood tool handle for 3 or 4 feet, listening for changes in sound. The predominant hollow thunking sound indicates stud cavities; a sharper rapping sound indicates studs. Also look for visual clues. Electrical receptacles almost always have a stud on one side or the other. Many wallboard installations have telltale nail depressions or joint outlines along studs; shining a light from the side accentuates their faint outlines. Nails along the upper edges of a baseboard go into the studs.

The most reliable way to locate studs is by probing. One technique is to drill a ⅛-inch-diameter hole into the wall, angled toward one side, and probe through the hole with a piece of stiff wire. When the wire hits a stud, mark the wire where it enters the wall by holding your thumb against it, slide the wire out, hold the wire against the outside of the wall in the same position, and note where the end of the wire falls. You can also find studs by drilling a series of small holes along the wall, spaced 1 inch apart, until you hit a stud, or by driving a 6d finishing nail into the wall at 1-inch intervals. All of these probing techniques leave holes that you'll have to fill with spackling compound when you are finished.

You can also locate studs with stud sensors. Magnetic stud finders work best on old lath-and-plaster walls, where lots of nails were used to fasten the lath to studs. A density gauge works better for wallboard walls; it uses sound waves to locate solid objects behind the wall surface.

Finally, you may be able to pinpoint the location of a stud if you already know where a nearby stud is located. The walls of most homes built since the 1940s have studs centered every 16 inches, although studs next to windows, doors, and corners may not fall into the 16-inch pattern.

Locating studs

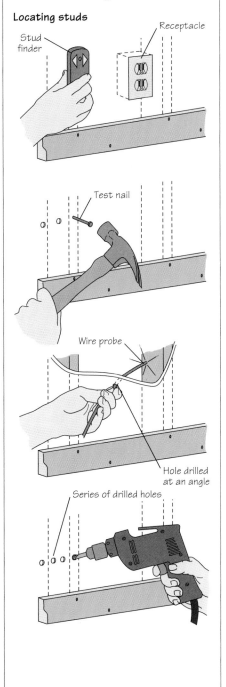

▶ Wall needs fasteners for hanging objects.

If the object you are hanging is light (1 to 2 pounds), any fastener is adequate, whether secured to a stud or not. An ordinary 1-inch screw will handle most needs. Don't be afraid to put a hole in the wall—it's easy to patch.

For medium loads (2 to 7 pounds), your choice of fastener will depend on whether you are attaching it to a stud. The easiest fastener for attaching to studs is an ordinary screw or nail. It should penetrate the stud at least ¾ inch. To hang something on a wall between studs, use a hollow-wall fastener. Expansion bolts and plastic, drive-in, and screw-in anchors leave a device in the wall that can be reused a number of times. A toggle bolt is the strongest fastener for hollow walls, but you must thread the bolt through the object to be hung, or through a hanger, before inserting the bolt and toggle into the wall—you cannot take the bolt out of the wall without losing the toggle.

Heavy loads should always be attached directly to studs, usually with lag screws.

For masonry walls use a fastener designed for masonry. When you drill into the brick or concrete, use a masonry bit of the same diameter as the outside of the fastener.

▶ Hanger comes out of wall.

The original hole might have been too large for the hanger, or the wall covering may be too soft. Do not return the hanger to the same hole. Replace it with a type that spreads out wider on the backside of the wall, such as an expansion bolt or toggle bolt.

Tip Framing for a standard 8-foot-high wall consists of a 2x4 <u>soleplate</u> resting on the floor, 94¼-inch <u>studs</u> nailed to the plate every 16 inches, and a <u>double top plate</u> consisting of two 2x4s nailed to the tops of the studs. Walls sometimes have 2x4 <u>blocking</u>, called fire blocking, between the studs halfway up the wall. Windows, doors, and other openings have a <u>header</u>, or beam, across the top that carries any loads above the opening. Each end of the header rests on short <u>trimmer studs</u>, which are nailed to full-length <u>king studs</u> that flank both ends of the header.

► Object seems too heavy to hang.

Use several hangers, all attached to studs. If the object is too narrow to span at least two studs, use several expansion bolts, or attach a 1x2 furring strip to the wall, bolting it into studs, and hang the heavy object from it.

► Hanger leaves mark or hole in wall.

Patch the hole with spackling compound and, if necessary, sand it smooth. Touch it up with paint to blend in with the wall.

► Plaster wall has cracks.

Widen the crack, undercutting the edges. Fill it with patching compound, smooth the compound with a 3-inch knife, and let it harden. Cover the crack and compound with self-sticking fiberglass-mesh tape. Apply compound over the tape with a 6-inch knife, let it harden, sand it smooth, and apply a thin top coat with a 10-inch knife, feathering the edges. Let it dry, sand it, and texture the patch to match the rest of the wall; then paint. *Note:* Some commercial patching kits require different techniques (for example, applying mesh first, then compound). Follow manufacturer's instructions. (For additional information, see page 12.)

► Plaster wall has hole.

For a small hole (less than 3 inches in diameter), first remove all the debris. Then wet the lath and surrounding plaster and fill the hole with patching compound or plaster of paris (mix according to instructions) to just below the level of the wall surface. Let it harden. Cover with fiberglass-mesh tape, then more patching compound, and texture the surface.

For a larger area (3 to 12 inches), you will need two coats of patching compound. Chip out weak plaster and clean out the area to expose the original lath. If necessary, secure the surrounding plaster with perforated plaster washers and 1⅝-inch wallboard screws. Apply a bonding agent (or mix of 2 parts water to 1 part white glue) to the edges of the old plaster. Moisten the lath. Apply the first coat of patching compound, scratch to texturize, and let dry. Then apply the finish coat. (See also page 13.)

For a huge hole or for extensively cracked areas, patch with wallboard. Cut out a large patch of ⅜-inch wallboard, sized so its edges will center over studs or other framing members. Use it to trace a cut line on the wall. Carefully cut out old plaster, using a saw or hammer and cold chisel; avoid jarring the plaster loose. Wear a dust mask. Screw the wallboard patch to the framing and lath. Tape joints with fiberglass-mesh tape; cover joints with compound. Texture the patch to match the surrounding area, then prime and paint.

Repairing a large hole in a plaster wall

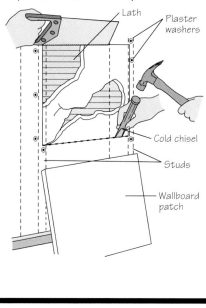

Lath

Plaster washers

Cold chisel

Studs

Wallboard patch

► Plaster wall is a mess.

Walls with extensive cracks or multiple layers of paint or wallpaper are not worth patching. Cover the area with canvas underliner material, and paint or paper over it, according to manufacturer's recommendation. Install the underliner with vertical seams slightly out of plumb, so wallpaper seams won't align over them. Or, for a smoother surface, forgo the underliner and cover the wall with wallboard. Be warned, however, that this is a big project that involves extending electrical boxes and door and window jambs, removing trim, lugging large sheets of wallboard, taping seams, and texturing. (See page 14.)

Applying underliner

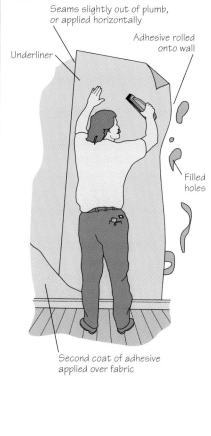

Seams slightly out of plumb, or applied horizontally

Adhesive rolled onto wall

Underliner

Filled holes

Second coat of adhesive applied over fabric

Tip *Although patching is quite simple, practice on closet walls and back bedrooms before taking on living room and dining room walls.*

Tip *Hairline cracks are inevitable. Patching other kinds of cracks is futile if you don't find out the cause and eliminate it. Moisture damage, indicated by water stains, must be fixed at the source. Stress cracks, usually around windows and doors, may be caused by house settling, or seasonal expanding and contracting of lumber. If the cracks are severe or continue to widen, consult a professional. Other cracks can be stabilized by patching with self-sticking fiberglass-mesh tape, as described above.*

▶ *Wallboard has hole.*

Small: Make sure the wall is free of dust, grease, and loose paint. Cover the hole with wallboard tape (or cloth soaked in thinned compound) and compound, using a knife wide enough to bridge the entire hole—otherwise, the corner of the knife will push the tape into the hole. (See also page 13.)

Medium: First cut the hole into a square shape. Install a small scrap of wallboard or plywood behind the hole, attaching it with wallboard screws driven through the wall. Cut a wallboard patch to fit into the square hole, attach it to the backing with one or two wallboard screws, tape the joints, and finish the patch and screw depressions to match the surrounding wall surface.

Large: Enlarge the hole by cutting the damaged area back to the framing, then install a new piece to fit the enlarged hole. Tape the joints and finish the patch to match the surrounding area. If you aren't confident about your taping skills, try to plan the cutout so that joints will be hidden behind furniture or cabinets, or locate joints at floor, ceiling, or corners.

▶ *Wallboard joint tape is coming loose.*

If the peeling tape is in only a small area, remove the loose section in a boat-shaped cutout. Fill the cutout with joint compound and smooth it with a 3-inch taping knife. If the tape is peeling in a large area, remove the tape (slice carefully with a sharp knife) and redo the area with new tape and compound.

▶ *Texture of new patch doesn't match wall.*

You probably won't be able to match the original texture perfectly because techniques, materials, and individual skill vary so much. However, before calling in a professional plasterer, experiment with the following techniques on some scraps of wallboard. To achieve a coarse, lumpy texture, apply slightly thinned finishing compound with a sponge and mold contours into it. For a uniformly bumpy texture, apply thinned compound with a large-nap roller. For a texture with variable bumps, use rollers with different nap sizes. For an orange-peel texture, use a small-nap roller or, with a texture sprayer, spray a mixture of thin compound and extrafine sand onto the area. To produce a random pattern of raised flat spots, spray or trowel thinned compound onto the surface and lightly flatten the high spots with a wide (24- to 36-inch) trowel. Stippling fresh compound with a stiff brush, fine broom, or crumpled newspaper also creates textured effects, all of which can be further enhanced by flattening high spots with a wide trowel.

Patching a medium hole

Cutting out damaged area

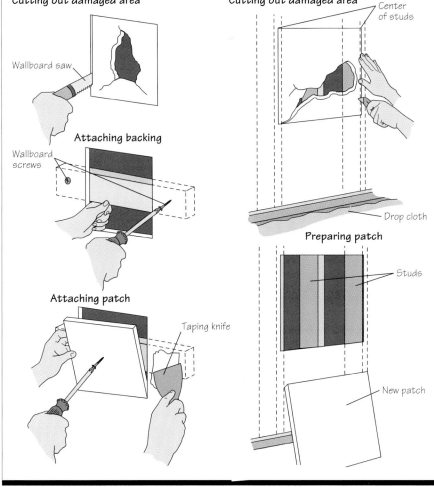

Wallboard saw

Attaching backing

Wallboard screws

Attaching patch

Taping knife

Patching a large hole

Cutting out damaged area

Center of studs

Drop cloth

Preparing patch

Studs

New patch

Tip *Wear eye protection and a dust mask when sanding or chipping.*

Tip *Can't tell if wall is plaster or wallboard? Wallboard has a layer of thick paper just beneath the paint or wallcovering; probe with a knife or nail. Other telltale signs of wallboard are faint nail depressions along studs and joint tape over seams. Plaster has a hard surface over a crumbly brown coat.*

▶ Wallboard nails are popping out.

Just hammering the nails back in won't work. Pull out the nail and replace it with a 1⅝-inch wallboard screw, or hammer the popped nail back in and secure it with a second nail driven close enough so its head overlaps the first. Be careful not to drive the screw or nail in so far that it breaks the paper facing on the wallboard. If this happens, remove the fastener altogether and drive a new one 2 inches away. Cover the dent and tear with compound and then spot-paint the area.

Removing popped nail

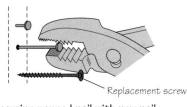

Replacement screw

Securing popped nail with new nail

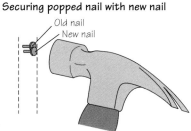

Old nail
New nail

▶ Wallboard panels don't join evenly.

When installing large patches (or full panels) of wallboard, sometimes you can't avoid butting the beveled edge of one panel against a full (unbeveled) edge of another, creating a discrepancy in thicknesses. A twisted stud may also cause an uneven joint. Before taping the joint, build up the low side. Use the type of joint compound, sometimes called "hot mud," that hardens by chemical reaction (hydration) rather than

evaporation (which causes shrinking). Hot mud is available in 30-, 60-, and 90-minute setting times; use 90-minute to allow adequate working time. Apply it on the low side only, feathering it out from the joint 10 to 12 inches. After the compound hardens, lay a long straightedge (such as a 4-foot level) across the joint to see if the low side is built up evenly; if not, build up the low spots with another layer. After it hardens, tape the joint like any other: Apply a coat of compound and embed wallboard tape into it. After it dries, sand the joint smooth and apply two to three light coats of compound, sanding each coat after it dries before applying the next. Coats should be successively wider—for example, 6, 12, and then 18 inches wide. Prime and paint to match.

▶ Wall feels cold to the touch.

If the exterior walls in a heated home feel uncomfortably cold, they do not have enough insulation. New insulation can be blown in, or you can remove siding and install rigid insulation under the new siding (which is a big job). As a simple alternative, try baseboard heaters set at a low temperature.

▶ Wall feels damp to the touch.

This problem is caused by a combination of humidity, cool wall surface, and lack of ventilation. Try to control all three by warming the room and providing increased air circulation. A baseboard heater along the wall should provide sufficient heat and create convective air currents, but it may be too expensive to operate for extended periods of time. If operating it for short periods doesn't control dampness, supplement with a small fan set at a low speed and run it continuously, or as long as necessary.

▶ Wall is discolored and smells musty.

The problem is mildew. Eradicate with mildew remover, either a commercial preparation or a homemade solution: ½ cup vinegar, ½ cup borax, and 3 gallons of water; or 1 teaspoon washing soda and ½ cup chlorine bleach in 1 gallon of water. Wash with a sponge, then rinse with a sponge and warm water. If you need to repaint, have the dealer add mildewcide to the paint. In any case, eliminate the source of the problem: lack of ventilation and high humidity.

▶ Walls are not soundproof.

There is a progression of steps you can take to soundproof walls, each involving a more complicated process. Start by plugging up or muffling all areas where air (and sound) can get through the wall. First remove covers from electrical fixtures and receptacles (on both sides) and seal cracks around the boxes with spray insulating foam. Seal holes inside the boxes as well. (Be sure to deaden each outlet first by turning off the circuit breaker.) Next install sound-deadening liners inside heating ducts shared by two rooms. Look for cracks along the floor and ceiling and seal them. Add weather stripping around doors, and a door sweep on both sides of each door. Replace hollow-core doors with solid-core doors. If sound persists, install resilient channels horizontally along one side of the wall, 16 inches on center, and attach new wallboard to the channels. Sound-deadening board is an alternative to the channels; you can install either over the old wallboard, but you may prefer to remove it to reduce wall thickness. Adding insulation between

Tip *The secrets to successful patching of holes and cracks are as follows. (1) Multiple layers. Don't try to build up a deep crack or hole in one layer; use several. Let each layer dry, then sand, and apply a new layer. (2) Feathering. To make sure that the patch won't show, finish with a loose skim coat of topping compound feathered 2 to 3 feet beyond the crack or hole. (3) Spot-prime before painting.*

the studs is not an adequate deterrent by itself; it is effective only when used with sound-deadening board or resilient channels.

Sealing openings

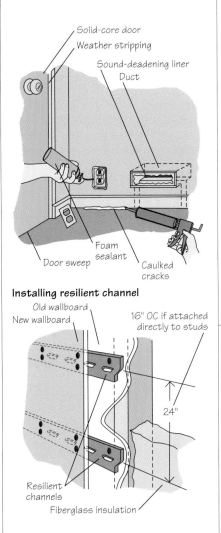

Solid-core door
Weather stripping
Sound-deadening liner
Duct
Foam sealant
Door sweep
Caulked cracks

Installing resilient channel

Old wallboard
New wallboard
16" OC if attached directly to studs
24"
Resilient channels
Fiberglass insulation

▶ Bathroom walls and ceiling have colored spots.

If not mildew (see opposite page), the problem is condensation that leaves an accumulating residue of dissolved pigments and dirt. Common in bathrooms, condensation is more likely with latex-based

paint than with alkyd-based. It can be removed by wiping down the walls and ceiling with a damp cloth, using a mild cleaning solution, if necessary. Try to improve ventilation in the bathroom.

▶ Fingerprints and smudges show on walls.

Enamel paints (glossy, hard) and flat paints (dull, rubbery) require different cleaning techniques.

Enamel paint: Clean with a sponge and a solution of 1 gallon lukewarm water mixed with 1 teaspoon washing soda. Wear rubber gloves. Do not use ammonia or all-purpose cleaners with ammonia— they can dull and etch the paint. For fingerprints and nongreasy stains, increase the amount of washing soda to ¼ cup, *or* use TSP or an all-purpose cleaner that does not contain ammonia. Rinse with a damp sponge. For greasy stains rub lightly from the center of the stain

outward, using a cloth dipped in alcohol and a dry cloth to blot as you go until the stain is gone.

Flat paint: Clean with a solution of 1 gallon lukewarm water mixed with 2 tablespoons washing soda, *or* use TSP. Wear rubber gloves. Rinse with plain water. Overlap sections to avoid streaks. Use only a white cloth because colored sponges may leave a dye. Don't scrub—it will leave marks. For greasy stains first blot with a crumpled paper towel, then cover the spot with two or three clean pieces of paper towel and go over it with a warm iron. Repeat until the stain is almost gone, changing the paper towel each time. Then blot with a commercial wall-cleaning paste, or make your own by mixing a cleaning fluid, such as liquid laundry detergent, with fuller's earth (for dark surfaces) or with cornstarch or whiting (for light surfaces). Apply the paste to the stain, let it dry thoroughly, then brush it off.

▶ New paint doesn't cover old paint or new patch.

The following chart shows which primer and paint to use over what surface. Problems often result from omitting primer over enamel, trying to cover red colors with one coat, not washing the walls first, using low-quality paint (not enough pigment and resins), and rolling out the paint too thinly.

Surface	Primer	Paint
Latexed walls and ceilings	Spot-prime spackled and patched areas; seal stains and smoke marks; if using different color, cover with tinted primer.	Latex flat
Bathroom/kitchen walls and ceilings	PVA primer for new wallboard; tinted oil-based or latex for painted surfaces.	Oil-based latex gloss, or latex eggshell
Enameled trim	Enamel primer	Oil-based or latex gloss
Masonry (concrete/brick)	Latex flat masonry paint	Latex flat

Tip *High-gloss paint and light colors accentuate wall bumps. Flat paint in neutral or dark tones minimizes imperfections.*

▶ New paint doesn't cover stains.

If scrubbing the stain with a solution of water and TSP doesn't remove it completely, seal it with white-pigmented shellac containing at least 65 percent titanium dioxide. Prime and paint after the shellac dries.

▶ Old paint layers make wall uneven.

Remove all loose paint with a putty knife. Wash the walls with TSP for proper adhesion. Skim-coat a thin layer of joint compound over the entire wall with a wide (24- to 36-inch) putty knife to fill in the depressions. After it dries, sand lightly; repeat if necessary. Seal/prime the wall with PVA sealer, then paint. Apply an undercoat primer if you plan to wallpaper. See also page 24.

▶ Textured paint needs removing.

The technique you use will depend on whether the textured paint is latex-based or oil-based. (You may not be able to tell until you try; assume [hope] it's latex. Test on an inconspicuous area.) For latex paint, buy a paint stripper specifically designed to remove textured paint and follow the instructions. For oil-based paint, try a homemade solution of 1 gallon water, 2 cups liquid fabric softener, 1 cup white vinegar, and proper ratio of enzyme-based wallpaper remover, according to label instructions. (The typical bottle size is 16 to 22 ounces.) With a clean garden sprayer, apply the solution to one small area at a time. Wet the area, wait five minutes, wet it a second time, wait five minutes, spray it a final time, and wait five minutes more. Then scrape the area with a 6-inch

putty knife. Clean the smoothed wall with a solution of 1 gallon water and ¼ cup white vinegar. After it dries, seal the walls with white-pigmented shellac.

If strippers don't work, your options are to skim-coat the wall to install new wallboard, or to apply wallpaper liner and wallpaper (see page 18).

▶ You want to paint over wallpaper.

It is never advisable to paint or wallpaper over an old wallcovering. The paper may not be adhering well to the wall. Paint wets the wallcovering, and it may pull away. Also dyes in the underlying wallpaper may bleed through the paint, and some wallcoverings include flocks or foils to which paint will not adhere. Finally, paint will exaggerate any seams, blisters, tears, or other imperfections in the wallpaper. If at all possible, remove the old wallpaper before you paint the walls (see opposite page).

▶ Wallpaper is dirty and needs cleaning.

Washable wallpaper: Clean with a solution of mild soap and cool water. Rinse with cold water and blot the paper dry with a clean cloth. Remove fingerprints and nongreasy stains with an art-gum eraser. For greasy stains first blot with crumpled paper towels, then hold several clean towels over the spot and press with a warm iron. Repeat until the grease is absorbed. Remove mildew with a light application of commercial mildew remover, or sponge with a cloth dampened in alcohol.

Nonwashable wallpaper: Clean with a solvent, because the wallcovering is vulnerable to water. Dampen several terry cloth towels with kerosene. Allow them to air-

dry. Wrap one of the towels around the head of a broom or mop, securing it with tape. Wipe the walls from the ceiling down, overlapping the strips as you move around the room. Turn or change the towels as they become grimy.

▶ Wallpaper seams are loose or curling.

With a razor or utility knife, cut slits above and below the loose area, starting at the seam and slicing away from it diagonally for 2 to 3 inches. Carefully peel back the loose section of wallpaper and apply wallpaper paste onto the exposed back. Press the paper into place to spread the paste onto the wall, then peel the paper away again. Let the paste dry slightly until it's tacky. Then carefully press the paper into place again. Gently apply pressure with a damp sponge, and use the sponge to remove any paste that oozes out of the seams. If a long section of seam has curled, do this process in short segments of 4 to 6 inches each.

Pasting a loose seam

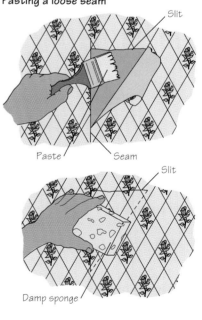

Slit

Paste　　　Seam

Slit

Damp sponge

▶ Wallpaper has blisters or bubbles.

If the blister is small, slit it and inject acrylic wallpaper adhesive under the blister with a glue syringe (available from a wallcovering store). Smooth the paper with a damp sponge. If the blister is larger than a quarter, cut an *x* over the blister with a razor or utility knife and peel back the wallpaper in four sections. Apply paste to the exposed back of each section. Press the sections into place, peel them away again, and let the paste dry until tacky. Then press the sections back into place, using a damp sponge to apply gentle pressure and to mop away any excess paste.

Repairing a small blister

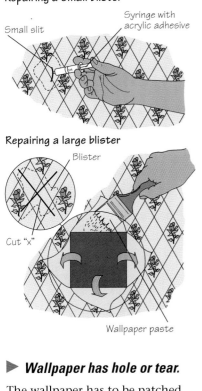

Small slit

Syringe with acrylic adhesive

Repairing a large blister

Blister

Cut "x"

Wallpaper paste

▶ Wallpaper has hole or tear.

The wallpaper has to be patched. Start by taping a scrap of wallpaper over the hole or tear, matching the wallpaper pattern; use masking tape or other tape that won't damage

paper. With a utility knife and straightedge, cut a clean-edged shape through both the scrap material and the installed wallpaper. With hot water and a putty knife, remove the damaged section of wallpaper from the wall and discard it. Apply paste to the back of the patch, press it into place, remove it to let the paste dry until tacky, then press the patch into place again. Smooth the patch and clean up with a damp sponge.

Cutting scrap and damaged wallpaper

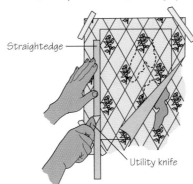

Straightedge

Utility knife

Removing damaged wallpaper

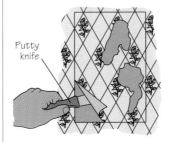

Putty knife

Pasting patch in place

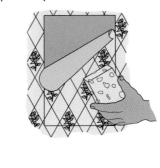

▶ Wallpaper is peeling off in large sections.

The wall wasn't prepared properly before wallcovering was applied. Strip off the paper and start over (see below).

▶ Wallpaper needs removing.

Remove old paper first. If it's a strippable type, you should be able to lift up a corner and peel strips right off the wall. Remove paste residue with hot water and a scraper. If it's a solid vinyl type, the vinyl will peel off but the backing paper needs to be stripped. To remove the backing paper or non-strippable wallpaper, start by scoring the surface with a wire brush or a spurlike perforation tool designed for this purpose. Don't press too hard or you will damage the wall. Then mix a solution of 3 gallons very hot water, ¼ cup liquid fabric softener, 2 tablespoons baking soda, and the appropriate proportion of enzyme-based wallpaper remover, according to label instructions. Observe all instructions printed on the product labels. Pour 1 gallon of the solution into a clean garden sprayer. Working from floor to ceiling, one section at a time, spray the walls with a fine mist. Immediately repeat the process two more times, then wait 15 minutes. Then, section by section in the same order you sprayed, scrape the wall-covering with a 6-inch taping knife, and peel off, working from the bottom up. Remove residue with a sponge soaked in the remover solution. Then rinse the walls with 1 cup white vinegar in 1 gallon water. Clean up. Now you're ready to prep the walls for the new paint or wall-covering. Wash walls with a mild household cleaner, patch holes and

Tip *If you don't know whether you'll be painting or wallpapering the wall, apply undercoater. You can have it tinted, so it will look like painted walls if you decide not to install wallpaper. Use two coats.*

gouges, smooth the wall surface (skim coat or underliner—see right), dust, and finally prime with acrylic primer designated as wallcovering undercoater.

Removing strippable wallcoverings

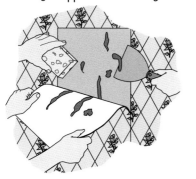

Removing nonstrippable wallcoverings

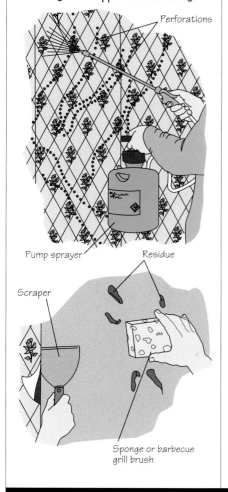

Perforations

Pump sprayer

Residue

Scraper

Sponge or barbecue grill brush

▶ Wall is too uneven for new wallpaper.

Textured or cracked walls and walls with many years' accumulation of paint and wallcoverings are poor surfaces for new wallcoverings. Removing them and installing new wallboard is sensible only if extensive wiring, insulating, plumbing, or structural changes make it necessary to expose the wall cavities. Installing thin wallboard over the walls is only slightly easier, as it requires altering electrical boxes and molding, and taping all the joints. The better do-it-yourself options are to apply a canvas underliner, or to skim-coat the walls.

Canvas underliner is available from wallcovering outlets. Apply according to manufacturer's instructions.

To skim-coat (or "float") a wall, start by scraping off loose and peeling paint (not textured surfaces). Then sand the walls with 40-grit sandpaper (wear a respirator); clean up by damp-mopping. Seal the walls with two coats of white-pigmented shellac, according to label instructions.

Mix a batch of joint compound, thinned with water to the consistency of stiff cake batter. Apply it to the walls with a 10-inch taping knife, working up from the base of the wall in 4-foot-square sections. Let dry overnight, then sand with 120-grit sandpaper and apply a second coat. Let dry, sand again, then seal the walls with one application of oil-based undercoater.

▶ New wallpaper won't stick to wall.

The wall probably was not primed correctly. For brand-new wallboard or plaster walls, use PVA primer. For walls painted with latex paint, use latex undercoater. For walls painted with oil-based paint, use acrylic undercoater.

▶ Paneling is worn and dirty.

If the paneling has a factory-applied lacquer or plastic finish, you can clean it with warm soapy water and a sponge; then wax it, if desired. If the paneling has a wax finish (one you can scratch with a fingernail), restore it by rubbing with a beeswax- or carnauba-based paste wax. If the paneling has an oil finish (which has a soft sheen, rather than shiny, and feels oiled), clean by rubbing with boiled linseed oil or lemon oil (light finishes) or Danish oil (darker finishes); remove any excess to avoid leaving a dust-attracting film. Do not use furniture polishes containing silicone for factory-finished paneling; it may break down the finish. Instead, spot-clean and dust, using lemon oil on a cloth, or follow paneling manufacturer's recommendation.

▶ Paneling has scratch or nick.

Apply furniture paste wax (for wax finishes) or furniture oil (for oil finishes) to the blemish and rub it in. If that doesn't work, dab it with a putty stick that matches the color of the paneling. Remove excess putty with a cloth. You may also be able to match the color with a felt-tipped pen, shoe polish, or wood stain (experimenting first in an obscured corner).

Tip *How can you tell if paint on a wall is latex or oil-based? A flat (not shiny) surface is latex; a glossy surface could be latex or oil-based. Hold a wet sponge to the wall for a few minutes. If the paint bubbles or dissolves, it's latex; if it stays intact, it's oil-based.*

▶ Paneling has darkened with age.

Some solid-wood paneling, especially pine, may have darkened with age. If cleaning with warm soapy water does not lighten it enough, try to renew the finish by rubbing it with fine steel wool (#4/0) dipped in mineral spirits; experiment in an inconspicuous area. If this doesn't work, you will have to strip off the old finish completely. Use a paste furniture stripper and apply according to instructions. Finish the bare wood with a urethane or oil finish, staining or bleaching the wood first, if desired.

▶ Paneling has stains.

Clean stains on lacquered, waxed, or plastic-coated paneling with warm soapy water or by rubbing with paste wax. If this doesn't work, use a commercial furniture-restorer product (available at home centers), following label instructions. Clean oiled wood by gently rubbing lemon oil into the stain with fine steel wool. Reoil, then wipe off excess. If the stain was caused by moisture, be sure that the source of the problem has been located and eliminated.

▶ Edge of paneling has come loose.

With a flat pry bar and a padded woodblock for a fulcrum, carefully pry the entire loose edge away from the wall, inserting wood spacer blocks between the wall and the panel edge as you work your way down. With the seam completely opened, apply a generous bead of paneling adhesive to the exposed bearing surfaces (such as wallboard or furring strips). Wait for the adhesive to get tacky but not hard, then remove the spacer blocks and press the panel edge into place.

Slide the padded block along the seam, tapping it with a hammer to ensure a tight bond. Clean off any adhesive residue with a clean cloth dipped in mineral spirits. For additional strength, add paneling nails (grooved finishing brads) along the seam. *Note:* If there's a chance that the seam will leave a slight crack between panels, first paint the wall behind the seam black, so the crack will be dark and less visible. Let the paint dry before applying the adhesive.

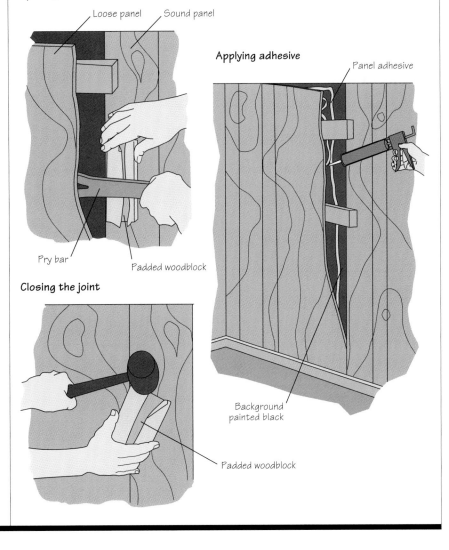

Opening the seam

Loose panel   Sound panel

Pry bar   Padded woodblock

Closing the joint

Applying adhesive   Panel adhesive

Background painted black

Padded woodblock

Tip   *Traditional paneling in most period homes consists of wide boards, or panels, with flat trim applied around each panel. This arrangement, called frame-and-panel, is capped by a continuous ledge built up of molding pieces. An alternative type of paneling consists of tongue-and-groove boards with beaded edges, of random or uniform width, installed vertically and capped by a continuous band of molding.*

SOLVING INDOOR PROBLEMS

▶ *Paneling is damaged or coming loose from wall.*

Remove the panel. (You may need to remove the baseboard first; see right.) If it is secured by nails, pry around the edges with a pry bar and padded fulcrum. Pull the panel away from the wall, and use pliers to pull out any nails left in the wall. If the panel is glued in place, start by chiseling through the panel along a line 2 to 3 inches in from one of the edges. Remove the larger section, breaking the adhesive bond by prying with a wrecking bar or flat shovel. Work carefully along any seams with other panels. Then gingerly remove the smaller strip of paneling remaining along the original seam; break the adhesive bond by hammering lightly on a taping knife or putty knife. Scrape off adhesive residue in the same way.

Inspect the wall for moisture or other damage and eliminate the cause of the problem. Replace loose plaster or wallboard, patch holes, scrape off flaking paint, and seal the wall with primer.

To install the new panel, apply adhesive to the furring strips, stud faces, or wall surface (around the edges of the opening and down the center every 16 inches in a zigzag pattern). Press the new panel into place and immediately secure the top with four finishing nails. Pull the bottom of the panel about 10 inches away from the wall, so the adhesive breaks full contact, and insert blocks every 10 inches to hold it for 10 minutes. When the adhesive gets tacky, remove the blocks and press the panel into place. Secure the bottom and edges with finishing nails, setting the heads and filling the holes with putty colored to match the paneling.

▶ *Baseboard needs removing.*

When replacing an entire panel, you probably have to remove baseboard and other molding strips to get full access to the panel. Pry them loose with a flat pry bar. Use two pry bars in stubborn areas, applying gentle pressure on one, then the other. After removing the molding, pull out any nails left in the wall. Remove any nails left in the molding by pulling them through from the back with pliers or nippers. If the face has any nail holes, touch them up with a putty stick after you install the new panel and nail the molding strips back in place.

▶ *Paneling has crack or hole.*

If the paneling is solid wood, not sheet, you will need to replace the entire damaged board (see left). If the paneling is sheet, you can patch it as follows: From a scrap of identical paneling, cut a rectangular patch slightly larger than the damaged area. Plan the patch so that the grain pattern will align with the pattern in the wall around the hole. Cut out the patch with a sharp utility knife and straightedge, rather than a saw, to ensure straight, clean edges. (Practice elsewhere on the scrap first.) Next tape the patch over the damaged area with masking tape, aligning the grain patterns. Carefully trace the outline of the patch with the knife, then set the patch aside. With the utility knife, cut through the paneling along the scored outline. Make several passes with the blade, cutting deeper each time. Then remove the damaged piece, gently prying it away from the wall, if necessary,

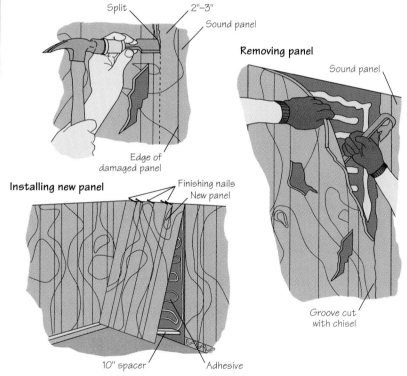

Scoring the edge

Split   2"–3"
Sound panel
Edge of damaged panel

Removing panel

Sound panel
Groove cut with chisel

Installing new panel

Finishing nails
New panel
10" spacer
Adhesive

Tip *Always scrub walls and woodwork before painting them. They accumulate an invisible greasy film over the years that prevents paint from adhering properly. If warm soapy water does not remove the film, mix a solution of 1 gallon water, ½ cup low-phosphate TSP substitute, and 2 tablespoons liquid fabric softener. Apply it with a clean garden sprayer, let stand for five minutes, then scrub with a damp sponge (wear latex gloves). Rinse with a solution of ¼ cup white vinegar in 1 gallon water.*

with a putty knife or pry bar. If the paneling is applied over furring strips, center 1x3 cleats under the edges of the cutout. Attach them with paneling adhesive and, if possible, nails. Apply paneling adhesive to the back of the patch, wait for the adhesive to get tacky, then press it into place. Over cleats, attach the patch with paneling nails (grooved finishing brads) as well.

Cutting the patch

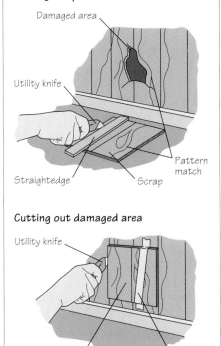

Damaged area

Utility knife

Straightedge

Pattern match

Scrap

Cutting out damaged area

Utility knife

Patch

Tape

Adhering the patch to cleats

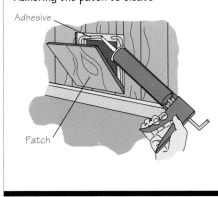

Adhesive

Patch

▶ *You want to paint paneling.*

First scrub the walls with warm soapy water and a sponge. Let dry. Fill cracks and holes with patching compound, let it dry, then sand it flush with the wall surface. Roughen the paneling surface with 150-grit sandpaper so the primer will adhere. Brush or vacuum away the residue and wipe the paneling with a damp cloth. Spot-prime all knots with a shellac-based sealer, then apply a base coat of latex or alkyd primer. Finish with two coats of latex paint—flat or semigloss, depending on your preference.

▶ *Solid-board paneling is damaged.*

Replace the entire damaged board. First remove the baseboard. Next, using a circular saw with the blade depth set to the thickness of the paneling, rip the board in half along its entire length. (Finish the ends of the cut, where the saw won't reach because of the floor or ceiling, with a chisel.) Pry both halves of the board away from the wall, starting with the half that has the groove edge. Be careful not to break the tongue of the adjacent board. The half of the damaged board with the tongue edge may be blind-nailed, so don't force it because the sudden release of the blind nails may cause the adjacent board to split. Instead pry under it enough to lift both the damaged board and adjacent board away from the wall, then change the direction of pressure so you are prying the damaged board away from the neighboring board as well as from the wall.

Prepare the replacement board. Cut it to the same length as the damaged board. Then, with a chisel or a circular saw with the blade set at a shallow depth, remove the back flange along the groove edge of the board (the groove is formed by two

flanges—one in front, that always shows, and one in back, that is always hidden).

To install the new board, fit the tongue into the corresponding groove of the adjacent board and snug it into place by hammering on a padded woodblock along the entire length of the board. Nail it with 8d finishing nails, set the heads, fill the holes with putty, then finish the board to match the rest of the paneling. Replace the baseboard.

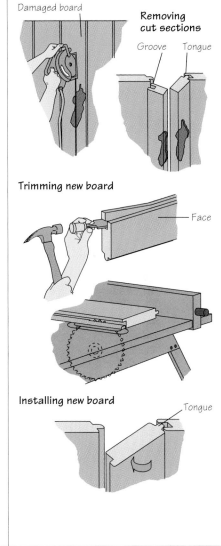

Sawing damaged board

Damaged board

Removing cut sections

Groove   Tongue

Trimming new board

Face

Installing new board

Tongue

Tip   To dull a finished wood surface for painting, you can sand it, or, wearing latex gloves and eye protection, you can apply a liquid deglosser, following manufacturer's instructions.

Tip   If you are painting frame-and-panel paneling, paint the recessed panels first. Drag the paint out from the corners and edges toward the center of the panel, then finish with vertical strokes in the direction of the wood grain.

SOLVING INDOOR PROBLEMS

▶ Insects are behind paneling.

Paneling that has been installed over old walls without protection from external moisture provides a natural haven for insects, especially termites and wood-boring pests. Look for small piles of fine sawdust, tunnels, or holes near the bottom of the paneling. If you suspect insects, call a qualified exterminator to conduct an inspection and recommend treatment.

▶ You can't tell whether wall is a bearing wall.

All exterior walls are considered bearing walls. For interior walls, look for clues in the attic or basement. In the attic note the direction of ceiling joists; if they run perpendicular to the wall, it is probably bearing, especially if the joists are overlapped or spliced. In the basement or crawl space, look for the main girders; walls located directly over them are probably bearing. Also doubled-up floor joists probably support bearing walls. Posts and footings within the perimeter of the foundation usually support bearing walls as well.

If a central hallway runs the length of the house, only one wall is the bearing wall. Look in the attic to see where the ceiling joists overlap. Short walls running perpendicular to ceiling joists, such as closet walls, are probably not bearing, especially if parallel walls are close by.

▶ Mitered joints of casings have opened up.

Miter joints will open up as the wood expands and contracts with changes in humidity. The wider the casing, the greater the problem. (This is one reason why wide casings in Victorian homes always have butt joints or block joints, not mitered joints.) This problem can

be minimized by priming every side and edge of each board before installing the casings. If a joint has opened up, lock-nail the joint from both directions and fill the gap with caulk, which works better than spackling compound because it's flexible. Be sure the caulk label specifies "paintable." If the casings are stained and not painted, use a wood filler—not caulk—that can be stained to match them.

Lock-nailing

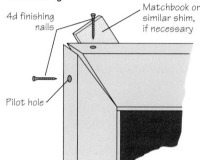

Filling gap

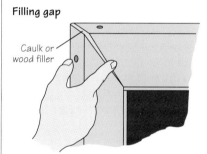

▶ Molding piece is missing or damaged.

Replacing most molding pieces is a matter of cutting a new piece to the right length and nailing it into place. There are some tricks of the trade, however, that will ensure precise, tight-fitting joints.

• When butting two pieces end-to-end, cut the ends at matching 45-degree bevels (rather than 90-degree straight cuts) so if the joint opens up it won't create a gap.

• When cutting miter joints for door and window casings (picture-frame joints), don't automatically cut two 45-degree angles—the corner may not be a perfect 90 degrees. Instead cut the first piece at 45 degrees and nail it in place. Then lay the second piece of stock in place, overlapping the first piece, and mark where the two ends of the miter angle of the first piece intersect its edges. Join the marks and cut along the line.

• Lock-nail all miter joints, using glue and 4d finishing nails (drill pilot holes first).

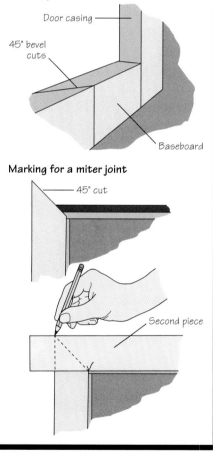

Joining pieces end-to-end

Marking for a miter joint

▶ Replacing molding requires coped cut.

When joining baseboard or similar molding at an inside corner, use a coped joint. Square-cut the first piece of molding to butt against the wall. The second piece of molding abuts the first, but because molding has irregular profiles the end of the second piece must be shaped to fit tightly to the face of the first piece. Create this shape with a coped cut. First cut a 45-degree bevel on the *face* side of the board. Then, with a coping saw, follow the irregular outline created by the bevel cut, angling the saw backward slightly. Test how well the coped cut fits against the first molding and make adjustments. Then, at the opposite end, cut the second piece of molding to length (add 1/16 inch), and nail into place.

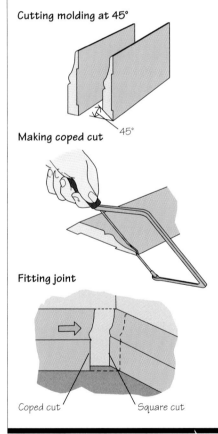

Cutting molding at 45°

45°

Making coped cut

Fitting joint

Coped cut   Square cut

▶ You can't find replacement molding to match original.

Look for a lumberyard that has been in business for a long time. If they don't have the material, they may be able to make a piece if they still have cutter blades to match your pattern. Other places to look are cabinet shops and hardwood dealers who do their own milling. Look for contractors who specialize in restoration work, and ask where they get hard-to-find moldings. Another place to look is a recycling center that specializes in used building materials or "architectural salvage." Finally, look in closets or back bedrooms of your own house (or even a willing neighbor's) and use an existing piece that you can replace with something reasonably close to it.

▶ Crown molding is missing.

Crown molding is the most difficult to cut and fit because it is installed at an awkward angle, plus you must also compensate if the walls and ceiling are not square or the ceiling isn't level. Install the corner pieces first. They require compound bevel cuts (the end of the board is cut with 45-degree angles going in two different directions), so once they are in place it will be easier to get the lengths right on pieces requiring less complicated cuts. Make corner cuts at a textbook-perfect 45-degree angle first, then make gradual adjustments by testing the pieces in place and shaving the cuts as needed. (A power miter saw makes precise trimming easy.) Cut the piece to length only after the corner cut is completed. Install crown molding by nailing into the "flats" along

both the ceiling and the wall edges. Gaps due to irregularities in the wall or ceiling surface may be filled with spackling compound.

Fitting a compound bevel cut

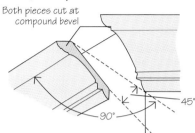

Both pieces cut at compound bevel

45°

90°

Cutting with compound miter saw

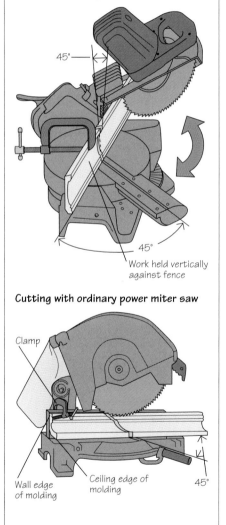

45°

45°

Work held vertically against fence

Cutting with ordinary power miter saw

Clamp

Wall edge of molding   Ceiling edge of molding   45°

Tip   *Types of moldings used to trim a room: Casings, which are the trim around windows and doors that resembles a picture frame; baseboards, which may be a single piece or may be built up with a base cap and base shoe; chair rail, which is a continuous strip of molding around the room at the height of a chair back; picture rail, which is a continuous strip of molding around the room approximately 1 foot below the ceiling; and crown molding, which covers the joint between walls and ceiling.*

SOLVING INDOOR PROBLEMS

▶ *Floor squeaks.*

Squeaks are annoying but rarely indicate major problems. They occur when a board rubs against a nail or another board. No movement, no squeak. First pinpoint the squeak by observing the floor closely while a helper walks, stands, and moves on the floor. The problem may be with finish floor boards that you can see, or it may be with boards hidden from view.

If you can see surface boards rubbing together, sprinkle talcum powder or squirt WD-40® into the joint for a temporary fix. For a permanent solution, secure the boards by driving wallboard screws up into them through the subfloor. Have your helper stand on the floor to force the board down, or predrill screw holes through the subfloor (but not through the finish floor); screws should penetrate only halfway into the finish floor. Use washers if the subfloor is soft or spongy. If there is no access from below, or if the finish floor is face-nailed, secure the board from the top with 6d (for 5⁄16-inch flooring) or 8d (for 3⁄4-inch) annular-ring finishing nails (or 16d finishing nails if you can nail directly into a joist). Predrill pilot holes to prevent splitting; set the nail heads and fill the holes with wood putty. If the flooring was installed directly over joists with no subfloor, screw 2x2 cleats to the sides of the joists and secure the squeaking floorboards to them by driving long wallboard screws up through the cleats (predrilling first), or secure from the top, as described above.

If the squeak is hidden from view, the movement could be subfloor boards or it could be finish boards covered by carpet or other floor covering. Make observations from below the floor while your helper squeaks the board from

above. If the subfloor or joists don't move, the problem is in the finish floor, hidden between the subfloor and floor covering. Secure the suspect board(s) by driving wallboard screws from below, or nails from above (through the carpet), as previously described. If you detect movement of the subfloor boards or joists, secure the boards in one of the following ways: (1) insert (don't force) shims into gaps between the joist and moving subfloor boards (dab construction adhesive on both sides of the shim first); (2) screw a 2x2 cleat into the side of the joist; or, if you don't have a 2x2, (3) snug (don't force) a 2x4 cleat up against the creaking subfloor next to a joist, and screw it securely to the joist (apply construction adhesive to the top and side of the cleat first).

Securing loose boards to subfloor with nail or screw

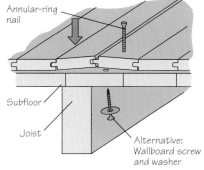

Annular-ring nail

Subfloor

Joist

Alternative: Wallboard screw and washer

Securing subfloor with shim or cleat

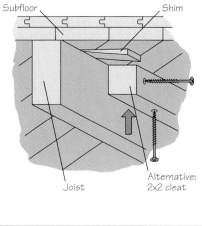

Subfloor Shim

Joist

Alternative: 2x2 cleat

▶ *Floor sags or bounces.*

If the problem occurs in a small area, inspect under the floor for a cracked joist or missing bracing between joists. If you have a cracked joist, temporarily shore it up on both sides with joist material; splices should extend 12 to 18 inches beyond the crack in both directions. Apply construction adhesive to the splice pieces first, then secure them to the joist with 16d common nails or 2¾-inch decking screws, spaced 12 inches apart along the tops and bottoms of the splices and randomly across the middle. Replace missing braces with solid blocking cut from lumber the same dimension as the joists (for example, 2x8, 2x12, and so on).

If the problem exists across the entire floor, the joists are undersized or poorly supported and need reinforcement. Consult a remodeling contractor, architect, or structural engineer.

Splicing a floor joist

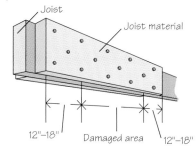

Joist

Joist material

12"–18" Damaged area 12"–18"

Replacing blocking or bridging

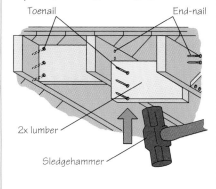

Toenail End-nail

2x lumber

Sledgehammer

Tip *Anatomy of a floor system. Most residential floors have three layers: a finish floor of wood, carpet, resilient sheet material, or other floor covering; a subfloor of plywood, 1-by boards, or other material that provides a structural membrane; and a supporting framework of joists that rest directly on foundation sills, girders, or bearing walls. The joists, which are 2-by lumber set on edge, are stabilized by blocking that is placed between them at the ends and at the midpoint of long spans.*

▶ *Subfloor has hole or rot.*

If the subfloor has a moisture problem, eliminate the source first. Then cut out the damaged area of subfloor. The cutout should be rectangular, it should extend at least 12 inches beyond any rotted wood, and its edges should be centered over floor joists. Use a circular saw with the blade set to the depth of subflooring. Next saw a replacement patch out of plywood of the same thickness as the subfloor, cutting it ¹⁄₁₆ to ⅛ inch smaller around the edges to allow for expansion. Glue and nail 2x4 cleats between the joists so all four edges of the patch will be supported. Apply a bead of construction adhesive to the exposed tops of the cleats and joists, set the patch in

place, and nail it with 8d annular-ring finishing nails. In some cases you may have to make a second patch for a layer of underlayment over the subfloor. If the rotted area is around a closet flange (toilet drain), cut the patches in two, as shown.

If rot has damaged a floor joist, support the joist at both ends of the rotted section with temporary shoring and cut the section out. Then install a new joist next to the truncated joist. The new joist should be long enough to rest on the girders or other bearing members. If this is not possible, it should at least extend 4 feet beyond the cutout section in each direction. Nail the two joists together with 12d or 16d common nails along the top and bottom edges.

▶ *Floor over unheated crawl space is cold.*

Carefully fit R-19 fiberglass insulation batts between the floor joists, vapor barrier facing up. Use wire insulation supports to hold the batts in place. Be sure insulation fits against the rim, or band, joists but does not cover the foundation vents. In colder climates insulate the inside face of the foundation and kneewalls as well. First cover the bare dirt with a vapor barrier of 6 mil polyethylene sheeting. Bring it up the wall 6 inches, lap all joints at least 6 inches, tape them securely, and weight them down with stones. Then hang R-19 fiberglass batts against the foundation or kneewall, securing them by nailing wood lath along the top, into the foundation sill or rim joist. Each batt should extend down the wall and out onto the plastic vapor barrier 2 feet or more. Batts should butt together snugly. Insulate the rim joist. Lay lengths of 2x6 on the batts to prevent movement.

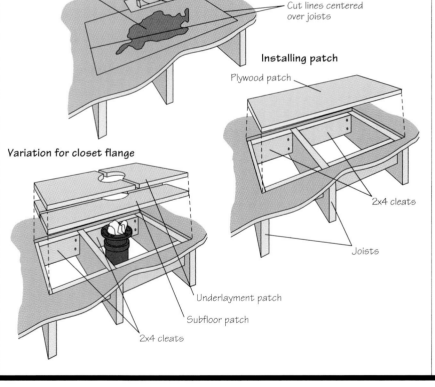

Cutting out damaged area

Damaged area

Cut lines centered over joists

Installing patch

Plywood patch

2x4 cleats

Joists

Variation for closet flange

Underlayment patch

Subfloor patch

2x4 cleats

Insulating a crawl space

Mudsill

Lath

Joist

Insulation

Subfloor

2'

2x6

Stones

Tape

Tape

Foundation

Vapor barrier

Tip *The areas most likely to have moisture problems are around the tub and toilet.*

Tip *When reinforcing a joist by nailing another one next to it, use 12d or 16d common nails spaced no farther than 12 inches apart along the top and bottom edges and 16 inches apart in the middle area. Drive the nails at opposing angles to keep the boards from separating. As you drive each nail, be sure the boards are clinched together; if necessary, use clamps to draw them together before nailing.*

▶ Floor over basement or garage is cold.

Install carpeting over insulating panels of high-density hardboard. These panels, designed for this purpose, are ½ inch thick and 4 feet square. Do not install them in bathrooms, over concrete, or on other surfaces where moisture may be present. Following manufacturer's recommendations, nail them to the floor, then install the pad and carpet.

▶ Concrete slab is cold.

Install carpet over a thick, dense urethane foam pad. Consult a local carpet dealer for additional recommendations. If you prefer a different floor covering, it is possible to install a false wood floor over 2-by sleepers with rigid foam insulation between the sleepers. Consult an experienced builder or floor specialist for specific details; moisture must be controlled or the wood will warp and eventually rot.

▶ Carpet is dirty.

If you want your carpet cleaned professionally, look for a reputable, bonded, and insured company that is willing to guarantee its work. Ask what methods they employ—the most common are steam/extraction, shampooing, and absorbent (dry) cleaning—and whether any chemicals they use might be irritating to crawling babies, pets, or other family members. If they use a steam/ extraction method, ask what percentage of the water and chemicals will be removed; it should be 85 to 95 percent. If they use water, ask how long it will take for the carpet to dry completely. If they use a dry compound or solution that dries to a powder, ask if they remove all of it; any residue will quickly attract dirt.

If you are cleaning carpets yourself, the best approach is to rent a heavy-duty deep-cleaning machine: steam/extraction, shampooing, or absorbent cleaning. All are effective, but each has distinct disadvantages with certain types of carpet. Steam uses water, which must be removed almost completely to prevent mildew and quick resoiling. It is risky to use on wool carpets and may take the twist out of some other fibers. Shampooing machines have a rotary action that may damage plush, shag, cut-and-loop, or frieze (twist) carpets. Dry cleaning requires a very strong vacuum cleaner to remove the absorbent cleaning material afterward, which would otherwise attract dirt quickly after cleaning. Get complete instructions from the rental agent. Also be sure that you vacuum your carpets thoroughly before cleaning them.

▶ Carpet has spilled liquid.

Spills happen. Be calm. With most spills the trick is to act quickly, before they dry and become stains. Blot the spot gently with white paper towels or a soft, clean cloth. (For nongreasy liquids you could also use a large, moist sponge). Do not rub! It only loosens the nap and makes the carpet yarn better able to absorb stains. Change towels or rinse out the sponge and repeat several times. When the towel or sponge no longer absorbs any liquid from the carpet, pour some cold water on the spot to dilute any colored residue. Blot to remove as much water as possible. To be sure all the color from the spill is out of the carpet, blot (don't rub) the wet spot with a white cloth or paper towel. If a stain does emerge, see right. Otherwise, cover the spot with a stack of white paper towels, weight them down, and leave them for four to six hours.

▶ Carpet has spilled mess.

Scrape up as much material as possible and follow procedure for liquids. To reduce odors apply a solution of 1 tablespoon ammonia in ¾ cup water; blot it up. Wash the area with a detergent-and-vinegar solution (see below); then blot, rinse with cold water, and blot dry.

▶ Carpet has mud tracks.

Use none of the procedures for other kinds of damage. Rather, let the mud dry and vacuum it up. If stains are left, see below.

▶ Carpet has candle wax.

Uh-oh. Try placing a cardboard blotter or small stack of paper towels over the wax, then use an iron or hair dryer to heat the wax so it will melt into the blotter. Watch the temperature carefully to avoid overheating or even burning the carpet fibers.

▶ Carpet has chewing gum.

Freeze the gum—several ice cubes in a plastic bag work well. When the gum is frozen, break it into pieces and lift them away from the carpet.

▶ Carpet has stains.

Determine the cause. Water-soluble stains can be washed out with a mild solution of 1 teaspoon white vinegar, 1 teaspoon powdered (or equivalent liquid) detergent, and 1 quart warm water. Pour some over the spot and scrub gently with a soft brush. After scrubbing, blot up as much liquid as possible (see

Tip   *Vacuum your carpets at least once a week (some experts recommend daily). The best types of vacuums have a beater bar, not just straight suction. Take six or seven strokes over each section of carpet—long, slow strokes if the vacuum has a beater bar, short strokes if not. Once or twice a year move heavy furniture and vacuum under it.*

opposite page). Rinse with cold water and blot again.

Greasy stains, including lipstick and crayon, require solvents or stronger cleaners. An all-purpose household cleaner may work; read the label and follow directions. For a stronger cleaner, try trichloroethylene. Ready-made carpet solvents also work but are risky to use because they can dissolve the latex backing glue. In all cases test the product first on an inconspicuous section of the carpet. Wipe it up with a damp sponge.

Urine, vomit, and pet messes leave very persistent stains. If they are not cleaned up immediately before they dry, try treating the stain with ammonia. Apply a solution of 1 tablespoon ammonia in ¾ cup water; blot it up. Follow with a solution of 1 part vinegar in 2 parts water. Then rinse with cold water and blot dry. If you have several such stains, it is best to have the carpet professionally cleaned.

▶ Carpet has burn spot.

If the burn is superficial, you may be able to trim off the charred fiber tips with scissors and clean the area with liquid detergent. Follow up by cleaning again with a solution of 1 part white vinegar in 2 parts water.

If a small area is badly burned, use a sharp knife to cut away the tuft of charred fibers by carefully slicing it off flush with the backing material. Cut a replacement tuft from a scrap or hidden section of identical carpet. Glue it in place with hot-melt or all-purpose glue. Then carefully trim the top of the replacement to match the height of surrounding fibers.

Replace larger burns with a patch (see right).

▶ Carpet has damaged area.

Replace the damaged area with a patch. First, with a sharp utility knife and framing square, cut out the damaged section in a rectangular shape, parting the nap first so it will be easier to slice through the carpet backing without shredding yarn unnecessarily (the more threads intact, the better the seam). Cut a replacement patch from a carpet scrap or the back of a closet, using the damaged section as a pattern. Cut the patch with the pile leaning the same direction as the original. Check for fit.

The easiest (but not strongest) way to seam the patch is with double-faced carpet tape. Stick the tape to the floor or pad, centering it under the edges. Peel off the protective paper and press the patch into place. You can strengthen the bond by applying carpet-seam cement to the edges of the backing before setting the patch in place. You can also seam with needle and thread or, for the strongest and cleanest seam, heat-bond tape. See page 34.

For small areas obtain a circular cutting tool from a carpet supplier, plus a few adhesive disks. The tool works like a cookie cutter and ensures that the cutout and patch are identical. Cut out the damaged area, then cut out a patch. Adhere the adhesive disk, sticky side up, to the bottom of the hole and press the patch into place.

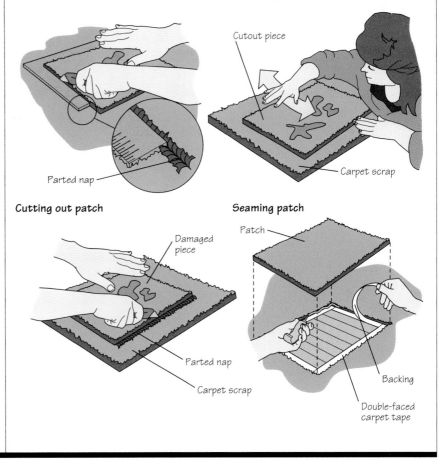

Cutting out damaged area

Parted nap

Checking pile

Cutout piece

Carpet scrap

Cutting out patch

Damaged piece

Parted nap

Carpet scrap

Seaming patch

Patch

Backing

Double-faced carpet tape

Tip *Some stains are very difficult to remove, especially those with pigments (paint, stain), dyes (ink, nail polish), or tannins (grape juice, red wine). Use only a stain removal method recommended for that stain, or call a professional.*

▶ Carpet has large faded or worn areas.

Try a new furniture arrangement or cover the areas with accent rugs. If you have a large scrap of identical carpet, you can probably have the worn area patched, although a perfect color match may not be possible due to fading and wear. Consult a professional installer.

▶ Carpet has tear or loose seam.

Sew up the rip with a heavy curved needle and linen carpet thread or fishing line. Thread the needle with about 5 feet of thread, double the thread, and knot it. Starting at one end of the tear, push the needle into one edge of the seam and pull it up through the opposite edge. Pliers will help you push and pull the needle through the tough carpet backing. Work along the length of the tear, using a basic loop stitch. The carpet nap should cover the seam; be sure to keep the nap out of the stitches. Tie off the thread and groom the seam with small scissors.

For long rips and seams, use heat-bond tape, available through carpet suppliers. You will also need to rent a carpet-seaming iron, or use an old iron (steam is not necessary). First tidy up the tear so the two edges can be pressed together with no debris or carpet nap between them. Then cut a strip of tape slightly longer than the tear. Tuck it under the seam so it lies on the carpet pad, glue side up, with the seam centered over it. Heat the iron to 250° F and, starting at one end, separate the carpet so you can set the hot iron directly on the tape; then slowly glide the iron along the tape. As you do this, reach back with your other hand and pinch the carpet seam together,

pressing it down onto the heated glue of the tape. Have a helper set heavy objects on the bonded seam as you press it together. When you reach the end of the seam, pull the iron away from the tape carefully to avoid getting hot glue all over the carpet. Quickly set it down on a board (placed in position ahead of time) and finish pressing the seam together and setting weights on it. Remove all the weights after 5 to 10 minutes and groom the seam with small scissors.

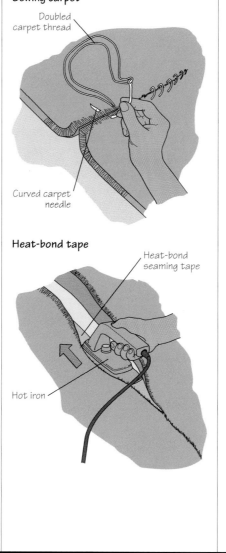

Sewing carpet

Doubled carpet thread

Curved carpet needle

Heat-bond tape

Heat-bond seaming tape

Hot iron

▶ Carpet is loose.

If a small area is wrinkled or loose, have a helper assist in pulling a section of carpet loose from the nearest edge. Then stretch the carpet tightly back to the wall and force it down on the tack strip. You may be able to rent a knee kicker to make this easier. With a putty knife or other wide, blunt tool, tuck the carpet edge in between the wall and nailing strip, making sure that the tucking operation does not force the carpet off the pins of the tack strip. If there are several loose areas, or the carpet is too stiff to stretch, rent a knee kicker. Pull a short section of carpet up along the edge, as described above, but use the kicker to force it back onto the tack strip instead of doing it by hand. If the entire carpet is loose, call an installer.

Stretching carpet by hand

Putty knife

Using a knee kicker

Knee kicker

Knob adjusts bite

Tip *To brighten dull-looking carpet, liberally sprinkle cornstarch over it and leave it alone for about an hour, then vacuum.*

▶ Padding is bunched up under carpet.

If the problem is extensive or is near the center of the room, call a carpet installer. Either the pad was not installed properly or it is disintegrating. If the problem is small and located near a corner, pull back just enough carpet to expose the problem area. Straighten out the pad and staple or tack it securely to the floor. If the problem was a loose seam between two pieces of pad, place duct tape over the seam. Then flop the carpet back in position and stretch it onto the tack strip (see opposite page).

▶ Carpet has depressions from heavy furniture.

The bent and compressed fibers should straighten out with the help of moisture. Place an ice cube on each depression. The gradual release of moisture will help the fibers to expand slowly as the moisture evaporates from them. If this does not work, periodically direct steam onto the dents from a steam iron or humidifier without soaking the carpet. Gently coaxing the carpet strands with a soft brush may also help.

▶ Carpet causes static electricity.

This is a common problem with older nylon carpets (but not with newer generations of nylon). For short-term relief, apply antistatic spray to the carpet, according to directions on the label. Be careful— oil-based sprays might attract dirt. A longer-lasting solution is to use a humidifier.

▶ Carpet is wet from flooding or leaks.

Synthetic carpets (such as nylon, polyester, and acrylics) will not mildew, but their jute backings will. Therefore, pull up the wet sections of the carpet and turn them over, exposing the backs to air circulation. For best results get them off the floor so air can also circulate underneath. Improvise a drying frame with chairs, sawhorses, or boards. A portable heater or heat lamp also helps; keep it from direct contact with carpet or other materials.

Carpets of organic fibers, such as wool or cotton, mildew easily. They should be dried more quickly. Use a clothesline, large dryer, or professional cleaner, depending on the type and value of the carpet.

A wet pad should also be pulled up in order to ventilate the floor itself. Rubber and foam pads can be dried out and saved, although they are inexpensive to replace and may not be worth the effort. Jute and horsehair pads are very difficult to dry out and are probably not worth the effort.

▶ Glued-down carpet needs removing.

If you're removing a cushion-backed carpet and not replacing it, there will probably be scraps of backing and adhesive residue left after the carpet is pulled up, which can be difficult to remove. Be sure the floor is worth preserving before you go through all the effort to restore it (it may be easier to lay down a new subfloor and floor covering).

First try scraping off the scraps with a flat shovel or floor scraper. If that doesn't work, rent an industrial floor buffer with a fiber pad. Get instructions for using the buffer

from the rental agent. Have a helper vacuum the floor as you buff it, to eliminate flying dust. After buffing, you may still need to rent a floor sander to remove the adhesive residue or stains. (See page 41.)

Removing residue of glued-down carpet

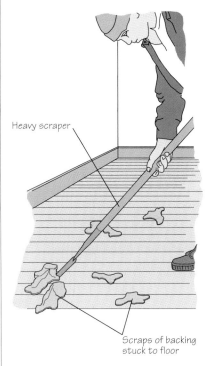

Heavy scraper

Scraps of backing stuck to floor

▶ New carpet has strong odor.

The odor is caused by chemical emissions from the adhesives and other components used to manufacture the carpet. Most, if not all, manufacturers subscribe to strict industry standards to ensure that these emissions remain at safe levels, although they may be obnoxious. To remove the odor as quickly as possible after installation, ventilate the room for 48 to 72 hours. Leave doors and windows open, if

Tip   *The most common type of carpet padding used today is rebonded foam rubber, which looks like bits of rubber floating around in a blue, gray, or green soup. Quality varies with the density and weight of the material.*

possible, and increase the flow of fresh air by placing a fan where it will exhaust room air through a window. If your home has a ventilating system that exhausts air to the outside (rather than circulating it within the house), run that too.

If the new carpet has not been installed yet, vacuum the old carpet just before removal; then vacuum the floor immediately after the carpet and pad are removed. Open windows and run exhaust fans during installation. If you or someone else in the house is unusually sensitive to the emissions, request that the dealer or installer unroll the carpet in a well-ventilated area for a day or two prior to installation, and make arrangements to be away from the house during installation and for a day or two after installation, if recommended.

▶ Resilient flooring looks dirty or dull.

If dust mopping or damp mopping with clear water doesn't spruce up the floor enough, apply a coat of water-based vinyl floor wax (unless the flooring is no-wax vinyl, which should be polished with a no-wax finish). Do not use a paste wax or other solvent-based finish on a vinyl floor. If the floor still looks dull, you will have to strip off all the old layers of wax or polish and start over. Apply a solution of 1 gallon warm water, 1 cup ammonia, and ½ cup TSP to the floor. Let it soak into the wax for a few minutes, then scrub with a brush or floor polisher. Wipe up the solution with a sponge mop, or squeegee it into a dustpan. Rinse the floor with clean water and let it dry thoroughly before rewaxing.

▶ Resilient flooring is scratched.

You can "erase" a small scratch by rubbing over it lightly with the edge of a coin. Fill deeper scratches and gouges (on unpatterned floors) with a homemade paste. Grate or scrape flakes from an identical scrap of flooring, grind or chop them into a fine powder, and mix the powder with white glue (clear nail polish, acetone, shellac, or polyurethane might also work). Protect the area around the gouge with masking tape and, with a putty knife, smooth the paste into the crevice. When dry, sand smooth with fine steel wool. Restore the shine with clear nail polish or floor wax. Acceptable substitutes for the paste are tub-and-tile caulk (mixed with latex paint to match color) or epoxy glue mixed with acrylic paint.

Making paste for repairing resilient flooring

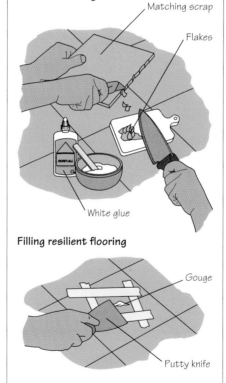

Matching scrap

Flakes

White glue

Filling resilient flooring

Gouge

Putty knife

▶ Resilient flooring has stains.

Try your usual floor polish, following its instructions. Ammonia, vinegar, or undiluted liquid laundry detergent might also work. Other stain removers include charcoal lighter fluid, liquid bleach, paint thinner, and rubbing alcohol. Test the cleaner in an inconspicuous place before using it. Wipe it up quickly to avoid damaging the floor finish.

▶ Resilient flooring has chewing gum or paint.

Scrape up as much as possible with a putty knife or spatula. Remove what remains with a small amount of dry-cleaning fluid or paint thinner (except on rubber tile—try buffing lightly with fine sandpaper).

▶ Resilient flooring has blister.

Blisters or bubbles are sometimes caused by poor installation, but more often by moisture wicking up through the subfloor. First inspect under the floor for a moisture source and, if you find one, eliminate it. To repair a small bubble, poke a tiny hole in the center with a large sewing needle or sharp wire to let out trapped air; allow any moisture to evaporate. Then lay a towel or aluminum foil over the area and press it with a warm iron to soften and flatten the bubble. The heat will also soften the old adhesive. Place wax paper on the area and weight it down for a few hours to get the area to adhere. If the old adhesive doesn't stick, inject glue through the hole with a glue syringe, place wax paper over the area, and replace the weights.

To repair large blisters, place a towel or foil over the area and press it with a warm iron to soften the flooring. With a sharp blade, slice across the blister and ½ inch beyond on each side; allow any

Tip *When trying any cleaning or repairing technique, experiment in a hidden corner first to see how it affects the floor material.*

Tip *If the old floor looks dated and replacing it is too expensive, get creative. Resilient sheet flooring and tile lend themselves to patchwork. Buy a small remnant of sheet flooring or a few bright tiles and inlay a border, an accent strip, or some brightly colored squares to liven up a dull, monotonous floor.*

moisture to evaporate. Scrape and vacuum away any specks of debris, then dab some adhesive into the cavity with a putty knife. Press down on the blister and remove adhesive residue with lacquer thinner. Cover the repair with wax paper and weight it down. After 24 hours remove the weights and apply seam sealer to the slit.

Repairing small blister

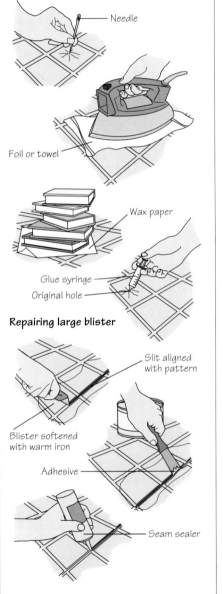

Needle

Foil or towel

Wax paper

Glue syringe

Original hole

Repairing large blister

Slit aligned with pattern

Blister softened with warm iron

Adhesive

Seam sealer

▶ *Resilient flooring is torn, burned, or damaged.*

Repair damaged area with a replacement patch. Lay a scrap of identical flooring over the damaged area, with patterns aligned, and tape it to the floor. With a sharp utility knife and straightedge, cut through both layers of flooring at the same time. Where possible, align cut lines with pattern lines. Set the patch aside. Remove the remaining scrap and the damaged cutout, carefully scrape away the adhesive residue, and vacuum away all debris. With a notched trowel, spread flooring adhesive onto the underlayment, then press the patch into place. Clean off excess adhesive with recommended solvent, then, following label instructions, carefully apply seam sealer to seams.

Cutting patch

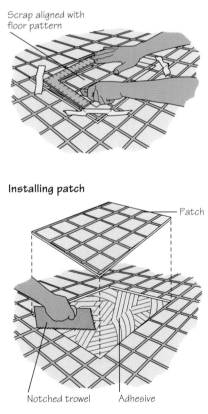

Scrap aligned with floor pattern

Installing patch

Patch

Notched trowel   Adhesive

▶ *Resilient flooring telegraphs bumps or cracks.*

Because they're thin, resilient flooring materials easily "telegraph" subsurface imperfections to the surface. Cracks between underlayment panels, nail heads, even specks of grit create grooves, dimples, and bumps on the floor surface. There is no way to smooth them out because they are trapped under the flooring material. All you can do is wait until you install new flooring to create a perfectly smooth underlayment. Until then, try to minimize their effect by balancing or changing light sources (shading windows, changing location of lamps, adding new lights).

▶ *Edge of resilient flooring is coming loose.*

First check for moisture problems, especially around bathtubs and sinks, and fix the source of the problem. Then carefully clean out any old caulk or other debris from under the flap and press it down gently. Some materials are supple enough that you can simply staple or tack down the edge and cover it with baseboard. If the edge is too stiff to force down easily, you will have to heat it first. Use a warm iron over aluminum foil, a heat gun, or a hair dryer. Soften the flooring enough to press down; then tack it with HDG annular-ring nails, or, if the material is flexible enough, with adhesive instead of nails. Recaulk the joint if the flooring abuts a bathtub.

▶ *Resilient tile is loose, damaged, or missing.*

To remove a damaged tile, cover it with a clean towel and heat with a hair dryer, heat gun, or hot iron. Pop the tile up with a putty knife. Scrape off adhesive residue from the

Tip *Flooring materials have varying tolerances for cleaning agents. If the flooring is vinyl or vinyl-asbestos, do not use nail polish remover. If the flooring is asphalt or rubber tile, do not use nail polish remover, turpentine, or lighter fluid. If the flooring is cork, do not use chlorine bleach. Avoid using abrasive scouring powder on any resilient flooring.*

underlayment and vacuum up all debris. With a notched trowel, spread the adhesive recommended for the replacement tile; set the new tile in place. If you don't have a re-placement tile that matches, remove one from a closet or hidden corner (under the refrigerator, perhaps).

▶ Resilient flooring needs removing.

Old flooring may contain asbestos fibers; to be safe, assume it does (today's products do not). These fibers are classified as "encapsu-lated," not "friable," which means that they are locked into the floor-ing material and present no danger of becoming airborne so long as the flooring is not cut, torn, abraded, or broken up. For this reason it is preferable to install new flooring over old, rather than run the risk of releasing the asbestos fibers. How-ever, if removal is necessary, there are certain precautions you must follow. The following work prac-tices include recommendations by the Resilient Floor Covering Insti-tute; check local regulations for additional requirements.

• Never work with asbestos-containing materials without wear-ing a MSHA-NIOSH–approved respirator for asbestos.

• Seal off interior doorways with plastic sheeting. Transfer the debris directly to the outdoors as you remove it.

• Never sand or abrade the flooring surface or backing.

• Never remove flooring, back-ing, or residual adhesives dry. Before pulling up or scraping an area, cut it into strips with a utility knife, then moisten the backing with a solution of 1 ounce liquid dishwashing deter-gent in 1 gallon water, applied by sprayer. The detergent must contain anionic, nonionic, and amphoteric surfactants. Check the label.

• Never sweep up debris; use a tank-type wet/dry vacuum cleaner (shop vac) with a disposable dust bag, a metal floor attachment (no brush), and a HEPA filter. Position the vacuum so the outtake air blows away from your work area, prefer-ably out a window. If you absolute-ly must sweep, wet the floor area with the detergent solution first.

• Place all debris in heavy-duty polyethylene bags (6 mil), seal the bags tightly, label them clearly as containing asbestos, and dispose of them at an approved site.

• Wear gloves at all times when handling the material. When fin-ished, remove and shake out your work clothes out of doors and shower immediately.

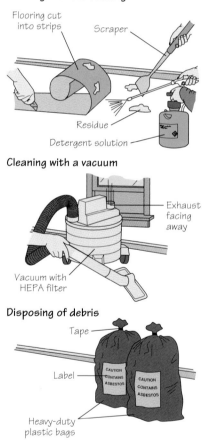

Wetting resilient backing

Flooring cut into strips
Scraper
Residue
Detergent solution

Cleaning with a vacuum

Exhaust facing away

Vacuum with HEPA filter

Disposing of debris

Tape
Label
CAUTION CONTAINS ASBESTOS
Heavy-duty plastic bags

▶ Old adhesive remains on the floor.

If adhesive residue remains on a finish floor after you remove the old flooring, try eradicating it with an adhesive remover available from flooring dealers. Follow all direc-tions on the label, especially regard-ing ventilation, protective clothing, and flammability.

▶ Old wood floor is dull and worn-looking.

If routine waxing does not renew the luster of an old wood floor and you are considering sanding and refinishing it, you may be able to restore it by removing all the layers of old wax and grime. To check, rub a small (hidden) area with steel wool dipped in alcohol until all layers of wax are removed. Then damp-mop the bare wood and apply a paste wax. If the results are satisfactory, clean the entire floor with a commercial wax stripper made for wood floors, or a solution of 1 gallon warm water, 1 cup de-natured alcohol or ammonia, and ½ cup TSP. Test the solution in a small area first. Apply the solution to the floor and let it soak in for a few minutes, then scrub with a brush or floor polisher. Wipe up the solution with a sponge or sponge mop. Rinse with clean water, or vacuum with a wet/dry shop vac. Allow to dry thoroughly, then apply a paste wax. *Note:* Floors that have a urethane finish should not be waxed.

▶ Waxed wood floor has marks or stains.

For water or alcohol marks try buff-ing with a damp cloth and mixture of 1 part toothpaste and 1 part baking soda; or rub the spot with fine steel wool and floor polish or wax. If the mark persists, rub

Tip *Routine care to keep your wood floors looking new: (1) Dust-mop frequently with an unoiled mop (unless your floors are oiled instead of waxed; then use an oiled mop). (2) Remove spots, marks, or stains as soon as they happen. (3) Wax periodically (one to six times per year, as necessary), but only in high-traffic areas to avoid waxy buildup over entire floor. Buff the entire floor.* Note: *Floors that have a urethane finish should not be waxed.*

with steel wool and odorless mineral spirits. Wash and rewax.

For black heel marks rub with fine steel wool and floor polish or wax.

For minor burns sand lightly, wash, dry, and rewax.

For chewing gum, wax, crayon, or tar, cover with ice cubes in a plastic bag. Scrape up the frozen material with a putty knife or spatula. Rub any residue with fine steel wool and odorless mineral spirits. Rewax.

For dark stains remove the wax or polish with TSP or a commercial wax stripper. Wash with vinegar and allow to soak in; then wipe dry. Repeat, if necessary. If the spot still remains, apply 1 tablespoon oxalic-acid crystals (read the label carefully for cautions and directions) dissolved in 1 cup water. Allow to soak until spot disappears; then wipe up with a damp cloth and rinse well. To see if the wood is still sealed, sprinkle with a few drops of water. If it beads up, the sealer is undamaged. If the drops soak into the wood, reseal with a wood sealer, then refinish with the appropriate wood stain. Rewax.

For grease or oil spills, wipe up immediately. Sponge with undiluted liquid dishwashing detergent. Sprinkle with baking soda and leave overnight. Wash with a general household cleaner containing ammonia. Rewax.

▶ Wood floor has scratches or gouges.

For superficial scratches try a putty crayon that matches the color of the floor. Deep scratches and gouges can be filled with wood filler matched to the color of the floor. (You can also make a paste of wood glue mixed with sawdust from a spare floorboard.) Clean the area to remove all the wax or oil.

With a putty knife, fill the gouge; after the filler sets, sand it smooth, and wax.

▶ Nails are protruding from wood floor.

Pull them out and replace them with annular-ring nails, matching the existing nailing pattern (see illustration below), and set the nail heads. Fill the holes with quick-drying wood filler stained to match the floor, or use a putty crayon of matching color.

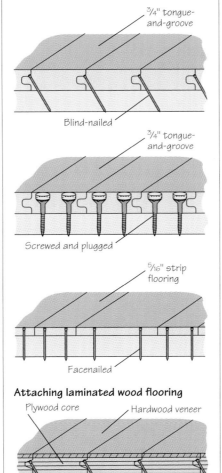

Attaching solid wood flooring

¾" tongue-and-groove

Blind-nailed

¾" tongue-and-groove

Screwed and plugged

⁵⁄₁₆" strip flooring

Facenailed

Attaching laminated wood flooring

Plywood core

Hardwood veneer

Blind-nailed   Subfloor

▶ Decorative plugs are missing from wood floor.

You may be able to obtain replacement plugs from a flooring dealer who specializes in wood floors. Otherwise, make plugs from hardwood dowels of the same diameter as the hole. Cut each plug slightly long, spread a thin layer of glue around the base, and tap it into place; wipe away excess glue immediately. After the glue sets, make the plug flush with the floor by sanding or by shaving it with a sharp chisel or a fine-toothed saw. (A hacksaw blade is flexible enough to bend, so you avoid scraping the floor around the plug; protect the floor with a piece of thin sheet metal.) Sand the plug smooth, stain it to match other plugs, and wax the area.

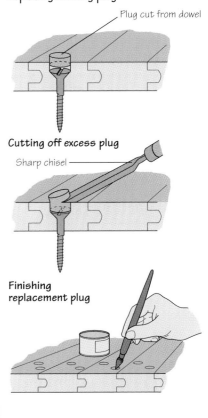

Replacing missing plug

Plug cut from dowel

Cutting off excess plug

Sharp chisel

Finishing replacement plug

Tip *How to wax a wood floor: (1) Move furniture out of the room or out of the high-traffic area you are waxing. (2) With a large cloth, rag mop, or wax applicator, spread the wax on 3-foot sections at a time. If using paste wax, apply a second coat to heavy traffic areas. Apply only one coat under large area rugs to reduce danger of slipping. (3) Buff by hand or with a buffing machine, following the grain of the wood. Labels generally advise that you allow paste wax to dry completely before buffing, but recommend you buff liquid waxes while they are still damp.*

SOLVING INDOOR PROBLEMS

▶ Floorboard is damaged and needs replacing.

If the damaged board is short, you can remove the entire board. Carefully split it and remove sections with a chisel and pry bar. If it is tongue-and-groove, remove the tongue with a sharp knife and pry up the entire board. If it is face-nailed square-edge (strip) flooring, simply drive the nails through the board with a nail set to release it.

If the damaged section is in a long board, mark a cut line square to the long edges of the board and bore large holes across the board inside the line (do not drill into the subfloor). Split out pieces of the damaged board and remove them, being careful not to damage adjacent boards. Carefully trim the board to the cut line with a sharp chisel. Sweep and vacuum away the debris. Cut a replacement board to the same length as the cavity and, if the flooring is tongue-and-groove, remove the bottom flange of the groove side of the replacement board. Set the board into place and check the fit. If the floor has been sanded and refinished in the past, the new board will be thicker than adjacent boards. Sand it down to match the level of adjacent boards before installing it. Predrill pilot holes for flooring nails or finishing nails at both ends of the new board, following the existing pattern. Nail, set the nail heads, and cover them with stainable putty (or with color-matched putty after finishing). Stain and finish the new board to match the old flooring, testing stains first on scrap pieces of wood, especially if the replacement board is a different species of wood from the original floor (red oak versus white oak, for example).

If adjacent boards are damaged, stagger the cut lines so the replacement boards won't look like an obvious patch.

Removing a short board

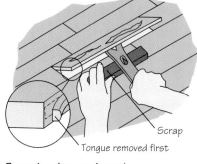

Scrap

Tongue removed first

Removing damaged section of a long board

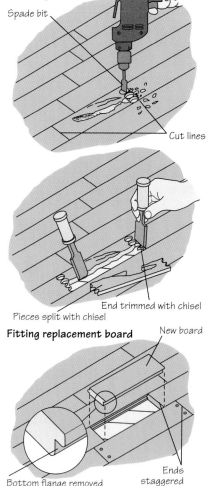

Spade bit

Cut lines

Pieces split with chisel

End trimmed with chisel

Fitting replacement board

New board

Bottom flange removed

Ends staggered

▶ Large area is damaged and needs replacing.

The best-looking repair is to cut out and replace each board individually (see left), so you can stagger the joints to avoid a patched look. A quicker fix is to cut out and replace the entire section as a rectangular patch of new boards. Use a framing square to mark the cut lines. If the floor is blind-nailed (tongue-and-groove boards), mark the cut lines slightly inside the board joints to avoid sawing into nails. Set the saw blade just deep enough to cut through the flooring but not into the subfloor. Cut carefully to avoid running the saw blade past the corners. You'll have to chisel out the parts of boards that the blade does not cut through.

After removing the damaged boards and cleaning out the debris, cut new floorboards to length and install them. If the boards are tongue-and-groove, remove the bottom flange (groove side) of the last board before installing it.

Cutting out damaged area

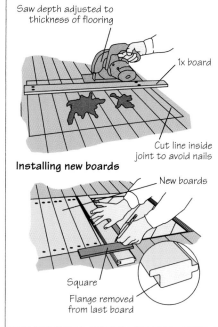

Saw depth adjusted to thickness of flooring

1x board

Cut line inside joint to avoid nails

Installing new boards

New boards

Square

Flange removed from last board

Tip *If removing floorboards reveals rot or damage to the subfloor, repair it before patching the finish floor.*

▶ *Wood floorboard is cupped or warped.*

Remove wax or finish and lay a damp towel over the board; keep it damp for 48 hours to moisten the wood and make it supple. Then force the board down with heavy weights and secure it to the sub-floor with screws. Screws can be driven into the flooring from below (see page 30) or from above (drill pilot holes and countersink the screws). Drive the screw as far as is possible without straining the board, then tighten it a half turn or so each day until the board is flat. Use enough screws to flatten

the board, spacing them approxi-mately 3 to 8 inches apart, then cover them with plugs or wood filler to match the flooring.

If two adjacent tongue-and-groove boards are warped enough that the joint has buckled, it may be impossible to realign the tongue into the groove. Instead, with a hooked knife or a saw set to a shal-low depth, remove the tongue from the moistened board and pull the resulting wood strip out of the joint. Then insert screws as just described.

Moistening floorboards

Screwing down floorboards

Fixing warped tongue-and-groove floorboards

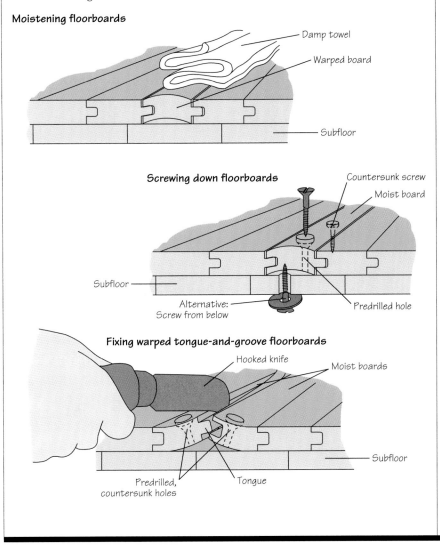

▶ *Wood floor needs sanding and refinishing.*

Sanding and refinishing a wood floor is a major undertaking, best done when the house is vacant or during a major renovation.

You will need a drum sander and a floor edger. Both machines are heavy-duty and require some strength to operate. Have the rental agent show you how; machines are not all alike. Pay attention to proce-dures for changing the sandpaper, lowering the drum, and emptying dust bags. You will need several grades of sandpaper in both sheets and disks. Take home plenty—you won't be charged for what you return unused.

Before sanding make sure the flooring is at least ¼ inch thick by inspecting the board ends at a floor register or by pulling up an incon-spicuous board. Then remove all furnishings, including curtains. Cover built-in units and doorways with plastic sheeting secured with masking tape. Remove baseboards. Fill deep holes, replace damaged boards, and set protruding nail heads. Make sure you have a dust mask and shoes with clean soles (not black rubber). You may also wish to wear ear protectors.

Strip floor: Start with a drum sander and the coarsest sandpaper (medium grade for new floors). Al-ways sand with the grain. Because the drum is constantly rotating, never let it engage the floor unless you are rolling the machine for-ward. Start near the center of one wall and a few inches away from it, standing with your side to the wall. Proceed toward the wall you are fac-ing and stop just before you reach it. Disengage the sanding drum and roll the machine back so the next pass will overlap the previous one by half the width of the drum. Continue, always starting at the

Tip *Estimated time for sanding and refinishing the floor of an average-sized room: Day 1 (two to five hours): Remove furniture, remove baseboards, make repairs, seal off room from the rest of the house, and rent equipment. Day 2 (three to four hours): Sand floor, return sanding equipment, vacuum, wipe floor with tack cloth, and apply stain or sealer. Day 3 (two hours): Rent floor buffer, buff floor, vacuum, wipe with tack cloth, and apply first coat of finish. Day 4 (one hour): Buff finish and apply final coat(s).*

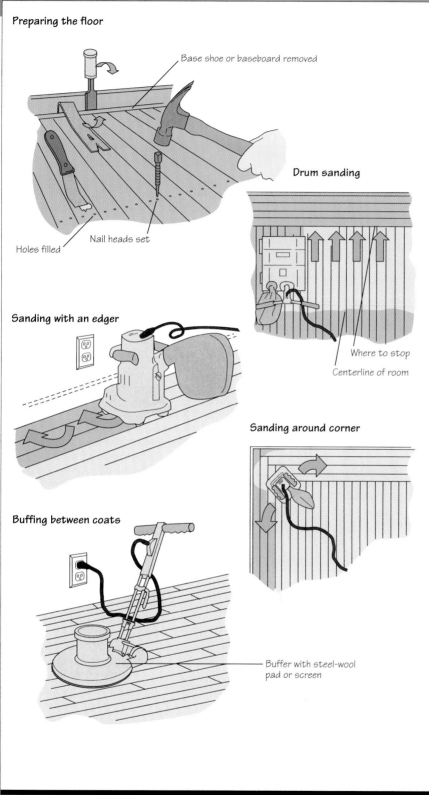

Preparing the floor

Base shoe or baseboard removed

Nail heads set

Holes filled

Drum sanding

Where to stop

Centerline of room

Sanding with an edger

Sanding around corner

Buffing between coats

Buffer with steel-wool pad or screen

midpoint and overlapping passes until you have finished half the room. Turn to face the opposite direction and complete the other half in the same way. Sand the border separately—with the grain—after you finish the main area.

After sanding the entire floor, repeat with the next finer grade sandpaper. Replace the paper when you no longer see any results; the finer paper wears out more quickly. When this second sanding is done, fill any remaining open cracks or nail holes with wood filler. When it dries, sand the entire floor with the fine-grit sandpaper.

Use an edge sander to sand along walls and in tight spaces. This rotary sander uses sandpaper disks, is faster than the drum sander, and is more prone to gouging. It also sands across the grain. Start out in closets or other hidden spaces until you get the feel of it. Using a scallop motion of small semicircles rather than a straight back-and-forth motion helps to avoid gouging. In corners where the border joins at right angles, turn the edger to go with the grain, and go back and forth around that turn several times. Again, sand first with the coarsest paper, then with medium, filling cracks and nail holes before the final sanding with fine-grit paper. Use a hand scraper and sanding block to get into awkward corners that the edger misses.

Parquet floors: Using coarse paper, sand the entire floor diagonally in one direction. Then sand diagonally at a right angle to the first direction with medium paper (thus forming an *x*). Finish with a fine grit, sanding parallel to one set of walls. Sand twice (make two passes) with each grit, always in the

Tip *Fine sanding dust, most floor finishes, and finish fumes are all flammable. Keep the room ventilated, extinguish pilot lights, and do not smoke while working. Empty dust bags and dispose of rags according to instructions from the rental agency or on the product labels.*

same direction. Use the edger as for strip floors. A parquet floor is likely to need a lot of filler, so buy a 1-gallon can and goop it on liberally before the final sanding.

All floors: Seal or stain the floor the same day that you finish sanding to prevent it from absorbing moisture from the air. Vacuum the floor and all horizontal surfaces in the room thoroughly, then wipe the floor with a tack cloth. Apply the sealer or stain with a sheepskin applicator, wiping away all excess after 10 or 15 minutes.

After the stain dries, buff the room with fine steel wool (#2/0)—unless the finish is water-based, in which case use window screening or very fine sandpaper; steel wool leaves particles that rust. Then vacuum and dust with a tack cloth. Apply the finish, according to instructions. Oil-based finishes require two coats, with 24 hours of drying time between coats; water-based finishes dry more quickly but require more coats. Lightly buff between coats.

▶ Heat registers don't match wood floor.

Warm-air heating systems often have vents, or registers, located in prominent places. If the appearance of an ordinary metal grille is not acceptable, you can obtain handsome wood grilles from flooring dealers or installers. They come in a variety of sizes and wood species. You can stain the unfinished wood to match your flooring, or choose a contrasting color. The grille fits flush with the surface of the floor, so you may have to trim the floor opening if the edges are ragged. The edges of the grille can also be trimmed to fit. Decorative brass grilles are also available, but usually only in standard dimensions.

▶ Wood floor on concrete slab is warped.

Wood floors installed over concrete slabs, especially in basements, are often exposed to moisture and unstable conditions that cause the wood to expand and contract, leading to warping, splits, and other problems. Solid-wood flooring is particularly sensitive to these conditions and may continue to be so even if you replace individual warped boards.

The best solution, if you want a permanently durable wood floor, is to install prefinished, laminated (veneer) wood flooring in place of the solid-wood floor. Because it is thinner (⅜ inch) than most solid-wood flooring and because the veneers (plies) are oriented in different directions, this type of flooring does not expand and contract easily. Tongue-and-groove joints on the edges and on the ends, consistent dimensions, and adhesive bonding make this flooring easy to install. Some types may be attached directly to the

concrete slab with a recommended adhesive (so long as the concrete is structurally sound and free of moisture problems). Where there is any danger at all of dampness coming through the basement floor, install the wood floor by "floating" it on a ⅛-inch-thick foam pad laid over 6 mil plastic sheeting. The boards are glued together at their edges, but not to the floor—hence, a "floating" floor. Install according to manufacturer's instructions.

A second way to install a wood floor if there's danger of dampness is to install a wood subfloor over the concrete: Lay down a moisture barrier of 6 mil polyethylene sheeting; attach 2x4 pressure-treated sleepers to the floor with a nailing gun; nail ¾-inch plywood to the sleepers (leave ¹⁄₁₆- to ⅛-inch expansion gaps around the panels). If the floor needs insulation, install foam panels between the sleepers.

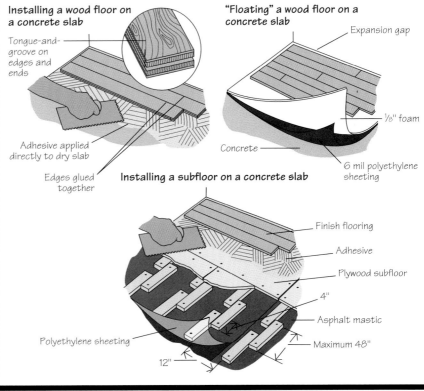

Installing a wood floor on a concrete slab

Tongue-and-groove on edges and ends

Adhesive applied directly to dry slab

Edges glued together

"Floating" a wood floor on a concrete slab

Expansion gap

⅛" foam

Concrete

6 mil polyethylene sheeting

Installing a subfloor on a concrete slab

Finish flooring

Adhesive

Plywood subfloor

4"

Asphalt mastic

Maximum 48"

Polyethylene sheeting

12"

Tip *The most popular wood-floor finishes are polyurethane, which are available in oil-based or water-based forms. The water-based ones emit fewer volatile organic compounds (VOCs) and are easier to touch up or recoat, but they are harder to spread and require more coats. Follow label directions carefully and, to ensure compatibility, use sealers, stains, and finishes from the same manufacturer.*

▶ Wood floor has carpet adhesive on it.

See page 35.

▶ Slate floor needs cleaning.

For routine cleaning, vacuum thoroughly and wash with a mild solution of water and washing soda or laundry detergent. Do not scour with abrasive pads and powders. If the floor is dull from waxy buildup, remove the old wax with a commercial floor wax remover. Experiment in a hidden area first. If it doesn't work, TSP or a water-based paint stripper may work; test first. After scrubbing the floor and letting it dry, apply a penetrating tile-and-brick sealer. If you prefer a softer sheen, apply a paste wax instead; use one with carnauba (test first; some stone is not porous enough to hold the wax and it will just come off on people's shoes). However, you will have to renew it every few months and remove the wax buildup when it becomes dull and dingy.

Clean stains with phosphoric acid diluted in water, following label directions.

▶ Quarry tiles need cleaning.

Use the same techniques as for a slate floor (see above).

▶ Ceramic-tile floor is old and needs replacing.

Before you tear it out and replace it, consider painting the tiles or installing new tiles directly over them. The present floor must be free of cracks and the subfloor structurally sound.

For painting, the surface must be roughened, usually by sanding (which you can do yourself), or by acid etching (which requires a professional). Then you can paint the floor with epoxy paint.

If the present installation is sound and the new tiles will not create a height or weight problem, install new tiles over old with epoxy adhesives. Roughen the old tiles, as described above, and remove the dust with a damp sponge. Fill in grout depressions with new adhesive. Install the new tiles.

▶ Floor tile is cracked and needs replacing.

See page 46.

▶ Baseboard doesn't touch flooring.

Unless the gap is more than ⅛ inch, this condition is desirable. It prevents the baseboard from interfering with the normal expansion and contraction of resilient or wood flooring materials. If the gap exceeds ⅛ inch, nail a base shoe into the baseboard—not the floor. Place cardboard shims under the shoe while nailing it, so there will still be a ⅛-inch gap.

▶ Corner joint of baseboard has gap.

Corner joints may open up as the house settles or the baseboards shrink. Outside corners, which are mitered, are more prone to reveal a gap than inside corners, which are usually coped. If a miter joint gap is small, fill it with plastic wood filler, or, if the board is painted, nonshrinking spackling compound. Work the patching material into the crack and roughly contour it with a putty knife or your finger. After it sets, sand it to the same shape as the baseboard profile and finish it to match the baseboard. Larger gaps may require replacing

one or both sections of baseboard. See page 29 for instructions on making corners.

▶ Baseboard is damaged.

See page 28.

▶ Baseboard is too plain.

If the baseboards are a modern style with simple lines and you want something more traditional and ornate, you may not have to replace the baseboards completely. You may be able to add molding strips to the existing baseboards to create a more elaborate profile. Obtain samples of small molding strips, such as base shoe, chair rail, picture molding, or fluted bead, and experiment with various arrangements to see if they can be combined with existing baseboard to create a more appropriate style. If so, install them using techniques described on page 28. Be sure to nail all the pieces into the baseboard or wall, not the floor.

Adding molding to baseboard

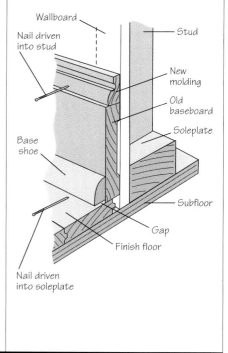

Wallboard
Nail driven into stud
Stud
New molding
Old baseboard
Soleplate
Base shoe
Subfloor
Gap
Finish floor
Nail driven into soleplate

Tip *When painting baseboards that have carpet installed against them, use a paint shield (or thin sheet of metal or stiff plastic; a spare slat from miniblinds works well) to hold the carpet tufts away from the baseboard as you paint it. Wipe off the shield every time you move it.*

▶ Tile is dirty, stained, or mildewed.

For general cleaning of glazed tile, use a commercial scrubbing foam, a mild detergent, or a solution of ½ gallon water and ¼ cup ammonia. For stains caused by mineral deposits, wipe with vinegar or a solution of equal parts ammonia and water; then rinse. For other stains, mix TSP or washing soda with just enough water to make a paste. Apply it to the stain, holding it in place with tape if it won't stick. Leave it for several hours, rewetting when necessary. Remove the cleaner by rubbing it with vinegar. For stubborn stains, use oxalic acid, following label directions carefully. For mildew, spray with commercial mildew cleaner or a chlorine bleach solution, as recommended on the bleach label. Then wipe with a solution of baking soda and water to remove the chlorine odor. Most of these treatments involve agents that contain acids or alkalines, which can break down the portland cements used in grout, so use them sparingly. Use mild detergents or tile cleaners for routine cleaning. For unglazed tiles, such as quarry tile, always use mild detergent. Avoid acid-based cleaners.

▶ Marble or other stone tiles are dirty or stained.

Clean with a mild solution of soap flakes or marble cleaner. Rinse well with water and let dry. Do not use ammonia, vinegar, or any cleaners with acids or alkalines.

To remove stains from marble, make a paste of soap flakes and hydrogen peroxide. Spread it on the stain; rub in the direction of the grain. Rinse well with water and let dry. Repolish, if necessary, with whiting powder (calcium carbonate).

▶ Grout is dirty or stained.

To clean stubborn dirt from grout, use a stiff brush (a grout brush or old toothbrush works well) with scouring powder that does not contain bleach. Test the cleaner in a concealed area to make sure it doesn't discolor the grout. For stubborn stains use a mild solution of water and phosphoric acid, according to label directions; increase the concentration of acid, if necessary. Wear rubber gloves and avoid spilling the acid solution on glass shower doors; it may etch them (but not your skin—this type of acid shouldn't irritate any but the most sensitive skin, if you follow all label precautions).

▶ Grout is deteriorating or missing.

For small touch-up work, replace missing areas of grout with color-matched caulk. To replace large areas of damaged or missing grout, first remove all remnants of the old grout with a grout saw. This is a tedious job; there is no shortcut. Work it back and forth along each grout line. After removing the grout, vacuum out the cracks. Look for loose tiles, deteriorating subsurface, or other damage that may have caused the grout to fail; fix before proceeding.

Remove soap scum and other residue from the tile surface by washing it with phosphoric acid and water, mixed according to label directions (see above). Wait until the area dries completely to mix the grout.

Grout comes in many colors, so you should be able to match the existing grout by checking samples at a tile shop. For installations with wide grout lines, use sanded grout. For wet installations (showers, tubs, countertops), mix the grout powder with a latex or vinyl additive instead of water. For kitchen countertops use epoxy worktop grout; it's waterproof and resists dirt, bacteria, and stains.

Apply grout with a rubber float, spreading it diagonally in both directions across the joint lines and packing it firmly into the cracks. Remove the excess with a damp sponge. After about 30 minutes shape the joints with the damp sponge to match the original grout. Wait another hour, then polish the tile with a soft cloth. After the grout sets (usually 24 to 48 hours), apply a grout sealer according to label directions.

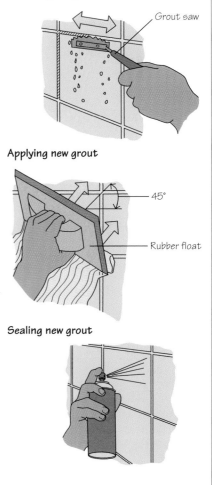

Removing old grout

Grout saw

Applying new grout

45°

Rubber float

Sealing new grout

Tip *Ammonia or cleaners containing acid should never be mixed with chlorine; it makes a poisonous gas. Never mix chlorinated laundry bleach with other cleaning products.*

Tip *Extend grout life by applying a grout sealer once or twice a year, according to label directions. Use silicone-based sealers in tubs and showers, but not on kitchen surfaces where food is prepared. Use natural lemon oil instead. For most sealers, the grout must be completely dry before sealing and must not be wet for a certain time after sealing, which will prevent use of the shower or tub. For greatest convenience, do only one bathroom at a time, or plan this procedure around vacations.*

▶ Grout around bathtub is missing or damaged.

The joint around a bathtub where the wall meets the tub is an important moisture seal and must be maintained to prevent structural damage. It should be sealed with caulk, not grout. (The vertical corners above a bathtub or shower floor, where tiled walls join at an angle, should also be sealed with caulk.) To renew a joint, scrape out all of the old grout (or caulk) with a grout saw, screwdriver, or similar tool. Then vacuum away the debris and clean the area thoroughly with vinegar or a phosphoric acid solution of 1 part acid in 10 parts water. Let it dry. Apply a bead of tub-and-tile caulk (specified as 100 percent silicone) to the joint. Smooth the caulk with a moistened finger or old spoon dipped in soapy water. Wipe away excess with a rag. While you are at it, recaulk any gaps around faucet handles, spouts, and showerheads. Moisture that leaks into these gaps can cause serious problems.

Removing old grout or caulk

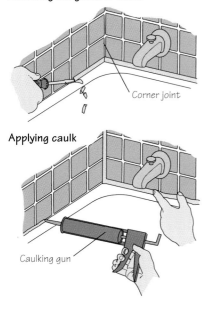

Corner joint

Applying caulk

Caulking gun

▶ Grout color is unappealing.

The most reliable way to change the color of grout is to replace it (see page 45), but you may be able to stain grout if it has not been sealed. Choose an acceptable stain color and experiment in a hidden area. Using a nylon-bristled brush, clean the grout with scouring powder or a mild solution of phosphoric acid and water. Let it dry. With a small artist's brush, apply the stain to the grout. Keep lines straight and avoid getting stain on the tile surface. After the stain dries thoroughly, apply a penetrating sealer that can be used over colored grout, following label directions.

▶ Tile is cracked or loose.

Remove the old tile. If it's loose, you should be able to pop it up with a screwdriver (don't wedge the screwdriver against adjacent tiles). If not, you'll have to break the old tile and chip out the pieces. Wear heavy gloves and eye protection—broken tile is very sharp. Cover any drains and protect surrounding surfaces with newspaper or cardboard. First remove the grout around the damaged tile (see page 45) so hammer blows won't jar adjacent tiles. Then break up the tile with short, sharp hammer blows; chip away the pieces with the hammer and a cold chisel. Carefully chisel away all adhesive residue and any leftover grout. Don't use chemical removers to clean off the old adhesive; it will weaken the bond of the new and surrounding adhesive. Fill depressions in the backing with patching compound and paint it with latex primer.

Dry-fit the replacement tile to make sure that it doesn't protrude above the surrounding tiles. Attach it with the same type of adhesive as the original (thin-set resembles cement mortar; organic mastic resembles hardened rubber). Apply adhesive to the back of the tile with a notched trowel to within ½ inch of each edge. Twist the tile slightly as you position it. Use a rubber mallet or a hammer and woodblock to tap the tile firmly into place. Remove excess adhesive, especially from inside the joint crack. To keep the tile aligned as the adhesive sets, place matchsticks, shims, or tile spacers in the joints; on vertical surfaces, secure the tile with tape. After the adhesive sets (24 to 48 hours), remove the shims and grout the joints (see page 45).

Removing broken tile

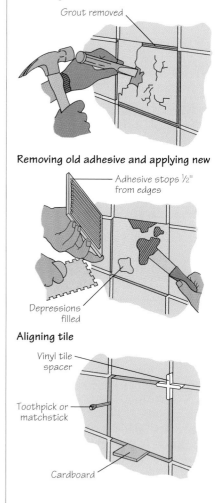

Grout removed

Removing old adhesive and applying new

Adhesive stops ½" from edges

Depressions filled

Aligning tile

Vinyl tile spacer

Toothpick or matchstick

Cardboard

Tip *If you can't find an exact replacement for a missing tile, create an accent by buying a decorative tile or a tile of a contrasting color. Replace several tiles, if necessary, to establish a pattern or to create a small mosaic. You may be able to match bathroom tiles by removing some from behind the toilet tank and replacing them with something else. This is a last resort, as you'll have to remove the toilet tank, remove all grout around the tiles, and then take your chances trying to pop them off without breaking them by striking a broad chisel under the edge of each tile.*

▶ *Tile is chipped.*

If it's only slightly nicked and not in a conspicuous place, try covering the nick with appliance touch-up paint. It adheres well and dries very hard. If you have trouble matching the color (only white and almond can be tinted with paint), try acrylic or epoxy paint. If painting doesn't work, replace the tile.

▶ *Trim pieces are falling off of counter edge.*

The procedure is the same as for replacing a missing tile (see opposite page), except that you'll have to improvise a way to hold the trim piece in place while the adhesive sets (masking tape works well). If several pieces have fallen, it's probably because they didn't have enough support. Remove the rest of the trim pieces and attach a wood strip to the edge of the countertop substrate with glue and screws. It should be just thick enough for the L-shaped trim pieces to clear. Prime or seal the wood strip, let the sealer dry, and reinstall the trim pieces over it.

Supporting trim pieces

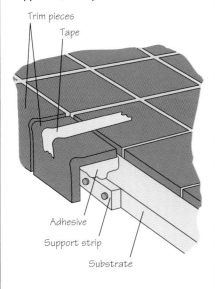

Trim pieces
Tape
Adhesive
Support strip
Substrate

▶ *Tile surface has adhesive stuck to it.*

Old adhesive bonds so tightly to tile that it is almost impossible to remove. You may be able to chip it off carefully, but pieces of glazing and tile will probably come off with it. Muriatic acid may work, if the adhesive is a cement-based compound, such as thin-set. Combine 1 part acid with 10 parts water and apply a tiny amount directly to the adhesive, following label directions. Wear rubber gloves and eye protection and protect nearby surfaces; the acid will eat into grout. If this doesn't work, replace the tile or paint the adhesive to match the tile.

▶ *Tile color is unappealing.*

Tile can be painted with epoxy paint that is designed for this purpose. Consult a tile supplier and follow label directions. Roughen the tile surface with 120-grit sandpaper, then clean thoroughly before painting. Plan to paint the grout lines as well, unless you have great patience and a steady hand (and the grout is worth leaving exposed).

▶ *You want to install new tile over old.*

If the old tile is sound and the new tile won't create a thickness or weight problem, install it directly over the old. Otherwise, remove the old tile and prepare a new underlayment. Several adhesives are suitable for installing tile over tile; consult a dealer and check product labels. Before installing the new tile, roughen the old tile with a masonry rubbing stone and level the grout joints with adhesive.

▶ *You want to install tile over laminate countertop.*

Look for delaminated edges or other loose places and glue them down. Clean the plastic laminate thoroughly with TSP or a similar all-purpose cleaner that will remove grease and other residue. Roughen the surface with sandpaper and wipe clean with a damp sponge. Fill cracks or gaps with epoxy adhesive. Use epoxy adhesive to install the tiles, using the same setting method as for any new tile installation.

▶ *You want to drill a hole through tile.*

Use a variable-speed drill with a glass- or tile-drilling bit. Some bits are shaped like traditional twist drills; others have spear points. Either type should have a tungsten carbide-hardened tip. To keep the bit on target as you start drilling, scratch a small *x* into the tile surface with a glass cutter, machinist's file, or other hardened steel tool. Run the drill at a very slow speed and lubricate the bore with antifreeze as you drill. After you drill through the tile, change the bit if you want to extend the bore into wood.

Drilling hole in tile

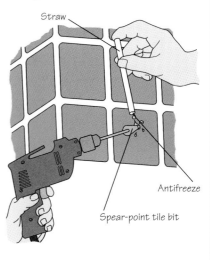

Straw
Antifreeze
Spear-point tile bit

Tip   *Update an old countertop by replacing the trim pieces around the edge. This is much easier than replacing the entire countertop.*

Tip   *If paint is stuck to the surface of tile, apply a water-based commercial paint remover, leave it on for an hour, then scrape off the softened paint with a putty knife or razor blade. Do not use steel wool; it scratches the surface and leaves steel fragments in the grout that may rust later.*

▶ *Cabinet drawer is tight or stuck.*

If a drawer sticks all of the time, sand or plane down the high spots on each side of the drawer. These spots will look worn and smooth, or can be located by rubbing chalk all along the drawer edges and seeing where it wears off first. Do not sand or plane too much wood or the drawer may wobble.

If the drawer has mechanical guide rails on the side or center, clean out any dust or grease that might cause sluggish movement. Lubricate the guides with a nonsticking lubricant, such as graphite. If the guides are badly worn or bent, replace them with identical hardware. If the guides are wood, check for a loose guide that binds the drawer and secure it with screws (predrill pilot holes).

If the drawer sticks only during wet or humid weather, it is swelling temporarily but will shrink back to normal size. For temporary relief rub a bar of soap, a candle, or a silicone grease stick along the drawer edges and runners. Then, during dry weather when the drawer works normally, paint or seal the sides (all faces and edges) to stop them from absorbing moisture.

▶ *Drawer is loose and wobbly.*

Remove it and check to see if the center guide is broken or out of alignment. If so, reattach it to the cabinet frame with screws or, if it's broken, replace it with a new one. Use a framing square to install the guide perpendicular to the cabinet face. If there is no center guide, check to see if the support rails inside the cabinet have channels for keeping the drawer aligned. If not, attach a strip of wood to each rail, just outside the path made by the bottom edge of the drawer side. Tack it in place after

sliding the drawer in and out to make sure the strip will guide the drawer properly. Then glue and nail or screw the strips in place. In addition check for excessive wear on the bottom of the drawer and on rails inside the cabinet. Replace worn parts, or cut away the worn sections of wood, cut new strips of wood to replace them (hardwood is best), and attach the strips with carpenter's wood glue and short paneling nails (grooved finishing brads); predrill to prevent splitting. An alternative to cutting new strips of wood is to build up the worn area with self-sticking (or iron-on) veneer strips used for edging plywood or particleboard.

Attaching center guide

Attaching guide strips

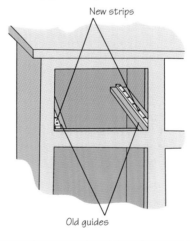

New strips

Old guides

▶ *Drawer won't stop and falls out.*

Remove the drawer. Screw a scrap of wood or metal to the inside of the drawer back. The scrap should protrude about 1 inch above the top of the back—high enough to bump against the front rail of the cabinet frame when the drawer is pulled open, but not high enough to scrape against the bottom of the countertop or drawer above.

▶ *Drawer bottom is loose; contents fall out.*

Remove and empty the drawer and inspect it. Most drawer bottoms are held in place by grooves cut into the drawer sides and front, with tacks holding the drawer bottom to the bottom of the drawer back. The tacks may have come loose, allowing the drawer bottom to sag and pull free from the grooves in the drawer sides. To reattach the bottom, slide it out of the grooves and turn it upside down (or replace it with a new bottom cut from plywood). Then nail it to the bottom of the drawer back with paneling nails (grooved finishing brads).

If the bottom fell out because the drawer sides have separated from the drawer back and spread apart, disassemble the drawer by knocking the loose joints apart with a rubber mallet or hammer and woodblock. Glue the sides and back together with carpenter's wood glue, clamp the drawer together (or use string and tape as shown on opposite page), and let the glue dry overnight. Then slide the drawer bottom into the grooves and tack it in place with paneling nails.

If the bottom fell out because part of a side split away (the part below the groove), remove all of the remaining drawer side below the groove with a plane or fine-toothed saw. Cut a new strip of

---

Tip *Some drawer problems may be a simple matter of the wrong drawer in the slot. Before starting a repair, switch around drawers of identical size to see if they'll work better.*

wood to replace the old runner (straight-grained hardwood works best), and attach it with glue and paneling nails (drill pilot holes for the nails; the sides are probably brittle).

Tacking bottom

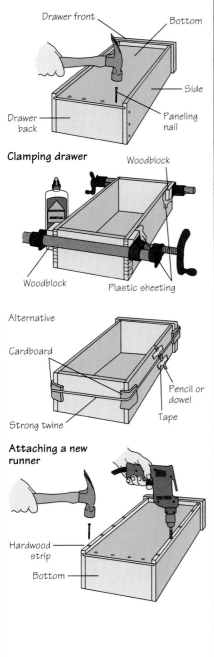

Clamping drawer

Woodblock

Woodblock

Plastic sheeting

Alternative

Cardboard

Strong twine

Pencil or dowel

Tape

Attaching a new runner

Hardwood strip

Bottom

▶ Handle has pulled off.

The threads in the handle have probably been stripped, so the bolt or screw that holds it to the drawer face can no longer get a grip. If you can't find a replacement handle, try squirting some adhesive or silicone caulk into the threaded hole of the pull; then reassemble and wait 24 hours before testing it. If the handle is plastic, you could also replace the screw with a slightly larger sheet-metal screw.

▶ Drawer and door handles need changing.

Buying new drawer and door pulls is an easy and inexpensive way to upgrade kitchen cabinets. Although looks should be your main consideration in choosing new handles, also consider the alignment of screw holes—the job is much easier if the screw holes for the new handles line up with the holes in the cabinet faces. If not, try to use at least one of the holes in the cabinet face, then drill a new one for the second handle screw. If you're left with a blank screw hole in the cabinet face, fill it with wood filler stained to match the cabinets, or use a putty stick that already matches. Some handle designs include a face plate that will cover unused screw holes in the door or drawer front.

Replacing cabinet handles

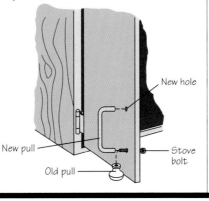

New hole

New pull

Old pull

Stove bolt

▶ Cabinet doors don't align.

Cabinets built recently should have adjustable hinges for fine-tuning the alignment of the door. Just by rotating one or more adjusting screws, or loosening and tightening a sliding setscrew, you can tilt the door from side-to-side or front-to-back. While you make adjustments, count the number of screw rotations for each setting you try, in case you need to go back to a previous setting.

If the hinges don't have adjusting screws, you can still make adjustments by loosening screws and inserting cardboard shims behind a hinge leaf. To tilt the door from side-to-side, place shims behind leaves attached to the cabinet frame; to tilt it front-to-back, place shims behind leaves attached to the back of the door.

Aligning doors with adjustable hinges

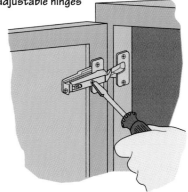

Shimming nonadjustable hinges

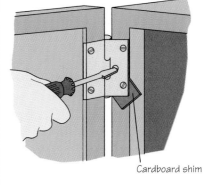

Cardboard shim

Tip *Avoid scouring pads or abrasive powders on laminated plastic finishes.*

▶ Cabinets have fingerprints and smudges around handles.

Apply mechanic's hand cleaner to a rag and scrub lightly (heavy-duty bar soap specified for hands also works). For stubborn buildup, use mineral spirits or paint thinner. Restore the finish with furniture oil or paste wax.

▶ Cabinet door sticks.

Note the exact places where the door edge sticks to the frame; look for worn spots. Hold a straightedge against these areas, first on the door edge and then on the corresponding area of door frame, to see which side has the high spots. Smooth down the high spots with a plane or, if dust will not be a problem, a belt sander. Finish with fine sandpaper and touch up with paint or stain to match the cabinets.

▶ Cabinets don't provide enough accessible storage space.

There are dozens of space-saving organizers that you can install in, on, or near existing cabinets to increase storage capacity and access. Install heavy-duty lazy susans or half-susans (semicircular shelves attached to the door) in lower corner cabinets, and multitiered lazy susans in upper corner cabinets. Mount shallow spice racks on the inside of doors, or store spices in a drawer (in a spice tray) to free up cabinet space. Convert the front panel of a sink cabinet to a tilt-out tray. Equip drawers with two-tiered utensil trays. Install pullout shelves or baskets in lower cabinets to make the contents more accessible. Utilize space under the sink by installing slide-out baskets, trash containers, or shelves; or attach storage trays, a trash container, or a towel rack to the inside of the sink cabinet doors. Free up cabinet space for pots and pans by installing a pot rack on the wall or ceiling near the range. Hang stemware from racks mounted below the wall cabinets.

If organizers aren't enough, look for places to install new cabinets that match existing ones. Consider a deep cabinet above the refrigerator, a pantry unit on a blank wall, a tall pantry unit to replace narrow upper and lower cabinets at the end of a counter, or an appliance garage on a corner of the countertop or recessed into the wall behind a straight section of countertop. Consider a portable kitchen island with a cutting-board top and storage shelves.

▶ Upper cabinets are cold in the winter.

Probably, the soffit above the upper cabinets opens directly into the attic and is not insulated. From the attic, install ½-inch wallboard over the soffit cavity (use screws to avoid pounding and raising dust). Cover the wallboard with insulation batts equal to the thickness required in your area (typically 8 to 12 inches).

▶ Stained wood cabinets need painting.

Remove the doors and drawers. With TSP or a similar cleaning product, wash the doors, drawer fronts, and cabinet frames thoroughly and let dry. Roughen the surfaces with 120-grit sandpaper, vacuum them, and wipe them with a tack cloth. Prime all surfaces with a high-quality white-pigmented shellac, following label directions carefully. Use a high-quality oil-based enamel for the finish coats. Make sure the room is well ventilated and free of dust.

Sand between coats with 220-grit sandpaper; remove dust with a thorough vacuuming and then a tack cloth. Doors and drawer fronts should be horizontal when you paint them, to eliminate sags and droops. Spray painting gives the smoothest finish, then foam rollers, then brushes, then conventional rollers. *Note:* If the cabinets are oak or other porous wood, the grain will show through the paint. To get a smoother finish, use 150-grit sandpaper when roughening the surface and let the dust fill the pores—don't vacuum or wipe it all out. Then seal it with two coats of primer.

▶ Wood cabinets need bleaching or pickling.

Remove the doors and drawers and strip all cabinet surfaces to bare wood by removing the finish with a solvent-based or water-based stripper. Follow label directions carefully, including safety precautions, working times, disposal instructions, and specifications for the types of scouring pads to use. If there are still traces of the old finish, apply two coats of wood bleach. After stripping off the old finish, clean the surfaces as specified on the product label and, when dry, sand them with 120-grit sandpaper. Then apply a white pickling stain over the bare wood, according to label directions.

▶ Plastic laminate cabinets need painting.

Plastic laminate surfaces can be painted using epoxy paints, but it should be done professionally. Consult a local painting contractor who has experience painting this type of cabinet.

Tip   *When painting, stripping, or staining cabinets, test a small section first to make sure you will be satisfied with the results before you take on the entire kitchen.*

▶ Cabinets are too plain.

If changing the handles or painting the cabinets isn't enough, you can try dressing up the fronts of cabinet doors and drawers with decorative moldings. Buy samples of several different sizes and profiles, then experiment with various combinations to create borders and designs. Try duplicating cabinet fronts that you've seen before and liked. Don't make a final selection until you've mocked up a sample of a complete door (one of the actual doors or a plywood substitute), painted it, and looked at it in the kitchen over the course of several days.

Another option is to have all of the cabinets refaced. Most areas have local contractors that specialize in this process.

▶ Solid-surface countertop has scratches, burns, or stains.

"Erase" the mark by scouring it lightly with household cleaner and a damp cloth, or with very fine (600-grit) wet/dry sandpaper dampened slightly. Some countertops require a coarser grade of sandpaper (320- to 400-grit). If the stain is deep, you can keep sanding without danger of rubbing away a veneered surface; the color goes all the way through the material. Feather the sanding so it doesn't create a noticeable depression. Finish by buffing with a soapless synthetic scouring pad. For deep gouges or damage, consult a professional countertop installer.

▶ Cultured marble countertop has burns or stains.

Most types of cast polymer (cultured marble) countertop have a protective surface that is only a thin veneer. Abrading it too much removes the coating and exposes the inner core, which is a softer material usually a different color than the surface. If very light scouring with household cleaner or 600-grit wet/dry sandpaper doesn't remove the stain, your only recourse is to replace the countertop. If light sanding removes the stain, renew the countertop by applying a coat of auto-body polish—except on surfaces where food is prepared, which should be treated with mineral oil, or left untreated.

▶ Tile countertop has stains, chips, cracks, or missing tiles.

See pages 45 and 46.

▶ Plastic laminate countertop has light scratches.

Scratches can't be eliminated, but if normal wear doesn't soften the unsightliness, try hiding the scratches by painting them with an acrylic paint. Take a sample of the laminate to the paint dealer to get a custom-mixed color to match. If you can find an appliance or auto-body touch-up paint that matches, it will dry harder. Apply the paint with an artist's brush.

▶ Plastic laminate countertop has stains.

Remove stains by rubbing mild liquid detergent or a paste of baking soda and water onto the stain with a soft brush; don't scour or use a household cleaner. If this doesn't work, lighten the stain by applying chlorine bleach or denatured alcohol with a damp cloth; rinse the area immediately.

▶ Plastic laminate countertop has burns or severe stains.

Burns and severe stains cannot be repaired. Although it's possible to patch the damaged area or replace a large section of laminate with a new piece, the easiest solution is to cut out the damaged area and replace it with an inset of a different material, such as decorative tiles or a synthetic cutting board (kits with mounting hardware are available).

Start by selecting the material and determining the exact size of cutout it requires. Then mark lines on the laminate surface for the cutout. Place masking tape over the cut lines to minimize chipping and to protect the surface, and trace the cut lines on the tape. Empty the drawer or shelf contents below the cutout area.

Drill 1-inch holes at two opposite corners for starter holes. Clamp or brace straightedge cutting guides to the countertop to guide the tools; you will be cutting through both the laminate and the substrate below it, which is typically ¾-inch material, either particleboard or plywood. To keep the cutout from breaking off and falling through the hole too soon, lay a 1x2 swivel stick across it and drive one screw

Tip *The National Kitchen and Bath Association recommends the following minimum countertop dimensions: Total frontage (length of countertop fronts) for kitchens smaller than 150 square feet—132 inches; total for kitchens larger than 150 square feet—198 inches; on each side of a sink—24 inches and 18 inches; for food-preparation area—36 inches; on latch side of refrigerator—15 inches (or a 15-inch landing space no more than 48 inches from refrigerator); on each side of a cooktop flanked by a wall—15 inches on open side and 3 inches on wall side; on each side of an open cooktop—15 inches and 9 inches; beside an oven—15 inches (or a 15-inch landing within 48 inches of oven if it does not open into a traffic lane); for a microwave oven—15 inches above, below, or beside the oven.*

through the stick into the laminate top, centered inside the cutout. Rotate this board out of the way as you cut around the opening. Make the cut with a jigsaw (teeth should be pointing downward), a compass handsaw (12 teeth per inch or finer), or a router with a deep, straight bit. Cut the corners carefully; you don't want to overcut them and leave kerf marks.

Clean up the edges of the cut with a file or rasp. Cover the bottom of the hole with a piece of plywood, screwed into the bottom of the countertop from below; this will hold the inset. Seal it with primer or sealer and add shim material as necessary to flush the inset surface with the countertop surface. Attach the inset material with adhesive and seal all gaps with grout or caulk.

Cutting out damaged section

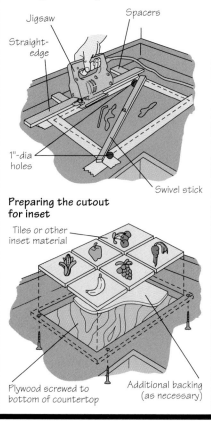

Preparing the cutout for inset

▶ Butcher-block countertop is dirty and worn.

For routine cleaning scrape with a plastic scraper, then rub with salt; rinse well and wipe dry. Rub surfaces used for food with vegetable oil; rub other surfaces with mineral oil. Let sit for 5 to 15 minutes, then wipe up excess oil.

To renew a butcher-block top, sand thoroughly with a reciprocating (or orbital) sander. Start with medium grades of sandpaper (100-grit) and finish with fine grades (200-, then 400-grit). Vacuum the block and remove all dust with a tack cloth. Protect with vegetable or mineral oil; heat the oil in a double boiler first, so it will penetrate the wood more easily.

▶ Vanity countertop is loose.

You will have to remove the countertop and reset it with caulk. To remove it, close the shutoff valves below the sink, disconnect the risers from them, and remove the P-trap. Lift the vanity top, with faucet and drain fitting attached, and carefully set it aside.

With the top removed, make sure the vanity is securely attached to the wall. If not, secure the back to the studs with screws. Then replace the countertop on the vanity to see if it wobbles. If so, mark the high spots around the top of the vanity where the countertop makes contact. Remove the countertop and plane down the high spots along the edge of the vanity; test-fit the countertop and replane as necessary until the top no longer wobbles. Apply a bead of silicone caulk around the top edge of the vanity, set the countertop in place, and press down on it. Let it set for an hour or two before reconnecting the plumbing or using it.

▶ Plastic laminate is loose and lifting.

Scrape out all debris and old adhesive from under the loose section (lift carefully). To make sure that the area is thoroughly dry, prop up the loose laminate for a day or two. Spread contact cement under the laminate, lower the laminate flap onto the cement long enough to coat it, and pull the flap up immediately. Prop up the laminate (toothpicks or matchsticks work well) long enough for the cement on both surfaces to get tacky, then press the laminate in place and smooth it down with a rolling pin.

Holding cemented surfaces apart

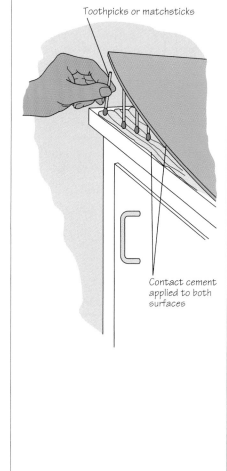

Tip *If other techniques don't remove a stain from a plastic laminate countertop, look for a cleaner specified for plastic laminates, usually with a tylol-exyol base. Such cleaners are available from paint dealers, full-service hardware stores, or suppliers that sell plastic laminates.*

▶ Stairs squeak.

Fix squeaks by tightening loose stair parts that are rubbing together. First pinpoint the squeaks by observing the stairs closely while a helper steps on them. If a tread moves and rubs against the riser below it, drive 8d or 12d finishing nails down through the tread (and through any carpet) into the riser. If possible, force some construction adhesive into the gap before nailing it shut. For greater strength use trimhead screws (wallboard screws with small heads). To conceal the heads, slice a small flap of the tread with a knife or sharp chisel, lift the flap, drive the screw beneath it, then glue the flap down over the screw head. Drive the nails in pairs set at oppos-ing angles. To prevent splitting, drill pilot holes before nailing. Have your helper stand on the tread while you nail.

If squeaks are caused by the back of a tread rubbing against the riser above it, insert glue-coated shims between the tread and riser. Trim them flush with a knife or fine-toothed saw and cover the gap with thin molding.

If a tread or riser is loose at either end, reattach it to the stair stringer with nails or screws, as described above. If you have access to the treads from underneath the stairs, snug wood blocks against the loose joints and attach them with glue and screws, or insert glued wedges.

▶ Handrail is coming loose from wall.

Most handrails are supported by brackets screwed into wall studs. If one comes loose, fix it immediately. A handrail must be able to support 200 pounds in any direction, along its entire length. If the screws won't retighten, replace them with longer screws that will. If the original bracket was secured with hollow-wall fasteners between studs, detach the bracket from the handrail and attach it to the closest stud with lag screws or wood screws that pene-trate at least 1½ inches into the wood. Add another bracket along the span created by moving the first bracket.

▶ End of handrail is open.

A handrail that terminates without butting into a wall or newel post is dangerous; it could snag someone's sleeve and cause a fall. Fix this problem by attaching a "return" to the end of the handrail so it bends into the adjacent wall. Short sec-tions of curved handrail that match the most common handrail styles are available for this purpose. To attach one to the handrail, make sure the ends of both pieces are cut square. Detach the handrail from the last wall bracket so you can pull it away from the wall to provide clearance for screwing in the curved section. Drill pilot holes for a dou-ble-ended screw and drive the screw halfway into the hole in the old rail. Spread carpenter's wood glue on one of the surfaces to be joined and screw the handrail extension onto the screw until it is tight. Stain the curved piece and touch up the joint to match the handrail. Re-attach the handrail to the wall bracket. If the bracket is not within 3 inches of the new end piece,

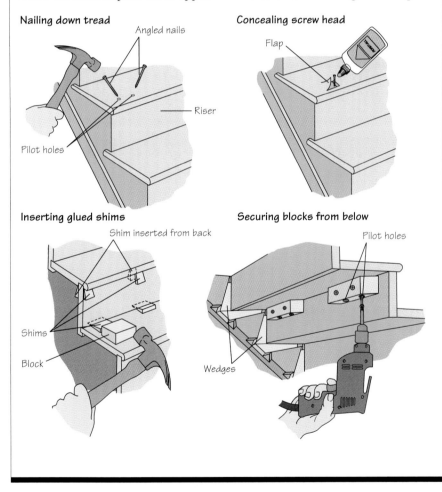

Nailing down tread

Angled nails

Riser

Pilot holes

Concealing screw head

Flap

Inserting glued shims

Shim inserted from back

Shims

Block

Securing blocks from below

Pilot holes

Wedges

Tip *Stairways that change direction may have winders (wedge-shaped stairs) to get around the corner, instead of a level platform. This type of stairway can be dangerous because treads are so narrow at the inside corner. Codes, when they do allow such stairs, require that the narrow end be no less than 6 inches wide and that the winder be at least as wide as the regular treads at a point 12 inches from the narrow end. Make winders safer by painting the nosings white so they are easy to see, providing additional lighting, or building a banister or other barrier out from the wall at the inside corner to divert traffic away from the dangerous narrow ends of the winders.*

secure the end piece to the wall with toenailed 16d finishing nails (if there's a stud or blocking behind the wallboard), or a toggle bolt.

If you can't locate a section of curved handrail, buy a short length of straight handrail to match the existing one. Cut miter angles on the short piece and the end of the handrail. Then cut the short piece to length and attach it to the end of the railing with wood glue and finishing nails. Attach the end to the wall, as described previously. Sand the joint smooth and finish the new wood.

Attaching curved end

Toggle bolt

Bracket

Double-ended screw

Attaching mitered end

Finishing nails

▶ *Stairs lack handrail.*

Codes vary, but most require a handrail for any set of stairs with four or more risers (some local codes require one for *any* step). It must be on the open side (or sides) of the stairs, or on one of the walls if neither side of the stairs is open. It should be located at a constant height above tread nosings, usually between 30 and 34 inches. It should be able to support 200 pounds in any direction, have at least 1½ inches of clearance from the wall, and have proper termination at both ends. A balustrade on the open side of stairs must have no openings wider than 6 inches (4 inches for some codes).

To install a handrail along a wall, you will need a straight length of handrail long enough to span from top tread to bottom, two curved sections for the ends, and enough brackets to support the handrail at least every 4 feet. Measure and mark a point 30 to 34 inches up from the bottom-tread nosing. Do the same above the top-tread nosing. Stretch a string between the two points (or snap a faint chalk line if you'll be painting the wall). Attach brackets to studs every 3 or 4 feet along this line and as close as possible to the top and bottom marks. Cut the handrail to length and attach a curved section to each end. Stain and finish the rail. When it dries, attach it to the brackets.

For open stairs you can buy prefabricated handrail pieces and assemble a balustrade, have one custom-made that you can install yourself, or have a stair specialist build one for you.

Meeting handrail requirements

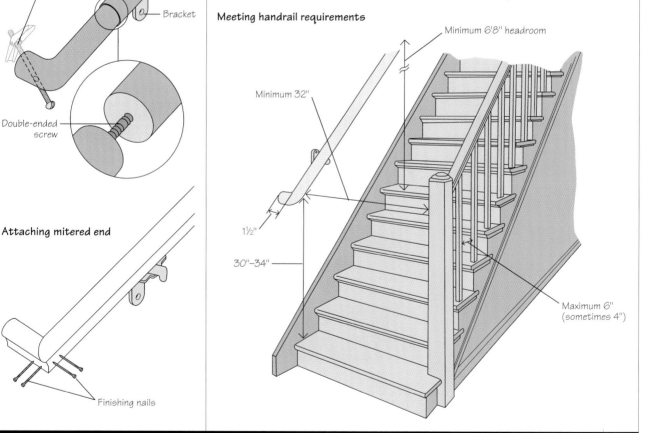

Minimum 6'8" headroom

Minimum 32"

1½"

30"–34"

Maximum 6" (sometimes 4")

Tip *Typical stair requirements: (1) the maximum height of a riser (distance from tread to tread) is 7½ inches; (2) riser heights cannot vary more than 3/16 inch; (3) two times the riser height plus the tread width, added together, should equal 25 inches; (4) the distance between handrails or between a handrail and wall must be at least 32 inches; (5) there must be at least 6 feet, 8 inches of headroom above each riser (7 feet is optimal).*

▶ *Baluster is loose.*

If a baluster is loose at the top, force a glue-covered shim into the gap, let it dry, and trim it flush; or drive a trimhead screw (wallboard screw with small head) up through the baluster (drill a pilot hole first) into the handrail. Conceal the head by first slicing a small flap of wood, lifting it and driving the screw beneath it, then gluing it back in place.

A baluster that is loose at the bottom can be secured to the tread with a trimhead screw driven into the side at an angle (drill first), or by removing a piece of molding from the end of the tread and securing the dovetail tenon of the baluster to the tread with glue and a screw (drill first). Replace the molding.

Securing baluster at top

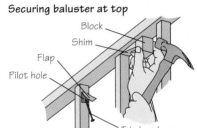

Securing with angled screw at bottom

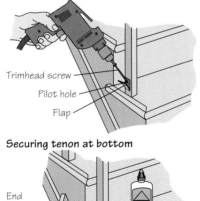

Securing tenon at bottom

▶ *Baluster is broken or missing.*

Remove the broken baluster. If it's held in place by dowels in the top and bottom, saw the baluster in half. Lock a pipe wrench onto the bottom half, twist it sharply to loosen the glue, and lift it out. Do the same for the top. Scrape and sand old glue out of the holes in the tread and handrail. Cut a replacement baluster to length. Apply glue to the tread hole and the top dowel (not the bottom dowel). Insert the top dowel into the handrail hole, then carefully slide the bottom dowel across the tread and into the hole.

If the baluster is attached to the tread with a tenon, remove the end trim from the tread. If the tenon is loose, tap it out. Otherwise, saw the baluster flush with the tread and remove it. Then saw or chisel the tenon out of the tread cutout and sand or chisel away the old glue. Cut a new baluster to length. Check for fit, then glue and screw it into place (drill pilot holes first). Replace the tread end molding.

Removing a dowel baluster

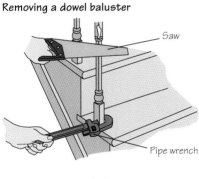

Removing a tenon baluster . . .

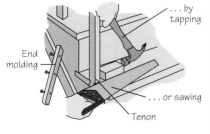

▶ *Tread is cracked or broken.*

Replacing a tread can be an ambitious job, depending on how the stairs are built. Some staircases are built like fine furniture or cabinetwork, with wedges, dadoes, and interlocking joinery. Others are built like a simple set of shelves. Proceed slowly and study how things are jointed together before you pry them apart.

To remove the damaged tread, first carefully pry off any moldings and balusters attached to the tread. Pry up the tread far enough to release nail heads, then force the tread back down, pull the nails, and remove it. If it won't budge, carefully saw or split it in half and remove it in pieces. Aligning nosings, carefully trace the outline of the old tread onto new tread stock. Cut the stock to size and install it with glue and 16d finishing nails or trimhead screws. Replace the balusters and molding pieces.

Removing tread

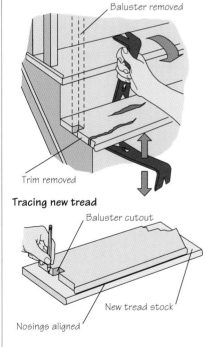

Tracing new tread

Tip *If carpet is coming loose at the back of a tread, fix it immediately; this is a dangerous condition. Stretch the carpet back from the nosing and reattach it to the tack strip across the back of the tread by forcing a broad putty knife into the crease. If the carpet doesn't stay, tack it to the back of the tread with a row of carpet tacks.*

▶ *Newel post is loose.*

Check in the basement or crawl space to see if the newel post extends through the floor and is anchored to a floor joist. If so, tighten the bolt or screws holding it in place. If not, wiggle the post and observe carefully. If the bottom slides back and forth on the floor, secure it to the floor by squeezing carpenter's wood glue under the post and angling two 2-inch trim-head screws (wallboard screws with small heads) through the side of the post and downward into the floor. Repeat on the other exposed sides. If the post is attached solidly to the floor and wiggles against the stair tread, secure it to the tread with a ⁵⁄₁₆ by 4-inch lag screw with ¾-inch washer. First countersink a hole into the newel post with a ¾-inch bit, aiming it back toward the stair stringer. Extend the hole through the newel post with a ⁵⁄₁₆-inch bit, then complete the bore into the finish stringer and support stringer with a ⁷⁄₃₂-inch bit. Slide the washer onto the lag screw, dab some adhesive onto the threads, and screw it into the hole snugly with a socket wrench. Glue a short piece of dowel into the countersunk hole, trim and sand it flush, and finish it to match the post.

Tightening joist connection

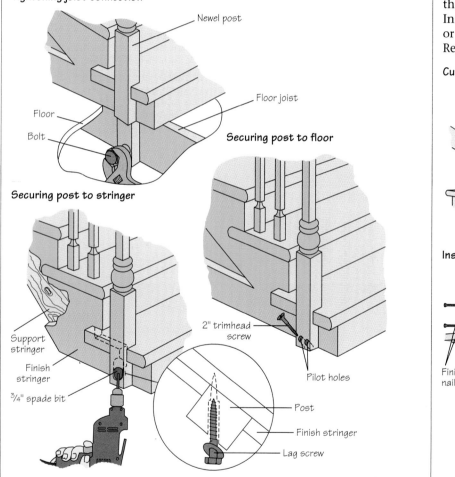

Newel post

Floor joist

Floor

Bolt

Securing post to stringer

Securing post to floor

Support stringer

Finish stringer

¾" spade bit

2" trimhead screw

Pilot holes

Post

Finish stringer

Lag screw

▶ *Riser is cracked or broken.*

Like replacing a tread, installing a new riser can be a big job. Study the stairs to be sure you can replicate the construction. If you want to go ahead, remove the tread (see page 55). If it won't pry loose from the riser, drill a pair of ⅜-inch starter holes into one side of the riser near the top, and use a compass saw or keyhole saw to cut the riser into two pieces horizontally. The tread should lift out, with the top piece of riser attached. Remove the rest of the riser. Note whether wedges were used to hold it in place; if so, salvage the old ones or buy new ones. Cut a new riser out of similar material, using the old riser pieces for dimensions. Install it with glue, finishing nails or screws, and wedges (if used). Replace the tread and related parts.

Cutting riser to release tread

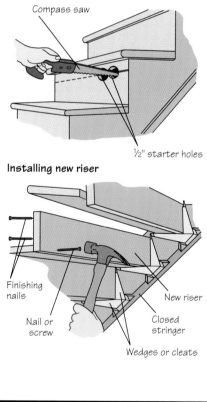

Compass saw

½" starter holes

Installing new riser

Finishing nails

Nail or screw

New riser

Closed stringer

Wedges or cleats

Tip *Carpeted stairs should be vacuumed at least once a week, more frequently if possible. Whether you use a stair-cleaning attachment or a minivacuum, it should have a beater brush built into it for agitating dirt out of the carpet as you clean.*

▶ Stairway is too dark.

All stairways must have a light that can be operated by a switch at both the top and the bottom. If none exists, have one installed. Avoid pendant lights that hang below the level of the upstairs ceiling. If the stairway has a light and only one switch, a second switch should be installed and the first switch replaced. There are two ways to connect the switches. One is with normal house wiring, installed behind walls or inside surface conduit. The other is to install a pair of remote-controlled switches, linked by low-voltage wiring or by radio signals. Consult an electrician or electrical-supply house.

Stairways can also be illuminated during the day with natural light. Consider a skylight above the stairwell, a window placed at the top of the stairs, or inserting wall openings between the stairwell and an adjacent room that has plenty of natural light. All require structural changes; seek help.

▶ Stairway is weak and sagging.

Building new stairs requires advanced carpentry skills, but there is a simple way to reinforce a weak stairway if all the parts are sound. Install a central 2x6 brace underneath the stairs. First remove any plaster or wallboard attached to the underside of the stairway. Cut a 2x6 to fit, on edge, under the center of the stairway along its entire length. It should be firmly supported at the top and bottom ends. Snugging it against the floor will take care of the bottom; attaching it to a joist hanger will secure the top. Use a bevel gauge to duplicate and mark the correct angles for cutting. To

install the brace, slide the bottom end into place first, then lift the top to a corner (not the center) of the top header and pound it over to the center with a sledgehammer. Slide a joist hanger under the top end, force the brace up as far as it will go, and nail the hanger to the header and brace. Toenail the bottom end of the brace to the floor.

To provide support for each tread, set a ¾-inch plywood cleat against the 2x6 brace and snug it up against the bottom of the tread. Screw it to the 2x6 with three 2-inch wallboard screws and secure it to the tread with finishing nails toenailed from the bottom or face-nailed from above.

Installing a 2x6 brace

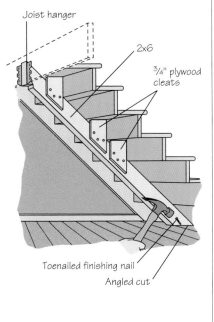

Joist hanger

2x6

¾" plywood cleats

Toenailed finishing nail

Angled cut

▶ Stairway lacks sufficient headroom.

If a bulkhead is only an inch or two below the minimum height, you may be able to gain the headroom by beveling the bottom corner. Otherwise, the stair will need to be rebuilt—a major job.

▶ Stairway is too steep, tilted, or narrow.

Codes vary, but typical requirements for stair dimensions are: maximum riser height 7½ inches, no variation greater than 3⁄16 inch; minimum tread depth 9 inches, plus 1-inch nosing; minimum headroom 6 feet, 8 inches above all nosings; minimum width 32 inches between handrails, 36 inches between walls; and minimum depth of landings 36 inches. Check your local building code for specific requirements.

Altering stairs to conform to these requirements usually means rebuilding the entire stairway, because changing one small dimension affects others, and many small changes have an incremental effect of changing the dimensions of the entire stairway. Consult a contractor or carpenter who specializes in stair building.

Meeting stair requirements

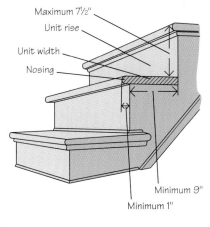

Maximum 7½"

Unit rise

Unit width

Nosing

Minimum 9"

Minimum 1"

Tip If your stairway is boring, try these ideas to liven it up: (1) Paint the risers a bright color or stencil a simple design onto some of them. (2) Replace a run-of-the-mill balustrade with a new one created from stock stair parts. (3) Install strip-lighting (used for theater and airplane floors) along the stair stringer. (4) Install a skylight over the stairwell or a window at the top of the stairs. (5) Freshen up the walls with new wallpaper or faux painting techniques such as rag painting, raking, marbling, or sponging.

▶ *Fire won't draw; smoke enters room.*

Open the damper (handle should be forward). Make sure the flue is not blocked with debris (leaves, bird nest, jolly fat fellow), soot, a clogged spark screen, or a chimney-top damper of which you are not aware. If smoke enters the room only for the first few minutes, stuff crumpled paper up into the chimney and light it before starting a fire. Also use more paper and kindling to start the fire; a quick, roaring blaze may be all that's needed. Exhaust fans (such as a range hood or vented clothes dryer) should not be on when you start the fire, nor a warm-air heating system if the return-air grille is nearby.

Apart from these possibilities, a smoky fireplace is most likely caused by poor chimney or fireplace design. A chimney must be at least 11 feet tall (floor to top) and rise 3 feet above the roof ridge or, if the ridge is too high, 3 feet above the highest point on the roof within 10 feet of the chimney. Exterior chimneys, especially on the north side of the house, draw less efficiently than chimneys enclosed within the house; and chimneys that terminate above eaves are less efficient than those that terminate above gables. No other appliances should share the same flue as the fireplace. The firebox should be at least 20 inches deep at the base. The optimum height depends on several variables, but if it's too high, smoke will escape into the room.

Extending a chimney involves adding sections of matching flue liner, bricks, and a cap; it should be done by a professional. You may be able to improve fireplace performance without having the firebox rebuilt by raising its floor with a new layer of firebricks or installing a metal smoke deflector or shallow hood across the top of the fireplace opening. Never use a wood "smoke board." If the fireplace is used regularly, the chimney should be serviced by a professional chimney sweep every year.

Meeting chimney requirements

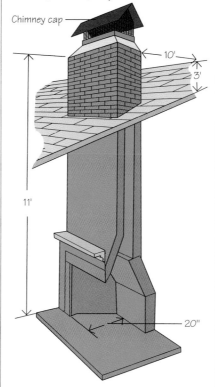

Altering a firebox that's too high

Metal smoke deflector

Firebricks

▶ *Fire is too hot or not hot enough.*

Fireplaces don't warm rooms very well. Most of the heat goes up the chimney or is absorbed into the bricks. At the same time, it draws huge quantities of warmed air out of the house. With most fireplaces the heat you feel is radiant heat from the fire itself, although some fireplaces are equipped with convective devices that circulate air around the firebox and distribute it back into the room. A fire may not feel hot because the radiant heat is blocked or deflected away. Arrange furniture for maximum exposure to direct heat, no closer to the fireplace opening than 3 feet. Build the fire closer to the front of the firebox (unless it smokes). Experiment with lowering or raising the grate.

To prevent warm room air from escaping up the chimney, have glass doors and a combustion air duct installed so the fireplace uses air from the outdoors rather than from the house.

To improve the fire itself, burn a mix of softwoods and well-seasoned hardwoods; avoid green wood. Stack logs vertically against the back of the firebox (as Europeans do). Keep kindling on hand to give the fire a boost from time to time.

If the fire burns too hot, change to softwoods. Avoid constant burning of those with high resin and pitch content; red cedar and Douglas fir burn fairly clean. Close the damper slightly to regulate draft. Install glass doors; the glass will block infrared radiation (warmest heat rays) and transmit only the "cooler" heat conducted through it. Or have a gas lighter and decorative logs installed and stop burning wood altogether.

Tip   *Install a smoke detector in the same room as a fireplace or wood-burning stove. Ideally this alarm should be wired to other smoke detectors throughout the house. Never start a fire with gasoline, kerosene, or lighter fluid. Keep a fire extinguisher nearby. Never burn trash in a fireplace or woodstove, especially plastics, colored inks, or treated wood. Never leave children unattended near a fire. Don't close the damper until the fire is extinguished. Read instructions before using artificial logs. Install a carbon monoxide detector in a room with a woodstove. Empty ashes into a closed metal container. Make sure a fire screen spans the entire fireplace opening, and keep combustibles at least 3 feet from the opening.*

▶ Cold air enters room through fireplace.

Shut the damper whenever the fireplace is not in use. Install a glass enclosure (required in most new installations). Cover the fireplace opening with a decorative shield.

▶ Damper is stuck.

Wear gloves and eye protection. Pull (to open) or push (to close) hard on the handle. If it won't budge, slide a 20- to 30-inch length of pipe over the handle for greater leverage. If you can't move it, strike the pipe sharply with a sledgehammer (you may need a helper). Aim the blow straight—a glancing or angled blow could bend the handle to the side—and avoid excessive hammering. Once you've opened the damper, work the handle back and forth a few times to loosen it. Clean the rotating pins with a wire brush; apply high-temperature lubricant.

Opening a stuck damper

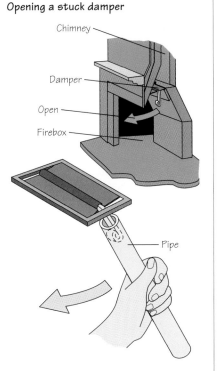

Chimney

Damper

Open

Firebox

Pipe

▶ Damper is missing.

See page 120.

▶ Rain comes down chimney.

Rain causes significant damage inside a chimney. It combines with the creosote present in most chimneys to produce acids that break down the flue lining and mortar. Install a metal chimney hood, or have a masonry hood custom-built. Both types should include a spark arrester (metal screening around the open areas). Measure the flue opening before buying a metal hood. Most are installed by pushing them down into the flue and require a tight fit.

Protecting chimney with metal hood

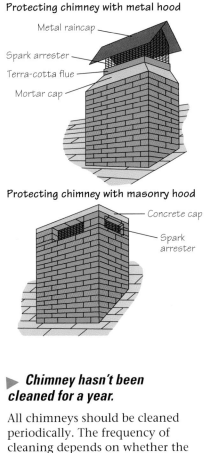

Metal raincap

Spark arrester

Terra-cotta flue

Mortar cap

Protecting chimney with masonry hood

Concrete cap

Spark arrester

▶ Chimney hasn't been cleaned for a year.

All chimneys should be cleaned periodically. The frequency of cleaning depends on whether the chimney vents an open fireplace, enclosed fireplace, or wood-burning stove; how often you burn fires; and on the type of fuel burned.

The culprit is creosote, which is formed when smoke and hot gases cool and make contact with even cooler surfaces. It builds up rapidly inside a chimney if the smoke is relatively cool to begin with (which is common with slow-burning stoves), and the fire never burns hot enough to heat up the chimney and force the smoke out quickly. Built-up creosote is a fire hazard.

When creosote builds up to $\frac{1}{8}$ inch on flue walls, the chimney should be cleaned. If you burn hot, blazing fires in an open fireplace, such accumulation may take a year or more. If you have a woodstove and burn slow fires, soot and creosote may build up to dangerous levels as quickly as every two weeks, depending on the type of fuel used. Have your chimney inspected and cleaned by a professional.

▶ Sparks fly onto rug or floor.

All fireplaces should have a protective screen or glass doors that cover the entire fireplace opening. Many homes have a freestanding, portable screen open at the top. This may not be sufficient protection; replace it with a permanent screen attached to the fireplace. Follow manufacturer's installation instructions. Most require boring two to four holes into the brick with a masonry bit and inserting expansion bolts or lead shields. If you drill on the inside of the firebox, wear gloves, goggles, and a hat for protection from falling soot and debris.

If the draw mechanism for a screen is fouled or stuck, clean the track and any wheels with a stiff brush. Apply a high-temperature lubricant recommended by a fireplace dealer.

Tip   To burn efficiently, firewood should be seasoned. Most woods take from nine months to two years to season. Ways of recognizing green wood and seasoned wood are: (1) Seasoned wood is much lighter in weight. (2) When struck together, two sticks of green wood will sound dull; two sticks of seasoned wood will resonate with a light ring. (3) The ends of seasoned wood are darker colored than green wood and they have slight cracks. (4) The bark of seasoned wood peels back easily, revealing no greenish wood underneath.

▶ Hearth is too small.

A fireplace hearth should extend 20 inches into the room in front of the fireplace opening and 12 inches to each side (16 and 8 inches for openings less than 6 square feet in area).

Extending a hearth is more complicated than removing some floorboards and gluing a few tiles or bricks to the subfloor. Most codes require at least ½ inch of noncombustible backing under the tiles or other masonry material, which means removing some of the subfloor and providing structural support to install new subflooring at a lower level. Consult a professional familiar with local requirements.

Meeting hearth requirements

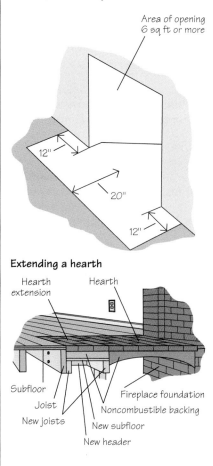

Area of opening 6 sq ft or more

12"

20"

12"

Extending a hearth

Hearth extension

Hearth

Subfloor

Joist

New joists

Fireplace foundation

Noncombustible backing

New subfloor

New header

▶ Fireplace is old and hasn't been used in years.

Have it inspected by a licensed fireplace specialist, such as a chimney sweep, fireplace contractor, or brick mason, before using it. If you've never used it, the inspection may turn up such surprises as a missing or blocked chimney, a chimney that terminates in the attic, or a gas-burning fireplace that was never intended for fires.

▶ Firebox bricks are cracked or crumbling.

Firebricks and fireclay mortar are intended to withstand extreme temperatures, but eventually deteriorate and must be replaced. If only a few mortar joints are failing, scrape out the loose mortar with a cold chisel or similar tool. Mix some mortar with fireclay and water, according to label directions for fireboxes. Pack mortar into the open joints with a trowel, then smooth the joints with a jointer or an old spoon (see page 125).

If the bricks are deteriorating (tapping them with a metal tool produces a dull thud instead of a sharp retort), the firebox needs to be rebuilt. This is best left to a professional brick mason, unless you have considerable experience laying bricks yourself. Use firebricks and fireclay mortar, and observe the layout pattern as you remove the old firebricks.

▶ Fireplace is too small.

Fireplaces in many older homes, especially Victorians, are small because they were intended to burn coal. Provided everything is in safe working order, you can build in such a fireplace a reasonably sized wood fire that generates the same amount of heat and ambience as a larger fireplace. You could also burn coal.

If you want the firebox enlarged, it will most likely involve rebuilding the entire fireplace and chimney as well. Consult a fireplace specialist.

Never enlarge a small firebox or fireplace opening without enlarging the chimney flue. (The area of the fireplace opening should not exceed 10 to 12 times the area of the flue opening.)

If you want to make the fireplace appear larger by extending or rebuilding the facade, plan it carefully. A large facade may overwhelm the smaller firebox. In general, stepped designs or variations in materials are more successful than a large, unrelieved expanse of the same material. Be sure not to place anything flammable too close to the firebox (see opposite page).

▶ Glass doors are dirty and smoky.

Buy some stove-glass cleaner, which contains chemicals for cutting through soot and creosote that ordinary glass cleaners don't have, and use according to label instructions. If you can't find it at a hardware store, try a fireplace or woodstove dealer.

▶ Fire screen is damaged.

If it's a freestanding screen, replace it with glass doors or a new fireplace screen that attaches to the fireplace. If you already have that type of screen and it doesn't work properly, dismantle as much of it as you can and look for replacement parts at a hardware store or fireplace dealer.

Tip *Fireplaces with gas lighters should have a removed or permanently propped-open damper to ensure a safe vent for combustion fumes or leaking gas. Brush ashes away from the holes of the gas burner after each use.*

▶ *Gas lighter doesn't light.*

Most lighters consist of a gas valve located outside the fireplace and operated by a removable key, and a perforated gas/air mixing chamber (burner) located in a decorative log inside the fireplace. If the log won't light when you turn on the valve, the holes in the perforated chamber are probably blocked by accumulated ashes. Instead of trying to unclog them, buy a replacement chamber at a home center or other supplier. It looks like a pipe with holes in it. Be sure to get one specified for your fuel source, either natural gas or LP. Make sure the valve is shut off when you remove the original chamber and install the replacement.

Some lighters, usually installed in a prefabricated fireplace, have a standing pilot light or electronic ignition that enables them to light automatically. If the unit won't light, consult the manufacturer's operating instructions or call a fireplace technician.

▶ *Mantel is too close to fireplace.*

All combustible materials, such as a wood mantel, must be at least 12 inches from the fireplace opening. Check local codes for required clearance above a wood-burning stove installed in a fireplace; it may be more than 12 inches.

If the mantel is attached to the face of the wall, you can probably detach it and move it up. Look for bolts, screws, or brackets under the mantel and remove them (a helper or brace should support the mantel). Move the mantel to the required height, mark where holes should be drilled or brackets attached for installing the support hardware, and reinstall it. Patch

holes and cracks from the original installation.

If the mantel rests on a brick shelf or it is otherwise impractical to detach and move it, install a sheet-metal deflector between the mantel and the fireplace opening. Have a sheet-metal shop cut a rectangle from 20-gauge sheet metal, 4 to 6 inches wide and long enough to span the fireplace opening. It should be bent lengthwise at a 135-degree angle, 1½ inches from one edge. This creates a flange that can be bolted to the face of the fireplace. The rest of the shield flares upward for 3 or 4 inches, enough to shield the mantel from direct heat. Have the exposed edge and corners folded; otherwise they're too sharp. To paint the shield, etch the metal with vinegar, rinse, and wipe dry. Spray-paint it flat black or a color to match the fireplace facade.

Attaching metal shield

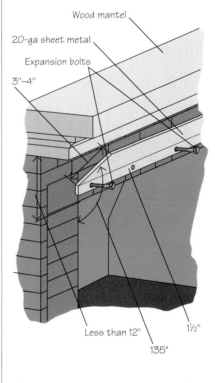

Wood mantel
20-ga sheet metal
Expansion bolts
3"–4"
Less than 12"
1½"
135°

▶ *Mantel is loose.*

Some mantels rest on the brick fireplace facade, some are supported by wood posts (pilasters) attached to the sides of the fireplace opening, and some hang on the fireplace wall supported by decorative brackets (corbels) or hidden hardware. Methods of attachment vary, so inspect closely to determine what fasteners have come loose and need tightening or replacing. The connections most likely to fail are wall fasteners, such as lag screws, angled through the mantel top or bottom and driven into wood framing inside the wall. If the hole drilled through the mantel is still sound, try drilling through it into the wall at a slightly different angle to create a new pilot hole for the lag screw. If the hole is not sound, drill a new one nearby and angle it toward the stud, or drill holes between studs and attach the mantel to the wallboard with expansion bolts. After tightening existing screws, create additional support by adding more lag screws (there may be other framing members hidden inside the wall), an unobtrusive cleat under the mantel, or decorative brackets at the ends of the mantel.

Boring for lag screw

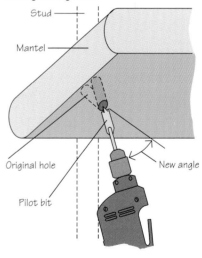

Stud
Mantel
Original hole
Pilot bit
New angle

Tip   *To protect carpets and flooring in front of a fireplace from occasional sparks or embers, place a fireproof hearth rug in front of the hearth. They come in a wide variety of decorative patterns and colors.*

▶ *Wood-burning stove is old and needs upgrading.*

Have it inspected by a professional such as a licensed chimney sweep, stove installer, or local building inspector. Safety and air-quality regulations are constantly being upgraded, and wood-burning stoves are not foolproof devices that you simply install and forget about. Having it inspected will make you aware of innovations in safety and efficiency, especially for installa-tions made prior to July 1992. Some of the things to inspect for include: a noncombustible base; minimum clearances to combustible walls and furniture; proper size and type of flue; allowable horizontal runs and changes in direction of the flue pipe; condition of the doors, legs, hinges, grate, and draft louvers; combustion efficiency; and the installation of an insulated chim-ney liner for fireplace inserts.

Meeting wood-burning stove requirements

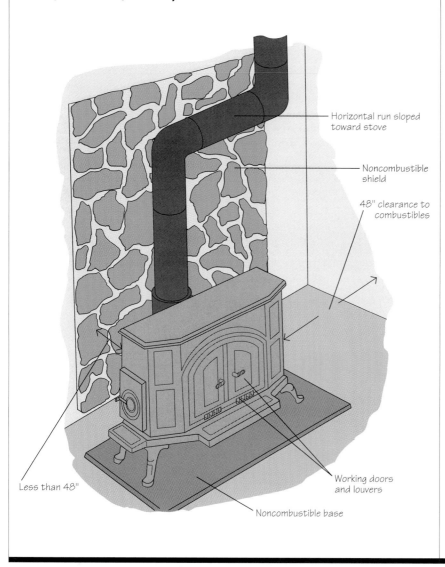

Horizontal run sloped toward stove

Noncombustible shield

48" clearance to combustibles

Less than 48"

Working doors and louvers

Noncombustible base

▶ *Brick facade is painted an undesirable color.*

Removing paint from bricks is diffi-cult because it penetrates deeply and gets partially baked on by the heat. The easiest way to solve this problem is to repaint the bricks a more desirable color. Scrape off loose or flaking paint, wash the surface with TSP, and paint with a high-quality latex masonry paint.

If the paint is already deteriorat-ing, you may have success with a paste-type paint stripper; follow label directions. You will need to make several applications, and still may not remove all the paint. Try staining the residue with a wood stain to match the exposed brick. Or give up and paint the mortar a mor-tar color and the bricks a brick color with flat latex paint. Paint the mor-tar first with a brush, then the bricks with a sponge or short-nap roller.

If the paint has not deteriorated and you do want it removed, have a professional sandblast the bricks.

▶ *Wood-burning stove with catalytic combustor emits dark smoke.*

The catalytic combustor, located at the base of the flue pipe, is intend-ed to "clean" the smoke by remov-ing pollutants before it goes up the flue. To work properly, the combus-tor must be cleaned regularly and replaced after 10,000 to 12,000 hours of use (three to eight years). Always follow manufacturer's in-structions. Most suggest cleaning the combustor with a soft-bristled brush at least twice a year and re-moving it for a major cleaning every two to three years. Follow the removal and cleaning instructions carefully; combustors are very frag-ile and should not be scraped, hit, washed with compressed air or a high-pressure hose, or returned to use until they are completely dry.

Tip *Transform an ordinary brick facade by covering it with tile, facing bricks, marble, cultured stone, plaster, or other noncombustible material. Then add a mantel. You can make one from a slab of marble, solid-surface countertop material, or wood boards and molding (at least 12 inches from the fireplace opening); order a kit; or look in architectural salvage yards.*

▶ Foundation has cracks.

Hairline cracks are normal for concrete foundations. Larger cracks, up to ⅛ inch wide, may indicate settling but should not be of concern unless they widen and shift over time. To test, glue a glass microscope slide over the crack with epoxy glue and check in a few weeks to see if concrete movement breaks it. If so, consult a foundation specialist. Patch small cracks on the outside of the foundation with a concrete patching compound. Apply a latex bonding agent to the area first, and feather the compound as you apply it over the crack. Cracks wider than ¼ inch and any crack that is wider at one end than the other require attention. Consult a professional.

▶ Foundation has white powder.

Efflorescence is a white powdery substance left on concrete and brick walls by moisture migrating through them. In and of itself it is insignificant; it does little damage to the masonry and can be removed with a stiff brush (avoid wire brush for brick). A new wall may have this problem temporarily while the concrete or mortar cures. If efflorescence is recurrent, it might indicate the presence of leaks or excessive moisture that could cause structural problems. Block the source of moisture by plugging cracks in specific areas, or by installing a drainage system on the outside of the foundation wall and sealing it.

▶ Foundation is sagging, leaning, or uneven.

The cause is poor foundation design and/or unstable soils. Consult a qualified foundation specialist, such as a structural engineer, a soils engineer, or a general building contractor experienced in foundation repair.

▶ Sill is not bolted to foundation.

Install anchor bolts no more than 6 feet apart (4 feet in earthquake or hurricane areas) and within 12 inches of each end of every sill board. To install the bolts, drill through the wood sill with a ½- or ⅝-inch spade bit, depending on the size of bolt. Then drill a 5-inch-deep hole into the concrete with a rotary hammer, using the same size bit. Use a piece of flexible tubing or an old basting syringe to blow concrete dust out of the hole (wear eye protection). Insert an expansion bolt into the hole and tighten the nut until the washer digs into the sill.

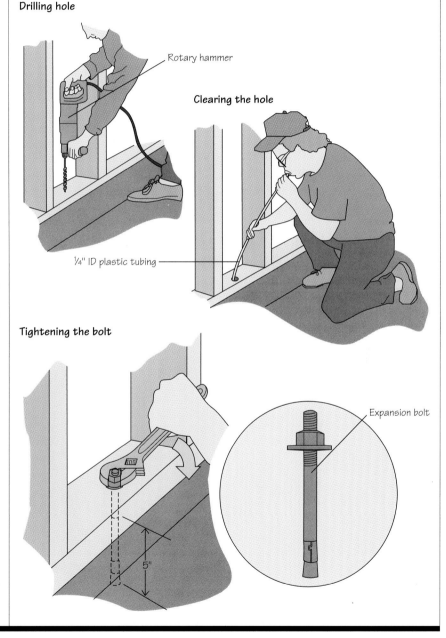

Drilling hole

Rotary hammer

¼" ID plastic tubing

Clearing the hole

Tightening the bolt

5"

Expansion bolt

Tip *When working in a crawl space, make sure lights and power tools are plugged into a GFCI-protected receptacle. Wear gloves and heavy clothing, such as a jumpsuit, to protect against insulation fibers, insects, dust, and chill.*

▶ Sill is rotted.

Replacing an entire rotted sill should be left to a professional, but you might be able to replace 2 or 3 feet of affected wood yourself. First make sure the cause is eliminated (termites, earth contact, moisture). Remove enough siding and sheathing on the outside of the house to expose the damaged sill. With a helper, two jacks, two short posts, and a 6-foot 4x4 beam, shore up the floor joists that bear on the damaged portion of sill. Set the jacks on 2x12 scraps, about 18 to 24 inches from the foundation wall. Rent jack posts if you're working in a basement. Raise the joists just enough to take pressure off the sill. With a reciprocating saw or handsaw, cut through the sill at both ends of the rot and remove the damaged portion. Cut a piece of pressure-treated 2x6 to the same length, coat the ends with preservative, apply three beads of caulk along the bottom, and tap it into place with a sledgehammer. Seal gaps with caulk. If the new sill is thinner than the old, place cedar shims under the joist ends to make up the difference. Remove the shoring and replace the siding and sheathing.

Replacing rotted section of sill

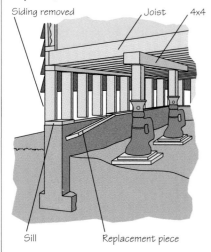

▶ Wood is within 8 inches of the ground.

Building codes require that all wood, except pressure-treated lumber specified for ground contact and certain grades of redwood or other durable species, be at least 8 inches above the ground. If siding, framing lumber, posts, or other wood members are closer than 8 inches to the ground, fix the problem by excavating soil away from the wood, replacing exposed wood with pressure-treated lumber (LP-22 for ground contact), or building up the foundation wall or piers with new concrete. Because these tasks may require shoring up parts of the house, building forms, or pouring concrete, consult a foundation specialist before proceeding.

If you are excavating soil from around the outside of the foundation, the ground should slope away from the house 1 inch per foot for 10 feet. If this is not possible, create a concrete gutter against the foundation that can carry water away.

Meeting clearance requirements

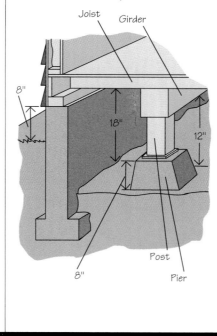

▶ Post is not centered on concrete pier.

The post will exert uneven pressure on the concrete footing and eventually cause it to lean. It is not difficult to move the post over to the center of the pier so long as it remains plumb and stays centered under the girder. First provide temporary shoring by jacking up short posts on each side of the main post; set the jacks on scraps of 2x12 or similar pads. Raise the beam just enough to take pressure off the original post. Then remove the toenails, brackets, or other connecting hardware from the post and tap it into place with a 5-pound sledgehammer (not a claw hammer). If the post is rotted or split, replace it with a new one cut just a hair longer than the space. With a level, plumb the post in two directions. Secure the post with new brackets or 12d HDG common nails toenailed into the support pier and girder. Remove the shoring.

If moving the post would move it off center under the girder, don't move it. Leave it alone or, if the pier is tilting, have a new footing and pier installed.

Moving post

Tip *All decay problems associated with wood structural members under the floor, such as termites, rot, and fungus damage, can be traced to a single cause: moisture. The moisture, however, can come from sources far above the crawl space or basement area. Leaky roof gutters, open cracks in the siding, rotted windowsills, unsealed porches, poorly caulked shower stalls, and leaking pipes can contribute to serious structural damage. Solving foundation and crawl-space problems includes addressing these conditions.*

▶ Post is not attached securely to pier or beam.

Attach posts to beams (girders) with metal framing connectors, available in a variety of sizes. Choose a post-to-beam bracket that fits the size of post (for example, a rough 4x4 is slightly wider than a surfaced 4x4) and can be attached after the post and beam are in place. Nail with 16d joist-hanger nails. For earthquake reinforcement, add a ¾-inch plywood triangular brace to each side of the post. Nail it to the post and beam with 8d or 10d common nails.

Securing post to beam and pier

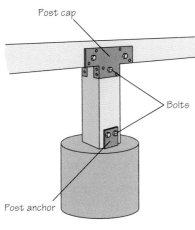

Post cap

Bolts

Post anchor

Adding plywood braces

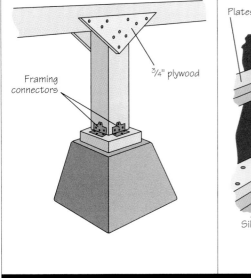

Framing connectors

¾" plywood

▶ Cripple wall does not have earthquake bracing.

In areas that require earthquake reinforcement, the short walls between a foundation and first floor should be well braced. If solid sheathing was not installed on the exterior side of the wall, nail ½-inch plywood panels to the crawl-space side. First be sure the sills are bolted to the foundation (see page 63). Then install 2x4 blocking between the studs along the sill to provide a nailing surface flush with the studs and plates. Nail each block to the sill with at least six 12d HDG common nails. Then cut sheets of plywood to fit horizontally along the wall; they should rest on the sill, not the foundation, and extend to the floor joists. Center vertical joints over studs. Nail the plywood to the studs, plates, and bottom blocking with 8d common nails, spaced every 4 inches along the edges, every 8 inches in the field. To provide air circulation, cut a 3-inch-diameter hole in the plywood at the top and bottom of each stud bay.

Installing plywood bracing

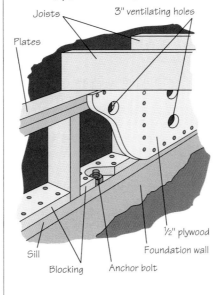

Joists

3" ventilating holes

Plates

½" plywood

Foundation wall

Sill

Blocking

Anchor bolt

▶ Powder-post beetles may be present.

While you are inspecting for termites, look for small piles of fresh powdery sawdust (frass) or random patterns of tiny holes in wood. They indicate powder-post beetles, which are structurally harmful and very difficult to control. Some types prefer hardwood and will attack flooring, furniture, and cabinets; others enjoy any type of wood. If you find such activity, call an exterminator.

▶ Termites may be present.

Inspect the foundation area for signs of termites and other insects once a year when the soil temperature is 50° to 55° F. The most obvious signs of infestation are earth tubes between the soil and wood. They are usually found along the foundation wall or interior piers but can be freestanding. They should be knocked down, but consult an exterminator first.

If you don't find tubes, it may mean that termites have found easier access to the wood structure. These paths are often hard to detect. Look for joints and cracks in the foundation, especially on the outside where stucco or brick veneer extends to the ground. Look for concealed posts or columns, such as porch or stair supports. With an ice pick or sharp awl, probe any wood near these points of access. The surface may appear sound, but the inside may be riddled with hollow channels and pockets. Other signs of termites are weakened wood, discarded insect wings on the ground, fresh coarse sawdust, and wood that has a hollow sound when tapped. If

Tip *Clear away all wood and other cellulose debris (paper, cardboard) from the crawl-space area. It attracts termites and other pests. Do not stack firewood or lumber close to the house. Remove nearby tree stumps. Trim tree limbs that touch the house.*

SOLVING INDOOR PROBLEMS

you find any suspicious signs, call an exterminator.

Even if you find no evidence of insect pests, you should be aware of conditions that promote them. Examine any wood for evidence of moisture or rot. Remove all wood and related material from the ground. Eliminate sources of crawl-space moisture. Patch or plug foundation cracks, gaps around pipes, and other potential passageways between the earth and wood.

Inspecting for termites

Stucco or brick veneer

Firewood

Buried wood debris

Earth tube

Wood on ground

Foundation crack

▶ *Wood structural members have streaks, stains, or rot.*

Several types of rot thrive in moist, unventilated areas. Once established, its growth is accelerated by humidity. If you discover rot, find the source of moisture and eliminate it first. Spongy or crumbly wood indicates severe rot and should be replaced immediately. Whitish streaks or cottonlike fibers indicate dry rot, a type of fungus that spreads rapidly and attacks wood. Dark gray or blue streaks indicate a faster-growing but less harmful type of fungus; its presence, however, indicates conditions that will attract the slower-growing but more dangerous types. Brownish streaks or stains indicate previously wet areas.

To treat rotted wood, eliminate the cause of moisture, allow the wood to dry, scrape or wipe away the rot, and apply preservative to the area, according to label directions. If the rot has caused more than surface damage, cut out all the infected wood at least 12 to 18 inches beyond the rotted section and replace it with pressure-treated wood. (For information on repairing joists, see page 30.)

▶ *Wires are sagging below floor joists.*

House wiring presents a danger in crawl spaces if it is not attached safely to floor joists or other framing members. Reattach sagging wires with staples approved for electrical cables, nailed no more than 42 inches apart. Use caution around wires, no matter how harmless they appear. Make sure the circuit is grounded and that wires terminate in electrical junction boxes or fixture boxes. Wear gloves,

use tools with wood or rubber handles, and avoid moist ground. Call an electrician if you are not comfortable with doing this yourself. Some local codes prohibit running house wiring across the bottoms of floor joists or require that it be protected by metal conduit. Other wires (telephone wires, TV cables) should also be securely attached.

▶ *Floor above crawl space needs insulation.*

See page 31.

▶ *Insulation is falling.*

Push the insulation up between the joists and support it with wire insulation supports, sometimes called "tiger tails" or "tiger teeth." Place one under the insulation every 16 to 24 inches, wedging it between the joists.

▶ *Insulation is installed upside down.*

In most climates floor insulation should be installed with the vapor barrier facing up toward the living space. If your insulation was installed with the paper on the bottom, first check to make sure that the exposed paper is indeed the vapor barrier—some insulation has paper on both sides. It should be labeled clearly. Also, in climates with warm winters it's preferable to have the floor insulation reversed. If neither of these situations apply and your insulation is upside down, you can remedy the problem by cutting slits into the exposed vapor barrier to allow trapped moisture to escape.

Tip *There are three types of termites in the United States: subterranean, drywood, and dampwood. Most damage is caused by subterranean termites, which are found in all states except Alaska; they live in colonies in the ground. Drywood termites are found in states along the southern coasts and border, in a large arc sweeping from Virginia and the Carolinas to Florida and across the southern border area into California. Dampwood termites are found west of the Rocky Mountains, throughout the Southwest, and in southeastern Florida.*

▶ *Crawl-space area has puddles or moisture.*

This condition contributes to mildew problems in the house, cold floors, structural damage under the house, and even mold in the attic. For temporary relief, install a 6 mil polyethylene moisture barrier over the dirt floor of the entire crawl space. Overlap seams 6 inches and seal with duct tape. Run the sheeting up the foundation walls at least 4 inches and seal with tape. (See page 31 for more information about crawl-space vapor barriers.) A sump pump will remove excess water; many communities require one for a crawl space or basement. The sump pit should have a liner, and the outlet pipe should discharge water at least 15 feet from the house.

Eliminating the source of moisture depends on the cause (condensation from high humidity, leaky pipes, excessive groundwater, a high water table). Prevent condensation by improving ventilation. Add screened vents around the foundation (no more than 25 feet apart) so there is at least 1 square foot of vent area (allow for reduced airflow because of screens) for every 150 square feet of crawl space. Corners should have a vent on each wall, and vents should be placed across from each other to ensure airflow. Inspect under bathroom and kitchen areas, repair leaky pipes, seal the floor around bathtubs and toilets, and avoid overflowing fixtures. To keep external groundwater away from the foundation, grade the soil so that it slopes away from the house 1 inch per foot for 10 feet or more. Repair leaky gutters and downspouts, and divert water at least 8 feet away from the house with leaders or underground drainage pipes that open to daylight (but not onto a neighbor's property). Seal foundation walls. Avoid sprinklers and excessive watering around the foundation area; plant large shrubs at least 3 feet away. Provide diversion drainage, such as a splash block or dry well, for the condensate from an air conditioner placed next to the house. A final, drastic measure is to install footing drains around the perimeter of the house (consult a professional).

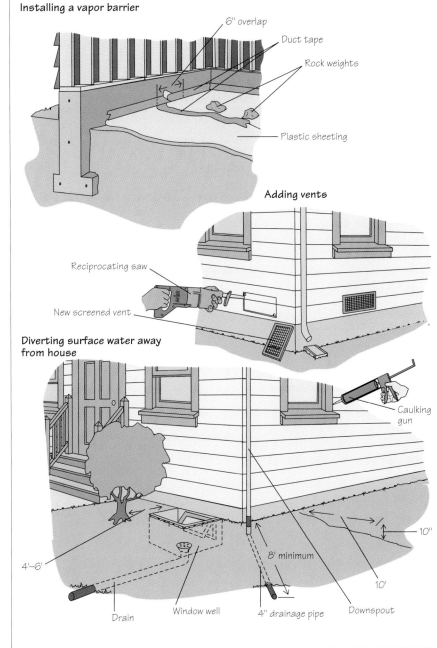

Installing a vapor barrier

6" overlap
Duct tape
Rock weights
Plastic sheeting

Adding vents

Reciprocating saw
New screened vent

Diverting surface water away from house

Caulking gun
4'–6'
Drain
Window well
8' minimum
4" drainage pipe
Downspout
10"
10'

Tip *Although excessive moisture in a crawl space usually comes from other sources, it is natural for some subsurface moisture to rise to the ground surface by means of capillary action, even if the water table is as deep as 10 feet below grade.*

▶ Basement walls have moisture.

Determine whether the cause is condensation or seepage; treatment varies. To find out, tape squares of aluminum foil or plastic sheeting to any suspicious areas of the wall, below grade level, when it is dry. When the wall is damp again, check the test patches. If they are damp on the surface, the problem is condensation. If they are damp underneath, it is seepage. (It could be both.)

To solve a condensation problem, increase ventilation and eliminate sources of vapor, such as from a clothes dryer or bathroom, by venting them directly to the outside. Insulate cold-water pipes. Keep basement windows closed on hot, humid days. On nonhumid days, raise the temperature slightly. If there is no seepage problem, finish the walls with insulation and wallboard as a long-term solution. As a last resort, install a dehumidifier.

Solving seepage problems requires eliminating the source. On the outside of the house, check all gutters, downspouts, windowsills, hose bibbs, and siding joints for leaks; repair any you find. Make sure window wells are sloped away from the house and have proper drainage. Provide leaders for the downspouts to divert water away from the house at least 8 feet (use solid, not perforated, pipe). Grade the soil around the foundation so that it slopes away from the house 1 inch per foot for 10 feet or more. Move plants and shrubs 4 to 6 feet from the foundation and replace them with grass or a 6-inch layer of packed clay, which is impermeable to surface water. Remove large tree roots next to the foundation. If you

suspect a leaky water pipe, turn off the valve at the meter before a vacation and check afterward to see if the seepage stopped. If so, excavate the pipe and fix the leak. If these measures don't solve the problem, it could be lack of adequate waterproofing and footing drainage around the foundation, a drain blocked by silt and debris, a high water table, or an overloaded community storm sewer. Consult a professional. See also page 67.

On the inside of the wall, repair obvious cracks, holes, and deteriorated mortar joints with an expansive mortar or hydraulic cement, according to label directions. Avoid using waterproofing paints unless seepage is eliminated completely, especially on block walls.

Testing for source of moisture

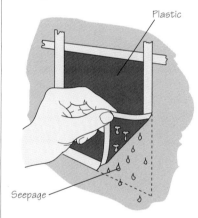

Plastic

Seepage

Patching cracks and holes

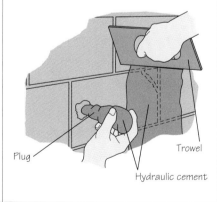

Plug

Trowel

Hydraulic cement

▶ Basement floor has moisture.

Water may be seeping imperceptibly through the walls and accumulating on the floor, so test and if necessary repair the walls (see left). If water regularly leaks in through the joint between the walls and floor, or up through floor cracks, the problem is most likely blocked foundation drains or a high water table. Try sealing the cracks with hydraulic cement, according to label directions, and installing a sump pump; avoid finishing the basement. A permanent solution, if possible, would require excavating around the foundation, waterproofing the walls, and installing a new drainage system, and perhaps installing a new basement floor over drain rock and moisture barriers. Consult a professional.

▶ Sump pump cycles on and off repeatedly.

A sump pump should cycle on and off no more than every 15 minutes, even after heavy rains. If it does, the water it discharges may be flowing right back to the basement, possibly undermining the soil beneath the foundation. Extend the outlet pipe as far as you can, at least 15 feet from the house or, if allowed, into a public storm sewer. If the pump continues to cycle rapidly, the problem is excessive moisture. See above for solutions.

▶ Basement floor has cracks.

There are many specialty products available for sealing cracks in concrete, such as expansive mortars, hydraulic cements, and epoxy-based sealers. Loosen and vacuum

Tip *Quick ways to make basement rooms more attractive: (1) Box in ducts or paint them bright colors. (2) Paint the ceiling with a light hue in graduating intensities, with the darkest shades around the edges and lightest tints in the center. (3) Paint the ceiling flat black and nail on wood lattice, stained or painted a light color. (4) Use one continuous floor covering in a light, neutral color to unify and simplify the space. (5) Cover a long wall with mirrors. (6) Stop paneling short of the ceiling to make the ceiling seem higher. (7) Conceal support*

away all debris in the crack. Some products require widening the crack and undercutting the edges with a hammer and cold chisel to provide better adhesion. Apply epoxy sealers to narrow cracks with the applicator supplied with the sealer. Apply hydraulic cement with a trowel, according to label directions.

If the floor has extensive cracking, sloping, or damage but is structurally sound, you can have a self-leveling compound (liquid underlayment) applied. It levels itself and hardens to a smooth, water-resistant surface without troweling.

Patching cracks

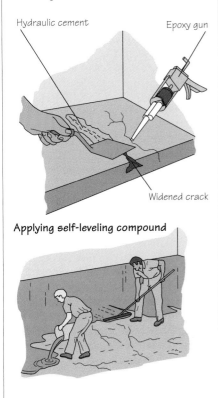

Hydraulic cement

Epoxy gun

Widened crack

Applying self-leveling compound

▶ Basement windows have moisture.

Moisture on the inside surface indicates condensation problems in the basement (see opposite page). If moisture collects between the panes of a double-glazed window, the moistureproof seal around the window glass has failed. Replace the glass unit. (See page 96.)

▶ Joint between floor and wall has gap.

In some cases this joint is intended as a weep joint to channel moisture to the base of the walls, where it collects in a trough and flows to a sump for automatic discharge. If a trough or other collection device is not present, the gap should be sealed. Use expansive mortar or hydraulic cement, applied according to label instructions.

▶ Stairs are too steep and narrow.

Most basement stairs are considered secondary stairs, which can be steeper and narrower than the primary stairs between the main floors of a home. If you convert your basement to living space, however, you may have to upgrade the stairs with safer dimensions. You may want to do this in any case. See page 57 for recommended stair dimensions. If there is not enough room for a straight-run stairway with wider treads and lower risers, consider adding a landing near the bottom and turning the stairs out into the room. Lengthening stairs also requires lengthening the stairwell ceiling opening; make sure

there is available space on the first floor. It may be more convenient to leave the present stairs and build a new stairway elsewhere.

Improving stairs

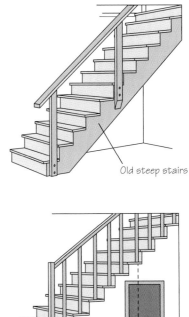

Old steep stairs

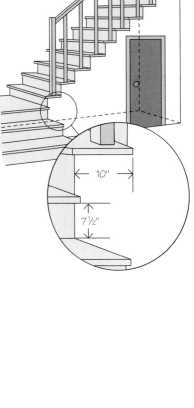

10"

7½"

posts in built-in cabinets or room dividers, or incorporate them into peninsula countertops. (8) Place lights on the floor and direct them upward against a wall to heighten it. (9) Replace ceiling lights with wall sconces to accentuate the walls rather than the ceiling. (10) Install a brightly colored metal or plastic handrail in the stairway. (11) Replace the door at the top of the stairs with a French door.

▶ *Basement has no emergency exit.*

All bedrooms must have an emergency egress. Some codes require an emergency exit for finished basements used for any purpose. The minimum requirement is either a door to the outside or a window with a clear opening at least 20 inches wide, 24 inches high, and 5.7 square feet in area; the sill can be no higher than 44 inches from the floor. Most basement windows must be enlarged by lowering the sill. To do this requires cutting through the concrete or masonry foundation wall, a job for professionals. The window well must also be enlarged, which offers opportunities for terracing or other landscaping, but may require a guardrail. It is also possible to add an exterior door by breaching the foundation wall and installing a prefabricated metal stairway with hatch cover.

Enlarging a window and well

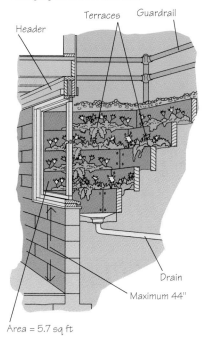

▶ *Basement ceiling is too low.*

Most codes require a minimum ceiling height of 7½ feet for habitable rooms (bedroom, family room, rec room, kitchen), and 7 feet for hallways and bathrooms. There should be 80 inches of clearance beneath ducts, headers, and other ceiling obstructions. (Measurements are from finished surface to finished surface.) If the ceiling is too low, the only solution for creating finished rooms is to lower the floor. This requires breaking through the existing concrete floor, excavating to the required depth (stopping 2 feet from the foundation), building short concrete retaining walls, and pouring a new concrete floor. This is major work, but the payoff is added living space and the opportunity to correct drainage, plumbing, and moisture problems.

Meeting clearance requirements

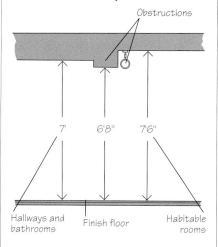

▶ *Basement is too dark.*

Strategies for brightening any room apply to basement rooms: Paint walls and ceilings light colors, install more light fixtures in the ceiling or on walls, and install large

mirrors on walls opposite windows. Maximize the natural light from small windows by clearing away shrubs, widening the window well (beware of creating a tripping hazard; add a guardrail or other barrier), and using light muslin or other gauzy material for curtains. To get the most light, add or enlarge windows—the most difficult solution. Take advantage of a basement in a hillside home by having large windows installed in the downhill wall. In conventional basements, cluster several small windows together in one area. Replace small windows with larger windows (and larger window wells); see left. You can also cut an opening in the ceiling to admit light from the room above.

▶ *Window wells present security risk.*

Install grates or plastic bubbles over the wells, or replace the window glass with panels of polycarbonate, a strong shatterproof plastic. Have the panels cut to size by a plastics supplier. Consider double-wall panels for additional strength and insulation, if you don't mind the fact that they obscure the view (they still admit light). If you wish, you can leave the window glass in place and install the polycarbonate panels on the outside like storm windows, although there is risk of condensation forming between the panes. First drill screw holes around the perimeter of the panel. Then apply a bead of silicone caulk around the window sash, and bed the panel in the caulk. Screw it in place with HDG wallboard screws. Run a second bead of caulk around the edge of the plastic. Gouge the screw heads to prevent unscrewing. Frame the edge with strips of mold-

Tip *If the basement has a furnace or gas water heater, the wood joists above the appliance should be protected with a layer of ⅝-inch, Type X wallboard or similar fire-resistant material.*

For quick (but unattractive) security, attach ½-inch hardware cloth (heavy screening) over the window; nail it to the sash with 1-inch HDG fencing staples.

Basement is too cold.

First take measures to keep cold out of the basement. Seal all gaps, cracks, and joints with caulk or weather stripping. Place fiberglass blanket insulation above the mudsill, against the rim joist. On the outside of the foundation wall, install foam insulation that is suitable for ground contact, from the floor line down to the frost line; or install insulation on the basement side of the wall if all moisture problems have been eliminated. Replace single-pane windows with double- or triple-glazed units. Install plastic shields (bubbles) over window wells.

If your home has a warm-air heating system, install one or two registers in the basement by tapping into ducts exposed in the ceiling. If the ducts are rigid, cut an opening in the sheet metal for a register boot: Trace the boot outline on the duct. With aviation snips, cut an opening 1 inch smaller than the outline, snipping slits around the opening to create tabs, and bending every other tab outward. Slide the end of the boot inside the bent tabs and reach inside it to bend the other tabs against its side. Secure three or four of the tabs to the boot with sheet-metal screws, seal the joint with metallic duct tape, and wrap duct insulation around the boot. Attach a register grille to the boot and adjust the heat level.

If the ducts are flexible, look for a joint between two sections, remove the tape and screws holding it together, and insert a Y-shaped fitting between the two sections.

Attach a register boot to the free branch of the Y fitting. Finally, install return-air vents for the basement in ducts that return cold air to the furnace plenum, as close to the floor as possible.

If there's no central heating system, install baseboard heaters or have a wood-burning stove or fireplace installed. Run the flue out the top of the basement wall and up the side of the house, then box it in.

Insulating a basement

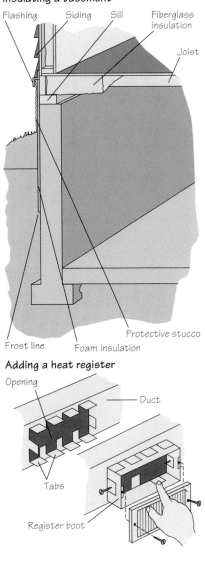

Flashing Siding Sill Fiberglass insulation

Joist

Protective stucco

Frost line Foam insulation

Adding a heat register

Opening

Duct

Tabs

Register boot

Basement needs finishing.

Do not install wallboard, insulation, flooring, or other finish materials unless all moisture problems have been eliminated completely and the basement remains dry for at least two seasons. The floor and walls should be installed over moisture membranes, such as 6 mil polyethylene sheeting or rigid foam insulation. Consult a qualified professional experienced in finishing basements in your area.

Window well traps animals.

If birds, squirrels, or other small animals get stuck in a window well from time to time, provide an escape ramp made from a 2x4 covered with carpet, chicken wire, or other material that offers secure footing.

Assisting trapped animals

▶ *Attic has moisture.*

First look for roof leaks. Active leaks during a rainstorm and points of daylight visible from the attic are obvious signs; you should also inspect the roof for damaged or missing shingles and deteriorated flashing, and make appropriate repairs (see page 110). Leaks in the winter may be caused by ice dams forming along the roof eaves and diverting melted snow under the shingles. Solve this problem by installing more ceiling insulation; this prevents heat inside the house from migrating through the ceiling and warming the attic enough to melt the snow on the roof.

Another source of moisture is condensation formed when warm vapor from inside the house rises through the ceiling and insulation, then contacts cold surfaces in the attic. Solve this problem by sealing cracks and gaps where pipes and other conduits penetrate the ceiling, by installing a vapor barrier between the ceiling material and insulation, or by providing more ventilation in the attic (see right).

▶ *Roof boards are rotted.*

Roof boards and framing members can rot from condensation formed in the attic during the winter. Prevent condensation by stopping the source of moisture, which is vapor migrating through the ceiling (see page 15), and increasing attic ventilation (see right and opposite page). Then replace the rotted boards.

▶ *Attic lacks ventilation.*

An attic should have 1 square foot of unobstructed attic vent for every 150 square feet of attic area. Vents should be positioned to promote cross-ventilation—for instance, two gable vents placed opposite each other. If prevailing winds are reliable, place the downwind vent higher than the upwind vent. Eave vents placed opposite each other allow some air circulation, but are much more effective when combined with several gable vents or a continuous ridge vent. Install attic vent chutes to improve circulation from eave vents. Vents should not be covered in the winter. Instead, use self-closing louvered vents, which open and close as breezes move air through the attic.

Installing gable vents

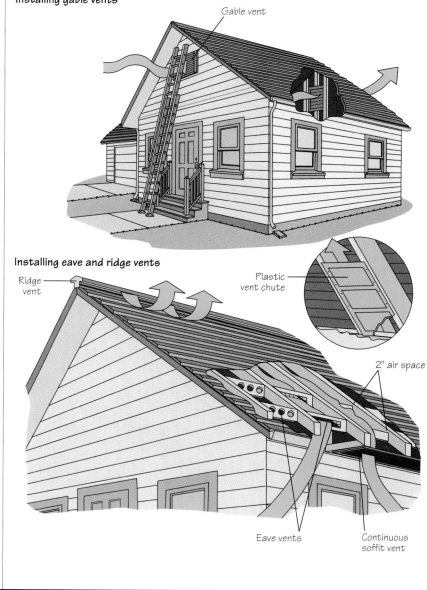

Gable vent

Installing eave and ridge vents

Ridge vent

Plastic vent chute

2" air space

Eave vents

Continuous soffit vent

Tip *Attics are exposed to severe temperature extremes. During hot weather, temperatures can reach as high as 150° F in a poorly ventilated attic. During cold weather, a poorly ventilated attic can turn water vapor to frost and ice, which eventually melts or forms condensation on attic surfaces.*

▶ *Attic overheats in hot weather.*

Install a roof fan, attic gable fan, or several roof turbines. Roof fans and turbines require cutting a hole in the roof. Mark the position, between two joists and near the ridge, by driving a nail up through the roof boards and roofing. From above, use the nail to lay out cut lines on the shingles. With a utility knife, cut through the shingles and under-layment and remove them. Cut through the roof sheathing with a reciprocating saw or compass saw, after drilling a starter hole with a ¾-inch spade bit. Set the fan or turbine housing into place by sliding the flashing under the shingles on the uphill side of the roof hole (you may have to remove nails). Replace any damaged or missing shingles. Secure the flashing with roofing nails; cover the heads with roofing cement.

Fans require electrical wiring. Most have automatic switches, so the minimum wiring requirement is a feeder line from any source directly to the fan. Many local codes, how-ever, require that you provide an override switch in a convenient location, either next to the attic access or downstairs.

Cutting roof hole

Shingles removed

Rafters

Securing housing

Roofing cement

▶ *Attic floor needs more insulation.*

At least 10 to 20 inches (R-30 to R-60) of ceiling insulation is now required for most climates, so you may need to add some. Con-sult your local code for the exact requirement. Before insulating, seal all gaps, cracks, and bypasses be-tween the living space and attic with caulk (use sheet metal for gaps around chimneys and flues). If the present insulation was installed with a vapor barrier, new fiberglass batts should be the kind without paper or foil facing, or else slit the facing in several places before lay-ing the batts over the existing insu-lation. If there is no vapor barrier present, consider pulling up the old insulation and installing the new over a vapor barrier, especially in climates with cold winters. Use 4-mil polyethylene, pressing it into place so it hugs the ceiling and sides of the joists. Then install batts or loose insulation over it. Install new batts at right angles to the old.

Do not block vents with insula-tion. Protect vents along the eaves with plastic-coated or foam baffles to maintain at least 2 inches of air space against the roof. Maintain 3 inches of air space around recessed light fixtures (unless they are clearly labeled for contact with insulation). Apply insulation to the scuttle hatch or attic door and weather stripping around the opening.

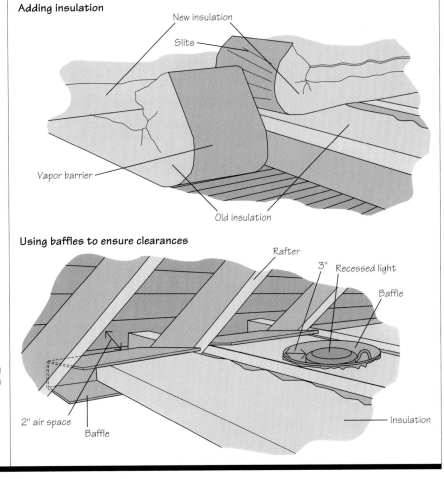

Adding insulation

New insulation

Slits

Vapor barrier

Old insulation

Using baffles to ensure clearances

Rafter

3" Recessed light

Baffle

2" air space   Baffle

Insulation

Tip *If an attic contains living space, the places that should be insulated are the walls around the living space, the ceiling of the living space, and the floor of the rest of the attic. If there is no living space in the attic, insulation should always go on the attic floor and not between the rafters.*

▶ *Attic has snow in it.*

Sometimes snow blows into a ridge vent, producing a line of powdery snow underneath. This is not a serious problem, but you can block the snow and still allow air to pass through the vent by inserting strips of 1-inch-thick fiberglass filter material (available in rolls, or cut from furnace filters) in the ridge vent openings. Replace it every few years when it gets clogged with dust and debris.

▶ *Insulation has dirty smudges.*

Smudges may appear where the insulation has filtered dust out of air leaking up from the rooms below. Such air leaks, called bypasses, contribute to heat loss and attic vapor problems and should be sealed; the smudges are a convenient way to find them. The most likely bypasses are around pipes, flues, electrical wires, light fixtures, chimneys, and wall intersections. Seal cracks with caulk, large gaps with foam insulation. Cover gaps around a chimney or flue with sheet metal and seal with high-temperature furnace cement.

Sealing bypasses

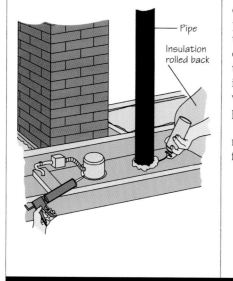

Pipe

Insulation rolled back

▶ *Attic is dark and stuffy.*

Attics should be well ventilated to prevent condensation problems during cold weather and overheating during hot weather. Provide gable or eave and ridge vents. Install a gable fan or roof fan. See also page 72.

▶ *Attic has limited access or egress.*

Most codes require a 22-inch by 30-inch scuttle if the attic has 30 inches or more of headroom. If you want to add another one, the best place is over a hallway or closet—joist spans in such a place are short and the location is accessible but out of the way. With a framing square, mark lines for a rectangular cutout. There should be no wires, ducts, or other obstructions over the opening. Cut lines should be on the inside faces of joists, not centered beneath the joists. Remove insulation from above the cutout and carefully saw along the cut lines with a handsaw. Set the cutout piece aside. Cut and remove the section of joist that passes over the opening and install 2x4 or 2x6 headers to support the cutoff ends of the joists, attaching with screws or a nailing gun; hammering might jar the ceiling. Attach molding to the ceiling around the edge of the opening so that it provides a lip for the cutout hatch to rest on. Apply insulation to the top of the hatch with adhesive; attach weather stripping around the opening.

If an attic is used for sleeping, it must have an emergency egress from the bedroom. A window that

has 5.7 square feet of unobstructed opening qualifies, so long as it is at least 20 inches wide, 24 inches high, and no more than 44 inches above the floor. If it doesn't open onto a section of relatively flat roof, provide an escape ladder that can be stored under the bed and hung from the sill in an emergency.

Cutting scuttle opening

Joists

Wallboard

Installing headers and trim

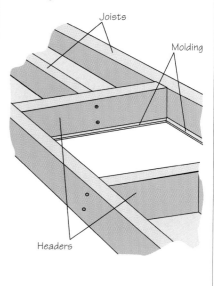

Joists

Molding

Headers

Tip *The old-fashioned storage attic is a bygone relic. Attics in modern homes are cluttered with insulation, vents, fans, baffles, truss framing, and other essential technology; stairs (if they exist) and scuttles are provided for service access, not storage access. Although you might be able to carve out some storage space, it is generally not worth the effort by the time you have built a floor above all the insulation and improved the access.*

▶ *Chimney has open gap around it.*

There should be at least 1 inch of clearance between a chimney and any combustible material, such as wood framing or sheathing. This clearance creates a gap around the chimney where it penetrates the ceiling and roof. Roof flashing takes care of the roof gap. The ceiling gap is usually filled with noncombustible material, such as plaster or fiberglass. The best way to seal the gap is with strips of sheet metal. Apply a bead of caulk to the tops of the framing members, then nail the metal strips to them so they butt tightly against the chimney. With high-temperature caulk, seal both the joint around the chimney and the joints between metal strips.

Sealing gap around chimney

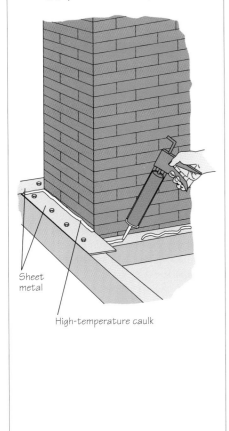

Sheet
metal

High-temperature caulk

▶ *Chimney bricks have white or black powder.*

White powder is probably efflorescence and indicates that the bricks have been in frequent contact with moisture. Inspect roof flashing around the chimney and take measures to eliminate attic moisture (see page 72).

Black powder is soot, caused by smoke escaping through joints or cracks in the chimney. This is a fire hazard. Have the chimney inspected and repaired before you use it again.

▶ *Attic floor sags or bounces.*

The floor is probably supported on ceiling joists not designed for an attic floor load. This is a structural problem; consult a professional.

▶ *You want to convert attic to living space.*

This is a major project. Before you involve an architect and contractor, you may want to do a quick feasibility check of your own. If the roof is supported by trusses, which create a web of braces and supports throughout the attic, go no further. Every member of this engineered roof system is vital and cannot be cut or moved.

Is there enough floor area and headroom? Codes specify the minimum size of a room intended for certain uses (80 square feet for a bedroom, for example); however, at least one-half of that area must also have the minimum headroom, which is 7½ feet for most habitable rooms. Furthermore, there is a minimum ceiling height, usually 5 feet. Any floor space outside that limit cannot be counted in calculating the room size. Finally, all of these dimensions are between finished surfaces; you must take into account alterations to the floor, ceiling, and walls. Dormers are one way to overcome height limitations, but as a rule of thumb there should be at least 9 feet of headroom in the unfinished attic to make a conversion feasible.

Other considerations are the size of floor joists, strength of the foundation and first-floor walls, availability of space for a stairway, location of plumbing and mechanical connections, and potential for windows and skylights.

Calculating floor area

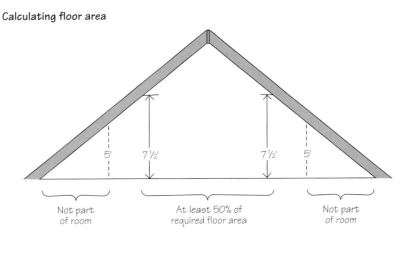

5'   7½'   7½'   5'

Not part
of room

At least 50% of
required floor area

Not part
of room

Tip *If your attic has a sleeping area, equip it with a smoke detector, a fire extinguisher, an emergency fire ladder close to an openable window, and a flashlight at each bedside. Instruct family members and guests on how to use the equipment during a fire or other emergency.*

SOLVING INDOOR PROBLEMS

▶ House has ants.

The most effective ant control is bait. Place ant baits where the ants are thickest and don't use any other controls for about a week. The ants will carry the bait back to their nest, which will poison it and stop the invasion from that nest. Another control is to apply an insecticide for ants (containing diazinon, chlorpyrifos, or propoxur) along baseboards, under the sink, around windowsills, and in other areas of access. Insecticides with pyrethrins have a repellent action; spray them across ant trails to control access. Follow label precautions.

To control ants permanently, follow trails to the central colony and destroy it. Apply a residual spray or granules (such as diazinon) around the perimeter of the house periodically to discourage future ant attacks. Be sure all cracks and openings on the outside of the house are caulked or otherwise sealed; this won't control ants by itself, but is essential for overall pest control. For limited control try spreading talcum or baby powder or cucumber peelings around areas that attract the ants.

▶ House has fleas.

Flea problems are linked to pets. As adults, fleas live on the host pet, but during the rest of their life cycle (egg, larvae, pupa), they inhabit various areas inside or outside the home, such as pet sleeping areas, baseboards, edges of rugs, and shady, moist areas under shrubs and along pet walkways. The simplest control is to apply an insect growth regulator to these areas, according to label directions. For more complete control, you must simultaneously treat the pet and all indoor and outdoor areas likely to harbor fleas.

Eradicate fleas on your pet with regular applications of a shampoo, spray, or dust product that contains a flea control agent such as carbaryl, tetramethrin plus sumithrin, pyrethrins, or malathion. Follow label directions and cautions exactly; be sure that the product is specified for use on animals. At the same time treat indoor areas by washing (or disposing of) the pet's bedding material; spraying or dusting the sleeping area with an insecticide specified for fleas; vacuuming all floors, carpeting, and furniture in rooms where the pet goes (dispose of the vacuum bag immediately); and treating the rooms with an insecticide spray or a total-release aerosol. Control fleas outdoors by applying insecticide to crawl spaces, pet sleeping areas, and other areas that animals frequent. Mint, garlic, cedar, and eucalyptus aromas may repel fleas. If infestations persist, consult a veterinarian or pest control specialist.

▶ House has cockroaches.

These pests infest kitchens, bathrooms, and other areas where food and water are available. They hide in walls, under sinks, behind refrigerators, within piles of grocery bags, around pipes, behind paneling or loose wallpaper, and in similar dark places; they rarely are seen during the day. To control cockroaches, eliminate all food and water sources (see right). Seal cracks around pipes, baseboards, sinks, cabinets, and other hidden areas with caulk or foam insulation. Remove all food and utensils from the kitchen. Then sprinkle finely powdered boric acid, which is very safe and effective, in cracks and other potential hiding places, following label directions. Reline the shelves with fresh paper, and replace the food and utensils.

▶ House has flies.

Flies feed on and lay their eggs in decaying organic materials, so the first line of defense is to maintain sanitary conditions in and around the home and garden, especially garbage cans. Keep cans clean by lining them with garbage bags or newspapers; attach a resinous pest strip to the bottom of the garbage can lid. Rinse bottles and cans thoroughly before placing them in recycling bins.

Next make sure that all doors and openable windows have tight-fitting screens that are in good repair. Inside the house control isolated flies with a flyswatter (and good aim). You can kill larger numbers of flies quickly with a spray containing d-trans allethrin, tetramethrin, pyrethrins, or resmethrin; follow label directions. For temporary control spray flies with hair spray—it doesn't kill them, but it immobilizes them so they can be disposed of easily.

Discourage flies from entering the house by spraying outdoor areas where flies land or congregate, such as around screen doors, lights, and south-facing walls, with a residual insecticide that contains chlorpyrifos, diazinon, or malathion. Pesticide strips work best in enclosed rooms where the vapors can build up; they are not very effective on porches or other well-ventilated spaces. Avoid using them near food or where infants or the elderly are confined. Control fruit flies (called vinegar flies) by removing any spoiled fruit or vegetables. If you leave fruit out to ripen at room temperature, control fruit flies with a simple trap: either a long-necked wine bottle with ½ inch of wine in the bottom, or a bowl of water with a small amount of apple juice and liquid detergent in it.

Tip *Good housekeeping is the best defense against pests (although occasional pests do not mean you're a bad housekeeper). Clean kitchen countertops, floors, shelves, and cabinets frequently, especially in corners and hidden areas. Store food (including pet food) in screw-top jars; wipe around lids after closing jars. Keep lids on garbage cans. Vacuum carpets frequently. Clean clothing before storing it. Close door and window screens tightly. Keep the house ventilated and moisture under control.*

▶ House has spiders.

Spiders are generally harmless and even beneficial. Only a few, particularly the black widow and brown recluse, are dangerous (but rarely fatal). However, because of the nuisance of webs and the disconcerting appearance of spiders, most people want them out of the house. Remove all spiderwebs and keep other insects (their prey) under control. Seal cracks and other entry points into the home; keep screens repaired. Remove debris from around the perimeter of the house and store firewood at least 10 feet away. Indoors, spray infested areas with an insecticide containing propoxur or chlorpyrifos, following label instructions carefully.

▶ House has silverfish.

Silverfish feed on starchy materials such as paper, book bindings, wallpaper paste, cotton or linen clothing (not wool or fur), and stored grains or cereals. They thrive in damp, humid conditions; some species prefer cool places like basements, others warm places near hot-water pipes or heaters. They are nocturnal. You are likely to notice them if you lift an object, such as a book or cardboard box, under which they've been hiding. To control, seal cracks around pipes, baseboards, and cabinets. Throw out unnecessary books, magazines, or papers. Move books around in bookcases periodically. Use a spray containing diazinon or chlorpyrifos to treat baseboard gaps, door and window frames, closets, behind drawers and shelves, behind and around the edges of bookshelves, and holes where pipes go through walls. Dusts such as boric acid or silica aerogel are also effective. Wait two or three weeks; if infestations recur, repeat the treatment. Bait packets also work, but are effective only when spaced no more than 1 to 3 feet apart. Follow all label instructions.

▶ House has clothes moths or carpet beetles.

Clothes moths and carpet beetles are not much nuisance themselves, but you'll know their presence by holes in sweaters, moth-eaten upholstery, and damaged carpets. The larvae (but not adults) damage household fabrics more often than any other insect pest. The adult moths, unlike other types of moths, prefer dark corners and are not attracted to light. The adult beetles resemble small ladybugs. Despite their names, neither pest infests only one type of material; they like it all.

Use the same control techniques for both pests. Start with a thorough search for the wormlike larvae in clothes, carpets, blankets, wool rugs, upholstered furniture, felt piano parts, animal-bristle brushes, feathers, animal skins, and accumulations of lint or pet hair in hidden areas. Eradicate the larvae by dry-cleaning or laundering the fabric, throwing out the damaged article (spray with insecticide first and seal in a plastic bag), or applying a spray with pyrethrins directly to the fabric, according to label instructions. To avoid staining, make sure it is specified for use with fabrics. To stem further activity, spray a residual insecticide containing propoxur, diazinon, or chlorpyrifos onto closet floors and corners, over empty shelves, along baseboards, behind heaters, and in cracks and other hidden places. Vacuum carpets frequently, moving furniture occasionally to vacuum underneath; dispose of the vacuum bag promptly if you suspect eggs or larvae. When storing clothes, blankets, and other susceptible items, clean them thoroughly first; then spray the garments with a moth-proofer containing tetramethrin and sumithrin and wrap them in plastic. Dry-clean or launder them before using again. Store woolen items in a tight container with mothballs, crystals, or flakes. Placing mothballs in a closet, or lining it with cedar, is not enough; the garments must be enclosed in a tight container. Wrap the mothballs in paper so they don't touch the fabric. Outdoors, remove or clean sources of hair, feathers, and animal debris.

▶ House has pantry moths or beetles.

Certain moths and beetles infest stored food, such as flour, spices, cereal, beans, nuts, dried fruits, candy, and even pet food. Although you may see the smallish moths (¼- to ½-inch wingspan) flying in your home in the evening, particularly in dimly lit areas, the reclusive habits of these pantry pests make it difficult to detect a problem unless you search. Telltale signs are tiny holes or webbing in food or packaging. Pay close attention to opened packages and boxes that have been on the shelf for a long time. If you find only one infested package, simply seal it in a plastic bag and throw it in the garbage. If infestation is widespread, you can save lightly contaminated items (throw out anything heavily infested). Kill the insects by freezing the food for three days or spreading it on cookie sheets and warming it in an oven set at 120° to 130° F for two hours. Keep an eye on it to avoid scorching the food. Boil dried fruit for about one minute, then spread it to dry before storing it again.

For serious infestation, remove all food, packages, and utensils from cabinets and shelves. Thoroughly

Tip   *How to handle and store poisons: (1) Read the label before using the product. (2) Store in a locked cabinet, never under the kitchen sink or near food. (3) Don't let insecticide sprays drift onto food or utensils. (4) Wash your hands and face immediately after using the product. (5) Keep the container handy in case you must identify the product for a doctor or poison control center if it gets in someone's mouth or eyes.*

SOLVING INDOOR PROBLEMS

clean the storage areas by vacuuming and scrubbing with soap and hot water. Dispose of crumbs in a sealed plastic bag. Spray corners and other hidden areas with a short-lived insecticide containing tetramethrin and sumithrin, or pyrethrins. It should be specified for food cabinets. Consider applying a residual insecticide containing chlorpyrifos or diazinon, but only to cracks and crevices. Allow it to dry thoroughly before replacing food and utensils. After an infestation clean shelves frequently and store all food in sealed containers.

▶ House has wood-boring insects.

Termites, powder-post beetles, carpenter ants, and carpenter bees are insects that bore into wood for food or nesting places. They should be eradicated when first detected. They are not restricted to the foundation and crawl-space areas—drywood termites infest attics, carpenter ants work throughout the structure, powder-post beetles invade hardwood furniture and flooring, and carpenter bees infest exterior siding and trim. Telltale signs of infestation are holes in the wood, small piles of fine sawdust (frass), weak wood, and discarded wings from swarming activity. The best control is inspections every 2 to 10 years, depending on where you live. Survey the foundation, outside and inside. Look for termite tubes, frass, small holes in wood, and soft, crumbly wood. For prevention: remove all wood debris from under and around the house; keep firewood piles as far from the house as possible; remove dead trees, branches, and stumps; eliminate sources of moisture from the crawl space, attic, and similar places; use pressure-treated lumber for ground

contact; and maintain 8 inches of clearance between all other wood parts of the house and the ground. See also page 65.

▶ House has dust mites.

All houses contain dust mites, which feed on human skin debris commonly found on mattresses and in house dust on floors. They produce asthma symptoms in sensitive people. It is impossible to eliminate them, but there are ways to control them. Try to maintain humidity below 70 percent (humans require 35 to 50 percent relative humidity). Do so by using exhaust fans in the bathroom and kitchen, controlling moisture in the basement or crawl space, venting gas heaters properly, and, if necessary, using a dehumidifier. Frequent vacuuming may control mites, but is also likely to stir them up. It is more effective to replace carpets with wood floors, area rugs, or other floor coverings. Consult an allergy specialist for other controls.

▶ House has mice.

Mice are difficult to control because they're nocturnal, can fit through cracks as small as ¼ inch, and can survive on meager food supplies. Practice general sanitation, remove debris from outside the house, and seal cracks and other openings on a regular basis. Droppings and greasy smudges along trails, such as baseboards, indicate the presence of mice. Eliminate them with traps or poison bait. Spring traps work best if you start by placing them baited but unset along trails and close to food sources for a few days. Experiment with such baits as peanut butter, dried fruit, gumdrops, or bacon to see what is preferred. When you set the traps, tie the bait to the trigger

or press it firmly in place. Use several traps (you may need as many as three per mouse) and space them no less than 6 feet apart. Make sure children or pets can't get to them. When placing traps along a wall, set single traps at right angles to it, with the bait toward the wall, or pairs of traps end-to-end, with bait facing opposite directions. Check traps daily; wear plastic gloves. Place carcasses in plastic bags and deposit them in the garbage or bury them. Poison baits are also effective, so long as they are specified for mice. The fastest-acting type, and safest to use around pets and desirable wild animals, is one with cholecalciferol. Place baits in the same kinds of places as traps, according to label instructions. If you have children or pets, place the bait in a wooden box with a lockable lid. Cut 2½-inch-square access holes in opposite ends of the box, then set the box against a wall so the holes are in line with the mouse trail. Check daily and replenish bait as needed. Cats that are skilled in hunting (most pet cats aren't) also help.

▶ House has rats.

Because rats are larger than mice, they are easier to exclude from the house by sealing openings. They are harder to trap, however, because they are more wary of new food or other items in their territory and, in the case of roof rats, can nest high in inaccessible places. Follow similar control procedures as for mice. Traps must be larger and can be spaced farther apart. Be especially careful where you place them if children or pets are in your home; you may need to set them in locked boxes, as with poison bait for mice (see above). For roof rats, place traps and bait up high, such as on tree limbs or fence tops, and tie them in place so they won't fall.

Tip *In cold climates subterranean termites live below the frost line and stay there during the winter. They can survive for months without a fresh food supply, which in their case is cellulose from wood materials.*

For safety, convenience, comfort, and appearance, all the doors and windows in your home should work properly and be in good repair. This chapter will help you solve more than 110 door and window problems, from a squeaking door to a broken drapery cord.

SOLVING DOOR & WINDOW PROBLEMS

▶ Door squeaks.

Oil the hinges with light penetrating oil or silicone spray. To get the lubricant inside the hinge, raise the pin slightly by placing a nail under the hinge pin and knocking it upward with a hammer. Then apply the oil around the pin at the top of the hinge. Wait a few minutes for it to penetrate, then hammer the pin back in place. If squeaking persists, open the door fully, prop the bottom so it won't sag, and remove the hinge pin by knocking it all the way out with a hammer and a 16d nail. Smooth the pin and inside of the hinge barrel with steel wool, lubricate them, and reassemble. Repeat for the other hinge.

▶ Door binds.

If the door binds on the hinge side, check the hinge screws first and tighten any loose ones (see Tip below). If a head protrudes because it's too large, use a longer screw with a smaller head. If part of a head protrudes because the screw is driven at an angle, remove the screw, fill the opening with glued matchsticks or toothpicks, and, after the glue dries, drill a pilot hole straight into the jamb and install the screw. If the door still binds, check for hinge leaves that are recessed (mortised) too deep and shim them out. To shim a leaf, loosen the screws, insert thin cardboard under the outside half of the leaf, and tighten the screws. Increase the shim thickness by folding the cardboard or adding layers. Use trial and error—slight increments amplify door move-

ment elsewhere. If removing the bind causes sticking elsewhere, see following.

Straightening an angled screw

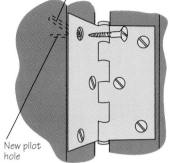

Old screw hole filled with glued toothpicks or matchsticks

New pilot hole

Shimming a hinge leaf

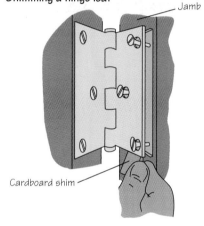

Jamb

Cardboard shim

▶ Door sticks on latch side.

First check for loose hinges and tighten the screws (see Tip below). If there's a gap along the hinge edge when the door is shut, keep it shut, remove the pin of the hinge closest to the gap and, with pliers, bend the hinge knuckles of the jamb leaf slightly toward the jamb; replace the pin. Another way to move the knuckles toward the jamb is to place a shim under the jamb hinge leaf along the edge closest to the doorstop (do this with the door open).

If the gap is too narrow (thinner than a dime) to move the door any more and the door still sticks, it's time to lubricate, sand, plane, or saw the edges—in that order. First locate exactly where the door sticks or binds. If it barely sticks, rub a candle over the bulge or apply silicone lubricant. If it still sticks, wrap coarse-grit sandpaper around a woodblock and ease the high spots with it, allowing for a layer of touch-up paint or finish. If the bottom sticks, tape a sheet of coarse sandpaper to the floor and work the door back and forth over it. As the sandpaper wears, place thin cardboard under the new paper so it will remove more of the door bottom.

To remove more wood, plane or saw the edge. Mark how much wood must be removed with the door in place; then remove the door (see Tip, opposite page) and stabilize it on edge (to plane) or lay it on sawhorses (to saw). Try to rent or borrow a power planer. It is easier to control than other tools, works quickly, and leaves a smooth edge for repainting. Whether using a hand plane or power planer, work with the grain and start at the corners, working toward the center. If you use a saw or you must plane an entire edge, trim the hinge edge instead of the latch edge; you won't have to take off the latch hardware and you don't run the risk of cutting off the 5-degree bevel that a latch edge must have. Trimming an edge with a saw may also leave scarring marks, which are hidden more easily on the hinge edge. After trimming, deepen the hinge mortises with a sharp chisel, touch up the edge with sandpaper, and repaint.

Tip *If a screw turns but won't tighten, remove the screw. Then pack a few matchsticks, some toothpicks, or some short pieces of solder into the hole and replace the screw with a slightly longer one. For a more permanent repair, remove the hinge leaf, enlarge the hole to 3/8 inch by drilling, and glue in a 3/8-inch hardwood dowel. Let the glue dry, trim the dowel flush, drill a pilot hole in it for the screw, and replace the hinge leaf.*

Note: If the sticking problem is seasonal, be aware that adjusting the hinges or trimming the door may cause other problems during the off season.

Bending knuckles

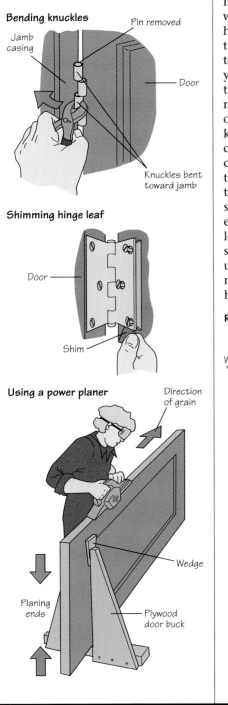

Shimming hinge leaf

Using a power planer

▶ *Door sticks against center of head jamb.*

Hold a level or straightedge against the head jamb to see if it is sagging. If so, it's probably because shims were placed between the jamb and header (overhead framing member), transferring weight from the header to the jamb. To solve the problem, you need to remove the shims. On the side of the door that is least noticeable, score the painted joints of the head casing with a utility knife, then carefully pry off the casing. Remove any shims from the cavity above the head jamb by splitting them with a chisel and pulling the pieces out. The head jamb should spring back toward the header. If nails prevent it from moving, locate the nail heads on the bottom side of the jamb and tap them upward with a nail set and hammer. Replace the casing, patch nail holes and cracks, and repaint.

Removing shims

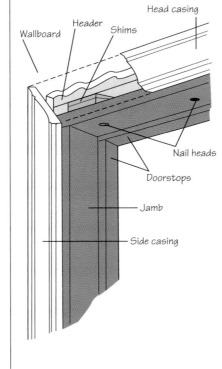

▶ *Door won't close tightly.*

If the door closes all the way but doesn't latch, the latch bolt isn't aligned with the strike plate. First close the door and check to see if the latch reaches the strike plate. If not, put enough shims behind the strike plate so that the latch bolt engages it. If they are not aligned, close the door and use a pencil to mark where the top and bottom of the latch bolt engage the strike plate. Compare these marks with the top and bottom of the strike plate hole. If the marks fall within the hole limits, the strike plate is too far back. If it's just a slight misalignment, enlarge the hole with a file. If a larger adjustment is necessary, remove the screws and plate, pack the screw holes with glued matchsticks, set the plate in the new location, drill pilot holes, and screw. You may also have to enlarge the hole in the doorjamb with a chisel to accommodate the latch.

If the marks show that the strike plate is too high or too low, measure the discrepancy. If it's less than ⅛ inch, enlarge the strike plate hole with a file. Otherwise, move the plate up or down the required distance by removing the plate, trimming away wood with a knife or sharp chisel, and reattaching the plate in the new location. Patch the resulting gap with spackling compound or wood putty, and touch it up with paint or stain. Bear in mind that this problem may be seasonal and the repair may cause misalignment during the off season.

If the latch bolt is aligned with the hole but doesn't engage it, the spring that drives the bolt is broken or jammed. Disassemble the lockset and clean all working parts with a

Tip *To remove a door, open it about halfway and slide a shim under the latch edge to stabilize it. Remove the lower hinge pin first, then the upper, by grabbing the top of the pin with pliers and pulling upward, or tuck a chisel under the top of the pin, or insert a 16d nail below it, and knock it upward with a hammer. With the pins removed, slide the door away from the hinges and carry it out. If the door is solid-core, have someone help you stabilize and lift it.*

SOLVING DOOR & WINDOW PROBLEMS

light solvent. Lubricate them with a silicone or other nonstick lock lubricant and replace the spring if broken. See page 95.

Marking latch bolt position

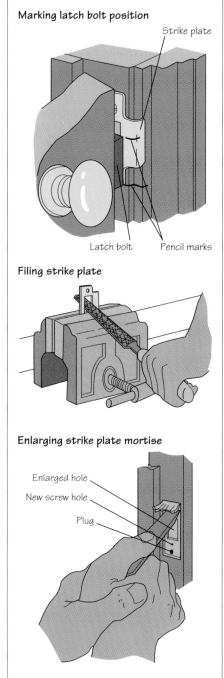

Strike plate

Latch bolt   Pencil marks

Filing strike plate

Enlarging strike plate mortise

Enlarged hole
New screw hole
Plug

▶ Door sags.

Check the screws in the top hinge and tighten any that are loose. If they are tight, shut the door and, while observing from the side where the hinge knuckles are exposed, check to see if there is a wide gap between the door and jamb near the top hinge. If so, remove the door (see page 80) by pulling the hinge pins and, using pliers, bend the knuckles of the top hinge back toward the jamb. Rehang the door. If it still sags, realign the hinges (see below), or trim the bottom.

▶ Door wanders and won't stay still.

The door wanders because the hinges are not aligned plumb. To steady the door, try stiffening the hinges by removing the pins, one at a time, striking them with a hammer to bend them slightly, and replacing them. If the door still wanders, you'll have to realign the hinges by working on the door-jamb leaves. Pull the hinge pins and remove the door. Suspend a small plumb bob from the first knuckle on the top hinge to the lowest knuckle on the bottom hinge and note the direction(s) in which the hinges are out of alignment; or hold a 6-foot level vertically against the hinges, checking it in two directions (a shorter level with a straightedge also works). Move one of the leaves away from the jamb (by inserting shims behind it) and/or move one farther out from the doorstop (by enlarging the mortise with a chisel and plugging old screw holes so screws won't drift back into them—see Tip, page 80). Before rehanging the door, straighten the bent hinge pins or buy replacements.

Note: Because moving hinges far enough to make them plumb may cause other problems, such as a sticking door or misaligned latch, it may not be worthwhile to make them perfectly plumb; adjusting them slightly may be enough.

Checking plumb alignment

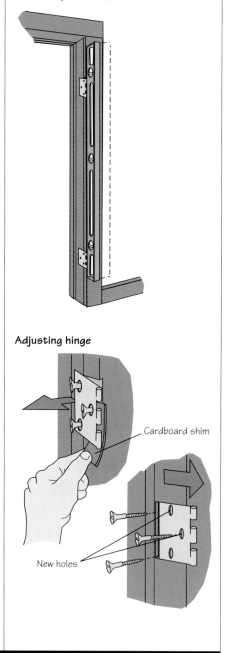

Adjusting hinge

Cardboard shim

New holes

Tip *Most interior doors are either "flush" (the face is plain and smooth) or "panel" (individual panels are set into a cross-shaped frame). Flush doors are hollow, with two "skins" (veneers) of thin lauan plywood. Panel doors vary in style and number of panels. Traditionally they were made from solid wood, which meant they were costly. Panel doors with hardboard facings made to resemble traditional panel styles are now available at much cheaper prices—about the same as flush doors.*

▶ *Door bottom needs trimming.*

At one time or other almost every home has a door that needs to be trimmed at the bottom: it drags on new carpet; it won't clear a new threshold; the door frame has shifted over time; or central heating requires airflow under the doors. If the door has not been removed, open it and measure ½ inch above the finish flooring at both bottom edges of the door (½ inch clears most carpets; ¾ inch is recommended if the home has central warm-air heating). Remeasure with the door closed. Remove the door (see page 80). If the door has been removed, measure from the head jamb down to the finish flooring along both sides of the door frame and transfer these measurements to the door, less ½ inch or ¾ inch for clearance. Allow for any gap that existed at the top of the door. (This method assumes that both the frame and the top of the door are square and that the floor level at the doorway is the same as where the door swings open; if not, adjust measurements accordingly.)

Run a length of masking tape along the bottom edge of the door face, to prevent the saw from splintering the door face, and scribe a cut line over it, between the marks. Lay the door on sawhorses with the best side facing up if you trim with a handsaw, down if you trim with a circular saw or jigsaw. To minimize splintering with a handsaw, duplicate the cut line on the side of the door that faces down and score that line with a utility knife. For a circular saw or jigsaw, score the cut line and clamp a straightedge to the

door to guide the saw. After sawing, sand the cut edges smooth and apply sealer or paint to the bare wood.

Measuring from floor

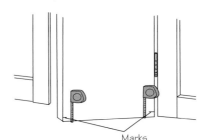

Marks

Marking door for trimming

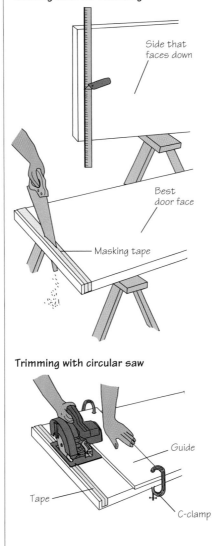

Side that faces down

Best door face

Masking tape

Trimming with circular saw

Guide

Tape

C-clamp

▶ *Door has gaps around edge.*

When they are shut, interior doors normally have about ³⁄₁₆ inch of clearance around the edges (thickness of a nickel). The door should "float" within the opening, rather than fit snugly all around; however, it should fit snugly against the doorstops.

If the gap is too wide, it may be unsightly. Remove the door (see page 80) and take the hinges off it. Plug the hinge mortises with wood strips. Attach a strip of wood (wide enough to reduce the gap to ³⁄₁₆ inch) along the hinge edge of the door with glue and nails. Then cut new hinge mortises into the strip, sand the strip smooth (especially along the joint), and finish it to match the rest of the door.

▶ *Door is warped or coming apart.*

It's often easier to buy a replacement door than to repair one; you may be able to find a used door or a door second at a reasonable price. If not, remove the door (see page 80). To repair a bowed door, set it on sawhorses, convex side up, and distribute weights (books, bricks) near the center of the door. Leave it there for two or three weeks. For warped doors that are twisted as well as bowed, attach wires and a turnbuckle to eye hooks screwed into opposite corners. Place a 2x4 under the wire and increase tension daily for three or four days. After it's straight, remove the hooks and fill the holes with putty. If the door is still warped when you hang it, install a third hinge midway between the top and bottom hinges.

To repair a panel door that's coming apart, remove the door and set it on sawhorses. Try squeezing the door parts together with bar clamps—paint and debris may have

Tip   *Most doors have butt hinges, which have two leaves of identical size that open flat. For interior doors, the most common size is 3½ inches. The leaves are recessed flush into mortises cut into the doorjamb and door edge. Most mortises are now cut with a router, which leaves corners rounded because the bit rotates in a circular motion. For this reason, butt hinges are available with rounded corners, in addition to the traditional kind with square corners for mortises cut with a chisel.*

clogged the cracks. Remove the clamps, separate the pieces as far as you can without breaking the joints, and inject aliphatic adhesive (carpenter's wood glue) into the joints with a glue syringe. Clamp the stiles together with a bar clamp placed at each rail on alternating sides of the door. Use 2x4 fillers to avoid marring the door. Alternately tighten clamps a little bit until the joints are all tight. Wipe away excess glue, let dry overnight, remove the clamps, and paint or seal the door.

Straightening a warped door

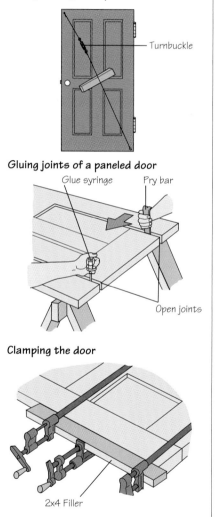

Turnbuckle

Gluing joints of a paneled door

Glue syringe   Pry bar

Open joints

Clamping the door

2x4 Filler

▶ Door is hard for children or an elderly person to open.

Replace the doorknobs with lever handles, which come in many attractive styles. With some styles, you may need to replace the entire lockset. There are also lever handles that clamp onto an ordinary doorknob. To make opening a door convenient for a person in a wheelchair, you can have automatic door openers installed on certain interior doors. They can be activated by a remote-controlled device, much like an automatic garage-door opener.

▶ Door opening is too narrow for wheelchair.

If the opening is wide enough without the door itself blocking part of it, replace the existing hinges with offset hinges. They let the door swing out of the way when it opens fully, so it clears the opening. If the opening is still too narrow, the only solution is to widen the doorway and install a new door. Consult a carpenter.

Using offset hinges to swing door out of the way

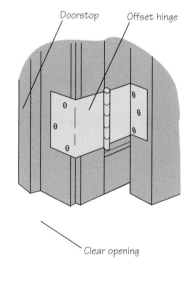

Doorstop   Offset hinge

Clear opening

▶ Door needs replacing.

Buy a new door the same size as the opening or slightly larger. The standard height for new doors is 6 feet, 8 inches; widths range in 2-inch increments from 2 feet to 3 feet. If the old door fits perfectly, use it as a template for trimming the new one to size. If one edge of the new door is beveled, make it the latch edge and trim the other edge. If not, make the trimmed edge the latch edge and bevel it 5 degrees. If the old door does not fit well or is missing, measure the doorway dimensions and use them to mark cut lines on the new door. Check the door opening for square by measuring the diagonals, or by holding a framing square against each corner; adjust dimensions accordingly. Allow for 3/16-inch clearance at the top and each side, 1/2 to 3/4 inch for the bottom. Score the cut line with a utility knife, or cover it with masking tape to minimize splintering; clamp a straightedge to the door as a saw guide. Use a power saw to trim the door. If you are trimming the latch edge, set the saw blade to a 5-degree bevel.

After trimming the door, measure and mark for the hinge mortises. Take measurements from the old door or measure the distance from the head jamb to the hinge mortises in the door frame, then subtract 3/16 inch to allow for the top clearance. Cut the mortises with a 1½-inch chisel; start by scoring and deepening the cut lines, then chisel away enough waste so that the hinge leaf will recess flush into the mortise. Next drill holes for the doorknob or other latching hardware. Instructions supplied with the doorknob should provide dimensions for the diameter and centering of the holes. Install the hinges and doorknob, and hang the door to test it for fit; make adjustments as necessary.

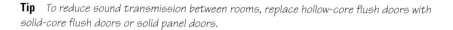

Tip   To reduce sound transmission between rooms, replace hollow-core flush doors with solid-core flush doors or solid panel doors.

Take down the door, remove the hardware, and paint or finish as desired. When the finish dries, install the hardware and hang the door.

Measuring door opening without square corners

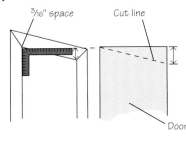

Trimming door edge

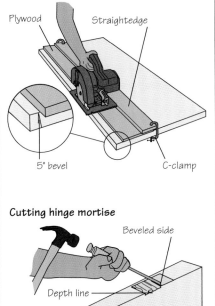

Cutting hinge mortise

▶ Edge of door seems to be wrong color.

If the whole door is painted one color, the edges should be the same color. If the two sides of the door are painted different colors, paint the edges to match the rooms they face when the door is open—hinge edge one color; latch edge, top, and bottom the other.

▶ Bifold doors bind or won't close.

First shut the doors as far as possible and see if there are gaps between the doors and side jambs. If there are, move the bottoms of the doors toward the jambs by lifting up on them and sliding them over. To move the tops, locate the pin holder at each end of the overhead track, and loosen the setscrews that lock them in place; slide the holders toward the jambs and retighten the screws. If the doors still bind, they are too wide for the door opening. Trim one of the center panels along its nonhinged edge.

Adjusting bifold door at top

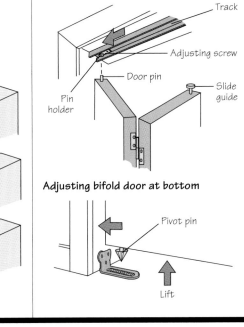

Adjusting bifold door at bottom

▶ Bifold doors don't align at the center.

This problem is prevented by a pair of guides attached to the backs of the center panels, near the floor. One or both may be missing or loose. To find replacements at the hardware store, look for bifold hinges.

If the gap where the two doors meet is uneven, adjust it by moving the pivot pin at the bottom outside corner of either door toward the jamb or away from it.

▶ Bifold door scrapes head jamb.

Move the bottom outside corner of the door toward the side jamb by lifting up on it and sliding the pivot pin a few notches toward the jamb. You will have to adjust it by trial and error. If adjusting the door causes the bottom edge to bind against the side jamb, adjust the top instead. Locate the pin holder at the end of the door track, and loosen the setscrew that locks it in place. Slide it slightly toward the center of the track and tighten the setscrew.

Straightening bifold door

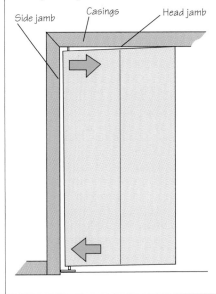

Tip   Door talk: A "two-eight by six-eight" (2-8 x 6-8) door is 2 feet, 8 inches wide (not 28 inches wide) and 6 feet, 8 inches high. Door widths from 2 feet to 3 feet are 2-0, 2-2, 2-4, 2-6, 2-8, 2-10, and 3-0.

▶ *Bifold doors scrape carpet.*

If there is enough clearance above the doors, raise them by rotating the threaded pivot pin that is located at the bottom outside corner of each door. If the turning knob does not rotate easily, lift up on the door while you turn it, or use pliers to rotate it. If the top of the door hits the track before the bottom clears the carpet, you will have to trim the bottoms of the doors. See page 83.

▶ *Bipass doors rub together.*

First make sure that the rollers for each door are attached securely and centered in the overhead track. Then check the door guide, which is a small cleat attached to the floor that keeps the doors separated from each other at the bottom. If it's missing or the center divider is broken, buy a replacement and screw it to the floor in the center of the door opening. If the doors still rub together, one door must be warped. Remove both doors and reverse them.

▶ *Bipass doors drag on floor or don't hang straight.*

If a door hangs too low or is tilted, you can adjust it by raising or lowering it where it hangs from the roller. Look behind the door where the hanger is attached. If it has a cam-type adjusting mechanism, loosen it with a wrench or screwdriver and adjust the cam. If not, the hanger should have slotted screw holes for the screws holding it to the door. With a helper, loosen the screws, move the door edge up or down so the screws change position in relation to the hanger, and tighten them. If you don't have a

helper, improvise a foot lever or use wedges to raise the door as you adjust the hanger screws.

Adjusting door height

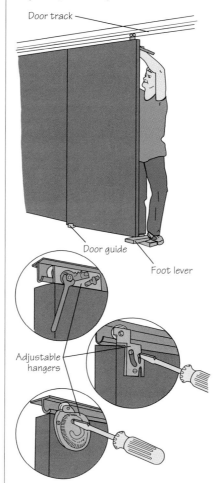

Door track

Door guide

Foot lever

Adjustable hangers

▶ *Bipass doors rattle.*

Lightweight hollow-core doors move easily with breezes or vibrations, causing them to rattle. The noise is usually caused by the door bottoms bumping against the door guide, but check other places as well. To muffle the noise, attach short pieces of self-sticking weather stripping to the guide where the doors rub against it.

▶ *Bipass doors have gap in center or on sides.*

If the doors aren't wide enough to cover the entire opening (they should overlap at least ¼ inch), widen one of the doors by attaching a strip of wood to the edge that rests against the side jamb. Use lattice for a narrow gap (up to ¼ inch) or 1x2 for wider gaps. Doors are 1⅜ inch thick, and most wood strips are 1½ inch wide; therefore, you will have to rip the strip to size. Attach it with glue and finishing nails, and smooth the joint by filling gaps with wood putty or spackling compound and sanding it. Then paint or finish the strip to match the doors. Another solution to the gap problem is to attach thick doorstops or other molding strips to the side jambs, in front of the doors, so they conceal the gaps. Attach bumpers to the door edges to keep the doors from closing too far.

▶ *Pocket door rattles.*

Check the bottom of the door pocket to see if the door guide or anchor is missing; it's a small shoe or pair of bumpers that stabilizes the door and keeps it from scraping against the sides of the pocket. If there is none, you may be able to find a new one where pocket-door hardware is sold. Otherwise, improvise one from a door guide for bipass doors (see left), or buy two glide buttons intended for the bottom of chair legs. To install the guide or glide buttons, you will need to remove the door. First pry the doorstop from the side jamb; then pull the door all the way into the opening, lift it, and tilt it (as shown) to release the rollers from the overhead track. With the door removed, center the guide in the door pocket

Tip *Properly installed bifold doors have ½ inch of clearance at the bottom, ⅛ inch between each door and the jamb at its side, and 1/16 inch between the doors when they are shut. The door fronts should be set back from the face of the casings approximately ¾ inch.*

and screw it to the floor; or nail the glide buttons to the sides of the pocket at the floor. Replace the door and doorstop.

If there is a guide and the door rattles against it, attach self-sticking weather stripping to its inside edges to muffle the sound and limit door movement. If it rattles against the doorstop, stick the weather stripping on the inside edge of the stop.

Removing a pocket door

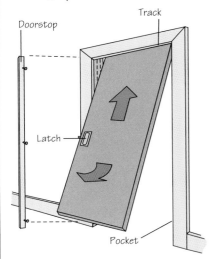

Doorstop · Track · Latch · Pocket

Installing door guides

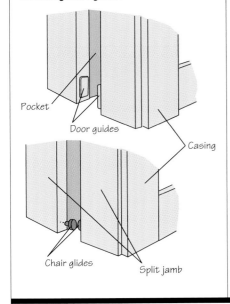

Pocket · Door guides · Casing · Chair glides · Split jamb

▶ Pocket-door latch won't align with strike plate.

If the door latch is too low to align with the strike plate, push up on the overhead track to see if it is loose and sagging, causing the door to droop. If so, push the door into the pocket and tighten the screws that attach the track to the framing. If the track is secure, see if you can adjust the hanger screws to move the door up or down. If not, you will have to enlarge the strike plate hole with a file so the door latch fits into it, or move the strike plate up or down (see page 81).

▶ Pocket door doesn't glide easily.

Remove the door (see opposite page). Inspect the rollers attached to the top of the door for worn, sticking, or broken wheels. If a wheel is defective, replace the whole roller mechanism. If the rollers spin freely, inspect the track for debris, looseness, cracks, or dents. Clean out all debris. If the track is loose, tighten the screws that hold it to the framing. This is a good job for someone with long, thin arms, as access to some screws is only through the 2-inch-wide door pocket. If the track is dented or cracked, replace it.

▶ Pocket door doesn't recess all the way into pocket.

Remove the door (see left) and inspect the back of the pocket for debris that might block the door. Then inspect the track for dents or other obstacles that might limit door movement. If the pocket and track are clear, measure the width

of the door and the depth of the pocket; the door might be too wide. If not, remove the bumper from the back edge of the door and replace it with something thinner, such as a plywood scrap, to allow the door to travel farther into the pocket. Rehang the door and reattach the doorstop.

▶ Pocket door doesn't block sound.

Pocket doors are not effective at blocking sound because of the loose fit, the hollow pocket cavity, and the need for clearance at the bottom to allow the door to slide back and forth. To reduce sound transmission, apply weather stripping to the doorstop and, if necessary, against the jamb where the door latches. Then apply it to the sides of the jamb where the door slides into the pocket when it's opened. Use the vinyl-cushion type of weather stripping for both places, and paint it to match the trim. To reduce sound transmission at the bottom, lower the door as much as possible by adjusting the hangers. At least one of the rooms adjacent to the door should have carpet; if only one room does, the carpet should terminate under the door, not in front of it. Replacing a hollow-core door with a solid door will also reduce sound transmission, but it may be necessary to reinforce the track for the heavier door (most track and door hardware is designed to hold doors up to 125 pounds).

Tip *Installing a pocket door requires a framed opening larger than other door openings because there can be no studs, wires, pipes, or other obstructions inside the recessed pocket area of the wall. Twice as much wall covering must be removed, and a header twice as long as an ordinary door header must be installed. Consult a carpenter or building contractor.*

▶ Pocket door comes off track.

An obstruction may be causing a roller wheel to jump the track, or the bottom of the door may be too low to clear the floor completely. First check the track by opening the door all the way and feeling along the track for debris or dents. Remove any debris. Repair dents by removing the door and the track, then pounding out the dent with a hammer, using a sledgehammer or other heavy block of metal in back of the track as you pound on it. If the track is clear, raise the door to clear the floor by adjusting the hanging mechanism. If the door still jumps the track, a roller wheel is probably worn or broken. Remove the door and inspect the rollers. If a wheel is defective, replace the whole roller mechanism.

▶ Exterior door admits drafts.

Install weather stripping around the top and sides, and a door shoe with vinyl gasket seal on the bottom (see right). If the door fits loosely between the jambs, install vinyl V-strip or metal spring-type weather stripping; it won't show when the door is shut. Install the top piece first, fitting it flush to the side jambs. Install the side pieces next, cutting the tops at an angle to fit snugly against the top strip; the nailed edge faces outward. Don't cover the strike plate; install a short piece of stripping against the doorstop instead. If the door fits snugly, apply gasket weather stripping to the doorstop around the outside of the door. The tubular vinyl type is easiest to install; the nail-on type lasts longer.

▶ Exterior door leaks at bottom.

To prevent water from coming under the door, install an aluminum threshold on the floor and a door shoe with a metal drip shield and vinyl gasket on the bottom of the door. First take down the door (see Tip, page 80), then remove the old threshold. If it is metal, remove the screws and lift it out; if it is wood, saw through the threshold at both ends, pry out the middle section, and remove the remaining end pieces. Mark the new threshold for cutting by setting it against the door opening and transferring measurements onto it. Cut it with a hacksaw. Set the threshold in place and mark the screw locations on the subfloor for drilling pilot holes. Remove the threshold, drill the holes, dab some caulk into each one, and set the threshold back in place. Drive the screws part way in, dab some caulk under the heads, then drive them tight.

With the threshold in place, rehang the door and close it to check for clearance between the threshold and bottom of the door. If the bottom clears, measure the height of any gap. Subtract that distance from the thickness of the new door shoe when you trim the bottom of the door for the shoe. If the bottom doesn't clear, mark on each edge of the door a point that is level with the top of the threshold. Measure above these marks a distance equal to the thickness of the shoe and make new marks; connect the new marks with a line. Remove the door and trim the bottom along that line (see page 82).

Cut the shoe to length with a hacksaw (cut the vinyl gasket with a knife), attach it to the bottom of the door with the screws provided, and rehang the door.

Cutting old wood threshold

Measuring for new threshold

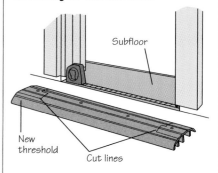

Subfloor

New threshold

Cut lines

Installing door shoe

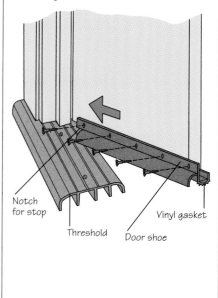

Notch for stop

Threshold

Door shoe

Vinyl gasket

Tip *To increase the effectiveness of gasket weather stripping with a nail-on flange installed around a door, apply a thin bead of acrylic latex caulk under the flange before screwing it in place.*

Tip *If you are installing adhesive-backed rubber or foam weather stripping around a door, be sure the temperature is above 50° F. If the temperature is lower, the adhesive may not stick.*

▶ *Exterior door leaks at top.*

An exterior door not protected by a porch or overhang is exposed to direct rain and any water running down the wall above it. Install a drip cap and drip flashing to divert water away from the top of the door. First remove a strip of siding and underlayment paper from above the door casing. Measure the siding cutout carefully. It should be as wide as the drip cap material is high, and long enough to extend ¾ inch beyond the door on each side. Then cut a piece of drip cap (or a strip of 1x2 redwood with a beveled top) and a piece of galvanized drip-cap flashing, both long enough to fit within the cutout. Set the flashing in place first, slipping the back flange up under the siding and underlayment paper. Then tuck the drip cap up under the flashing and attach it to the wall sheathing with 8d HDG nails driven up at an angle from below. Set the nail heads, fill them with caulk, and paint the drip cap to match the house trim. If leaking persists, have a small sheet-metal shield fabricated and installed above the door, or have a permanent overhang constructed.

Cutting siding

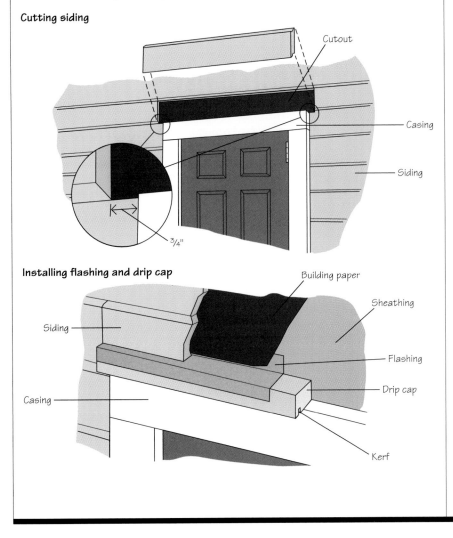

Cutout

Casing

Siding

¾"

Installing flashing and drip cap

Building paper

Sheathing

Siding

Flashing

Casing

Drip cap

Kerf

▶ *Exterior door sticks.*

First check the hinges for loose screws and the edges for excessive gaps, as with an interior door (see page 80). If it still sticks, do not trim the door unless you are sure that the problem is permanent and not seasonal. If the weather is humid or rainy, wait until a drier season. If the door still sticks, trim it. If not, make sure the gap is wide enough for a new coat of paint; remove the door and reseal all four edges and both sides with two coats of sealer or one coat of primer and one of paint. If the gap is too narrow for the buildup of paint, trim the door before resealing it.

▶ *Exterior-door jamb is cracked.*

Even for cracks as long as 2 feet, it is easier to splice in a new section of jamb than to replace the entire damaged jamb. First remove the exterior casing next to the damaged area. Then, with a pencil and square, mark cut lines across the jamb above and below the crack. If damage is confined to the outer half of the jamb, make a vertical cut line between these marks along the doorstop. With a circular saw or reciprocating saw, cut through the jamb at both horizontal lines; if you made a vertical line at the doorstop, stop the cuts there and use a jigsaw to complete the cuts. Remove the damaged section of jamb. Next nail or glue shims or a filler block behind the cut ends of the jamb, leaving enough shim material above and below the cuts to fur out the new patch. Cut a patch from identical jamb stock or other replacement lumber, apply glue to the back of it, set it into the cutout area, and nail it with 16d

Tip   *A wood door exposed to the weather can soak up water like a sponge, especially at the bottom, unless all surfaces are sealed. The most vulnerable surfaces are the top and bottom edges, which are also hidden from view. If a door has not been painted in some time, it is worthwhile to remove the door entirely and paint all six surfaces (two sides and four edges) with a clear sealer or a coat each of primer and paint.*

SOLVING DOOR & WINDOW PROBLEMS

finishing nails; set the nail heads well below the surface. Plane or sand the patch so it is flush with the rest of the jamb, then finish to match.

Cutting out damaged section

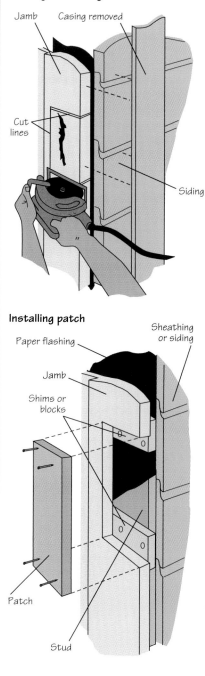

Installing patch

▶ Exterior-door panels are cracked.

An old door may not be worth repairing; consider buying an insulated steel-clad door to replace it. For slight cracks or surface damage, sand the area, apply wood filler with a putty knife, let it dry, sand it smooth, and touch up the repair to match the rest of the door. If the joints are coming apart and you feel the door is worth repairing, repair it in the same way as an interior door (see page 83).

▶ Exterior door needs painting or varnishing.

Start early in the day so the paint will be dry by evening. Remove the door (see Tip, page 80), set it on sawhorses, and remove all hardware. Thoroughly scrape and sand away all loose paint and varnish; wear a dust mask and eye protection. If you wish to refinish a painted door with a stain or natural finish, use a water-soluble paint stripper, following label directions carefully. When the old finish has been scraped or stripped, vacuum the door and remove any remaining dust with a tack cloth or solution of TSP and water, mixed and applied according to label directions. Then prime, seal, or stain both sides and all four edges of the door. Let the first coat dry, sand it lightly with 200-grit sandpaper or fine steel wool, and apply the finish coat. When it dries, replace the hardware and rehang the door. If the finish isn't dry, leave the door ajar overnight. Screw a panel of ½-inch plywood to the inside of the door opening for security.

▶ Threshold is damaged or rotted.

Remove the old threshold by sawing through it at both doorstops, prying out the center section, and chiseling away the short end pieces. Next mark the new threshold for cutting. Use the pieces of the old threshold as a template for marking the new, or hold the new threshold against the door opening and transfer cut marks onto it with a pencil and square held against the sides of the door opening. Cut out the new threshold and finish it with a sealer or paint. When the finish dries, apply caulk to the bottom of the threshold, set it in place, and nail or screw it to the floor. To install a metal threshold, see page 88.

▶ Threshold gasket is missing or worn.

Some metal thresholds include a vinyl gasket that may get worn or damaged. Buy a replacement gasket where thresholds are sold. Slip the old one off, vacuum out the channels in the threshold, cut the new gasket to length with a utility knife so it fits flush against both door jambs, and press it into place so the flanges are locked into the two channels in the threshold.

▶ Threshold screws won't tighten.

Try longer screws. If they won't tighten, the screw holes for the threshold are probably lined up over a gap between the subfloor and wall sheathing, leaving little wood for the screws to bite into. Remove the screws and, with the threshold in place, insert a thin pencil (or a nail with chalk on the

Tip *Many exterior doors have a sill under the threshold, which slopes downward away from the house. Be sure that the joint between the sill and threshold is sealed tightly with a bead of caulk and that both pieces of wood are well sealed with paint or a clear wood finish.*

point) into each hole to mark locations on the subfloor. Remove the threshold. If the problem is a gap, widen it to ¾ inch and insert a 1-by board into the gap. It should be deep enough to rest on the rim joist or other framing below the subfloor. Nail it to the framing with 8d or larger nails (predrill first). Caulk any gaps around the strip. Set the threshold in place, mark where the holes line up over the new strip, and remove the threshold. Drill pilot holes into the marks, moving them toward the center of the wood strip if they align over a crack or open joint; dab caulk into the holes, and set the threshold in place. Drive the screws in most of the way, dab some caulk under the heads, and then tighten them.

Inserting filler strip

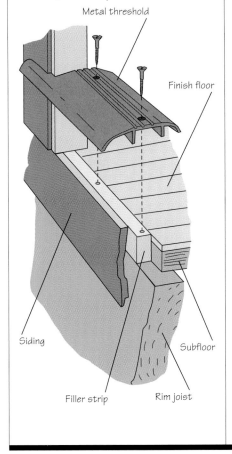

Metal threshold

Finish floor

Siding

Filler strip

Subfloor

Rim joist

▶ Double French doors don't align.

The latch in one door may not be aligned with the strike plate in the other door, keeping them from shutting securely. To solve this problem, start by shutting the doors and observing how wide the gaps are around the tops and sides. Knowing where the gaps are will help you make adjustments later. If the alignment is only slightly off and the door gaps are not objectionable, simply enlarge the hole in the strike plate with a file. For larger adjustments, move the latch edge of each door up or down by slipping cardboard shims beneath the hinge leaves or bending the hinge knuckles. (See page 80 for specific techniques.)

▶ Double doors have exposed gap between them.

If there is a gap between double French or patio doors that are exposed to the exterior, a strip of molding on the exterior will keep out rain and keep the doors aligned. Attach it to the fixed door if the doors open inward; to the moving door if they open outward. Flat molding, such as a doorstop, is the easiest type to install. Cut a piece the same length as the door, prime or seal all sides and edges, apply a bead of caulk along one side, and nail it to the exterior side of the door so half of it extends beyond the edge of the door.

An astragal, which is T-shaped in profile, is stronger than flat molding, but you will need to trim back the door edge to install it. After cutting the astragal to the same length as the door and priming or sealing it, remove the lockset hardware from the door (or the strike plate if the doors open inward). Then measure the width of

the astragal flange and trim that amount from the edge of the door. Set the saw blade at the same bevel as the flange. Apply a bead of caulk to the back of the astragal near the front edge, and nail the flange into the edge of the door with 6d finishing nails. Bore out the astragal where it covers the hole in the door edge for the lockset, paint the astragal, and replace the door hardware when the paint is dry.

Installing molding

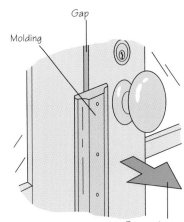

Gap

Molding

Door swing

Installing an astragal

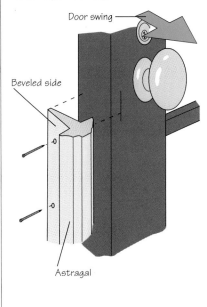

Door swing

Beveled side

Astragal

Tip *According to the National Association of Home Builders, the life expectancy of an exterior door protected by a porch or overhang is 80 to 100 years. The same door, without such protection, would last from 25 to 30 years.*

SOLVING DOOR & WINDOW PROBLEMS

► Double glass doors don't lock securely.

With a pair of French doors, one door serves as a fixed panel and the other door opens and closes against it. Install heavy-duty throw bolts at the top and bottom of the fixed door; they should be long enough to slide at least 1 inch beyond the strike plates or cleats attached to the head jamb and floor. Install a lockset in the moving door that includes a 1-inch dead bolt. A single lock assembly, called a cremone lock, includes lock bolts at all three points—top, bottom, and latch. Avoid locks that require a key to open from the interior side as well as exterior; many codes do not allow them because they present an escape hazard during emergencies.

► Sliding glass door doesn't glide smoothly.

Start with routine maintenance by giving the bottom door track a thorough cleaning; dig out stubborn debris with a screwdriver, vacuum out the track, and buff the channel with fine steel wool. Apply a light coating of silicone spray or aerosol furniture polish to the top track. If the door still balks, inspect the top and bottom tracks for bent or dented areas. Bend such spots back into shape with a hammer; place a woodblock in the track to back up the blows. If the tracks pass inspection, the problem is faulty door wheels. Loosen the adjusting screws for the wheels and, with a helper, remove the door by lifting it up and pulling the bottom outward (you may need to hold the wheels up until they clear the track). Place the door on padded sawhorses, supporting the frame so

the glass doesn't take the weight. The wheels should feel solid and spin freely. Remove worn or loose wheels by loosening or removing the setscrews that hold them in place; replace them with roller units from the same manufacturer.

Hammering out a dent

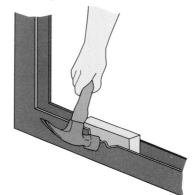

Replacing a wheel

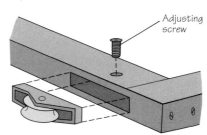

Adjusting screw

► Sliding glass door lacks safety glass.

Codes developed in recent years require that doors have safety glazing such as laminated safety glass, tempered glass, or plastic panels (except panes less than 3 inches wide). Check to see if your glass door is labeled as safety glass in one of the corners. If not and the doors are standard height (6 feet, 6 inches for 6-foot 8-inch openings), you should be able to buy replacement doors with safety glass that will fit in the same frame. To conserve energy, consider buying double-glazed units.

► Sliding glass door lacks security lock.

The style of latch in most older patio doors is not very strong. For extra security install a keyed lock or thumb latch designed for installation near the top of the door. Mount it on the face of the metal frame farthest from the latch side; drill holes for the two sheet-metal screws that hold it, and screw it to the frame. Then shut the door and mark where the lock bolt strikes the top metal jamb. Drill a hole at the mark, slightly larger than the diameter of the lock bolt. Mark and drill a second hole with the door open 2 to 4 inches; this allows you to lock the door with it opened slightly for fresh air. Another way to lock the door is with a "charley bar," an adjustable rod that lies in the floor track and blocks movement of the door.

► Screen/storm door opens too far or not far enough.

To limit door travel and prevent a storm door or screen door from blowing against the house wall, install a chain retainer. Attach one end to the head jamb, then open the door as far as you want it to reach, and stretch out the chain to determine where to attach it to the door frame. Close the door and attach the chain. If the door has a chain that doesn't allow it to open as far as you'd like, loosen the chain from the head jamb and reattach it at a point closer to the hinge end of the jamb.

Tip *French doors and other glass doors should have safety glass. Doors in most older homes don't. It is possible to replace each of the panes with tempered glass or laminated safety glass (double-glazed for energy conservation and sound control), especially if the outside putty is already loose and deteriorating. It may be easier, however, to buy a replacement door.*

▶ Screen/storm door closes too fast or too slow.

Regulate the speed of the door by adjusting the automatic door closer. If it's the pneumatic type, which has a horizontal tube or piston, close the door and turn the adjusting screw at the end of the tube. If it doesn't have a screw, remove the pin that holds the tube to the door. Holding the tube in one hand, use pliers to rotate the plunger that was held by the pin—clockwise to increase tension and door speed, counterclockwise to slow the speed. If the door has a hydraulic closer (vertical barrel), use a screwdriver to rotate the adjusting screw at the bottom of the barrel to change speed.

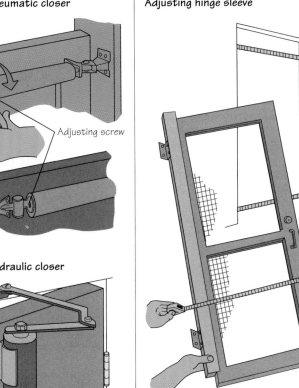

Adjusting a pneumatic closer

Adjusting screw

Adjusting a hydraulic closer

Adjusting screw

▶ Screen/storm door won't fit in opening.

A door opening may be too narrow for the new screen door or storm door closest to it in size. If the door is wood, trim it along the hinge edge, allowing for a ³⁄₁₆-inch gap on both sides. Most aluminum doors have a sleeve on the hinge side that makes it possible to adjust the door to any width within a 1- to 2-inch range.

Measure the width of the door opening at the top and bottom, and subtract ¼ to ⅜ inch from each dimension. Adjust the hinge sleeve so the width of the door is the same as these dimensions at the top and bottom, drill pilot holes, and secure it with the screws provided.

Adjusting hinge sleeve

▶ Screen/storm door frame is tarnished.

Restore tarnished aluminum with aluminum or copper cleaner, following label directions. Do not scrub with abrasive powders or a scouring pad.

▶ Screen/storm door sags.

If the door is wood, buy a cable-and-turnbuckle kit for reinforcing sagging screen doors. With the turnbuckle fully open, attach one end to the top corner of the door on the hinge side, the other end to the bottom corner on the latch side. Tighten the turnbuckle until the door sag is gone. An aluminum door can be fixed in the same way, but you may also be able to fix it by replacing a bent or broken corner key. This is a metal reinforcing bracket located inside the door frame at each corner. (Not all aluminum doors have them.) A buckled corner reveals which key needs to be replaced. Remove the door and disassemble the buckled corner. Look for a replacement key at door shops or hardware stores that sell the type of door you have.

▶ Doorknob is loose.

If the lockset is an old-fashioned mortise style with a porcelain, glass, or heavy brass doorknob, loosen the setscrew on the side of the knob that secures it to the square spindle. Back off the setscrew far enough for the knob to turn freely without operating the latch. Screw the knob clockwise until it is snug but not tight against the door, then tighten the setscrew. Be sure the screw is tightened against a flat side of the spindle, not a pointed corner (you may have to back the knob away from the door one-eighth turn).

If the lockset is the cylindrical type, one of the knobs will have a

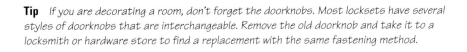

Tip *If you are decorating a room, don't forget the doorknobs. Most locksets have several styles of doorknobs that are interchangeable. Remove the old doorknob and take it to a locksmith or hardware store to find a replacement with the same fastening method.*

slot on the side of the shank, just behind the knob. Push a screwdriver into the slot to release the knob. Then remove the decorative rose that covers the lockset by depressing a spring clip at the edge. This will expose a mounting plate with two screws. Tighten the two screws, snap the rose back in place, and push the knob onto the spindle so the keeper snaps back into the slot on the shank.

Locating setscrew for mortise lock

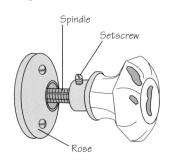

Spindle
Setscrew
Rose

Removing knob from lock cylinder

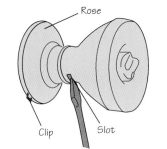

Rose
Clip
Slot

Tightening screws of cylindrical lock

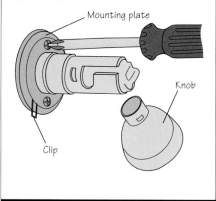

Mounting plate
Knob
Clip

▶ Key doesn't slide into lock smoothly.

First check to be sure it's the right key and that the key isn't bent. If the weather is cold, the lock could be jammed with ice formed from accumulated moisture. Start by chipping away as much ice from the keyhole as possible. Then heat the key with a match and insert it in the lock; you may have to repeat this operation until it goes in all the way. Turn the key carefully; don't force it. If the problem is not ice, lubricate the keyhole and key with a nonsticking lubricant such as silicone spray or powdered graphite. If that doesn't work, look inside the keyhole for a foreign object. Remove it with a piece of thin, stiff wire.

▶ Latch bolt gets stuck in lock.

Check to see if the latch bolt is binding against the latch plate in the edge of the door (see page 81 for adjusting the alignment). If so, inject some graphite powder or silicone spray into the latch mechanism to lubricate the edges of the plate. If the latch bolt still binds, insert a thin screwdriver between the latch bolt and plate and carefully enlarge the gap by prying them apart. If necessary, dismantle the lockset to remove the latch assembly so you can lubricate it and adjust alignment of the bolt.

▶ Key is broken in lock.

If enough of the key is protruding, pull it out with needle nose pliers. If the pliers can't grip it, try raking out the broken piece with the blade of a coping saw, or pulling it out with stiff wire formed into a hook. If none of this works, try to dismantle the lockset and push the piece

out from the backside with a piece of thin, stiff wire. *Note:* Some locksets can't be disassembled while the door is shut.

▶ Key turns and nothing happens.

The mechanism connecting the lock cylinder to the tailpiece or spindle may be broken, or the tailpiece has snapped off. Disassemble the lockset and check to see if the tailpiece is intact. If it is not, buy a new cylinder with tailpiece. If it's intact, turn the key in the cylinder to see if it moves the tailpiece. If not, take the assembly to a locksmith and have it repaired or replaced. If the key does turn the tailpiece, the tailpiece is not engaging the deadbolt assembly or the dead bolt is defective. Try reassembling with the tailpiece properly engaged in the dead-bolt hole. If it still does not work, replace the dead-bolt assembly or the entire lockset.

Checking lock assembly

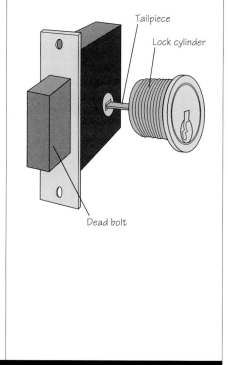

Tailpiece
Lock cylinder
Dead bolt

Tip *Lock your house whenever you leave. An unlocked home is an invitation to burglary. In fact, many insurance policies will not honor a claim for theft if there was no evidence of forced entry.*

▶ Key won't turn in lock.

Don't force it. If it's a newly made replacement key, check it against the original for minor discrepancies; get a new key made. If it's not new, the problem may be that the lock cylinder is turned slightly from a vertical position. Open the door from the inside and locate the setscrew on the door edge that holds the cylinder in place (with some models you may have to disassemble the lockset), loosen it, and return the cylinder to its original position; tighten the screw. If the key still won't turn, the tumblers are probably damaged; have the cylinder replaced.

▶ Latch bolt of mortise lockset retracts but won't extend.

A mortise lock has a one-piece rectangular body that is recessed into a large cavity cut into the edge of the door. Occasionally the spring inside breaks, eliminating the thrust that forces the latch bolt back after you retract it by turning the handle. To remove the lockset, remove one of the doorknobs by loosening the setscrew that holds it to the spindle and screwing off the knob. Remove the other knob and spindle from the other side of the lockset. If the lockset has a dead-bolt knob, remove it by loosening the setscrew and sliding it off the spindle; then loosen the setscrew for the lock cylinder (located on the latch plate), and pull the lock cylinder and spindle out from the other side of the door. Next remove the two mounting screws from the latch plate and remove the lock assembly. One side has three screws; lay down the lockset so the screws face up, loosen them, and remove the cover plate. Locate the broken spring and take it to a locksmith to get a replacement. Set the new spring in place, holding

it under tension with needle nose pliers so it fits behind the latch linkage. Carefully reassemble the lockset and reinstall it in the door.

Removing mortise lockset

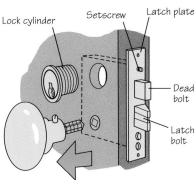

▶ Security bolt doesn't align with hole.

First tighten any loose mounting screws. They are located on the lock housing if the lock is surface-mounted, and on the latch plate if the lock is inside the door. If the lock is secure, you may need to adjust the strike plate as described on page 81. However, consider the possibility that this is a temporary problem due to a change in the weather or slight shifting of the house. If the door gradually starts to bind, leave it locked and do not use the door for a week or two—it may fix itself.

▶ Dead bolt is keyed on both sides.

This type of dead bolt, which requires a key to open it from the inside, is intended to discourage intruders from breaking nearby glass and reaching in to turn the lock handle. However, such locks also prevent occupants from making a quick escape in case of emergency and are often prohibited by local codes. Replace the double-key dead bolt with a conventional dead bolt. To improve security, replace glass in the nearby window with breakproof glazing.

▶ Lock is not heavy enough.

A dead-bolt lock should have at least a 1-inch throw, be constructed of solid (not stamped) metal, and have a heavy-gauge strike plate with screws long enough to reach the stud behind the jamb. If the existing lock lacks these attributes, buy a lock designated as "heavy-duty" to replace it. First remove the old lock to use as a template in selecting the new lock so you can use the same holes bored in the door. If you have to enlarge a hole, use a hole saw.

▶ Bathroom door is locked and someone's inside.

If a child is locked in the bathroom or someone falls and is unable to reach the door for help, you need to be able to unlock the door from the outside. If the doorknob is the type with a small hole in the center, push a nail or similar device into the hole to unlock the door. If the doorknob cannot be unlocked, remove the door by extracting the hinge pins, if they are exposed. If they aren't, pry loose the doorstop on the latch side just enough to slip a plastic credit card against the latch to force it open.

Tip *Fumbling for extra keys is awkward and unnecessary. You can have both locks in one door—or all locks in the house—keyed to a single key if they have compatible cylinders. For one door, remove the dead bolt or lock, whichever is easier, and take it to a locksmith along with both keys. Have the locksmith replace the lock cylinder and key it to the same key that operates the other lock. If the cylinder can't be changed, buy a dead bolt with a compatible cylinder and have it keyed to the key of the other lock.*

▶ Window glass is broken.

Wooden frames: Work from the outside, except for windows that have removable wood strips on the interior side of the glass. First, wearing gloves and eye protection, remove all loose pieces of glass; then remove the glazing compound by chipping it away with a putty knife. If it doesn't chip easily, heat it with a hair dryer or heat lamp to soften it. With a putty knife or needle nose pliers, pry out the metal points that hold the glass in place. As you work, the remaining pieces of glass will loosen; be wary and remove them as you work your way around the window. Pull out the rest of the glass, using pliers for stubborn pieces. Scrape away all old putty and paint, and brush out the rabbet (groove) thoroughly. Measure the width and height of the opening for a new pane of glass, subtracting ⅛ inch from each dimension for clearance. Before you go to the glass dealer, paint any bare wood in the rabbet with fast-drying primer. Bring a scrap of glass to the store to be sure the replacement glass is the same type (see Tip on opposite page for windows that require safety or tempered glass).

To install the new pane, first make a thin rope (¼ inch) of glazing compound and press it into the rabbet; this cushions the glass and provides a tight seal. Next press the new pane firmly into place and secure it with glazing points, spacing them 4 to 6 inches apart; push them into the wood with a stiff putty knife. Apply new glazing compound around the window; work it into a rope and press it into place with your fingers, then smooth it with a putty knife held at a 45-degree angle. Check other panes to see how far to extend it onto the glass. Let it cure for at least a week, then paint it.

Aluminum frames: Remove the sash. If the glass is held in place by beveled strips around the outside edges, pry them off, remove the broken glass, apply sealing mastic around the interior perimeter of the new pane, press it into place, and reinstall the strips. If the frame consists of U-shaped channels with no removable strips, disassemble it by loosening the screws from both corners of one side and removing the side. Pull out the broken glass and vinyl gasket surrounding it. Slip the gasket around the new glass, slide it into the frame, and replace the side piece.

Removing putty

Sash

Applying glazing compound

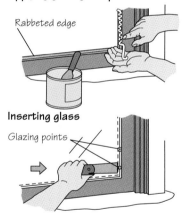

Rabbeted edge

Inserting glass

Glazing points

Smoothing compound

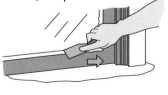

▶ Double-glazed window has moisture or haze between panes.

Air with water vapor has seeped into the sealed cavity between the two panes and has condensed on the cold glass. It is difficult, if not impossible, to have the window repaired. It is also difficult to replace only the glass unit; you'll probably have to replace the entire sash, unless the window is a fixed window fabricated on-site. Check to see if your window has a guarantee.

▶ Window glass is wavy or distorted.

Because it is technically a liquid, all glass eventually slumps and deforms. This condition adds to the charm of older homes; but if you find it annoying, you can replace the offending panes (see left). While you're at it, you might consider double-glazed replacement windows with low-E glass to increase energy efficiency, sound insulation, and sun control. The replacements should match the design and proportion of existing windows to retain the style of the home.

▶ Plastic glazing is faded or scratched.

Most plastic windowpanes collect scratches over time, and some types discolor or develop a haze. Replace older panes with new acrylic panes if you want plastic that stays clear longer. Use polycarbonate for windows vulnerable to burglars or active play (such as basement windows); it is more expensive than acrylic and tends to become hazy over time, but it is very durable and shatter resistant. Have either type of pane cut to size by a plastics

Tip   *To temporarily seal a cracked window until you can replace the glass, apply clear shellac to the crack.*

Tip   *If you have broken a double-glazed (insulating) window, replace the entire sash or have a professional glazier repair it.*

supplier and install it like a glass pane with glazing points and putty (see opposite page). To install it like a storm window, drill screw holes around the perimeter of the panel, apply a bead of silicone caulk around the window frame, bed the plastic panel into the caulk, and secure it with 1-inch HDG wallboard screws. The screw holes should be slightly larger than the screws so the plastic can expand and contract. Give it a finished look by covering the edges with molding.

▶ *Window admits too much sun.*

Direct sunlight coming through a window can cause glare, fading, and overheating problems. The most effective control is to shade the window from the outside. If an awning, overhead, or shade tree isn't feasible, provide exterior sun control with a sun screen or shading fabric. You can order a screen that will fit over the window and block 70 percent or more of the sunlight, or you can replace the insect screening with shading fabric.

Another way to block the sun is to apply sun-control film to the inside of the window. (Older films were applied to the outside; modern films applied to the inside perform much better.) Reflective films, which are silver or slightly tinted, block heat, glare, and ultraviolet rays, but reduce visibility from the inside. Low-E films also block heat, glare, and rays, but do not discolor the window and have the added benefit of reducing heat loss through the window during winter. Both types are self-sticking. To apply, first clean the window thoroughly, then measure it. With a utility knife and straightedge, cut the film 1 inch larger in both directions. Spray the window with soapy water (½ ounce clear dishwashing liquid to 1 quart water). With a

helper remove the protective backing from the film, being careful not to wrinkle the film or let it stick to itself, and spray the adhesive side of it with the soap solution. Stick the film on the window, spray the exposed side with soap solution, and use a squeegee to smooth it in place. Trim the edges ⅟16 inch in from the sash, and smooth the film again with the squeegee, working outward from the center.

Installing a shade screen

Smoothing window film

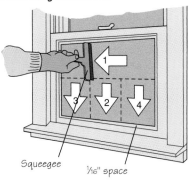

Squeegee   ⅟16" space

▶ *Window film is difficult to remove.*

If you want to remove old film and it doesn't peel off easily, start by loosening ¾ inch of film along the top with a razor blade. Then mix a solution of 1 part ammonia to 1 part water and spray it behind the

loosened flap to soften the stubborn adhesive. Wearing rubber gloves, start at one corner and pull the loosened flap downward diagonally, spraying behind it as you go. When the film is removed, spray the same solution onto any remaining adhesive and rub it in with your gloved hand for 3 to 6 minutes; then scrape it off with a razor blade. Wash the window with soap and water.

▶ *Single-glazed windows allow heat to escape.*

Single-glazed windows in older homes account for a significant amount of heat loss during cold weather (and heat gain in warm weather). One way to reduce heat loss is to replace the old windows with energy-saving, double-glazed, insulating windows. However, there are simpler, less expensive ways that are almost as effective. First apply weather stripping to eliminate infiltration of cold air. If the windows are double-hung or sliding (not casement), install storm windows on the outside. Choose a combination style that has operable windows and insect screens so you can leave the units in place all year. To install, measure the inside dimensions (jamb to jamb) of the window, and trim the mounting flange of the storm window to fit. Drill screw holes around the outside edge of the mounting flange, apply a bead of silicone caulk to the front edges of the top and side window stops, and set the storm window in place, pressing it against the caulk. Slide the storm window as high as it will go and secure it with screws. Force the adjustable windowsill down over the original sill, making sure the weep holes are clear.

Another type of secondary window, called an interior insulating window, is installed on the interior and is less obtrusive than a storm

---

Tip *Safety requirements for windows: (1) For emergency egress, bedroom windows must have 5.7 square feet of unobstructed openable area, be at least 20 inches wide and 24 inches high, and be no more than 42 inches above the floor. (2) Windows within 18 inches of the floor must be safety glass. (3) Windows at the bottom of stairs must be at least 36 inches above the floor. (4) Windows within 16 inches of a door must have tempered or safety glass. (5) Windows above a shower or tub must have tempered or safety glass.*

window. It can be used on any type of window. Installation kits include an acrylic panel that you cut to size and magnetic or self-fastening edging that you attach to the borders of the panel for sealing it against the window. Follow manufacturer's instructions carefully to ensure a tight seal.

Other ways to reduce heat loss are to apply low-E film to the interior side of the window glass (see page 97) and to install heavy floor-to-ceiling draperies. You can also eliminate some heat loss due to metal window frames by covering the insides of the frames with wood trim.

Installing a storm window

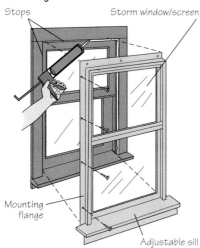

Stops

Storm window/screen

Mounting flange

Adjustable sill

Installing an interior insulating window

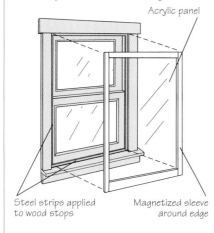

Acrylic panel

Steel strips applied to wood stops

Magnetized sleeve around edge

▶ **Window glass has condensation on surface.**

When warm, moist interior air contacts cold window glass, condensation forms. Install an interior insulating window to keep house air away from the cold glass (see page 97). If the house has high humidity, it is likely to be caused by things that you can control. Reduce the sources of water vapor, such as an unvented clothes dryer, bathroom shower, or stovetop. Increase air circulation to further reduce condensation.

▶ **Window sash is rotted or joints are coming loose.**

A broken or deteriorated sash should be replaced, but you can repair some damage. If the joints are slightly loose, remove the sash and gently squeeze the joints together by hand at the top and bottom of the window to see if they move. If not, clean them out as much as possible and try again. Then clamp the top and bottom together with bar clamps and apply gentle pressure. At each joint that is coming loose, drill two 3/8-inch-diameter holes through the stiles into the rails, vacuum out the holes, and glue dowels into them. Trim the dowels flush with the edge of the window and touch up with sealer, primer, and paint. Restore damaged glazing compound around the windowpanes and repaint it.

Fill rotted cavities with wood filler or epoxy compound. These materials are different from spackling or other patching compounds; they include potent chemicals and are applied in two steps that require mixing two materials (resin and hardener) each time. The wood must be dry. Remove loose and rotted material. Drill several 3/16-

inch-diameter holes through the rotted wood into sound wood. Vacuum, then paint sealer or primer onto the damaged section. After it dries, wearing rubber gloves, apply the first mixture according to label directions. Apply the second mixture, a paste filler, according to label directions and smooth it with a putty knife. After it dries, sand it smooth and touch up the area with primer and two coats of finish paint.

Doweling a sash joint

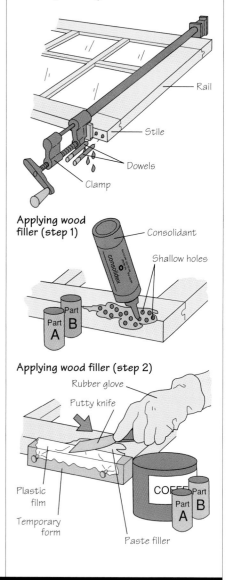

Rail

Stile

Dowels

Clamp

Applying wood filler (step 1)

Consolidant

Shallow holes

Part A

Part B

Applying wood filler (step 2)

Rubber glove

Putty knife

Plastic film

Temporary form

Paste filler

Part A

Part B

Tip *Window terminology: glazing is a pane of glass or plastic; sash is the frame, usually movable, that holds the glazing; divided lights are multiple panes within one sash; muntins are the strips of wood that divide the sash into panes; true divided lights are sashes with multiple individual panes, as opposed to a single pane with a grid placed over it to resemble individual panes.*

▶ Window sash is stuck and won't open.

The window is probably painted shut. Break the paint bond by scoring all the joints, inside and out, with a putty knife, paint zipper, or pizza cutter. If the sash still sticks, carefully pry it open by inserting a pry bar under both bottom corners and lifting (pry at top and bottom corners for casement windows). Work double-hung sashes up and down to loosen them. Scrape paint and debris out of the channels and coat them with candle wax, silicone spray, or white lithium grease (used for auto maintenance).

▶ Windowsill is rotted or split.

If the sill is badly damaged, replace it. Remove the bottom window sash and interior trim (casings, stops, apron, and stool). Work carefully; score the paint joints with a utility knife and pry gently. Use a hacksaw to cut exposed nails to release the trim pieces. Measure the dimensions of the old sill while it is in place. Then saw through it near both ends, remove the center piece, and pry away the end pieces. Save any wedges. Lay out the measurements on the new sill and cut it. If you use a circular saw, be careful not to cut past layout marks at the corners. Bevel the ends slightly so they will fit against the window jambs without binding. Test the sill for fit by sliding it into place or tapping it with a hammer and woodblock; don't force it. Remove it and sand the ends if necessary, then prime or seal the wood on all sides. After it dries, install it, and replace the wedges. Drive 12d HDG finishing nails through the bottom of the sill into the exterior casings; toenail 16d finishing nails into the interior edge and facenail them as needed. Caulk all joints on the exterior and apply the final finish.

If a sill is slightly damaged or cracked, repair it with wood filler or epoxy compound (see opposite page).

Removing old sill

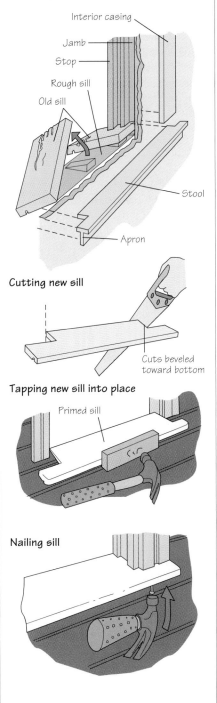

Interior casing
Jamb
Stop
Rough sill
Old sill
Stool
Apron

Cutting new sill

Cuts beveled toward bottom

Tapping new sill into place

Primed sill

Nailing sill

▶ Double-hung window sash sticks.

Brush and vacuum the side channels thoroughly, especially corners; remove built-up grit or paint with a sharp chisel and sand the wood smooth. Rub candle wax into the channels, or lubricate with silicone spray. If the channels are too narrow and pinch the sash, place a woodblock against the stops wherever they bind and tap it sharply with a hammer. In some cases you may have to pry off the stops and renail them farther from the sash.

▶ Window latches don't lock securely.

Windows provide easy access for intruders because they are often open or the latches don't lock securely. Double-hung windows are especially vulnerable because the ordinary butterfly latch that holds the two sashes together can be flicked open from outside with a table knife. Replace the latch with a safety lock or improvise a pin latch by drilling a hole through the sash into the side jamb, near the top; insert a 12d nail into it when the window is closed. To secure the window when it's open for ventilation, move the sash to the open position and drill into the jamb through the same sash hole. You can also install a ventilating window lock. It has a sliding bolt that stops the sash at a certain point or slides out of the way so you can open the window fully.

Secure a sliding window with one of several devices that clamp into the top or bottom track and stop the sash from sliding any farther. Casement windows latch fairly securely when they're shut because exterior trim covers the joint

Tip *Technically, a windowsill is the sloped ledge outside the window. Inside, the sill is not visible, as it is covered with a ledge called the window stool. Most people refer to the stool as the sill, however.*

SOLVING DOOR & WINDOW PROBLEMS

between sashes, but you can fortify them with sliding bolts at the top and bottom of both sashes. Basement windows provide convenient access. Cover the window glass with polycarbonate plastic or decorative safety bars. At least one window should have movable bars that can be unlocked from the inside and swung out of the way in an emergency.

Securing a double-hung window

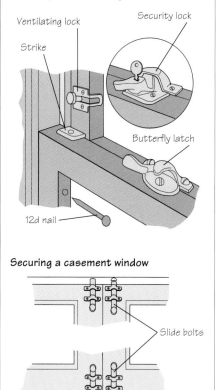

Ventilating lock
Security lock
Strike
Butterfly latch
12d nail

Securing a casement window

Slide bolts

Securing a sliding window

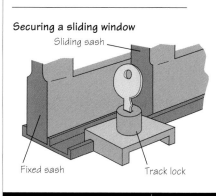

Sliding sash
Fixed sash
Track lock

▶ Double-hung window sash is too loose and rattles.

To prevent side-to-side movement, install weather stripping in the sash channels, either vinyl V-strip or the metal spring-type (see opposite page). If the window has weather stripping on the outside, install spring tension devices in the side channels. Screw them to the channels or the edge of the sash, depending on the type. They press against the sides of the sash and hold it steady.

If the sash rattles back and forth, move the stops closer to it. To nudge a stop less than 1/16 inch, set a woodblock against the stop and strike it with a hammer along its entire length until the paint breaks loose and the stop moves. Drive three or four finishing nails into it to hold it in the new position. To move a stop farther (1/16 inch or more), pry it loose, scrape the jamb smooth with a chisel, and renail the stop closer to the sash. Place a thin cardboard shim between the stop and sash as a temporary spacer.

▶ Double-hung window is hard to lift or won't stay up.

If the sash glides easily (see page 99), the lifting mechanism is faulty. For most windows installed before 1940, the mechanism consists of a counterweight, pulley, and sash cord on both sides of the window. One or both cords may be broken, or the pulleys jammed. Buy new sash cord to replace broken cords. To install it, remove the lower sash by prying off one of the side stops and easing out the sash. If an unbroken cord is still attached, free the knotted end from the sash groove, keep tension on it while

the counterweight pulls it upward, and insert a nail through the knot to hold it against the pulley.

To tie new cord to a weight, or to rescue a dropped weight, remove the access plate located in the jamb. If it's covered by the parting bead that separates the upper and lower sashes, pry out the bead with a chisel, or pull it out with pliers (using wood strips to pad the jaws). Now you can remove the upper sash, if necessary. Inspect the pulley and replace it if the wheel won't turn. Thread new sash cord over the pulley and down the weight cavity; tie the end to the weight. Rest the sash on the sill and pull the free end of the cord far enough down the sash groove to lift the weight within 2 inches of the pulley. Cut the cord where it touches the sash 2 inches below the groove and knot it. Replace the access plate, repeat the operation for the other broken or missing cord, and reassemble the window. If you use chain instead of cord, attach it to the sash groove with screws.

There are several types of lifting mechanisms in post-1940 windows, including tension-spring and spiral lift units. To repair a tension-spring unit, remove the lower sash and unhook the pull tapes from it. Remove the faulty spring unit from the side jamb, replace it with a new unit, reattach the pull tapes to the sash, and reassemble the window. A spiral lift mechanism has a spiral rod inside a long tube located in the sash channel. To adjust tension, swing the lower sash outward, detach the spiral rod from the sash (keep a tight grip on it), and tighten or loosen it a few turns; then reattach it. To replace a unit, detach the spiral rod from the sash and the

Tip *Types of windows: A* fixed window *doesn't open; a* double-hung window *has two sashes that move up and down; a* single-hung window *has only one sash (the lower) that moves up and down; a* casement window *opens like a door, with hinges on the sides of the sash; a* double casement window *has two sashes that open like double doors; an* awning window *swings outward at the bottom; a* hopper window *swings inward at the top.*

tube from the jamb; then attach the new tube to the jamb, wind up the spiral rod, and attach it to the sash.

Removing lower sash

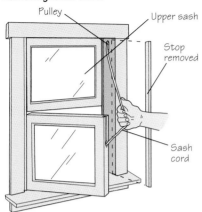

Attaching cord

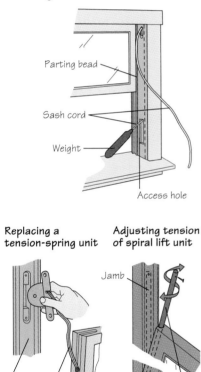

Replacing a tension-spring unit   **Adjusting tension of spiral lift unit**

▶ Double-hung window is missing access plate or parting bead.

You may find an access plate at a used-window dealer or architectural salvage yard. Take the remaining cover plate out of the window and bring it along as a sample. If you can't locate a replacement, take one from a less conspicuous window (closet or back room) of the same kind. Using it as a pattern, fabricate a replacement out of a scrap of wood, then install them both.

If a parting bead is missing or broken, buy a new bead at a lumberyard. Bring along a scrap piece of the remaining bead to make sure the new one is the same size. If not, look for a salvage yard or used-window dealer who has the same size bead.

▶ Double-hung window admits draft and needs weather stripping.

For double-hung windows, use metal spring-type weather stripping, in either a V shape or an offset angle; it is durable and unobtrusive. Attach it with nails provided with the material; the nailed edge should face out. First raise the lower sash and install strips in the side channels beneath it. They should extend 1 inch above the sash when it is shut. Lower the upper sash. Nail strips into the side channels above it, extending them 1 inch lower than the sash when it is shut. Nail strips to the top of the upper sash and bottom of the lower sash. Check for gaps around the edges and pull the free side of the strip out with your fingers to fill the gaps.

If the windows fit too tightly along the edges to install weather stripping in the channels, apply

tubular vinyl weather stripping to both sashes around the outside edges. Seal the joint between the two sashes by applying a strip under the bottom of the upper sash.

Applying metal spring-type weather stripping

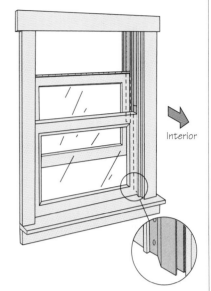

Applying tubular vinyl gasket

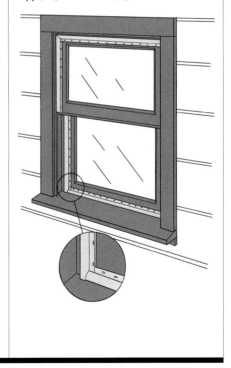

Tip   An open double-hung window without a screen is a temptation for young children to crawl through. To childproof such a window: add a screen; secure the lower sash and open only the top sash; or limit how far the lower sash can open (4 inches is safe) by attaching a safety lock to the top, or drilling a hole through the sash into the side jamb near the top and inserting a nail through both holes.

▶ Double-hung window latch won't lock.

Make sure that the sashes are aligned horizontally. If the upper sash is stuck, score the painted joints and lower it slightly, then try to slide it all the way into the top channel. If it won't go all the way up, paint buildup and grit are probably blocking it; chisel them away and smooth out the channel with sandpaper. Make sure the lower sash is not binding against the interior stool. If the sashes are aligned and the latch still won't lock, loosen the piece attached to the upper sash and move it to the right or left. Plug the old screw holes with glue-coated matchsticks and drill new pilot holes. If the latch is defective, replace it with a safety lock.

▶ Casement window sash flies open in wind.

Install a casement operating mechanism that will hold the window open in any position. One type is operated by a crank, the other by loosening and tightening a thumb knob attached to a sliding rod. Both types have a primary bracket that attaches to the interior stool with screws, and a secondary bracket that attaches to the bottom rail of the sash.

▶ Casement window sash sticks or binds.

Look for paint buildup between the sash and frame; remove it by scraping with a sharp chisel or paint scraper. Sand the area smooth, touch up bare wood with primer or sealer, and apply candle wax or a nonsticking lubricant. If the problem isn't paint, open and shut the window a few times and mark any places where it binds. Remove the sash and the weather stripping,

then plane 1/16 to 1/8 inch of wood from the marked areas. Touch up the bare wood with sealer or primer and finish paint.

▶ Casement window sash is loose.

If it has conventional hinges, inspect them for loose screws and tighten them (see page 80). Replace faulty hinges. If the sash pivots on levers at the top and bottom, check them for loose joints and replace a defective unit (see opposite page). If a replacement is not available, repair loose joints with new rivets. Remove a loose rivet by chiseling off the head, or drilling through it and driving out the body with a punch. Insert a new aluminum hollow rivet and squeeze it with a rivet tool.

Removing rivet

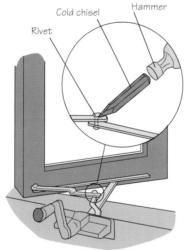

Cold chisel — Hammer — Rivet

Installing a new rivet

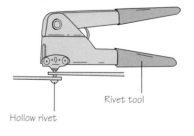

Rivet tool — Hollow rivet

▶ Casement window crank interferes with blinds.

Replace the handle with a more compact type such as a disk handle (a small disk with a knob) or butterfly handle. Both are harder to crank because of reduced leverage.

▶ Casement window mechanism doesn't work properly.

If it's just hard to crank, replace the handle with a longer one that offers more leverage. First make sure the sash isn't sticking or binding. Then, to remove a handle, loosen the setscrew at its base; pull off the handle. Slide on the new one and tighten the setscrew. If a crank turns and nothing happens, loosen the setscrew, rotate the crank slightly, and tighten the screw in the new position. If that doesn't work, remove the handle and inspect the teeth on the shaft. If they are stripped, replace the operating mechanism. If not, replace the handle.

The mechanism itself may be corroded or worn and need replacing. Models vary, but removing most operating mechanisms involves unscrewing the cranking unit from the window frame or stool and slipping the arm out of a track at the bottom of the sash. Some models have a wood stop that covers the gears; carefully pry it off to gain access to the mounting screws. After removing the operating mechanism, secure the loose window sash by shutting and latching it. Inspect the gears and arm of the operating unit. If they are stripped or damaged, take the unit to a window dealer or home center and buy a replacement. If they appear sound, clean the unit with kerosene, wipe it dry, and coat moving parts with silicone spray or other nonsticking lubricant.

Tip Most casement windows open outward, making it possible to decorate them with almost any type of window treatment. If they open inward, the decorative treatments are restricted to those that don't interfere with window movement. Curtains or blinds attached to the window sashes, traditional draperies installed alongside the windows, and Roman shades mounted high enough to clear the window are options that work well.

Straighten the arm if it is bent. Clean out the track, lubricate it, and reassemble the window.

Unscrewing handle

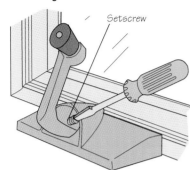

Setscrew

Removing older-type operator

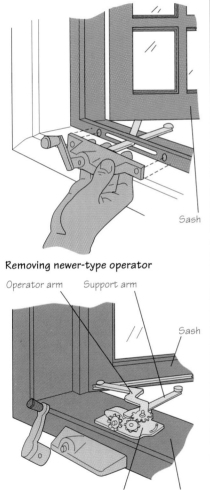

Sash

Removing newer-type operator

Operator arm   Support arm

Sash

Cranking mechanism   Stool

▶ *Casement window admits draft and needs weather stripping.*

Metal spring-type weather stripping is the least conspicuous and most durable type for casement windows. Install the side strips first, cutting them flush with the sill and head jamb. Nail along the exterior edge so the free edge faces inward. Cut the ends of the top and bottom strips at a slight angle, so they don't force the side strips shut, and install them, concealing the bottom strip by applying it to the bottom of the window sash. If the window is too tight for weather-stripping the channels, apply tubular or cushion vinyl stripping (which is less attractive) to the window stops.

For steel casement windows, which have narrow frames, you can buy weather stripping that slips over the metal flanges. Miter the joints by cutting the ends at 45-degree angles, and attach the strips with an adhesive recommended by the manufacturer.

Applying weather stripping

Metal spring-type weather stripping   Sash

Stop

Stop

Tubular gasket   Viewed from indoors

▶ *Gliding-window sash sticks and won't slide easily.*

Remove the sash by lifting it up and swinging the bottom out from the tracks; you may need to adjust a setscrew at the top of the sash before lifting it. Clean out the tracks. Scrape away accumulated grit and debris with a toothbrush or nylon scouring pad, and vacuum thoroughly. Hammer out any dents; back up the blows with a woodblock to keep from denting the track more. Inspect the bottom of the sash for debris, loose screws, nicks, or worn wheels; clean it and remove obstructions. Free stuck wheels with a few drops of penetrating oil, or remove them and buy replacements from a window dealer. Apply silicone lubricant to the tracks and reassemble the window.

▶ *Gliding-window latch won't catch.*

Check to see if the latch is aligned with the strike hole. The sash may be riding up on accumulated debris or an obstruction, raising the latch too high to engage the strike hole. If so, clean out the track, as described above. If the latch is faulty, remove the screws that hold it in place and take it to a window dealer for a replacement.

▶ *Aluminum window frame is tarnished.*

Clean with aluminum cleaner, a mild abrasive cleaner, or fine steel wool and mild detergent. The oxidation that forms on aluminum does not deteriorate the metal—it actually forms a protective surface that inhibits further oxidation—so you're cleaning the metal for cosmetic purposes only. If you wish to paint aluminum window frames, you do not have to remove the oxidation. Lightly sand the frame

Tip   *Many gliding windows are vulnerable to break-ins even when locked, because the sashes can be removed simply by lifting them up and inward. To avoid this possibility, slide the movable sash open and install a sheet-metal screw in its upper track. Adjust the screw until it protrudes enough to prevent the sash from being lifted when it is shut.*

to smooth it, then prime with zinc chromate or a water-based metal primer specified for aluminum.

▶ Jalousie window is vulnerable to break-in.

Jalousie windows, where allowed, should not be placed near doors or where an intruder can reach them easily; they are easy to break into. The intruder simply reaches in, bends back the holding clips, and removes all the panes. If a window is vulnerable, replace it with a more secure type, install security bars on the inside, or have the holding clips soldered or secured so they can't be bent back to release the panes.

▶ Jalousie windowpane is broken, missing, or loose.

To remove a damaged pane, crank the window open until all of the panes are horizontal. Both ends of the pane rest in a channel with a clip wrapped over the top edge. Push the clips downward and slide the glass out of the channels. Buy a replacement pane or have one cut from tempered glass and buffed around the edges. Slide the new pane into place and bend the clips over it. If a pane is loose, remove it. Then bend the clips with pliers and pull them down as small a distance as possible while you slide the pane into place.

Sliding jalousie pane into place

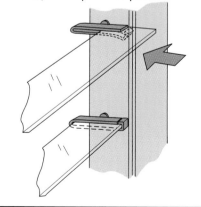

▶ Jalousie window won't close tightly and admits drafts.

Although grooved gaskets that slip over the edges of individual panes are available, it is difficult to seal a jalousie window. The best solution is to remove the window and replace it with a double-hung or sliding window. Because jalousies can't be sealed tightly and the panes are susceptible to coming loose and falling out, many communities don't allow them for house windows except for enclosing porches or in climates where energy performance of windows is not a concern.

▶ Windows need upgrading or replacing.

Replacing old windows with new ones can solve many problems, including heat loss and gain, air infiltration, noise, condensation, carpet fading, and tired-looking windows. Replacing old windows is also very expensive, however, and in some cases may jeopardize the historical integrity of a home. Before you elect to replace windows completely, consider the following options for upgrading your present windows. Although most of the repair techniques are described in this chapter, some of the projects are beyond the scope of this book, and you should consult a professional.

For improving energy performance, consider weather stripping, an interior film, an exterior storm-window/screen combination, an interior insulating window, heavy draperies, or an insulating shade.

To upgrade performance, consider overhauling or replacing the lifting mechanism of a double-hung window, repairing or replacing the cranking mechanism of a casement window, and overhauling the track and sash of a gliding window.

To improve the appearance of a window, consider replacing cracked or distorted glass;, repairing rotted wood with an epoxy filler; painting a metal window frame; adding snap-on muntins to a plain window; exchanging old, dull hardware for decorative replacement latches, cranks, and lifts; cleaning or replacing screens; installing exterior shutters; or adding a flower box.

If you choose to replace old windows, consider all of the replacement options when talking with a dealer or contractor. They include: new sash only (fits inside old jambs); new sash and side-jamb liners (fit inside old jambs); new sash and side jambs (fit inside old jambs); new sash and jamb set (remove old jambs); and complete window unit (sash, jambs, and casings—requires complete tear-out).

▶ Window opening is too small for new window.

Although replacements for most windows may be ordered in custom sizes to fit any opening, there are times when you may want to install a new window that is larger than the existing opening. In planning such an installation, keep in mind that making an opening longer by lowering the sill is fairly easy to do; making it wider by more than 1 or 2 inches is very complicated and involves replacing the header above the opening.

▶ Screening is torn or has hole.

Seal a tiny hole or tear with a drop or two of waterproof glue that dries clear. Apply it in layers; wipe away excess. If the screen is metal and the wires are not torn, simply restore the original weave by pushing individual wires back into place with an awl or sharp nail. You can also repair a small hole by darning it with a few strands of screening.

Tip   If the window screens in your home are showing their age, replacing all of the screening at one time will give your home an immediate face-lift. Screening fabrics of fiberglass and other materials come in many attractive patterns and colors. Replacing the screening also provides a good opportunity to repair and repaint the frames.

Cover larger holes with a patch. If the screen is plastic or fiberglass, sew the patch in place with a few strands taken from the same kind of screening. (You can also iron on a fiberglass patch: set the iron at a high temperature, lay the screen on solid backing, place a cloth over the patch, and press it; practice on scraps first.) To patch a metal screen, cut the patch 2 inches wider than the hole, remove some strands from around the edge of the patch, and bend the protruding ends 90 degrees. Lay the patch over the hole, push the bent ends through the screen, and crimp them.

Patching small holes

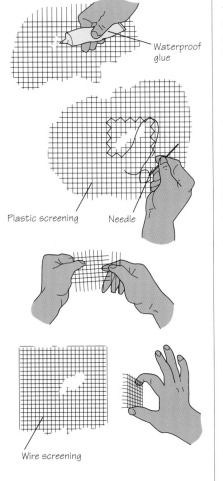

Waterproof glue

Plastic screening   Needle

Wire screening

▶ Screening in wood frame needs replacing.

To replace the screening in a wood frame, pry off the screen bead (wood strips) from the frame, and remove the staples that hold the screening. Remove the screening and dust out the groove. For doors or large window screens, bend the frame by setting a piece of 1-by lumber under each end and holding down the center with clamps on both sides. Lay new metal screening over the frame and staple or tack it to one end. If the screening is fiberglass or vinyl, fold it under to make a 1½-inch hem before stapling it to the frame. Stretch the screening taut and staple it to the other end. Remove the clamps and 1-by pieces and staple the sides, starting at the center and working toward the ends. Nail the screen bead to the edges with 3d HDG finish nails. If the old bead is damaged, replace it with new bead; prime and paint it first.

Removing screen bead

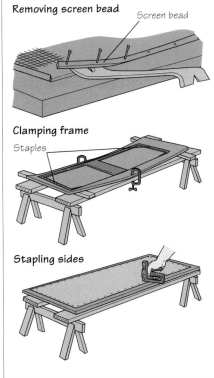

Screen bead

Clamping frame

Staples

Stapling sides

▶ Screen is hard to see through.

Remove the screen from the window. Clean it with soapy water and a brush (brass bristles for metal screening, nylon bristles for plastic or fiberglass screening). Let it dry in the sun. Although all screens distort the view somewhat, changing the screening fabric to a different color may improve visibility. A black screen is the least obtrusive; it seems to recede into the background. It also changes the look of the window dramatically, however; so if you want your screens to match, you'll have to change them all. Light-colored screens can be difficult to see through when they are new because the shiny surface attracts the eye, but as they age they become darker and less distracting.

▶ Screening in metal frame needs replacing.

To replace the screening in a metal frame, buy a piece of fiberglass, aluminum, or vinyl screening at least 1½ inches larger all around than the old screen. Lay the old screen on sawhorses with the interior side facing up. Remove the vinyl spline that holds the old screening in place; start at one end and pull carefully to avoid breaking it. (If it's damaged or brittle, buy a new length of spline.) With the spline and screening removed, vacuum out the groove. Lay the new screening over the frame and trim off the corners diagonally. If the new screening is metal, use the convex wheel of a screen splining tool to press the screening into the groove along one side of the frame. Then, using the concave (grooved) wheel, press the vinyl spline into the same groove. Use short, choppy motions. Repeat the process for one end, then the second side, and finally the other end, keeping the

Tip   *When replacing window screens, you can get sun control by using shading fabric instead of traditional insect screening. Some types reduce visibility; others allow almost as much visibility as regular insect screening while blocking as much as 60 percent of the sun's rays. Shading fabric will also keep out insects.*

screening taut. If the screening is fiberglass or vinyl, use the grooved wheel to press both it and the spline into the groove in one pass.

Removing old screening from metal frame

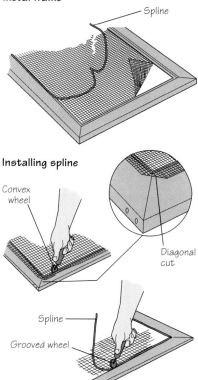

Spline

Installing spline

Convex wheel

Diagonal cut

Spline

Grooved wheel

▶ *Aluminum screen frame is tarnished or bent.*

Clean tarnished frames with aluminum cleaner, a mild abrasive cleaner, or fine steel wool and mild detergent. It is normal for aluminum to oxidize, so the frames will stay clean only a short time. A frame that is bent or damaged can be repaired, but it is easier to find a replacement. Window dealers and most home centers carry replacement screens in standard sizes. If you can't locate one, have a window dealer fabricate a new one.

▶ *Wood-frame screen is weak or loose at joints.*

Renew old screens by reinforcing the joints with metal angles or straps available at any hardware store. Place them on the inside, and paint them to match the screen.

▶ *Screen doesn't fill opening or fit snugly.*

Even small gaps around a screen allow insects to enter. If a wood-frame screen is too small, fill the gaps with wood strips nailed to the edges. If the screen has an aluminum frame, look for a replacement screen at a window dealer or home center. One of the standard sizes may be just what you need. If not, you can have a window shop fabricate a larger screen, or you could build out the frame by attaching strips of extruded aluminum framing stock. Buy it at a window shop, cut pieces to length with a hacksaw, and screw them to the frame.

▶ *Shade rolls up too quickly.*

Roll up the shade, leaving it in a locked position. Carefully lift the flattened pin (spear) out of the slotted bracket. Make sure the little flipper (pawl) is locked against the ratchet teeth and the spear is not exerting tension on the bracket as you lift it out; if it is, stop, unroll and then roll up the shade again until it locks, and lift the spear out of the bracket. With pliers, rotate the spear counterclockwise a few turns while steadying the shade with your other hand. Make sure that the ratchet teeth are locked by the pawl at the end of each turn; start each turn by twisting the spear clockwise a bit to release the pawl before turning it counterclockwise to release spring tension. Return the shade to the brackets and test it. If it is too

fast, repeat the process. If it is too slow, tighten the tension by rotating the spear clockwise a few turns.

▶ *Shade doesn't catch.*

A shade catches when the ratchet teeth at the end of the roller are locked in place by a little flipper (pawl) that falls against them. If the shade doesn't catch, it's usually because the pawl is gummed up and can't move freely. To clean it, roll up the shade and carefully remove it by lifting the end with the flattened pin out of the slotted bracket. Brush the grit and grease away from the pawl and lubricate it with graphite powder or silicone spray. With a pair of pliers, wind the flattened pin (spear) a few times and return the shade to the brackets.

Cleaning out the pawl

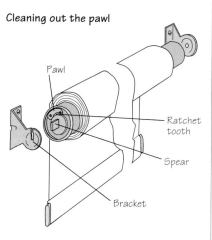

Pawl

Ratchet tooth

Spear

Bracket

▶ *Shade winds up too slowly or not far enough.*

You can control the speed of a shade by adjusting the tension of the internal spring. To do this, roll up the shade as far as possible and leave it in a locked position. Lift the end with the flattened pin (spear) out of the slotted bracket. With pliers, turn the spear clockwise a

Tip   *To clean a plastic or plastic-coated window shade, remove it from the window and lay it flat. Scrub both sides with hot water and an all-purpose cleaner. Sponge to rinse, then dry. Roll up at once to smooth the fabric, then unroll and air-dry. Spot-clean with an art-gum eraser.*

few turns while holding the shade with your other hand. Make sure the pawl is locked against the ratchet teeth each turn before releasing the pliers, or the spear will unwind completely and you'll have to start over again. Return the shade to the brackets and test it. If it's still too slow, tighten the spear some more; if it's too fast, release the tension by backing off the spear a few turns.

Increasing tension on the spring

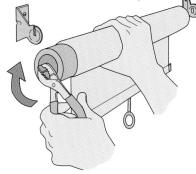

▶ Shade wobbles or doesn't wind up straight.

If the shade winds up crooked, check to see if the brackets are level. Roll up the shade, leaving it in a locked position, and set a level on it. Note which bracket is lower and how far; decide whether it should be moved up or the other bracket moved down. Remove the shade by lifting the end with the flattened pin (spear) out of the slotted bracket. Remove the nails or screws of the bracket to be moved, set it in the new position, and secure it with nails or screws. Replace the shade and test it. If it still wobbles (or was level in the first place), check for bent pins, worn bracket holes, or a loose spear. Straighten bent pins with pliers; replace worn brackets. Replace the shade if the spear is loose or the roller is faulty.

▶ Shade is loose or needs replacing.

If the fabric has become detached from the roller but is otherwise in good condition, restaple it to the roller. First roll the shade up, leaving it in a locked position, and remove it from the brackets. Then, without releasing the ratchet from the pawl, unroll the shade onto a long table or the floor by turning the roller. Staple the loose end of the shade to the roller with a staple gun, or attach it with tacks. Carefully roll up the shade by hand without releasing the ratchet, and return it to the brackets.

If the shade fabric is torn or otherwise needs replacing, take the whole shade, roller and all, to a shade store and have it repaired.

▶ Shade comes loose from brackets and falls.

The brackets are too far apart. Try bending them toward each other. If they are loose, remove the nails and secure them with screws or hollow-wall fasteners (see page 17). If the shade still comes loose, remove one of the brackets and move it closer to the other one.

▶ Blinds have worn cords and tapes that need replacing.

Buy new ladder tapes and cord at a hardware, variety, or drapery store. Be sure the new tapes are appropriate for the slat width. Remove the blinds from the window and lay on a work surface. Release the tapes and cords from the bottom bar. Untie the knots at the bottom of the lift cords and pull the ends of the cords up just to the headbox. Remove the slats, wash them, and set them aside to dry. Release the tapes from the tilt tube; some loop over prongs, others are held by clips. Cut the new tapes to the same

length and number of slats as the old, including any loops you need to sew for attaching the tops to the tilt tube. Attach the new tapes to the tilt tube and slide the slats into position.

To replace the old cords, which are still in the headbox, cut the loop at the bottom of the lift cord and remove the equalizing buckle. Attach each end of the replacement cord to the two cut ends of the lift cord by butting the ends together and wrapping tape around them. Then find the two free ends of the lift cord in the headbox and thread them down through the slats. As you pull on them, the old cord will pull the new cord into place. Pull until the looped end of the new cord is at the same height as the old one was. Cut the free ends of the new cord and attach them to the bottom bar the same way as the original cord was. Attach the tapes to the bottom bar as the old ones were. If the blinds have a tilt cord instead of a vertical bar, replace it with new cord—just lift it off the pulley and loop the new cord over it.

Replacing cords and tapes

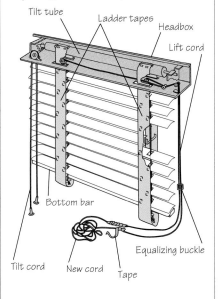

Tip *To clean miniblinds, wash them in the tub or shower with mild detergent and water. Dry metal parts with a hair dryer and coat them with mineral oil to prevent corrosion. To clean larger venetian blinds, wipe both sides of each slat with a mild detergent, an all-purpose cleaner, or a venetian blind cleaner. Scrub the tapes with a soft brush and warm soapy water, then rinse.*

SOLVING DOOR & WINDOW PROBLEMS

▶ Blinds rise unevenly or don't operate smoothly.

Pull on one side of the lift cord, then the other, until the bottom bar of the blinds is level. Then adjust the equalizing buckle on the cord so it hangs evenly. If the blinds still rise unevenly, the cord is not threading through one of the pulleys properly. Remove the cover from the headbox at the top of the blinds and inspect the pulleys and cord channels for obstructions. Have repairs made by a window-covering specialist.

▶ Curtain rod sags.

Rods over 48 inches long should have a center support. Wire hooks for this purpose are available from hardware stores or fabric stores that have drapery supplies. To screw in the hook at the right level, stretch a string between the bottoms of both ends of the curtain rod and mark the wall at the midpoint of the string. Measure up from the mark a distance equal to the depth of the hook; screw the hook into the wall at that point.

▶ Curtain rod bracket has come loose from wall.

If the bracket is attached to wood trim and the screws have pulled loose, deepen the hole by drilling all the way through the trim and wallboard and slightly into the stud or header behind it. Reattach the bracket with longer screws (1½ inches for wallboard walls, longer for plaster walls). If the bracket is attached to wallboard or plaster where there is no wood framing to back up the screws, use expansion bolts or other hollow-wall fasteners (see page 17).

▶ Traverse rod has broken or excess slides.

Drapery hooks hang from slides in the traverse rod; there should be a separate slide for each hook (except end hooks, which are attached to the corners of the rod and the carriers). To remove a broken or extra slide, take down the draperies. Push down on the gate at the end of the rod and slip the slide out. Replace a broken slide with an exact duplicate. The slides on decorative rods are attached to a ring; replace the entire ring. Rehang the draperies.

▶ Traverse rod cord is loose and lacks proper tension.

Locate the pulley yoke attached to the wall at the bottom of the window. Raise the tension pulley and hold it in place with the lock button on the side of the yoke or, if it has none, insert a nail through the hole in the pulley shaft. Then locate the master carrier in the traverse rod and pull the knotted end of the cord to take up the slack. Tie a new knot in the cord and trim the excess. Release the tension pulley.

▶ Draperies don't draw evenly.

If two-way draperies don't part evenly in the center, the cord has probably slipped position in the underlap carrier. Release the cord from the bridge under which it is hooked, slide the carrier to the proper position (the same distance from the center of the rod as the master carrier), and rehook the cord under the bridge.

▶ Traverse rod cord is broken or frayed.

Replace a damaged drapery cord with new cord, available where drapery rods are sold. First unhook and take down the draperies. Then remove the old cord by untying both ends from the master carrier and releasing it from the bridge (a friction hook) of the underlap carrier. Thread one end of the new cord through either hole in the master carrier, knot it, and thread the rest of the cord through the rod, pulleys, and tension pulley (as shown). Secure the second end of the cord to the master carrier with a temporary knot. With the underlap carrier and master carrier at equal distances from the rod ends, secure the cord to the underlap carrier by hooking it under the bridge. Before tying a final knot in the second end of the cord, raise the tension pulley in the pulley yoke as far as it will go and secure it with the lock button or a nail. Then pull all of the slack out of the cord, tie the final knot in the end, and trim off the excess. Release the tension pulley and hang the draperies.

Threading drapery cord

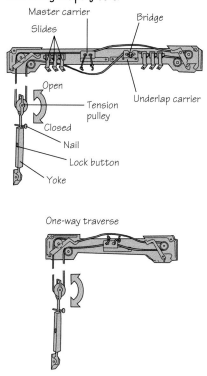

Master carrier
Slides
Bridge
Open
Tension pulley
Underlap carrier
Closed
Nail
Lock button
Yoke

One-way traverse

Tip *A considerable amount of heat can be lost through windows on a cold night. Various types of window coverings are available that insulate as well as decorate. Pleated shades, which have an insulated air space between two layers of fabric, compress into a very tight formation when they are raised, much like miniblinds. Window quilts, which insulate like blankets, can be concealed in a valance when they're rolled up.*

From roof shingles to patio paving, the areas outside your home develop problems that often need immediate attention. This chapter provides information for solving more than 180 such problems.

▶ Roof leaks.

The first step in fixing a roof leak is to find it. The actual leak is seldom directly above the area where the ceiling is dripping. To pinpoint the source, inspect the attic during a storm or, at a more convenient time, have someone spray the roof with a hose while you search the attic. Look for water migrating along rafters, pipes, or other attic features and follow it upstream.

When you find the point where water penetrates the roof sheathing, mark it clearly with bright chalk for future reference. Transfer the location of this point to the surface of the roof. One way is to drive a 16d nail straight up through the leaking area, but only if you'll be fixing the leak right away. Otherwise, take two measurements—one from the roof ridge down to the leak, the other laterally from the leak to a nearby feature on either side, such as a pipe, chimney, or gable wall—and transfer the measurements to the surface of the roof.

Once on the roof, examine the area around the nail or measured coordinates for broken shingles, loose flashing, cracked caulk, or other problems. If none is apparent, look for those problems farther up the roof slope. (For especially mysterious leaks, wait for dry weather and then have someone watch the chalked area in the attic while you spray the roof with a hose, working slowly upslope and wetting small areas until water flows into the attic.) Once you have verified the source of the leak, mark it, and repair it during dry weather. You can temporarily protect it during a storm by covering the leak area with a tarp; it should extend up and over the roof ridge. Anchor it well with bricks, timbers, or similar weights, or by tying it down.

▶ Roof leaks around chimney.

Deteriorating chimney flashing, or a chimney that was not flashed properly in the first place, is a source of many roof leaks. Such a leak may not be noticed for many months if the chimney is enclosed by interior walls. If you suspect a leak, make an attic inspection during a storm or while someone sprays water on the roof, and note where water runs down the chimney bricks. Then climb up onto the roof and check that side of the chimney for defective flashing. (Inspect other areas also, as the leak may originate upslope from where it penetrates the roof.) If the chimney leaks on the side, it may have the wrong kind of flashing. It should have step flashing—a series of L-shaped pieces installed over shingles and covered by the shingles above them. (See page 121.) If the upslope side of the chimney leaks, the roof may lack a cricket (a peaked bulge that diverts water away from the chimney). If so, whatever flashing protects the upslope side of the chimney may not extend far enough up the slope under the shingles to repel the rapid buildup of water behind the chimney. Replace it with a cricket, new flashing, and new roofing material.

Another cause of leaks around a chimney is lack of counter flashing, or cap flashing, to protect the top of the primary flashing. To install new counter flashing, buy a 10-foot length from a sheet-metal shop. Cut and install in stair-step fashion short sections that overlap the primary flashing and each other. The top of each section should be anchored in the mortar joints between bricks. First chisel out ¼ to ½ inch of mortar. Then run a bead of roof caulk into the deepened joint, press the bent top of the flashing into it,

and secure it to the mortar with two 1-inch concrete nails. Hold the nails with needle nose pliers and drive them sharply with a 2- or 3-pound hammer. See also page 119.

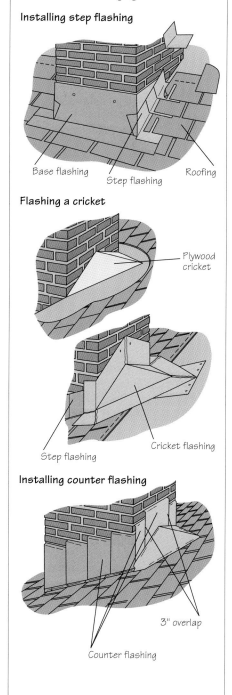

Installing step flashing

Base flashing
Step flashing
Roofing

Flashing a cricket

Plywood cricket

Cricket flashing

Step flashing

Installing counter flashing

3" overlap

Counter flashing

Tip *Roof safety: Wait until the roof is dry. Wear sneakers or other soft-soled shoes. Inspect any ladder for damage or weakness before using it. Set the feet on solid ground at a distance away from the house equal to one-quarter the total height. Don't place the ladder near power lines. When you climb to the top, tie the ladder to the gutter or another anchorage so it won't slide to either side. If the roof slope is greater than 5 in 12, use a safety rope. Tie one end to a tree or post on the side of the house opposite where you'll be working; toss the other end over the roof to the ladder.*

▶ *Composition shingle leaks.*

For a temporary repair, slide a flat piece of aluminum or galvanized flashing under the damaged shingle. It should extend 4 inches beyond the crack or hole on each side. Secure it with roofing cement or a nail, or by bending the metal slightly so it is held in place by friction. If a nail has popped up and poked a hole through the shingle, pull the nail, fill the nail hole with caulk, and drive a new nail nearby.

Inserting metal flashing

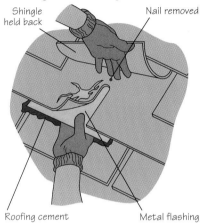

▶ *Roof valley leaks.*

Valleys are prone to leaking because water rushes into them from different angles and accumulates with great force near the bottom. Sometimes it's easy to locate the source of a leak, such as a hole in the valley flashing. Repair a crack or small hole by cleaning the area with a wire brush, filling the hole with gutter sealant or butyl caulk, and smoothing it with a putty knife moistened with paint thinner. Repair larger holes (2 to 3 inches) by applying a layer of roofing cement around the hole, embedding an aluminum or galvanized metal patch into it, and covering the area with more roofing cement.

For additional protection, paint the repair with aluminum paint.

If the flashing and roofing look sound, the valley may leak due to improper installation. If the leak is near the bottom of the valley, the adjacent shingles may be too close together, trapping water under them. Trim the shingles alongside the valley so they are farther apart at the bottom of the valley than at the top; the distance across the valley should widen ⅛ inch per foot, top to bottom. (This repair applies to roofs with metal valley flashing, not shingles that are woven across the valley.) Next inspect the edges of the shingles along the valley; they should be sealed with roofing cement. Then lift a few shingles to inspect under

them. The top corners should be "dubbed" (cut off at a 45-degree angle) so they don't have sharp edges that could catch water flowing across the valley. Also inspect the flashing itself for holes or rust. Fill small holes with butyl caulk or gutter sealant. If the valley is flashed with roll roofing, repair holes and cracks with roofing cement. Cover larger holes with a temporary metal patch (composition shingle for roll roofing); spread roofing cement over the area, lay the patch in place, and cover the patch with more roofing cement. If the shingles aren't dubbed or the valley is not flashed properly, have the shingles and flashing stripped away and replaced with new materials by a professional roofer.

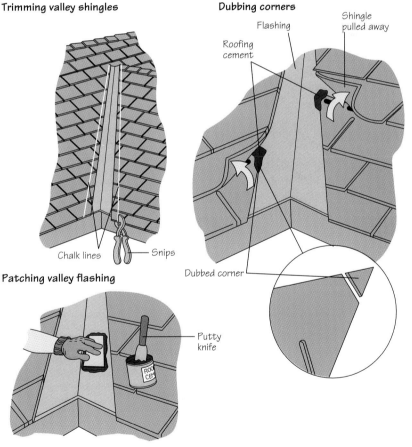

Tip *The most common places for roof leaks are: (1) chimney flashing, (2) vent flashing, (3) valleys, (4) skylight flashing, and (5) eave areas where ice dams form.*

Tip *Inspect your roof every year. Use binoculars if you can't get onto the roof. Look for exposed nail heads; loose, curling, cracked, or missing shingles; loose flashing; dried caulk; and accumulated debris. These problems can be solved with a handful of roofing nails, some roof caulk, a few metal shims, and a broom.*

▶ Composition shingle is damaged or missing.

Repair a crack by spreading roofing cement under it, nailing down both sides of the crack, and covering the repair with more cement.

To replace a damaged shingle, carefully lift the shingle tabs above it far enough to slip a pry bar under the nails holding the damaged shingle in place. Pry out all nails (most composition shingles are 36 inches wide and have four nails) and, if shingles are installed close

Removing old shingles

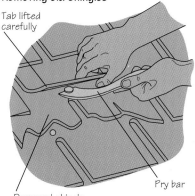

Tab lifted carefully

Damaged shingle

Pry bar

Nailing new shingle

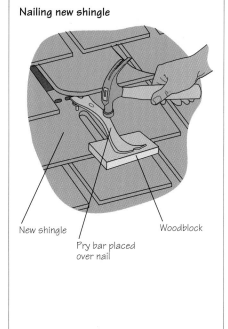

New shingle

Pry bar placed over nail

Woodblock

together, nails from the two courses above the damaged shingle. With the nails removed, pull the damaged shingle out and slide a new shingle into the same place. If the new shingle is metric (39 inches long), trim it to 36 inches so it will fit. To nail the new shingle, carefully lift the tabs above it and avoid placing the new nails in the old nail holes. If the tabs above the new shingle are too brittle to lift enough to allow for hammering, lift them just high enough to set the new nails in place. Then set one end of a pry bar on the nail head and the other on a woodblock; hammer the bar, not the nail.

▶ Roof leaks around plumbing vent or flue.

Pipes and flues that penetrate the roof require vent flashing around them. When it rusts or comes loose, a leak develops. If the flashing is loose around the top but otherwise sound, seal the top by removing old roofing cement and debris, applying new roofing cement between the top of the flashing and the pipe, and wrapping metallic duct tape around the joint. If the vent has a storm collar above the flashing, apply a bead of silicone caulk between the collar and pipe.

If the flashing itself is rusted or cracked, replace it with new vent flashing. Buy the type with a neoprene gasket that fits around the vent pipe or flue, in a size specified for the diameter of the pipe and the slope of the roof. To remove the old flashing, carefully remove roof shingles above the flashing, starting two courses above and working down until the sides of the flashing are exposed. Remove the nails from the flashing and slide it off the pipe. Slide the new flashing over

the pipe, tuck the top edge under the shingles, and nail down the top corners and middles of both sides with roofing nails. Daub the nail heads with roofing cement, then replace the shingles.

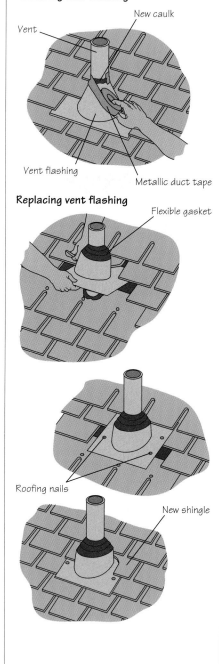

Resealing vent flashing

New caulk

Vent

Vent flashing

Metallic duct tape

Replacing vent flashing

Flexible gasket

Roofing nails

New shingle

Tip   *Codes limit the number of times new roofing material can be installed over old without removing the old; most codes allow two layers of roofing, some three.*

Tip   *Composition-shingle roofs can last from 10 to 25 years, depending on the quality of shingles and the weather conditions. If many of the shingles are curled, have crumbling edges, are brittle, have lost most of the mineral coating, or have protruding nail heads, it is time for a new roof.*

▶ *Wood shingle or shake leaks.*

If the shingle is split, slip a flat piece of aluminum or galvanized flashing under it to shed any water that seeps through the crack. If the problem is a protruding nail, pull it out, drive a new one next to the old hole, and cover the head and hole with roofing cement.

▶ *Wood shingles or shakes are weathered or stained.*

Cleaning cedar shingles and applying a preservative every few years can extend the life of a wood roof, so long as the shingles aren't damaged or cracked. Consult a professional roofing company that offers this service. The process involves having the roof sprayed with a high-pressure washer and then coated with a solvent containing copper naphthenate or a similar preservative.

▶ *Wood shingle or shake is damaged or missing.*

If a shingle is broken, split the remaining part into lengthwise sections with a hammer and chisel and pull out the pieces. Then slip a hacksaw blade under the overlapping shingle above, cut off the nails, and remove them.

To install a new shingle or shake, cut it to the same width as the old, allowing a ¼-inch gap on each side. Then slide it into place, but leave ¼ to ½ inch of the butt extending below the adjacent shingles. As close as possible to the bottom edge of the overlapping shingle above, drive two 5d HDG box nails into the new shingle (8d for shakes) at an angle. Drive the nail heads snug, but don't embed them in the wood. Then, with a nailing block and hammer, strike the bottom of the new shingle, driving it upward

so it is flush with the adjacent shingles. As the shingle slides upward, the exposed nail heads will move with it, up and under the protection of the overlapping shingle. For added protection tuck a piece of metal flashing between the new shingle and the overlapping one, to cover the nail heads.

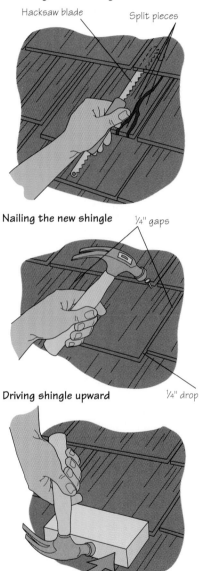

Removing a wood shingle or shake

Hacksaw blade   Split pieces

Nailing the new shingle   ¼" gaps

Driving shingle upward   ¼" drop

▶ *New cedar shakes don't match color of old.*

To "weather" new cedar shakes or shingles quickly, apply a solution of 1 pound baking soda in ½ gallon water. The new shingles will turn gray in a few hours.

▶ *Tile roof leaks.*

Because tiles are brittle and have interlocking pieces, most repairs should be done by a professional roofer experienced with tile. If the problem is a broken tile that you can reach from a ladder or open window, slip a piece of aluminum or copper flashing under it to stop the leak. Bend or curve the metal to match the profile of the tile.

▶ *Metal roof leaks.*

Seal a pinhole leak with roofing cement. If there are extensive pinhole leaks, coat the roof with liquid sealant specified for metal roofs, according to manufacturer's instructions. If leaks occur around fasteners, it is probably because they were installed without allowance for expansion. The same problems will persist unless the roofing is reinstalled correctly.

Repair a larger hole, except in aluminum, by soldering a patch of the same kind of metal over it. Cut a rectangular patch at least 2 inches larger than the hole. Snip off the corners of the patch, fold the edges under ½ inch, and crimp them. Then clean the damaged area of the roof with a wire brush or steel wool, especially where the edges of the patch will touch; polish the edges of the patch with sandpaper. Coat the cleaned edges of the patch and roof surface with flux—acid flux for copper, noncorrosive resin flux for steel or terne metal (steel roofing coated with a tin/lead alloy). Lay the patch over the damaged area and set

Tip *How to measure roof slope: (1) Hold a level so one end rests on the roof. (2) Mark a point on the level 12 inches from the end that is resting on the roof. (3) Hold the level steady and measure the distance between that point and the roof surface, straight down. This distance is the slope of the roof, and is expressed as n in 12—for instance, 3 in 12 or 5 in 12.*

weights on it. Solder by heating the metal with an electric soldering iron and touching the solder to the metal long enough for solder to flow into the joint, working your way around the patch slowly.

To repair a hole in aluminum, spread roofing cement over the damaged area and lay a fiberglass patch over the cement. Then apply a second layer of cement over the patch, lay a second patch over it, and cover the repair with a final coat of cement.

Soldering a patch

▶ Tar-and-gravel roof leaks.

Because a tar-and-gravel (or built-up) roof is fairly flat, the leak is usually directly above the wet ceiling area. Look for a hole, crack, tear, or blister on the roof surface. Sweep gravel aside to expose the roofing material. If the problem is a blister, slit it with a utility knife to relieve the pressure. With a putty knife apply a generous coating of roofing cement inside the blister, over it, and around it for 2 to 3 inches. Cover the area with a patch of roll roofing, press it into the cement, and nail it around the edges with roofing nails. Apply another layer of cement over the patch, let it partially dry, and spread gravel over the area.

If the problem is a hole or tear, use a utility knife and straightedge to cut a rectangular outline around the damaged section, then remove it. Cut a patch to fit into the cut-out area. Spread a generous layer of roofing cement onto the cutout area, working the cement under all four edges and extending it 2 inches over the surrounding roof surface. Press the patch into place and secure the edges with roofing nails. Apply more roofing cement over the patch and surrounding border. Cover this layer of cement with a new, larger patch; nail it in place, cover it with roofing cement, and spread gravel over it when the cement begins to dry.

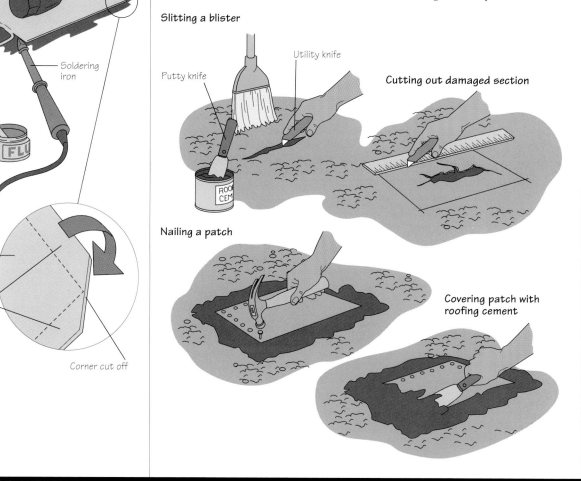

Tip *The purpose of gravel on a tar-and-gravel roof is to protect the tar from exposure to direct sunlight. Otherwise, the solvents in the tar would evaporate very quickly, causing the tar to crack and become brittle.*

▶ Roll roofing is worn or damaged and needs replacing.

Repair a hole or blister in the same way as for a tar-and-gravel roof (see opposite page). If the entire roof is worn, replace it with new roll roofing, following manufacturer's directions. Roll roofing is available in "single coverage," which leaves 32 inches of the 36-inch-wide roll exposed, or "double coverage," which has a 17-inch exposure and 19-inch selvage. Double coverage offers better protection.

▶ Snow avalanches off roof.

In areas of heavy snowfall, when snow slides off a roof in one large chunk it can damage gutters, ruin decks, break exposed pipes, collapse lower roofs, imperil pedestrians, and cause other problems. Various types of snow guards, or snow bucks, either hold back the snow or prevent it from sliding off the roof all at once. Some are fabricated from wire, others from bent metal. Depending on the type of guard and slope of the roof, space them 2 to 8 feet apart in staggered rows. Attach them directly to the roof decking, under the shingles, with HDG nails or fasteners supplied by the manufacturer.

▶ Ice dams cause leaks near edge of roof.

When attic heat melts snow near the ridge of the roof, the water runs toward the gutters, encounters colder roof temperatures on the way, and freezes into ice. This ice isn't generally noticed because it's hidden and insulated by the snowpack, but it creates dams that back up more meltwater, forcing it under shingles and causing leaks.

The best solution for this problem is to prevent attic heat from escaping through the roof by adding substantially more ceiling insulation and attic ventilation. Another solution is to install eave flashing when you have a new roof put on. It is a wide, rubberlike membrane that extends up the roof at least 3 feet from the eave. As shingles are nailed over it, the membrane seals around the nails, blocking off potential leaks. Electric heat tapes and cables are partial solutions at best: They only prevent icicles from forming on the gutter.

Controlling ice dams

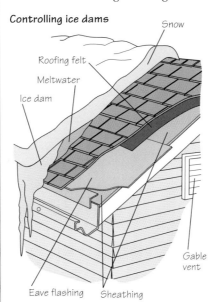

▶ Moss or fungus is growing on shingles.

Although moss can grow on almost any type of roof, wood roofs are particularly vulnerable to damage from moss and fungus. Moss, usually restricted to shaded areas, acts like a sponge and retains moisture, accelerating decay of the shingles. Fungus, which blackens the shingles and affects the entire roof, also retains moisture and causes decay.

Unchecked it helps to account for wood roofs lasting only 15 years in some climates, instead of 80 years or more in areas where harsh winters control fungus growth.

Fallen leaves, dirt, pine needles, and other debris encourage fungus growth, so sweeping a roof often will discourage (but not prevent) it, as well as removing large clumps of moss. Use a stiff broom that clears the joints between shingles. If the roof has composition shingles, wet it with a hose first so the broom doesn't remove the surface granules. Total fungus control starts with bleaching the roof or washing it with a high-pressure washer, then repairing any loose or broken shingles, and finally applying a nonflammable wood preservative. Because this treatment involves the entire roof, it is an ambitious task for a homeowner. You may prefer to have a professional roof maintenance company provide the service every 5 to 10 years.

If the roofing material is composition shingles, remove fungus by spraying the roof with a solution of ½ ounce sodium arsenate (available from garden centers) in 10 gallons water. A solution of 1 part chlorine bleach to 4 parts water may also work, though not as well. Follow all label instructions about mixing, applying, and storing these products. Spray with a clean garden sprayer. First cover shrubs and plants below the eaves with plastic sheeting; protect the house siding by wetting it thoroughly, and have someone stand by to rinse off areas that get spattered as you work. Wear soft-soled shoes on the roof, gloves, and eye protection. Standing partway up the roof and always

Tip *Several roofing products are available that inhibit fungus growth. One is shingles with zinc granules, available from most manufacturers of composition shingles. Another, common on the West Coast, is a strip of zinc metal that is installed at the ridge of the roof. Rainwater washing over it distributes metallic residue onto the roof. Copper wires installed on the roof every 3 to 4 feet, parallel to the eaves, have the same effect.*

moving up, start spraying at the bottom of the roof and work upward, staying above the slippery, freshly sprayed areas. After applying the solution, rinse it off with a hose, working from top to bottom. Avoid touching or spraying power lines.

Spraying a roof

Plastic

▶ Roof is not fire resistant.

Roofing materials and application techniques are classified by fire-resistance ratings. Class A materials are noncombustible, Class B partially combustible, and Class C combustible. Check with the building-inspection department for local requirements; many communities prohibit certain types of roofing materials. If you have wood shingles or shakes that were not pressure treated with fire retardant prior to installation, there is no reliable way to make the roof fire resistant. You'll have to replace the untreated shingles with Class A materials (or Class B where allowed).

▶ Roof is vulnerable to lightning.

In an area of frequent storms, almost any home is vulnerable to lightning strikes, even if it's surrounded by taller structures. Any building, tree, or structure that is sufficiently ionized (has a certain electric charge) during a storm can attract lightning, no matter how tall it is. Some protection systems neutralize a home so it won't attract lightning; others divert a strike to the earth so it doesn't cause damage to the building. All systems are tailored to the individual home, so take a sketch or photo of yours to a lightning-protection equipment dealer to have an individual system designed for your home. You may be able to install it yourself, depending on the type of system and your skills. You may want to consult your homeowner's insurance agent first to assess the level of risk in your area and to see what kind of rate discount you would be eligible for if your home had a lightning-protection system.

▶ Ridge is sagging.

Most roofs sag slightly over time, but a "swayback" roof sagging more than 2 inches over its length indicates a structural problem. Consult a competent building contractor, structural engineer, or architect to see if the roof can be stabilized by minor reinforcement or if major structural changes are needed.

▶ Roof looks worn and unappealing.

Sooner or later almost every type of roof, with the exception of tile, slate, and some metals, needs replacing. New materials, such as lightweight concrete tiles and spray-on foam, and improved older materials, such as random-thickness fiberglass shingles, offer many attractive

alternatives to just getting a new covering of the same material. Consult knowledgeable roofing professionals about the required roof slope, feasibility of covering the old roofing, weight, durability, fire rating, and cost of each option before you choose replacement materials for your roof.

▶ Gutter is clogged and doesn't drain.

First remove twigs, leaves, and other debris from the gutter, starting at the downspout. Wearing gloves, loosen crusted debris with a stiff brush and scoop out matted debris with a garden trowel. If you notice any problem areas that will need fixing later, mark the location with chalk on the outside of the gutter so it will be easy to find. After cleaning the gutter, flush the downspout with a garden hose. If the pipe is clogged, insert the hose from the bottom of the spout, pack rags around the outlet, and turn on the water full force to loosen the blockage. If that doesn't work, clear the pipe with a drain auger. After clearing the downspout, hose down the gutter. Watch for leaks or sluggish flow, and make repairs.

▶ Gutter overflows but is not clogged.

The gutter doesn't have enough slope for the water to flow properly; it might even slope backward. It should be sloped toward the downspout at a rate of 1/16 inch per foot of run. Do not gauge slope by the roof eave; it may not be level. Instead set a 6-foot level (or a short level on top of a long straightedge) on top of the gutter at several points to check where the gutter is improperly sloped. To adjust it,

---

Tip *A continuous gutter screen is an excellent way to keep leaves and debris from clogging gutters. Most home centers or building-supply outlets have kits that include a roll of screening material, snap-on fittings to attach the screen, and instructions for installing it. If you can't locate such a kit, buy 1/4-inch hardware cloth (galvanized screening with a wider mesh than ordinary window screen). With metal-cutting snips, cut it into strips just wide enough to wedge between the top edges of the gutter.*

loosen the hangers and reset them at new positions (L brackets can be moved only by removing the gutter first). If you have to adjust the entire gutter, remove it to align the top of the gutter. Use a hydrolevel or a series of measurements with a long level to establish the correct height for each end of the line. First mark points at each end that are level with each other; then, at the down-stream end, measure down from the mark enough distance to ensure a slope of 1/16 inch per foot of run. Snap a chalk line along the fascia board or rafter ends to this measure-ment. When attaching the gutter, slide the backside under the drip edge—the L-shaped roof flashing that bends down over the fascia.

Hanging gutters

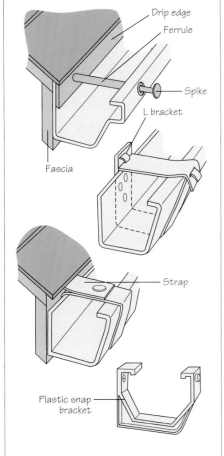

Drip edge
Ferrule
Spike
L bracket
Fascia
Strap
Plastic snap bracket

▶ Seamless gutter leaks at corners.

Long sections of aluminum gutter expand and contract in length through the seasons, causing stress at the corners. Caulk the open joints with gutter sealant. If the problem recurs every year, buy for each corner a gutter connector that fits the profile of the gutters. Con-nectors are like sleeves; you slide a section of gutter into each end. To install, cut the long section of gut-ter near the leaky corner, apply sealant around the inside edges of the sleeve, and slip the connector between the cut ends.

▶ Gutter leaks.

Repair tiny holes and hairline cracks with gutter sealant specified for the type of gutter—aluminum, vinyl, or galvanized metal (you may have to buy it through a siding or roofing supplier). First dry the area around the hole or crack thoroughly and buff it with steel wool or a wire brush enough to loosen debris but not remove the zinc coating of galvanized metal. Then apply the sealant and work it into the hole or crack with a putty knife.

If a seam leaks and it wasn't joined with solder, disassemble it by removing the sheet-metal screws or pop rivets used to hold the two gutter pieces together. Clean off the mating surfaces, apply a generous bead of sealant to the lower surface, and press the gutter pieces back to-gether. Secure them with new sheet-metal screws or pop rivets. Seal leaky connector joints in a similar manner, but use screws or rivets only if the repair doesn't work without them.

The best way to patch a large hole or deteriorated area in a metal gutter is to solder a patch over it (see page 113). If this is not feasible, clean the area with a wire brush or abrasive pad; be sure to remove rust completely. Wipe the area with a rag soaked in paint thinner and let it dry. Then coat the area with a 1/8-inch-thick layer of gutter sealant and press a fiberglass-mesh or metal patch into it. Smooth the sealant where it oozes out around the edges of the patch, then cover the patch with another layer of sealant and smooth it with a putty knife. If a section of gutter has several holes, or the gutter is a modular, snap-together style, replace the section instead of trying to patch it.

Sealing a leaky joint

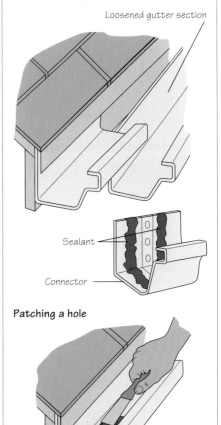

Loosened gutter section
Sealant
Connector

Patching a hole

Patch
Sealant

Tip *Clean leaves and debris out of gutters at least twice a year (spring and fall) and flush the gutters with a garden hose. Inspect for leaks, excessive rust, broken brackets, and improper alignment, and repair as necessary. If leaves clog downspouts frequently, install leaf strainers above the downspout openings, or, for greater protection, stiff leaf screens over all the gutters. Install leaf screens by curving them and letting friction hold them in place, or by slipping one edge under the roof shingles.*

▶ Gutter spikes or brackets are bent.

Bent spikes distort the gutter and force it out of alignment. Straighten a bent spike by prying it up with an improvised "sky hook"—a strong lever with a hook in the middle. For the lever use a short length of angle iron or a crowbar with a notch in the straight end. For the hook use a chain link or a bungee-cord hook. Place one end of the lever over the ferrule (spacer tube that the spike goes through) where it abuts the house. Slip the hook over the bar and attach it to the ferrule where the spike is bent. Lift up on the bar until the ferrule and spike are straight.

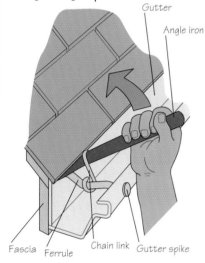

Straightening a spike

Gutter

Angle iron

Fascia Ferrule Chain link Gutter spike

▶ Gutter is loose.

First remove the spike or hanger that is loose and prop up the gutter so it is straight. Then pour water in the gutter to see if it slopes properly. If it does, reattach the loose hanger, moving it 2 to 3 inches away from the original location. If it's a spike, drill a ¼-inch pilot hole through the face of the gutter first, then slide the ferrule in place and drive the spike through the hole and ferrule. If the hanger is an L bracket, pull the gutter down and away from the fascia board or rafter tail so you can attach the bracket first, then snap the gutter into it. If the gutter does not slope toward the downspout, see page 116.

▶ Gutter needs painting.

To paint new galvanized gutters, etch off residual oils from the manufacturing process by brushing distilled vinegar or other mild acid onto the gutters and rinsing it off; follow label precautions for acid. Then paint the gutters with a coat of zinc chromate green or yellow primer. (This oil-based product is the best choice, but if it's not available, use a latex galvanized-metal primer—etching won't be necessary.) Then paint the gutters with oil-based or latex exterior trim paint. If ungalvanized gutters have weathered and turned a dull gray, they have etched naturally and can be primed and painted after cleaning with a mild solution of TSP and water. Do not sand them or wire-brush them; it removes the zinc coating.

If the gutters were previously painted, scrap off loose or flaking paint and spot-prime bare metal with zinc chromate or latex galvanized-metal primer. Then prime the old painted surfaces according to label directions for the final coat of paint, and complete the painting.

Paint bare aluminum gutters in the same way as galvanized metal. If the gutters have a baked-on enamel finish, prime them with an oil-based exterior primer, then apply the final coat of exterior trim paint.

Vinyl gutters are intended to need no painting, but if you want to change the color and are willing to maintain the paint every few years, you can paint them. Check with the manufacturer about specific recommendations, or follow these steps: First clean the gutters with rubbing alcohol, following label precautions about wearing gloves and avoiding fumes. Then prime them with vinyl-siding primer and apply a final coat of latex house paint.

▶ Gutter is missing or needs replacing.

Replace worn or missing sections of gutter with the same type. If you are installing all new gutters, the choices are vinyl, galvanized steel, and aluminum. Vinyl gutters snap together and come with installation instructions for do-it-yourselfers. Some aluminum gutters are available in modular units that can be snapped together; others are fabricated on-site by professional installers. Galvanized-steel gutters require soldered seams, although if you need to make only a few connections, you could use gutter sealant and sheet-metal screws.

▶ Downspout deposits water against foundation.

Water from gutters and downspouts should be diverted away from the foundation at least 8 feet. There are several ways to do this. The easiest is to slip a length of 3- or 4-inch-diameter pipe (nonperforated), at least 8 feet long, over the end of the downspout. Make sure the outlet of the pipe discharges water where it will flow away from the house (but not into a neighbor's yard). A less obtrusive arrangement (although a bigger project) is to bury the pipe, sloping it at least 1 inch per 8 feet of run. You will probably have to make the run much longer to find a discharge point low enough to maintain the slope. If you can't discharge the pipe to daylight, run it into a dry well—a hole in the

Tip *Gutters have an important job to do in diverting water away from the foundation. The roof surface of a 2,000-square-foot home is approximately 2,500 square feet. In an area with 30 inches of annual rainfall, the gutters of this roof must handle more than 55,000 gallons of water every year, the equivalent of three average-sized swimming pools.*

ground 4 feet in diameter and 6 to 8 feet deep, filled with rocks and gravel. The dry well should be at least 10 feet from the house. Fittings are available for connecting the downspout to the drainage pipe. Also make sure that the soil slopes away from the house all around, at a rate of 1 inch per foot for at least 10 feet. Where this is not possible, slope it at least a foot or two toward a buried drainage pipe, or to a shallow concrete surface gutter installed parallel to the house and sloped toward drainage. If there's no low point to discharge the drainage pipe or gutter, and a dry well is not feasible, have a sump and sump pump installed which discharges water into the backyard or the street (consult municipal codes).

Installing a drain pipe

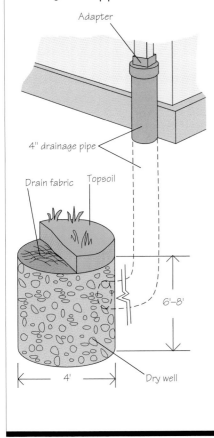

▶ *Chimney flashing leaks.*

Check for loose joints where the flashing attaches to the chimney. Clean out old caulk and debris from around the top of the flashing, especially behind it. Pull the top of the flashing away from the chimney far enough to apply new caulk behind it. Then press the flashing back into the mortar joint and secure it with 1-inch concrete nails driven through the top of the flashing into the mortar. Use a 2- or 3-pound hammer and hold the nails with needle nose pliers. Patch small holes or rusted areas in the flashing by wire-brushing the weak area and painting it with rusty-metal primer. After the paint dries, coat the area with butyl caulk or sealant, press fiberglass mesh into the sealant, and smooth a second layer over the mesh. If flashing is deteriorated or has large holes, replace it with new flashing, making sure that it is overlapped by roofing or other flashing in the same manner as the original piece. Avoid aluminum flashing, as mortar will corrode it. See also page 110.

▶ *Chimney has cracks.*

Seal hairline cracks with butyl caulk. For larger cracks that don't span the width of the chimney, clean out loose and broken mortar and repoint the joints (see left). Long vertical cracks down the center of the chimney result from inadequate air space between the flue and chimney bricks, causing the bricks to heat too much. Although they should remain stable and not pose a threat to the structure of the chimney, they are a fire hazard and should be sealed with fireplace, or refractory, cement. Very large cracks that break bricks, span the chimney horizontally, or distort alignment are dangerous and should be inspected by a brick mason or foundation contractor specializing in chimney repair. It may be necessary to reinforce the chimney with corner brackets, a roof brace, or shoring.

▶ *Chimney mortar joints are crumbling.*

Remove the crumbling mortar with a cold chisel and hammer, to a depth of 1 inch (see page 125), and wire-brush away all debris. Wear safety goggles; mortar dust can irritate eyes. Mix an all-purpose mortar (Type N) according to label directions, slightly stiffer than for laying bricks. Moisten the joints with a fine spray from a garden hose, then pack mortar into the cracks. For horizontal cracks, slide mortar off a hawk (small mortarboard) and into the crack with a pointing trowel or joint filler. For vertical joints, slice some mortar off the hawk with the back of a pointing trowel and force it into the crack. Fill deep joints with two or three layers, letting it stiffen each time. When joints are filled and the mortar is just stiff enough to hold a thumbprint, use a jointing tool with a profile that matches the existing joints (V-shaped or rounded) to compress and smooth the mortar. Remove excess mortar from the bricks with a soft brush.

Tip *Before you have new roofing installed, consult the roofer about removing the old chimney flashing and installing new flashing. Common practice for many roofers is to leave the old flashing in place and simply adhere new flashing over it with mastic. This application will not last long and should not be accepted.*

SOLVING EXTERIOR PROBLEMS

▶ Chimney brick is loose or damaged.

Individual bricks can be chipped out and replaced quite easily, although structural problems may exist if many bricks are involved. Remove the old brick by chiseling out the mortar around it (or scraping it out with a mortar rake); then chisel out the brick and clean out the cavity with a brush. Obtain premixed mortar or mix a small batch using 1 part cement to 3 parts sand. Wet the cavity, then place mortar on the bottom, back, and sides. Steady the brick by setting it on a board in front of the cavity, then shove it into the cavity so it beds in the new mortar. Pack additional mortar around the brick, as necessary, and tool the joints.

Pushing brick into cavity

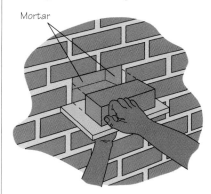

Mortar

▶ Chimney lacks spark arrester or weather cap.

Both are required by building and safety codes. A spark arrester keeps embers from flying out of the chimney; a chimney hood, or weather cap, keeps rain from entering the flue and combining with creosote to form acids that eat away the brick and mortar.

Measure the width of the flue (inside dimension) in both directions and buy an arrester, with a hood over it, for that size. Most types can be installed simply by shoving the bottom sleeve part of the arrester into the flue. Some have clamps that are tightened onto the flue walls. If the style of a prefabricated hood doesn't suit your home, have a local sheet-metal shop fabricate a custom one.

▶ Chimney is leaning away from wall.

A chimney and fireplace are on a foundation of their own, independent of the rest of the house, and may settle differently. In some cases settlement occurs early and then stabilizes for many years. In other cases new movement can occur over time. Consult a general contractor, structural engineer, or other professional experienced in foundation and chimney repair to see if reinforcement is necessary.

▶ Concrete chimney cap is cracked or crumbling.

A cracked or crumbling mortar cap should be repaired as soon as possible; otherwise, moisture can soak into it and cause serious damage to the chimney bricks through cycles of freezing and thawing. If the cap is sound and has only a few cracks, widen them with a cold chisel and fill them with butyl or silicone caulk. Smooth the surface with a putty knife moistened with soapy water. If the entire cap is deteriorated, break it up with a brick chisel

and heavy hammer; wear goggles and gloves. Remove the pieces carefully so you don't damage any roof shingles, and clean away all debris. Prepare a sack of ready-mixed concrete to a stiff consistency. Moisten the bricks and flue, and trowel wet concrete onto the bricks, packing it around the flue pipe. Build up the cap in several layers, sloping it away from the flue. Smooth the final layer with a steel trowel. Keep the concrete moist for 4 to 5 days by spraying it daily or covering it with plastic sheeting.

▶ Chimney cap is separating from flue.

The difference in materials between a terra-cotta chimney flue and the concrete cap that surrounds it may cause the two to separate. Seal a thin crack with butyl caulk. For larger cracks, clean the crack thoroughly and brush some latex modified bonding agent into it, then seal the crack with mortar. (*Note:* There should be a 1-inch gap around the flue farther down the chimney and closer to the fireplace to allow the flue to expand with heat.)

▶ Chimney should have a damper.

If the fireplace lacks an operable damper, you can buy a chimney-top damper from a masonry supplier or fireplace store and install it on top of the flue. It is operated from the fireplace by a long chain that hangs down the chimney. Installation varies, but most slide over the flue; others are attached to the flue by forming a new concrete cap (see left) and embedding the anchoring lugs of the damper into the fresh concrete.

Tip   *Some experts recommend sealing chimney bricks with a thin coat of liquid silicone. It dries to a clear, dull finish and prevents the brick and mortar from absorbing moisture that can deteriorate the joints.*

▶ *Skylight admits too much sun.*

Install a standard window shade directly beneath the skylight and run a long cord from the bottom of the shade, through an eyehook on the frame or trim at the other end, and down a nearby wall. This type of shade works best on skylights that can be opened to release hot air that builds up above the shade. For more efficient shading, especially for fixed skylights, install a shade screen on the outside. Check with the manufacturer to see if a kit is available. Otherwise, consult a window dealer about weather-resistant shading fabrics.

▶ *Skylight needs cleaning.*

Most people are resigned to waiting for the rain, but if a trip to the roof is worth it, wash glass skylights in the same way as a window. Do not wash plastic skylights, such as acrylic bubbles, with anything that has ammonia in it; use a solution of water and mild dish soap, or special cleaning solutions available from a plastics supplier. If you can't get onto the roof, hose off the skylight from the ground or a ladder, or try reaching the skylight with a mop attached to a long pole. Some skylights pivot and can be cleaned from inside.

▶ *Skylight leaks.*

Wind can drive rain through un-sealed cracks, so if the skylight is operable (opening type), check all seals, overhangs, and flanges to be sure that the lid shuts tightly, especially if the roof slope is less than 3 in 12 (3 inches of rise for every 12 inches of horizontal run). The next most likely source of leaks is improper flashing. The top collar flashing should have soldered seams at the corners. There should be no nails in it for 6 inches above the skylight curb; it should lap over the side flashing and extend upward under at least two courses of shingles. The flashing on the sides of the curb should be step flashing, with each L-shaped piece installed over a shingle and covered by the next course of shingles above it. Check the tops of the step flashing to be sure that the skylight flange extends down over them. If not, loosen the tops, apply caulk behind them, and then renail. If the skylight is on a flat roof, have the leak repaired by a professional roofer.

Flashing a skylight

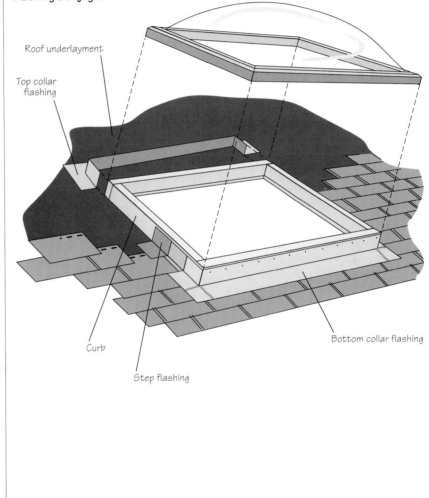

Roof underlayment

Top collar flashing

Curb

Step flashing

Bottom collar flashing

Tip *A skylight should never have ordinary window glass, which can break into sharp pieces. All skylights must be glazed with safety glass, such as tempered, laminated, or wire glass, or with plastic.*

Tip *Most plastic skylights are dome-shaped because plastic expands and contracts with temperature changes. The dome allows the material to move without disrupting the watertight seal around the edges.*

▶ *Siding board is cracked or split.*

Prop the lower half of the split piece away from the siding with a chisel. Coat both exposed edges with epoxy resin cement, then slide the chisel out. Nail each half of the split piece to the sheathing or to a stud with HDG casing or finishing nails; predrill holes and countersink the heads. Then use exterior spackling compound or linseed oil putty to fill the nail heads.

For larger holes replace the damaged section of the board. For lap siding drive a wood shim under the siding at one end of the crack; then, while protecting the board below with a scrap of wood, use a backsaw to cut through the exposed part of the cracked siding. To finish the cut, drive two shims under the board above; cut through the rest of the cracked board with a compass saw. Repeat the procedure at the other end. To loosen it, pry out exposed nails with a nail puller; cut off hidden nails with a hacksaw blade. Cut a replacement piece. Prime the front, back, and ends, then tap the piece into place. If the

siding is the 3½-inch-wide style, fasten it with HDG nails ½ inch up from the bottom. Wider siding should be nailed 2 inches from the bottom. Predrill before nailing.

To replace a section of flush tongue-and-groove siding, make pocket cuts with a circular saw centered over the studs on each side of the damaged section. Split and pry out the damaged section. Cut a new piece of siding the same length and chisel off the back half of the groove. Prime all edges and faces of the piece. Let dry, then run a bead of acrylic latex caulk along the edges. Predrill the nail holes and nail the piece to the studs with 8d HDG common nails. Countersink the nails and fill with exterior spackling compound.

For vertical siding, follow the same procedures as for repairing a crack or hole, except if you install a new piece, bevel the horizontal cuts in the old board and the new piece 30 degrees so that any water is directed outward and downward.

▶ *Siding board is warped.*

Warped wood siding can be straightened with screws. Predrill holes through the siding and drive HDG screws, at least 2 inches long, through the holes and into the wood sheathing or wall framing beneath. Drive the screw heads slightly beneath the surface of the siding, then fill with putty or compound and touch up with paint that matches the color of the siding.

▶ *Siding board is missing.*

Missing siding boards should be replaced as soon as possible with a matching type of siding. Cut the new board ⅛ inch shorter than the opening. Prime or seal the front, back, and edges of the new piece. After it dries, apply a bead of paintable caulk to each end, tap it in place, and secure with 8d HDG common nails. Countersink the nails, cover them with linseed oil putty or exterior spackling compound, then paint or stain to match.

▶ *Nails have caused rust stains.*

Sand the rust stains off the siding. Then, wearing rubber gloves and eye protection, brush the nail heads with a phosphoric acid solution to remove the rust and to prevent future rusting. Follow all label directions. Leave the solution on for about 20 minutes, then rinse. For painted siding, repaint the sanded area and the nail heads. Clear siding that's badly rust stained may look better with an opaque stain applied to the sanded areas and nail heads.

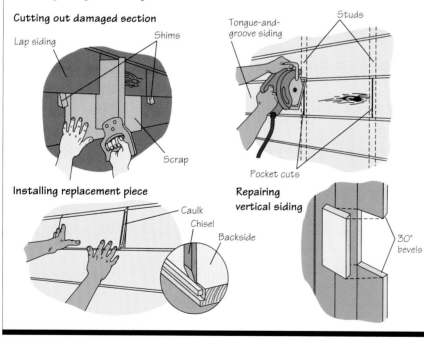

Cutting out damaged section
Lap siding
Shims
Scrap

Installing replacement piece
Caulk
Chisel
Backside

Tongue-and-groove siding
Studs
Pocket cuts

Repairing vertical siding
30° bevels

Tip *Caulks and sealants come in a bewildering variety of types. When choosing caulk, have your requirements in mind: the type of material the caulk will adhere to (wood, glass, masonry, metal); whether the two surfaces meeting at the joint are the same or different; whether the caulk will be painted; the range of temperatures the caulk will be subjected to; whether it will be exposed to direct sunlight (ultraviolet rays); and the amount of caulking to be done (how important cost is).*

▶ Mildew has formed on siding.

Use a solution of 1 part chlorine bleach to 3 parts water. Spray it on the siding with a hose-end spraying canister. When working with bleach, make sure to wear protective goggles and rubber gloves, and read all directions on the label. For areas with stubborn mildew, a long-handled scrub brush can be helpful. Make sure to clean off all the mildew or it will grow back. Let the bleach solution dry on the siding; don't rinse it off. Mildew often grows in shady areas; if this is the case, consider trimming tree branches that shade the problem surfaces.

▶ Siding has soft, spongy spots, especially near base.

This is a definite sign of rot. Soft sections should be replaced (see opposite page). If the rot is widespread, check the humidity levels inside the house, especially in the rooms where the siding is soft. Constant indoor humidity can result in moisture working its way through walls and condensing on the backside of siding. Rot on siding near the base of a wall may indicate that runoff water from the roof is splashing the siding. Check the gutters for leaks or clogs and provide tubing at the bottom of downspouts to divert water away. If siding is within 6 inches of the ground, the ground should be graded, sloping away from the house, or the foundation wall raised by capping. Consult a general contractor or foundation repair specialist.

▶ Termites are present.

A sure sign of termites is mud shelter tubes that lead from the ground, along a concrete foundation, and up into the siding. Other signs include wings on the ground near the foundation or inside a basement or crawl space. Likely areas of infestation are any place there is wood-to-earth contact or where wood has become soft. Termites can cause expensive structural damage. Hire a licensed pest-control specialist to perform a complete inspection as soon as possible. See also page 65.

▶ Replacement siding is hard to locate.

Always bring along a piece of the old siding when you look for replacement boards. If the local lumberyard or home center doesn't stock the same type, look for a lumberyard that has been in the area for a long time; they may have cutter blades for milling new boards. If not, try an architectural salvage yard that has old siding. You might also ask neighbors with similar siding if they have extra pieces. Or, remove one or two siding boards from the garage, back of your house, or other inconspicuous area and replace them with new boards of the same size, if not pattern. Styles and names may vary according to geographic region and historical period.

▶ Nails have caused rust stains on wood shingles.

See opposite page.

▶ Wood shingles at corners are curled, rotted, or missing.

Replacing a pair of corner shingles is similar to replacing a midwall shingle, with a few exceptions. First remove the damaged shingles; then cut one new shingle to fit, making sure it extends slightly past the corner. Next cut the second shingle so that it butts snugly against the first shingle. Finally, use a block plane to shave down the overhanging edge of the first shingle. If you're repairing more than one course of shingles, alternate the overlapping edges from course to course.

Replacing corner shingles

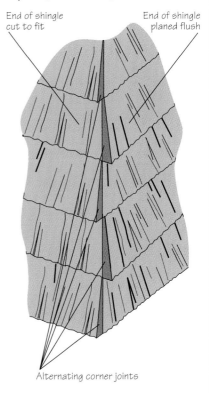

End of shingle cut to fit

End of shingle planed flush

Alternating corner joints

Tip   Liquid chlorine bleach is an effective agent for many household tasks besides laundry. Use it for removing stains, sanitizing surfaces like the inside of garbage cans and pet houses, and controlling mold and mildew (it has a residual effect that discourages future growth). For most uses mix it in a ratio of 4 tablespoons bleach to 1 quart warm water. Never store it in a metal container. Never mix it with ammonia, which creates a gas that produces a choking, burning sensation and can be deadly. If you get chlorine bleach in your eye, flush it with cool water for 10 to 15 minutes and see an ophthalmologist immediately (harmful effects are unnoticeable at first).

▶ Wood shingles are split, broken, or missing.

Broken or split shingles should be replaced. First split the damaged shingle into a few long pieces with a wood chisel. Then remove the pieces and cut off the hidden nail heads with a hacksaw blade. Cut a new shingle ¼ inch narrower than the opening by scoring the shingle several times with a utility knife, then snapping off the excess. Tap in the shingle ½ inch shy of its final position. Then drive two 6d HDG box nails into the shingle at a slight angle, positioned directly below the butt edge of the shingle above. Snug the heads to the shingle but don't embed them in the wood. Finally, with a hammer and woodblock, tap up the shingle the last ½ inch to hide the nail heads. See page 113.

▶ Cedar shingles look weathered and dull.

Cedar shingles will always turn gray. To slow the process, apply a clear penetrating finish (also called a clear water-repellent preservative) with an ultraviolet protector to the shingles immediately after they are put up. Use a rough-surface bristle brush, not a roller or sprayer. Follow manufacturer's instructions. If the shingles are new, apply two coats; then apply another coat one year later. Shingles that have been up at least two years will need a coat of finish about every two years. To determine if the shingles need a new coat, splash water on them— if it soaks in, it's time to reapply the finish. If the shingles are dirty, scrub them first with a mild solution of dishwashing detergent followed by a rinse with clear water. Another option that will keep the shingles about the same color as they were originally is to apply a semitransparent stain that matches the cedar color.

Applying finish to shingle siding

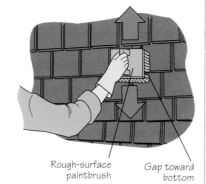

Rough-surface paintbrush

Gap toward bottom

Coating shingle edges

Bottom coated by small bristles

▶ Mineral fiber shingles are split, broken, or damaged.

To remove the damaged shingle, loosen the exposed nail heads with a nail puller or pry bar. The shingle should drop out. To install a new one, first cut it to the correct width. For just a few shingles, use a utility knife fitted with a carbide blade; for a lot, rent a shingle breaker. Slip the new shingle in place, then fasten it with 3d HDG nails. Predrill for the nails.

▶ Asbestos replacement shingles are not available.

Shingles made with portland cement and reinforced with fiberglass are a close match for asbestos shingles. Look for them at a local roofing-supply house.

▶ Asbestos shingles are split, broken, or missing.

Repairing asbestos shingles is not a job you should take on yourself. Doing extensive work with asbestos-containing material can create large amounts of dangerous dust. If you are not sure if the shingles contain asbestos, take a small sample of the damaged shingle to a local testing lab or health department to have it evaluated. Then, if asbestos is discovered, hire a local asbestos abatement firm to remove the damaged shingles. You can replace them with a mineral fiber look-alike.

▶ Nails in asbestos shingles have worked loose.

Most likely, the nails are either not driven into solid framing or are corroded. When you are working with asbestos-containing materials, always wear a MSHA-NIOSH–approved respirator for asbestos. These inexpensive face masks are available through building-supply centers. Carefully pull out the nails, then drive in new 4d HDG box nails at a different angle. This avoids using the existing nail hole.

▶ Color of old asbestos shingles is undesirable.

Paint over the shingles with an exterior latex or oil-based paint. First clean the siding with a solution of laundry detergent and chlorine bleach (3 parts soapy water to 1 part

Tip *When caulking: (1) Apply caulk in the spring or fall, when temperatures are between the extremes that cause joints to expand and contract. (2) Clean surfaces and let them dry thoroughly before caulking. (3) If you plan to paint after caulking, prime the surface before caulking. (4) Apply caulk so it adheres to both sides of the crack and the bottom. (5) Clean the tip of the tube often to prevent clogging. (6) At the end of a run, push the caulk into the crack and disengage the tube with a sharp twist. (7) Smooth joints with a plastic spoon or old butter knife.*

bleach). Use a car-washing brush attached to a garden hose to prevent harmful fibers from becoming airborne. When working with asbestos-containing materials, always wear a MSHA-NIOSH–approved respirator for asbestos (available at home centers). Let the shingles dry, then apply the paint.

▶ Hardboard siding panels are coming loose at edges.

If the nails pull out easily, they probably weren't nailed into solid framing. Remove them and fill the holes with exterior spackling compound or linseed oil putty. If the nails are driven in too deep or not deep enough, check the illustration below for the proper course of action. When you replace missing nails, use hardboard panel siding nails. They should be long enough to penetrate the wood framing beneath by at least 1½ inches.

Correcting nailing problems in hardboard siding

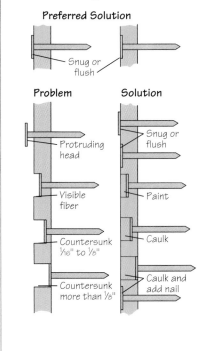

Preferred Solution

Snug or flush

Problem / Solution

Protruding head → Snug or flush

Visible fiber → Paint

Countersunk ¹⁄₁₆" to ⅛" → Caulk

Countersunk more than ⅛" → Caulk and add nail

▶ Hardboard siding panels are delaminating.

Water that soaks into unpainted panel edges causes delamination. Either cut away the damaged areas and patch with new siding (see below), or replace the entire damaged panel, making sure to paint all the edges before installing it.

▶ Nails are causing rust stains on panel siding.

Apply a phosphoric acid solution (rust dissolver) to the nail heads. Wait 20 minutes, then rinse it off. Scuff-sand the siding if it has a glossy finish. Then apply a primer/sealer to the stains, followed by a paint that matches the existing color.

▶ Z-bar flashing on hardboard panel siding is rusted or missing.

Use a wire brush to remove any rust. Then sand the area and prime it with an oil-based rusty-metal primer. Finish with an acrylic latex paint that matches the siding color. First apply the primer and paint to a small area and let dry to ensure that the color matches. Adjust the color as necessary and complete the touch-up.

    If the flashing is missing and the panel edges aren't swollen from water damage, prime any gaps less than ½ inch wide and fill with acrylic latex caulk. For wider gaps, install new Z-bar flashing. Carefully remove nails from the bottom edge of the top panel, tuck the Z-bar into place, and nail with new 3d HDG box nails. If the panel edge has water damage, cut away at least 1½ inches of the damaged siding and install new pieces. Paint all edges with a paint recommended for hardboard siding. Install Z-bar above and below the filler piece,

leaving a ½-inch gap between the bottom hardboard edge and bottom Z-bar bend.

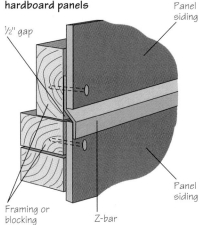

Installing Z-bar between hardboard panels

½" gap

Panel siding

Framing or blocking

Z-bar

Panel siding

▶ Brick mortar is crumbling or missing.

Crumbling mortar should be removed and replaced with new mortar, a process called pointing. To remove the old mortar, use a handheld sledgehammer and a tuck pointing chisel. Wear safety goggles and heavy gloves. Chip out the mortar to a depth of about 1 inch, making sure to make the back of the trough flat, not V-shaped. Be careful not to chip the brick. Next, brush out the joints with a stiff-bristled brush, followed by a light misting with water. To fill the joints, mix a small batch (about enough to fill a 1-gallon paint can) of prepackaged mortar mix with water. Place the mix on a hawk. Using a pointing trowel or a joint-filling tool, first pack the vertical (head) joints, then the horizontal (bed) joints. Joints deeper than 1 inch should be filled in two successive passes. Let the mortar dry enough to hold a thumbprint between fillings. When all the mortar

Tip *The ideal consistency of brick mortar is moist enough to adhere, dry enough not to slump. Mix it so there is no residual water puddling on the surface. Test it by making a "snowball"—it should hold its shape but water shouldn't drain out of it when you squeeze it. Experienced brick masons can tell good mortar by the sliding sound it makes on the trowel.* <u>Caution:</u> *Mortar can irritate skin, so wear gloves.*

is stiff, finish off the joints with a jointing tool. Jointing tools come in different profiles; use a style that matches the existing joints. Spots of mortar that remain on the brick may be removed after a few days with a stiff-bristled brush.

Removing old mortar

Filling head joints and bed joints

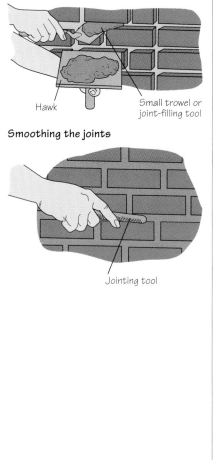

Hawk

Small trowel or joint-filling tool

Smoothing the joints

Jointing tool

▶ Brick wall has long, vertical cracks.

If a house foundation doesn't settle evenly, brick veneer siding often cracks in a staircase-shaped pattern. Although the crack itself isn't serious, you should fill it as soon as possible to stop water or insect penetration. Cracks that occur through mortar joints may be repaired with pointing (see page 125). Brick cracks may be filled with masonry crack filler, which is available in tubes and applied with a caulking gun. If the cracking recurs, there may be a foundation problem, which should be examined by a structural engineer.

▶ Bricks above window or door are sagging.

If the lintel that supports the brick over a door or window is badly rusted or rotted, it can weaken and allow the bricks to sag. You can replace a lintel in a one-story building, but consult a professional if there is a second story above it. To replace a lintel, first remove the sagging bricks carefully with a hand-held sledgehammer and a narrow masonry chisel; wear eye protection and gloves. Next cut out the mortar around the lintel and remove it; be sure to remove all metal or wood pieces. The new lintel should be primed and painted steel. Slip it in place and pack mortar around the embedded ends. Next install a strip of galvanized-steel flashing over the lintel. Bend the back of it up against the wall sheathing and lap the front edge over the lintel about ½ inch. Then replace the brick, applying mortar to the top, back, and sides of each brick before slipping it into place. When installing the course of brick that rests

directly on the lintel, omit mortar from every third vertical joint to create weep holes. In these holes, stuff rope made of fiberglass or polypropylene. It will wick decay-causing moisture from the wall cavity while preventing insects from getting in.

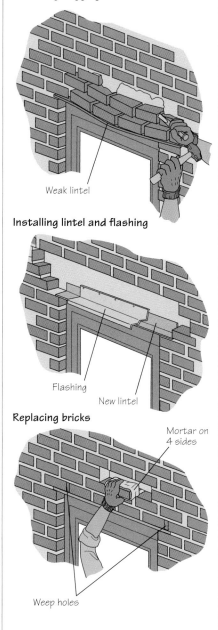

Removing sagging bricks

Weak lintel

Installing lintel and flashing

Flashing

New lintel

Replacing bricks

Mortar on 4 sides

Weep holes

Tip *When laying bricks, wet the bricks before setting them in mortar. Dry bricks absorb moisture from the mortar before it can set up, thus weakening it.*

▶ Brick surface has white powder on it.

The whitish powder found on some brick surfaces, known as efflorescence, is salt that's present in some brick and mortar. When moisture in the brick or mortar migrates to the surface and dries, it leaves behind this white powder. Remove it, with a dry stiff-bristled brush; follow up with either a TSP solution or a heavy-duty hand soap that contains pumice. For stubborn stains, scrub on a mild solution of 1 part muriatic acid to 20 parts water. Be sure to wear eye protection and rubber gloves. When mixing the solution, add the acid to the water, not the water to the acid. Recurring efflorescence may indicate that water is leaking into the wall through defective flashing (see page 89) or cracks in window molding (see page 128).

▶ Brick veneer is leaning away from wall.

This can be caused by a number of things, including poor construction methods or moisture damage. To correctly identify the cause and determine the appropriate repair, contact a structural engineer.

▶ Cracks have opened up between brick and stucco.

First make sure that all surfaces are free of dirt and loose debris. Then fill the cracks with a clear silicone caulk. Cracks wider than ¼ inch should first be filled with foam backer rod, compressible filler material that comes in long strips. The diameter of the rod should be 25 to 50 percent more than the width of the crack.

▶ Bricks above windows on outside wall are cracked.

This is often caused by a deteriorated lintel. See opposite page.

▶ Paint won't stick to galvanized metal.

First, before painting, clean galvanized metal thoroughly, using sandpaper, a wire brush, or a wire wheel mounted on an electric drill. Make sure all rust, corrosion, and flaking metal are removed. Then wipe down the surface with mineral spirits or lacquer thinner. Make sure the surface is clean by wiping it with a white cloth. Finally, use a galvanized-steel primer or a metal etch compound (sold in paint stores), followed by a finish coat.

▶ Paint is chalking, blistering, or peeling.

Wash away chalky paint, blisters, and peeling with a high-pressure washer. Rent a gas-powered model, which creates up to 2,500 psi of pressure. Handle it carefully and wear gloves, eye protection, and rain gear. Do not spray up under lapped shingles or siding. Blisters or peeling that remain after pressure washing may be removed with a hand scraper. Feather the scraped edges before repainting, then prime the bare spots and apply the paint.

If paint problems are caused by moisture coming through the walls from the inside of the house, install ventilating fans in the bathrooms and kitchen. Also paint the interior sides of peeling walls with a vapor-retarder paint, such as oil-based enamel, and seal around window and base moldings with caulk. If peeling and blistering problems

persist, add ventilating plugs to exterior walls to provide a path for moisture inside the walls to escape.

Installing ventilating plug

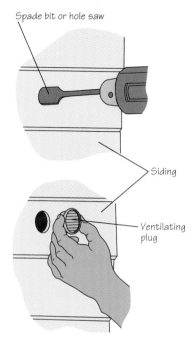

Spade bit or hole saw

Siding

Ventilating plug

▶ Paint is splotchy and discolored.

This may be the result of mildew growth or because the paint has worn out. First try washing the paint with a mild solution of laundry detergent or a solution of 4 tablespoons bleach to 1 quart warm water. If that doesn't solve the problem, repaint the affected area.

Tip *Many paint problems are caused by poor application techniques. Prepare the surface thoroughly by washing the siding with a solution of 3 parts detergent/water solution and 1 part chlorine bleach, scraping off old paint, eradicating mildew with a bleach solution, sealing knots with pigmented shellac, filling holes and cracks, and priming. When painting: (1) avoid working in direct sunlight, (2) allow paint to dry thoroughly before recoating or adding a second color next to it, (3) apply flat paints before gloss paints, and (4) paint up to visual breakpoints before stopping work.*

▶ Paint won't cover knots.

Knots are probably the densest part of a piece of wood. As such they don't take paint as well as the surrounding surface. To ensure that the paint will hide them, spot-prime knots with a pigmented shellac and then with an oil-based primer/sealer before painting.

▶ Paint on wood shingles is badly cracked and worn.

If there are many layers of paint, take the surface down to bare wood by either sanding or stripping with chemical strippers. Paint applied prior to 1972 probably has lead in it; take special precautions by wearing a dust mask, capturing the residue in plastic sheeting, and disposing of it in an approved landfill. If the paint layer is not exceptionally thick, first wash the shingles with a pressure washer, directing the stream from above or from the side, but not from below. Wear waterproof clothing and eye protection, cover nearby bushes with plastic, and tape plastic over outdoor electrical receptacles and loose-fitting windows and doors. Next scrape away any loose paint and feather the chipped edges with sandpaper. Prime any bare wood. Then repaint the shingles with exterior latex paint, using a rough-surface brush.

▶ Oil-based stain applied with power sprayer is peeling.

Stain can peel if the surface was not sufficiently prepped before the stain was applied. Other possible causes are a low-quality grade of stain or a moisture problem behind the affected area. Once you've determined the problem and corrected it, scrape off all loose stain with a broad putty knife, prepare the wall according to label direc-tions on the new stain, and apply a fresh coat. If you spray it on, after spraying go over the surface with a brush or roller (backbrushing) to work the stain into the surface.

▶ Paint is peeling off outside trim.

First solve any interior moisture problems (windows that fog frequently are a sign). On a problem wall, painting the interior surface with a vapor-barrier paint and caulking around interior window and base moldings can help. Also make sure that flashing around doors or windows isn't leaking. Then scrape off the loose paint and feather the scraped edges with sandpaper. Pry out all old caulk around the trim and clean off dirt and chalking paint. Prime any bare wood with latex exterior wood primer. Fill all cracks between trim pieces and between the trim and the siding with acrylic latex or butyl rubber caulk. Then apply two coats of exterior trim paint.

▶ Caulk has dried, shrunken, or cracked, or is missing.

First scrape out the old caulk with a molding scraper, thin putty knife, or lever-type can opener. Next remove any dirt or chalking paint from the surfaces to be caulked by sanding or scraping. Fill any gaps wider than ¼ inch with foam backer rod. Finally, refill the gaps with a bead of caulk. Use acrylic latex or butyl rubber caulk over painted surfaces, silicone caulk on clear finished surfaces, and elastomeric terpolymer caulk on masonry surfaces.

▶ Caulk won't adhere.

Most likely the surface has dirt or chalking paint on it. Clean off the dirt or chalk and apply a primer appropriate for the particular surface. Let dry, then apply the caulk. Follow label directions—some caulk won't adhere if applied in cold weather.

▶ Paint doesn't adhere to caulk.

Most types of silicone caulk form a smooth surface that doesn't take paint well. First pull off and scrape out all the caulk. Then refill the gaps with an acrylic latex caulk, butyl rubber caulk, or other caulk specified as paintable. Let dry, then apply the paint.

▶ Weather is too hot or cold to apply caulk.

Different caulks tolerate different temperature ranges. Newer, more expensive caulks may be applied in extremely hot or cold weather. If you must apply caulk now, buy a type tolerant of the extreme temperature.

▶ Stucco has lost color.

If the stucco is painted, first wash the surface, scrape off any loose paint, and patch the cracks. Then apply a new coat of exterior latex paint with a long-nap roller or a rough-surface brush. If you use a roller, follow up with a dry roller or brush to remove drips. An unpainted surface can get a new coat of colored stucco. Apply a mixture of 2 parts white portland cement, 3 parts silica sand, and powdered pigment to create the color of your choice, all mixed to a thick soupy consistency. Use a long-bristled brush. Finish the stucco in your choice of surfaces (see opposite page).

Tip *The main difference in composition between high-quality paint and ordinary paint is that high-quality paint has a higher ratio of vehicle (the oil or latex agent that allows the paint to remain liquid in the can and then harden when applied) to solvent (the thinning agent, either mineral spirits for oil-based paint or water for latex paint). Also, high-quality paint has a lower ratio of fillers and extenders (various materials, such as clay, added for bulk) than ordinary paint.*

▶ *Stucco has cracks.*

If the cracks are very narrow, use a thin bead of elastomeric caulk, such as a terpolymer type, to fill them. Then paint the caulk to match the stucco. If the wall has extensive small cracks and is otherwise sound, coat the entire wall with an elastomeric sealant according to label directions. (Unlike latex paint, these sealants are impermeable to moisture vapor and will blister if moisture migrates from inside the wall toward the outside, so be sure there are no internal sources of moisture.) For wider cracks, scrape the crack with the point of a lever-type can opener, undercutting the edges. Wet the crack, then fill it with stucco mortar mixed to a creamy consistency. Either use a mortar color that matches the existing stucco, or paint the patch when it's dry. If the crack keeps reopening, have the house checked by a structural engineer.

Cleaning the crack

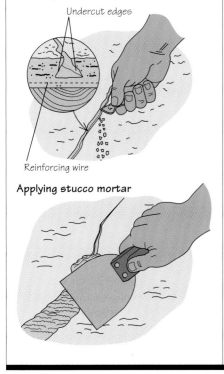

Undercut edges

Reinforcing wire

Applying stucco mortar

▶ *Stucco has holes.*

Fill tiny holes with elastomeric terpolymer caulk. Small holes, up to 1¼ inches in diameter, can be filled with stucco patching material. Slightly larger holes can also be filled with stucco patch, but not quite flush with the surface. Finish filling the hole with a flexible patching compound, spread out around the hole to make a good seal and to give the compound a larger surface to grip.

Larger holes should be filled with new stucco. First determine the type of stucco it is by placing a small piece in a muriatic acid solution. Lime mortar will dissolve; portland cement won't. Next determine to what extent the stucco has to be removed. Tap around the hole, moving progressively farther away from it until you reach stucco that's solid and doesn't move. Remove all cracked and loose stucco from the patch area, down to the building paper or concrete block. Leave the stucco wire (reinforcing mesh known as stucco lath) intact. If it is damaged or missing from the patch area, expose the stucco wire for 3 additional inches around all sides. Cut a new piece of galvanized stucco wire to fit in the hole, overlapping the old wire, and nail it with stucco nails that have fiber spacers to hold the mesh away from the sheathing. Concrete-block walls should be brushed off, sprayed with water, allowed to dry, then coated with a masonry bonding agent.

Next moisten the hole lightly and spread on a ⅜-inch-thick layer of the appropriate type of stucco. Let it firm up, then score deep scratches in it with a nail. Allow it to dry overnight, then apply the second coat to within ⅛ inch of the surface. Finally, apply a finish coat that matches the texture and color of the existing wall.

Patching a hole in stucco

Applying scratch coat

Building paper

Applying second coat

Stucco wire

Applying final coat

Scratched surface of previous coat

Applying different finishes

Modern American finish

Spatter finish

Snap brush against stick

2x4

Standard smooth finish

Old English finish

Wood float

Round-nose trowel

Tip   *Most older stucco has permanent color added to the final coat. If you want to paint over stucco, wash the wall thoroughly to remove dirt and any loose or flaking material. Then coat the wall with a primer specified for stucco surfaces, and topcoat it with latex paint. Apply the paint with a thick-nap roller (½ inch). Look for missed spots and touch them up with a brush.*

▶ Stucco surface extends into ground.

Building codes now require that stucco applied over a wood-frame wall terminate at least 4 inches above the ground. Otherwise, moisture can get trapped behind it against the foundation sill. If you have an older home with walls stuccoed to the ground, make sure that the gutters and downspouts are not leaking and are successfully channeling water away from the house. Also check nearby drains to ensure that they aren't clogged. Seal all cracks in the wall, especially around door and window trim, and be sure that the stucco is sound. Finally, make sure that the ground against the foundation slopes away from the house.

If you're having new stucco applied, make sure it ends at least 4 inches above the ground and has a metal stop bead along the bottom.

▶ Stucco around windows and doors is cracked.

First wipe away any dust and dirt from the crack edges. Then, for cracks that are wider than ¼ inch, stuff a length of foam backer rod into the crack. Then fill the cracks with either an acrylic/silicone caulk that matches the stucco or trim color, or a clear solvent-based caulk. Acrylic caulk cleans up with water; solvent-based caulk requires something other than water, such as mineral spirits or paint thinner.

▶ Stucco isn't sealed.

Stucco siding should not be sealed. By design it's supposed to allow some moisture in and out, and if it needs to be recoated, any sealer on it would first have to be sandblasted off. If you paint the stucco, use a latex-based paint, which is porous and will allow water to pass through.

▶ Vinyl siding needs cleaning.

The best tool for washing vinyl siding is a power washer. You can rent or purchase one. Homeowner-grade models that produce up to 1,200 psi, useful for many outdoor cleaning projects, are now available. When renting a power washer, choose a small unit for general washing, a large unit for extensive paint scraping. Choose a model with interchangeable nozzles that alter the spray patterns and pressure. To use the sprayer, first seal off any electrical receptacles, vent openings, and light fixtures with plastic and duct tape. Cover nearby shrubs. Then spray the siding with a mild solution of laundry detergent and water. Use a low-pressure nozzle and work from bottom to top to prevent staining and dirt buildup. Shoot the water across the siding, not up into it. Then use a medium-pressure nozzle and plain water to rinse off the solution, working from top to bottom. Whenever possible, work on a shady side of the house—warm, sunny surfaces can dry before you have time to rinse off the dirt and soap.

Power washers produce a high-pressure jet of water that can be dangerous. Observe all manufacturer's warnings and cautions. Do not point the nozzle at unprotected skin, as it can cause a puncture wound. Wear eye protection. Be careful when working from a ladder—the spray wand starts and stops with a bit of a kick.

Cleaning vinyl siding

Goggles

Spray wand

Gloves

Rain gear

Pressure washer

Water supply hose

Tip   *To apply stucco, place a small amount on a hawk (mortarboard). Holding the hawk in one hand and a trowel upside down in the other, scoop some of the stucco onto the bottom of the trowel and then onto the wall in a continuous, upward-pushing motion. Regulate the depth of stucco by varying the pressure. Plan on having much of the stucco end up on the ground as you learn to scoop it off the hawk and onto the wall.*

▶ Vinyl siding has faded.

You can paint vinyl siding just like aluminum or wood siding. First clean the siding (see opposite page). Then lightly sand the surface and remove the dust. Next apply an oil-based primer with a brush. Let dry, then apply two coats of a high-quality (high solid content) acrylic latex paint. Be sure to use a color as light as or lighter than that of the siding; darker colors can cause the siding to overheat and warp.

▶ Vinyl siding is difficult for one person to install.

Long pieces of siding can be unwieldy to handle, especially when a small gust of wind kicks up. If you don't have a helper, position one end of the siding in place and hold it there with strips of duct tape while you work toward it from the other end.

▶ Vinyl siding is damaged.

You can replace an entire piece of vinyl siding or, if seams won't be objectionable, just the damaged section. First choose a time when it's not too cold (below 50° F) or you'll crack the vinyl. To remove a damaged section, make vertical cuts on either side of the damaged area with a utility knife. Then, for the damaged section or a full piece, unsnap the siding by pushing up on the cut piece and pulling down on the piece above it. If that does not work, use a zip tool (available at a siding supplier or home center) to unlock the siding. Hook the end of

the tool into the locking strip of the upper piece of siding and, while maintaining firm downward pressure on the tool, slide it the length of the lower piece. Then lift the upper piece, prop it in place with woodblocks, pull out the nails with a pry bar, and remove the damaged section or full piece. Cut a new piece so it will overlap 1¼ inches at each end. Snap the bottom edge in place and nail in the top. Then press the upper piece down, or use the zip tool to relock it in place.

Unsnapping vinyl siding

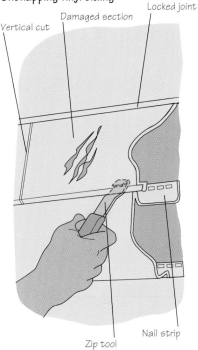

Vertical cut · Damaged section · Locked joint · Nail strip · Zip tool

▶ Vinyl siding has crack.

Using a zip tool (available at a siding supplier or home center), carefully unlock the bottom edge of the siding immediately above the damaged piece. Then use a nail puller to remove the nails from the top of the damaged piece. Remove the piece and lay it facedown. Cut a patch out of scrap vinyl siding to fit

over the crack. Clean around the crack with PVC cleaner, then coat around the crack with PVC cement. Attach the patch, good side down. When the cement dries, reinstall the piece.

Adhering patch behind crack

PVC cement · Backside · Patch

▶ Corner of vinyl siding is damaged.

See page 132.

▶ Aluminum siding needs cleaning.

Clean as for vinyl; see opposite page.

▶ Aluminum siding has faded.

Aluminum siding can be painted to give it a fresh, new color. First scrape off any loose flakes, then lightly sand the surface to provide adequate adhesion for the new paint. Wash the siding (see opposite page). Prime any patches of bare metal with an oil- or water-based primer made for metal. Finish

Tip   *There are several ways to cut vinyl siding. If you use a utility knife, use medium pressure to score the vinyl on the face side, then snap the vinyl in half. If you use tin snips or aviation snips, you'll get a cleaner cut if you avoid closing the blades at the end of each stroke. If you use a power saw, install the blade backward for a cleaner cut (this works especially well in cold weather). Be sure to turn the blade around before cutting any other material.*

SOLVING EXTERIOR PROBLEMS

by applying a coat of high-quality (high solid content) acrylic latex paint. If you use a sprayer or roller, go back over the surface with a brush (backbrushing).

▶ Aluminum surface is corroded.

If a small area is corroded, sand or wire-brush the area to bring it down to bare metal. Then mask off the area, spray on a metal primer, let dry, and brush on two coats of matching paint. For larger areas, see page 131.

▶ Aluminum siding is damaged.

To pull out small, round dents, fit a rubber grommet or several washers on the end of a small sheet-metal screw and drive the screw into the center of the dent. Using a pair of pliers, grasp the head of the screw and pull outward until the dent has popped or flattened out. Remove the screw from the panel and fill the hole with plastic aluminum, available in hardware stores. Apply it as neatly as possible, then let the material harden. Sand and touch up with matching paint.

For larger dents use the sheet-metal screw and washer procedure over a few areas of the dent. Then roughen the dented surface with sandpaper and apply auto-body filler over the area. Before the filler dries, smooth it flush with the siding. Finish by masking off the area, spraying on a metal primer, then brushing on two coats of matching paint.

If the panel has a large hole or gash, first get a new piece of matching siding that's at least 2 inches longer than the damaged area. To cut away the damage, mark two vertical lines, one on each side of the hole. Mark a horizontal line above the hole, 1 inch beneath the butt edge of the panel above. Drill

pilot holes where the lines meet, cut along the marks with tin snips, and remove the cutout. Next remove enough of the top of the new piece so that when locked in place, its top edge will touch the butt edge of the panel above. For a straight edge, score it with a sharp utility knife, then bend it back and forth until it breaks off. Run a bead of butyl rubber caulk along the back of the new piece, then lock it in place so the ends overlap the cutout 1 inch on each side and the top abuts the piece above it.

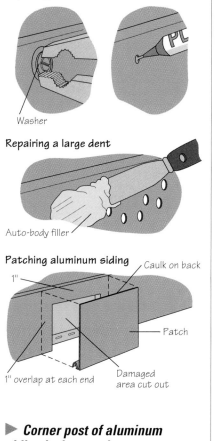

Repairing a dent

Washer

Repairing a large dent

Auto-body filler

Patching aluminum siding

1"

1" overlap at each end

Caulk on back

Patch

Damaged area cut out

▶ Corner post of aluminum siding is damaged.

First make a vertical cut along one side of the corner post with a sharp utility knife. It may require a few strokes to cut through completely.

Then score the other side of the post and bend the piece back and forth until it breaks off. Cut the nailing flanges off a new corner post by scoring and bending. Apply a bead of butyl rubber caulk to each of the existing nailing flanges and to the replacement post (as shown below), and set the post in place. Secure both ends of the new corner with pop rivets.

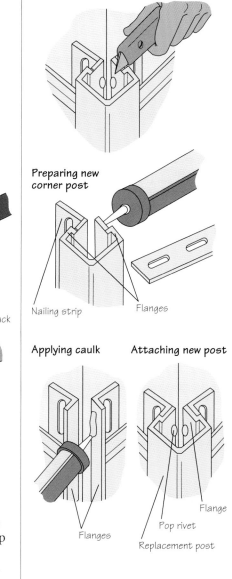

Cutting off old corner post

Preparing new corner post

Nailing strip

Flanges

Applying caulk

Attaching new post

Flanges

Flange

Pop rivet

Replacement post

Tip *When placing a ladder against a wall, a quick way to test if it's leaning at a safe angle is to stand on the ground with your toes against the ladder feet and your arms outstretched to the front. The ladder is at the safest angle if your fingertips comfortably touch the ladder sides.*

▶ *Floorboards are rotted.*

Rotted floorboards should be replaced with new boards, but first the condition that caused the rot should be corrected. Causes include inadequate ventilation under a porch floor, floorboards with exposed end grain that hasn't been sealed, and settlement (porches that were once sloped to shed water may level over time, allowing puddles to collect).

To increase ventilation, replace solid siding under the floor with lattice, or add screened vents to allow cross-ventilation, especially near corners. If the porch floor does not slope away from the house at least ⅛ inch per foot, consult a contractor experienced with porch restoration about the best technique for restoring proper slope. If the slope and ventilation are adequate and only a few boards need to be replaced, use the same techniques as for replacing interior floorboards (see page 40). Prime or seal each board, including ends, before installing, and use HDG nails.

▶ *Wood floor needs painting.*

Specialized paints are available for porches and decks that are highly resistant to abrasion and high traffic. Unfortunately, they're available in only a limited range of colors. If the floor is bare wood, coat the boards with a water repellent/preservative before applying a primer. A previously painted floor should be scraped and sanded first to provide a solid base and tooth for the new coating.

▶ *Concrete porch floor is settling.*

See page 143.

▶ *Porch roof post is rotted and needs replacing.*

Shore up the porch roof with a temporary 4x4 brace. First nail a temporary 2x4 cleat to the underside of the roof header immediately next to the rotted post. Cut the 4x4 brace about 6 inches longer than the distance between the cleat and the ground; it should rest on a 2-foot-long pad of 2x8 scrap. Set up the brace with the top under the cleat and the bottom on the pad. Then tap the bottom of the brace with a sledgehammer until the header is raised about ¼ inch. Secure the brace in place by driving a wedge under it and toenailing it to the scrap. Then remove the old post.

The new post should be the same size as the old one. Most lumberyards and home centers stock decorative posts in many styles. If you have difficulty matching the post, try an architectural salvage yard. Prime or seal the new post, and attach an aluminum pedestal bracket to the bottom to prevent trapped moisture from rotting the base. Set the new post in place. Secure the top by toenailing it with two 8d HDG common nails on each side (predrill, and countersink the heads with a nail set). Attach the bottom bracket with 3-inch HDG decking screws. Remove the brace.

Replacing porch roof post

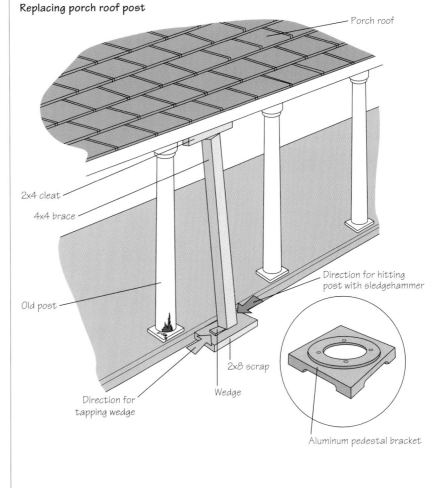

Porch roof

2x4 cleat

4x4 brace

Old post

Direction for tapping wedge

Direction for hitting post with sledgehammer

2x8 scrap

Wedge

Aluminum pedestal bracket

Tip *If your porch feels dark and uninviting, paint the ceiling white. If it's still too dark, paint the floor white with latex deck paint specified for floors, or have the floor whitewashed.*

Tip *Recessed ceiling fixtures are an excellent lighting choice for porches, provided there is some attic space (because it's not insulated, even a low attic usually has enough access). The lights are unobtrusive to neighbors, provide plenty of useful illumination, and maintain privacy by directing light downward into focused pools instead of bouncing it off walls and occupants. Space lights 8 feet apart.*

SOLVING EXTERIOR PROBLEMS

▶ Wood tread is cracked or rotting.

Weak treads are dangerous and should be replaced immediately. First loosen the tread from the cleat or stair stringer by tapping it from below with a sledgehammer. Then pull out the nails with a claw hammer or pry bar. If the stairs have a closed stringer and there's no access from below, dig out the nails with a nail puller. Using the old tread for a pattern, cut a new tread from pressure-treated lumber; brush wood preservative on the cut ends. Then install the new tread with HDG nails, using two nails on each end of the tread. Paint or stain to match.

Replacing tread

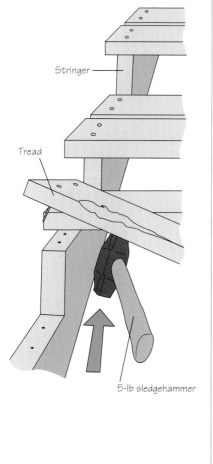

Stringer

Tread

5-lb sledgehammer

▶ Stringer is splitting.

Support the stringer with a temporary brace. Then add a cleat to the inside of the stringer; it should be 6 inches longer than the split. Bore pilot holes in the cleat and use HDG wood screws every 4 to 6 inches. Then remove the brace.

Bracing the stringer

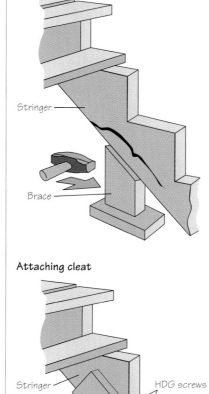

Stringer

Brace

Attaching cleat

Stringer

Cleat

HDG screws

▶ Stair treads are slippery.

If water puddles on the treads, drill ⅜-inch-diameter holes for drainage. If moss makes the treads slippery, scrub it off with bleach diluted in water, according to label directions. If the treads are painted with a high-gloss paint, redo them with a latex paint specified for porches and decks. Follow all directions on the paint label. To make the treads even more skidproof, add a small amount of silica sand to the paint—enough to produce a slightly abrasive surface.

▶ Treads lean to one side.

Either the base of the stringer is decayed or the footing has settled. If the stringer is decayed, install a temporary brace to support it near its base. The brace should raise the staircase back to the level position. Draw a level line on the stringer above the rotted area, then use a saber saw or circular saw to cut off the damaged section. Measure a new piece of pressure-treated lumber to fit under the stringer by holding it against the stringer and marking the level cut line on it. Then, with a straightedge held along each stringer edge, mark cut lines parallel to the stringer on the front and back edges of the block. Cut the block to fit, and brush wood preservative on the cut ends. Slip the block under the stringer; then use at least two HDG nails to hold it in place, dulling the nail heads to prevent splitting the piece. To strengthen the repair, attach a short piece of lumber (a cleat) on the inside of the stringer and block (see left). Drill pilot holes in the cleat and attach it with HDG screws.

If the footing has settled but is still sound (neither cracked nor below grade), raise the stringer with a temporary brace, and shim the gap below the stringer with a block of pressure-treated wood cut to fit.

Tip *The best way to keep moths, mosquitoes, and other insects away from porches is with screens. Using 1x2s, build frames that fit snugly into all of the openings of the porch. Prime and paint the frames. Then stretch insect screening over them, staple it to the faces of the frames, and nail primed and painted decorative molding around the frame to conceal the edges. Drill pilot holes for screws into the frame sides every 3 or 4 feet for attaching the screens to the porch posts.*

Tip *Black screening fabric provides daytime privacy, is easiest to see through from the inside, and gives the house a strong design accent.*

If the footing has deteriorated or has sunk below grade, raise the stringer with a temporary brace and remove the footing. Build forms and pour a new concrete footing as described on page 143.

Cutting off the rotted section

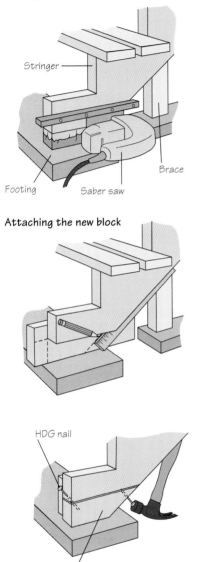

Attaching the new block

▶ *Railing is loose.*

If the staircase is made of wood, use two galvanized-steel strap brackets for each railing post. Slip the brackets around the post base and bolt them to the stringer with ⁵⁄₁₆-inch by 1½-inch lag screws; then drive 1½-inch HDG wood screws through the bracket and into the post.

If you are unable to locate brackets, use carriage bolts. Bore 2⅜-inch-diameter holes through the stringer and post, spacing the holes 4 inches apart with one near the top edge of the stringer. Then install the bolts with malleable washers, which are large washers designed to distribute the bolt tension over a wider area. The bolts should not be so tight that the washers crush the wood fibers of the post.

If the railing is metal and embedded in concrete steps, the attachment may have worked its way loose. Remove the damaged concrete around the metal post base, then refill around the post with a soupy mixture of quick-drying concrete patching material. This patch, which is mixed with water, comes in a small tub or cardboard box and is sold at most home centers. If the hole is too close to the edge of the stairs to hold the patching material, anchor the bottom of the railing laterally by drilling a ½-inch-diameter horizontal hole through the metal post, then extending the hole into the concrete with a rotary hammer and ½-inch bit. Blow dust out of the hole with a tire pump, insert an expansion bolt, and tighten the nut against the metal post.

Reinforcing a wood post   Bolting a metal post

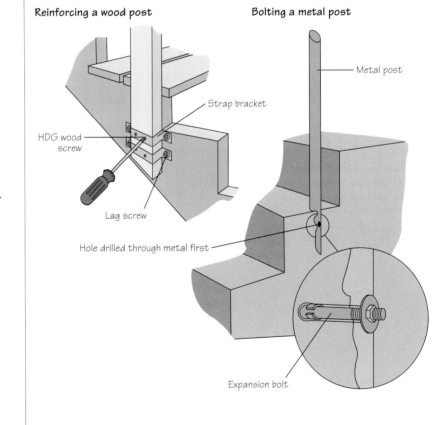

SOLVING EXTERIOR PROBLEMS

▶ *Garage doesn't have enough storage space.*

If you have basic carpentry skills, you can build a storage system on any length wall using the basic modules illustrated below. The dimensions and arrangement shown maximize the use of 4x8 sheets of plywood, but you can adjust the dimensions as desired. If you space the modules more than 4 feet apart, you will have to reinforce the shelves between them. Cut the sides, tops, and shelves from ¾-inch plywood, mark shelf locations on the inside faces of the two sides, and scribe corresponding nailing lines on the outside faces. Assemble each module with glue and 8d box nails. Cut back pieces out of ¼-inch plywood or hard-

board and attach them with glue and 4d box nails. Attach the modules to the wall studs with 2-inch screws, using a level and shims to make them square and plumb. Cut shelves as desired for the spaces between cabinets. If you use plywood, cut the shelves so that the long dimension runs the same direction as the long edge of the plywood (with the grain, not across it). Attach them with glue and 8d box nails, or install shelf track to make them adjustable. Install sliding-door track as shown, and attach roller brackets to the tops of full sheets of ¾-inch lumbercore plywood, which will stay flat, to make the doors.

▶ *Garage roof has too many cross members for storage.*

The roof is probably framed with prefabricated trusses. All of the parts of a truss work together to hold up the roof; each truss is rated to carry a certain amount of weight. Storing items on a truss can over-stress it and may permanently damage the roof. Under no circumstances should any member be cut or removed.

▶ *Perfboard hooks fall off board.*

Perforated board is sold in ⅛-inch and ¼-inch thicknesses; the ¼-inch type has larger holes. Make sure you have the correct pegs for the thickness of the board. Regular steel hooks loosen from everyday use; check a local home center for locking pegs. Two common types of locking pegs are steel pegs with a locking plate and heavy plastic pegs that lock in place when installed.

▶ *Large garden tools have no storage area.*

If wall space is limited, make a narrow rack that will store several tools. Use two pieces of ½-inch plywood attached to either side of an exposed wall stud. Cut them 16 inches long and graduate the width from 12 to 16 inches. Attach the 12-inch width to the stud sides with four 2-inch wood screws each.

If you have more wall space (3 to 5 feet), hang garden tools from nails driven into a scrap of ¾-inch plywood. First lay the plywood on the floor and arrange the tools with their heads on the plywood and all handles hanging in the same direction. Stagger tools to maximize the space. With the tools in place, drive two nails below each head. Remove

Building modules

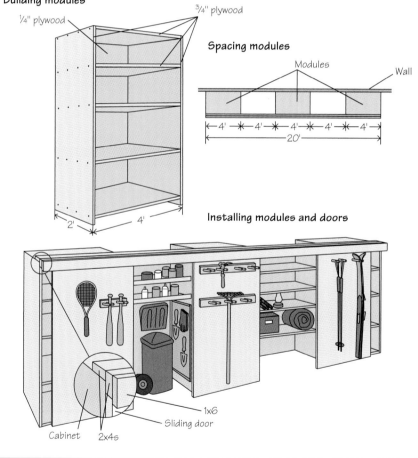

¼" plywood
¾" plywood

2'   4'

Spacing modules

Modules   Wall

←4'→←4'→←4'→←4'→←4'→
←——————20'——————→

Installing modules and doors

1x6
Sliding door
Cabinet   2x4s

Tip   *Garages are often a weak link in a home's security system. Be sure all entrances to the garage are locked and that the door between the garage and house is locked. Don't leave the garage door open for long periods of time, allowing passersby to notice what's stored in there. Don't leave keys to the house in a conspicuous place in the garage; hide them where only you can find them.*

the tools, attach the plywood securely to the wall with lag screws and washers, and hang each tool from its pair of nails.

Building a narrow rack for garden tools

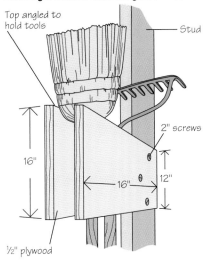

▶ Long objects, such as molding, pipe, and some tools, are awkward to store.

Organize and store such objects in sections of vinyl rain gutter. Attach the gutter support brackets to the studs, then snap the sections in place.

Storing long objects

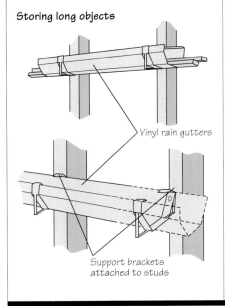

▶ Garden hose is awkward to store.

Do not hang the hose from a peg or narrow hanger; instead, make a sturdy hose hanger from a large cylinder, such as a plastic plant liner. Secure it to the wall with 1½-inch wood screws and fender washers. Or check a home center for a hook-and-loop hose-carrying handle that can easily be hung on the wall.

▶ Garage lighting is inadequate.

One or more pairs of 4-foot fluorescent lights provide adequate lighting for most garage needs. If you have a workbench, position one pair directly over it. As a safety measure, slip clear plastic tubes over the bulbs; these will contain the glass if the lights are accidentally broken. Plastic tubes are available at lighting stores.

▶ Garage is too cold.

First check the garage door. Make sure the weather stripping on the bottom of the door is in good shape and that there isn't any debris preventing it from sealing completely. If the garage has windows, they should be shut tightly and not have any cracked or missing panes. Insulating the walls and ceiling will also help. Finally, if the floor is cold, bury insulation around the foundation. Dig a narrow 2-foot-deep trench around the foundation and place beadboard insulation (rigid foam panels specified for ground contact or burial) against the footings.

▶ Garage access to attic lacks solid door.

Garages without ceilings often have an access opening to the attic, located high up on the common wall with the house. This opening must have a solid door rated at one-hour fire resistance to prevent a fire in the garage from being sucked up into the attic. To make such a door, buy a damaged solid-core door and cut it to size, or attach ⅝-inch wallboard to a piece of ¾-inch plywood.

If the garage has a ceiling with a pull-down staircase, there should be a fireproof cover over the hatch. Cover kits are available from home centers and ladder manufacturers. There are two kinds: premolded fiberglass or an assemble-it-yourself foam cover that fits over the ladder when it's in the closed position.

▶ Concrete floor is stained.

Remove oil, rust, and other stains from concrete with a solution of 1 part muriatic acid to 10 parts water. You can mix a small batch in a plastic watering can. Add the acid to the water, not the water to the acid. Wear rubber gloves, eye protection, a long-sleeved shirt, long pants, and work shoes. Sprinkle the solution on the stain and work it in with a long-handled scrub brush. Wait five minutes, then rinse the surface thoroughly with water. You can also purchase a premixed concrete cleaning solution from a home center or hardware store.

▶ Concrete floor is cracked.

See page 142.

Tip   All electrical receptacles in a garage should be protected by ground fault circuit interrupters (GFCIs). An exception is the overhead outlet for an automatic garage-door opener (check local codes).

Tip   To help you navigate your car into the garage, paint markers on the back wall to aim headlights at, and hang a tennis ball or other harmless object where the windshield will touch it when you've pulled in far enough.

▶ Garage floor is slippery from melting snow and ice.

If snow and ice melting from the car spread out over the garage floor, confine the mess to the area under the car by gluing two continuous strips of garage-door weather stripping to the floor, about 1 foot away from each side of the car. Attach each strip with a bead of outdoor construction adhesive. If you're planning to build a garage, install a concrete floor that's sloped slightly toward a central drain.

Controlling meltwater

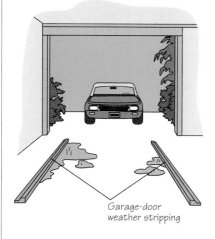

Garage-door
weather stripping

▶ Manual door gets stuck.

Check for objects stored overhead that may be interfering with the door, then make sure that all hinges are securely fastened to the door. If that doesn't help, see right.

▶ Garage-door locking bar doesn't catch in side latches.

An object or debris under the bottom of the door, such as a small stone or some leaves, can prevent the door from closing fully. Check along the garage floor and on the door bottom. Also make sure that the locking bars aren't bent and that the locking-bar guides are

properly positioned. Straighten the bars or realign the guides as needed.

Realigning locking-bar guide

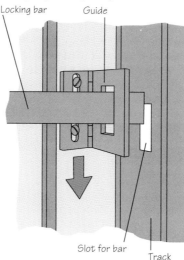

Locking bar   Guide

Slot for bar   Track

▶ Sectional door doesn't open easily.

The hardware may be out of alignment, broken, or in need of cleaning and lubrication. If the rollers bind in the tracks, the tracks may be out of alignment—either not straight, not perfectly parallel to each other, or not perpendicular to the door. To align a track, loosen the mounting bracket and tap it back into alignment with a hammer and woodblock. If only one roller drags or jams, try shimming or remounting the roller bracket. If the door is still difficult to lift, try cleaning and lubricating all of the door hardware. Start with the rollers and hinges. Remove one at a time and soak it in kerosene; use a paintbrush to work the kerosene into cracks. Take off rust with steel wool or a liquid rust-removing paste. Then wipe off the parts and apply a light lubricating oil, especially on the hinge knuckles and where the rollers and shafts make contact. If you've installed weather

stripping around the sides of the door, it should seal against the door without jamming tightly against it; adjust the strip if necessary. Finally, check the springs for breaks or looseness; there should be slight tension when the door is fully open. See opposite page.

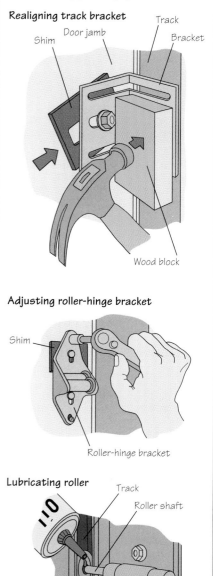

Realigning track bracket

Shim   Door jamb   Track   Bracket

Wood block

Adjusting roller-hinge bracket

Shim

Roller-hinge bracket

Lubricating roller   Track

Roller shaft

Roller

Tip *If your garage is cluttered with tricycles, wagons, and similar children's toys that are constantly on the move, designate a parking space for each one by outlining boxes on the floor with colorful floor and deck paint. While you're at it, do the same for lawnmowers, wheelbarrows, and similar equipment that competes for space.*

▶ *Springs need adjustment.*

Don't attempt to adjust torsion springs, which are mounted crossways above the opening of a roll-up door. They are extremely dangerous to work on. Contact a professional garage-door mechanic.

Springs located along the door track that operate by stretching, which are called tension springs or extension springs, can be adjusted. First raise the door fully and hold it in position by attaching a clamp or locking pliers to one of the tracks, below the last wheel. Make sure that the spring has a safety cable or chain strung through it. Then release the end of each lifting cable from its mounting bracket at the top of the track or the bottom door panel, tighten the slack, tie a new knot in the cable, and reattach it.

Tightening slack in lifting cable

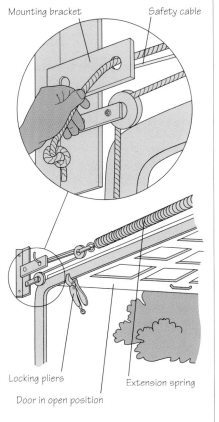

Mounting bracket
Safety cable
Locking pliers
Extension spring
Door in open position

▶ *One-piece door sags in middle when open.*

Purchase a bracing kit from a garage-door company; it consists of two threaded steel rods and six mounting brackets. To install it, use carriage bolts to attach the brackets to the back of the garage door, three brackets along the top of the door and three at the bottom. Position the threaded rods in the brackets, secure them with washers and nuts, and tighten the tension until the door straightens.

Straightening a garage door

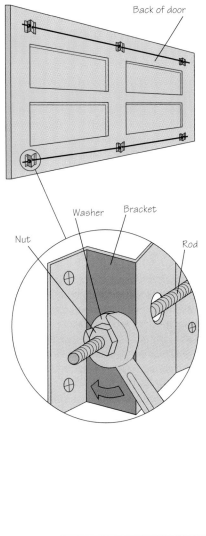

Back of door
Washer
Bracket
Nut
Rod

▶ *Automatic door opener doesn't turn on.*

First check the transmitter battery. If it's cold, warm it up. Then make sure that the opener is plugged in and that there's power going to the plug. Next check that the wall button operates the opener; if it does not, replace the opener button and wiring with a standard doorbell button and wire. If the transmitter still doesn't open the door, check for objects, such as boxes or lumber, that are blocking the path of the transmitter signal. Replace a broken or missing receiver antenna with a new one from the opener manufacturer. Finally, make sure that the code settings on the transmitter and receiver match.

▶ *Automatic door opener works but door doesn't open.*

Most likely, the problem is with the door. First pull the emergency disconnect cord and try to open the door manually. If it's difficult to open, see opposite page.

▶ *Automatic door doesn't reverse soon enough or reverses as soon as it shuts.*

Test the safety reverse by placing a scrap of 2x4 in the doorway and closing the door on it. If the door reverses upon impact, it is adjusted properly. If the door does not reverse, find the front-limit switch located on the overhead rail near the door opening, or check for a knob to adjust the automatic-reversing switch (see page 140). Move an overhead-rail switch forward in 1/16-inch increments until the door reverses upon impact. If it reverses too soon, move the switch back. If the door closes fully but reverses after a few seconds, adjust the down-limit screw or knob, located on the motor, to relieve

Tip *If your garage door has an automatic opener and the power fails, you can get your car out of the garage simply by pulling the emergency disconnect cord and then lifting the garage door manually.*

Tip *The Consumer Product Safety Act of 1990 requires that all automatic door openers manufactured after January 1, 1993, meet certain safety standards. Among other things, the standards require that a door have a safety reversing mechanism that reopens it automatically if it hits any obstruction higher than 1 inch above the floor.*

pressure. Some turn by hand; others require a screwdriver or wrench.

▶ Automatic door reverses before cycle ends.

Remove any ice, snow, or debris buildup under the door. Also check the door opener rail; if it bows when the door is closed, decrease the down limit. Look for a down-limit adjusting screw or knob on the power unit and adjust it so the door opener doesn't try to force the door down quite so far. If there's no down-limit adjustment on the power unit, look for a front-limit switch along the rail that gets triggered when the traveler arm reaches it. Slide it back toward the power unit slightly so the opener will shut off sooner.

Checking for a bowed rail

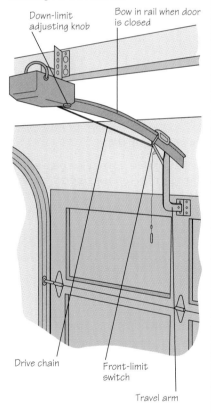

Down-limit adjusting knob

Bow in rail when door is closed

Drive chain

Front-limit switch

Travel arm

▶ Automatic door opens for no reason.

Check the transmitter button to see that it's not stuck. If it is, either unstick the button or replace the transmitter. If that doesn't work, try changing your code. An intermittent short in the button wire can also cause the door to open. Check the wire for continuity and, if it's broken, replace it. If the problem persists, purchase a new transmitter and receiver set. Get one that uses two codes simultaneously.

▶ Automatic door lacks autoreverse.

Recent updates in the safety code mandate that new openers have a number of built-in sensing devices to protect against entrapment. First check with the manufacturer to see if an upgrade kit is available. If not, replace the unit with a new, safer one that complies with UL standard number 325. It will include a photoelectric sensor to be mounted on the door jambs, or a sensing edge to be attached to the door bottom.

▶ Garage ceiling is too low for an automatic door opener.

Most standard openers need about 12 inches of clearance between the top of the door and the garage ceiling. There are low-clearance kits that need about 3 inches of headroom. If you have less than 3 inches of clearance and have a wood door, you can cut off some of the top of the door. Just don't trim too much, or when the door is closed, there will be a gap between the top of the door and the stop molding.

There are openers that require no clearance; they utilize a motor that mounts on the back of the door and a drive wheel that runs in

the door track. A power cord connects the motor to a control panel mounted on the garage wall. A specialty item, this may not be available in home centers. Contact local garage-door companies to find one.

Installing an opener that attaches to the door

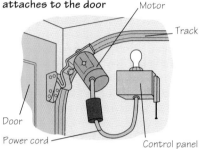

Motor

Track

Door

Power cord

Control panel

▶ Water and drafts leak in around door.

First make sure that no debris, snow, or ice is preventing the door from closing completely. If that's not the problem, add or replace the weather stripping at the door bottom. Rubber weather stripping specially made for this purpose is sold in most home centers. If the floor under the door is uneven, nail on a strip of ¾-inch-diameter pipe insulation with the slit facing downward. Attach the strip near the back edge of the door, using 4d HDG box nails.

Attaching foam pipe insulation

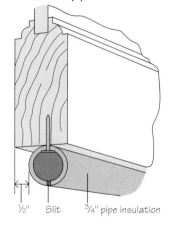

½" Slit ¾" pipe insulation

Tip *Occasionally, a garage door with an automatic opener may open when the transmitter has not been activated, even when nobody is home. The cause may be a neighbor or a passing car with a transmitter coded the same as the opener. This problem can be solved by recoding the transmitter; check the manufacturer's directions. Another cause might be a short in the wire between the door opener and wall button, which can activate the opener at the slightest jiggle. Replace the wire.*

▶ Automatic-door drive mechanism binds or slips.

If you have a chain-drive system, open the door halfway and measure the chain sag at the carrier; it shouldn't exceed ½ inch. If it does, tighten the chain-tension adjusting screw on the power unit. If you have a screw-drive system and live in a cold area, the grease on the drive may not be made for low temperatures. Spray a penetrating solvent on the carrier and screw shaft to remove the grease. Then lubricate them, using a lightweight oil or silicone spray. For track-drive systems, make sure that the track is clean and that the sections aren't bent. Replace any plastic guides that are broken.

Measuring chain tension

Rail Carrier Chain
Door open halfway

Removing built-up grease from drive screw

Penetrating solvent

Cleaning grease from a drive track

Rag with solvent

▶ Light doesn't go on when automatic door opens.

Check the bulb to see if it's burned out. If it is, purchase a bulb that's recommended by the opener manufacturer; often it's one made for heavy-duty use, such as in a car repair drop light. If the problem is not the bulb, consult a professional garage-door specialist.

▶ Bottom of sectional wood door gets wet.

First make sure that the bottom of the door has been sealed or painted, has weather stripping, and is not cracked. Add or replace as needed. Then seal the long joints between the bottom rail and the panels, running a bead of clear caulk along the joint according to label directions.

▶ Varnish on outside of garage door fades quickly.

Clear finishes won't last on outdoor surfaces. Resign yourself to a yearly job of scraping and sanding, followed by another coat of finish. Use marine-grade spar varnish, or refinish the door with a heavy-bodied stain or paint.

▶ Asphalt driveway is cracked or damaged.

Seal cracks as quickly as possible to prevent further damage from moisture or freezing-and-thawing cycles. Fill large cracks with a premixed asphalt crack filler, which comes in squeeze bottles, 1-gallon containers, and caulking-gun tubes; it's available at home centers and hardware stores. First remove any vegetation growing in the cracks and, if you have a compressor or shop vac, blow out or vacuum the debris. Then fill the crack according to label directions. Next spread a liquid sealer over the asphalt. (You should apply sealer every three to four years, according to label directions.) Use a high-quality sealer with a high solid content. Note that the average life of an asphalt driveway is 20 years; if it's older, it may need to be replaced.

▶ Asphalt driveway has holes.

First remove all loose asphalt and other debris. Then scrape around the hole with a trowel until you reach solid material. Fill the hole to within 1 inch of the surface with cold-mix asphalt patch, which comes in 60-pound bags. Tamp the patch with the butt end of a 4x4, then overfill the hole with more patch and tamp it flush with the driveway surface.

▶ Driveway has oil spots.

First soak up any standing oil with an absorbent clay, such as cat litter. Work the clay into the stain with a stiff-bristled brush, sweep clean, then scrub the stain with scouring powder and water. If the stain has penetrated deeply, mix a paste of talc and kerosene and smear it on the stain. When it dries, scrub with scouring powder and water, then rinse.

▶ Concrete driveway has rust and other dark stains on it.

See page 137.

▶ Concrete driveway has hole.

Follow the procedure for cracks wider than ⅛ inch, described on page 142.

Tip *If a water heater or other appliance with a pilot light is located in the garage, it should be on a platform that raises the pilot light 18 inches above the floor. Gas vapors from the car gravitate to the floor and, if they come in contact with a flame before dissipating, may explode.*

▶ Brick is broken.

If the brick is laid in mortar, use a brick chisel to break up the surrounding mortar joints and the brick. Use a pry bar to remove loose pieces, then chip any loose mortar from the cavity and brush out the particles. Wet the cavity and the new brick. Mix mortar according to label instructions, then line the base and sides of the cavity with mortar. Press the new brick in place, smooth the joints to match the rest, and clean off any excess mortar.

To replace a broken sand-laid brick, remove the broken pieces with a flat pry bar. Then refill the base with sand, dampen it, and tamp it down with the butt end of a 2x4. Use a paving-grade brick for a replacement. Sweep sand in around the crack.

Removing damaged brick

Brick chisel

Pry bar

Setting new brick

Cavity lined with fresh mortar

▶ Bricks are uneven.

If the bricks are laid in sand, remove the tilted brick and relevel the sand or tamp in new sand to bring the base back up to level. Then replace the brick and sweep sand into the surrounding joints. Poor drainage around laid brick, such as from a badly situated downspout, can cause a sand base to wash away. Relocate the downspout or install diversion drainage, if necessary. Bricks can also settle unevenly if they do not have a firm border, such as a concrete curb or 2x4s held in place with stakes. To make a simple but effective border, excavate a shallow trench around the bricks and lay pressure-treated 2x4s on edge against the bricks. Hold the boards in place with 1x2 stakes, 12 to 18 inches long, driven 1 inch below the tops of the boards. Nail the stakes to the boards with 8d HDG common nails.

▶ Bricks have moss.

Scrape off the moss with a trowel, then scrub the bricks with a solution of 1 part household bleach to 3 parts water. Use a stiff-bristled brush and wear eye protection and rubber gloves. Let the solution dry on the bricks. To prevent a return of the moss, make sure the area has proper drainage and that it isn't shaded by tree branches.

▶ Brick has fresh mortar glops.

Avoid smearing them by waiting until the mortar is almost dry, then remove them with a trowel. Mix a solution of 1 part muriatic acid to 15 parts water, making sure to add the acid to the water, not the water to the acid. Wear rubber gloves, eye protection, a long-sleeved shirt, and long pants when working with acid. Wipe the solution on the brick(s), wait three to four minutes, then flush it away with clear water.

▶ Brick has dried mortar on the surface.

Chip off the dried mortar with a trowel or putty knife. Then mix a solution of 1 part muriatic acid solution to 10 parts water; add the acid to the water, not the water to the acid. Wet the brick, then apply the solution with a stiff-bristled brush, scrubbing it until the mortar is gone. Immediately rinse the bricks with clear water. Remember to wear eye protection, a long-sleeved shirt, rubber gloves, and long pants.

▶ Bricks to be laid on sand need to be evenly spaced.

Set the bricks in plastic grids, available in many home centers; they ensure uniform spacing and stabilize the bricks. Set them on a packed sand base, snapping their edges together to create the layout you want. They come in various sizes to accommodate modular bricks, standard bricks, and patio blocks.

▶ Concrete is cracked.

Scrape out and vacuum away any debris. Lightly mist the crack with a garden hose so that it's damp but not dripping wet. If the crack is ⅛ inch wide or less, fill it with either a soupy mixture of 1 part portland cement to 3 parts concrete bonding liquid, or a masonry crack filler that comes in a tube and is applied with a caulking gun. If the crack is wider, use a cold chisel and a hand sledgehammer to chip away any loose material. To keep the patch locked in, chisel the crack so that edges are undercut. Remember to wear eye

Tip *Ordinary bricks, called common bricks, are sufficient for most garden projects, but for patios, walks, and especially driveways, use paver bricks. They are more durable than common bricks.*

Tip *The most common width for brick joints is ⅜ inch. When estimating the number of bricks needed for a project, allow for the joint space between bricks. Also keep in mind that brick sizes are irregular and vary from the nominal brick size (2x4x8 inches) by as much as ⅜ inch.*

protection. Mix 1 part portland cement to 3 parts sand, then add enough concrete bonding liquid to make a stiff mixture. Set aside a small part of the mixture and add more liquid to it until it's soupy. Brush the soupy mixture into the crack, then pack in the stiff mixture and trowel it smooth. Over the next week lightly spray the crack with water twice a day to help cure the patch.

Undercutting the edges of a wide crack

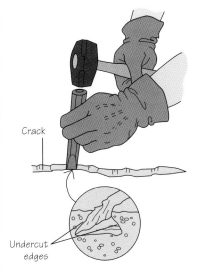

Crack

Undercut edges

▶ Concrete is spalling.

Spalling is chipping or breaking up beneath the surface that causes pieces of the surface to lift. Symptoms of spalling include circular or oval depressions. To repair the concrete, use a cold chisel and hand sledgehammer to chip out the damaged area to a depth of 1 inch, undercutting the sides of the hole. Then clean out the hole and patch it as you would a crack (see page 142).

▶ Corner of concrete slab has settled.

Concrete slabs list from settling or washing away of the underlying soil. You can build the slab back up to level with a topping compound. It mixes like tile grout and can be built up to a thickness of 1 to 1½ inches.

If the concrete is severely settled, the slab can be "pumped" back up to level by a process known as mudjacking or slabjacking. A contractor first bores holes in the concrete slab, then pumps a cementious grout into the holes. Slowly, the slab begins to rise until it's level again. When the grout sets, it creates a solid support base. Companies that specialize in mudjacking can be found in the Yellow Pages under "Concrete, Repairs" or through a local building inspector or engineer.

Raising a slab by mudjacking

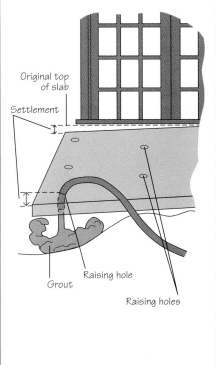

Original top of slab

Settlement

Grout

Raising hole

Raising holes

▶ Section of concrete walkway needs replacing.

First use a sledgehammer to break up the damaged section. Remove all debris and gravel to 4 inches below the walkway surface. In freezing climates, make sure there is at least 4 inches of gravel subsurface below the cavity. Dig a shallow trench along each side of the section and install forms flush with the top of the walkway. Then mix and pour new concrete. Strike off the concrete so it's level with the surrounding surface by dragging a 2x4 across the tops of the forms with a back-and-forth motion. Wait one or two hours for it to set up—when all float water has evaporated and the concrete holds its shape. Then finish the surface: Use a wood or magnesium float for a rough surface, a steel trowel for a smooth surface, or a push broom for a textured surface. To help the concrete cure, cover it with a plastic sheet for about a week. Spray the section once a day to keep it moist.

Pouring concrete

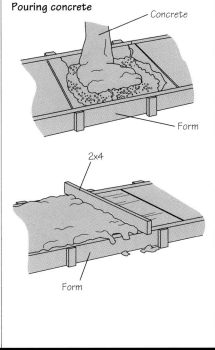

Concrete

Form

2x4

Form

Tip   An alternative paving material to bricks is interlocking pavers. Unlike bricks, which are made from clay, pavers are usually made from cast concrete. They have shapes (usually based on a hexagonal design) that allow them to lock into place for more stability than rectangular units.

Tip   When working with muriatic acid, as with any acid, follow all label cautions carefully. To dilute, always add acid to water; never add water to acid, as it may cause the acid to spatter. Wear rubber gloves, eye protection, and clothing that protects all of your skin.

SOLVING EXTERIOR PROBLEMS

▶ Deck needs more seating.

The easiest way to build new deck benches is to attach them to the railing posts. First make sure that the railing posts are solid. Then use three ⅜-inch by 7-inch carriage bolts to attach a pair of 2x12 seat supports to each post. Cut the 2x12 pieces 18 to 20 inches long (longer at a corner; measure first) and taper them for leg clearance. If the posts are spaced farther than 3 feet apart, bolt an intermediate 4x4 support post to the outside of the rim (end) joist, positioned halfway between the railing posts. Attach 1x4s across the tops of the seat supports for the bench seat; space them ¼ inch apart and secure them with 1½-inch HDG decking screws. Trim the front edge with a 1x2, 1x3, or 1x4 attached to the ends of the supports.

Attaching bench supports

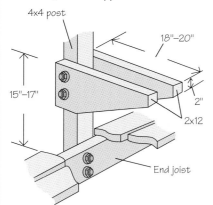

4x4 post
18"–20"
15"–17"
2"
2x12
End joist

Attaching seat boards

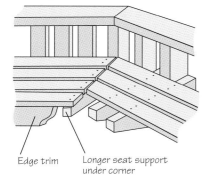

Edge trim
Longer seat support under corner

▶ Post bottom is rotted and footing is too low.

You'll need to remove the rotten post section and build up the footing. First install a temporary 4x4 post to shore up the deck. Find the beam that is supported by the rotted deck post, then drop a plumb line from this beam to the ground, as close as possible to the footing. Measure the distance between the underside of the beam and the ground; cut the temporary post 1 inch shorter than this distance. Place this temporary post in position, resting it on a scrap of 2x8. Toenail its top to the underside of the beam; then, using a sledgehammer, drive the post vertical. It should be plumb. Toenail its bottom to the 2x8 scrap.

Next mark a level line on the rotted post immediately above the rotted section. Cut on the line with a handsaw or circular saw. Drive several concrete nails into the top of the footing, spaced 3 inches apart. Build a form around the footing high enough to bring the top of the footing up to the bottom of the dangling post, then nail a post anchor to the bottom of the post. Coat the old concrete with a liquid concrete bonding agent, then pour new concrete in the form. Use a trowel to slope the top of the new concrete slightly away from the post. Let the concrete cure for a week before removing the shoring and forms.

▶ Deck boards are sagging or bouncy.

The joists are spaced too far apart. Add additional joists, spaced halfway between the existing ones. Toenail them in place with 12d HDG common nails where they rest on a beam; use galvanized joist-hanger brackets to support the ends where they abut a header.

▶ Pier is tipping or sliding away.

Shore up the deck with temporary posts (see left). Remove the existing post and pier, then drop a plumb line to locate the center of the new pier location, which will most likely be where the old pier was. Dig a hole for a new pier footing, 18 inches square and 12 to 24 inches deep (or below the frost line, depending on the soil conditions and local building code). Fill the hole with concrete up to ground level, then insert four 1-foot-long pieces of rebar 6 inches into the concrete. When the concrete dries, on top of the footing and around the rebar build a pier form that's 6 inches high and 12 inches square. Fill the form with concrete, sloping the top slightly to shed water. When the concrete starts to stiffen, embed a galvanized post-anchor bracket in it, located directly under the plumb line. Allow two to five days for the concrete to cure; then install a new post, soaking the bottom with preservative first. Stay off the deck until the repair is complete.

▶ Deck fasteners rust or stain the deck.

When building or repairing outdoor structures, always use corrosion-resistant fasteners. For nails, avoid electrogalvanized (EG) and "bright" nails; hot-dipped galvanized (HDG), aluminum, and stainless steel are the best choices. Galvanized nails are the most economical, but the coating on the head can sometimes chip off when hit with a hammer. Recoat chipped heads with a dab of galvanized paint. Screws are available in HDG or stainless steel. Stainless steel screws are much more

Tip *Keep your deck clean. Sweep (even vacuum) it regularly to eliminate dust and grit that can get ground into the finish, causing it to break down faster and destroying the coating that protects the wood.*

Tip *When applying a stain or sealer to a deck, avoid spraying it on. Brush it instead, to ensure better penetration and buildup for longer-lasting results.*

expensive than HDG, but they are more durable and weather-resistant. Screws are more reliable than nails, but take more time to install because pilot holes must be drilled at the board ends to prevent splitting. Stainless steel nailing strips and nailing clips are also available for attaching deck boards. Both types are attached to the deck before the deck boards are placed. If you can't find them in a local hardware store or home center, ask a local deck-building professional for the name of a supplier. Bolts, brackets, hangers, and other framing devices all should be galvanized.

▶ Gaps appear between pieces of wood as deck ages.

It's normal for boards to shrink across their width, creating gaps. For most deck joints this is not a structural problem, but it may be unsightly and, in the case of decking, dangerous for people wearing high-heeled shoes. The only solution to this problem is to pull up the boards and reinstall them closer together. Wood that was not dried sufficiently can also shrink lengthwise. Gaps most often open up at the ends of very long deck boards; sometimes they are wide enough that the boards creep off the joists. To close a gap, remove the long deck board and replace it with two shorter boards.

▶ Parts of the deck are rotting.

Trapped moisture will cause a deck to rot. Probe any suspicious areas with an ice pick or awl. The best remedy is to replace the rotted board, especially if it's load-bearing. To replace the ledger board, post, or joist you will have to shore up the deck temporarily (see opposite page). A

new ledger board should have a ¾-inch to 1½-inch space behind it to allow air to circulate between it and the house siding. Replace rotted sections of decking by removing the entire board or cutting out the rotted section. Any individual board should span at least 2 joist bays. Cut along the inside face of joists. To support the new piece, attach pressure-treated nailers to the faces of the joists with 3-inch HDG nails, then cut and nail the new decking in place. At nonstructural points, such as the cantilevered (overhanging) joist ends, solidify the rotted area with an epoxy-based wood-hardening compound. Depending on the brand, it can be brushed on, injected into ⅛-inch-diameter holes bored in the rotted area, or formed as a putty that will rebuild a missing piece. The compound is expensive and appropriate only for small areas. See also page 98.

▶ Clear wood finish is damaged by sunlight.

Most clear finishes allow UV (ultraviolet) rays from the sun to pass through and damage the wood. Film-forming finishes such as polyurethane eventually lose their bond to the wood, become brittle, crack, and peel. To remove them, scraping and sanding is the solution. (Rent a floor sander to do the deck surface.) A better finish for a deck is a penetrating clear finish that has a built-in UV blocker and mildewcide. For the best penetration, apply it with a bristle brush. To maintain the natural color of the wood, expect to apply the finish every year or two.

▶ Deck needs cleaning.

A high-pressure washer with an output of 750 to 1,000 psi can clean a deck with plain water. A washer with this capacity can be rented or purchased and is also handy for other chores, such as cleaning siding, patios, and walkways, and washing the car. Another way to scrub a deck is to rent an electric floor cleaner/polisher fitted with stiff-bristled brushes. Use a deck-cleaning solution and follow label directions. Make sure that the polisher is plugged into a GFCI-protected receptacle.

▶ Deck has mildew.

Scrub the deck with a solution of 1 part bleach to 3 parts water; a long-handled scrub brush is helpful for working the solution into the wood. Let the solution dry on the deck surface. For stubborn stains, apply a solution of 1 pound oxalic acid mixed with 1 gallon of water. To prevent further mildew growth, make sure the protective coating that you apply to the deck, such as a clear water repellent or semitransparent or opaque stain, contains a mildewcide. Mildewcide additives are also sold in paint stores. Mildew has a tendency to grow in heavily shaded areas, so consider trimming overhanging branches or bushes.

▶ Nails are popping up from deck boards.

Carefully remove the old nails. Replace them with 3-inch HDG decking screws, or drive new 16d HDG nails in the original holes, but at a new angle to avoid the old holes in the joists below.

Tip *Whenever building an outdoor structure, such as a deck or overhead, observe these tips to ensure long-lasting results: (1) Use pressure-treated lumber or heart lumber of a durable species such as redwood, cedar, or cypress. (2) Use corrosion-resistant fasteners, such as HDG, stainless steel, or aluminum. (3) Apply preservative to the cut ends of boards. (4) Do not nail boards together lengthwise, as this creates a moisture trap—space members at least ½ inch apart to allow air circulation. (5) Cut the tops of vertical members at an angle to facilitate water runoff, or cover them with horizontal boards. (6) Drill pilot holes for nails at the ends of boards to prevent splitting. (7) Stagger nails along the grain of the wood to keep it from splitting.*

SOLVING EXTERIOR PROBLEMS

▶ *Gate won't shut.*

First check the latch. Spray silicone lubricant on all moving parts that don't operate smoothly. Next make sure that the strike and latch are properly aligned; if they aren't, reposition them. A sagging gate that won't close should be resquared with a turnbuckle.

Adjusting a turnbuckle

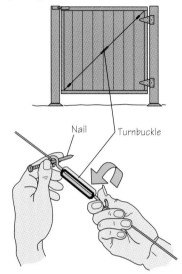

Nail
Turnbuckle

▶ *Fence is sagging or falling.*

First straighten and brace the fence with 2x4s and stakes. Then, if the sagging post is set in soil, install sister posts. Use a pressure-treated 2x4 half as long as the fence post, with one end bevel-cut. Position it next to the post with the bevel end down, facing out. Drive the post halfway into the ground with a sledgehammer. Leaving 18 inches exposed, bevel-cut the top of the post. Repeat this procedure on the other side of the post. Then bore holes through all three posts

and join them with HDG carriage bolts. Remove the bracing. If the fence posts are set in concrete, drive pressure-treated shims into the gaps between the post base and the concrete. Replace broken concrete footings.

Bracing the fence

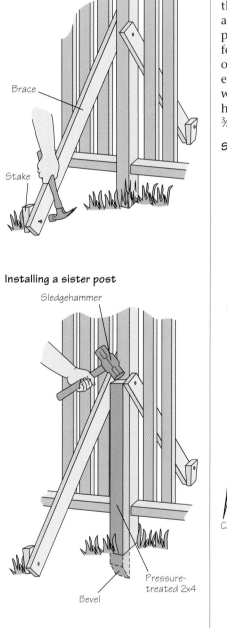

Brace

Stake

Installing a sister post

Sledgehammer

Bevel

Pressure-treated 2x4

▶ *Post is rotted.*

First support the adjacent fence sections and detach them from the rotted post by pulling or cutting the nails. If the rotted area is within 3 feet of the ground, replace the post. If the rotted area is 3 feet or more aboveground, cut away the rotted section. Splice a new post to the remaining section of post with a lap joint. On the remainder of the post, cut away a vertical half for 2 feet. On the new post, remove half of the bottom 2 feet. Angle the ends of the cuts downward to repel water. Mate the pieces together, drill holes, and bolt them with three $\frac{3}{8}$-inch by 4-inch carriage bolts.

Splicing a post

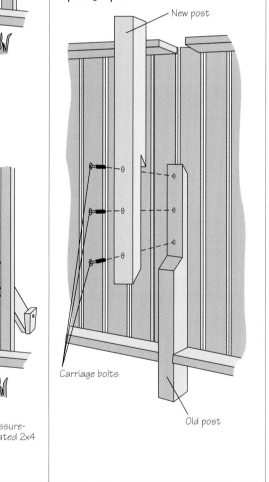

New post

Carriage bolts

Old post

Tip Be sure to verify the property line location before building a new fence. Property lines are defined on a survey that should be attached to the deed for the property. If you can't find the deed, check with the local county clerk's office. To determine exactly where the property line is located, hire a surveyor to stake out the property lines.

Tip When buying lumber for fences, choose pressure-treated lumber or heart grades of a durable species for posts and other fence members that will be in contact with the ground. Avoid lumber with sapwood (nonheart grades of lumber) for such members. Use the lesser grades with sapwood for nonstructural parts of the fence, such as the infill panels.

▶ New posts might lean.

Before setting the post and filling the hole with concrete, drive three 3-foot lengths of pipe horizontally into the sides of the hole, leaving a few inches protruding into the hole. Space the pipes evenly and drive them in at a slightly downward angle. Then set the post in place and pour the concrete.

Anchoring the concrete footing

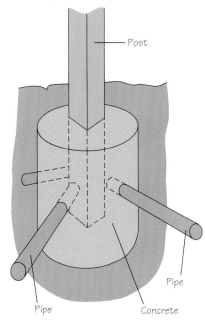

▶ New posts must be perfectly plumb.

To get posts plumb (vertical), use a regular level and alternately check all sides as you secure the post in its final position. Or else use a special post level—the most common type available consists of a pair of level vials mounted on a right-angle bracket, sometimes with an elastic retaining strap. It's sold in home centers and hardware stores, and is often included in packaged deck-building tools.

▶ Tops of fence posts need to be shaped with points.

Use a handheld circular saw and a 2x4 collar that fits snugly around the fence post. Slip the collar over the top of the post and rest it on a C-clamp. Then set the saw blade at 45 degrees. Holding it vertically and resting on the collar, cut each side of the post.

Sawing pointed fence post

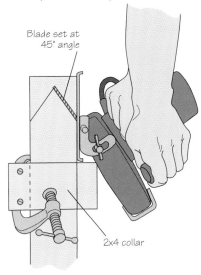

▶ Masonry retaining wall has cracks.

This is an indication that the wall doesn't have proper drainage. First make sure that the weep holes at the base of the wall are draining properly. Use a long-handled screwdriver or bent coat hanger to clean out any clogging debris. If the wall does not have weep holes, add a drainage system behind it: Dig a trench along the back of the wall, then lay in perforated PVC pipe bedded in drain rock. Cover the pipe with filter fabric and ¾-inch crushed stone.

▶ Masonry retaining wall is leaning or falling over.

This is most often caused by the force of shifting soil pressing against the back of the wall. It will have to be rebuilt. Masonry supply yards now sell retaining-wall block that solves the problem. These blocks interlock to form a solid, mortar-free wall that sets back automatically. A vertical wall of stone, brick, or block should have drain rock or filter fabric placed between it and the soil behind it, with weep holes or drainage lines installed behind the wall along the base.

Providing proper drainage

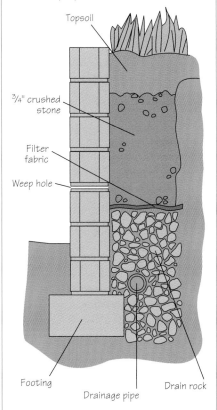

Tip   *Garden walls may be made from brick, stone, wood timbers, concrete, concrete block, or adobe. Except for those made of loose-laid stone or wood, all garden walls should be supported by a continuous concrete footing. Most walls lower than 3 feet are within the homeowner's ability to build, so long as there is someone to help with handling the materials.*

Tip   *When mixing mortar for a stone wall, make it richer than the mortar for a brick wall. Mix 3 parts sand to 1 part portland cement, with ½ part fireclay added for better consistency. The mortar should not contain lime, which might stain the stones, and it should be dry enough that it balls up in your hand but not so dry that it crumbles.*

▶ Pool filter motor won't run.

First make sure that the motor is plugged in and the timer is operating and set properly. Also check the electrical panel to ensure that the circuit breaker isn't tripped. If neither is the problem, check the filter to see if it is clogged with debris. If the motor still doesn't run, consult a pool service or repair specialist.

▶ Automatic pool sweep won't run.

Pool sweeps that run on the outflow of the circulation pump or a booster pump, such as a floating-head sweep, an in-floor hose jet sweep, or a vacuum-head roving sweep, won't run properly if the outflow pressure is down. First see if the filter is clogged. If that's not the case, have your filtration and circulation system checked by a professional pool mechanic.

Vacuum sweeps run on suction, either through the filtration pump and skimmer basket or from a self-contained motor. Check the skimmer basket and filter to make sure they're clean. On a motor-driven robot sweep, the power cord should be plugged into a GFCI-protected receptacle; also check the breaker switch—it should be in the *On* position.

▶ Pool sweep is sluggish and follows same pattern.

See above. Also consult the manufacturer's operating manual for instructions on adjusting the drive mechanism, which usually consists of rotating gears or adjusting control knobs to vary the cycles that determine changes of direction.

▶ Bubbles or air pockets appear in pool pump strainer.

Most likely, a gasket in the circulation pump is leaking. Have a professional pool mechanic pressure-test the system to locate and replace it. Air may also be entering through a leak or break in the piping, which is usually underground. Locating and repairing such a leak is very difficult. Consult a professional leak-detection service.

▶ Pool water is murky.

Failure of the filtration system or irregular maintenance can cause this problem. If the filter tank pressure reading is higher than normal, or if there is less water circulating through the system, the filter needs to be cleaned or replaced. Water will also become murky because of a chemical imbalance, sometimes caused by acid rain. Check the water with a test kit and adjust it accordingly by adding the proper chemicals.

▶ Brown or black spots appear on pool sides or bottom.

Algae or iron stains will cause these spots. Increase the chlorine in the water to remove them, monitoring the levels carefully for safe concentrations. Scrub algae spots with a stainless steel brush, then spot-treat immediately with an algaecide specified for swimming pools to prevent dislodged spores from attaching to the pool side or bottom.

▶ Water level of in-ground pool goes down rapidly.

A cement or gunite pool can leak through cracks caused by slight shifts in the surrounding soil. If the crack is thin, lower the water level to below the crack, then fill the crack with plaster, caulk, or epoxy putty. Large cracks may indicate a major soil shift or a drainage problem and should be diagnosed and corrected by a pool professional.

Tears of less than 3 inches or punctures in a vinyl-lined pool can be repaired with a kit from the pool manufacturer. Some kits allow you to work underwater, so check before you drain the pool. Large tears may be difficult to fix properly. Call a pool professional for help.

Another cause of rapid water loss is leaks in the circulation system. Ask a pool professional to perform a pressure check on the system. There are also companies that specialize in locating leaks in underground pipes.

▶ Pool is expensive to maintain.

First make sure you regularly filter, backwash, and chemically balance the pool, according to the maintenance instructions. Keep the pool covered when it's not in use; a solar cover cuts down substantially on heating costs as well as evaporation. A wind barrier may help somewhat as well. You can also discourage splashing caused by water fights and diving. Maintain the pool at 78° F, which, according to the National Spa and Pool Institute and the American Red Cross, is the most healthful temperature. An increase in temperature by 1 degree can add 10 percent to your fuel costs. Also make sure you have an accurate thermometer to check it. On days

Tip *If you live in an area where weather doesn't allow you to use and maintain your pool all year, winterize your pool to make it easier to start up in the spring. Begin by cleaning out leaves and debris, scrubbing the pool walls and bottom, and vacuuming the pool. Then add winterizing chemicals, according to label directions (most suggest running the filter for 24 hours). If you live in a cold climate where temperatures drop below freezing for extended periods, lower the water level so ice has room to expand. Completely drain the pump, filter, heater, exposed pipes, and other equipment by blowing out the water; add antifreeze specified for swimming pools where any water may remain.*

when you aren't using the pool, lower the thermostat by 10 degrees.

You can save money on electricity by operating the filter during off-peak hours and only as long as necessary. Usually, electric rates are cheapest between 6:00 a.m. and noon. To determine the optimum run time for the filter, lessen the duration it runs in half-hour increments until the clarity and chemical balance of the water begin to deteriorate. Then increase the run time until the water normalizes. Switch the automatic run cycle to manual during periods of high use.

To save on chemicals, add disinfectant during the evening; or consider adding an ionizer or ozone generator, each of which can pay for itself in just a few years. Also trim back excess foliage around the pool to minimize debris and organic materials that require stabilizing.

▶ Pool cover is not childproof.

Use a safety cover that passes ASTM (American Society for Testing and Materials) standards and is labeled accordingly. It will be strong enough to walk on. Safety covers, which are different from pool covers intended only for retaining heat, are heavy plastic and run on a motorized system with rails, or are manual systems that attach to concrete-embedded anchors with heavy springs. Consult local codes for specific requirements.

▶ Acrylic or Centrex® (Rovel®) spa surface is scratched, nicked, or damaged.

Both of these types of surfaces are made from a single sheet of plastic. Extremely durable, they rarely need repair. However, if they do, check the owner's manual that came with the spa or contact the manufacturer for a touch-up kit made specifically for your spa.

▶ Pool filter hasn't been cleaned for a year.

Procedures for cleaning a filter vary, depending on its type. A diatomaceous earth (DE) filter will have to be backwashed, the filter elements cleaned with an acid wash, and the spent DE replaced. A sand filter should be backwashed and the sand replenished. Make sure you use the type of sand recommended by the filter manufacturer. You may be able to reuse a cartridge filter; soak it in an appropriate filter-cleaning solution and clean the filter housing. If it still doesn't work adequately, replace the filter.

Identifying pool filters

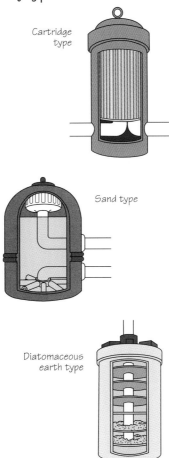

Cartridge type

Sand type

Diatomaceous earth type

▶ Gelcoat or fiberglass spa surface is scratched, nicked, or damaged.

Small blemishes, such as a surface chip, gouge, or crack, you can probably fix yourself. Get a repair kit from a large paint-supply store, boat shop, or the spa manufacturer; it should include some gelcoat that closely matches the color of your spa, and a catalyst. Follow directions carefully, which should include the precise ratio of gelcoat to catalyst as well as the acceptable air temperature and humidity in which to work. You'll also need a razor blade, squeegee, sanding block, sandpaper, wax paper, and polishing compound. If the damage exceeds the gelcoat surface and affects the fiberglass backing, also get some strands of fiberglass. If you prefer to have the repair done by a professional, contact a spa-shell refinisher or boat repair firm.

▶ Spa pump doesn't run.

Inspect the electrical panel and switches. Make sure the switch is in the *On* position. If it is, see if the water-pump circuit breaker has tripped; if so, reset it. If it trips again, there is probably a major problem somewhere in that circuit. Don't jam a circuit breaker in the *On* position or bypass it with a pigtail. Deaden the circuit and check all connections and wires for continuity, or call a licensed electrician.

▶ Spa heater doesn't work.

Check the shutoff valve and pilot light (for a gas heater); someone may have turned it off by mistake. If this isn't the problem, check for any loose or disconnected electrical wires leading to a thermostat

Tip *Local codes have specific provisions for security fences to prevent toddlers from wandering into the pool area. Typically, the fence should be a minimum of 48 inches high, have no horizontal bars that facilitate climbing, and surround the pool on all sides that don't adjoin the house. The gate should be self-closing and self-latching. If you have a patio door that opens directly onto the pool area, install a latch high on the door frame, and consider installing a door alarm.*

or control panel. Or call a licensed electrician to troubleshoot the problem.

▶ Spa lacks rigid cover.

You can purchase a rigid spa cover that provides insulation, prevents water and chemical evaporation, keeps small children and pets from falling in, and protects outdoor spas from dirt and debris. Some of the better rigid covers can be locked in place, which provides peace of mind since the spa is childproof when the cover is installed. If well maintained, a rigid cover will last a long time. It must be cleaned inside and out; and if it is made of a hard surface like Centrex® thermoplastic, it must be waxed periodically. If you have just added chemicals to the spa, wait about 30 minutes to an hour before installing the cover to allow some of the vapors to dissipate; if the cover is installed too soon, the inner surface may start to deteriorate.

▶ Spa water level goes down rapidly.

The cause may be a leak in an underground pipe or fitting. Call a leak-detection service, which can trace a water leak without disturbing the ground surface—even under concrete, asphalt, and cement slabs—with its sonar system and ultrasound field tester.

Once the leak is detected, the company will drain the spa and apply a sealant in a flow-coating process that seeks out the leak and seals it off. When the sealant has cured, the spa can be refilled with water.

▶ Backyard pond lacks a circulation system.

Before you build the pond, get a pool skimmer and install it on the inside of a plastic garbage can by cutting a square hole in the can and bolting the skimmer face plate around the opening. Then bury the can next to the pond deep enough that the water level of the pond is about two-thirds of the way up the skimmer opening. Build the pond, draping the liner over the can. Unbolt the skimmer face plate. Insert the liner so that it's sandwiched between the gasket and the can surface. Reattach the skimmer face plate and cut out the liner from the face plate opening. Install a grounded electrical plug near the can. Finally, lower a submersible pump into the can with a return-water line running back to the other end of the pond.

Installing a pond filter

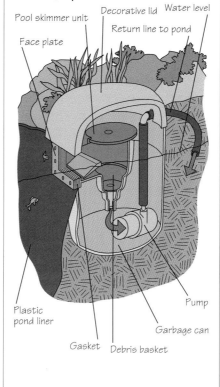

Pool skimmer unit
Decorative lid
Water level
Face plate
Return line to pond
Plastic pond liner
Pump
Gasket
Debris basket
Garbage can

▶ Garden pond has too much algae.

Algae grows where there is abundant sunlight and no competition for nutrients. These conditions are common in early spring, before the water warms up. With warmer weather, however, other plants get established and create shade, stifling algae growth and causing the algae to die and sink to the bottom. If excessive algae persist into the summer, experiment with a balance of surface plants, submerged plants, marginal plants, and fish to keep algae under control. For temporary control use an algaecide. Read labels carefully and choose an algaecide suitable for your pond. Some algaecides are safe for fish but not plants; others are safe for plants but not fish.

▶ Fishpond freezes over.

If a garden pond containing fish is covered by ice for more than a few days, the fish may suffocate. For a quick, emergency fix, clear a breathing hole by boiling water in a pot and setting the pot on the ice until it melts through. Do not try to bash a hole; shock waves may kill the fish.

In mildly cold regions a submerged circulating pump may keep the surface ice-free. The intake port should be close to the bottom, and the discharge outlet 2 to 3 inches below the surface. Another technique for preventing ice is to cover one end of the pond with clear plastic sheeting stretched over a wood frame a few inches above the water.

Where winters are more severe, install a thermostatically controlled deicer or remove fish from the pond and keep them indoors in cool, well-aerated water treated to remove chlorine compounds.

Tip *If you have excess pool chemicals you want to dispose of, there may be local agencies or individuals that could use them. Contact local water treatment or waste treatment plants (for excess chlorine), public swimming pools, apartment or condominium associations, pool services, or pool installers to see if they could use your leftovers.*

The plumbing system in most homes moves water and waste so efficiently that it's easy to take the system for granted. Problems do occur, however, and are often urgent. This chapter covers 130 plumbing problems that you can either solve yourself or diagnose well enough to know when to call for help.

▶ *Plumbing leak is coming from unknown source.*

To fix a leak, you have to find the source. Sometimes this can be a frustrating search, but be persistent and don't dismiss the impossible (for example, water flowing uphill, pipes having invisible cracks, and tile installations not being waterproof). Start your detective work by considering sources other than a leaking pipe. Water that splashes around sinks often works its way down walls or into cabinets. A sink may also have a crack or loose drain fitting that dribbles a hidden stream of water. Tubs and showers are likely sources of leaks, especially at joints along the floor, at joints between the tub rim and walls, and at tiled corners inside a shower stall or tub surround. All of these areas, as well as joints between sinks and walls and around sink faucets, should be sealed with flexible caulk specified for tubs or bathrooms. To apply, first remove old caulk and loose debris; then dry out the joints with a hair dryer or portable heater and apply the caulk according to the manufacturer's instructions. (See page 183.)

If those aren't the sources, and clues point toward a leaky pipe, look for a pattern in the telltale drips, water stains, or musty smells. A steady leak, especially when plumbing fixtures aren't used, is almost certainly from a water supply line and should be repaired immediately (see right). A leak that fluctuates between a trickle and a gush is probably from a leaking drainpipe. You can temporarily stop this type of leak by not using the fixture(s) served by the pipe. If moisture appears only when certain fixtures are used or if the leak dries up when you're away on vacation, the problem is most likely a leaking drain pipe or water being regularly splashed on the floor.

If you still can't verify whether the leak is from a drainpipe or supply line, turn off the main water valve, open faucets in the house to relieve pressure, and let the area around the leak dry out for a while. Then close all faucets and open the main valve. If signs of leakage reappear, you can figure that you have a supply leak because you haven't let any water into the drain system or used any fixtures. You can also detect a supply-line leak, especially one that you may not be aware of (for example, in an underground pipe), by turning off all faucets in the house and then monitoring your water meter for a while (don't forget to turn off an automatic ice maker and other appliances hooked directly to water pipes).

To verify a drainpipe leak: Fill some buckets with water, shut off the main water supply, wait a while, then pour buckets of water down drains near the suspected pipe; watch for signs of leaking after each pour. For ambiguous leaks (such as water on the sidewalk that could be from your drain or your neighbor's), add fluorescent tracer dye (available from plumbing suppliers) to the water before pouring it down drains.

▶ *Supply pipe leaks.*

To temporarily fix a pinhole leak, jam a toothpick into it or tighten a piece of rubber over it with a hose clamp; for cracks or larger holes try wrapping the pipe with electrical tape or resin-coated fiberglass cloth. Another quick fix is a repair clamp. Buy the same size as the leaking pipe (usually ½ inch or ¾ inch), lay the rubber gasket over the leak, and tighten the clamp onto it.

For permanent repairs replace the pipe or fitting or, if it's a small hole, patch it with a dresser coupling. To install a dresser coupling, turn off the water and cut through the pipe at the leak with a hacksaw (if there's no "give" in the pipe you will have to make two cuts—far enough apart to slip the coupling onto one of them but close enough for the coupling body to bridge the gap). Separate the pipes enough to slip the disassembled coupling components, in sequence, onto the cut ends of the pipe. Align the pipe and center the coupling body over the cut(s); then snug the gaskets and retainers into place, screw the nuts onto the coupling body, and tighten them with two wrenches. If you find a leak in a buried pipe, you may be able to patch it, but it could be a sign that it's time to install a new line.

Using a dresser coupling

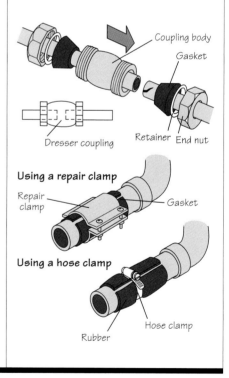

Coupling body
Gasket
Dresser coupling
Retainer   End nut

Using a repair clamp

Repair clamp
Gasket

Using a hose clamp

Hose clamp
Rubber

Tip *Pipes in the drain-waste-vent (DWV) system are 1½, 2, 3, and 4 inches ID (inside diameter). At one time virtually all DWV pipes were cast iron or galvanized steel. More recently, copper pipes were used for the smaller sizes (1½ and 2 inch). Now almost all systems use plastic pipes, either ABS (black) or PVC (white or beige).*

Tip *Supply pipes, which bring hot and cold water to fixtures, are easy to distinguish from drainpipes because they are smaller (usually ½ inch or ¾ inch ID). The hot-water and cold-water pipes are often (but not always) installed parallel to each other, about 8 to 12 inches apart, and don't have to slope downward on horizontal runs as drainpipes do.*

▶ Drainpipe leaks.

Drainpipes can be frustrating to repair because of difficult access, bulky materials, and rigid pipes with no "give" to them. However, the advent of plastic piping and no-hub couplings eases much of the work, and you can take your time because you don't have to shut off the water (although nobody can use fixtures affected by the leak). After you've found the leak (most drainpipe leaks are in joints), remove any ceiling or wall materials necessary to gain full access to it; then warn everyone in the house not to use fixtures that drain into the leaking pipe. If you trace the leak to a bathtub drain, see page 184.

For temporary repairs, seal a leaky joint in cast iron or steel pipe with plumber's epoxy putty (available at plumbing-supply stores). Follow label directions carefully and wear gloves. Use the same putty to patch cracks and small holes in pipe, or cover the hole with a rubber patch cut from an inner tube or similar material. Wrap a piece of sheet metal over the patch and secure it with hose clamps. Seal a leaking joint in plastic pipe with epoxy putty or the bonding solvent used to join plastic pipes. First dry the pipe with a hair dryer or heat lamp. Use solvent specified for the type of plastic—ABS (black pipe) or PVC (white or beige pipe)—and follow directions on the label. Apply a thick layer and press it into the joint with a toothpick. Work quickly and wear gloves.

For permanent repairs, cut out the leaky section of pipe or fittings and replace it with new pipe and fittings. Make cuts where exposed pipe ends will be accessible and will leave room for new pipe to be jockeyed into place. For cutting plastic pipe use a carpenter's handsaw; for copper, a hacksaw; for steel, a reciprocating saw with bimetallic blade; and for cast iron, a pipe snapper (which you can rent) or circular saw with metal-cutoff blade. Make cuts square (mark by wrapping a piece of paper around the pipe and tracing along one edge). After cutting out the leaky section, carefully examine the remaining pipe ends for cracks. If an end is cracked, cut off more pipe (make sure the stub is long enough to fit into the new fitting or coupling).

When measuring for the new pipe and fittings, allow for a ⅛- to ¼-inch gap at each end. To join plastic pipe to fittings, see page 154. To join steel or cast-iron pipe, or to join plastic pipe to either one (or itself), use a no-hub coupling. It has a stainless steel sleeve with a neoprene gasket inside and tightening bands around the outside, and comes in 1½-, 2-, 3-, and 4-inch diameter sizes. Make sure the coupling is specified for the type of pipe you are joining (cast iron, steel, plastic, or copper), which all have different wall thicknesses even though the nominal pipe size is the same. Use a transition coupling for joining two different types of pipe. Tighten any coupling to 60 foot-pounds of pressure (rent or borrow a plumber's torque wrench).

Before positioning pipes for the last joint, slide the stainless steel sleeve of the coupling onto the old pipe; then slip the neoprene gasket onto the pipe until it is halfway on, and roll the loose end back over itself (like rolling a sock inside out). Position the new pipe and secure it at the other end. Then unroll the gasket onto the new pipe and center it over the joint. Slide the sleeve over the gasket and tighten the bands.

If wet spots in your yard make you suspect that you have a leaking sewer line, or perhaps a hole in your septic tank, pick up a bottle of tracer dye at a local plumbing-supply store. Flush some down the toilet and watch for signs of the dye in the yard. If it shows up, you will need to have repairs made on your sewage system right away.

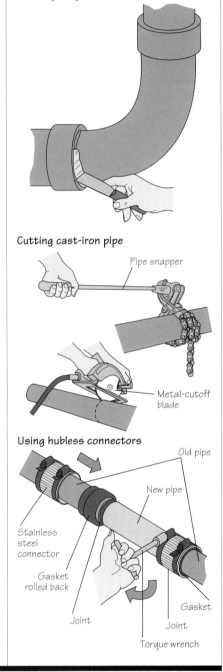

Using epoxy putty

Cutting cast-iron pipe

Pipe snapper

Metal-cutoff blade

Using hubless connectors

Old pipe

New pipe

Stainless steel connector

Gasket rolled back

Joint

Gasket

Joint

Torque wrench

Tip *Terminology for drain-waste-vent (DWV) fittings may seem confusing but is really quite logical.* Couplings *join two pipes of the same size.* Adapters *join fittings and pipes of different sizes or materials.* Elbows, *called ells or bends, are named by their angle or by the fraction of a full circle they turn (for example, a 90-degree bend or quarter bend, a 45-degree bend or eighth bend).* Tees *(T shaped) and* wyes *(Y shaped), which have three openings, are referred to by the size of their openings as well as type of fitting (for example, 2-inch wye). If the opening sizes vary, they are listed in this order: downstream outlet, upstream inlet, branch inlet (for example, a 3X3X2 wye or 2X1½X1½ sanitary tee).*

SOLVING PLUMBING PROBLEMS

▶ *Steel pipe needs replacing.*

Turn off the water supply. Cut through the damaged section and unscrew both sections of cut pipe. Take them to the hardware store or plumbing supplier and buy a union fitting, one short nipple, and a threaded section of pipe long enough so that the new assembly, when tightened, will be the same length as the original section of pipe. If you can't find threaded pipe the right length, you will need to have one cut and threaded. You can rent pipe threaders, but you should be able to get it threaded at a hardware store, at a plumbing supplier, or by a cooperative plumber.

Before screwing a pipe into a fitting, coat the male pipe threads with pipe joint tape or compound. (Do not coat the male half of the union fitting that the ring nut tightens onto.) To assemble, tighten the two halves of the union onto the new pipes. Then slip the ring nut onto the pipe that has the non-threaded union half on it, with the threads of the ring nut facing the union fitting. Screw each pipe into one of the fittings in the water line. You'll have to push the first pipe over slightly to get the second one in; be careful not to loosen any joints. Tighten each joint with two wrenches (one on the pipe, one on the fitting for opposition).

Once the pipes are in place, align them so the union halves mate without binding, spin the ring nut onto its corresponding half of the union, and, with two wrenches, cinch it tight.

▶ *Plastic pipe needs replacing.*

Shut off the water (if a supply pipe) or warn people not to use upstream fixtures (if a drainpipe). You will need to cut out the leaky section of pipe; use a carpenter's handsaw for drainpipes, a hacksaw for supply pipes (smaller diameter). Locate cuts where the remaining pipe ends will be accessible and will allow you to jockey the new pipes into place. On large pipes, to be sure cuts are square, mark cut lines by wrapping a piece of paper around the pipe and tracing along one edge. When measuring between fittings to cut new pipe to length, include the full depth of each hub in your measurement, less ⅛ inch per hub, to make sure "slip-in" dimensions are included. After cutting, sand off any burrs or rough spots.

If the assembly includes bends or tees, dry-fit the pieces together before gluing them to make sure everything aligns. If you're dry-fitting ABS (black) pipe, the pipe will slip only about halfway into each hub when dry (it goes all the way when cemented), so make allowances. PVC (white or beige) pipe will slip into hubs the full distance, with or without solvent cement. With pipes aligned, use a nail to scratch a line across each joint so you can quickly align the pipe and fitting when you glue them together.

When you are sure everything will fit, pull the pieces apart and glue the assembly together, joint by joint. If you are joining PVC pipe, coat each mating surface with primer first, then solvent cement (both specified for PVC pipe). For joining ABS pipe, use just ABS solvent cement (no primer). Use the applicators attached to the can lids and follow all label directions. After coating the outside of the pipe and the inside of the fitting hub with

Replacing leaking pipe

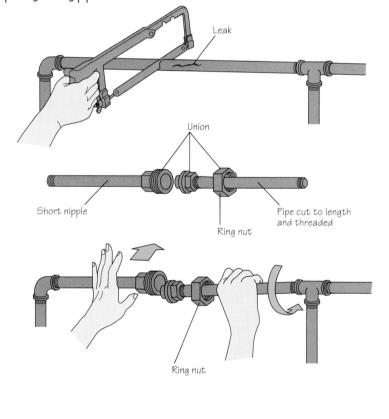

Leak

Union

Short nipple

Ring nut

Pipe cut to length and threaded

Ring nut

Tip *DWV fittings differ from water supply fittings in two important ways. First, fittings that change the direction of flow allow for the slope that horizontal pipes must have. For instance, a 90-degree bend turns slightly more than 90 degrees. Using this fitting to change the direction of flow from vertical to horizontal gives the horizontal pipe a slight downward slope away from the vertical pipe. Using the same fitting to change direction of flow from horizontal to vertical allows the horizontal pipe to slope toward the fitting. The second difference is that tee fittings have the direction of flow built into them: The two openings that form the straight "through" part of the fitting are an inlet and an outlet and must be oriented accordingly. (Vent tees are an exception and can be installed either way.)*

cement, insert the pipe into the fitting and turn it so the scratch marks align; then shove the pipe so it bottoms out in the fitting and hold it until the cement sets. Work quickly; setup time is less than 10 seconds.

If there's not enough flexibility in the drain line to separate pipes far enough to slip them into fittings, use no-hub couplings, at least for the last joint you make (see page 153).

Joining plastic pipe

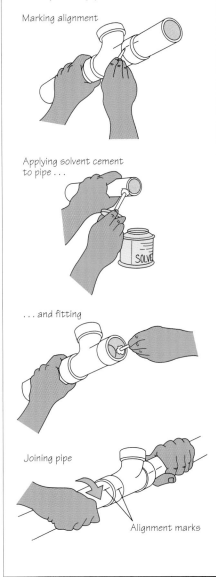

Marking alignment

Applying solvent cement to pipe . . .

. . . and fitting

Joining pipe

Alignment marks

▶ *Soldering copper pipe may present fire hazard.*

The flame from a propane torch can ignite wood framing in a matter of seconds. Be prepared! Keep a fire extinguisher or a spray bottle filled with water close by. Whenever possible, prefabricate assemblies by soldering joints before putting the assembly in place. When soldering joints in place, protect all flammable surfaces with a piece of sheet metal—a double thickness of standard flue pipe works well. You can also buy fireproof pads at a hardware or plumbing-supply store. Make sure you can access the back of the joint as well as the front, and bend the solder into a curve or hook to reach those awkward areas before you start the flame.

▶ *Copper pipe needs replacing.*

For an assured permanent repair to a leaking copper pipe, replace it with new copper tubing. First turn off the water supply or, for a drain-pipe, stop upstream usage. Cut out the leaking section with a tubing cutter or hacksaw. Cut a new piece of the same size tubing to length; include the hub depths of both fittings in your measurement (hub depth equals the nominal size of the pipe—for example, ½ inch or ¾ inch). Using the appropriate fittings, such as a straight coupling or an elbow, dry-fit the assembly to make sure all the pieces fit. If it is a complex DWV assembly, use a nail to scratch a line across each joint so it will be easy to align when you solder it.

To prepare a joint for soldering, shine both mating surfaces so the copper has no oxidation (discoloring) marks: Use sand cloth to shine the end of the tubing, and a fitting brush to scour the inside of the fitting. To be successful, soldering must be done on dry tubing. If

there is any water remaining in the pipe, plug the pipe with a piece of white bread or a dissolvable plug made for this purpose. The bread or plug will disintegrate and pass out of a faucet (you might want to remove aerators until it does).

To solder, spread a small layer of flux on the mating surfaces and assemble the joint. Light a propane torch and heat the fitting uniformly. As you heat, touch the solder against the joint. It will melt and be drawn into the joint when the metal is hot enough; when it starts to melt, remove the flame and run the solder all around the joint, forming a continuous bead. Let the joint cool before touching it or turning the water back on.

Joining copper pipe

Tubing cutter

Brush

Sand cloth

Flux

Flame on fitting

Solder melting into joint

Tip   *Gas lines are always steel, so when you work on a steel water pipe you want to be sure it's not a gas line. The best way to tell is to trace the pipe to a fixture or other known component of the plumbing system. If that's impossible, you certainly know it's a water pipe if water is leaking from it. If there are no active leaks, look for rusty spots near joints. If the pipe is black (ungalvanized) or coated uniformly with rust, it is probably a gas line. However, note that gas lines may have galvanized fittings and even galvanized pipe for short runs. Finally, pipes in pairs indicate water piping for hot and cold water.*

Tip   *Solder with lead in it cannot be used for making plumbing joints. Buy lead-free solder.*

▶ *Pipe is frozen.*

Shut off the water supply to the pipe. Open the nearest faucet to allow melting ice and steam to escape. Using a hair dryer or, on a metal pipe, a propane torch, apply heat to the frozen pipe, starting at the open faucet and working back. (Be careful not to overheat the pipe.) Alternatively, wrap the pipe with electrical heating tape or a securely tied towel and pour hot water on the tape or towel. Once the ice has melted, turn on the water supply, then close the faucet after water flows freely. If freezing persists, insulate the pipe or permanently wrap it with electrical heating tape.

Thawing a frozen pipe

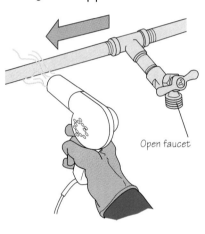

Open faucet

▶ *Fixture has no vent pipe.*

Plumbing codes require that every fixture drain within a specified distance of the fixture trap (P-trap) be connected to a vent pipe that terminates above the roof. The vents have two purposes: to vent sewer gases from the drain/waste system and to equalize pressure in the drain system so water won't siphon out of the fixture trap every time a fixture is used, thereby admitting sewer gases into the house.

If a sink or other fixture drains slowly or periodically releases sewer gas through the drain, it is probably not vented properly. You can tell for sure only by inspecting the drain line behind the wall or under the floor; it should have a vent pipe that branches off from it and eventually terminates above the roof. Consult a plumber to see if a vent pipe is needed and to have one installed. There are strict code requirements governing vents—where and at what angle it should connect to the drain line, what size pipe is required, what fittings are allowed, whether the same pipe can be a vent for one fixture and a drain for another ("wet vent"),

and what type of pipe is allowed if exposed to sunlight and weather.

If you have experience with rough plumbing and want to install a vent yourself, the most difficult part of the job is finding a pathway for a vent configuration that satisfies code requirements. The easiest vent to install is an individual pipe from the fixture all the way to the roof, one size smaller than the drain pipe size, but there may be windows and other obstacles in the way. Look for closets and corners where the pipe could be boxed in. Limit horizontal runs to half the total vertical rise. Horizontal runs should slope ¼ inch per foot back toward the drain. Some local codes

Venting fixtures

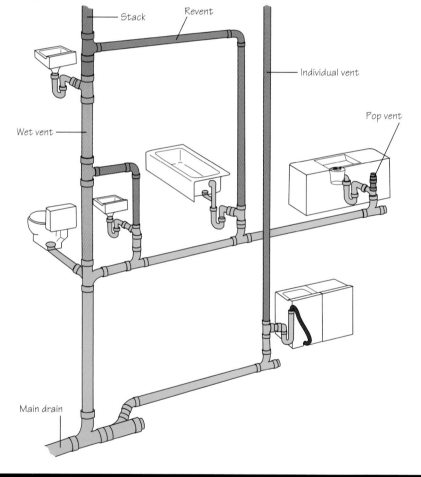

Stack

Revent

Individual vent

Pop vent

Wet vent

Open faucet

Main drain

Tip *An important part of the venting system is the trap that every fixture must have, which functions as a seal to keep sewer gases out of the house. The trap is a semicircular section of pipe that retains a small amount of water after each use of the fixture. Most traps have a horizontal outlet and are thus shaped somewhat like the letter P—hence the term "P-trap." Some, such as sink traps, are visible. Tub and shower traps are located under the floor. Washing-machine traps are located inside the wall above floor level. Toilet traps are integrated into the fixture. Double traps (two traps serving one fixture—for instance, if a trap is plumbed into the waste outlet of a toilet) are prohibited.*

allow vents to be run outside the house. If an individual vent is unworkable and wet-venting is allowed, is there a stack (main vent for house, usually 4-inch pipe) close by that you can tie into? If not, can you "revent" by tying the new vent pipe into a stack above the point where its highest branch drain connects to it? Some codes allow the use of indoor vents, sometimes called "pop vents." These can save you the trouble of having to run a vent up through the roof. Check with the local building-inspection department about these and other requirements before you begin.

▶ Pipes are corroded on outside.

If old galvanized-steel or iron pipe looks corroded but is not leaking, poke at it with an awl or a small screwdriver to see if the walls seem solid. If the pipe seems strong, there's probably no reason to take any remedial action—just keep an eye on the pipes from time to time. If you detect severe corrosion, you can cover the damaged area with plumber's epoxy or a clamp (see page 152), or you can cut out the old pipe and replace it with new (see page 154).

Copper tubing is unlikely to corrode unless the water supply is particularly acidic. If this is the case, keep an eye on the pipes—especially joints—and be prepared to replace leaky copper pipes with plastic supply pipes (PVC for cold water, CPVC for hot) as the need arises. Consult a plumber about replacing all the pipes at once and other remedies.

▶ Vent pipe is frozen or clogged.

As water vapor from draining hot water exits a vent pipe and contacts frigid air, it causes frost and ice to form. On small-diameter vent pipes (1½ and 2 inches), it can build up enough to form ice across the opening. If you can get on the roof, dig out the ice with a stick or chipping tool; if not, look for a cleanout or use the closest plumbing fixture to run a drain auger up the vent. To prevent the problem in the future, have vent "reducers" (they actually enlarge the vent size) installed at the top of small vents. Other clogs, such as bird nests or leaves, should be cleaned out by hand (barbecue tongs work well for reaching down the pipe). Then flush the pipe using a garden hose.

▶ Drainpipe is clogged.

First locate the blockage by noting which fixtures are backing up and tracing the drain system from there. If only one fixture is clogged, the blockage is probably very close to it. First try clearing it with a plunger. If it's a sink or tub, remove the strainer or stopper, and plug the overflow opening with a wet rag. Make sure there's at least a couple of inches of water in the bottom. Coat the bottom of the plunger with petroleum jelly, plunge vigorously, wait, then plunge some more.

The traps on sink drains often have a cleanout plug. If the plunger fails to open the drain, place a bucket under the trap and remove the plug. Use a piece of wire to try to detect a clog in the trap and if so, to break it up.

If the problem persists, try "snaking" the pipes with a drain auger. Push the auger down into the drain until it meets resistance. Tighten the thumbscrew on the crank handle so it's about 1½ inches from the drain hole; rotate

the handle back and forth while pushing it down, until you can push the handle all the way to the drain with no resistance. To determine whether the auger tip broke up the clog or merely turned a tight corner, turn on the water to see if it drains quickly. If so, remove the auger and flush the drain. If not, plunge onward by releasing the thumbscrew and reeling out some more auger until you meet resistance again. Repeat the process until water flows. On tub drains, remove the overflow plate and run the auger down the overflow opening.

If all fixtures are blocked, the clog is probably in the main drain. If upstairs fixtures are blocked and downstairs fixtures aren't, the clog is probably located in an upper portion of the soil stack. Look for a cleanout plug near the affected fixtures. Cleanouts are located at the upstream ends of horizontal runs, usually where a branch drain connects to the main drain. Even if you can't find exposed drainpipes, you may find an exposed cleanout protruding from an exterior wall, in a stairwell, or behind a laundry area. Remove the cleanout plug and try to open the drain using an auger. Have buckets, rags, and newspapers handy. If there is no cleanout near the fixtures, run the auger down the vent pipe or down the drain of the fixture that is farthest downstream of all the affected ones.

Chemical drain cleaners should be used only as a last resort. They are potentially dangerous to the user and if on the first try they don't dissolve the blockage completely, it may harden and won't dissolve again. They work best for periodic cleaning or for clearing pipes that are only slightly blocked. If you must use one, follow directions carefully, and avoid using a

Tip *When buying and installing DWV fittings, pay attention to the direction of flow built into tee and wye fittings. Unlike supply fittings, which are reversible, DWV fittings can be installed backward by mistake.*

SOLVING PLUMBING PROBLEMS

plunger on a drain after you have dumped chemical drain cleaner down it.

If all of this fails to remove the clog, call a plumber or drain-cleaning service. (See also entries for specific fixtures: sink, page 174; bathtub, page 185; toilet, page 189.)

Using a drain auger in a sink

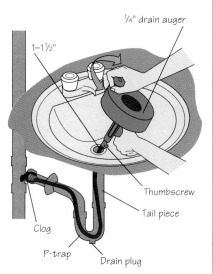

¼" drain auger

1–1½"

Thumbscrew

Tail piece

Clog

P-trap

Drain plug

▶ *Drainpipes are noisy.*

Drainpipes located inside walls and ceilings can transmit the sound of rushing water into adjacent rooms, especially if the pipes are plastic and the walls thin. The remedies are drastic—you will have to open up the walls and either replace the plastic pipes with cast iron or wrap them in sound-absorbing insulating material. It also helps to isolate pipes from the framing with sound-deadening pipe hangers or with cushioning material packed around the holes where they penetrate the framing. Also check any drains where the noise is noticeable

to see if they are properly vented (see page 156). If so, check the vent opening on the roof to see if it is clogged. If that doesn't fix the problem, consult a table of drain and vent sizes to make sure that the drainpipes and connections are properly sized (see page 304).

▶ *Supply pipes are noisy.*

All water pipes create a certain amount of sound when the water is on; it's usually a low murmur (different from the sudden sloshing sound of drainpipes) that is easy to get used to. When pipes are in direct contact with the house framing, this sound is magnified and may become annoying. If so, trace as many water pipes as you can and look for the straps and hangers that secure them to the house framing. Remove old hangers and secure the pipes with plastic or plastic-coated straps and hangers. Where pipes go through holes drilled in the framing, force pieces of insulation, rubber matting, rubber gloves, or other sound-deadening material between the pipe and wood.

Supply pipes make another sound that is much more annoying: "water hammer," a loud hammering noise whenever a faucet is turned off, especially automatic valves in a dishwasher or washing machine. To reduce the sound, first insulate the pipes from the house framing with insulated straps and hangers, and pack insulation between pipes and wood framing. If that doesn't fix the problem, install air chambers at each offending fixture. These are devices installed on the hot- and cold-water pipes that function as shock absorbers to cushion the sudden change in water pressure created by a faucet being turned off. You can make air chambers from pipe one size larger than the supply pipes you are

muffling. Turn off the main water supply and drain the pipes. On a horizontal section of each supply pipe near the fixture, cut out enough pipe to install a tee fitting, pointing up. Attach a short nipple, a reducing coupling, and a 12- to

Insulating pipe from framing

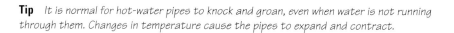

Plastic-coated hanger

Rubber scrap

Plastic strap

Fiberglass insulation

Installing an air chamber or shock absorber

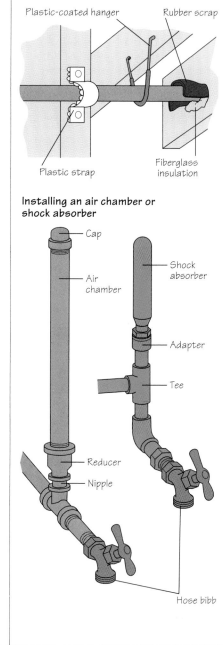

Cap

Air chamber

Shock absorber

Adapter

Tee

Reducer

Nipple

Hose bibb

Tip *It is normal for hot-water pipes to knock and groan, even when water is not running through them. Changes in temperature cause the pipes to expand and contract.*

18-inch length of larger-diameter pipe (this is the air chamber) to the tee. Cap the pipe.

You can also buy water-hammer arresters, or shock absorbers, at a plumbing-supply house. One type is connected to the supply piping, the same way as an air chamber. The other type, which is more expensive but much easier to install, fits between the washing-machine hose and hose bibb. If several fixtures have water-hammer problems, it is due to high water pressure throughout the house. Rather than install several air chambers, a better solution would be to install a pressure-reducing valve near the water meter (see right).

▶ Pipes bang even after air chambers have been installed.

Air chambers act as shock absorbers in pipes. They rely on a cushion of air that is in contact with water under constant pressure. Eventually, the air cushion dissolves into the water. To restore air to the chamber, turn off the main water supply to the house and open all faucets. When the pipes have completely drained, turn off the faucets and turn the water supply back on. with air. If you want to avoid this chore, replace the air chambers with water-hammer arresters, which can't become waterlogged (see opposite page).

▶ Water flow is restricted.

If the problem is not due to chronic low water pressure (see right), check any aerators at the affected faucets to see if they are clogged. If not, and if the fixture has a shutoff valve, turn off the valve, disconnect the supply riser (rigid or flexible tube that connects the shutoff valve to the faucet) from it, and temporarily connect a flexible riser that can be aimed into a bucket. Turn on the shutoff valve and observe the flow of water into the bucket. Test both valves. If water pressure is low, pipes supplying water to the affected fixture are undersized or clogged. They should be at least ½ inch in diameter. If they are old galvanized-steel pipes, they are probably clogged and should be replaced. If the whole house has been hit suddenly with low pressure, suspect a leak in an underground supply line (see page 152).

▶ Water pressure is too low or too high.

If low pressure is a problem throughout the house, it may be completely unrelated to the plumbing in the house. Have the water company come out and check the pressure at the meter. If it tests normal (30 to 55 psi), the problem is in the supply pipes for the house. It could be caused by an undersized feeder pipe from the meter or by clogged pipes. The supply pipe should be at least ¾ inch in diameter, 1 inch if your house is upslope from the street. If you have galvanized-iron water pipes, and especially if your water is "hard," the pipes may be clogged by scale and rust. In this case consider replacing the clogged pipes with copper tubing, which won't clog up like galvanized, and/or upsizing the main supply line. Replacing the pipes involves digging a trench from the water meter to the house foundation, turning off the meter, removing the old pipe, installing new pipe in the trench, and connecting it to the meter and house piping inside the basement or crawl space. If you use copper pipe, check with your local building department to see if Type L or Type K is required, and if underground connections must be made using different soldering techniques from those used above ground. (Silver solder or brazing may be required.)

If the low pressure exists at only one fixture or in one wing of the house, see left.

If the water pressure is too high, it can damage pipes and fixtures. Telltale signs are banging and chattering pipes, spurting water when you turn on a faucet, and excessively forceful water from a faucet only partially opened. To reduce pressure, install a pressure-reducing valve on the house side of the main shutoff valve. Turn off the water supply, cut the pipe, and install the valve as you would a replacement pipe (see page 152). However, you will probably not need to install a union fitting because the valve has coupling nuts at each connection. After you install it and turn on the water, adjust the pressure to between 30 and 45 psi, or until clanging noises in the pipes cease.

Installing a pressure-reducing valve

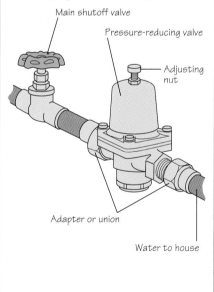

Main shutoff valve

Pressure-reducing valve

Adjusting nut

Adapter or union

Water to house

Tip *After you repair or replace a water pipe, let water run through a nearby faucet for several minutes to flush out any debris that may have been dislodged into the pipes. Remove the aerator from the faucet first.*

▶ *Basement lacks a below-grade drain.*

If you want to install a new bathroom or plumbing fixture in a basement with no drain below the floor, install a sewage ejector or sump pump. Check local code for your exact needs. Normally, a sump pump will be sufficient to dispose of gray water (the waste water from a sink or bath). If the bathroom contains a toilet, you will need a sewage ejector, which is designed to pump solids as well as liquids. In either case the pump requires a pit under the basement floor into which you install an airtight tank. Then run a waste line from the bathroom to the tank, venting it

properly, and a discharge pipe from the tank to the sewer line. This line is plumbed differently from ordinary waste lines because it's under pressure; it must also have a check valve to prevent the waste from flowing back into the tank.

In addition to digging a hole through the basement floor for the sump, you will need to dig a trench for a 4-inch drainpipe. Cutting through concrete will probably require a jackhammer or concrete-cutting saw. Because of the scope of this project and the unusual plumbing requirements, you should consult a plumber before attempting the installation yourself.

Installing a sewage ejector

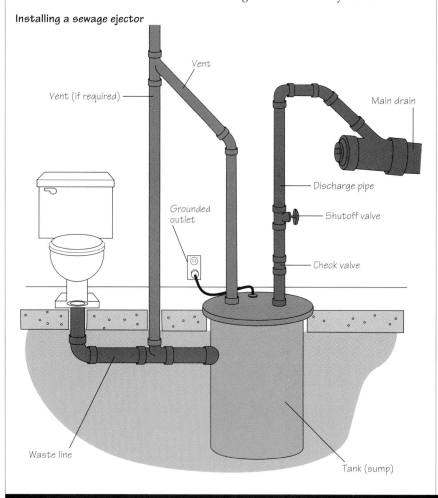

Vent

Vent (if required)

Main drain

Grounded outlet

Discharge pipe

Shutoff valve

Check valve

Waste line

Tank (sump)

▶ *Gas lines emit fumes.*

If you notice a strong gas odor or if your gas detector is going off, open some windows and doors and evacuate the house. Turn off the main gas supply, which should be near the meter on a natural-gas system or on the propane (LP) tank. Call the gas supplier or 9-1-1 from a neighbor's house.

If the gas smell you notice is faint and seems to be limited to certain rooms, check valves and pipe joints around that area by spraying them with a soapy-water solution. If you find some bubbling, carefully tighten the connection with two wrenches, then retest. If the main supply has been turned off recently, it may be that some pilot lights weren't relit and are emitting gas. Check the pilots in all the gas appliances and, after ventilating the room, light any that are off, following instructions on the appliance.

If you have any gas appliances in your house, you should have a gas detector as well. It operates like a smoke detector and will alert the household to a dangerous concentration of natural gas, propane, or carbon monoxide. Contact your gas company for a supplier in your area.

▶ *Gas line has flexible connector in the middle of a run.*

Flexible connectors are generally permitted only at the end of a run to connect an appliance directly to the gas piping (some codes won't allow any flexible gas lines). If you have a flexible line anywhere else, have it replaced with rigid pipe. There are strict requirements for gas piping regarding type of fittings (no unions), size of pipe, length of runs, changes of direction, and the use of certain materials, so have the work done by a qualified professional.

Tip *If you aren't sure whether a pipe is a gas line or water pipe, have someone run hot and cold water at the nearest faucet. Listen to the pipe, holding an empty can or other small container against it to magnify the sound. If it's a water pipe, you should be able to hear running water in it very clearly.*

▶ Gas line has manual shutoff valve in middle of a run.

Gas valves (or cocks) are generally allowed only at the end of a line serving an appliance (except the main valve located at the gas meter). If you have one anywhere else, it should be removed because it presents the possibility of gas being inadvertently turned on and off. Also, valves are not entirely leakproof and become a weak link in an otherwise reliable run of rigid gas piping. To replace a fitting in the middle of a run of threaded pipe means working backward and unscrewing all the connections to that point, or cutting the adjacent piece of pipe to unscrew the valve, then replacing the valve and cut pipe with new fittings. However, plumbing and mechanical codes prohibit the use in gas piping of a union normally used to join threaded water pipes in the middle of a run; a left/right nipple and coupling must be used instead. Because gas piping has stricter requirements than water pipes, have the work done by a qualified professional.

▶ Gas lines are corroded.

Gas lines are most often run with black iron pipe, not galvanized pipe (some fittings and nipples may be galvanized, but pipe for long runs cannot be because the inside has a rough surface that inhibits the smooth flow of gas). Black pipe is susceptible to a little surface rust, which isn't necessarily a problem unless the pipe is in direct contact with the ground. Poke the corrosion with a sharp point; if the corrosion is thick and the pipe seems less than sound, call the gas company or a plumber.

▶ Gas line for a new appliance needs installing.

This work should be done by an expert. Gas lines need to be sized properly. If you were to simply tap into an existing branch line to serve the new appliance, you might overload the line, which could result in the other appliances on that line not working safely. A new line will normally be run from the large-diameter trunk line, but if the trunk line isn't large enough, it will have to be run from the gas meter.

In most areas, homeowners are not allowed to run or service gas lines. Plumbers are permitted to do gas piping in some areas, but not in others. Your gas supplier should be able to inform you.

▶ Gas line is in the way of other work.

If gas piping interferes with some other work (carpentry, plumbing, wiring), try to find some way to re-route the new job. Having to reroute threaded iron pipe, which is what gas piping most often is, can be intensive work. If it is not possible to avoid the piping and it has to be disconnected temporarily or rerouted permanently, the work should be done by a professional. Codes have very strict rules for running gas lines; for instance, they usually won't allow gas piping to run through air ducts, laundry chutes, dumbwaiters, or vents.

All concealed gas lines must be rigid pipe and solid fittings. If you decide to conceal piping that was previously accessible, rather than move it, make sure it is rigid pipe and has no unions, fittings, couplings, bushings, or flexible connectors.

For tying into existing gas lines, there are some restrictions that differ from what is allowed with water piping. For example,

vertical branches run from horizontal pipes should connect to the top of the pipe, not the bottom. A branch that is taken from the side must run at least 6 inches horizontally before dropping from an elbow. Also, if you need to add offsets to the piping to get around an obstacle, it should be made with 45-degree elbows, not 90-degree elbows. This provides for less friction in the gas flow. Other requirements must be observed, but these three examples are most often overlooked, even by professional plumbers.

Changing direction of gas piping

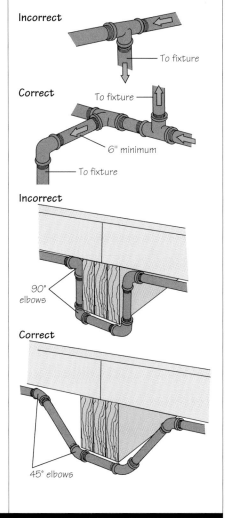

Incorrect

To fixture

Correct

To fixture

6" minimum

To fixture

Incorrect

90° elbows

Correct

45° elbows

Tip   *Threaded pipe and fittings are normally right-handed; that is, they are tightened to the right (clockwise). There are situations with gas piping, however, where left-handed pipe threads or fittings are used. A left/right nipple or a left/right coupling, for instance, has right-hand threads at one end and left-hand threads at the other; when it is turned, both ends tighten or loosen simultaneously. Brass coupling nuts with small notches around the edge indicate left-hand threads; they are often used for connections around LP tanks.*

▶ Scalding water or steam comes out of faucet.

Water heaters are pressurized tanks that can explode. Leave the faucet open to relieve pressure. Immediately turn off the main gas valve for the house (if water heater is gas) or main circuit breaker (if water heater is electric) and get out of the house. Wait at least 15 minutes to re-enter. Shut off the faucet that was steaming. Before restoring gas or electricity to the rest of the house, turn off the gas valve or circuit breaker for the water heater and the shutoff valve on the cold-water inlet pipe above the tank. Then repair or replace the unit, depending on the age of the water heater and type of problem.

With a gas water heater, the scalding water, steam, and excess pressure indicate that the thermostat wasn't turning off the burner. Replace the water heater or have a plumber install a new control unit. Get an estimate first; buying and installing a new tank yourself may be cheaper. With an electric unit, the heating elements didn't shut off in time. The problem could be a faulty upper thermostat and high-temperature cutoff; replace it (see page 168). For either type of heater the TPRV should also be replaced; it should have released steam and scalding water through the discharge pipe before they had a chance to build up in the pipes and faucets (see right).

▶ Temperature-pressure relief valve (TPRV) leaks.

The TPRV is supposed to open in an emergency—that is, when the temperature and/or pressure in the water heater gets dangerously high. If it is constantly dribbling water, the thermostat may be adjusted too high. For a gas unit, turn down the temperature knob on the control unit near the bottom of the heater; for an electric unit, turn down the dial or small screw on the side of the water heater. If water still dribbles from the TPRV, it may be stuck open slightly. To loosen it, lift the lever on top of the valve several times and let some water run out (the discharge pipe should direct it to a sink, drain, or outside). If the problem persists, replace the valve.

To replace a TPRV, first buy a new one that matches the BTU and pressure rating of the original. Shut off the electric power or gas supply and close the cold-water inlet valve. Drain about 10 gallons out of any hot-water faucet. Remove the discharge pipe from the valve and, with a pipe wrench, loosen and remove the valve from the water heater. Coat the male threads of the new valve with pipe joint tape or compound and screw it tightly into the tank. Reattach the discharge pipe (coat the male threads first). Turn on the inlet valve and restore power.

Installing a TPRV and discharge pipe

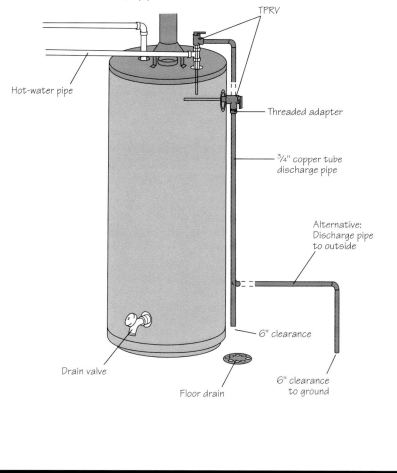

Hot-water pipe

TPRV

Threaded adapter

¾" copper tube discharge pipe

Alternative: Discharge pipe to outside

6" clearance

Drain valve

Floor drain

6" clearance to ground

Tip *In a home with young children or elderly adults, set the water-heater thermostat to 120° F to prevent accidental scalding.*

Tip *Test the TPRV every six months by lifting the lever and letting some water run out. If, when you lift the lever, no water comes out, tap on the valve lightly with a hammer and try again. If that doesn't fix the problem, replace the valve right away. Water heaters lacking TPRV valves or with nonfunctioning ones have been known to explode, sending the tank up through the roof like a rocket.*

▶ *Tank leaks.*

To find the source of the leak, check and tighten all connections (cold- and hot-water pipes, drain valve, anode rod, TPRV, thermostat, heating elements). If a leaking drain valve is brass, replace the stem washer or packing washer (see page 170). If it is a plastic dough-nut-shaped knob, replace the valve (see next paragraph). For leaks at threaded fittings, remove the fit-ting, clean it, wrap it with pipe joint tape, and then reinstall. If the threads appear damaged, replace the fitting or pipe (see page 154).

To replace the drain valve, the tank doesn't have to be drained but the pressure must be removed from the tank. Close the cold-water inlet valve and open any hot-water faucet just long enough to let water flow. Shut it off and make sure no one uses any water while you work. Turn off electric power or turn the gas control to *Pilot*. Place a pan under the valve and unscrew it. Wrap pipe joint tape around the nipple on the water tank, then screw on the new valve.

If water is leaking through the tank itself, pronounce the tank dead and replace it as soon as possible.

▶ *Tank hasn't been drained in six months.*

A water heater should be drained regularly to prevent sediment from accumulating on the bottom of the tank, which shortens the life of the heater. One good strategy is to drain off 1 gallon every month. Some recommend that the tank be completely flushed every six months; this requires turning off

the inlet valve and draining the tank completely, then turning on the inlet valve while the drain hose is connected and running water through the tank at full force.

To drain a heater tank, shut off the cold-water inlet valve and the source of power—for an electric heater shut off the circuit breaker; for a gas heater turn the burner control to *Pilot*. Open the hot-water faucet that is at the highest level in the house, and leave it open. Screw a garden hose onto the drain valve at the bottom of the water heater and run it outside or to a drain. Open the valve. If the heater is in a basement and there is no drain, you will have to drain it off one bucket at a time.

To flush the tank after it's drained, keep the drain valve open and open the cold-water inlet valve for a couple of minutes to give the bottom of the tank a good flushing.

Close the drain valve and let the tank fill; keep the upstairs faucet open until water comes out of it for a few minutes to purge all the air from the pipes. Turn off the faucet and start up the water heater.

If sediment buildup is a com-mon problem with your heater or in your neighborhood, replace the straight dip tube in the heater with a curved one. This will force the incoming water to swirl around the bottom of the tank, flushing it out when the drain valve is opened. To replace the tube, turn the con-trol knob to *Off*; shut off the cold-water inlet valve and drain off a few buckets of water from the drain valve. Then disconnect the pipe or fitting from the cold-water inlet and pull out the plastic dip tube. Replace it with a curved one, then reassemble the inlet fitting. There

are also chemical products that can help remove certain kinds of sedi-ment. Check with the water-heater manufacturer for recommendations.

Replacing a dip tube

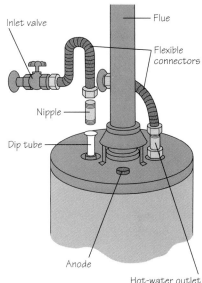

Inlet valve — Flue

Flexible connectors

Nipple

Dip tube —

Anode

Hot-water outlet

▶ *Hot water is rusty.*

There are several possible causes. First check the water coming into the tank by closing the inlet valve, disconnecting the pipe from the tank, and capturing a few buckets of water from the inlet pipe. If it's rusty, the problem is rusty water supply lines; have them replaced. If the water is slightly rusty but not as much as the hot water is, the anode in the water heater may have deteriorated and is no longer able to clear mineral deposits from the water. Check it and, if it is worn, replace it (see page 163). If the water is still rusty, the glass lining in the

Tip   *If water is leaking from a plastic drain valve—a common occurrence—consider replacing it with a ³⁄₄-inch ball valve or hose bibb, which will assure you of a sound fit and easier maintenance.*

Tip   *A clue that sediment has accumulated in an electric water heater is if the lower heating element burns out. A clue for a gas heater is if the burner remains on for excessively long periods of time; the sediment creates a barrier between the water and the flame, which slows down heating.*

tank may have deteriorated—especially if the water heater is quite old. To check, drain a few buckets of water from the drain valve and compare it with hot water from a faucet. If the tank water is as rusty as, or more rusty than, the faucet water, the tank lining has worn through; replace the water heater. If the tank water is less rusty than the faucet water, and the hot-water pipes are galvanized steel, the pipes are probably deteriorating and need to be replaced. Finally, certain bacteria ("iron bacteria") in the water can also give it a rusty appearance. Have the water tested.

▶ Hot water has a strange odor or taste.

If there is a taste of plastic in the water, it may be due to a deteriorating plastic dip tube; replace it. Another cause might be sediment accumulating on the bottom of the tank. If you suspect this, drain and clean the tank (see page 163).

▶ Hot water takes too long to reach faucet.

First make sure that the hot-water pipes are thoroughly insulated.

If the problem is confined to a single bath or shower located far from the water heater, the best solution is to have a small 4- to 10-gallon electric heater installed at the point of use. A 120-volt heater can be plugged into normal household current, and it will supply hot water where you want it, when you want it.

If there are several remote locations, it might be more cost-effective to have a recirculating loop installed that constantly runs hot water to the remote locations and back to the water heater, or have a plumber run small-diameter pipes directly to each point of use rather than a main line with branches. This will reduce the volume of water in the plumbing and speed up the arrival of hot water. Consult a plumber about these options.

▶ Recirculating system is using too much energy.

A recirculating system provides instant hot water at the faucets. It eliminates water waste, but it requires the water heater to heat water more often, and most systems have a small circulating pump that runs constantly. You can control energy usage by installing a timer to shut the pump off when it's not needed and/or a thermostat to control water temperature in the loop. Consult a plumber.

▶ Water heater uses too much energy.

First turn the thermostat down to 120° F. If your dishwasher requires 140° F, consider installing a small point-of-use water heater for the dishwasher. Note that many newer dishwashers are sold with their own built-in water heaters, allowing you to keep the household water heater at a lower temperature. Next drain the tank if that hasn't been done in six months or more, and check the pipe connections and bottom of the tank carefully for leaks.

Insulate the water heater and the hot-water pipes. Ready-made blankets are sold to fit over water heaters specifically for this purpose. Insulate pipes with closed-cell foam insulation, which can be bought preslit and is easy to install. Just make sure you get the right size for your pipes; most are ½ inch or ¾ inch.

Add low-flow showerheads and faucet aerators.

If you have an electric heater, you can install a timer, which will run it during less expensive, off-peak hours. Check with the local electric company for details.

If you use a lot of hot water at a point far from the heater, install a point-of-use water heater there, or have a recirculating loop installed if it can be done efficiently.

Next time you have to replace your water heater, buy an energy-efficient unit. Study the labels on the sides. If you buy a tank that has been insulated to R-16 or more, you won't have to add an insulation blanket after it's installed. If your water comes from a well, consider installing a holding tank, in which the water can warm up before going to the heater.

Installing insulation on a gas water heater

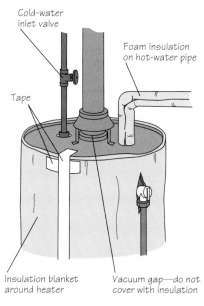

Cold-water inlet valve

Foam insulation on hot-water pipe

Tape

Insulation blanket around heater

Vacuum gap—do not cover with insulation

Tip *Check the anode rod of your water heater every three or four years—more often if you have particularly hard, softened, or acidic water. This is a "sacrificial" rod that is intended to deteriorate over time so that the tank doesn't. If the anode is corroded, replace it by shutting off the power, closing the water inlet valve, draining a few gallons of water from the tank, unscrewing the rod from the top of the tank, and screwing in a new one.*

Tip *When insulating a gas water heater, consult the manufacturer's recommendations. Some prohibit the use of insulating blankets on certain models. In all cases, never cover the vent on the top, the air intake on the bottom, or the temperature-pressure relief valve.*

▶ Pilot light won't light or goes out.

If it won't light, check the gas supply (valves are open, propane tanks aren't empty). If there is no supply problem, the pilot line may be clogged. To check it, turn off the gas supply, remove the pilot burner assembly, and run a thin wire through the line. If the pilot still won't light, the problem is in the gas supply line or the automatic control valve. Call a plumber.

If you can light the pilot but, when you release the gas control valve after holding it down for at least one minute, the pilot doesn't stay lit, the thermocouple is not transmitting heat to the automatic valve that regulates the flow of gas to the pilot light and burner. First see if the tip of the sensor is completely surrounded by the pilot flame. If not, with pliers bend the bracket that holds the sensor so that it is centered in the pilot flame. If the pilot still won't stay lit, replace the thermocouple.

First turn off the gas supply. With two wrenches, unscrew the nuts that hold the thermocouple to the burner bracket and the control unit (you may have to remove the whole burner assembly to access the burner bracket). Remove the thermocouple and install the new one in the same way; make sure it's the right one for your water heater. Light the pilot while pushing on the pilot button (see right). Then check that the thermocouple is properly aligned with the flame. After a minute or two, release the pilot button and turn the gas control valve from *Pilot* to *On*.

If you can light the pilot successfully but it goes out frequently, check for drafts along the floor and seal them off. There may also be dirt in the thin tube that supplies gas to the pilot, causing the pilot flame to burn low and go out easily. Clean out the blockage with a thin wire, as described. A low flame may also be caused by insufficient pressure in the gas lines. The gas company should be called to check this.

Clearing pilot supply line

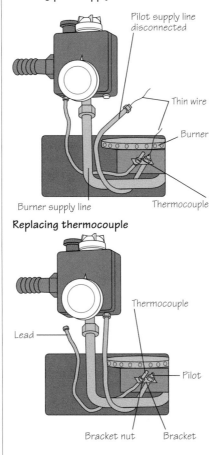

Pilot supply line disconnected

Thin wire

Burner

Burner supply line

Thermocouple

Replacing thermocouple

Thermocouple

Lead

Pilot

Bracket nut   Bracket

▶ Gas burner will not fire.

Make sure the pilot is lit, then turn the temperature knob to the highest setting. If the burner does not fire, the gas supply doesn't have enough pressure to activate the automatic control valve, or the thermostat is defective. Make sure the gas shutoff valves for the water heater and the house are fully open (handles parallel with pipes). If they are, the gas flow may still be impeded by dirt in the burner line or orifices. Shut off the gas, remove the burner, and clean out the supply tube and orifices with a piece of soft copper wire (see page 166). If the burner still doesn't fire, the thermostat in the control valve is probably not functioning. Call a plumber and get an estimate; it may be more economical to replace the whole water heater than to have it repaired.

▶ Gas water heater isn't heating the water.

First see if the pilot light is lit. If not, relight it following the instructions on the tank. (For models with electronic ignition, see below.) If you can't get a flame at the pilot light, check the gas shutoff valve for the water heater and the main shutoff valve for the house to be sure they are open (the handles should be parallel to the pipes). If gas supply is propane, check the gauge on the tank to make sure it isn't empty. If the pilot won't stay lit, the orifice may be clogged. Turn off the pilot, let it cool, and carefully clean out the tip with a toothpick, old toothbrush, or thin wire. If that doesn't fix the problem, replace the thermocouple (see left).

If the pilot light is on and the water doesn't heat up, check to make sure that the control knob is turned to *On*, not *Pilot*. Also turn up the temperature-control knob. If neither of these start the burner, the burner fuel line or ports may be clogged (see left), or the thermostat in the automatic control valve may be faulty (call a plumber).

If the gas heater has electronic ignition instead of a pilot light

Tip *Newer, more efficient gas water heaters have electronic ignition devices instead of pilot lights. You can tell by looking inside the burner compartment (use a flashlight): a pilot light has a small fan-shaped hood that emits a steady flame; an electronic ignition device is contained in a small box with electrical wires attached.*

Tip *The temperature settings on thermostats aren't always accurate. The best way to measure how hot the water is getting is to run hot water out of a faucet near the water heater, fill a glass, and then quickly test the temperature with a thermometer that goes up to 180° F, such as a meat or confection thermometer.*

(which you can identify by a conspicuous box-shaped device on the side of the tank or in the burner chamber, or by checking the printed instructions to make sure there is no mention of lighting a pilot), you will have to have the unit replaced. Call a plumber.

Identifying water heater components

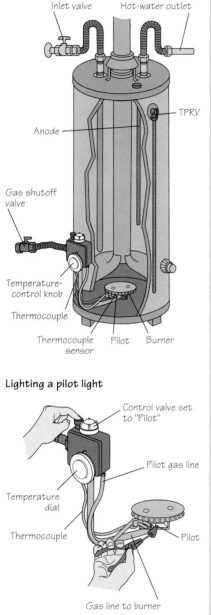

Lighting a pilot light

▶ Gas water heater makes water too hot or too cool.

Turn the temperature-control knob higher or lower to adjust the temperature. Experiment with slight increments over the course of several days. For most conditions 120° F will be adequate. If you want the water hotter but it fails to reach at least 140° F, even at the highest setting, the tank may have sediment on the bottom or the water may be cooling off in the pipes because of inadequate insulation or excessively long runs (see page 164). Also make sure that all valves to and from the water heater are open fully. If the tank is located outdoors or in an un-heated space, it should have an in-sulating blanket and insulated pipes (unless it's a newer model that should not be covered by a blanket).

Adjusting temperature knob

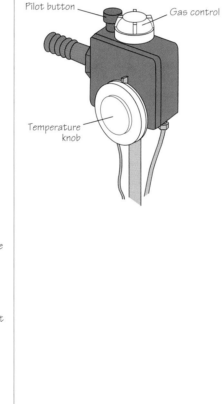

▶ Gas water heater doesn't provide enough hot water.

Check the temperature knob or measure the temperature of the hot water (see page 165). Perhaps a setting of 120° F is too low, in which case set the temperature to 130° F or even 140° F. Check the holding size of the water heater. A 40-gallon gas heater will satisfy the requirements of most families, but large households or unusually high hot-water needs may require a larger tank. Also make sure that hot-water pipes are well insulated, especially on long runs.

Perhaps you are just wasting too much hot water. Make sure that you don't have any leaking hot-water faucets. The dip tube may have fallen or corroded. This plastic tube hangs down inside the tank directing the incoming cold water to the bottom of the tank so that it doesn't mix with (and thereby cool) the heated water at the top of the tank. Many a water heater has been replaced simply because this inexpensive element was broken. To check, shut off the cold-water inlet valve and then disconnect the inlet below the valve. Remove the dip tube (or what is left). If it's not intact, replace it with a new plastic one, or have your plumber make a more durable copper dip tube by flaring one end so it will seat in the inlet opening and not fall through the hole. See page 163.

The burner may not be burning at full capacity due to clogged orifices. Observe the burner in oper-ation. If you see weak or broken flames, shut off the heater, wait for it to cool (or wear oven mitts), and

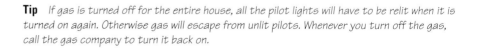

Tip *If gas is turned off for the entire house, all the pilot lights will have to be relit when it is turned on again. Otherwise gas will escape from unlit pilots. Whenever you turn off the gas, call the gas company to turn it back on.*

clean out the clogged orifices with a thin wire (you may have to remove the burner); or call the gas company for service.

If you get your water from a well, the problem may be due to a very cold source of water, which forces your water heater to work overtime and perhaps fail to keep up with household demand. If this is the problem, you can install a holding tank between the well and the water heater inside the house that allows the water to warm up before it reaches the water heater.

Cleaning burner orifices

Wire

Burner

Pilot

Thermocouple

Gas supply

▶ Gas water heater makes strange noises.

Sizzling or popping noises are caused by drops of water falling on the burner. First check the sides of the tank for condensation; it can form on the outside of a tank if the water is cool enough, such as when the tank fills rapidly after all the hot water has been used. This is a temporary condition that will stop after the water heats up. If the sound persists, check for leaks (see page 163).

If the water heater sounds as if rocks are being shattered inside when it fires up, the bottom of the tank has a layer of minerals and sediment that have accumulated and hardened over the years. Although the sediment buildup has an insulating effect that compels the burner to stay on longer, the problem is not as serious as it is loud, and there is little you can do about it. When sediments have built up to this extent, they are too solid to be flushed out. You can, however, slow down the natural buildup by flushing out the water heater every six months (see page 163). When you replace the tank with a new one, it will have an anode that also helps to control sediment buildup.

▶ Gas water heater emits fumes or strange odors.

The flue may be clogged or broken. While the water heater is on, hold a smoking match or candle near the vacuum gap (draft diverter or flue hat) on the water heater. If smoke is drawn into the flue, the flue is fine; the fumes are most likely caused by inefficient operation of the burner due to low air supply or low gas pressure. Call the gas company. But if smoke is pushed away, the flue is not drawing properly and fumes are being backdrafted into the house. The flue may be blocked or

have too many turns—have it inspected by a heating contractor; or the house has negative air pressure due to tight insulation and poor ventilation (see pages 260 and 261).

If you smell fumes around a gas water heater, coat the connections with soapy water; you will see bubbles if there is a gas leak. If there is, carefully tighten the connection with two wrenches and check again, until no bubbles form. If tightening doesn't stop the leak, shut off the gas at the water heater valve or house shutoff valve, depending on where the leak is. Disconnect the pipes and coat the male threads with pipe joint compound specified for gas lines; then reassemble and tighten the connections. If you turned off the gas at the heater, turn it back on. If you turned it off at the main house valve, call the gas company to turn it back on. If there are no leaks, light the pilot. *Note:* Do not coat pipe threads of compression fittings, which are part of flexible gas connectors and consist of a brass coupling nut that tightens onto a threaded brass fitting with a rounded tip.

Testing for backdrafting

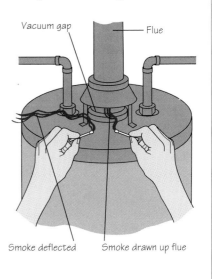

Vacuum gap

Flue

Smoke deflected

Smoke drawn up flue

▶ Electric water heater makes strange noises.

Scale buildup on electric heating elements can cause noise. Check and clean the elements, if necessary, by turning off the power to the heater, draining the water, removing the elements, soaking them in vinegar, and removing the scale with a soft brush. If the noise is a chattering thermostat, replace the thermostat. For other noises, see page 167.

▶ Electric water heater doesn't provide enough hot water.

Check the size of the tank; a 50-gallon electric heater will satisfy the requirements of most families, but large households or unusually high hot-water needs may require a larger tank.

If you suddenly start running out of hot water sooner than you used to, the cause may be a burned-out lower heating element due to sediment piling up around it in the tank. This can and does happen even on tanks that are "glass lined." You will have to drain the tank and replace the heating element. (See right and page 166.)

▶ Electric water heater makes water too hot or too cool.

Most electric heaters have two thermostats, an upper and a lower, controlling two heating elements. On some newer heaters, the upper thermostat can't be adjusted; instead it is preset at 120° F and will shut down if water exceeds 190° F. Once shut off, it can be reset by pushing the reset button. If it keeps kicking off, the heater is consistently overheating the water; the upper thermostat is defective and should be replaced. If the water is getting much too hot, perhaps with steam coming out of the faucet, see page 162.

If water is not hot enough, first check all valves to and from the water heater to make sure that they are fully open. Then try adjusting both thermostats to a higher temperature. On a dual-element water heater, one of the heating elements may be defective. If the water won't heat up sufficiently, the upper is probably at fault; if it heats up but not for long, the lower is at fault. See right for instructions for testing and replacing an element or for replacing a thermostat.

Scale from mineral deposits may also build up on heating elements, causing them to overheat. If you remove the elements and find some scale on them, soak them in vinegar and use a soft brush to remove the scale. Scale buildup on the elements can indicate that you need a new anode. (See pages 163 and 166.)

Adjusting a thermostat

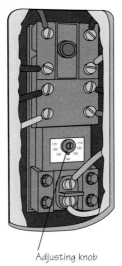

Adjusting knob

▶ Electric water heater isn't heating water.

First check for a tripped circuit breaker or blown fuse; if that is the problem, reset the circuit breaker or replace the fuse. If the breaker trips or fuse blows again, have an electrician determine the cause.

If the power is OK, push the reset button on the water heater, which cuts off power when the temperature exceeds a certain limit, usually 190° F. To gain access to this button you may have to remove the cover panel and push insulation aside. If so, *turn off the power first!* Wire terminals will be exposed, with the potential of a 240-volt shock if the two feeder terminals are touched simultaneously.

If the heater works somewhat but not at full capacity, one of the two heating elements has failed. If there is no heat, the water heater is most likely an old style with a single heating element that has failed. In either case the heating elements need to be tested and, if necessary, replaced. If the heater works temporarily, then shuts off again, the thermostat is defective and should be replaced (see opposite page).

To test the heating elements, turn off power to the heater. Remove the panel cover and push aside any insulation to expose the thermostat and heating-element terminals. *Avoid touching wires or screw terminals until you have tested all combinations—especially the two wires at the top of the upper thermostat—with a voltage tester to be absolutely certain that power is shut off.* To locate the heating-element terminals, look for the large tightening nut (some models have four small bolts instead) with two wire terminals attached. Disconnect

Tip *An electric water heater is a 240-volt appliance and can deliver a fatal shock from exposed wires. Be absolutely certain that the power is off before you work on it. Post a warning sign on the circuit breaker or lock the breaker panel box so somebody won't inadvertently reset the breaker.*

the wires from the terminals and, with a continuity tester or volt-ohmmeter (set at 4 × 1 ohms resistance), touch the probes to the two terminals of each element, in turn. If an element shows no electrical continuity, replace it. If it shows continuity, repeat the test (with the ohm setting at 4 × 1000), this time touching one probe to the tank side or a bolt attached to the tank, and the other probe to each terminal, in turn. If there *is* continuity on this test, the element has a short and should be replaced.

To replace an element, drain the tank (see page 163). Unscrew the tightening nut with a pipe wrench (or remove the bolts securing a mounting flange) and pull out the element carefully. The replacement should be identical. Coat the new gasket on both sides with pipe joint compound; carefully thread the new element through it, and tighten the bolt (or bolts) to the tank. Connect the wires, set the temperature, restore the power and the water supply, and press the reset button.

To replace a thermostat, make sure the power and water are shut off; then remove the panel cover and push the insulation out of the way. Remove wires from the screw terminals. Loosen the bracket bolts and lift the thermostat out of the bracket, or clip. Slip the new one into the clip and reconnect the wires. Then set the temperature, turn on the water, restore power, and press the reset button.

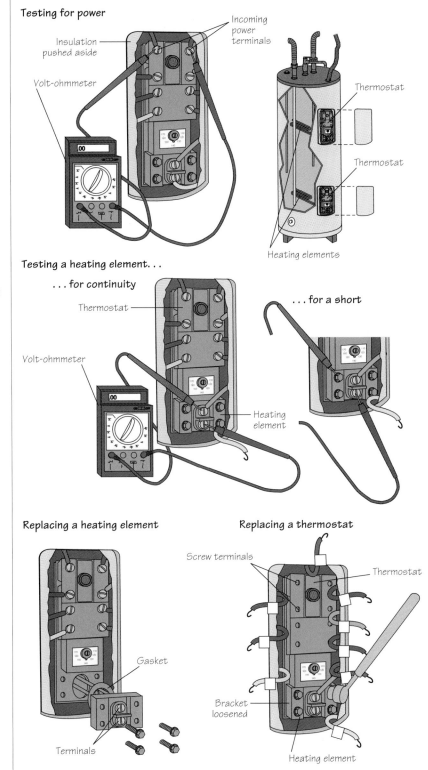

Testing for power

Testing a heating element. . .

. . . for continuity

. . . for a short

Replacing a heating element

Replacing a thermostat

Tip *Before disconnecting any wires, draw a color-coded sketch of which wires go where and use the sketch to assist you in reconnecting the wires.*

SOLVING PLUMBING PROBLEMS

▶ Faucet drips or won't shut off.

Different types of faucets require different repair techniques (see right). Buy replacement parts and kits for only your specific brand and model. Many repair kits will contain specialized tools needed to disassemble the faucet. The kit will probably include more parts than you intend to replace, such as washers and gaskets; always replace all parts included in the kit. If you take the faucet apart before buying any replacement parts, take the assembly with you to the hardware store or plumbing supplier.

Begin by closing both shutoff valves (also called angle stops) below the sink. Some water will remain trapped in the faucet and supply risers, so have a bucket and rags available before you start to work. Cover the drain and clear off enough counter space so you can set down the parts in order. Work slowly and study how each part is positioned before you disassemble it; if you don't trust your memory, make a sketch of each part as you remove it. When using metal tools on a polished surface, protect the surface with a rag or several layers of tape. Remove all grit and debris from faucet parts as you work.

▶ Faucet leaks around handle stem.

This problem is restricted to compression (washer-style) faucets. Depending on the specific type, replace the packing washer, O-ring, or packing string wrapped around the stem. See below.

▶ Compression (washer-style) faucet drips or won't shut off.

First see left. Remove the handle screw (it may be hidden under a decorative cap or behind the handle), and pull the handle off the valve stem. If it is stuck, don't force it off by prying; use a faucet handle puller, available from a hardware or plumbing store. Next, with an adjustable wrench or pliers, unscrew the nut or nuts holding the valve stem and lift the stem out. Replace the washer and screw at the end of

Repairing a compression faucet

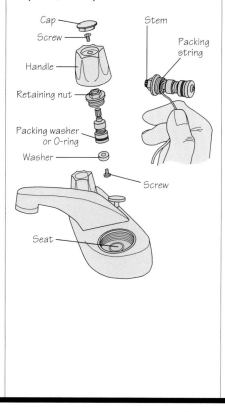

- Cap
- Screw
- Handle
- Retaining nut
- Packing washer or O-ring
- Washer
- Stem
- Packing string
- Screw
- Seat

the stem; tighten the new screw firmly. If the holding cup (recessed end of valve stem that holds the washer) is broken, buy a replacement valve stem or file off the cup and buy an appropriate replacement assembly. Before reassembling the faucet, feel the valve seat for pits, cracks, and wear. If it is damaged, remove the seat with a valve-stem wrench or allen wrench and replace it. Reassemble the valve. The spout may still drip until the washer has had a few days to work in. *Note:* Some compression faucets have a cartridge assembly that contains the washers and moving parts. Simply replace the whole assembly.

▶ Ball faucet drips or won't shut off.

First see left. With an allen wrench loosen the setscrew on the handle and remove the handle. Slightly loosen the adjusting ring on top of the dome-shaped cap to relieve pressure from the internal ball mechanism (a special wrench is provided with the manufacturer's repair kit). Unscrew the cap (with the adjusting ring still attached), remove the plastic cam holding the ball in place, then the gasket and ball. Use needle nose pliers to gently lift out the small rubber seals and springs that were under the ball. Remove any loose debris and put replacement springs and sleeves back into the seats. While you're at it, lift off the spout and replace the two O-rings. Remove the old rings with a sharp knife, being careful not to scratch the metal faucet body; apply a light coating of valve grease to the new rings before installing them. Reassemble the faucet and tighten the adjusting ring just enough to prevent leaks with-

Tip *To drain water out of a faucet before working on it: (1) shut off the main house valve, (2) open both the hot and cold sides of the faucet, (3) find another nearby faucet lower than the faucet you're working on, (4) open the other faucet for a short time to allow the faucet you're working on to empty, (5) shut off all faucets, (6) close the shutoff valves below the sink, and (7) turn the main house valve back on. Now you're ready to work.*

Tip *While you're at it, replace the washers for the other side (hot or cold) of the faucet.*

out making the handle difficult to operate. Leave the handle half open and turn the shutoff valves (angle stops) back on. Let the water run for a few seconds before shutting off the faucet.

Repairing a ball faucet

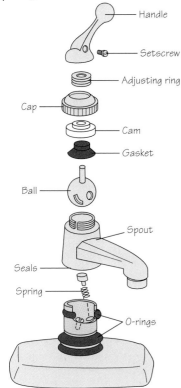

Handle

Setscrew

Adjusting ring

Cap

Cam

Gasket

Ball

Spout

Seals

Spring

O-rings

▶ Cartridge faucet drips or won't shut off.

First see opposite page. Pry off the handle cap with a small screwdriver. Remove the exposed screw, handle, and handle assembly, then remove the spout (you may first need to remove a retaining nut or retaining ring with pliers). If the faucet has a sprayer, there will be a collar-shaped diverter beneath the spout housing; remove it. Next use needle nose pliers to pull out the horseshoe-shaped clip that holds the cartridge

in place. Remove the cartridge by pulling up on it firmly with pliers (you may need a special puller made by the faucet manufacturer, often included in the replacement kit). Flush out any debris from the faucet body, then apply a light coat of valve grease (included with the repair kit) to the new cartridge and push it into the faucet body firmly, compressing any trapped air. Make sure the notch in the stem faces the sink. Use the retaining clip to secure the cartridge. While you're at it, replace the faucet O-rings with new O-rings provided in the kit. Remove the old rings by cutting them with a sharp knife (don't scratch the metal faucet body). Then reassemble the faucet.

Repairing a cartridge faucet

Cap

Handle assembly

Retaining pivot nut

Cartridge

Spout

Retaining clip

Faucet body

O-rings

▶ Ceramic-disk faucet drips or won't shut off.

First see opposite page. Although this type of faucet has a replaceable disk assembly that may become worn, the cause of most leaks is worn rubber (neoprene) seals located under the disk assembly. Find the setscrew in the handle, which may be hidden under a cover, loosen it, and lift off the handle. Remove the escutcheon, cap, or retainer ring. Then remove the disk assembly as a unit by unscrewing the mounting screws and pulling it out; turn it over and remove the rubber seals. Clean the inlet holes and filter cones (if included), flush out all debris, install new seals, and reassemble the faucet. Leave the handle half open when you turn the angle stops back on and let some water flow before turning off the faucet. If the faucet still leaks, replace the disk assembly with a new one.

Repairing a ceramic-disk faucet

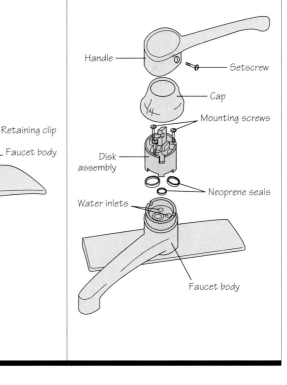

Handle

Setscrew

Cap

Mounting screws

Disk assembly

Neoprene seals

Water inlets

Faucet body

Tip *If you aren't sure which type of faucet you have, here's how to tell: If the faucet has separate handles for hot and cold, it is compression or ceramic disk. Compression faucets require several turns of the handle and tighten gradually. Ceramic-disk faucets, which are more modern, require only a quarter turn and shut off abruptly. Single-handle faucets are cartridge, ball, or ceramic disk. Cartridge faucet handles slide outward as well as rotate to the right or left. Ball and ceramic-disk handles rotate but don't slide. Handles of ball faucets usually have a wider range of travel than ceramic-disk handles. Once you remove the handle, you can tell the difference immediately. Single faucets, such as hose bibbs, are the compression type.*

▶ Faucet is noisy.

Whistling, rattling, or vibrating noises that you can trace to the faucet itself are caused by loose or misaligned parts. Disassemble the faucet (see pages 170 and 171) and restore or replace any loose parts. Noises not from the faucet itself, such as banging that occurs when you shut off the faucet or loud humming within the walls or floor, are caused by poorly secured or insulated pipes, excessively high water pressure, the absence of air chambers near the suspect faucets, or air chambers that have become waterlogged (see page 158).

▶ Water flow is restricted.

Make sure the shutoff valves (angle stops) below the sink are open. If they are, the problem is probably a clogged aerator. Unscrew the aerator from the spout; to get a grip on it, use rubber gloves or pliers (with tape or a rag around the jaws to protect the finish). Run the faucet without the aerator to see if the pressure is adequate. If it is not, you will need to investigate further. In either case flush out the aerator parts; be sure to keep the parts in order. Remove all debris, using a fine needle if necessary. If the parts look damaged or hopelessly clogged, buy a new aerator.

If a clogged aerator wasn't the problem, get under the sink with a flashlight and inspect the bottom of the faucet. Some models have copper inlet tubes that constrict easily if they are kinked. If a tube is kinked, close the shutoff valve (in case the tube comes loose as you work on it) and carefully straighten the kink with your hands. Then squeeze the sides of the kink with pliers to restore the tube to full roundness. Turn the water back on and check.

If the problem was not kinked tubing, check for blockage within the faucet itself. Close the shutoff valves and disassemble the faucet (see pages 170 and 171). Look for trapped debris or misaligned parts, make adjustments, and reassemble the faucet.

Finally, if none of the above works, the problem is blockage within a shutoff valve, supply tube, or pipe. If the problem is restricted to just hot water or just cold water, close that shutoff valve and place a bucket under it. Remove the supply tube and check it for blockage. Then attach a flexible supply tube (not all tubes are flexible; use the old one if it is, or buy one) to the shutoff valve and aim it into the bucket. Open the shutoff valve enough to check whether it has full force. If not, call a plumber. If it does, the problem is in the supply tube or faucet; replace them.

▶ Brass surface is tarnished.

Most brass faucets have a clear protective coating to prevent tarnishing. Once the coating is scratched or begins to peel off, the brass tarnishes rapidly. Recoating is difficult and seldom satisfactory. Instead peel off all of the coating with your fingernails or a toothpick and either let the brass age gracefully or polish it regularly with brass cleaner. A paste of lemon juice and salt works well. Avoid scouring pads and abrasive powders.

▶ Chrome surface is tarnished.

Remove stains by rubbing with ammonia or a paste of baking soda and water. Avoid abrasive scouring pads and powders, salt, harsh metal cleaners, and acids such as vinegar. Polish with silver polish, rinse, and dry immediately.

▶ Faucet wobbles or is separating from sink.

With a helper centering the faucet while you work, crawl under the sink with a flashlight. If there is no rubber gasket between the sink and faucet to prevent water from seeping between them, apply silicone bathroom caulk or plumber's putty under the outside edge of the sink base. You may first need to loosen the faucet-mounting locknuts to be able to lift the faucet base high enough to inject caulk under it. Now tighten the locknuts, using a basin wrench to reach up into the awkward cavity behind the sink. Be sure to tighten the locknuts (the ones snugged up to the sink bottom), not the coupling nuts that connect the water supply tubing to the faucet.

Tightening faucet under sink

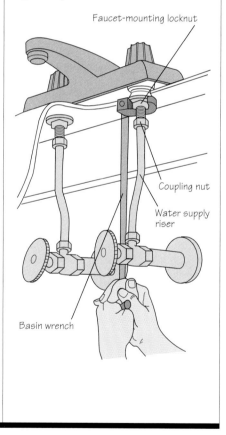

Faucet-mounting locknut

Coupling nut

Water supply riser

Basin wrench

Tip *If you're replacing an old faucet with a new one, be sure the faucet fits the hole configuration of the sink. If the sink holes are spaced 4 inches apart, buy a centerset faucet for 4-inch centers. If the sink holes are spaced 8 inches apart, buy a wideset faucet or a faucet with handles separate from the spout. Kitchen sinks often have extra holes for sprayer attachments and other accessories.*

Tip *If you need a light while working under a sink, use a flashlight. It could be dangerous to work on water pipes or plumbing fixtures with a light, cord, or appliance that's plugged into the electrical system.*

▶ *Shutoff valve is hard to turn.*

To get a good grip, use channel lock (tongue-and-groove) pliers, but don't force a stuck valve. The packing around the valve stem may have dried and can crack, causing a leak. To lubricate it, place a few drops of light machine oil on the valve stem next to the nut. Next loosen the nut one turn, then tighten it finger-tight. Wait for the packing to absorb oil, then try turning the valve handle. If it works, tighten the packing nut; if not, repeat the process.

▶ *Shutoff valve leaks.*

Dry it off and inspect it carefully to pinpoint the leak. If water comes from the compression nut at the top of the valve, tighten the nut. Use two wrenches, one for the nut and one to hold the valve (channel lock pliers also work). If the leak persists, turn off the valve, unscrew the compression nut, slide the tubing away from the valve, and wrap pipe joint tape around the brass ferrule (ring) at the base of the tubing. If it's an older style of valve with a slip-joint connection (rubber cone washer instead of a brass ferrule), replace the washer, then reassemble, using two wrenches to tighten the nut.

If water leaks from behind the valve where it is connected to the water pipe, tighten that compression nut with two wrenches. If the valve is an older style without a compression nut, the leak is due to a loosened valve or a badly corroded joint. You can try tightening the valve, but at the risk of breaking off a corroded connection or loosening pipe joints behind the wall. Call a plumber, unless you are willing to open up the wall and replace the valve altogether if necessary.

If water leaks from around the handle stem, see left. If water leaks from a crack in the valve body, call a plumber; the valve needs to be replaced.

Stopping a leak in a shutoff valve with compression connections

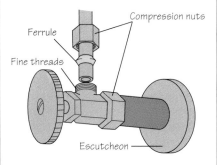

Stopping a leak in a shutoff valve with slip-joint connections

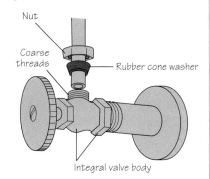

▶ *Outdoor faucet (hose bibb) leaks.*

Close the main shutoff valve, then open the faucet to drain water from the nearby pipes. Use the same repair technique as for a compression faucet (see page 170), or, because hose bibbs are inexpensive, simply unscrew the entire faucet and replace it. Apply pipe joint tape or compound to the male threads before screwing on the new bibb.

▶ *Outdoor faucet (hose bibb) is hard to reach.*

If shrubs or other obstacles block a faucet, have a new one installed in a better location, or "extend" it temporarily by mounting a second faucet in a more convenient place, such as elsewhere on the house or on a sturdy post driven in the ground. Since there won't be a rigid pipe to help support the faucet, buy one with "ears" (mounting flanges with holes drilled through them for screws) so it's easy to attach. If the faucet has no ears, secure it to the house or post with a pipe clamp or plumbing strap. After it's mounted, connect the two faucets with a short, heavy-duty garden hose, using a hose-to-pipe adapter to attach the male end of the hose to the inlet side of the new faucet. To prevent leaks, new washers in the hose couplings, apply pipe joint compound to the threads, and tighten all joints securely. Inspect the connections periodically and turn off the original faucet during the winter and when you go on vacation. Most hardware stores carry complete kits for this project.

▶ *Outdoor faucet (hose bibb) freezes.*

Replace it with a freezeproof bibb. This type of faucet has a longer shank than ordinary bibbs, so you will have to cut back some of the water pipe that the old bibb is connected to. You will need access to the pipe, which is probably located in the floor joist cavity above the crawlspace or basement ceiling. To mark where the pipe should be cut, measure the shank of the freeze-proof bibb and transfer that distance onto the pipe, measuring from the outside face of the house

---

Tip *When loosening nuts around faucets and sinks, you may find one or two that are corroded and difficult to turn. Instead of forcing the wrench, spray some penetrating lubricant onto the threads around the nut. Let it soak in for a few minutes before you try to loosen the nut.*

Tip *When sealing the joint between a faucet and marble sink, don't use plumber's putty; it will deteriorate the marble. Use silicone bathroom caulk instead.*

siding. Mark where you need to cut the supply pipe, allowing for whatever transition fittings or threaded nipples are needed. If necessary, your local hardware store can cut and thread a short piece of iron pipe to replace the existing one. (If a shutoff valve was installed on the water pipe to protect the old bibb from freezing, it won't be needed with the freezeproof bibb; don't worry if you have to cut it out.)

Before cutting the pipe make sure you have all of the pipe and materials you'll need. Then shut off the main house valve, cut the pipe, and remove the old bibb. Insert the new bibb through the same hole and solder or thread the bibb, fittings, and pipe together. Coat all threaded joints with pipe joint tape or compound. Seal any openings in the wall with caulk and attach the bibb flange to the wall with brass screws. If the freezeproof bibb is the type with a vacuum breaker next to the valve, make sure the bibb is level when you connect it.

Installing a freezeproof outdoor faucet

▶ *Drain is clogged or drains slowly.*

If the sink has a pop-up stopper, lift it out of the drain hole to see if the clog might simply be hair and other debris trapped by it. If the stopper won't lift out, release it by unscrewing the retaining nut under the sink that holds the stopper pivot arm in place, and sliding the arm out of the drain fitting (see page 176). Since this may release water from the stopped-up sink, be sure to place a bucket under the drain first. If removing the stopper doesn't clear the drain, leave the stopper out, replace the pivot arm and retaining nut, and proceed.

Next try clearing the drain with a plunger. For the plunger to work effectively, you must first seal off the overflow hole and second drain (if it's a double sink) by holding a wet rag over each opening (you may need a helper). If the sink has a disposer with a dishwasher hose attached to it, seal the hose to the air gap shut with two woodblocks squeezed in a C-clamp. Next lightly coat the rim of the plunger cup with petroleum jelly and place the plunger over the drain. The drain should be covered by 1 to 2 inches of water to provide a tight seal. Over a period of two or three minutes, work the plunger up and down vigorously 10 to 12 strokes at a time.

If plunging isn't successful, look for a clog in the P-trap. First place a bucket under the trap to catch water. If the trap has a cleanout plug, remove it and poke around the trap with a wire to find and remove any clogs. If it doesn't have a cleanout, you will have to disassemble the trap. With channel lock pliers loosen the slip nuts; then, holding the trap with your free hand, unscrew the nuts, remove the trap, pour out the water, and remove any debris.

If the trap wasn't clogged, leave it off and run a drain auger into the drainpipe (see page 157). After clearing the obstruction, reassemble the trap, tighten the slip nuts with a quarter turn of channel lock pliers, and run hot water down the drain for five minutes to flush away scum and residue from the clog.

Locating drain components of a kitchen sink

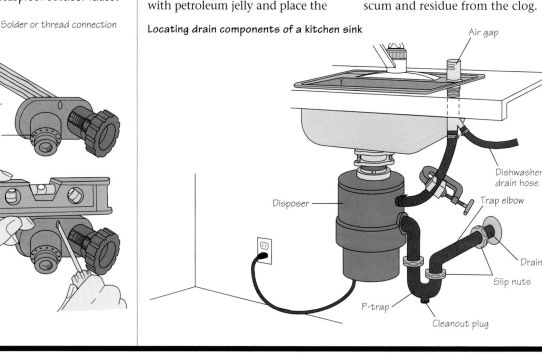

Tip *The space under a sink is awkward and often underutilized. There are many types of pull-out shelves, storage containers, and trash receptacles designed for under-sink use that will help you keep the space organized. These are widely available at home centers and other hardware outlets. To make choosing components easier, bring along a sketch of the area under your sink, with accurate measurements. Choose components that are easy to move out of the way in case you need access for repairs.*

▶ *Water puddles under the sink.*

To find the source of the leak, fill and then drain the sink. If the leak seems most apparent during filling, the leak is probably on the supply side. Look closely at the shutoff valves (angle stops) and faucet connections under the sink. Dry off any wet areas and observe them. If leaking occurs around a loose connection, tighten it (use two wrenches, not just one). For faucet leaks, see page 170. If no leaks occur until you drain the water, check the drain assembly (see right).

If the leak is in a sink with a garbage disposer, run the water and disposer while you investigate for the source. Vibration from the disposer can loosen slip nuts on the drain connections; these can be tightened.

Water may also be seeping under the faucets or through gaps along the wall or around the edge of the sink. If a faucet is loose, get under the sink with a basin wrench and tighten the mounting locknuts (not the coupling nuts that connect the faucet to the supply risers). If this doesn't help, loosen the locknuts enough that you can raise the faucet and apply silicone tub caulk around the bottom of the faucet base; have a helper center the faucet as you tighten the locknuts. On rim-type sinks and on self-rimming stainless steel sinks, the cause may be loose or missing hold-down clips. These are located under the countertop around the edge of the sink and can easily be tightened or replaced. Make sure that the sink is sealed under the rim with plumber's putty or caulk. If not, loosen all of the hold-down clips enough to raise the rim and apply a bead of silicone tub or bathroom caulk under it; then retighten the clips.

On sinks that have been set in mortar, water may be leaking through the grout. Apply a grout sealer to the joints, according to manufacturer's instructions, and seal the gap around the sink with caulk specified for tile. A permanent solution may require resetting the tile, using an epoxy grout. Consult an experienced tile setter.

▶ *Water leaks from the drain.*

For bathroom sinks, if water is leaking from around the drain fitting where it's connected to the bottom of the sink, either the putty seal under the sink flange inside the bowl has failed, or the rubber gasket on the underside of the sink has deteriorated. Replace both. First disconnect the P-trap, then loosen the locknut that holds the drain assembly against the bottom of the sink. Unscrew the flange above the sink while holding onto the tailpiece below the sink (you may need a helper; loosen the flange with a strainer wrench or a woodblock shoved into the drain hole). With the drain disassembled, remove the rubber gasket and take it to the hardware store to buy an exact replacement (along with a supply of plumber's putty).

To reassemble, first clean off the bottom of the drain flange and apply a fresh bead of plumber's putty to it. Thread the body of the drain fitting up through the sink hole and screw the flange down onto it as far as possible without rubbing off the putty. Slip the new gasket (and fiber or brass friction washer, if included) over the drain fitting from below the sink and screw the locknut onto the fitting to force the gasket up against the sink. Tighten the locknut while holding the flange steady from above with a strainer wrench or woodblock shoved into the drain hole. Reassemble the P-trap.

Pop-up assemblies can leak at the connection between the drain and the pivot rod. Tighten the retaining nut. If this doesn't stop the leak, unscrew the nut, spread some plumber's putty onto the threads, and tighten it again; or replace the washers or gaskets surrounding the pivot-ball assembly (see page 176).

If a kitchen sink drain (called a basket strainer) leaks, try tightening the large locknut under the sink with channel lock pliers (some basket strainers have a retainer with setscrews; tighten them with a screwdriver). If the fitting is tight but still leaks, replace the gasket between the sink and locknut (or retainer). The procedure is the same as for a bathroom sink, except that the entire strainer body lifts out of the sink hole from the top.

The locknut on a basket strainer may be too large for any wrench you own. You could buy a spud wrench for the job, or large channel lock pliers if you have other uses for them around the house; otherwise you can usually loosen the nut by tapping on it with a hammer and a small woodblock. To hold the body of the strainer in place from above, strainer wrenches are available, or you can stick the handles of a pair of pliers (held upside down) into the strainer and wedge a screwdriver between the handles for leverage.

Leaks can occur in the P-trap assembly. Before working on one, have a bucket handy to catch water in case you have to disassemble the trap. If there is a cleanout plug at the bottom of the trap, make sure it is tight. Loose slip nuts should be tightened. If a slip nut is tight but still leaks, loosen the joint and inspect the washer. If it is cracked, stiff, or deformed, replace it. If the new washer still leaks, coat the inside of the slip nut with plumber's

Tip *Use mechanical means to clear a drain before resorting to chemical drain cleaners. Avoid using a plunger on a drain after dumping chemical drain cleaner down it; it may spatter caustic material around. Chemical cleaners work best for periodic cleaning or for clearing pipes that are only slightly blocked. If the pipe is fully blocked and the chemicals don't dissolve the blockage completely, the clog can harden and become impossible to remove, requiring replacement of the blocked section of pipe.*

putty. If you overtighten a slip nut and strip the threads, or if the trap is cracked, replace it (wrapping the trap with waterproof tape may stop the leak temporarily). When buying a new trap, be sure to get the right size—traps in bathroom drains are usually 1¼ inches in diameter (with a 1½-inch outlet); in kitchens, they are always 1½ inches.

Replacing a drain gasket in a bathroom sink

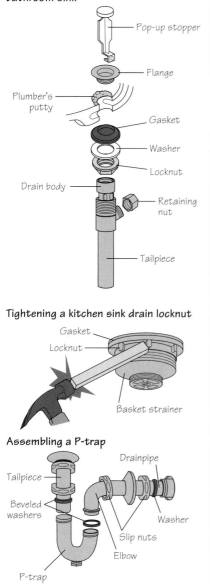

Tightening a kitchen sink drain locknut

Assembling a P-trap

▶ Stopper leaks and doesn't hold water.

If it's a rubber stopper, it may be dried and cracked; buy a new one (make sure it's the right size). If it's the pop-up stopper of a bathroom sink, see if the stopper is dropping all the way down into the drain. If not, lower the stopper by adjusting the linkage under the sink (see below), or by removing the stopper and rotating an adjusting nut that regulates the length of the stopper. If the stopper covers the drain hole but still leaks, replace the O-ring on the stopper; take the stopper with you to the hardware store when you buy the new ring. If the stopper still leaks, the drain hole or stopper may be slightly out of round or have a crack or burr on it. Inspect carefully and replace any damaged parts.

If the basket strainer of a kitchen sink leaks, check the rubber seal on the bottom. If it appears worn, buy a new strainer. You can also buy a flat disk stopper that covers the strainer completely.

▶ Pop-up stopper is out of alignment.

If a stopper wobbles, doesn't travel far enough, or comes to rest in a cockeyed position, you can make adjustments to bring it back into alignment. First make sure that the stopper is correctly engaged with the pivot rod. This will depend on the type of stopper you have. Some simply lift out, others must be twisted on and off the pivot rod, and a third type requires that the pivot rod be threaded through a hole in the bottom of the stopper (if it's not attached, you have to remove the pivot rod by unscrewing the retaining nut, then insert the rod through the hole at the bottom of the stopper before tightening the nut again).

With the stopper resting firmly on the pivot rod, or securely connected to it, push the lift rod up and down to see if the stopper opens and closes far enough. To raise the stopper higher, loosen the screw that secures the clevis strap to the lift rod (you may need pliers); slide the strap farther down the rod and tighten the screw. To lower the stopper, slide the clevis strap farther up the rod. If adjusting the stopper one way limits it the other way, increase the total distance (range) the stopper can travel by moving the clevis strap down the pivot rod, closer to the drain fitting. To do this, simply squeeze the spring clip and slide the strap along the rod. Finally, by tightening or loosening the retaining nut you can adjust the stiffness, or resistance, of the stopper mechanism so that it glides more smoothly.

Adjusting a pop-up assembly

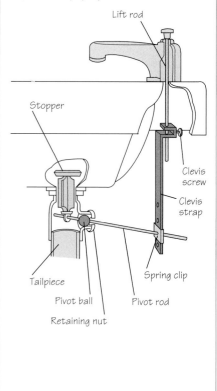

Tip   *When disassembling a sink trap, stuff a rag into the trap arm or drainpipe to prevent sewer gas from escaping.*

Tip   *To maintain the beauty of a sink, clean it daily. Use mild cleaning powders or paste cleaners, not heavy-duty abrasive cleaners. Avoid steel wool; scour with a nylon brush or cleaning pad. Rinse with clear water.*

▶ *Wall-mounted sink is coming loose from the wall.*

Look under the sink for visible screws anchoring the sink to the wall. If there are some, tighten them. If there are none, or if the sink is still loose, you will have to remove it to tighten or replace the support bracket. Close the shutoff valves under the sink and disconnect the supply risers from the valves by unscrewing the compression nuts. Disconnect the P-trap by unscrewing the slip nuts (have a bucket of water handy to dump the water from the trap). Stick a rag into the drainpipe to block sewer gas. If the sink has been screwed to the wall, remove the screws. If the gap between the sink and the wall has been caulked, cut the caulk with a utility knife.

Now carefully lift the sink straight up until it clears the wall bracket; set it aside on its back. If the bracket is loose, tighten the screws; if the bracket is worn or corroded, you will need to replace it with an exact duplicate (contact a reputable plumbing-supply house or the sink manufacturer).

If the screws won't tighten, you will have to open up the wall and install new blocking to support the bracket. First measure the height of the bracket above the floor, then remove it. Remove a swath of wall covering the same width as a 2x6 and long enough to expose two studs; it should be at the same height as the bracket. Cut notches in the studs to recess a 2x6. Screw the 2x6 to the notched studs, then repair the wall and screw the bracket into the 2x6 blocking. Carefully position the sink on the bracket, tighten anchor screws through the sink into the wall (if the sink back has holes for them), and reconnect the water supply and drain.

An easier solution in some cases might be simply to install leg supports under the front corners of the sink; the legs must be the right type for your sink. Attach them according to manufacturer's instructions.

Removing sink to expose wall bracket

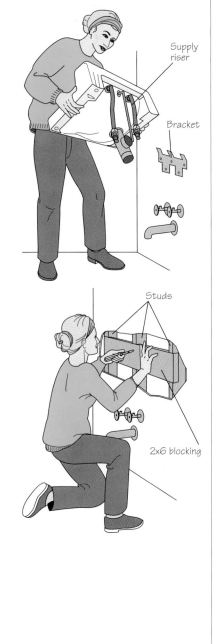

Supply riser

Bracket

Studs

2x6 blocking

▶ *Sink surface is chipped or scratched.*

If the sink is cast iron (heavy, with thunking sound) or enameled steel (lightweight, with tinny sound), you can repair the porcelain enamel surface with compounds or repair kits available at hardware stores. However, they work best on parts of the sink that are not frequently wet. You can mix the compound with alkyd paint to match the color of the sink. To repair, first carefully smooth the area around the chip or scratch by sanding it with emery cloth (medium grit); then clean it with a cloth dampened with rubbing alcohol. After it dries, apply the compound, according to label directions. Using a small putty knife or razor blade, keep it flush with the enamel surface. Let it dry thoroughly and then smooth the surface using a cotton swab and some fingernail-polish remover. These repairs are not likely to last long if the damage was in the basin itself, where it is regularly exposed to water. In this case you may want to find a professional refinisher (check in the Yellow Pages under "Bathtub Refinishing"), or replace the sink.

Scratches in a stainless steel sink are almost impossible to remove. You can try polishing the sink with automotive polishing compound to restore the overall sheen.

▶ *Sink made of solid-surface material is cracked.*

Some sinks, known by various brand names, are made from synthetic materials such as cast or compression-molded modified acrylic. Some are continuously molded into one piece as a sink and countertop; others are just the sink and are installed in a conventional countertop. It is best to call a professional

Tip *If you plan to replace the kitchen sink, consider the wide range of materials, sizes, and configurations available to you. Besides cast iron, stainless steel, and enameled steel, sinks are manufactured from solid-surface synthetic materials and lightweight composites. The most common size is 22x33 inches, but you can get narrower sinks to utilize more counter space, or wider sinks that have multiple compartments. Consider where the deck is located for mounting a faucet on the sink, and how many holes will be needed for the faucet, sprayer, and other accessories. Finally, if you have an awkward space where the sink will be placed, or want to take advantage of a corner window, consider a double-bowl sink that wraps around the inside corner of two intersecting counters, allowing you easy access to both bowls.*

to repair these sinks. If the crack is at the drain hole, the sink may have to be replaced, but other cracks can be repaired with plugs and/or joint adhesive.

▶ Stainless steel sink is too noisy or bouncy.

Get underneath the sink and, with a screwdriver, tighten the screws on the clips holding the sink to the rim or counter. If there is a garbage disposer in the sink, tighten its connections as well. Lighter sinks, which are made from 22-gauge steel, are prone to be noisy and show scratches, dents, and stains. Higher-quality sinks are made with thicker steel (20 and 18 gauge) and have an undercoating applied to the bottom that retains heat and reduces noise. If you have a persistent problem, consider replacing the sink.

▶ Sprayer hose leaks or is stiff and cracked.

Buy a new sprayer kit, or, if the spray head is working fine, replace only the hose with a new nylon-reinforced vinyl one. First close the shutoff valves under the sink. Then with a basin wrench loosen the nut connecting the sprayer hose to the bottom of the faucet. You might find it easier to cut the hose first to get it out of the way. Then remove the spray head by unscrewing it from the coupling. Take the head and the old hose to the hardware store to make sure the new hose will fit; also pick up a new washer for the spray head.

To install the new hose, start at the attachment under the faucet. Wrap some pipe joint tape on the male threads, then screw on the hose coupling nut and tighten it

with a basin wrench. Bring the other end of the hose up through the hole in the sink and slide on the coupling, retaining ring, and washers (or plastic rings). Apply pipe joint tape to the male threads of the sprayer head and attach it to the coupling ring on the hose. Restore the water supply and test the sprayer.

Attaching a new sprayer hose

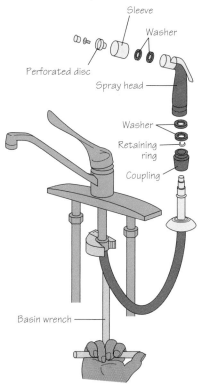

Sleeve

Washer

Perforated disc

Spray head

Washer

Retaining ring

Coupling

Basin wrench

▶ Sprayer head leaks.

Close the shutoff valves under the sink. If the sprayer head leaks where it is connected to the hose, unscrew the head from the hose coupling and replace the washer in the head (there may be two). Also make sure that the retaining ring that holds the coupling onto the hose is properly seated in the groove on the fitting at the end of the hose.

If the leak is from the nozzle, remove the nozzle from the head. On some models you pry off a small cover over the screw; on other models the whole nozzle housing screws onto the head. Carefully remove the parts. You should find either a standard washer (or washers) or a flexible seat. Replace these and reassemble.

▶ Sprayer won't spray.

If you have hard water, the head may be clogged with minerals. Wrap a rubber band around the handle to keep it in the open position, and drain all the water from the hose. Fill a small glass with a solution of equal parts vinegar and water. Let the spray nozzle soak in the solution for a couple of hours. Then, with hot water, try to use the sprayer. If the clog remains or the spray is inconsistent, take the nozzle apart and examine the perforated disc. Remove any debris with a pin or small wire. Reassemble the nozzle and test the sprayer again.

If it is still clogged, the problem is probably in the diverter valve under the spout. Turn off the water supply and remove the spout (see pages 170 and 171). Most often you'll need to remove a nut at the base of the spout (double-handled faucets) and unscrew the diverter from the top; or you will have to remove the spout sleeve (single-handled faucets) and pull the diverter out from the side of the assembly. Use a wire to clean debris from the inlet holes, or soak the assembly in a solution of 1 part vinegar to 1 part water. Reassemble. If the cone on the diverter is loose, replace the diverter.

Tip   *Always retract a sprayer hose back into its housing after use. Leaving it in the sink subjects the water supply to potential contamination, especially if there is standing water.*

▶ Disposer won't start and makes no sound.

If the disposer suddenly shuts off while running, wait a few minutes and then press the reset button, usually on the bottom of the disposer. If it won't start, try the on-off switch in both positions. If it does not start in either position, check the circuit breaker or fuse. If none of the switches or breakers is off, check the instruction booklet that came with the disposer. Call a plumber or electrician for more-involved repairs.

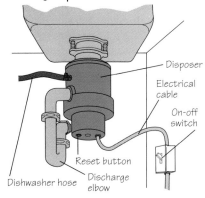

Locating disposer switches under sink

▶ Disposer makes a humming noise but won't grind.

Most likely something is stuck between the impeller (a rotating plate at the bottom of the waste chamber) and the grind ring (a stationary collar). Turn off the electric power at the on-off switch or at the circuit breaker or fuse box. Most disposers today are sold with a wrench that fits into the bottom of the disposer, allowing you to turn the motor back and forth until it is free. An alternative method is to carefully insert a dowel or broom handle into the disposer and rotate the impeller until it spins freely. Remove the material that jammed the impeller, restore power, push in the reset button on the bottom of the

disposer, and let it run for a few minutes with the cold water on.

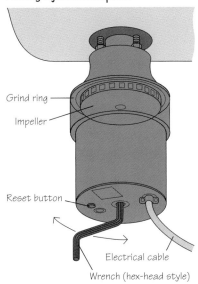

Freeing a jammed impeller

▶ Disposer runs slowly.

Turn off the electric power at the circuit breaker. Remove the rubber shield from the sink drain and look for undisposed material in the drum. If you find some, remove it and see if that solves the problem. If the problem persists, the impeller may be damaged or the cutting edges on the grind ring dulled. Replace them according to manufacturer's instructions, or call a plumber.

▶ Disposer makes strange or excessive noise.

Turn off the electric power and check for undisposed material in the drum. Also examine the impeller; if it is broken, replace the turntable, following manufacturer's instructions. If the problem persists, the motor bearings may be worn or damaged. You may find that it costs

you little more to replace a malfunctioning disposer than it does to repair it.

▶ Disposer smells.

Foul odors from a garbage disposer often indicate that you are letting food sit in the drum too long before turning on the disposer. To remove the smell, grind up some raw potatoes or citrus rind. For a preventive treatment, when replacing the box of baking soda in your refrigerator, pour the old soda down the drain rather than throwing it away. Always use only cold water when running the disposer; hot water will liquefy grease, allowing it to cling to surfaces. Grinding a handful of ice cubes from time to time will congeal any greasy buildup and allow it to be carried away.

▶ Disposer leaks at sink flange.

From under the sink tighten the mounting flange that attaches to the sink drain and holds the disposer in place. Some models have a large ring that can be turned with a spud wrench or channel lock pliers, or can be tightened by hammering a woodblock held against it; others have three setscrews that you can tighten with a screwdriver. If tightening the flange doesn't fix the problem, replace the gasket or gaskets.

First shut off power to the disposer by turning off the circuit breaker or by unplugging the unit. Then disconnect the P-trap from the disposer outlet and the dishwasher drain hose from the inlet located on the disposer body. While supporting the disposer with one hand, loosen it from the mounting bracket under the sink by turning the locking collar with a screwdriver or hex-head wrench provided with the disposer; lower the disposer to the cabinet floor (it may be heavy; use a helper). With the mounting flange

Tip *Before turning on a disposer, check for silverware, scrubbers, and other items that may jam it. Avoid putting stringy or fibrous materials into the disposer, such as onion skins, banana peels, artichoke leaves, or celery. Don't put large bones, pits, or grease into the disposer (but do put small bones, such as chicken bones, into the disposer; they clean out the chamber with a scouring action).*

exposed, disconnect it from the sink drain by loosening the lockring or setscrews and remove the gasket. Replace it with a new one. Apply a fresh bead of plumber's putty under the sink flange before you insert it back into the sink drain hole (see right). Then reassemble the disposer in the same order as you removed it.

Detaching the disposer

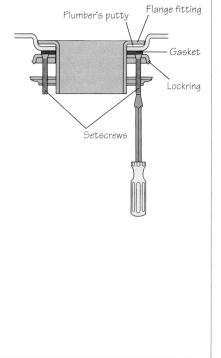

Locking collar

Dishwasher drain hose

P-trap

Disconnecting the mounting flange

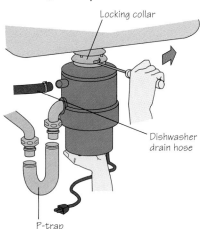

Plumber's putty

Flange fitting

Gasket

Lockring

Setscrews

▶ *Disposer needs replacing.*

Turn off the electricity at the circuit breaker or fuse. Make sure that the electrical wiring is sound (see page 200) and up to code (a garbage disposer should have its own circuit with a switch wired into it). Disconnect the wiring by unplugging the disposer from the wall receptacle, or by removing the cover plate on the bottom of the disposer and disconnecting the cable connector and cable from the unit. Disconnect the P-trap or other drain fitting from the disposer outlet pipe, then disconnect the dishwasher drain hose from the disposer. Remove the disposer from the mounting flange by loosening the locking collar with a screwdriver and lowering the disposer to the cabinet floor (see page 179). Remove the mounting flange by loosening the lockring or setscrews that secure it to the sink. Remove the sink gasket, any hardware securing the mounting plate to the sink, and the sink flange.

Reverse the process to install the new unit. First install the mounting flange. Apply a bead of plumber's putty underneath the flange and lower the fitting through the drain opening. From under the sink, place the gasket, mounting ring, and any other mounting hardware onto the body of the sink flange extending down through the sink hole (different models of disposers have different parts). Tighten the screws on the mounting ring to seat the flange and then remove excess putty from the sink.

Remove the electrical cover plate from the bottom of the disposer. Attach the feeder cable (armored conduit, nonmetallic cable) or power cord that was attached to the old disposer to a cable connector (connector for attaching electrical cable to the knockout hole of an electrical box). Run the wires into the junction box through the knockout hole and secure the connector to the disposer. Connect the wires (white to white, black to black) using electrical wire connectors. Attach the ground wire to the green screw. Replace the cover plate.

If a dishwasher drain hose will be attached to the disposer, remove the plug from inside the dishwasher inlet tube on the side of the disposer. Attach the drain fitting (usually an elbow) to the disposer. Lift the disposer up to the mounting flange, turn it so the drain fitting will line up with the P-trap, and secure the mounting hardware. Attach the P-trap to the drain fitting and connect it to the drainpipe in the wall. Turn on the electricity, press the reset button, and test the disposer.

Making electrical connections

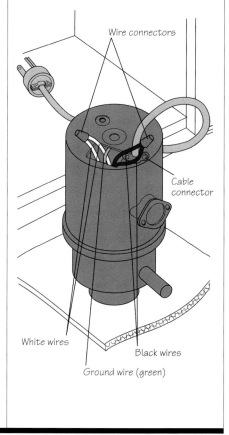

Wire connectors

Cable connector

White wires

Black wires

Ground wire (green)

Tip *Scrape small amounts of waste into the disposer; don't pack it in. Always turn on a strong flow of cold water before you start the disposer. Let it run another minute or two after grinding to be sure all waste is flushed away.*

Tip *If food is stuck in a disposer, turn off the power at the circuit breaker and remove the food by hand or with tongs. Avoid clearing a disposer with chemical drain cleaners containing lye or acid.*

▶ *Tub or shower faucet drips.*

Tub and shower faucets (called valves) have either separate handles for hot and cold water, or a single handle. Two-handled faucets have a compression washer or a ceramic-disk operating mechanism in each handle. You may be able to tell which side is leaking by the temperature of the dripping water; but for a compression faucet, at least, you should repair both sides while you're at it.

To repair a compression faucet, first turn off the water supply (at shutoff valves behind an access door behind the wall or under the floor, or at the main house valve). Next remove the setscrews that hold the handles onto the stems (they may be under decorative caps) and pull off the handles (you may need to use a handle puller, or pry carefully on each handle with two screwdrivers from opposite sides). If there's an escutcheon (collar) block-ing the stem, remove that. Remove the packing nut (if it's recessed too far for an ordinary wrench to reach, use a bonnet wrench or a deep socket wrench). You may have to chip away some tile with a hammer and cold chisel to gain access. With the nut off, rotate the valve stem out of the valve body. Replace the washer and screw at the end of the stem, and any O-rings elsewhere on the stem (take the stem with you to the store and buy replacements for the stems on both faucets). Examine the holding cup (recessed end of valve stem that holds the washer) and the valve seat. If the holding cup is broken, buy a replacement valve stem or file off the cup and buy an appropriate replacement assembly. If the valve seat is damaged, remove the seat with a valve-stem wrench or allen wrench and replace it. As you reassemble the valve, wrap some packing string around the stem a few times before threading the packing nut back on.

A single-handled faucet will be of cartridge, ball, or ceramic-disc design. Obtain a replacement kit for the type you have. The repair procedure is the same as for a sink faucet, except that there is no spout attached to the faucet for you to remove (see pages 170 and 171).

▶ *Faucet leaks around stem.*

Turn off the water supply to the tub or shower, then remove the handle and escutcheon (or stem cover). You may have to pry a cover plate off the handle to gain access to the screw. Two-handled faucets will be either a compression or a ceramic-disk type. On a compression faucet tighten the packing nut, using an adjustable wrench if you can, or a deep socket wrench or bonnet wrench if the nut is recessed. You may have to chip away some tile with a hammer and cold chisel to gain access. Now turn on the water. If the leak persists, turn off the water and remove the packing nut. Unscrew the stem and replace any O-rings it has and, while you're at it, the stem washer (see page 170). Screw the stem back in and wrap some packing string around the top (two to four wraps should do) before threading the packing nut back on.

A two-handled ceramic-disk faucet, or a single-handled faucet, will very rarely leak around the handle. If it does, the problem is probably a worn O-ring or gasket under the retaining cap or escutcheon. Buy a replacement washer kit for the model of faucet you have. Turn off the water, remove the handle, and loosen the screws or retaining ring holding the cover in place. Remove it to expose the gasket or O-ring. While replacing it, look for scratches around the gasket seat or loose grit

Identifying the parts of a . . .

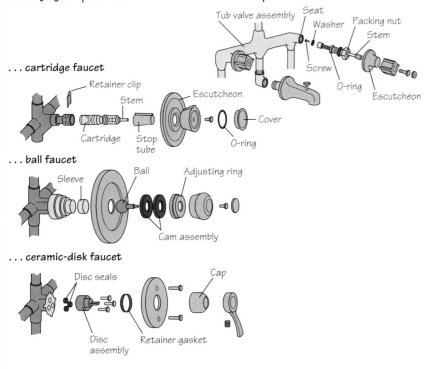

. . . cartridge faucet

. . . compression faucet

. . . ball faucet

. . . ceramic-disk faucet

Tip *A shower valve, tub valve, and combination tub/shower valve are essentially the same. Some combination tub/shower valves have diverter handles built into them to divert the water to the spout or showerhead, but valves without this feature can be used interchangeably. These valves have two outlets—one on the bottom for a tub spout and one on the top for a showerhead. Either or both can be used.*

that may prevent a tight seal. Flush away any grit and smooth rough edges around scratches. Apply valve grease to the seat and reassemble the faucet.

▶ Tub spout drips when shower is turned on.

If the shower is turned on and water still dribbles from the tub spout, the diverter mechanism is not working properly. For some tubs, the diverter is located in the tub spout and is operated by pulling up on a knob. To fix this type of diverter, replace the entire spout with a new diverter spout. To remove the old spout, unscrew it from the nipple hidden in the wall behind it. If it doesn't loosen by hand, insert the handle of a hammer, wrench, or large screwdriver into the spout for leverage (you may first need to loosen a set-screw under the spout with an allen wrench before the spout will turn). After removing the spout, look inside to see if the diverter is blocked by grit or debris and remove it; if this doesn't solve the problem, replace the spout. Make sure that the

Loosening tub spout

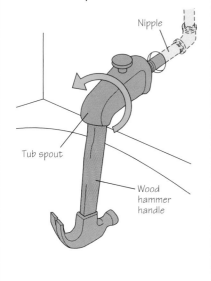

Nipple

Tub spout

Wood hammer handle

threaded inlet hole on the new spout is in the same position and of the same diameter as the one in the old spout. Before screwing on the new spout, fill the gap between the wall and nipple with caulk, and apply a thin bead of caulk to the back edge of the spout.

If the shower flow is controlled by a diverter knob that is part of the faucet, remove the handle and packing nut, and replace washers, O-rings, and packing. If the leak persists, the entire faucet may have to be replaced. This is a major job, probably not equal to the nuisance caused by a dribbling tub spout.

▶ Scalding water sometimes comes out of spout or showerhead.

Either turn down the water-heater control to 120° F or less (see page 166), or install an antiscald faucet. Two types are available: One contains a built-in control that will prevent the water temperature from rising to a dangerous level; another type allows the user to choose the desired temperature, which the valve will maintain within a very close range.

▶ Showerhead wastes water.

Install a low-flow showerhead. Look for one with a maximum flow of 2½ gallons per minute or less, with a built-in on-off button. Unscrew the old showerhead, apply pipe joint tape or compound to the threads of the shower arm, and carefully thread on the new head.

▶ Showerhead is at an inconvenient height.

You can alter the height by installing a shorter or longer shower arm. To raise the height of the shower-head significantly, get an S-shaped arm. These easily thread into the

fitting in the wall. If you want to be able to change the height of the showerhead, get an adjustable arm, which allows as much as 20 inches of height flexibility. You can also install a handheld sprayer, either as an addition to your regular showerhead, by placing a diverter valve between the shower arm and head, or as an addition to the tub spout, by replacing it with one that has a side outlet. Both allow the water flow to be directed to either the showerhead or the handheld unit. Be sure to apply pipe joint tape or compound to the male threads. If you have to drill through tile for mounting a bracket on the wall, see page 47.

Adding a handheld showerhead

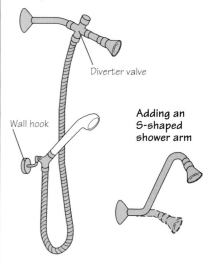

Diverter valve

Wall hook

Adding an S-shaped shower arm

▶ Showerhead drips.

If the faucet is turned off completely and the showerhead drips, the valve in the faucet doesn't seal properly and needs to be repaired (see page 181). If the shower is on and water drips from around the knurled tightening nut, creating a nuisance, remove the showerhead and replace the washer in the nut. Apply pipe joint tape or compound

Tip *Many single-handled shower or tub faucets have shutoff valves built into them. After removing the handle and escutcheon or cover plate, look for a setscrew on each side of the valve near the connection to the cold- and hot-water supply pipes. Tighten both screws to shut off the water supply. You can also regulate the rate of flow with these screws.*

Tip *Fixtures with chrome finishes can be restored by rubbing with ammonia or a paste of baking soda and water. Avoid abrasive scouring pads and powders, harsh metal cleaners, salt, and acids such as vinegar. Polish with silver polish, rinse, and dry immediately.*

to the threads on the shower arm. Replace the showerhead. If water dribbles out of clogged spray holes, see below.

► Showerhead seems to be clogged.

Remove the showerhead and, if possible, disassemble it. Rinse out loose debris and clean out water holes with a pin. If you find mineral deposits, soak the showerhead overnight in a solution of equal parts water and vinegar. Reassemble and reinstall the showerhead, using pipe joint tape or compound on the threads. If it's too difficult to remove the showerhead, you can mix the solution in a heavy plastic bag and strap the bag over the showerhead so it can soak in the solution overnight.

► Enamel tub surface is stained.

First scrub with a household cleaner. To remove mineral deposits, use a solution of equal parts of vinegar and water. Special cleaners are available to remove lime buildup. Iron stains may require a rust dissolver or a cleaner containing oxalic acid. Mildew should be removed with a solution of chlorine bleach and water, mixed according to label recommendations.

► Enamel tub surface is chipped or scratched.

Compounds and repair kits for enamel surfaces are available at hardware stores. Be sure to read the product information carefully; some may not work on areas that get submerged or that are frequently exposed to water. They may need to be mixed with paint to match the surface (check product recommendations for the type of paint; most work with alkyd). The area around the chip or scratch must be cleaned and carefully sanded with

emery cloth. Apply the compound according to label directions, using a small putty knife or razor blade to keep it flush with the enamel surface. Let it dry thoroughly and then smooth the surface using a cotton swab and some fingernail-polish remover. For repairs that will get wet repeatedly, or for large scratches, you may want to find a professional refinisher (check in the Yellow Pages under "Bathtub Refinishing").

► Tub bottom has adhesive from old antiskid appliqués.

If the tub is enameled steel or cast iron, carefully remove the adhesive with a single-edged razor blade. Alternatively, buy a cleaner that is formulated to remove sticky residue, checking to be sure it is compatible with the surface to which you will be applying it.

► Enameled-steel tub is too noisy and cools the bathwater too fast.

If you can gain access through the wall behind the tub or through the floor from under the tub, install fiberglass insulation around the underside of the tub.

► Tub is leaking at tile joint around rim.

Remove the old caulk or loose grout from the joint with a small putty knife or screwdriver, being careful not to damage the tiles or tub surface. Clean the area with rubbing alcohol, which removes soap residue, and wipe away the cleaner with a dry paper towel before it evaporates. Dry the joint thoroughly using a heat lamp, or leave it to dry over several days.

For a crisp caulk line, mask off the joint with masking or transparent tape. Using caulk specified for bathtub and tile installations, apply a fresh, continuous bead of caulk to the joint. Cut the nozzle on the caulking tube to create a bead of caulk the same size as the joint, so the caulk will make contact with both sides of the gap and the bottom (three-point adhesion) and will fill the joint completely in one pass. Smooth the caulk with a plastic spoon moistened in soapy water. For a straight joint, cut the end of a flat stick (a paint stirrer works well) to a point with two 45-degree cuts, then square off the end of the point so it has a straight edge exactly the same width as the joint. Moisten it, then smooth the caulk by dragging it along the joint corner. Clean off excess caulk from around the joint as soon as possible, before it can set. For best results stand in the tub while caulking, or fill the tub with water; the extra weight will open the joint to its maximum size.

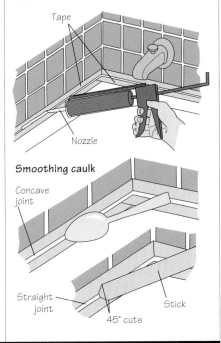

Applying caulk

Tape

Nozzle

Smoothing caulk

Concave joint

Straight joint

45° cuts

Stick

Tip *If the bathtub or shower stall finish is acrylic, fiberglass, gelcoat, or a similar product, avoid using abrasive cleansers on it. Contact the manufacturer for recommended cleaning products and procedures and for use specifications, such as avoidance of bath oils and other products.*

Tip *Soap film and mildew can usually be removed from a shower curtain by scrubbing it with full-strength vinegar and a wet sponge. The curtain can also be washed in a washing machine (put a bath towel in the load at the same time). Add a cup of white vinegar to the rinse water. Be sure to remove the curtain hooks before washing.*

SOLVING PLUMBING PROBLEMS

▶ Acrylic or fiberglass tub has a crack.

Buy a repair kit from the manufacturer or a local supplier of acrylic fixtures. Most repairs will require you to enlarge the crack and then mix and apply a filler compound. Pigment can be added to match the color of the tub. Once the compound has set, sand with progressively finer grits of sandpaper. Then apply a gel-type polish or some car wax and buff. If you want to be certain of a repair that blends in perfectly with the tub, call a professional bathtub refinisher.

▶ Shower pan made from synthetic material has stains.

Some pan materials, such as solid-surface synthetics, are the same color and texture throughout, and you can sand out the stain with emery cloth or fine sandpaper (according to manufacturer's recommendations). Other materials, especially older cast polymer (cultured marble) pans, have only a thin color veneer and must not be abraded in any way. For these materials, to remove mineral deposits from hard water mix ½ cup ammonia, ¼ cup vinegar, and ¼ cup baking soda with ½ gallon hot water. Wearing rubber gloves, apply the solution with a sponge to a small area first to make sure it does not harm the finish. If it causes no damage, apply it to the stained surface. After five minutes, rinse well.

For darker stains, try placing a cotton rag soaked with hydrogen peroxide on the stain for several hours. Rinse with cold water.

▶ Stopper won't hold water.

Tub drains are usually one of two designs. A trip-lever stopper seals by dropping a brass plunger into a seat in the overflow tube. Wear on the plunger, which causes it to leak, may be overcome by lengthening the linkage. Remove the screws in the overflow plate and lift out the whole assembly. To lengthen it, loosen the locknut and turn the threaded rod in the desired direction. Make only a small adjustment, counting the rotations, and then reassemble the mechanism and test.

On a pop-up drain, the stopper is visible in the drain hole. First check the O-ring on the stopper by opening the drain and pulling out the stopper and connected linkage; replace the O-ring if it appears worn. If the stopper isn't dropping far enough into the drain, remove the overflow plate and adjust the linkage as for a trip-lever stopper.

Adjusting a pop-up stopper

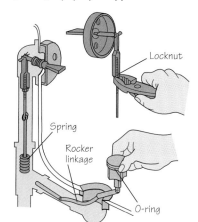

Locknut

Spring

Rocker linkage

O-ring

Adjusting a trip-lever stopper

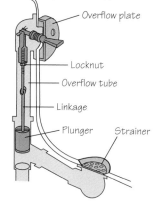

Overflow plate

Locknut

Overflow tube

Linkage

Plunger

Strainer

▶ Tub drain leaks.

Get below the tub and inspect the joint between the tub and waste arm (L-shaped drain fitting). If water leaks from this joint, replace the gasket. (You may need a helper so one person can work below the tub, another above.) First, from above, remove the stopper. Then insert a strainer wrench or a wedge-shaped woodblock into the drain hole and, with large pliers, turn it counterclockwise to loosen the fitting; unscrew it and pull it out. From below retrieve the gasket. Buy a new one and slip it into place. Then, from above, screw the drain fitting back in, first putting pipe joint tape or compound onto the threads of the fitting and plumber's putty under the flange. Tighten it snug but do not distort the alignment of the waste outlet.

If the leak is at the tee fitting where the horizontal waste arm joins the vertical overflow pipe, loosen the slip nuts and take the unit apart (to pull the assembly apart you may have to detach the overflow fitting from the tub; do this from above). Then reassemble the tee joint, applying pipe joint tape or compound to the male threads of the overflow pipe and installing new 1½-inch washers under the slip nuts. (Some plumbers solder the overflow pipe to the tee to ensure a leakproof joint.) When you reattach the overflow fitting to the tub, make sure the wedge-shaped rubber gasket is sound and seals completely around the overflow hole of the tub. If the leak persists, try taking the tee apart again and applying a ring of plumber's putty inside each slip nut, where it engages the washer. If this doesn't work, the problem is probably a crack or a leaking joint caused

Tip *Tub joints and corners are the places in a tile installation most vulnerable to water penetration; make sure they are sealed with flexible caulk. Replace the caulk periodically whenever it gets dried or cracked.*

Tip *Make sure your tub or shower drain has a strainer to keep out hair and debris.*

by the deformed end of a tube. Install a new waste and overflow assembly.

Disassembling a waste and overflow assembly

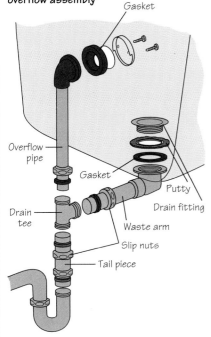

Gasket

Overflow pipe

Gasket

Putty

Drain fitting

Drain tee

Waste arm

Slip nuts

Tail piece

▶ Water drains slowly or not at all.

First try a plunger to clear the clog. Remove the drain strainer and run a little water into the tub. Hold a wet rag over the overflow hole (a helper makes this much easier), then begin pushing the plunger up and down. Start slowly, and gradually increase the speed of plunging; continue for several minutes.

If this fails, run an auger down the drain. In a tub, snake the auger down the overflow pipe. To gain access, remove the stopper linkage by unscrewing the cover plate and then pulling the assembly out. Check to see if the plug is covered with hair or other debris that could cause slow drainage. Then work the auger into the overflow hole and through the pipes until it contacts the blockage (see page 157). If the auger can't reach or break up the clog, the problem may be deeper in the drain piping (in this case, other fixtures may be backing up as well). If possible, follow the drain from the tub or shower (ideally in a basement or crawl space) to the nearest cleanout plug. Remove the plug and try the auger again. If you still can't remove the clog, call a professional drain-cleaning service.

Old bathtubs often had drum traps located next to the tub. These function as P-traps and can be the source of a clog. Take off the cover (you may need a hammer and cold chisel to unscrew it) and remove any visible clog, or probe with an auger.

Clearing a tub drain

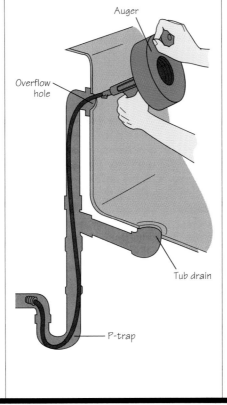

Auger

Overflow hole

Tub drain

P-trap

▶ Drain emits odor.

If it smells like sewer gases are coming out of the drain, the P-trap does not have enough water in it to seal them out. Run some water into the drain and see if the odor dissipates after a short period. If so, the water in the P-trap probably evaporated out; perhaps the tub or shower had not been used for several weeks. Otherwise, the P-trap might have a leak, or the vent system for that trap is not functioning properly. Inspect the P-trap from under the tub (see opposite page). If it has a leak, replace it. This is fairly easy if the P-trap has slip-joint connections; just loosen the slip nuts and remove it. If the trap is connected with pipe joints, it will have to be cut out and new piping installed; call a plumber. If the trap is sound, but the odor problem persists, a malfunctioning vent system is allowing water to be siphoned out of the trap when the tub is drained; call a plumber.

▶ Bottom is slippery.

Stick-on appliqués can be applied to the bottom of tubs and showers to prevent slipping, but they often begin peeling off and looking ugly after a while. For a tub, a better solution may be to purchase a replaceable rubber mat. A soapy buildup can create a particularly slippery surface. Clean the tub or shower regularly with a household cleaner (for acrylic or similar surfaces, consult the manufacturer's recommendations for cleaning).

Tip *Not all tub drains are easily accessible. If there's no access panel below the floor or behind the wall, you will have to cut into the downstairs ceiling or the back of the wall behind the tub drain. After you cut the hole and make repairs, fit the opening with an access panel. Glue molding around the edge of it to conceal the joint, and screw the panel to the framing around the cutout.*

▶ *Water in tub doesn't flow toward drain.*

The tub is probably not level. With a carpenter's level and long straight-edge, check whether the tub rim is level in several places, lengthwise and across the width. Measure discrepancies so you will know how far the foot end of the tub must be lifted and shimmed to level it. This seems like a major job because a bathtub is locked into place by the wall and floor finish materials, but the work is done in small increments and most of it involves just patching and repair work. However, there is no way to estimate how involved the work will be until you get into it. Ironically, the process is easier with a heavy cast-iron tub than a lightweight tub because the heavier tub is probably not attached to the walls with screws (its weight keeps it in place). In either case the joints between the tub and walls must be opened, some of the wall tile or other finish material around the rim must be removed, and the joint between the tub and floor must be opened. If the tub is nailed or screwed to the wall, the fasteners must be removed along the side and back, after the tile or other backing is removed to expose them. Then, with a pry bar or other lever, slightly raise the foot end of the tub and slip metal shims under the feet and between the tub rim and any ledger boards attached to the walls. After the tub is level, the wall and floor must be patched and the joints caulked.

If the tub is level to begin with, you may have a slightly deformed tub (from a less-than-perfect casting, for example). If shims can't make the water drain better, the tub should be replaced.

▶ *Old tub is too large to remove through the doorway.*

If you plan to discard the tub, break or cut it into pieces. A sledge-hammer will be needed on a cast-iron tub, whereas a reciprocating saw should do the trick on a steel or plastic tub. If you want to keep the tub in one piece, you will have to lift it and then turn it on its side. If it is a cast-iron tub, you will need several helpers. One trick for moving a heavy tub is to place it on several 24-inch rollers cut from 1½-inch plastic drainpipe.

▶ *Tub is difficult to get in and out of.*

Install grab bars. The recommended standard is four horizontal grab bars around a typical tub: one on each wall at a convenient height to use while showering, and a lower one along the side (long) wall. The bar at the foot of the tub can be omitted if the tub has a built-in transfer seat. Some individuals may prefer slight modifications, such as a vertical bar at the end of the tub.

Grab bars, which are available in a wide variety of colors to match bathroom decors, must be carefully selected and installed. Because they must be able to support a force of 250 pounds in any direction, they should not be attached to existing stud walls without first providing some blocking for reinforcement. If you are adding them to a finished wall, you can either open the wall and add blocking between studs, or you can install exposed reinforcement in the form of a wood cleat over the wall, bolted securely through the wall material into the studs. The wood must be of a durable species and sealed or painted thoroughly. Use stainless steel screws and bolts. Check the local building-inspection department for further requirements.

A tub seat also makes it easier to enter and use a tub. Some move back and forth and are removable. Built-in seats are safer and more stable; install according to the manufacturer's instructions.

Locating grab bars in a tub

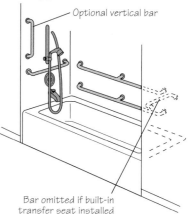

Optional vertical bar

Bar omitted if built-in transfer seat installed

Installing grab bars

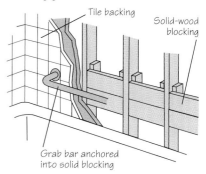

Tile backing

Solid-wood blocking

Grab bar anchored into solid blocking

▶ *Shower stall is mildewed.*

Clean with a solution of 3 tablespoons chlorine bleach to 1 quart water; follow label precautions carefully. You may need to increase the ratio of bleach for stubborn stains. If mildew is a persistent problem, fill a squirt bottle with the solution and keep it in the bathroom. On a weekly basis, spray the spots where mildew appears, then rinse.

Tip *To prevent water from seeping behind a tub spout into the wall, be sure the spout fits tightly against the tile behind it. If there is a gap, unscrew the spout and replace the pipe with one slightly shorter. Seal the space between the pipe and wall hole with a generous application of caulk. When you screw the spout back onto the pipe, apply caulk to the back of the spout along the top edge and sides, so it fills any gaps between the wall and spout.*

▶ Sliding glass door is hard to move.

Clean the tracks. Pour white vinegar into the tracks and let it stand for five minutes; then rinse carefully. Repeat as necessary, scraping away crusty material with a sharp stick (avoid screwdrivers or other metal objects that might scratch the finish). Use tweezers to remove any debris. If the door slides on wheels in the upper part of the frame, clean the wheels with a solution of equal parts vinegar and water and make sure that they are riding in their tracks.

▶ Shower leaks but source is hard to detect.

Don't use the shower for a few days, giving it a chance to dry out. Then remove the showerhead and screw on an adapter that will allow you to attach a garden hose to the shower arm. (On some units, you may have to remove the arm completely and install a long nipple to connect with the hose adapter.) Now run the hose out a window or into a different drain and turn on the water (hot and cold). If the leak reappears, you will know that it is coming from the valve assembly or piping (see page 181).

If no signs of a leak appear, insert the hose into the shower drain and run some water. If this produces the leak, you will know that the source is in the drain assembly (see page 184).

If you still haven't found the leak, start investigating all corners in the shower and other joints along the floor, walls, and shower door; apply new caulk to joints where it is missing, dried, or cracked (see page 183). Water often leaks over the shower curb or edge of a tub when the shower is on. This can be cured either by replacing the shower curtain with one that provides better coverage, or by installing a small dam to block the water. This can be a simple bead of caulk, or you may be able to find an adhesive-backed product at a home center designed specifically for this problem.

▶ Shower-door frame has come loose from the wall.

Tighten the screws securing the frame to the wall. If the screws aren't holding well enough, use longer ones or enlarge the hole for a hollow-wall fastener. (See page 17.) If that doesn't fix the problem, you can create new screw holes in the track. First, drill a hole into the wall through the track, then install the screws. If you have to drill through tile, see page 47.

If the frame is glued rather than screwed to the wall, you should remove the door or doors, then pry off the frame. Scrape the mating surfaces clean and smooth, and rinse with rubbing alcohol to remove soap residue. Wipe it dry with a clean cloth and apply a suitable waterproof sealant to both surfaces. Carefully reinstall the frame.

▶ Shower-door glass needs replacing.

Tempered glass and safety glass are labeled near one of the edges. If your shower-door glass is not so labeled, replace it immediately with acrylic or safety glass—don't wait for it to break. If you already have an acrylic door but it has become scratched, it is easy to replace. First take the door off its hinge. Remove the screws in the corner and gently tap the corners to separate them. Carefully remove the gasket, and clean it and the frame with a household cleaner and rag. Using ⅛-inch acrylic, cut a new piece to match the size of the old door. Most hardware stores will cut it to size for you, or you can carefully scribe a cut line with a utility knife (make several passes), then break the acrylic over a dowel or broom handle. Put the gasket around the new acrylic, reassemble the frame, replace the screws, and rehang the door.

Disassembling a shower-door frame

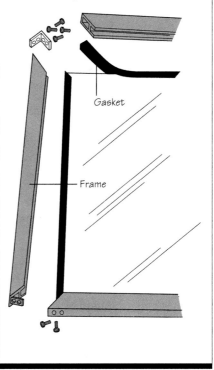

Gasket

Frame

Tip *If you have a shower door that is safe but lacks visual appeal, look for a stained-glass or window shop in your area that offers stained-glass appliqués. Some you can apply yourself; for others you may have to bring the door into the shop and leave it for a few days.*

Tip *If the curtain rod is falling off, tighten the screws on the flange holding the rod. If the screws are loose and don't grab, try longer screws; if they don't grip, rotate the flange 45 degrees and drive the screws in the new location. If there is no backing behind the wall, use hollow-wall fasteners behind the screws.*

▶ *Water runs constantly.*

Tap the handle a few times. If this works but the problem frequently recurs, there may be a mineral buildup on the handle mechanism. Take the cover off the tank, loosen the handle nut on the inside of the tank, and scrub the threads with some vinegar and a small brush with brass or nylon bristles (an old toothbrush might work in a pinch).

If jiggling the handle doesn't work, look for water flowing into the top of the overflow tube. If it is, the mechanism for adjusting the water level is set too high. If there is a float ball on the end of an arm, carefully bend the arm to force the float downward by placing both hands near the middle of the arm; try not to apply pressure to the float or ball-cock valve. After bending it, test by flushing. The float is correctly positioned when the water level stabilizes about ½ inch below the top of the overflow tube.

If your tank has a floating-cup ball cock, adjust the water level by squeezing the clip located on its side and moving the ball cock up or down.

If water is not flowing into the overflow tube, carefully lift the float a bit. If this shuts off the water flow, the problem is that the float isn't rising high enough in the tank. Carefully bend the float arm to raise the float. If this still doesn't fix the problem, unscrew the float and shake it to see if it's water-logged; if so, replace the float. If water continues to come out of the ball-cock valve and adjusting the float doesn't affect it, the washers in the valve probably need replacing. Shut off the water supply and flush the toilet to drain the tank. Then remove the screws or pins holding the float arm to the valve. Pull out the small plunger centered in the top of the valve, remove and

replace the washers, and reassemble the valve. Instead of repairing the valve, you may want to replace the entire valve assembly with a new floating-cup ball-cock kit.

Adjusting a conventional float ball cock and tank ball

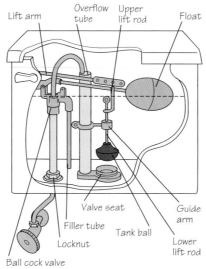

Adjusting a plastic floating-cup ball cock and chain-controlled flapper

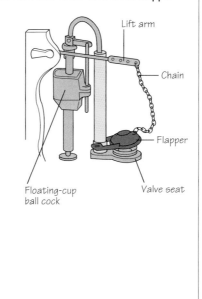

If the float and ball-cock valve seem to be operating correctly, water is probably running because the tank ball or flapper is not dropping fully into the valve seat (drain hole) in the bottom of the tank. Drain the tank before working on it. First close the shutoff valve under the tank; if there is no valve, turn off the main water supply valve. Then flush the toilet to empty the tank. If the toilet has a tank-ball assembly, make sure that the guide arm is aligned directly over the valve seat. If the guide arm needs adjustment, loosen the thumbscrew, move the arm to the right or left, then retighten the thumbscrew. Examine the tank ball; if it appears worn, unscrew it from the lift rod and replace it. If the lift rod is bent, causing the ball to drop crookenly into the valve seat, straighten it. If the ball doesn't drop far enough to seat tightly, move the upper lift rod to a different hole in the lift arm. If the ball or flapper is controlled by a chain, move the chain to a different hole, or hook it by a different link so that there is just a small amount of slack when the ball or flapper is seated.

If the tank ball seats properly but water continues to leak out, empty the tank and clean the bottom of the ball with detergent or a vinegar-and-water solution. Use water and a small wire brush or steel wool to clean the valve seat. Reassemble, turn on the water, and test.

▶ *Toilet doesn't flush completely.*

Check the water level in the tank. It should be about ½ inch below the top of the overflow tube. If it is lower than that, the tank may not be filling with enough water. To adjust the level, raise the float higher by bending the float arm, or replace the float if it is waterlogged (see left). If the toilet has a plastic

Tip *If the ball-cock valve or valve seat seems to require repair too often, replace both of them with a plastic floating-cup ball cock and a hinged flapper. Both are inexpensive and quite easy to install, following the simple instructions on the package.*

floating-cup ball cock, adjust the water level by squeezing the clip and raising the float.

If the water level is adequate, try to make the tank ball or flapper lift higher. If the overflow tube has an adjustable guide arm and it blocks the tank ball from rising any higher, loosen the thumbscrew and raise the arm about ½ inch. Also shorten the lift rods by bending the top hook over with pliers. If the ball or flapper is controlled by a chain, reduce the slack in the chain.

If the toilet never seems to flush completely, the problem may be a partial clog in the waste line (see page 157), inadequate venting (see page 156), or a low-flush model that requires a higher water pressure. Call a plumber.

▶ Handle is loose.

Tighten the nut inside the tank. If it is too corroded and you can't remove it, turn off the water at the shutoff valve and drain the tank by flushing it. On the inside of the tank, cut through the handle shaft with a hacksaw. Detach the inside piece from the lift arm, or if they are permanently connected, buy a new handle with a lift arm attached. To install the new handle, insert the shaft through the hole from the outside of the tank; attach the locknut or holding device from the inside. Because the handle is above water level, it doesn't require a tight-fitting gasket or seal around the hole. Tighten it enough to lift easily without wobbling.

▶ Toilet makes unusual noises when filling.

Take off the tank top, flush the toilet, and watch the ball-cock valve. The washers in the plunger may be worn, allowing water to squirt around it under pressure. If you see water squirting around the plunger, and you can confirm that it causes the noise, replace the washers on the plunger (see opposite page), or replace the ball cock with a floating-cup ball cock. If the noise is a splashing or gurgling sound, make sure the flexible filler tube is aimed into the overflow pipe and not the tank reservoir. There should be a clip on the end of the filler tube for attaching it to the top of the overflow tube. Adjust it so the water flows completely into the tube and does not splash out.

▶ Bowl is clogged.

If the toilet is the only fixture that is backing up, the clog is probably in the bowl trap. Use a plunger with a funnel cup to try to clear the blockage. If the problem remains after several minutes of regular plunging, snake a closet auger down the bowl. The bottom of the shaft of this kind of auger is protected to keep it from scratching the porcelain bowl surface. Retract the cable into the shaft by pulling up on the handle, then insert the shaft into the bowl and push the handle down to work the cable into the drain until it contacts the clog. Rock the handle back and forth gently while pushing and pulling slightly on it, keeping the shaft steady with your other hand. Be patient; it may take some time to break up the clog.

If the plunger and auger don't clear things up and you are certain that the clog is in the bowl, remove the toilet (see page 191). Be sure to drain the tank (if necessary, with a cup and bucket). If possible, carry the bowl outside and place it upside down. Use an auger or a piece of a wire clothes hanger to fish out the clog. Flush the trap with a garden hose. Put in a new wax ring when you reinstall the bowl.

Using a closet auger

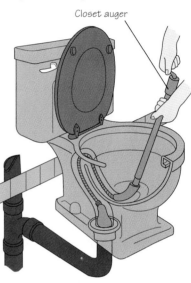

Closet auger

▶ Water leaks around the floor.

First make sure that the water is coming from under the base of the bowl and not dripping from condensation on the tank or a leak from the tank or supply line (see page 190). Lift up the caps covering the bolts on each side of the toilet base to see if the nuts are loose.

Tip *If the handle on the toilet tank droops, or if it doesn't rotate far enough to provide a complete flush, look for a setscrew inside the tank where the handle connects to the trip lever, or lift arm. Loosen the screw, adjust the handle to its proper position, and tighten the screw.*

If so, tighten them carefully; over-tightening will crack the entire bowl. If the nuts aren't loose or tightening them does not stop the leak, you will have to lift the bowl from the floor to see what the problem is. Most likely the wax seal between the closet flange and the toilet has slipped or is damaged and needs to be replaced. However, the subfloor around the drain flange may have rotted or collapsed enough to cause the flange to shift, requiring more extensive repair. To remove the bowl and install a new wax ring, see opposite page. If you discover that the old wax ring shifted because the closet flange has come loose from the floor or the soil pipe, call a plumber.

▶ Tank sweats.

Condensation forms when warm moist air strikes a cold surface. A toilet tank surface remains cool from the cold water stored inside the tank. If the air is humid and warm, condensation will form. First try to control humidity in the bathroom by providing adequate ventilation. You can also keep the tank surface from cooling off by installing an insulation liner inside the tank; liner kits are available at hardware stores and home centers. Proper installation usually requires that the tank be completely dry. Trim the liner pieces to size and adhere them to the tank sides with the adhesive provided with the kit. A more expensive alternative is to install a tempering valve below the tank. It is connected to the hot-water and cold-water supply lines, allowing you to adjust the temperature so warmer water enters the tank, thus keeping the tank surface warm. This is a job for a plumber.

▶ You can't tell if the tank is leaking or sweating.

If there is water on the floor and the underside of the tank is damp, the problem is most likely condensation. If the tank is dry, you can rule out sweating or condensation as the problem. Clean up the water around the bowl and thoroughly dry the area. Then flush the toilet. If water appears from around the base, the wax seal is leaking. If the source of the leak remains a mystery, carefully examine and tighten all connections from the shutoff valve up to the tank (inside and out). Do the same with the nuts securing the bowl to the tank, but only if they are loose; overtightening will crack the bowl. See if the water level in the tank is too high, causing water to leak through the handle hole; and check to see if the refill tube isn't shooting water some place other than straight down the overflow tube. Examine the ball-cock valve for a leak. Finally, look for cracks in the tank or bowl.

▶ Seat is loose.

Look under the top rim of the bowl for the tightening nuts connected to the seat bolts and tighten them. Check the rubber or plastic spacers that keep the nuts from tightening directly against the porcelain bowl. If they are missing, replace each with a rubber cone washer and fiber washer of appropriate size. Don't overtighten the nuts, as this will crack the porcelain. If the nuts are corroded and don't turn easily, squirt some penetrating oil on the bolt threads above the nuts and wait a few minutes for it to soak in. If the nuts are snug and the seat is still loose, check the screws that secure the hinges to the seat and cover; tighten any loose screws.

▶ Seat needs replacing.

To remove the old seat, loosen the nuts under the top rim of the bowl. If they are corroded and won't turn, apply penetrating oil to the threads above them and wait for it to soak in. If the nuts still won't turn, cut through the bolts with a mini hacksaw, being careful not to scratch the porcelain surface of the bowl (protect it with duct tape if necessary). With the nuts removed, lift off the old seat. Toilet seat sizes are highly standardized, but if you have a very old or unusual toilet, you might want to take the old seat along when you buy a new one. Seats are available in many styles, including solid wood, enameled wood, molded plastic, and fur. Install the new seat with the washers and nuts provided. Most seats have plastic bolts and nuts to prevent rusting. Tighten the nuts securely, but don't overtighten.

Replacing a toilet seat

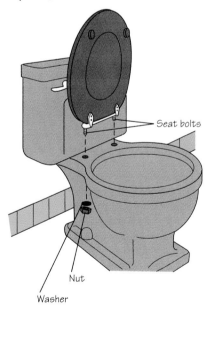

Seat bolts

Nut

Washer

Tip   *If the caps that cover the closet bolts at the base of the toilet are loose, there are two ways to secure them. One is to dab some caulk or plumber's putty inside the caps so they will adhere to the closet bolts and nuts. The second is to buy plastic caps that include a separate snap washer. Unscrew the nuts from the closet bolts, slide a washer over each bolt with the grooved edge facing down, screw the nuts back on, and snap the plastic caps onto the washers.*

▶ *Toilet needs replacing.*

Shut off the water supply and drain the water from the tank and bowl (flush the toilet, then use a siphon or a cup and sponge to scoop out the remaining water). Remove the locknut securing the water supply line to the bottom of the tank, and remove the nuts holding the tank to the bowl; lift the tank off the bowl. Now loosen the nuts at the base of the bowl (they may be hidden under decorative caps). Lift the bowl off the closet flange (you may need to rock it back and forth), and carefully carry the bowl outside (spread newspapers along your route beforehand to protect carpets and floors). Stuff a rag into the flange to prevent sewer gas from entering the bathroom.

Clean off the wax residue from the closet flange with a putty knife. Slide out the old closet bolts and buy new ones. Clean the flange. If it is an old cast-iron flange and is cracked or broken around the bolt hole, check with a plumbing supplier for a short, curved repair strap for bolting to the flange; otherwise you should replace the flange. You will probably have to cut off the soil pipe below the floor, add a new section of pipe, and attach the flange to it.

Slide the new closet bolts into the slots on the flange. Use a dab of plumber's putty to hold them in place until you can set the bowl. Set the new bowl upside down on a towel or piece of old carpeting, and press a new wax ring onto the horn of the bowl. Some wax rings have a plastic sleeve that extends into the flange when the bowl is mounted on it, ensuring a better seal. Use this type especially when the flange lies below the level of the finish floor; if

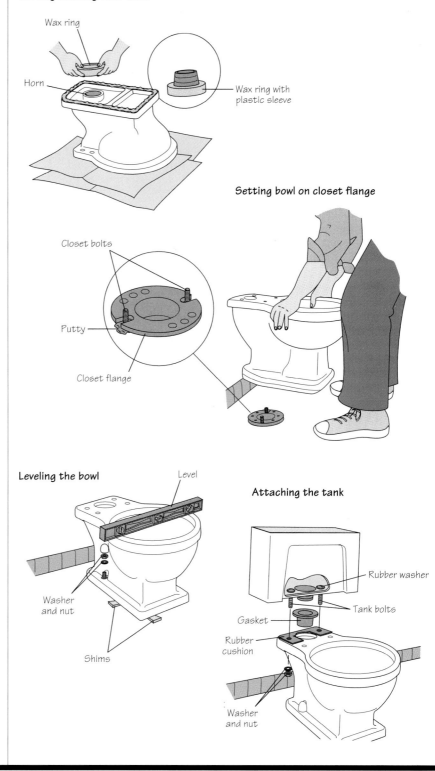

Setting wax ring onto horn

Wax ring

Horn

Wax ring with plastic sleeve

Setting bowl on closet flange

Closet bolts

Putty

Closet flange

Leveling the bowl

Level

Washer and nut

Shims

Attaching the tank

Rubber washer

Tank bolts

Gasket

Rubber cushion

Washer and nut

Tip *Some communities, in an effort to promote water conservation, have programs for replacing toilets with low-flush models (1.6 gallons or less), free of cost. If you plan to install a new toilet, or wish to reduce water consumption, contact the water department to see if it offers this service.*

the finish floor is more than ¾ inch above the flange, stack two wax rings to make sure the gap will be sealed. Next turn the bowl over and gently set it onto the flange, using the closet bolts as a guide. Push the bowl down into the wax ring. Place the washers and nuts that came with the new bowl onto the bolts and tighten carefully. If a plastic disk is included for snapping the bolt caps onto, place it over the closet bolt first. Tighten each side a little bit at a time. Once they are snug, kneel or sit on the bowl with all of your weight. Check it with a level, using shims to level it if necessary. Then tighten the nuts again. Once the nuts are snug, don't tighten them any more. With a small hacksaw, cut the excess from the bolts and put on the decorative caps.

Next set the tank on the bowl. Make sure to align any washers, gaskets, or cushions exactly as specified in the installation directions. Normally, you will need to tighten the nuts from underneath while securing the bolt in the tank with a large screwdriver. Finally, reattach the water supply line to the tank, turn on the water, and flush a few times to check for leaks.

After a few days' use, if there are still no leaks, especially around the base, run a bead of caulk between the base and floor to prevent water from leaking under the bowl and damaging the floor. Some plumbers run a snake of plumber's putty around the bottom of the bowl before setting it if they are confident that the wax ring will seal perfectly. (The putty prevents water from leaking out from under the bowl, a warning that the wax seal is defective.)

▶ Flushing uses too much water.

Toilets are responsible for a large amount of water consumption, an issue of concern in many communities. Older toilets can use as much as 5 to 7 gallons of water for each flush. There are devices available that can limit the amount of water an older toilet uses, but often these toilets aren't designed to provide a complete flush with less water. Low-flush toilets are available that require 1.6 gallons of water or less per flush. Your community may require that you install one of these anytime you replace a toilet or add a new bathroom (check with the local building department). If you don't plan to install a new toilet and are otherwise happy with the one you've got, you can try installing a toilet dam, available at home centers and plumbing-supply outlets. Generally two dams are installed in the tank, reducing the amount of water that the tank holds. Do not place bricks in the tank to reduce water consumption, as they will slowly deteriorate and release grit that can foul up the functioning of the toilet.

▶ Porcelain is scratched, cracked, or stained.

Try covering minor scratches with appliance paint or auto-body touch-up paint. You may be able to stop a leak through cracked porcelain by sealing the crack with epoxy, but the solution will be only temporary as the crack will have weakened the fixture. The best solution is to replace the toilet. If stains in the bowl resist common household cleaners, pour some chorine bleach into the bowl, let it sit overnight, then scrub the stains again. For rusty stains, use a rust remover recommended for plumbing fixtures. If all efforts fail, consider replacing the toilet.

▶ Water trickles into bowl between flushes.

The tank ball or flapper that seals the drain hole in the tank bottom is probably not seating properly. If enough water leaks out and into the bowl, the tank will refill on its own with a rush of water, sounding like a phantom flush.

To correct the problem, check the alignment of the tank ball or flapper to be sure it settles securely over the drain hole after each flush. Correct the alignment of a tank ball by loosening the thumbscrew holding the support arm in place and rotating the arm until the ball is aligned. If a flapper is out of alignment, make sure it isn't torn or broken and that the hingelike mounting flange is securely attached to the overflow pipe. If alignment is not the problem, inspect the tank ball or flapper for nicks or wear; replace it if it seems worn.

If the problem persists, check the valve seat that the ball or flapper fits into. It may have mineral deposits or scratches that prevent a tight seal. To clean it, empty the tank and scour the valve seat with steel wool (if it's brass) or a nylon pot scrubber (if it's plastic).

▶ Water seeps from under tank.

The bolts that hold the tank to the bowl may be loose, or their rubber washers may have deteriorated. Try tightening the bolts by turning the nuts located behind the toilet and beneath the tank. Be very careful—overtightening will crack the bowl. If the nut is stuck to the bolt and they both turn, steady the bolt with a screwdriver from inside the tank (you may need a helper). If the nuts don't need tightening, turn off the water supply, flush the toilet to drain the tank, and replace the tank bolts, nuts, and rubber washers with new ones.

Tip *If the tank doesn't empty completely after flushing, the flush valve is closing too soon. This problem occurs most often with toilets that have a flapper-type flush valve. To fix it, take some of the slack out of the chain that connects the flapper to the handle lever.*

▶ Septic system backs up.

The septic tank may need pumping. Tanks should be pumped out every two or three years. If yours hasn't been pumped out for a while, call a professional tank pumper. Before the tank is closed back up, flush the toilets and run water down the drain to see if the clog has been removed. If it hasn't, use an auger to find and remove the clog. Run the auger from the tank inlet pipe, or from the sewer-line cleanout near the house foundation (if there is one).

Septic systems can also back up if too much water is run into the tank too fast—it runs directly into the leach field, clogs the soil, and fills the pipes. A larger tank or drain field may solve this problem if it is recurrent.

Finally, the leach field may not be functioning properly (see right).

Pumping a septic tank

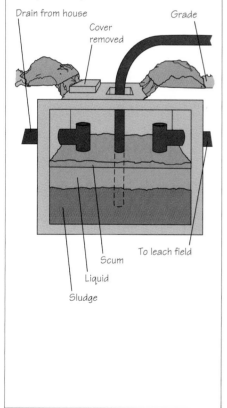

Drain from house
Cover removed
Grade
To leach field
Scum
Liquid
Sludge

▶ Odors emanate from ground.

Odors coming from the tank, or the house side of the tank, may indicate a crack or hole in the tank or a leaking drainage pipe. An expert should be called to try to determine the source of the leak and suggest corrective action.

▶ Leach field is marshy.

The leach field isn't draining properly. This will be particularly evident on dry days if you see patches of especially green grass above the leach pipes. If the problem is infrequent, and especially if it follows particularly heavy rainfall or spring thaw, if may not be worth fixing. But if it is persistent, the gravel in the leach field may have to be replaced and the pipes cleaned out.

▶ Pump cycles on and off erratically.

The pressure switch is probably defective and should be replaced. Drain the tank or, if there's a valve isolating it from the switch, close it. Turn off the power. Remove the switch cover and label the wires (or draw a sketch of the electrical connections). Then disconnect the wires from the terminals, unscrew the locknuts that attach the armored electrical cables to the switch box, and remove the cables. Unscrew the switch from its riser nipple, then wrap pipe joint tape on the nipple threads, and thread on the new switch. Reconnect the wires and turn on the power. The pump should shut off after it builds up pressure in the system. Open a faucet to test the switch; it should turn the pump on after a short time, when the open faucet has drained pressure from the system. Watch the pressure gauge while the pump runs; the switch should turn the pump

on when pressure falls below 40 pounds and shut it off when pressure builds up to 60 to 65 pounds. If the pressure gets too high because the switch leaves the pump on too long, or the pressure falls too low because the switch doesn't turn the pump on soon enough, adjust the pressure switch by turning the adjusting nut at the end of the spring.

Replacing a pressure switch

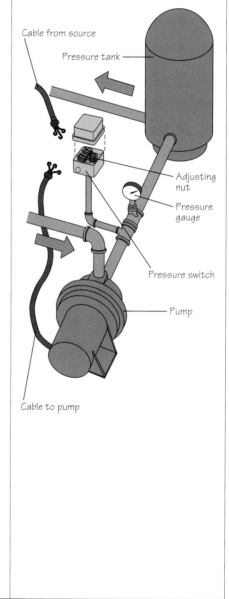

Cable from source
Pressure tank
Adjusting nut
Pressure gauge
Pressure switch
Pump
Cable to pump

Tip *The normal interval for having a septic tank pumped is between two and three years.*

Tip *Typical requirements for a septic-tank drain field: (1) minimum of 10 inches of soil above the drainage pipes, (2) no pipes within 10 feet of the house foundation or within 5 feet of any other structure, (3) no pipes within 10 feet of a property line, and (4) no pipes within 10 feet of a water supply pipe or within 100 feet of a well.*

▶ Pump cycles on and off frequently.

If the pump turns on every time you run water out of a faucet, the pressure tank isn't holding air pressure. First check the pressure with a tire gauge at the small threaded valve that looks like a tire valve. If it is less than recommended by the manufacturer, add the necessary amount of air with a tire pump. Add only a little at a time, checking regularly with the gauge.

If the tank is an older style of pressure tank without an air valve, it has probably lost air pressure from becoming waterlogged. To recharge the air, shut off power to the pump, then open the drain valve on the tank (attach a hose if necessary). Open a faucet in the house to drain the water out of the tank so it fills with air. Then turn off the faucet, shut the drain valve on the tank, and turn the pump back on. The water will compress the air into a cushion at the top of the tank, which pressurizes the system. Over time the air in such a tank does become waterlogged. If this happens frequently, replace the tank with a newer model that keeps the air separated from the water by an expandable bladder or diaphragm, which can be recharged without draining the tank.

If recharging the tank doesn't solve the problem, or solves it for only a short time, the tank is losing pressure because of leaks. First check for water leaks in the plumbing system: leaking faucets or pipes or a running toilet. Then check the pressure tank for an air leak. Spray soapy water around the tank surface. If you see bubbles indicating a leak, the internal diaphragm or the whole tank may need to be replaced. If you can't find a leak and the tank still does not hold pressure, the check valve for the pump, which keeps water from draining back into the well, may need replacing. This requires that the pump be pulled from the well if it is a submersible pump. Call for repairs.

▶ Pump won't run.

Check for a tripped circuit breaker or blown fuse. Well pumps require a large draw of amperage to start up and may overload the circuit. If the breaker trips frequently, have an electrician rewire the circuit. Also, with the power off, check that all wires are connected securely.

If a fuse or breaker isn't the problem, check the pressure switch, usually located near the pressure tank. The spring on the switch may have weakened over time; compensate by tightening the adjusting nut at the end of the spring. Also see if the switch contacts are dirty or discolored; if so, shut off the power and sand or file them (a nail file or very fine sandpaper works best). Restore power and draw some water. If the pump still doesn't come on, you probably need a new pressure switch (see page 193).

There may be an obstruction in the piping to the pressure switch or in the pump mechanism itself. Shut off the power and inspect the pipes and fittings. If they are clear, check the pump. Some kinds of pumps you can turn manually; if you encounter resistance while turning the shaft, there is some kind of obstruction in the impeller. Have the pump inspected and repaired by a professional.

If you have a well pump with a control box located near the pressure tank, the box may have a capacitor or capacitor coil that is the source of pump failure. If the pump is totally dead, both should be checked for an open relay or a short. Have a professional do this, as a capacitor can discharge a dangerously high level of voltage even when the power is off. If either component is defective, it will have to be replaced.

Cleaning pressure-switch contact points

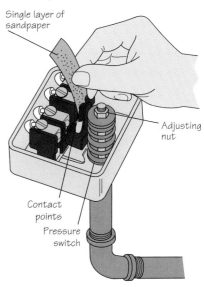

Single layer of sandpaper

Adjusting nut

Contact points

Pressure switch

▶ Pump won't stop running.

It's possible that the pump has lost its "prime" and is running continuously to try to catch up. Turn off power to the pump and restore the prime by pouring water into the priming hole. However, it's more likely the problem is in the pressure switch. It may be set too high; to adjust the setting, turn the adjusting nut at the end of the spring counterclockwise. If that doesn't work, turn off power to the pump and inspect the contact points; if they appear to be stuck together, gently pry them apart with a screwdriver and smooth them with sandpaper. If the switch still doesn't work, replace it (see page 193).

Tip *Wells run dry when the water table drops below the intake, often during severe drought or following particularly heavy usage. If the problem happens at other times, you should either have the well drilled deeper or have a new well drilled in a better location. Consult an experienced well driller.*

▶ Impeller on pump isn't working.

If you have a deep-well centrifugal pump, commonly called a submersible pump, the pumping suction is created by a rotating impeller, which is often made of either nylon or brass. If a centrifugal pump runs dry, heat buildup can quickly melt the blades. The pump will have to be pulled from the well and repaired or replaced.

▶ Well water may be contaminated.

There are dozens of biological and chemical contaminants that may be found in drinking water. Federal standards set allowable limits. Some contaminants can be detected by sight or smell, but most cannot. Some can cause acute health effects (diarrhea, nausea), whereas others can cause long-term, chronic problems. Contact the county extension service or a water-quality expert for advice on testing and treating. All water from wells should be checked periodically for coliform bacteria. Don't install any water treatment equipment until you have discovered what, if anything, you want to treat.

If you have had any work done on your well recently, you should chlorinate the whole system. Use regular, unscented laundry bleach. Mix at least 1 cup in 5 gallons of water, then pour the solution into the well casing. Turn on faucets in the house until you smell the bleach. Let the chlorinated water sit in the pipes for a couple of hours, then run the water out of each faucet until long after the bleach smell has disappeared. If your drains run into a septic tank, empty the chlorinated water into buckets, let them sit for a few days, then dispose of the water elsewhere (it shouldn't be harmful to any but the most sensitive lawn or garden plants).

▶ Water needs softening.

Water containing high amounts of calcium, magnesium, or iron, called "hard" water, should be treated with a softener. Water softeners filter water through a granulated resin that causes an ion exchange, trapping the hard ions of the minerals and exchanging them for soft sodium ions. Salt is then filtered through the resin to rejuvenate it. Salt must be added to the container on a regular basis.

A water-softening system contains a resin tank and a brine tank, sometimes combined inside one self-enclosed unit. An automatic water softener will also have a time clock control that is programmed to siphon the brine into the resin tank to replenish its effectiveness. Generally, the only work required of the homeowner is to add salt to the brine tank from time to time.

There are two methods of installing water softeners, and the one you choose may depend on the degree of hardness in your water. For moderately hard water, which prevents soap from lathering easily but does not stain fixtures, you can choose to soften only the hot water, providing softened water where it is most needed (laundry and bathing). This is the simpler option and it has the added benefit of not adding sodium to your drinking water, which can be a health problem for some.

If your water is hard enough to stain fixtures and build up scale in pipes, fixtures, and appliances, you'll have to soften the water in the whole house.

For a hot-water-only installation, install the softener on the cold-water inlet line that runs to the water heater. To soften water on the whole system, install the softener near the water meter, before the hot- and cold-water lines branch off, though you might wish to avoid softening lines to sillcocks, as softened water can damage lawns and gardens. Installation should be done by a professional, as water pipes may have to be resized or a bypass system added to keep the water pressure up—adding a softener usually reduces it.

You can also rent a water softener, which will save you from having to install one, but will cost more in the long run.

Typical water-softening unit

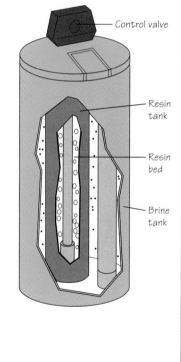

Control valve

Resin tank

Resin bed

Brine tank

Tip   *To see if your water is hard enough to require further testing or a softener, fill a jar halfway with cold tap water. Then sprinkle in a few flakes of pure detergent or soap (unscented, with no additives). Screw a lid onto the jar and shake it. If little or no lather forms, the water is hard. Hard water will also leave a residue on your finger if you dip it into the solution.*

SOLVING PLUMBING PROBLEMS

▶ *Sprinkler pipe is leaking.*

Most lawn sprinklers today are installed using plastic pipe, either flexible (polybutylene or poly-ethylene) or rigid (PVC or ABS). They can be damaged by digging in the yard or garden. First dig a trench to expose 1 to 2 feet of pipe around the leak, removing dirt from the sides and bottom of the pipe as well as the top. Shut off the water supply. If the pipe has a small hole or crack, you can make a permanent repair with a dresser, or repair, coupling (see page 152). First cut through the pipe where it is damaged. Then carefully pull the cut ends apart far enough to slide the coupling over one end (the coupling nuts should be loose). Slide the coupling over the other end, tighten the nuts, and turn on the water to test the repair.

If the damage extends along the pipe too far for a repair coupling to cover it (1 inch for ½-inch pipe, 2 to 3 inches for ¾-inch pipe), cut out the damaged section and replace it with tubing of the same size and material. If it is solid pipe with solvent-weld joints, see page 154 for joining techniques. If it is flexible polybutylene or poly-ethylene pipe, there are several types of fittings available to join the replacement section of tubing to the rest of the pipe. Choose the same type of fitting that was used on the rest of the sprinkler system. Join push-fit fittings by simply pushing the tubing into the fitting. To join clamp fittings, tighten the setscrew with a screwdriver. Join crimped fittings by squeezing them together with pliers.

▶ *Sprinkler head is clogged.*

Some heads can be cleaned by clearing out the holes with a thin piece of wire. Heads that include a large cartridge body have an internal screen that you can remove and clean by disassembling the cartridge. You may need to dig around the cartridge a bit to grip it so you can unscrew the head, and to keep debris from falling into the exposed cartridge chamber. If cleaning does not solve the problem, replace the head (see below).

▶ *Sprinkler head doesn't spray far enough.*

First check for clogs (see above). Then adjust the force of the spray: Some sprinklers have an adjusting screw in the middle of the head; others have an allen-head setscrew. If the head sprays far enough but doesn't cover the required area of lawn, it may not be the right head for that spot. Some heads cover a full 360-degree sweep, others cover 180 degrees (useful along the sides of buildings or walks), and yet others cover only 90 degrees (one quarter of a circle) and are used in corners. Some types of sprinkler heads can be adjusted for changing the coverage arc. They are usually plastic and have a canister extending into the ground below the head. Consult the manufacturer's instruction sheet for your type of heads to see if you can adjust them; otherwise replace the head with one that has the coverage you desire. To install it, turn off the automatic timer for the system. Remove a few inches of grass and dirt from around the sprinkler head and unscrew it from the riser pipe (use two wrenches or pliers). If the

head has a deep body, dig carefully around it to expose the connection to the riser pipe before unscrewing it. If the new sprinkler head is not identical to the old, attach whatever couplings or nipples are necessary to adapt it to the right height and screw it onto the riser pipe. (If you won't be installing the new sprinkler head immediately, screw a pipe nipple or pipe cap onto the exposed water pipe to keep dirt from falling into it.) Orient the new head, or adjust it according to manufacturer's instructions, so the spray will cover the desired area.

Removing old head

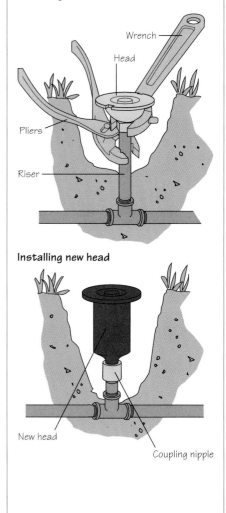

Installing new head

Tip   *A simple way to test the water distribution of a sprinkler head is to set up a gridlike pattern of small, equal-sized containers on the section of lawn surrounding the sprinkler head. Run the sprinkler for a set time and measure the contents of each container with a ruler. A lawn generally needs from 1 to 2 inches of water per week.*

Electricity deserves respect, but it is not necessarily mysterious. The electrical system can be one of the simplest and most logical areas to work on, so long as you understand a few basic principles and safety procedures. This chapter presents guidelines for solving more than 130 problems. Before you attempt to solve a particular problem, browse through a few others to be sure you understand the principles involved.

SOLVING ELECTRICAL PROBLEMS

▶ *Electricity needs to be turned off.*

If you're turning off power to do any work on the electrical system, test your voltage tester first to make sure it works by inserting the probes into a receptacle. To shut off power to the entire house, locate the main circuit breaker, which is usually in a metal box near the electric meter, and switch it to *Off*. (It may be inside the main service panel in the house.) If there is no main breaker, shut off all the branch-circuit breakers. Older homes may have a fuse drawer marked *Main* that you pull out, or cartridge fuses that you can disconnect by pulling down a lever on the outside of the box (do not try to pull out the cartridges unless you are wearing rubber gloves or have an insulated fuse-pulling tool, and

the circuit is not drawing power). In some service entrances (the meter, main disconnect, and the circuit-breaker panel) there may be one or two other large breakers besides the main, labeled *Range* or *Air Conditioner;* they control those appliances independently of the rest of the house, and should be switched off if you want all power off.

To shut off electricity to only one part of the house—to a light switch you are replacing, for instance—shut off the circuit breaker or unscrew the fuse (make sure that it is not drawing power) for that particular circuit; it will deaden other fixtures and outlets as well. Then test the light switch or other device you are working on with a voltage tester to make sure it is dead.

Shutting off main disconnect

Breaker type   Cartridge fuse type   Fuse drawer type

Main breaker panel   Main fuse panel

▶ *Power goes off in whole house.*

Check to see if the main breaker is tripped. Examine the immediate area first for loose or dangling power lines; don't stand on damp ground, wear gloves, and take a flashlight. If the breaker is not tripped, phone the power company. If it is tripped, don't reset it. First turn off all the branch-circuit breakers; then reset the main breaker and, one by one, reset the circuit breakers. (To reset a breaker, turn it to *Off* first, then to *On.*) If the main breaker suddenly trips when you reset one of the circuit breakers, that circuit may be the source of the problem. Leave that circuit breaker off as you continue resetting breakers. If power is restored successfully, tape the problem breaker in the *Off* position and call an electrician. If the main breaker trips again as you continue resetting circuit breakers, the problem is probably an overloaded main breaker. No individual circuit is at fault, but the combined load is too much for the main breaker. Call an electrician. In the meantime reduce the load by turning off or disconnecting as many appliances as you can, especially an electric range or heaters; if you have to use one, turn off another first.

Be aware that occasionally bad guys trip the main breaker to lure you out of the house. The box that contains the main breaker or fuse should be locked, and you should keep the key indoors.

▶ *Power goes off in part of house.*

Look for a tripped breaker in the circuit-breaker panel. The handle of a tripped breaker isn't always easy to notice; it may be in the center position, not the more conspicuous *Off* position. If the system has fuses instead of circuit breakers, shine a

Tip *Never replace a fuse with one that has a higher amperage rating. For protection, buy an S-type fuse of the proper rating and an adapter that matches it. The adapter screws into the fuse socket and will accept only S-type fuses of the same rating.*

Tip *For working with electricity safely:*
(1) Test your voltage tester before shutting off power.
(2) Always shut off power to any circuit you plan to work on and post a warning sign for others at the breaker panel.
(3) Test exposed wires or fixtures with the voltage tester before working on them.

flashlight into the glass center of each fuse until you see one that is smudged or has a broken internal bar. Do not reset the tripped breaker or replace the blown fuse yet; instead switch off or unplug all of the appliances and lights affected by the dead circuit, then reset the breaker or replace the fuse. If the breaker or fuse immediately trips again, call an electrician. If it does not, turn the lights and appliances back on, one by one, until the breaker or fuse trips. If it trips suddenly, the problem is almost certainly a short circuit in the last appliance turned on. To be sure, unplug it and reset the circuit breaker again; it should stay on. Turn on the rest of the appliances. If the breaker goes off again (there might be a delay), the problem is an overloaded circuit. Plug some of the appliances, especially those with heating elements, into other circuits. If the electricity stays on, the isolated appliance is the problem. Have it repaired.

▶ Power is off but breakers look fine.

If a few receptacles are dead (not necessarily in the same room), they may have been deadened by a tripped GFCI receptacle that they are wired into. These sensitive receptacles are subject to "nuisance tripping," and sometimes control outlets in other rooms. Check all GFCI receptacles, starting with the one closest to the dead outlets. Push the reset button on each one until electricity is restored.

If the problem isn't a tripped GFCI, there may be a subpanel of which you're not aware that controls the areas without power. Look in closets, under sinks, and in other hidden places. The main breaker

panel may have a breaker marked *Subpanel* or *Sub,* which confirms its existence if not its location. Even labels like *Addition, Basement,* or *Kitchen* are strong hints of a subpanel somewhere. If you can find it, look for a tripped breaker and proceed as described on opposite page. If not, call an electrician.

▶ Circuit breaker trips repeatedly.

The problem is probably an overloaded circuit. Follow the same procedure as for fuses (see below), except that the breaker gives no visible clues. Therefore, start with all appliances and lamps unplugged.

▶ Fuse blows repeatedly.

The problem is a short circuit or an overload. Examine the blown fuse to find out; if the window is blackened or discolored, the cause is a short circuit—either in the house wiring or in an appliance or fixture. Unplug all appliances and lamps on the circuit and try a new fuse. If it blows immediately, call an electrician. If it doesn't, plug in each device until the fuse blows again. The last appliance was the culprit. Replace or repair it.

If the fuse windows are clear but the internal link is broken, the cause is circuit overloading. It may be temporary overloading from a heavy motor starting up. Install a time-delay fuse of the same amperage; it allows temporary surges that aren't at dangerous levels. Or the overload may be caused by too many appliances plugged into the

same circuit. Redistribute the load by plugging some appliances into other circuits, or call an electrician. Do *not* attempt to solve the problem by installing a larger fuse.

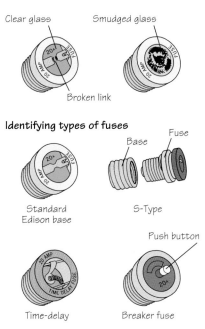

Reading a blown fuse

Clear glass   Smudged glass

Broken link

Identifying types of fuses

Base   Fuse

Standard Edison base   S-Type

Push button

Time-delay   Breaker fuse

▶ Circuit-breaker handle won't budge or flaps loosely.

A breaker can wear out. Replace it with a new one of identical amperage from the same manufacturer, or a compatible model. To remove the old one, first turn off the main circuit breaker. Take off the panel cover to expose the wiring inside. Remove the old breaker by pulling first one end straight out, then the other, until one of them comes loose. Loosen the setscrew that holds the wire in place. Insert the wire into the new breaker, tighten the setscrew, and snap the breaker into the panel. Replace the cover

(4) *Never stand on a wet or damp surface when working with electricity. Place dry rubber mats or boards over damp areas.*
(5) *Never touch plumbing, radiators, or metal duct work while working with electricity.*
(6) *Use a wood or fiberglass ladder (not metal) near overhead wires.*
(7) *Use tools with rubber- or plastic-coated handles.*
(8) *Wear safety glasses and, when working on service equipment (the main service entrance or circuit-breaker panel), gloves.*
(9) *Use only one hand when working on service equipment.*
(10) *Check your work with a voltage tester or receptacle analyzer.*

and restore power. *Caution:* Wear gloves, use tools with insulated handles, don't stand on damp floor or ground, and keep fingers away from wires inside the box.

Removing old breaker

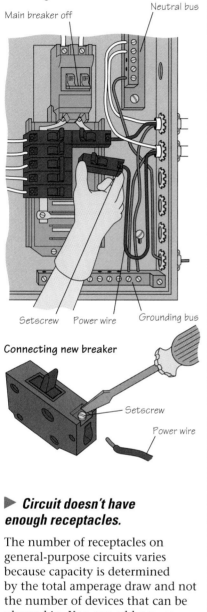

Main breaker off

Neutral bus

Setscrew Power wire Grounding bus

Connecting new breaker

Setscrew

Power wire

▶ Circuit doesn't have enough receptacles.

The number of receptacles on general-purpose circuits varies because capacity is determined by the total amperage draw and not the number of devices that can be plugged in. You can add new receptacles (see page 208) anywhere along a circuit (so long as it's not dedicated to a single appliance) by

running wire from any of the existing receptacles to the new one (provided the new wires don't crowd the electrical box; see "Number of Conductors Permitted in an Electrical Box" on page 303) or by splicing a junction box into the circuit wiring to provide a place to connect new wires. (You may have to install two junction boxes to make up for cable lost to splicing; see page 204.) Consult an electrician; obtain a proper permit.

Tying into receptacle at end of run

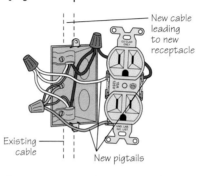

New cable leading to new receptacle

Existing cable

New pigtails

Tying into receptacle in middle of run

Existing cable

New cable

Existing cable

Box enlarged by ganging a second one onto the original

Tying into cable run

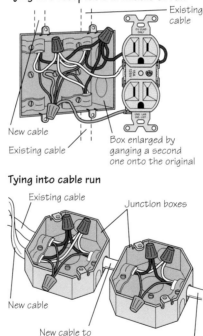

Existing cable

Junction boxes

New cable

New cable to join boxes

Existing cable

▶ Circuits are overloaded; not enough circuits.

If there are knockout blanks in the circuit-breaker panel or the breakers are the type that can be replaced with thinner ("wafer") versions, you can have new circuits run from the main breaker panel. If not, you will have to have a subpanel installed and run new circuits from it. In either case be sure that the increased load will not overload the main disconnect device (main breaker), that the new wire is sized large enough for the intended load, and that the circuit-breaker rating does not exceed the capacity of the wire size. The NEC® has specific requirements for various kinds of circuits. Consult an electrician or the local building-inspection department.

▶ Circuits aren't labeled clearly at breaker panel.

To prevent future annoyance during troubleshooting or to evaluate the house wiring system, map out the circuits by drawing a floor plan with all receptacles, switches, lights, and permanent (built-in) appliances. You'll need a helper and one or two plug-in lamps. If you work alone, use a radio that you can plug into different outlets throughout the house, turned up loud enough for you to hear from the circuit-breaker panel. If the circuits are not numbered, number them. Turn off the circuit breakers one by one and see which lights and receptacles don't work each time. On the floor plan, write the number of the circuit breaker next to each receptacle, appliance, or fixture it serves. Label the breakers themselves to identify which rooms or devices they control. Post a copy of the map inside or near the breaker panel.

Tip   *A tripped circuit breaker helps you diagnose the problem. If you switch it on and it suddenly trips with an angry buzzing sound, the problem is a short circuit where a hot (black) wire is in direct contact with a neutral wire or a ground wire; the short may be in a faulty piece of equipment, an electrical box, an electric fixture, or along a wiring run. If there's a delay before the breaker trips, it is an overloaded circuit.*

Note: You can also perform this test without turning off any breakers, by using a circuit-breaker locator tool. You may find it worth buying just so you won't have to reset digital clocks, VCRs, and other timers disturbed by turning off the circuits.

▶ Lights dim throughout house from time to time.

Occasional dimming may be caused by electrical storms or voltage drops in the power lines. More persistent dimming is probably due to heavy appliances, such as a refrigerator or washing machine, cycling on and off. These appliances should have their own circuits. Otherwise, try plugging them into a circuit that doesn't have lights on it.

▶ Appliances don't seem to run at full power.

The circuit that they are on is overloaded, but not to the point of tripping the circuit breaker or blowing a fuse. Reduce the load on the circuit by plugging some appliances into other circuits and using shorter extension cords wherever possible. If the problem continues, the entire electrical system should be inspected by a qualified electrician.

▶ TV picture shrinks.

The circuit is overloaded, probably by an appliance with a heavy-duty motor or a large heating element. Reduce the load on the circuit by plugging some appliances into other circuits, or plug the television into another circuit.

▶ System isn't grounded or is improperly grounded.

An electrical system must have a backup path that allows errant charges of electricity—from a disconnected wire, for instance—to flow at maximum available current so the circuit breaker or fuse can respond and shut off the circuit. Otherwise, the charged wire or appliance is a hazard to anyone touching it; it's also a potential fire hazard if the loose connection causes sparking. All receptacles, switches, lights, and built-in appliances should be connected to a ground wire (bare copper or green) or rigid metal conduit as part of their wiring. The entire system, in turn, should be grounded at the service-entrance panel by a continuous wire connected to at least two separate "grounding electrodes." These might be a metal water pipe (with bonding wires around the water meter and water heater), an 8-foot copper-clad ground rod, a 20-foot length of ½-inch-diameter reinforcing steel buried in the foundation (Ufer ground), or other approved means.

If your electrical system has partial or improper grounding, you should have it inspected and upgraded by a qualified electrician. In the meantime there is a stopgap measure you can undertake immediately: Replace ungrounded, two-prong outlets with GFCI receptacles, which work without a ground wire. They protect against shock by shutting off current so quickly that for all practical purposes the receptacle is dead *before* a hazard exists. If you can't afford one for each outlet, protect all outlets on the same circuit by installing a GFCI receptacle in the one closest to the breaker panel and attaching the wires that feed the other receptacles to the "load" terminals of the GFCI. Do not connect a ground wire between the GFCI and any downstream receptacles. See also page 210.

Providing grounding electrodes for a service panel

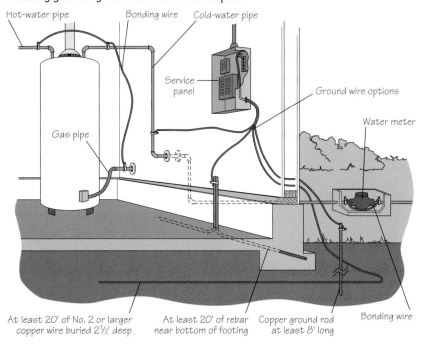

Hot-water pipe Bonding wire Cold-water pipe

Service panel

Ground wire options

Water meter

Gas pipe

At least 20' of No. 2 or larger copper wire buried 2½' deep   At least 20' of rebar near bottom of footing   Copper ground rod at least 8' long   Bonding wire

▶ Power surges from time to time.

Except for the potential catastrophe of a rare lightning strike, power surges were never considered a serious problem until recently. Now homes have computers, electronic entertainment systems, appliances controlled by microprocessors, and other delicate (and expensive) equipment that is vulnerable to power surges. Although utility companies monitor and adjust voltage constantly, surges are unavoidable and no community is immune. At the very least you should protect your most expensive equipment (especially a computer) with a surge protector, readily available at electronics dealers or computer stores. Get one with a response time less than 10 nanoseconds (10 billionths of a second), a "clamping voltage" (threshold at which it reacts) between 120 and 300 volts or as close to normal house voltage (120 volts) as you can afford, and an energy-absorbing capability of at least 100 joule (more where lightning is common). For cheaper but less reliable protection, hardware stores and home centers carry plug-in power strips with surge suppressors, which usually have multiple receptacles. It is also possible to have an electrician install surge-protection devices that protect your entire electrical system.

▶ System is grounded to water pipes, but some are plastic.

A system grounded to water pipes alone may not be grounded sufficiently. There is no assurance of a continuous path of uninterrupted metal piping to provide adequate contact with the soil; the path may be broken by sections of plastic piping or plastic bushings (sleeves or gaskets that separate metal pipes electrically) within some metal fittings (for instance, connections to water meters and water heaters have such fittings). Although bonding wires can and should be attached to metal pipes to bypass such obstructions, to be completely safe you should install a secondary grounding electrode. For most soil conditions you can use an 8-foot-long copper or copper-clad rod, ½ inch in diameter. Drive it into the ground next to the electrical service entrance until it is flush with the finished grade. Scoop some soil away from the rod and clamp No. 6 or larger copper wire to the top, then to the water pipe, and finally to the neutral bus bar in the circuit-breaker panel (which is bonded to the grounding bus bar if they are separate). Wear gloves and avoid touching both the ground wire and service equipment at the same time unless they are securely bonded together and the wire is grounded. Consult the local building-inspection department about permits and code requirements.

▶ Old service entrance is rated at less than 100 amps.

The minimum size for new service-entrance equipment is 100 amps—more if certain loads, such as air-conditioning or electric heating, are included. If your home has a smaller service entrance (30 amps is typical for many older homes), you are probably inconvenienced by frequent overloads. Unless you choose to revert to a 1920s life-style, you should have the service entrance changed by a qualified electrician. Aside from being undersized, a 30-amp system may have improper grounding, no 240-volt capability, and fatigued wires with worn or cracked insulation. Some older homes have a 60-amp service, which is almost always a three-wire service that was installed to accommodate an electric range. Such a system, if grounded properly, usually doesn't need upgrading unless you are adding electric heating loads. It often has sufficient capacity even for a major kitchen remodel; just replace the electric range with a gas one and use the range feeder wires for a new subpanel. Do not try to upgrade a system only by installing a larger main breaker or fuse. The entrance wires between the weatherhead and main breaker must also be replaced, and probably the mast as well.

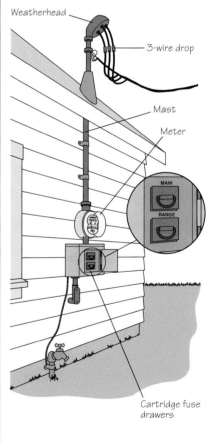

Identifying an older, 60-amp service entrance

Weatherhead

3-wire drop

Mast

Meter

MAIN

RANGE

Cartridge fuse drawers

▶ House is wired with aluminum wire.

Aluminum wiring, which was installed in many homes between 1965 and 1973, has been the cause of many residential fires, according to the Consumer Product Safety Commission. Symptoms such as warm cover plates, metallic odors, and even sparks or smoke can occur spontaneously. To tell if the wiring in your home is aluminum, look in the attic, basement, or garage for exposed wiring. If the cable has plastic sheathing that says *AL* or *Aluminum*, call the builder or an electrician certified to work on aluminum wiring. The system should be inspected and possibly replaced with copper wiring. Do not try to work with aluminum wiring yourself. Connections can corrode or overheat unless they are made carefully and with materials specified for use with aluminum wire.

This caution does not apply to aluminum wire used for the large service-entrance wires inside a mast or underground conduit. It is used widely and is not hazardous if connected properly. Aluminum wiring that poses the greater hazard is smaller-gauge circuit wiring inside the home, with multiple connections to receptacles, switches, and lights.

▶ House has old knob-and-tube wiring.

In this system, which was used in homes when they were first electrified, the wires are kept separate from each other and are fastened to the house framing with porcelain knobs and tubes. Most codes do not require replacing it, but any new wiring must use modern materials. Knob-and-tube wiring has the advantage of not overheating, but the disadvantage of no ground wire. If you tap into this type of wiring to extend a circuit, first verify that the two

wires are indeed a hot wire and a neutral wire by testing them with a no-contact voltage tester. (The wires aren't color-coded and two parallel wires aren't necessarily a hot and a neutral—they could be separate legs of a switch loop.) Then turn off the power and install two junction boxes close to the wires. Cut the wires, test them with a neon voltage tester to be sure they are dead, and thread them through knockout holes in the junction boxes. If the box is metal, slide some sheathing or "loom" over the wires to protect them. Run a short length of No. 14, two-wire NMC cable between the boxes. Then run the cable that feeds the new receptacles or lighting into one of the boxes and join the wires. If you tap into this type of wiring to feed new receptacles, use a GFCI receptacle in the first box, and wire all additional receptacles into it. No ground wire should be used with this arrangement.

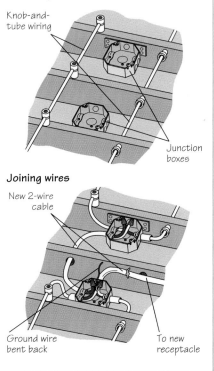

Installing boxes

Knob-and-tube wiring

Junction boxes

Joining wires

New 2-wire cable

Ground wire bent back

To new receptacle

▶ Ends of old knob-and-tube wiring are missing insulation.

The insulation on old wires eventually becomes brittle and frayed, especially near connections at the ends of wires. It can easily disintegrate when touched or rubbed, leaving wires dangerously bare. Turn off the power to affected wires, check them with a voltage tester, then wrap exposed ends with electrical tape. Where one wire crosses over another or enters a metal box, make sure it is enclosed in a length of loom (thick woven tubing used for insulation).

▶ Wire has splices or connections outside of electrical boxes.

This situation violates the NEC; all splices and connections must be made inside electrical boxes or other approved housings. Install a junction box in which to make the connections. First turn off the power to the wires; then disconnect them carefully and verify that the power is off by testing the exposed ends of both sets of wires with a voltage tester before proceeding. Mount a junction box where both sets of wires can be brought into it. Knock out a hole for each cable or wire, tighten the internal clamps over the wires, and connect the wires inside the box with wire connectors. If the wires aren't long enough to connect inside the box, move it toward one set of wires, install a second box for the second set, and join the boxes with new cable. (See page 204.) Screw a cover onto the junction box and leave it accessible (for example, do not bury it in a wall).

Tip *Treat electricity with respect. (1) Buy several neon voltage testers so you always have one handy; it's very cheap insurance. (2) Test the tester on a live receptacle before using it to test wires, just to make sure it works. (3) When testing, be sure that your fingers don't touch the metal probes of the tester or any other metal objects. (4) Consider all wires, terminals, and fixtures live until your voltage tester verifies that they are dead.*

▶ *Cable is not long enough to reach electrical box.*

Install a junction box at a convenient place along the cable run. Turn off the power and cut the cable so the "line" end of it (end originating at the power source) is long enough to be clamped into the box with 6 to 8 inches to spare. Discard the cutoff section. Thread the cable through a knockout hole in the box, strip off the sheathing from the portion inside the box, and tighten the box clamp onto it. With wire connectors, join a new cable to it inside the junction box, long enough to reach the receptacle, light, or switch box you are feeding. Attach a cover to the box and leave it exposed for access.

Using a junction box to extend cable

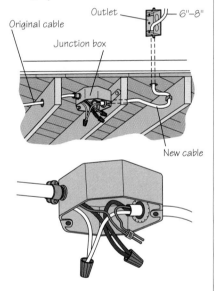

▶ *Junction-box cover shows and is obtrusive.*

Junction boxes (and covers) must be accessible. You cannot cover them with wallboard or other permanent coverings. Hang a picture over it.

▶ *Wire connector doesn't grip wires tightly.*

Check the chart on the connector package to make sure it is the proper size for the wires you are joining; you may need to use a smaller size. Also check manufacturer's instructions for how much insulation should be stripped from the end of the wire (strip length), and whether the wires are to lie side by side or be twisted together before screwing on the connector.

Joining wires with connector

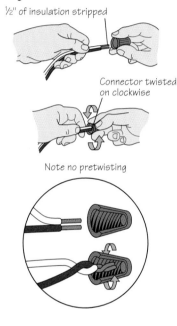

½" of insulation stripped

Connector twisted on clockwise

Note no pretwisting

▶ *Wires are not colored properly.*

Although common wiring practice is to use black or red wires for hot conductors, white wires for neutral, and green or bare wires for ground, you should never assume that you can tell the polarity of wire by its color. Occasionally a white wire is used as a hot conductor—when wiring a switch loop with nonmetallic-sheathed cable, for instance. Such wires are often wrapped with black tape or colored with a black pen at the ends to indicate that they are hot, but this practice is not universally observed or even required by the NEC. Sometimes all wires are black, as with knob-and-tube wiring or service-entrance conductors.

With a voltage tester you can check the polarity of a wire by touching one probe to it and the other probe to a ground wire or known ground, with the power on. (Be sure your fingers are not touching any metal, including the probes.) A hot wire will light up the tester; a neutral wire won't. To identify wires in the middle of their run, such as knob-and-tube wires, use a no-contact voltage tester.

▶ *Wire is not attached to anything; can't trace it to source.*

If you run across the end of a mysterious wire or cable that you can't account for, you should find the other end so you know whether to remove the wire or connect it properly. Treat it as a live wire until you are absolutely sure it is dead. Try to trace the wire visually; note its location on the wall and look directly above that location in the attic (or below it in the basement) to see if the wire emerges. If it does, continue tracing it; if it doesn't, poke a discreet hole in the wall next to the wire and use a flashlight to follow it as far as possible. Poke additional holes as necessary (to be spackled later) until you find the source. Then turn off the power to the house, disconnect the wire, and test it for continuity to verify that it is the wire you started with. If it is a cable with two or more wires, test continuity by joining two of them together at one end with a connector (with the power off). Then, at the other end of the cable, touch the two probes of a continuity tester (not a voltage tester) to

Tip *Wire connectors that twist onto the ends of wires, which are used to make connections inside electrical boxes, are often referred to as wing nuts or by the brand names Wire-Nut® or Scotchlok®. They have replaced soldering as a means of making such connections.*

the two wires that match the colors of those that you joined together. If the tester lights up, it's the same cable. Double-check by removing the connector and testing the same two wires again; the tester should-n't light up. To test a single wire, connect a long wire to one end and run it to the other end via the shortest route possible (the power should be off). Touch one probe of a continuity tester to this jumper wire and the other probe to the mystery wire. If the continuity test verifies that you have found both ends of the mystery wire or cable and it does not have a use, remove it. Otherwise, call an electrician.

Testing continuity

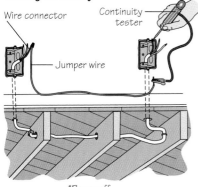

Wire connector

Continuity tester

Jumper wire

*Power off

▶ Wire is wrong size for new circuit wiring.

Never use wire that is too small for the fuse or circuit breaker of a given circuit. Most circuits are 15 or 20 amps, which require No. 14 and No. 12 wire, respectively. Because No. 12 wire is larger than No. 14, it could be used to wire a 15-amp circuit. On the other hand, No. 14 wire could not be substituted for No. 12 for a 20-amp circuit. If the wires for an existing circuit are too small for the breaker or fuse, replace the breaker or fuse with one that has the proper rating for the wire size.

▶ *Wires must be run inside a wall.*

Electrical wires or cable should be run through holes drilled in the centers of studs, which means removing portions of the existing wall covering. The least obtrusive area is along the floor. Remove the baseboard along the path between electrical boxes; then remove enough wall covering along the floor to expose all studs between the boxes. Drill a ¾-inch-diameter hole through the center of each stud near its base and pull cable through the holes, feeding it into the electrical boxes (or, for a new box, a hole cut into the wall covering). Connect the devices, test them, get any required inspections, patch the wall covering, and replace the baseboard.

Although the shortest distance between two points is a straight line, it may not be the easiest or best. The least disruptive run may be through the attic or the basement (or crawl space). For runs through the attic, drill a ¾-inch-diameter hole down from the attic through the top plate of the wall framing into the stud bay of each

of the electrical boxes to be connected. Feed fish tape (stiff wire for fishing cable through walls) down through this hole to one of the boxes, attach new cable to it, and pull the cable up into the attic. Drill holes through the centers of the ceiling joists. Run the cable through these holes to the hole in the plate above the other stud bay, then down to the electrical box. If you encounter an obstruction in the wall, drill a second hole next to the first. Shine a flashlight into the wall cavity while looking through the first hole. You may be able to guide the wire past it; if not, choose another stud cavity or remove wall covering at the obstacle and drill a hole through it. For running cable through the basement or crawl space, use the same process as for running cable through an attic. Avoid running wire through exterior walls. If you encounter the complications of insulation, windows, fire blocking, and limited access under eaves and above foundation walls, see page 206.

Running cable behind baseboard

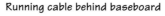

Existing receptacle

Wallboard cut out behind baseboard

New receptacle

Cable

Temporarily removed baseboard

Running cable through attic

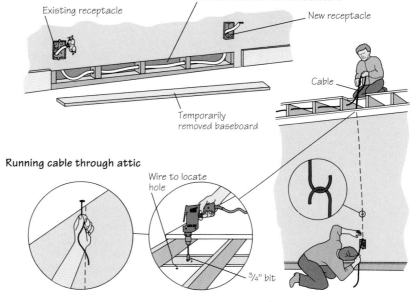

Wire to locate hole

¾" bit

Tip When using NM cable, be sure it is designated NM, Type B. This cable, which is rated for 194° F (90° C), is required by code and replaces older types of NM cable.

Tip Nonmetallic-sheathed cable (NM or NMC) run inside a wall must be protected from nails that might be driven into the wall in the future. When drilling through studs and other framing to create cable pathways, locate the holes as close to the center of the framing members as possible. If the hole is within 1¼ inch of the edge of the stud, or you are able only to notch the framing member, nail a metal plate (stud guard) to the stud to protect the cable before patching the wall.

▶ Wires must be run through ceiling or floor.

If the wiring runs parallel to a joist, fasten it to the side of the joist. If it runs across joists, drill holes in the approximate center of each and run cable through the holes. Cable strung below basement joists or across the top of attic joists must be protected by wood boards beside it or above it. Some communities allow an exception: In any area more than 6 feet from the opening to a "nonaccessible" attic (accessible only through a ceiling scuttle), cable can be strung across the tops of joists without guard strips. Check with local authorities.

Running wire parallel to joist

Joist

Cable straps no more than 4½' apart

Running wire perpendicular to joists

Subfloor

Joists

No protection needed

Running board

Guard strips

▶ Wires can't be run through wall, ceiling, or floor.

Run the wiring inside plastic or metal raceways that can be mounted on wall and ceiling surfaces. Systems designed for this purpose include channels, elbows, connecting devices, outlet boxes, and other components. Follow local code requirements and manufacturer's instructions—for instance, a system may require using individual wires and not sheathed cable; or surface-mounted wiring may not be allowed in certain rooms.

Using surface raceway

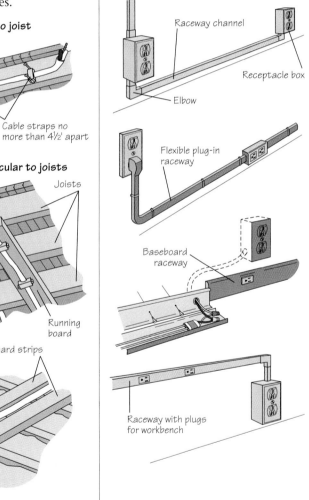

Raceway channel

Receptacle box

Elbow

Flexible plug-in raceway

Baseboard raceway

Raceway with plugs for workbench

▶ Wires must be run outdoors or through garage or basement.

Wiring in these locations is often exposed to possible damage, thus requiring metal conduit. Be sure to use liquidtight connectors (which are tightened onto the conduit by compression nuts) for outdoor work. Check local codes for other requirements.

To run wiring underground, use rigid metal conduit with liquidtight fittings or nonmetallic cable specified for direct burial (for example, SE or UF cable). You can also use PVC (plastic) conduit wherever it will be buried at least 18 inches (it cannot be used for vertical segments where wiring emerges from the ground). Never bury ordinary NM or NMC cable, ordinary metal conduit (EMT), or flexible conduit.

▶ Receptacle doesn't have hole for grounding prong of plug.

Don't remove the grounding prong from a plug to make it fit an ungrounded, two-slot receptacle. Instead, buy a grounding adapter or a plug-in GFCI. An adapter has a short pigtail, or ground wire, intended to be attached to the coverplate screw of the receptacle. However, this provides grounding only if the electrical box is metal and is itself grounded (look for a ground wire in the box or continuous metal conduit). If so, screw the pigtail to the cover-plate screw and leave the adapter in the receptacle for future use. If the box is not grounded, using the adapter will not provide grounding for the appliance. For immediate protection use a plug-in GFCI for the receptacle. Unless you plan to have all of the house wiring upgraded

Tip *If you are working with armored cable (AC, sometimes called BX), connect it to metal electrical boxes with cable connectors specified for armored cable, or use a box with internal clamps designed for armored cable. Before connecting the cable, remove 8 to 10 inches of armor at each end by cutting with a hacksaw through one of the raised corrugations in the armor, being careful not to cut too deeply, and then bending the cable to release the cut end. Before connecting each end to an electrical box, insert a plastic antishort bushing into the end of the armor, and wrap the end of the internal ground wire around the metal armor so it will be in contact with the box clamp.*

with a system ground, you can provide more permanent protection by running a No. 12 wire from the electrical box to a grounded metal water pipe and plugging in an adapter, or replacing the ungrounded receptacle with a GFCI receptacle.

▶ Prongs of plug won't stay in receptacle slots.

Unplug the cord and, with pliers, carefully bend the prongs of the plug closer together or farther apart so they grip the receptacle slots better. If this doesn't work because the clamps inside the slots are too loose, replace the receptacle.

▶ Prong of plug is too wide for receptacle slots.

At one time the prongs of all lamp and appliance cords were interchangeable—the appliance would work whichever way the plug was plugged into the receptacle. Now appliances and electronic equipment often have internal switches or other devices that require correct polarization of the electrical supply to work properly, and to accommodate this, the prong on one side of the plug is wider and will fit only the longer, or neutral, slot of a receptacle. The receptacle, in turn, must be wired so the neutral side is connected to the neutral wire (usually white) of the branch circuit. An older receptacle, however, doesn't have a longer slot to ensure correct polarity, so a polarized plug won't fit. Replace the receptacle and wire the new one for correct polarity. Connect the neutral (white) wire to the silver-colored terminal beside

the wider slot, connect the hot (black) wire to the brass-colored terminal, and attach the ground (bare or green) wire to the green grounding screw (see page 208).

Wiring a receptacle for correct polarity

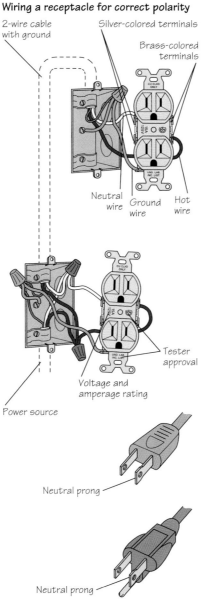

2-wire cable with ground
Silver-colored terminals
Brass-colored terminals
Neutral wire
Ground wire
Hot wire

Tester approval

Voltage and amperage rating

Power source

Neutral prong

Neutral prong

▶ Plug doesn't match receptacle.

Most household receptacles are rated 15 amps (even for 20-amp circuits), and accept almost any plug-in appliance or device intended for household use. Some large appliances and power tools have plugs that don't fit into an ordinary receptacle. This is to protect the circuit from overload and the equipment from insufficient power. Except for devices with 20-amp plugs, which can be plugged into any 20-amp receptacle wired into a 20-amp circuit, each appliance should be plugged into a matching receptacle on a dedicated circuit wired for that one appliance.

Matching plugs and receptacles

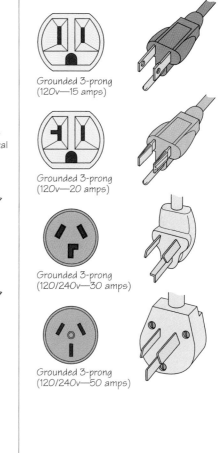

Grounded 3-prong
(120v—15 amps)

Grounded 3-prong
(120v—20 amps)

Grounded 3-prong
(120/240v—30 amps)

Grounded 3-prong
(120/240v—50 amps)

Tip *Receptacles with two outlets for plugs, which are the most common type available, are called <u>duplex receptacles</u>. Two duplex receptacles installed together in a double, or ganged, box provide outlets for four plugs. A <u>switch/receptacle combination device</u> has a single receptacle that is always hot, and a switch that controls a light or other device located elsewhere. Some receptacles are built into a light fixture or electrical appliance. A <u>clock receptacle</u>, for walls where a plug-in clock or other fixture will hang flush over the receptacle, has a recessed alcove for the plug.*

SOLVING ELECTRICAL PROBLEMS

▶ *Receptacle is dead; appliance or lamp won't work.*

After confirming that the receptacle itself is dead (not the entire circuit or the appliance), shut off power to the circuit, remove the screws holding the receptacle in place, and pull it free from the box. Then restore power to the circuit and carefully test the exposed wire ends with a voltage tester; if the tester lights up, the problem is the receptacle. Turn off the power and replace it with a new one.

If the tester indicates no voltage in the wires, the problem is a loose connection or defective receptacle somewhere else. Turn off the power and put the receptacle back. Then restore power and look for a nearby receptacle or light on the same circuit that does not work. If you find one, turn off the power and inspect that device for loose connections. Then repeat the diagnostic procedure for testing the receptacle and wires. If you can't find another dead receptacle or fixture, the problem is a loose connection or broken wire somewhere. Call an electrician.

Testing wires with voltage tester

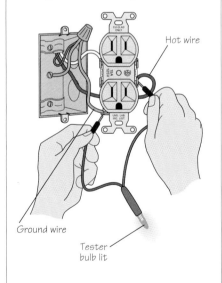

Hot wire

Ground wire

Tester bulb lit

▶ *Receptacle works only at certain times.*

In all likelihood, it is wired to a light switch. Plug a radio into the receptacle, turn it on, and test all the switches you can find to see which one operates the receptacle. Then label the switch so everyone will know what it's for, or rewire the receptacle (see opposite page).

▶ *Receptacle needs replacing.*

Turn off power to the circuit, remove the cover plate and screws holding the receptacle in place, and pull it out of the wall. If it has only two wires connected to it (besides a ground wire), disconnect them and wire the new receptacle to them in the same sequence: hot (black) wire connected to the brass-colored terminal, neutral (white) wire connected to the silver-colored terminal. To connect the wires, straighten the ends (make sure about ½ inch of insulation is removed) and push them into the round holes in the back of the receptacle. To release a wire from a push-in terminal, force a small screwdriver blade, finishing nail, or piece of No. 12 copper wire into the slot just above the terminal and pull the wire out.

If the old receptacle has two sets of white and black wires connected to it (a pair of incoming wires and a pair of outgoing wires), it means that the receptacle itself is part of the circuit. When attaching the new receptacle, connect only one wire to each screw, or wire the new receptacle to black, white, and grounding pigtails (short lengths of wire about 8 inches long). Then, using connectors, join each pigtail to the two wires of the same color that are in the electrical box.

After securing the new receptacle in the box, restore power and test it with an outlet analyzer—a small plug-in device that tests voltage, grounding, and polarity. If it indicates reversed polarity, the house wires were not properly color-coded. Turn off the power, disconnect the wires from the receptacle, and reverse them. Test again.

Connecting wires to receptacle in middle of run

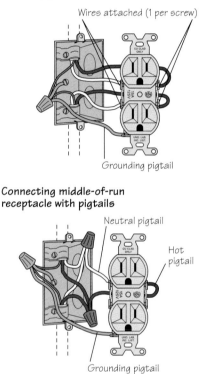

Wires attached (1 per screw)

Grounding pigtail

Connecting middle-of-run receptacle with pigtails

Neutral pigtail

Hot pigtail

Grounding pigtail

Using an outlet analyzer

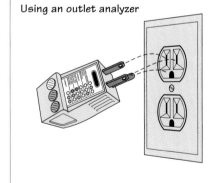

Tip *If you are replacing a receptacle in a location where a GFCI-protected outlet is required, such as in a bathroom or in a kitchen within 6 feet of the sink, be sure that the replacement receptacle is a GFCI type, even if the original receptacle was not. The electrical box does not have to be grounded in order for the GFCI to function.*

Tip *Whenever you run new wiring into an electrical box, leave at least 6 inches of each conductor extending out of the box to make it easy to connect receptacles and other devices.*

▶ *Polarity of wires to be attached to receptacle isn't clear.*

You can determine the polarity of a wire with a voltage tester. First make sure that the ends of the wires are exposed but not touching anything; then turn on the power. To test the polarity of each wire, hold one probe of the voltage tester on the ground wire; touch the other probe to one wire, then the second. The tester will light when it touches the hot wire; it won't light (or will only glow faintly) when it touches the neutral. Make sure your fingers don't touch anything metal, including the probes.

Testing for hot wire

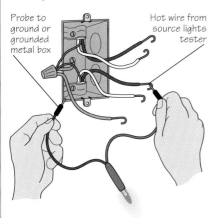

Probe to ground or grounded metal box

Hot wire from source lights tester

▶ *Receptacle makes sparks.*

It is normal for the prongs of a plug to arc slightly when you plug in or unplug an appliance that is switched on. However, if sparks occur around a receptacle at any other time, the problem may be caused by a defective receptacle or a loose wire. Turn off power to the receptacle and inspect it. If it's a loose connection with copper wire, tighten it. If it's aluminum wire, call an electrician. If the connections are not loose, replace the receptacle.

▶ *Switch-controlled receptacle needs replacing.*

Turn off the power. Verify that it is off by testing both the upper and lower halves of the receptacle with a voltage tester (insert one probe in each slot). Then remove the cover plate and screws holding the receptacle and pull it out. Wire connections will vary, depending on whether both halves of the receptacle are controlled by the switch (or just one), and whether the wires from the source come through the receptacle box or the switch box. Note how many hot (black) wires are attached to the brass-colored screws, and whether the tab between the screws has been broken off. Label or mark all wires so you won't get them confused, and note which end of the receptacle points up; then remove them. (*Note:* The hot wire for the switched half of the receptacle may be white because it is part of a switch loop and two-wire cable was used for the wiring.)

Breaking receptacle tab

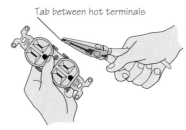

Tab between hot terminals

Connecting wires: power through receptacle

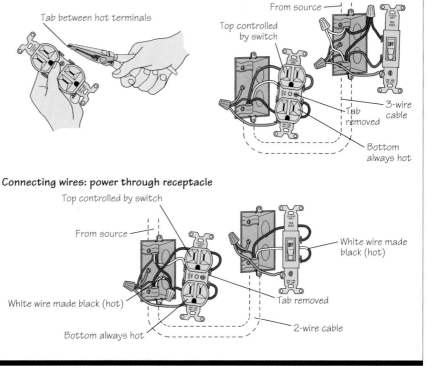

Top controlled by switch

From source

White wire made black (hot)

Bottom always hot

White wire made black (hot)

Tab removed

2-wire cable

Before connecting wires to the new receptacle, break the tab on the hot (brass-colored) side of the receptacle if it was broken on the old receptacle. This isolates the two halves so that one can be controlled by the switch while the other remains hot. Connect the appropriate black (or white-made-black) wire to each brass-colored terminal.

Because the tab on the neutral (silver-colored) side remains unbroken, only one neutral wire is necessary. If two neutral (white) wires were attached to the old receptacle, connect a white pigtail (8-inch length of wire) to one of the silver-colored terminals and join it to the other two white wires with a wire connector. Connect the ground wire, secure the receptacle to the electrical box, and restore power. Test both halves of the receptacle with an outlet analyzer (with the switch in both positions).

Connecting wires: power through switch

From source

Top controlled by switch

Tab removed

3-wire cable

Bottom always hot

Tip *The National Electrical Code requires that every habitable room, hallway, and stairway in a home have at least one light controlled by a wall switch at each entrance to that room. Most rooms fulfill this requirement with a permanently mounted ceiling or wall fixture, but a receptacle controlled by a switch, which is common in living rooms, dining rooms, and master bedrooms, is allowable in lieu of a light fixture (except in bathrooms and kitchens).*

SOLVING ELECTRICAL PROBLEMS

▶ *240-volt receptacle needs replacing.*

A 240-volt receptacle is controlled by a double circuit breaker. Make sure both toggles of the breaker are off—they should be connected—before proceeding. Pull the appliance plug from the receptacle and plug it into the replacement receptacle to be sure that it is the right kind—prong configurations vary according to amperage. Then remove the cover from the old receptacle, loosen the screws that hold it in place, and pull it out of the electrical box. Note which wires are connected to which terminals (mark them if necessary), then disconnect the wires by loosening the setscrews. Connect them to the terminals of the new receptacle, tighten the screws, and attach the receptacle to the electrical box. Plug in the appliance and restore power.

▶ *Receptacle needs GFCI protection.*

The NEC requires that receptacles in certain locations be protected by GFCIs, which protect people from shock hazards; grounding alone is not sufficient protection. These locations include bathrooms, garages, basements, the area above countertops within 6 feet of a kitchen sink, and anywhere outdoors. Although there are several ways to provide ground fault circuit protection with various kinds of devices, individual GFCI receptacles are now inexpensive enough that the most convenient way to protect existing receptacles is to replace each one with a separate GFCI. Install them according to manufacturer's instructions, which typically involve connecting the black and white GFCI pigtails marked *Line* to the black and white circuit wires, respectively. If the GFCI has two more pigtails marked *Load* (often

a gray and a red wire), cap the bare ends with small wire connectors—they will be live and shouldn't be exposed. If the old receptacle had two pairs of wires connected to it, you have to identify which pair (black and white) are the "line," or source, wires and which two are "load"—going to other receptacles (see page 209). Join the "line" wires to the GFCI pigtails marked *Line,* and the "load" wires to *Load.* If the system is grounded, attach a ground wire to the GFCI. Otherwise, leave it unconnected. Read the manufacturer's instructions about testing the GFCI.

Installing a GFCI

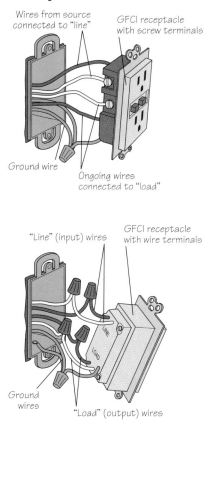

Wires from source connected to "line"

GFCI receptacle with screw terminals

Ground wire

Ongoing wires connected to "load"

"Line" (input) wires

GFCI receptacle with wire terminals

Ground wires

"Load" (output) wires

▶ *GFCI receptacle constantly trips or won't reset.*

It may be wired incorrectly. Turn off power, disconnect the GFCI, and make sure the wire ends do not touch anything. Restore power and test the wires for polarity (see page 209). If the wires were reversed, turn off power and reconnect the GFCI correctly. If the wires weren't reversed, the problem may be a worn GFCI; install a new one. If tripping persists, the problem is probably a constant ground fault in the circuit. Call an electrician.

▶ *Switch doesn't work.*

Make sure that the problem is not a burned-out light bulb or tripped circuit breaker (or blown fuse). If not, replace the switch. First shut off the circuit breaker that controls the switch and light fixture. Remove the cover plate and the screws that attach the switch to the electrical box. Gently pull the switch away from the box, being careful not to touch the screw terminals. With a voltage tester, verify that the power is off by touching one probe to the ground wire and the other probe to each screw terminal of the switch, in turn. If there is no grounding screw or wire, touch the probes to the two screw terminals with the switch in both positions (be sure the light fixture has a functioning bulb in place).

If the switch is one of two switches controlling the same light, it has three screw terminals. Touch one probe to the terminal marked *Common* (bronze-colored) and the other probe to one of the two brass-colored terminals, with the switch in both positions *and* the other switch in both positions each time (four combinations in all).

Tip *If you use power tools outdoors, be sure to plug them into a GFCI-protected receptacle. If one isn't convenient, buy a portable plug-in GFCI. You can plug it into any receptacle, then run an extension cord from it to the outdoor location where you are working.*

Tip *The most common mistake when installing a GFCI is failing to attach the source wires from the circuit-breaker panel to the two terminals marked "Line." If these wires are hooked up to the two "Load" terminals, the receptacle will appear to work normally but in fact the GFCI will not trip when it is supposed to.*

The tester should indicate no power. If not, trip the correct circuit breaker. With power off, remove the switch (mark the wire attached to the "common" terminal if switch is three-way), and replace it with the same type. If the new switch does not work, the problem is in the wiring. Turn off the breaker and call an electrician.

▶ Old switch needs replacing.

Turn off power to the switch, remove the cover plate and screws that hold it in place, and carefully pull the switch away from the box. With a voltage tester verify that the power is off (see opposite page). Note how the wires are attached to the switch (mark them so you can remember), and disconnect them by loosening the side screws or, if they're wired to the back, releasing them by forcing a small screwdriver into the slot just above or below each wire. Before connecting the wires to the new switch, snip the curved ends off the wires and strip the insulation to expose ½ inch of bare wire. If you use the push terminals in the back of the switch, use the stripping gauge printed on the back of the switch to make sure enough insulation is removed. Keep the wires straight. If you connect wires to the side screws, bend them with needle nose pliers or by inserting the ends into the small holes in the blade of a wire stripper. Wrap them clockwise around the screw, making sure they engage it fully when it is tight. When all connections are made, fold the wires so you can push the switch into the box without kinking them. Secure the switch with the screws provided and replace the cover plate.

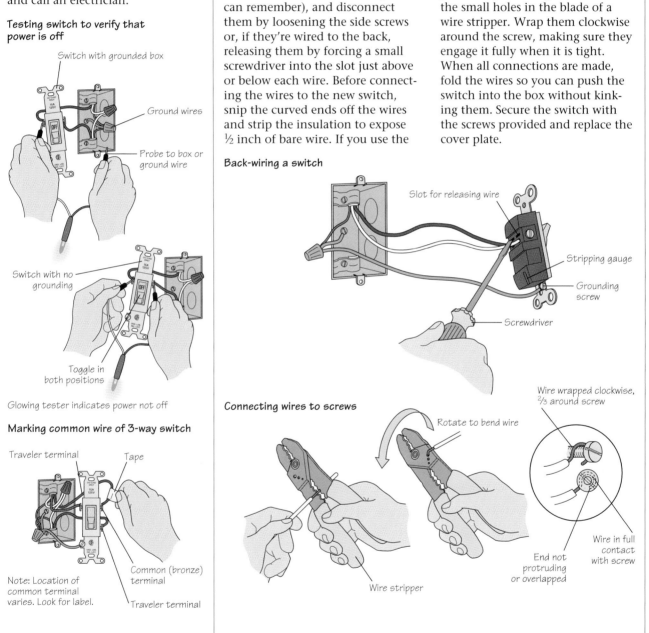

Testing switch to verify that power is off

Switch with grounded box

Ground wires

Probe to box or ground wire

Switch with no grounding

Toggle in both positions

Glowing tester indicates power not off

Marking common wire of 3-way switch

Traveler terminal

Tape

Common (bronze) terminal

Traveler terminal

Note: Location of common terminal varies. Look for label.

Back-wiring a switch

Slot for releasing wire

Stripping gauge

Grounding screw

Screwdriver

Connecting wires to screws

Rotate to bend wire

Wire wrapped clockwise, ⅔ around screw

Wire stripper

End not protruding or overlapped

Wire in full contact with screw

Tip *Switches should never be attached to neutral wires, thus interrupting a constant and safe path for electricity to flow back to the source. Only hot (black or red) wires should be connected to switches. In some cases white wires are used as hot wires and should not be confused with neutral wires; they often, but not always, have black tape or paint at the ends to designate them as hot wires.*

▶ Old and new switches have different number of terminals.

Both switches must be the same type: two-way, three-way, or (more rarely) four-way. In simplest terms, these designations refer to the number of terminals (not counting the grounding screw) on the back or sides of the switch. More accurately, a two-way (or single-pole) switch is for installations where only one switch controls a light or fixture (or multiple fixtures). It is the only switch with positions marked *On* and *Off*. It has two terminals, and the wires can be interchanged.

A three-way switch is for installations where two switches control a light or group of lights, and is always paired with another three-way switch. The toggle has no *On* or *Off* position because the light could be on or off in either position, depending on how the partner switch is set. A three-way switch has three wires connected to it (besides the ground wire); it is very important that the correct wire is attached to the bronze-colored terminal, marked *Common*. The brass-colored terminals are interchangeable for the remaining two wires.

A four-way switch is used together with two 3-way switches, so a light is controlled by three different switches. Additional four-way switches can be used to increase the number of control points, so long as they are all installed between two 3-way switches. A four-way switch has four wires (besides ground); it's important how they are attached.

You can use a replacement switch that has a different color, design, or specialty function (like a dimmer or pilot light switch), but it must have the same switching capability as the old switch. Use the switch diagrams that follow for hooking up the wires correctly.

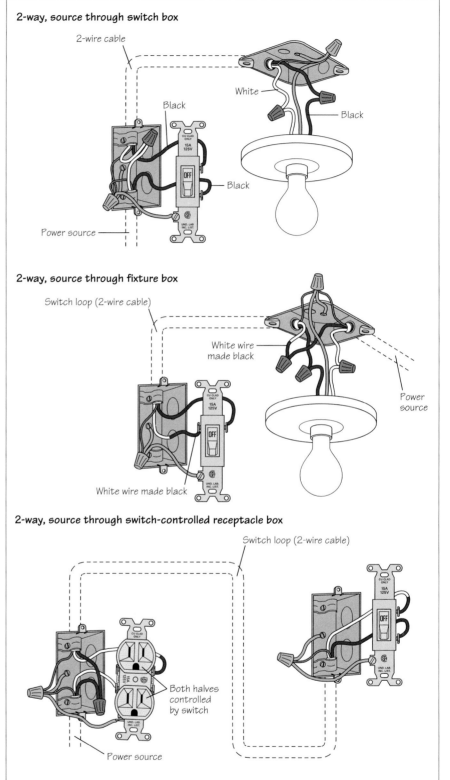

2-way, source through switch box

2-wire cable

White

Black

Black

Black

Power source

2-way, source through fixture box

Switch loop (2-wire cable)

White wire made black

Power source

White wire made black

2-way, source through switch-controlled receptacle box

Switch loop (2-wire cable)

Both halves controlled by switch

Power source

Tip *Some specialty switches: time-delay switches that go off automatically after a certain amount of time; timer switches that go on and off at preset times; motion-sensing switches that go on whenever someone enters the room; illuminated switches that are easy to find in the dark; pilot light switches with a light that shows whether they are on or off, for controlling fixtures or appliances out of view (such as an attic fan or a basement light); lockable switches for tamperproof control of dangerous or expensive equipment; remote-controlled switches that are controlled by low-voltage relay wiring from a master control panel; and photo cell switches that go on in darkness, off in daylight.*

3-way, source through central-fixture box

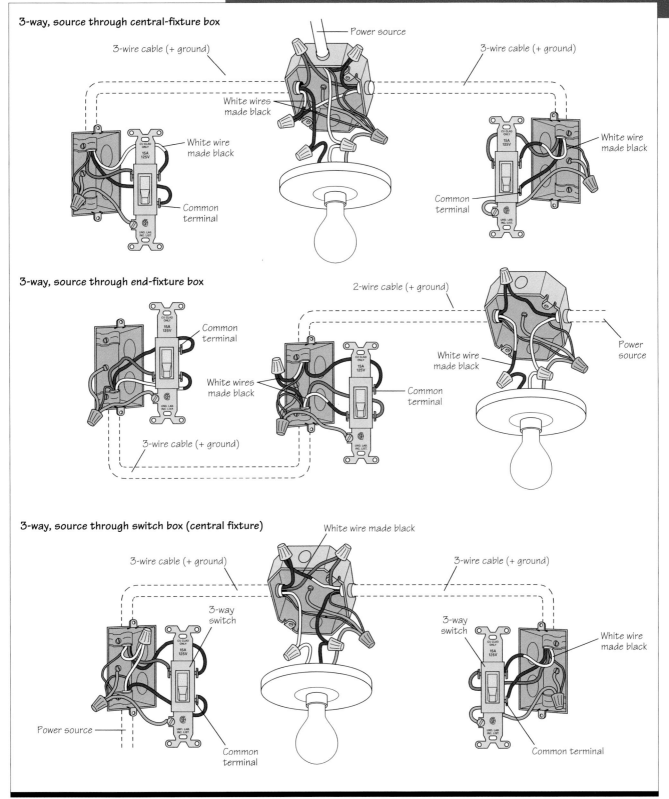

Power source

3-wire cable (+ ground)

3-wire cable (+ ground)

White wires made black

White wire made black

White wire made black

Common terminal

Common terminal

3-way, source through end-fixture box

Common terminal

2-wire cable (+ ground)

Power source

White wires made black

White wire made black

Common terminal

3-wire cable (+ ground)

3-way, source through switch box (central fixture)

White wire made black

3-wire cable (+ ground)

3-wire cable (+ ground)

3-way switch

3-way switch

White wire made black

Power source

Common terminal

Common terminal

Tip The wire connected to the "common" terminal of a three-way switch must be either the hot wire from the source or the hot wire connecting to the light fixture. It's never one of the travelers, the two wires connected to the partner switch.

3-way, source through switch box (end fixture)

3-way, source through switch box; receptacle beyond

4-way, source through fixture box

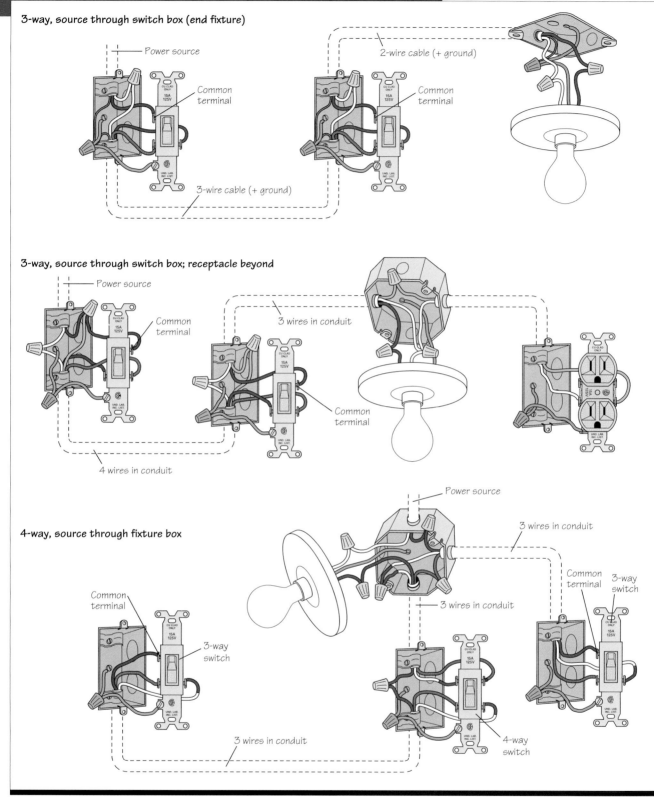

Power source

Common terminal

2-wire cable (+ ground)

3-wire cable (+ ground)

Power source

Common terminal

3 wires in conduit

Common terminal

4 wires in conduit

Power source

3 wires in conduit

Common terminal

3-way switch

3 wires in conduit

Common terminal

3-way switch

3 wires in conduit

4-way switch

Tip *If you are installing a switch that does not have a terminal screw for attaching the ground wire to the switch, wrap the ground wire around one of the mounting screws used for securing the switch to the electrical box.*

▶ Wires weren't marked for attaching to terminals.

If you lost track of which wires should be attached to which terminals of a switch, you can identify the wires with a voltage tester. The ground wire should be obvious; it should be bare or green and the only wire attached directly to a metal electrical box. For two-way switches, it doesn't matter which of the other two wires is attached to the top or bottom of the switch. Nevertheless, you can identify the "line" wire (from the source), if necessary, by turning on the power and touching one probe of the voltage tester to the ground wire and the other probe to the others, in turn. The "line" wire will light the tester. The other wire is "load" and goes to the light fixture.

For a three-way switch, hold one probe of the tester on the ground wire and test the other three wires, one at a time, with the partner switch in both positions (it's easier if someone helps). If one wire lights the tester no matter what position the other switch is in, it is the "line" wire and should be attached to the "common" (bronze-colored) terminal of the switch. The other two, which light the tester once each time, are "travelers" and are connected to the brass-colored terminals of the switch (either way). Be sure to turn off the power before making connections. If none of the wires lights the tester with the partner switch in both positions, identify the one that doesn't light the tester *at all*; this wire goes to the light bulb and carries power only when it's connected to the switch. It connects to the "common" (bronze-colored) terminal of the switch, and the other two wires to the brass-colored terminals. Turn off the power and connect them.

For a four-way switch, attach the two wires from one cable to the top two terminals, the two wires from the other cable to the bottom two terminals—in either order.

▶ New switch doesn't operate correctly.

If new wiring was involved, have a licensed electrician inspect the installation. If you replaced a working switch with a new one that doesn't work properly, there is the possibility that the new switch is defective. However, it is more likely, especially with three-way switches, that wires got reversed. This is almost certainly the case if the new switch works when the partner switch is in one position but not the other; the wrong wire is attached to the "common" terminal. To fix, turn off the power, remove the switch (test with a voltage tester first), and follow the procedure for identifying wires described at left.

▶ Light or fixture needs an additional switch.

Stairways, halls, and rooms with more than one entrance should have multiple switches so you can turn on the light no matter which way you enter. Adding a switch means running new three-wire cable between the existing switch, the light fixture, and the new switch location—most likely inside walls and through ceilings or floors. An alternative is to install a pair of radio-controlled switches. One of them replaces the existing two-way switch and requires no new wiring. The other switch is installed in the new location and requires no wiring; it communicates with the

master switch by radio frequencies. Look for this type of switch at a local electrical-supply house and install it according to manufacturer's instructions.

▶ Switch is behind door and is hard to reach.

Switches should be located on the latch side of doors where they can be easily reached. Sometimes doors are reversed after the house has been wired. The only solution is to install a new switch on the wall at the latch side of the door. Consult an electrician about running new wiring.

▶ Switch has no "click."

Old-style switches with a spring-activated toggle had a distinct snapping sound. New switches are quieter, although most have a distinctive click. If a switch has suddenly gone silent but still works, it should not be a problem. If the toggle flaps loosely, replace the switch.

▶ Switch is hard to find at night.

Replace it with an illuminated switch. The toggle contains a small light that glows when the switch is in the *Off* position. It requires that the electrical box or cable running to it be grounded, but the light operates at a slow, pulsating frequency that does not require a neutral wire, as lamps do.

▶ Switch is too high to reach.

Most switches are installed 48 inches above the floor, which may be too high for a child or a person in a wheelchair to reach easily. You can install another switch below it, using the original switch box for a junction box. If it's a two-way switch, replace it with a three-way one so you can operate the light

---

Tip *If you are replacing a switch with three or more terminals (a three-way or four-way switch), be sure to mark the wires with tape or other identification before you disconnect them from the terminals so you can attach the wires to the same terminals of the new switch. The important wire to distinguish is the one connected to the "common" terminal of a three-way switch.*

from either switch; the new switch must be a three-way switch also.

To install the new switch, first shut off power to the old one. Drill a small hole at the new location and probe with a wire for obstructions. If there are none, trace the outline of a new box and cut the opening with a keyhole saw or wallboard saw. Cut carefully; there may be wires inside the wall. Remove the cover plate and screws holding the switch in place and pull it out of the box. If it is a three-way switch (three terminals), mark the wire that was connected to the terminal marked *Common*.

Next remove one of the knockouts from the bottom of the switch box. Cut about 3 feet of No. 14 sheathed cable and attach a wire connector about 8 inches from one end. Use three-wire cable (with ground) if the old switch was a three-way switch or you are installing two switches; use two-wire cable (with ground) if the old switch was two-way and you want only one switch. Remove the tightening ring from the connector, strip the sheathing from 8 inches of cable, and thread the wires through the new wall opening and up into the bottom knockout hole of the old switch box. From inside the box place the tightening ring over the new cable and screw the ring onto the connector threads. Thread the other end of the cable through a knockout hole in the top of the new cut-in box (using a wire connector for a metal box). Set the box into the wall opening and secure it by tightening the clamps or other devices attached to the box.

For a two-way switch, join the new wires to the old wires inside the original box with wire connectors, and the other ends of the new wires to a two-way switch in the new box. Mark the white wires black with electrical tape or paint.

To install a three-way switch in the new box, use wire connectors to join the three wires inside the original box to the three wires of the new cable, noting which new wire is connected to the "common" wire. Attach the other end of that wire to the terminal on the new switch marked *Common*. Connect the other two wires to the brass-colored terminals.

If you are replacing the old two-way switch with a pair of three-way switches, connect one of the original wires to the "common" terminal of one switch, and join the other wire to the red wire of the new cable. Connect the other end of the red cable wire to the "common" terminal of the other switch. Attach the black and white wires to the brass-colored terminals of both switches.

Cutting hole for new box

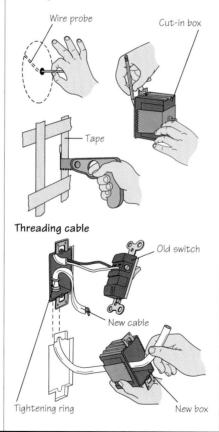

Wire probe

Cut-in box

Tape

Threading cable

Old switch

New cable

Tightening ring

New box

▶ *Closet has pull-chain light and needs switch.*

You can install a conventional switch on the inside or outside wall of the closet, close to the latch edge of the door; or you can install a door-activated switch that automatically turns on every time the door is opened. You can use the same pull-chain fixture (left in the *On* position) or replace it with a surface-mounted fixture approved for closet locations (see page 218). To wire the new switch, run two-wire No. 14 cable between the light fixture and the new switch location. Disconnect the hot (black) wire from the light fixture, attach it to one of the new wires, and attach the other new wire to the same light fixture terminal. Then connect the other end of the wires to a two-way switch; follow manufacturer's instructions for installing a door-activated switch.

▶ *Mysterious switch doesn't seem to control anything.*

Before testing the switch and analyzing wires, try some elementary detective work. If the switch is at the entrance to a room without a ceiling fixture, it most likely controls one of the receptacles in the room. Test every receptacle (both halves) by plugging a working lamp or radio into it and flipping the mystery switch to both positions. If none of the receptacles responds to the switch, one of them may have at one time been connected and then been rewired. Look for a receptacle that looks newer than the rest. If there is one, turn off the power, remove the cover plate and screws holding the receptacle, pull it out of the box, and look for unconnected wires in the box. To rewire the receptacle, see page 209.

Some switches, especially near doors to the garage, basement, attic,

Tip *When you remove a switch, you may find other wires in the electrical box that are not connected to the switch. There is no need to disconnect them or identify them for the purpose of replacing the switch. If all of the wires in the box are connected to the switch, it is at the end of a switch loop. The wires are all hot wires (not necessarily connected directly to the source, however), making the box an inappropriate one to tap into for extending the circuit.*

or outdoors, may control appliances that have timers or other automatic switching devices that must also be on for the appliance to work. Look for outdoor lighting with timers or motion-sensing devices, an attic fan that goes on only when the attic overheats, a furnace blower that can be switched on during hot weather, and receptacles for power tools.

If none of these investigations solves the mystery, carefully check the switch to see if it's hot. First turn off the power and pull the switch out of the box to expose the terminals, then restore power and touch one probe of a voltage tester to the ground wire and the other probe to all of the screw terminals of the switch, in turn. If the tester lights up, turn off the power, reattach the switch to the box, restore power, and call an electrician. If the tester doesn't light up, follow the procedure for tracing wires (see page 204).

▶ Bulb burns out too quickly.

Check the location for vibrations, such as a nearby door that slams frequently or a heavy appliance like a washing machine. Replace the bulb with an impact-resistant type designed for use in work lights for shops, available at lumberyards, auto-supply stores, or electrical-supply outlets. Another cause of frequent burnout may be overheating. The bulb wattage may exceed the limit recommended for the light fixture. Replace it with a bulb of less wattage. You could also

install a dimmer switch; running it at 90 percent capacity can double the life span of an ordinary incandescent bulb. On the other hand, dimming may reduce the life span of a halogen lamp.

▶ Bulb makes buzzing sound.

First be sure that it's the bulb and not a dimmer. If it's a dimmer, it may be overloaded and should be replaced with one that has a higher wattage rating. If a bulb is buzzing, especially in a recessed fixture that tends to amplify sound, replace it with a rough-service (impact-resistant) incandescent bulb; the tungsten filament won't vibrate as much. Otherwise, replace it with a compact fluorescent bulb; if there is a dimmer, be sure it's rated for fluorescent bulbs.

▶ Bulb is broken; base won't screw out.

Deaden the circuit, or unplug the lamp if applicable. Then, wearing gloves, remove as much glass from the bulb base as possible. With the glass removed, unscrew the base with needle nose pliers. You may have to deform the base with the pliers to get a good grip—just don't deform the socket.

▶ Bulb is hard to reach.

You can buy an extension pole with a device on the end for gripping light bulbs. The ones for flood-lights and spotlights work by suction; those for incandescent bulbs work by friction. Be sure to deaden the circuit first. Wear eye protection, and stay clear of overhead wires when changing bulbs outside. If you don't have access to such a pole changer, improvise one for incandescent bulbs by attaching a cardboard mailing tube to the end of a pole. Cut four slits

in the unattached end of the tube, as if sectioning an orange, and wrap a heavy rubber band around the end. Reach up and slip the tube onto the light bulb and unscrew it, then use the changer to install the new bulb.

▶ Ceiling light fixture heats up.

This is a problem that's difficult to detect but may be a serious fire hazard, especially with recessed fixtures. First make sure that the light bulbs do not exceed the wattage recommended for the fixture, which is usually written where you can read it after taking off the globe or removing the bulbs. If you aren't sure, use 60-watt (or less) bulbs. Next, if it's a recessed fixture, you should check the insulation in the attic. Most codes require that insulation be kept at least 3 inches away from the fixture on all sides, and that no insulation be placed above it. However, some fixtures are designed for zero-clearance insulation, and some codes allow you to insulate above the fixture under certain conditions. Check with the local building department and adjust the insulation accordingly.

Keeping insulation away from recessed fixture

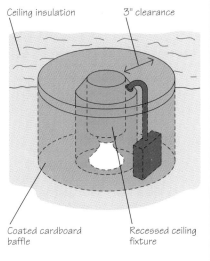

Ceiling insulation   3" clearance

Coated cardboard baffle   Recessed ceiling fixture

Tip *Because of higher efficiency standards now required for light bulbs, stores may be carrying bulbs that you aren't familiar with, such as compact fluorescent bulbs and various halogen lamps. Many of them have Edison bases, or standard screw bases, that make it possible to screw them into an incandescent bulb socket. When choosing bulbs, don't just compare wattages; look at lumens (amount of light output) as well so you can compare lumens per watt (the higher the better).*

▶ *Light in closet is too close to combustibles.*

The NEC requires that incandescent surface fixtures in clothes closets be at least 12 inches away from the storage area, and fluorescent or recessed incandescent fixtures at least 6 inches away. In addition, a surface-mounted incandescent fixture must have the bulb completely enclosed by a glass globe. Pendant fixtures and bulbs not completely covered by a protective globe are prohibited in closets. The usual places to install closet fixtures are on the wall above the door or on the ceiling as close to the door as possible.

Meeting requirements for closet fixtures

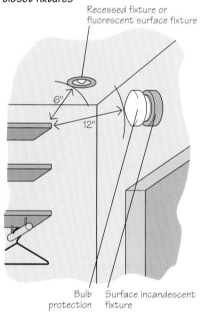

Recessed fixture or fluorescent surface fixture

6"

12"

Bulb protection

Surface incandescent fixture

▶ *Light won't go on.*

First check to see if the light switch is faulty (see page 210). If it works, the problem may be a loose wire in the light fixture. Turn off the circuit breaker and remove the globe and light bulbs from the fixture. Then loosen the screws or coupling nut that attach the fixture housing to the box; for a ceiling fixture have some coat hanger wire handy to hook onto the fixture and suspend it from the ceiling bracket after you loosen it. Inspect all of the wire connections between the light fixture and house wiring inside the box; tug at each wire to be sure it's not loose from its connection. If there are no loose connections, disconnect the wires from the fixture, restore power to them, and test with a voltage tester to see if the problem is in the wiring. Touch the probes to the hot (black) wire and the neutral (white) wire, or the hot wire and the ground wire. If the tester doesn't light up with the switch in either position, the wiring is at fault. Call an electrician. If it does light up, the problem is in the light fixture. Turn off the power and replace the fixture.

Testing wires for power

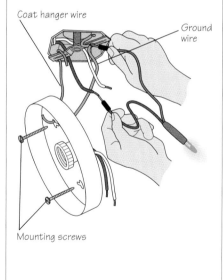

Coat hanger wire

Ground wire

Mounting screws

▶ *Light fixture needs replacing.*

Turn off power to the light fixture at the circuit breaker. Remove any globe or other decorative cover and the light bulbs. Loosen the mounting screws or coupling nut that attach the fixture to the ceiling box and lower the fixture. Attach a coat hanger to it and suspend it from the ceiling bracket while you reach above it and disconnect the wires. Now you can discard the fixture and install a new one, following these steps in reverse order. Be sure that the ground wire in the electrical box is connected to the box strap (if you use one) or the ground wire of the fixture, if it has one. Before joining the wires, install the mounting screws in the ceiling box or strap. Join the neutral (white) wires together and the hot (black) wires together with wire connectors; then slip the keyhole-shaped slots in the fixture housing over the mounting screws, rotate the housing, and tighten the screws. Install the bulbs, test the fixture, and attach the globe.

Connecting the ground wire

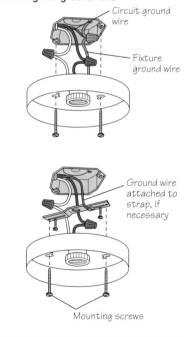

Circuit ground wire

Fixture ground wire

Ground wire attached to strap, if necessary

Mounting screws

Tip   *For general lighting choose full-spectrum fluorescent bulbs—either tubes or compact bulbs that can be screwed into ordinary fixtures. They are extremely efficient and create very little heat. For reading, illuminating artwork, lighting bathrooms, and lighting food-serving areas, choose halogen lamps. They provide a whiter light with more contrast than fluorescent lights, and therefore reflect colors more accurately. Both types of lamps contribute much less heat to a home than incandescent bulbs, although halogen lamps are intensely hot at close range.*

▶ Several lights on same circuit don't work.

This will take time. First make sure that there is not another circuit breaker in a subpanel or a GFCI receptacle that has tripped. Look for hidden subpanels in closets, behind furniture or pictures, under sinks, and behind doors. Push the reset button on all GFCIs in the house.

If this doesn't work, the wiring for part of the circuit may be going through a fixture that is defective or has loose connections. Turn off the circuit, then check for loose wiring connections at the fixtures. Also make sure that none of the fixtures has more than one circuit wire screwed to the same terminal. Wherever this condition exists, remove the wires from the terminal, screw a pigtail (8-inch length of No. 14 wire of the same color) to the same terminal, and use an electrical connector to join the pigtail to the wires that you removed.

If the lights still don't work, there could be a broken wire in the circuit wiring between them and the source. Tracing it requires deadening the entire circuit and testing the run of wires between the affected fixtures and the source with a continuity tester (not a voltage tester). That run may be hard to identify, so you'll probably have to test several runs. To test continuity of any given run, disconnect the fixtures or switches at both ends of the run and, at one end, join the wires of the disconnected cable (except ground) together with a connector. Then go to the electrical box at the other end of the cable and touch the probes of the continuity tester to the other end of the same cable wires. If you find a combination that doesn't light the tester, and you are sure that the run doesn't have a switch or other device along it, one of the wires is

broken and should be replaced. Remove the connector, identify the wires, and replace them. If all of the wires test successfully for continuity, call an electrician.

▶ Older pendant fixture may not have ground wire.

All light fixtures must be grounded, especially hanging fixtures that are easy to reach. A chain alone is not sufficient to provide a continuous ground. Look for a bare wire or, if the light hangs on a cord, a green ground wire coming out of the bottom end of the cord. To add a ground wire to a fixture suspended from a chain, turn off the power, then twine bare stranded wire through the chain; connect the bottom end to the metal housing of the fixture and the top end to the circuit ground wire above the canopy. For fixtures suspended by cord, turn off the power and replace the cord with No. 16 cable that has a ground wire; attach the bottom end of the green or bare ground wire to the metal fixture housing and the top end to the circuit ground wire above the canopy.

Connecting ground wire to pendant fixture

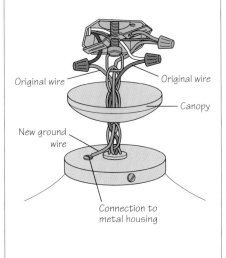

Original wire

Original wire

Canopy

New ground wire

Connection to metal housing

▶ Globe for light fixture attached to ceiling fan comes loose.

Vibrations from the fan can cause the setscrews that hold the fixture globe to work loose, causing it to rattle or even fall. With the power off, loosen the setscrews and remove the globe. Slip a wide rubber band around the outside of the neck of the globe, wide enough for the ends of the set screws to make full contact with it when the globe is in place. Tighten the screws snugly against the rubber band. It creates enough friction to keep the screws from backing out.

▶ One light of chandelier doesn't work.

Turn off the light, switch bulbs between the dead socket and one that works, and turn the light back on. If the socket still doesn't work, it probably has a broken or disconnected feeder wire. Mark the dead socket with tape. To fix it, you need access to where all the socket wires are joined, which is usually reached by removing the decorative cap under the center of the fixture; otherwise you must disconnect the canopy from the ceiling (have one or two helpers hold the chandelier). First turn off the power. Remove the cap to expose the wires and inspect the connections, tugging on each wire to be sure it is secure; if one is loose, remake the connection. Then restore power, test the light, and replace the cap. If none of the wires is loose or if the light still doesn't work, turn off the power. Touch one prong of a continuity (not voltage) tester to each end of the wire. If the tester doesn't light, replace the wire; attach the new wire to one end and

Tip   When using a ladder to change bulbs in a ceiling fixture, there's usually no place to set the bulbs and glass globe that must be removed first. To solve this problem, tie two straw baskets or plastic pails to the top of the ladder before you go up. Use one to hold the new bulb, the other for the globe.

SOLVING ELECTRICAL PROBLEMS

feed the new wire into the tubing by pulling the old wire out. If the tester lights for both wires, remove the socket itself and replace it with the same kind.

Replacing socket wires

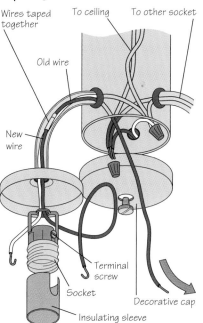

Wires taped together
To ceiling
To other socket
Old wire
New wire
Terminal screw
Socket
Decorative cap
Insulating sleeve

▶ Light is hard to turn on when arms are full.

Place a lamp with a touch-sensitive switch near the entrance to the room. Activate it by just brushing the base with your elbow. You can also replace a two-way switch with a motion-sensing switch that turns on the light as someone approaches. A number of additional features are available, such as manual override for normal operation, a dormant mode for deadening the switch during daylight hours, and options for setting the length of time the light stays on before turning off automatically. These switches are for indoor use and are similar to those used for outdoor security lighting.

▶ Fluorescent light flickers.

If it's a brand-new tube, leave it on for a few hours to stabilize. Cold temperatures (below 50°F) can also cause a bulb to flicker; allow several minutes for the bulb to warm up, or wait for the room to warm up before turning on the light. If flickering persists, the pins may be misaligned or have oxidation on them. Turn off the light, remove the tube, and clean the pins with a dry scouring pad or sandpaper. Install the tube again, rotating it in the pin holders a few times to clear the surfaces. Make sure all four pins snap into place securely. If the lamp still flickers, try a new bulb. If that fails, replace the fixture.

Aligning pins

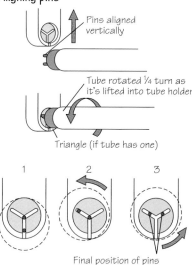

Pins aligned vertically

Tube rotated ¼ turn as it's lifted into tube holder

Triangle (if tube has one)

1   2   3

Final position of pins

▶ Fluorescent light blinks on and off.

If the bulb is old, replace it. If the bulb is new, check to see if the pins are aligned properly. If they are, the problem could be a defective starter; replace it (see opposite page). If a new starter doesn't solve the problem, turn off the power and inspect the wires for loose connections. Finally, replace the ballast or entire fixture.

▶ Fluorescent fixture hums.

Most ballasts inevitably create a low humming sound. If it's too loud, check the mounting screws that secure the ballast to the fixture and tighten any loose ones. If the ballast has an acrid smell besides the humming, it's defective and should be replaced. If not, be sure that the ballast is the right size for the number and wattage of the tubes in the fixture; check the rating plate. Also check the wiring diagram printed on the ballast and make sure that the wires are connected properly. You may also have to check the polarity of the circuit wires in the electrical box. With the power off, expose the ends of the wires. Then turn the power back on and touch one probe of a voltage tester to the ground wire, the other to the hot (black) wire. The tester should light when the switch is on but not when it's off. It should also light with one probe touching the neutral (white) wire and the other probe touching the hot wire when the switch is on. It should not light when one probe touches the ground wire and the other probe touches the neutral wire. If the wiring is correct and the humming persists, check the sound rating of the fixture. If it's not an A or B, which are the quietest on a scale of A to F, replace the fixture with one rated A.

▶ Fluorescent tube is dark at ends and glows in center.

Some grayness is normal an inch or two from the ends. If the ends are black and the tube is old, replace it. If only one end is dark, switch the tube around. If the tube is new, replace the starter. If this doesn't work or the fixture has no starter, check the wiring for loose connections. Finally, replace the ballast or entire fixture.

Tip *Compact fluorescent bulbs have an Edison base that screws into an ordinary (incandescent) light bulb socket. The ballast and other electronics are built into the bulb. Although costly, they use less than half as much energy as an incandescent bulb of the same brightness.*

▶ *Fluorescent light won't go on.*

First check the circuit breaker or fuse box, then try a different bulb, one from another fixture that you know is working. Make sure it is the same type of bulb—some have two pins at each end, others have one. Position the bulb so that the triangular marking on both ends is visible, not concealed by the sockets. Also check the specifications printed on the ballast, where the wires are attached, to make sure that the bulb is the correct wattage. If the light still doesn't work and the fixture is the preheat type with a starter, which is a metal cylinder about the size of a film canister, remove the starter (turn it counterclockwise) and replace it with a new one. It should have the same wattage rating as the tubes. If this doesn't work or the fixture doesn't have a separate starter, the problem is probably the ballast, which is a box inside the fixture that contains a transformer. You can replace the ballast, but it may cost no more to replace the entire fixture.

▶ *Fluorescent tube is dark in center and glows at ends.*

Try a new tube. If that doesn't work, replace the starter if the fixture has one. Finally, replace the ballast or entire fixture.

▶ *Fluorescent tube burns out too quickly.*

You may be turning the light on and off too frequently. Leave the light on for longer periods of time. If the bulb still wears out fast, replace the starter if there is one. Otherwise, check the wiring connections for loose wires. Finally, replace the fixture.

▶ *Fluorescent fixture needs a dimmer switch.*

Only certain fluorescent fixtures can be controlled by a dimmer switch. They must be rapid-start fixtures with a ballast designed for dimmers and a grounded reflector mounted within 1 inch of the tube. The dimmer, in turn, must be specified for fluorescent fixtures and labeled clearly as such. The dimmer can control more than one such fixture, but not a combination of fluorescent and incandescent fixtures. Also the wiring between the switch and fixture must have three conductors (besides a ground wire). Consult an electrician for other wiring requirements.

▶ *Fluorescent light makes things look ghastly.*

If the colors are too green or blue, change the tube to a warm white or deluxe warm white. If the colors are too orange or red, change the tube to a cool white or deluxe cool white. You may also find, with full-spectrum tubes, that things appear different because you are seeing things in true color rather than the familiar warm colors created by incandescent lighting.

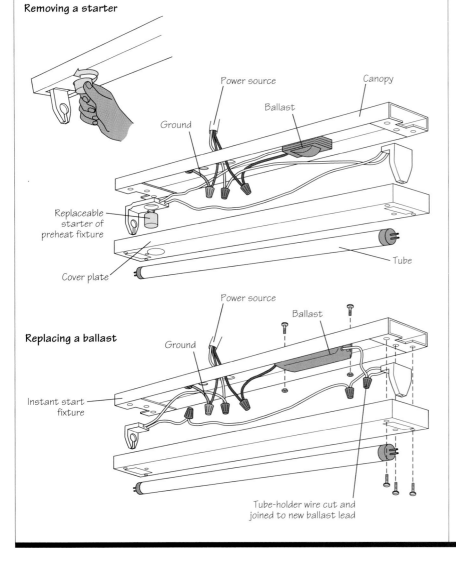

Removing a starter

Power source · Ground · Ballast · Canopy · Replaceable starter of preheat fixture · Cover plate · Tube

Replacing a ballast

Power source · Ground · Ballast · Instant start fixture · Tube-holder wire cut and joined to new ballast lead

Tip   *Wattage is not a measurement of light, but of power consumed. A 40-watt fluorescent bulb produces six times as much light as an ordinary 40-watt incandescent bulb (and lasts up to five times longer).*

Tip   *A fluorescent light consumes more energy when it is switched on and off several times during a short period than when it is left on the whole time.*

SOLVING ELECTRICAL PROBLEMS

▶ Lamp switch won't click.

Replace the socket-and-switch assembly. Unplug the lamp, remove the top half of the socket shell, disconnect the wires from the switch, unscrew the bottom half of the shell from the lamp base, and install the new socket-and-switch assembly. See below.

▶ Lamp doesn't work.

Be sure that the bulb isn't burned out, then check the circuit breaker. Plug the lamp into a receptacle in another room. If it still doesn't work, unplug the lamp and inspect the plug and cord for breaks; replace the plug or cord as necessary (see right and opposite page). If they appear sound, unscrew the light bulb and disassemble the lamp socket by squeezing where it says *Press*. Now check the cord for hidden breaks by testing each wire with a continuity tester. Touch one probe to a terminal screw and the other probe to each prong of the plug. One prong should make it light. The tester should also light when you touch the other terminal screw and the prong that didn't light the first time. If either wire fails to show continuity, replace the cord and plug.

If the wire tests for continuity, test the switch by touching one probe of the continuity tester to the silver-colored terminal and one probe to the brass-colored socket body. Test it with the switch in both positions. If the tester doesn't light either time, replace the socket-and-switch assembly. Be sure to attach the ribbed (neutral) side of the cord to the silver-colored screw of the

new switch. After connecting the wires, reassemble the socket by slipping the insulating sleeve over the switch and pressing the top shell into place until you hear it click.

Testing wire continuity

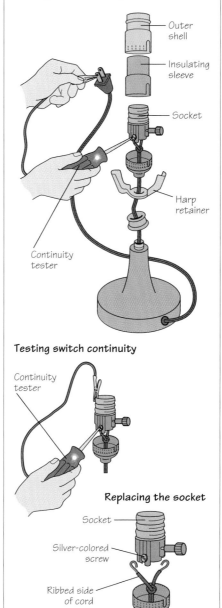

- Outer shell
- Insulating sleeve
- Socket
- Harp retainer
- Continuity tester

Testing switch continuity

- Continuity tester

Replacing the socket

- Socket
- Silver-colored screw
- Ribbed side of cord

▶ Plug makes sparks when plugged in.

It is normal for the plug to arc slightly if a lamp or appliance is on while being plugged or unplugged from a live receptacle. If sparks occur under any other conditions, inspect the plug for loose connections and tighten them. If it appears sound, try it in a different receptacle. If the problem recurs, replace the plug. If it doesn't, check the original receptacle (see page 209).

▶ Cord needs new plug.

Replace any plug that has cracks, twisted prongs, a missing grounding prong, or frayed wires. Be sure to use a grounded (three-pronged) plug for a cord with three wires. All grounded plugs and some two-pronged plugs are attached to the wires with terminal screws; other two-pronged plugs connect to wires with clamps. For either type, pull the plug from the electrical receptacle and cut the cord about 1 inch above the plug. If the new plug is self-connecting, split the wires apart for the first ½ inch to 1 inch, depending on the style of connection. You do not have to remove any insulation. To attach, open the plug clamp, slide the cord into the plug body, and close the clamp. If one side of the cord is ribbed or otherwise identifiable as the neutral side, attach it to the side of the plug with the wider prong.

To attach the cord to a plug with screw terminals, separate the wires about 1¼ inches at the end and strip about ½ inch of insulation off both wires. Remove the insulating barrier from between the plug prongs and slide the plug body off the prong assembly to expose the screws. Thread the cord through the body and attach the wires to

Tip *The old-fashioned round plug, with a cardboard insulator between the prongs, poses a hazard from potentially exposed wires and is no longer allowed. When replacing it, choose a plug with a plastic insulator.*

Tip *The cord of a lamp or small appliance is likely to wear out sooner than the plug. If the plug needs replacing, consider replacing both with a new polarized plug and cord.*

the screws—green wire to the green (grounding) screw, white or ribbed wire to the silver-colored (neutral) screw, and black or smooth wire to the brass-colored (hot) screw. To attach each wire, tightly twist the strands together clockwise, wrap the wire around each screw clockwise, and keep all of the strands together as you tighten the screw onto them. Slide the plug body back over the screw terminals and snap the insulating barrier between the prongs.

Attaching self-connecting plugs

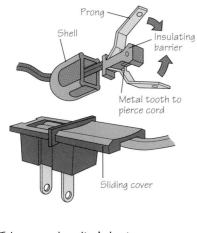

Tying an underwriter's knot

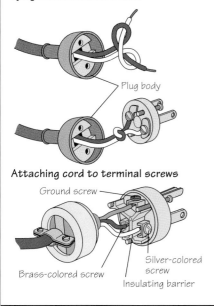

Attaching cord to terminal screws

▶ Cord needs switch.

Lamps, especially by bedsides, can be made more convenient by installing a thumb switch on the cord. The cord must be zip cord, which has a ribbed side and a smooth side. If it isn't, replace the entire cord first (see right). To attach the switch, unplug the cord. At the point where you'll install the switch, separate the cord wires for about 1 inch by slitting the groove between them. Cut the smooth (hot) wire of the cord, which should be attached to the narrower prong of the plug; do not cut the ribbed side of the cord. You do not have to strip insulation from the cut ends. Next separate the two shells of the switch by loosening the connecting screw. Place the cord into the bottom half of the shell so the cut side lies where the two sharp contacts will engage each segment of the wire. The ribbed (neutral) side of the wire should lie in a continuous groove of the shell and not be broken or punctured by the contacts when the two halves of the switch are joined. Then snap the two switch halves together and tighten the connecting screw. Test the switch.

Placing cord in switch shell

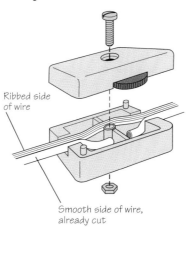

▶ Lamp cord is frayed, burnt, or too short.

Replace the old cord with zip cord, which has a ribbed side and a smooth side. Most lamp cords are 6 feet long. Buy a new plug to match the cord. (For three-wire grounding cord, see page 224.) Unplug the lamp, remove the shade and bulb, then remove the top half of the socket assembly by squeezing where it says *Press*. Disconnect both wires from the screw terminals. Tape the wire ends to one end of the new cord and pull the old cord through the lamp. Remove the old cord and split the end of the new wire for 2½ inches. Tie an underwriter's knot (see opposite page), strip ½ inch of insulation from the ends, and connect it to the socket terminals—ribbed side of cord attached to silver-colored screw. At the bottom of the lamp, pull the cord until the socket is snug. Reassemble the socket by slipping the insulating sleeve over the switch and pressing the top shell into place until you hear it click. Attach a plug to the new cord (see opposite page).

Pulling new wire through lamp

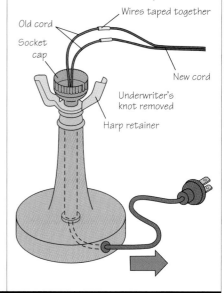

Tip *Lamp and small-appliance cord is referred to as flexible cord because the wires are multistranded, rather than single conductors. Most cords are 16 or 18 gauge and are called zip cord, fixture cord, or STP cord.*

SOLVING ELECTRICAL PROBLEMS

▶ *Cord for small appliance needs replacing.*

Unplug the cord and remove the housing from the appliance to expose the terminal connections for the cord. If it is connected to screw terminals, unscrew them. If the connections are soldered and the first 3 or 4 inches of cord are undamaged, cut the old cord about 3 inches from the connections and strip 1½ inches of sheathing from the cut end of the short piece (if the cord is sheathed); then strip ¾ inch of insulation from the end of each wire. Take the cord to the store and buy new cord of the same gauge, type (two-wire or three-wire), and length; buy a new plug to match the cord.

To connect the new cord, strip 1½ to 2 inches of sheathing from one end, if it is sheathed; strip ¾ inch of insulation from the wires. Thread the cord through the hole or grommet in the housing, if there is one, and tie an underwriter's knot. Then attach the wires to the screw terminals (wrap them around the screws clockwise)—green wire to the grounding screw, white wire to the silver-colored (neutral) screw, and black wire to the brass-colored (hot) screw. If you had cut the old cord because the connections were soldered, thread the new cord through the housing, tie an underwriter's knot, and splice each wire to the corresponding wire of the old cord with wire connectors. Wrap electrical tape around the connectors and wires. Attach the plug to the cord and plug in the appliance to test it.

Splicing new wire to old wire

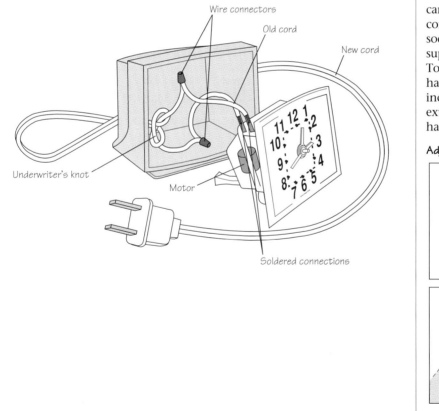

Wire connectors

Old cord

New cord

Underwriter's knot

Motor

Soldered connections

▶ *Lamp illuminates too much or not enough.*

For a table lamp the vertical height of the shade (called depth) should be about 2 inches less than the height of the base to keep the lamp from looking top-heavy. For floor lamps the bottom of the shade should be even with the bottom of the socket or harp. The shade should also control the spread of light upward and downward for the desired effect. If the bottom diameter of the shade is too small, the light won't reach the entire area you want to illuminate; if it's too large, the light will spread too far. If the top is too small, the ceiling may not receive enough light, creating a harsh pool of light under the lamp.

If the shade seems to be the right proportions but lighting is inadequate, the shade may be too high or too low in relation to the bulb. This can happen if you install a touch control or other adapter between the socket and bulb, or if the harp that supports the lamp shade is too large. To lower the shade, buy a smaller harp (sizes range from 7 to 13 inches). To raise the shade, buy an extension screw for the top of the harp, or buy a larger harp.

Adjusting light spread

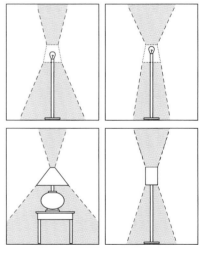

Tip *To get the most light from a lamp, choose a shade that is made of light-colored material that has high reflective value, with large openings at the top and bottom. Place the lamp near a corner, where it can reflect light off of two walls instead of one.*

▶ House lacks outdoor lighting.

Outdoor lights deter intruders, prevent people from tripping in the dark, make patios and backyards usable into the evening, and enhance the beauty of a home. With the widespread availability of low-voltage lighting systems, installing lights is inexpensive and relatively easy, especially if your home already has an outdoor receptacle. Pick the types of fixtures that best suit your needs. If you want to play nighttime badminton games in the backyard, mount a pair of floodlights under the eaves. If you're interested in subtle illumination to welcome guests, install low-voltage lights along the path to the front door. Use small spotlights to accent plants or sculpture. You can also sink lights into the lawn or recess them into a wall or into a riser on an outside step.

For safety, place lights at entrances and on each side of the house. Also light steps and pathways. Don't leave any shadows where intruders could hide, and make sure address numbers are well lit.

▶ Low-voltage lights need installing.

A typical low-voltage kit includes four to 14 or more fixtures, low-voltage cable, and a weatherproof transformer. The transformer plugs into a standard receptacle and reduces the 120-volt house current to a safe 12 volts. If you buy components separately, add the wattages of the fixtures and select a transformer that offers more than enough power.

Mount the transformer near a receptacle, either indoors or out. Attach the low-voltage cable to the terminal screw of the transformer, and plug in the power cord. Most fixtures, whether they are globes, floodlights, or tier lights, consist of a lamp head and ground stake.

Assemble the fixtures and wire them to the cable following kit directions. To avoid damaging the wire connections, don't drive the stake into the ground. Instead dig a hole, insert the stake, and pack the hole with dirt. Run the cable to the next fixture, covering it with mulch or burying it in a shallow trench. In places where the cable could be damaged by foot traffic or a lawn mower, bury it 1 foot deep. For best results, place lights no more than 200 feet from the transformer.

To turn lights on and off, install additional manual switches, a timer, a motion sensor, or a photoelectric eye.

Mounting transformer

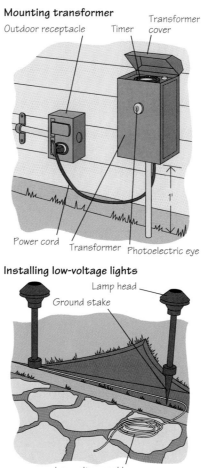

Outdoor receptacle   Timer   Transformer cover

Power cord   Transformer   Photoelectric eye

Installing low-voltage lights

Lamp head
Ground stake

Low-voltage cable

▶ Lighting is too bright and not broad enough.

Your yard doesn't need to look like a nighttime ballfield to deter intruders. Several well-placed, low-wattage bulbs are more effective and less irritating to neighbors than a single floodlight. If you do use a floodlight, place it under the eaves and point it downward, or on the ground pointing upward toward the house. If you aim it out toward the street, the glare will prevent others from seeing an intruder in your yard. Avoid placing it directly above or below a window.

Mounting floodlights under eaves

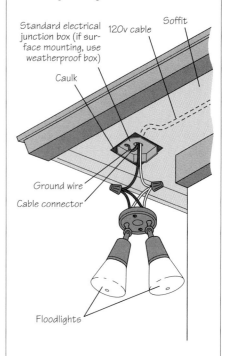

Standard electrical junction box (if surface mounting, use weatherproof box)   120v cable   Soffit

Caulk

Ground wire
Cable connector

Floodlights

▶ Yard or garden needs a receptacle.

To install a remote receptacle, tap into a circuit at an existing outdoor fixture such as a porch light, or install a junction box on an indoor circuit (preferably in the basement

Tip *Many low-voltage fixtures use halogen bulbs, which should not be touched with bare hands. The oil from your skin will leave a residue on the bulb, causing it to heat unevenly and burn out too soon. Handle the bulbs with gloves or tissue paper.*

SOLVING ELECTRICAL PROBLEMS

or attic) and feed cable to the outside through a hole in the wall.

None of the wiring can be exposed; it must be enclosed in walls or conduit or buried. If you run wires through conduit (along the house or a deck joist, for instance), use liquidtight connectors to join lengths of conduit, and secure it with straps every 10 feet and within 3 feet of any box. Check with the local building department about requirements for burying cable. In most regions you can bury rigid metal conduit (at least 6 inches deep) and plastic conduit (at least 18 inches deep) and fish Type TW or Type THW wire through it. Plastic conduit cannot be used for vertical segments where wiring emerges from the ground; use threaded rigid metal conduit instead. Type UF (underground feeder) cable can be buried directly in the soil so long as it's at least 12 inches deep. Cover the UF cable with sand or redwood boards. Where conduit turns to rise to a receptacle, lower a concrete block into the trench and bring conduit up through the hole in the block, stabilizing the conduit by filling the hole with gravel or concrete (see right); fill the trench with dirt. Enclose exposed UF cable in conduit where it exits the house and where it connects to the receptacle.

For the receptacle, mount a weatherproof box on a post or on the side of a shed. A box is not allowed to be supported by conduit only, unless there are two separate conduits connected securely to the box. Attach conduit to the box by screwing the end into the threaded holes in the box. Seal unused holes with coin-shaped screw-in plugs. Attach a receptacle to the wires (a GFCI receptacle if the circuit is not already GFCI

protected), secure it to the box, and attach a weatherproof cover with a hinged door that snaps shut.

Tapping into a light fixture

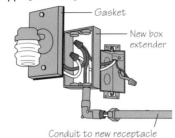

- Gasket
- New box extender
- Conduit to new receptacle

Running conduit underground

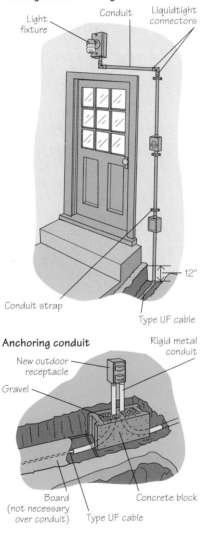

- Light fixture
- Conduit
- Liquidtight connectors
- 12"
- Conduit strap
- Type UF cable

Anchoring conduit

- Rigid metal conduit
- New outdoor receptacle
- Gravel
- Board (not necessary over conduit)
- Concrete block
- Type UF cable

▶ *House doesn't have outdoor receptacle.*

If you have to add a new receptacle outdoors, the easiest way is to install it on the side of the house. You can use an ordinary electrical box or a weatherproof surface-mounted box. The receptacle must have a weatherproof gasket and cover and a hinged door that snaps shut when the outlet is not in use. Outdoor receptacles must be GFCI protected.

To install, find a receptacle inside the house on an exterior wall, then shut off the power. Unscrew the cover, disconnect the receptacle, and remove one of the knockouts from the back of the box. Then, using a window or some other point of reference, measure and mark the location of the receptacle on the outside of the exterior wall. Make a second mark about 6 inches from the first (most walls are not thick enough to mount boxes back-to-back). Center the new receptacle over the second mark and trace its outline on the wall, making sure the outline isn't over a stud. If the house has board siding, position the box entirely on one board rather than on the joint between boards.

Cut the hole with a saber saw or reciprocating saw. On masonry walls use an electric drill and masonry bit to drill several holes within the outline, then knock out the remaining masonry with a hammer and cold chisel. Pull the cable from the indoor box through the new opening and into the outdoor receptacle box. Screw or mortar the box into the outside wall and caulk the gap between the box and wall. Wire the GFCI outdoor receptacle as you would an indoor

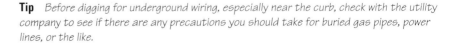

Tip *Before digging for underground wiring, especially near the curb, check with the utility company to see if there are any precautions you should take for buried gas pipes, power lines, or the like.*

receptacle (see page 210); connect the power supply cable to the receptacle leads marked *Line,* and connect the ground wires. Cap leads marked *Load* with wire connectors; tuck them into the box. Screw the receptacle into the box and attach the gasket and cover. Put the indoor receptacle back together and restore power.

Installing outdoor receptacle on an outside wall

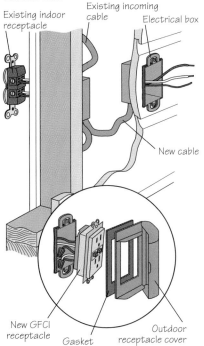

Existing indoor receptacle

Existing incoming cable

Electrical box

New cable

New GFCI receptacle

Gasket

Outdoor receptacle cover

▶ Outdoor receptacle or circuit is not GFCI protected.

The NEC requires that all newly installed outdoor receptacles be protected with a ground fault circuit interrupter (GFCI). The device prevents shocks by monitoring electricity flowing through the receptacle. If even a minuscule amount of voltage leaks, the device will "interrupt" or shut off the current within one-fortieth of a second. There are three ways to provide GFCI protection.

The easiest is to install a GFCI receptacle at each location where you need power. The second way is to use a GFCI receptacle at one location and protect all other receptacles that are on the same circuit and downstream from it by wiring them into its terminal screws or leads marked *Load.* A third way to achieve GFCI protection is to install a GFCI breaker at the circuit-breaker panel. Unlike normal breakers, the GFCI breaker includes a white neutral wire that must be connected to the neutral bus (the terminal strip in the breaker panel to which all the white wires are connected).

Protecting receptacles downstream from a GFCI device

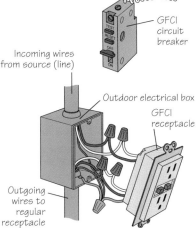

GFCI circuit breaker

Incoming wires from source (line)

Outdoor electrical box

GFCI receptacle

Outgoing wires to regular receptacle

▶ Outdoor wiring is too complicated.

Install solar-powered lights that run on rechargeable batteries. They don't boost the electricity bill and are simple to mount because they are not wired to an external power source. However, solar-powered lamps may not be a good choice if you need hours of brilliant light. They often use less-bright, low-wattage bulbs, and most will operate for only six hours after being charged for a full day in sunlight. They work best in sunny climates.

▶ Lights lack automatic switches.

There are several ways to control outdoor lights without flipping a switch. One way is to install a clock timer, which will turn lights on and off at preset times. Mount the clock in a junction box on an inside wall near where the outdoor cable exits the house. If the timer doesn't have one, mount a switch nearby so you can manually override the clock. Following manufacturer's instructions, wire the switch to the clock and connect the clock to the cable leading from the power source to the outdoor lights.

Another option is photoelectric eyes, which automatically turn lights on at dusk and off at dawn. These sensors, which detect daylight, come in a variety of styles and can be wired directly into any outside circuit. You can also convert most single fixtures with a small photoelectric unit that screws directly into the fixture socket. The bulb then screws into a socket in the photoelectric unit.

If you want illumination only when someone comes near your home, install a light with a built-in motion detector. Using passive infrared sensors, these lights turn on when a vehicle or person enters a preset radius, and remain on until the person or vehicle leaves. Small animals will not trigger the sensor, but large ones will. Generally, motion-detecting lights don't operate in daylight. They come in floodlamp styles and in a variety of decorative fixtures; most include a photoelectric eye. A conversion kit, available at most home centers, will turn any outdoor light into a motion-sensitive light. Some outdoor motion detectors can be set up to trigger additional lights indoors.

Tip *There are three types of conduit for wiring: rigid metal, EMT (electrical metallic tubing, also called thin-wall), and PVC plastic. Rigid metal conduit is available in galvanized steel or aluminum. It uses threaded or threadless compression couplings and connectors, and can be used above ground and below ground. EMT is easier to cut and work with, but is restricted in outdoor use: it cannot be buried and, in some areas, cannot be used outdoors at all. Connectors are threadless and come in two types: setscrew (for indoors only) and compression, or "liquidtight" (for outdoors). PVC plastic conduit can be buried but not exposed; it is cut and joined like plastic plumbing pipe.*

SOLVING ELECTRICAL PROBLEMS

▶ *Motion-detecting light comes on too often and stays on too long.*

If the motion-detecting light comes on with annoying frequency, shorten the range of the sensor using the control knobs on the fixture. Ranges among sensors vary from 1 to 75 feet. You can also adjust the time setting, which controls how many minutes the lamp remains on after it's been triggered.

If the lamp points at a busy sidewalk or street, unscrew the fixture and mount it in a different location or at another angle. If only an edge of the sensor field extends into a busy sidewalk, block that area by covering part of the sensor lens with duct tape or electrical tape. Have a helper walk in front of the sensor to isolate the part of the lens you should cover.

If the lamp on the fixture is mounted below the sensor, the heat from the bulb may be triggering the sensor. Replace the fixture with one in which the sensor is below the lamp. Power surges and vibrations can also trigger the sensor. Surges can't be controlled; vibrations might be if they're caused by a fan or some other appliance that you could move.

Adjusting time setting on motion-detecting light

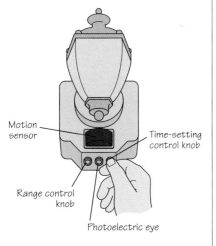

Motion sensor

Time-setting control knob

Range control knob

Photoelectric eye

▶ *Lights don't turn on at the right time.*

Timers must be reset periodically due to seasonal changes and daylight saving time. Because the timers are connected to the house current, they also need to be reset after power outages, unless the timer comes with a backup battery. If you don't want to reset the timer, consider installing a photoelectric eye, which automatically turns the lights on at dusk and off at dawn.

▶ *Lights don't come on.*

Check to see if the bulb has burned out; remove the bulb and screw in a new one that you know is working. If the problem is not the bulb, shut off power to the circuit and inspect the socket. Make sure it is clean and that nothing is preventing the bulb from making contact with the socket base. Remove the fixture from the wall to expose the wires. Make sure the black and the white wires from the house circuit are connected to the corresponding wires from the fixture. If the lamp includes a motion detector, make sure the red wire from the motion detector is connected to the wires from the lamp holders.

▶ *Outdoor bulb won't unscrew.*

Outdoor bulbs are prone to corrosion because the fixture is exposed to moisture and dirt. First shut off electricity to the fixture and try easing the bulb out of the socket again. If that won't work, break the bulb near the base, wearing thick gloves and holding a paper bag over the bulb. Then with needle nose pliers unscrew the metal base of the bulb from the socket. (See page 217.) To reduce sticking problems

in the future, smear petroleum jelly on the threads of the bulb before installing it, or use fixtures with coated-aluminum screw shells or ceramic sockets.

▶ *Bulbs burn out too often.*

See page 217.

▶ *Doorbell won't ring.*

First check to see if a fuse has blown or a circuit breaker has tripped. The problem may simply be no power. If the power is on, the trouble is in the push button, the bell, the transformer, or the wires. Inspect the push button first (you do not need to turn the power off to check the push button or the bell). Unscrew the unit from the wall and check the back to see if the two wires are touching. Connect any wires that may have come loose from a terminal screw. If the bell still doesn't ring, unscrew the wires and touch their ends together, holding them by the insulation; if the bell rings, the button is defective. Straighten and clean the contacts with fine sandpaper or an emery board; then rehook the wires and try again. If the button still does not work, replace it.

If touching the wires together produces only a faint ring or no sound at all, the problem is elsewhere. Unscrew the cover from the bell. Using a cotton swab and rubbing alcohol, clean off any dirt, paint, or grease that may have accumulated on the bell, the hammer, or the contacts. Also check for loose parts and inspect the wires where they connect to the screw terminals to see if any have broken or become loose.

If these steps don't solve the problem, check the transformer. (To find the transformer, see page 230.) This boxlike device reduces the 120-volt house current to a low-voltage

---

Tip *To make an outdoor bulb easier to remove, smear petroleum jelly on the threads of the new bulb before installing it.*

Tip *Replace standard incandescent bulbs with longer-lasting bulbs. High-pressure sodium or mercury vapor lamps last for years; fluorescent bulbs are also more energy efficient. All of these bulbs give off a quality of light different from incandescent bulbs, so check them in a natural setting before making a switch. Compact fluorescent bulbs screw into standard incandescent fixtures, but for other types of bulbs you will have to change the light fixtures too.*

current (usually under 20) for the doorbell system. You do not need to turn the power off to check the transformer or the wires. However, if checking reveals that you need to work on the transformer, you must

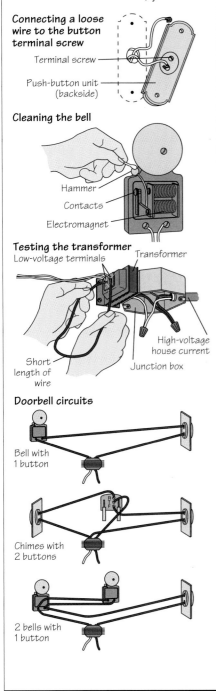

Connecting a loose wire to the button terminal screw

Terminal screw

Push-button unit (backside)

Cleaning the bell

Hammer

Contacts

Electromagnet

Testing the transformer

Low-voltage terminals

Transformer

High-voltage house current

Short length of wire

Junction box

Doorbell circuits

Bell with 1 button

Chimes with 2 buttons

2 bells with 1 button

turn the power off. Check the thin, low-voltage bell wires where they attach to the transformer screw terminals and tighten any loose connections. (The transformer wires that connect to the 120-volt current are usually enclosed in a junction box, safely out of the way; however, use caution, especially in older homes where connections could be outside of junction boxes.) If you have a voltmeter, touch a probe to each terminal screw; if the voltmeter doesn't measure any voltage, the transformer is broken and you'll need to replace it. You also can test for power by holding a length of wire to both terminals. If the transformer works, you will see a faint spark as you lift the wire on and off the screws (you may need to conduct this test in the dark). Just be sure that you are testing only the low-voltage wires.

If the button, bell, and transformer seem to be OK, check any wire you can easily get at. Wrap frayed areas with electrical tape and repair breaks by stripping the ends and twisting wires together or connecting them with wire nuts. If the bell is still silent, you'll have to replace all the wire.

▶ Chimes won't ring.

Most newer homes have chimes instead of a doorbell or buzzer. In a two-tone chime, when someone presses the front-door button, a striker hits the high-note chime. When the button is released, the striker springs back and hits the low-note chime, producing the familiar "ding-dong." The backdoor button sounds only the high-note chime. If the system isn't working, check the button, transformer, and exposed wires. (See opposite page.)

If all of these are unimpaired, remove the cover from the chimes. Clean moving parts and connect any loose wires. If you have a voltmeter, place one probe to the terminal marked *Front* on the chimes. This terminal connects to the front-door button. Place the other probe on the terminal marked *Trans*, which connects to the transformer. If you get a reading, it means the chimes are broken and need to be replaced. If you don't have a voltmeter, hook the chimes directly to the transformer with two short lengths of wire. Attach the *Front* chime terminal to one terminal on the transformer; connect the *Trans* chime terminal to the other. The chimes should ring if they are OK.

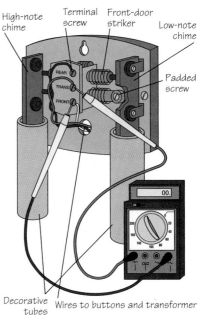

Checking chimes with a volt meter

High-note chime

Terminal screw

Front-door striker

Low-note chime

Padded screw

Decorative tubes

Wires to buttons and transformer

▶ Ding but no dong.

If your two-tone chimes deliver only a single tone, remove the cover from the fixture and check to see if a striker is sticking or missing (see illustration above). If it's sticking,

---

Tip *Connect doorbells to buttons with 18- or 20-gauge "bell wire," which has two insulated conductors wrapped around each other or encased together.*

lubricate it with powdered graphite. Never use oil; it attracts dirt, which muffles the sound. If the striker is missing, replace the chimes.

If the striker doesn't seem to be the problem, the trouble is either in the chimes or in the wires running to the buttons or the transformer. Try hooking the chimes directly to the transformer. If you get both tones, the chime unit is working fine, and you know the problem is in the wires. See page 228.

▶ Chimes ring but the sound is faint.

Remove the cover from the fixture and make sure the strikers that ring the chimes are not dirty or bent (see illustration, page 229). If that's not the problem, the transformer may be too weak to handle the doorbell system. Most bells require less than 10 volts, whereas many chimes need up to 24 volts. Someone may have replaced an old bell with a new set of chimes without installing a more powerful transformer.

Check how many volts the transformer delivers and how many volts the chimes need. The information should be written somewhere on the units themselves. If necessary, replace the transformer with a more powerful one. If the transformer is not the problem, you may need to shop around for louder chimes.

▶ Transformer is hard to find.

Most transformers are wired into one of the 120-volt house circuits at a junction box in the attic, basement, or a closet, often near a furnace or water heater. Check the wires coming from the bell. If they

head downward, the transformer is likely in the basement, mounted on one of the floor joists, possibly connected to overhead lights or receptacles. If the wires from the bell head upward, check for the transformer in the attic. If you still can't locate it, trace the wires from the button and see if you have better luck.

▶ Doorbell rings only sometimes.

Make sure all the wires are firmly connected at the button, bell, and transformer. There is likely a loose connection at one of these places.

▶ Doorbell rings continually.

Carefully unscrew the push button from the wall and check the back to see if bare sections of the two wires are touching. If they are, separate the wires. Wrap frayed areas with electrical tape.

If the wires are not touching, unscrew them from the terminals and hold them apart. If the ringing stops, the push button is likely stuck in a depressed position. Pry up the button and make sure the spring works. If it's old and bent out of shape, replace the entire button.

Occasionally, the ringing does not stop when you hold the wires apart. This means that somewhere along the run the wires between the button and the bell are touching those between the button and the transformer. Trace the wires and wrap bare spots with electrical tape.

▶ One button rings doorbell but the other doesn't.

Test the button first and replace it if it's broken (see page 228). If the button works, check for loose connections at the bell and transformer. Finally, inspect and, if necessary, repair the wires that run

from the silent button to the bell and transformer.

Don't bother checking the wires running from the working button to the transformer or those from the transformer to the bell.

▶ House has no doorbell.

To install a bell or chimes, you will need to wire a transformer to the house circuit. You'll also have to run 18- or 20-gauge wires inside walls or under floors to connect the transformer to the button and bell. Attach the transformer to an existing junction box in an accessible location (the basement or attic are likely sites). Make sure the power to the circuit is off before you start working. Tap out a knockout hole from the junction box, and pass the transformer wires into the box. Then secure the transformer to the box by inserting the threaded lug into the knockout hole and screwing the locknut onto it from inside the junction box. With wire connectors, attach one transformer wire to the black 120-volt wire and connect the other transformer to the white 120-volt wire.

Install the bell in a central location so the sound can be heard throughout the house. Chimes generally hang about 6 feet off the floor. To mount the push button, drill a hole in the exterior wall about 4½ feet up from the ground and about 4½ inches from the outer edge of the door. Run low-voltage wire from the transformer to the bell, from the bell to the button, and from the button to the transformer. Use different-colored wires for each stretch, and you'll have an easier time isolating problems later on.

Tip *If you're still living in a ding-dong world you should visit your local lighting store or electrical supplier to see the variety of chimes available. You may be amazed at the astonishing selection of sounds—and sights—available for announcing your visitors. Popular songs, classical melodies, tunes you program yourself, and flashing lights are some of the options readily available.*

Bell wires are permitted by code to be exposed, so you can run the wires along the molding or under the edge of a carpet, but most people prefer them hidden inside walls (see page 205). Anchor the wires to joists or beams with insulated staples about every 4 inches, being careful not to pierce the wires. Closely follow manufacturer's instructions for connecting the low-voltage bell wires. Hook up the button and the bell first. If you're installing chimes, make sure the wires are clear of the strikers. Finally, screw the bell wires to the transformer, flip the power back on, and test the new bell.

Securing transformer to junction box

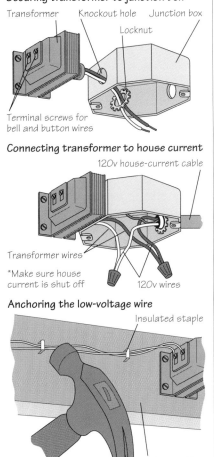

Transformer   Knockout hole   Junction box
Locknut
Terminal screws for bell and button wires

Connecting transformer to house current

120v house-current cable
Transformer wires
*Make sure house current is shut off
120v wires

Anchoring the low-voltage wire

Insulated staple
Joist or other framing

▶ Doorbell is too complicated to install.

If you want to avoid the effort of wiring a doorbell, consider buying a battery-operated "wireless" unit. This is also a good solution for renters who do not have their landlord's permission to drill holes in the wall. You can find battery-operated doorbells at most hardware or electronics stores. Simply mount the push button, called the "transmitter," on or next to the door, and plug the chimes, or "receiver," into an existing outlet. Some models use portable chimes that run off 9-volt batteries. These chimes can be hung anywhere in the house so long as they're within 100 feet of the button. When you press the button, a radio signal is sent to the receiver, and the chimes will ring. The signal doesn't travel well through metal, so don't put the button on a steel door.

If the chime unit goes off when no one is pushing the button, it may be picking up a signal from a neighbor's doorbell or garage-door opener. Follow manufacturer's instructions on how to set the doorbell code; this may prevent the interference.

▶ Bell can't be heard from certain rooms.

Install a new bell in the part of the house where you have trouble hearing the existing one. Pick a spot, measure the distance from there to the existing bell, and buy enough 18- or 20-gauge wire to cover this distance. Mount the new bell on the wall and connect it to the existing bell with the wire. Carefully follow manufacturer's instructions for connecting the wires to each terminal of the new bell. You do not need to attach the new bell to the transformer.

▶ Back door has no button.

Adding another button to a doorbell circuit usually involves attaching a new button next to a door and running wires to both the bell and the transformer. Follow manufacturer's instructions for hooking up the button. If the wire from the new button ends up running alongside the wire from the existing button on its way to the transformer, you can splice the two lengths together. Cut the existing wire where it's joined by the wire from the new button, and twist the loose ends together with a wire connector.

▶ Smoke detector is chirping.

Most battery-operated smoke detectors will chirp when their battery runs down. Replace the battery and test the alarm. Not all smoke detectors deliver a low-battery signal; you will know the battery is dead only by testing.

▶ Smoke detector goes off frequently.

Don't disconnect the detector from the power circuit or remove the battery; you will likely forget to hook it up again. Instead open a window or turn on a fan to clear the air. Then at a more convenient time, determine what's triggering the alarm. It could be fumes from a toaster or moisture from a shower or clothes dryer. Try moving the detector farther away from the source of the problem. If the unit is in the kitchen or garage, move it just outside the door to these areas. If the detector runs on a battery, unscrew the mounting bracket and simply install the unit in its new location. Moving a direct-wired smoke detector is more complicated because you need to connect it to the house current. Call an electrician, or see page 232.

Tip   If you add new chimes to a system that uses a doorbell or buzzer, you can use the old buttons but you will likely need to replace the old transformer with a larger one. Chimes need up to 24 volts, whereas bells and buzzers use less than 10 volts.

Tip   Keep smoke detectors away from cooking fumes, fireplaces, bathroom showers, water heaters, and clothes dryers. Don't mount them in drafty areas or in corners where the air never moves. Also keep them far from fluorescent lights, and do not mount them on exterior walls.

SOLVING ELECTRICAL PROBLEMS

▶ Smoke detector needs testing.

Smoke detectors either run off 9-volt batteries or are wired directly to the 120-volt house current. Some direct-wired units also use backup batteries. Change the battery once a year and test the alarm every two months. Most smoke detectors have a test button you can push, but this tests only the batteries. To test the entire unit, wave a lighted candle or cigarette under it and let smoke drift into the vent. If the alarm goes off, it's working. You can also buy a tester aerosol that simulates smoke (it doesn't deplete the ozone); spray it at the detector vents for a few seconds. Clean the unit periodically with the soft brush of a vacuum cleaner. If a smoke detector doesn't react to a test, replace it.

▶ Smoke alarm isn't loud enough.

People who are hard of hearing or who sleep soundly can buy a smoke detector with a louder horn. Some models on the market are twice as loud as the average 85-decibel alarm. You can also install additional alarms.

▶ Basement smoke alarm can't be heard upstairs.

Install a multiple alarm system in which each detector is linked to the others with low-voltage wire. If one goes off, they all will. To test, trigger each unit separately and check to see that all the others were set off. The indicator light will go off on the detector that is triggered first; the indicator lights on the others will remain on. To install this type of system, follow manufacturer's instructions.

▶ House doesn't have a smoke detector.

Every home should have a smoke detector in each bedroom and in hallways outside bedrooms. Homes with two stories or more should have a detector on each floor and at the top of each stairwell, including the one leading to the basement.

Alarm units use one of two detection systems. Photoelectric systems respond especially well to smoldering fires; smoke detectors of this type are best used in kitchen and bedroom areas. Ionization detectors are sensitive to rapidly developing fires. Use this type in furnace rooms and storage areas.

Installing a battery-operated detector is easy. Screw the unit into a wall or ceiling, slip in a battery, and snap on the cover. Wall installations should be within 12 inches of the ceiling.

To install a direct-wired detector, cut a hole in the wall or ceiling and mount a junction box. Making sure the circuit is shut off, extend a 120-volt house cable to the box. Attach the mounting bracket to the ceiling box. With wire screws, connect the black house wire to the black lead coming from the smoke detector, and the white house wire to the white lead. Finally, screw the detector into the mounting bracket.

If you are direct-wiring several smoke detectors, link them together in the same wiring circuit so that all of the alarms will sound if one of them is activated. Many codes now require that multiple detectors be interconnected in this way. Use "feedthrough," or "tandem," alarms. They have three wires: one black, one white, and one yellow or orange. Up to ten such units can be wired into the same circuit. Use three-wire cable for the circuit wiring, connecting the black and white wires to the black and white leads of the smoke

detectors, and the red wire to the yellow or orange leads of the detectors. Make sure that the circuit wiring is not controlled by a switch or protected by a GFCI outlet or circuit breaker. For maximum security at least one of the units should be equipped with a 9-volt battery to provide a backup in case the house wiring has a power failure.

Installing a single direct-wired smoke detector

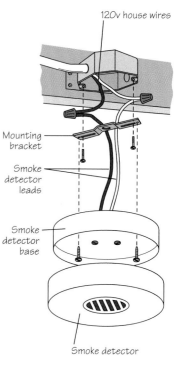

120v house wires

Mounting bracket

Smoke detector leads

Smoke detector base

Smoke detector

Tip *To provide extra protection for small children or people with limited mobility, consider a smoke detector that comes with a flashing red light. The unit is placed on the ceiling of the bedroom. The light attaches to a bedroom window with suction cups. When the alarm goes off, the light automatically starts flashing to indicate to rescuers the presence of someone in need of help. Another type of smoke detector includes a built-in light that comes on to illuminate an escape route when the alarm sounds.*

▶ Phone is dead.

Make sure none of the cords between the telephone handset, the telephone base, and the wall jack is loose. If the system uses square plastic modular plugs, check to see that they are securely snapped into place. If a cord has been chewed by a pet or otherwise damaged, replace it.

If the cords are in good shape, test the phone itself by plugging it into a jack that you know is working, either in another room or at a neighbor's house. If you still get no dial tone, have the phone repaired.

If you do get a dial tone, the problem lies in the wiring. Check where the telephone line first enters the house; you will find either a lightning protector or a test jack. If there is a jack, plug in the phone. No sound means the problem is in the outside wires, and the local telephone company will repair it.

If, on the other hand, the phone works in the test jack, you have a problem in the house wires. Unscrew the cover from the wall jack; you should see color-coded conductor wires. Make sure each wire is connected to the properly marked terminal screw. Also make sure no bare wires are touching; if any are, separate them and trim the excess wire. If a wire is broken (usually because it was nicked when the insulation was stripped), splice it or run a new length of wire.

Still no dial tone? Trace the phone wire (station wire) from the jack to where it enters the house, checking for breaks. If you find one, splice it or replace all the wire.

▶ Phone cord tangles easily.

Replace the phone cord between the telephone handset and base with a retractable cord. As you pull the handset away from the base, a small disc-shaped holder reels out up to 16 feet of cord. When you hang up, the cord automatically rewinds, much like a retractable tape measure. These can be purchased at hardware stores and at some office-supply stores.

▶ Phone reception is interrupted by static or humming.

Crackling sounds are usually caused by damp connections inside the jack. Dry the connections with a hair dryer. Remove the source of the moisture; if that's not possible, consider moving the phone jack.

If the phone hums, the red and green wires may be attached to the wrong screw terminals. Open the jack and reverse them. A loud humming sound that makes the phone unusable usually means that a bare phone wire is touching a metal water pipe or electrical conduit. Inspect the wires, especially where they run between floors. Staple them away from metal surfaces and wrap any bare spots with electrical tape. If that doesn't solve the problem, replace all the wires.

The poor reception could be caused by the phone itself. Make sure there are no kinks in the handset cord. Then check the contacts in the handset. Unscrew the mouthpiece, pull out the microphone disc, and gently bend the two contacts upward with your fingers or a small screwdriver. Clean them with a pencil eraser if necessary.

Phones that have additional features, such as automatic redial or call screening, are more sensitive to interference from radio frequency signals. Sometimes you can reduce static by using a couple of snap-on

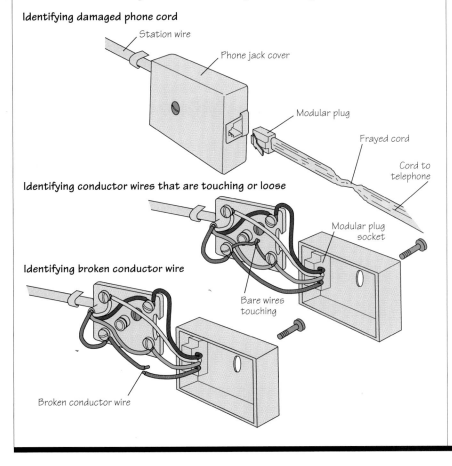

Identifying damaged phone cord

Station wire

Phone jack cover

Modular plug

Frayed cord

Cord to telephone

Identifying conductor wires that are touching or loose

Modular plug socket

Bare wires touching

Identifying broken conductor wire

Broken conductor wire

Tip *Phone wires conduct low-level electric current that is unlikely to cause harm. However, observe the following precautions: (1) Don't work on phones during thunderstorms or if you have a pacemaker. (2) Avoid touching bare wires or screws, and use tools with insulated handles. (3) Disconnect the house system from the company system before you work on a wall jack; if that's not possible, unplug all the phones in the house or take a phone off the hook while you're working.*

filter chokes, available at electronics or telephone-supply stores. Disconnect the handset cord, then wrap the handset end of the cord around one of the filter chokes as close to the handset connection as possible. Do the same with the second filter choke where the cord attaches to the base.

Cleaning mouthpiece contacts

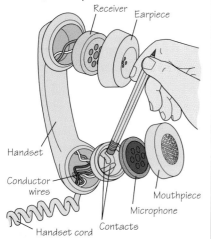

Placing filter chokes on handset cord

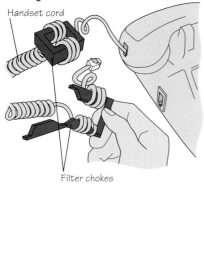

▶ *Phone dials out but doesn't ring on incoming calls.*

If the phone doesn't ring or has a muffled sound, something may be jammed. Open the phone and look between the bells for the recoil metal and clapper. Free the jammed part with a knife or small screwdriver.

If the phone rings when it is plugged into another jack, you may have too many phones. The phone company provides enough power to run five standard phones on each line. If you overload the system, one or more phones may not ring. The amount of power a phone needs is expressed as a ringer equivalence number (REN) written on the bottom of the phone. Most phones are rated at 1, but some are higher (a computer modem may be as high as 3). Add up the RENs of all the phones and equipment on your line. If the total is higher than 5, you may have to unplug a phone to get them all to work.

Freeing clapper with a screwdriver

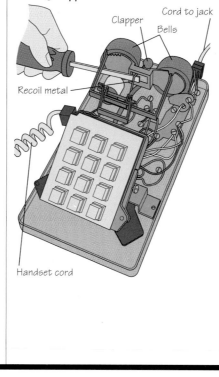

▶ *There is a dial tone but you cannot dial out.*

If you hear a tone while you dial and the phone is a push-button one dating from the early 1980s, the green and red conductor wires may be reversed. Remove the jack cover and reverse the wires. If that does not work, take it to a repair shop.

▶ *Portable cordless phone is dead.*

Batteries may not be charging properly. First check that the base is plugged in, then clean the metal charging points on the base and handset with a pencil eraser or alcohol and a cotton swab. Place the handset in the base and let it charge. If the handset is still dead after 24 hours, replace the batteries. If the base unit of the cordless phone is dead, check the telephone wires and the power supply cord. Repair any frayed areas and if necessary replace the wires. (See page 233.)

▶ *Portable cordless phone has noisy reception.*

Try a regular phone on the same jack. If the noise persists, check the phone wires for problems. (See page 233.) If you get clear reception, the problem is with the cordless phone.

Crackling on the line may be caused by fluorescent lights or by electrical appliances near the base; move the base. Radio signals from a neighbor's cordless phone can also cause static. Most cordless phones have a security code that you can program into the handset and base that will prevent interference from nearby units. Change this code,

Tip *Once a month leave the handset of a portable cordless phone off the base until the batteries completely run out of power, then recharge. This will prolong the life of the batteries.*

Tip *Unplug the base of a portable cordless phone when you leave for vacation and during electrical storms. Power surges caused by lightning can disable a cordless telephone.*

following manufacturer's instructions. Make sure you enter the same numbers into the base and handset, or you will get no reception at all.

If you hear beep tones, you are too far away from the base. Move closer and try again. If the base is sitting on a metal surface or is near metal such as foil-faced insulation, the range will be shortened.

▶ Other callers can be heard.

If you hear other people's conversations in the background on your phone, one of your outside phone wires is probably touching a neighbor's line. Call the local phone company; this is not a problem you can fix yourself. If you hear other callers when using a portable cordless phone, try changing the security code (see opposite page).

▶ Phone won't reach far enough.

Replace the cord between the telephone base and the wall jack with a longer one. Or buy an extension phone cord with a modular plug on one end and a modular socket on the other end. You can find these at consumer electronics or phone-supply stores. Unplug the cord from the wall jack, snap in the extension cord, then simply connect the two cords.

▶ Ringing phone near nursery wakes up baby.

Install a ring controller on the phone. This small, box-shaped device, which operates with a simple on-off switch, will silence the bell while still allowing you to answer a call on that phone if you hear another of your phones ringing. It can be used with rotary or push-button phones.

▶ New modular phone doesn't plug into old jack.

All new phone equipment uses square plastic connectors known as modular plugs. Older phones may be hard-wired into a wall jack—you can't unplug them. If so, buy a modular jack converter at a hardware store. Unscrew the cover from the old jack, leaving the base still attached to the wall. Snip off the wires that lead to the old telephone, making sure you don't cut incoming wires. Then snap the color-coded caps of the new cover onto the appropriate screw terminals. Screw the cover to the base, and plug in the new phone. Some converters may attach to the old base in a slightly different way—follow manufacturer's instructions.

Similar converters are available for hard-wired jacks that are mounted flush into the wall.

For older jacks that have four round holes, buy a modular adapter that plugs directly into the jack.

Converting to modular jack

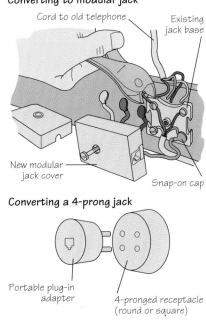

Cord to old telephone

Existing jack base

New modular jack cover

Snap-on cap

Converting a 4-prong jack

Portable plug-in adapter

4-pronged receptacle (round or square)

▶ Modular plug is broken.

To attach a new plug to a length of phone wire, you'll need a modular crimping tool. First lay the wire flat with the small lever on the damaged modular plug facing up. Mark the top side of the wire so you can attach the new plug in the same position. Next cut off the damaged plug with wire clippers, making sure the cut is at a 90-degree angle. Put the cut end of the cable into the wire stripper on the crimping tool; remove enough outer insulation to expose the colored wires. Then put a new modular plug into the crimping tool. Insert the trimmed phone wire into the plug and squeeze. Use this same method to shorten a phone cord.

Cutting off damaged plug

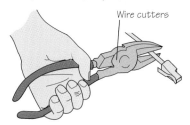

Wire cutters

Inserting new plug and wire into crimping tool

Modular crimping tool

New modular plug

Wire stripper blade

Trimmed phone cable

Tip *How many phones can you hook up? You may notice that newer telephones have an REN (ringer equivalence number) rating, which refers to the voltage required to ring the phone. A single phone line usually has enough power to ring the equivalent of 5 RENs. An older-style electromechanical ringer is equivalent to 1 REN; newer electronic ringers usually have lower RENs (for example, .5), but some are rated as high as 2 RENs. Therefore, one line could handle as few as three phones or as many as 10, depending on the total number of RENs of all the phones.*

SOLVING ELECTRICAL PROBLEMS

▶ *Room needs new phone.*

To install a phone you'll need to mount a new jack and connect it by wire to an existing jack. First choose a site for the new jack. For clear reception, keep it away from moisture, heat, and electrical receptacles. Situate it no more than 200 feet from the point where the telephone wire first enters the house.

Buy a new jack and a length of standard telephone cable, also known as station wire. While at the hardware store, pick up a phone-cable stripping tool if you do not already own one.

Mount the new jack first. Make sure no wires or plumbing lie behind the wall. Drill pilot holes and screw the base of the jack to the wall or baseboard. Next strip about 2 inches of sheathing from the phone cable, exposing the four color-coded conductor wires; strip 1 inch of insulation from each conductor wire. Then loop each conductor wire around the appropriately marked terminal screw on the jack (loop the wire clockwise so the wire will wrap around the post as you tighten the screw, ensuring a better connection). Next connect the jack cover to the base. The four color-coded wires running from the jack cover will end either in plastic caps or metal spade clips, depending on the type of jack. The caps snap onto the terminal screw heads; the spade clips slip under them. Attach the wires, and screw the cover onto the base.

Next run phone cable to the existing jack. You can conceal it under the edge of a carpet between the wall and tack strip, or along the top of a baseboard. Other places to hide cable are along molding, inside closets, or along the backs or bottoms of cabinets. Secure the cable with rounded staples every 8 to 10 inches; do not let the staples pierce the cable. Do not run

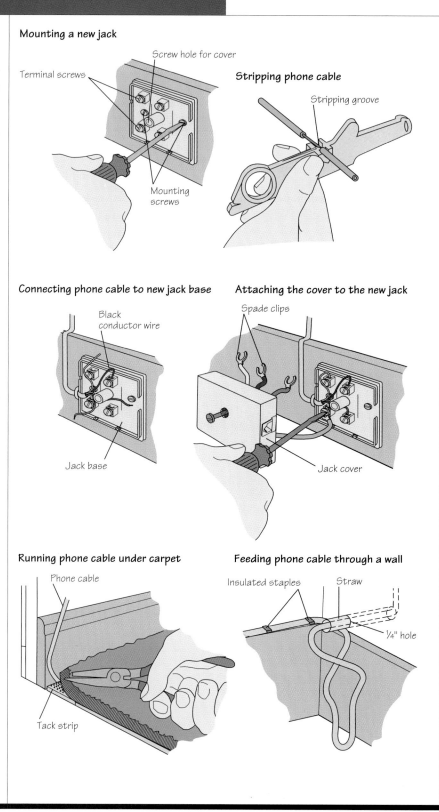

Mounting a new jack

Screw hole for cover

Terminal screws

Mounting screws

Stripping phone cable

Stripping groove

Connecting phone cable to new jack base

Black conductor wire

Jack base

Attaching the cover to the new jack

Spade clips

Jack cover

Running phone cable under carpet

Phone cable

Tack strip

Feeding phone cable through a wall

Insulated staples

Straw

¼" hole

Tip *AT&T publishes a booklet on how to install extra telephones. It's available at AT&T phone centers.*

Tip *Contact the local phone company before installing additional equipment. Some states require you to give the company the Federal Communications Commission (FCC) registration number and ringer equivalence number (REN) of your new phone. These numbers are usually printed on a manufacturer's label on the bottom of the phone.*

phone cable in a conduit with electrical wiring, or where the cable could touch water or hot pipes. You can completely hide phone cable by running it under the floor, through walls, or in the attic. Cut a hole directly behind the jack base and fish the cable through the walls (see page 205).

If you need to reach another floor, run the cable through a cold-air return or along the pipes that carry waste water from a sink or toilet. To pass cable through a wall, drill a ¼-inch hole just above the baseboard and insert a plastic drinking straw through the opening. Thread the cable through the straw.

Before attaching the cable to the existing jack, unplug the phones in the house or take one off the hook—this will prevent you from getting a shock. Unscrew the cover from the existing jack, strip the cable and each conductor wire, and attach them to the correct color-coded terminals.

Finally, plug the new phone into the new jack.

▶ Phone doesn't work on newly installed jack.

If you get no dial tone, open the new jack and look for loose or broken wires. Also check wires where they connect to the old jack. If the dial tone won't stop, you probably have reversed the red and green wires at one of the jacks. Attach them to the correct terminals.

▶ House needs security alarm system.

Most alarm systems consist of a control panel, sensors, and a siren. When a sensor detects something out of the ordinary such as movement or breaking glass, it signals the control panel, which in turn sounds the siren. Residents generally turn the alarm on and off using keypads, which are often mounted on walls near entrances and in the master bedroom.

You can save money by putting in an alarm system yourself. However, get professional advice from several sources before you buy and install the components. Or you can hire a security company to install the system for you. For a monthly charge, the company will also monitor the alarm. This means your control panel will automatically relay any alarm to the security company's monitoring center. Staff at the center will call your home to find out if the alarm was triggered accidentally. In most cases, if someone does not answer and give a prearranged password, the center will call the police, fire department, or an ambulance, depending on the type of emergency.

A system that is not monitored is known as a local alarm. The siren sounds only at the house, hopefully scaring off the intruder and prompting neighbors to call the proper authorities. Only a handful of alarm systems that you can install yourself offer a monitoring service.

Alarm systems are either hard-wired or wireless. Hard-wired systems run off the 120-volt house current; the control panel contains a transformer and is connected to the sensors and the siren with low-voltage wires. In wireless systems, the parts communicate via radio waves. When a sensor is triggered, a transmitter sends a radio signal to

a receiver at the control panel. The transmitter may be plugged into an electrical receptacle next to the sensor, or it may run on batteries that need to be checked and replaced regularly. You can usually add wireless sensors to hard-wired systems in places where it would be difficult to run wires. For example, you can use a battery-operated sensor on a skylight in a cathedral ceiling. Hard-wired systems are generally less expensive and slightly more reliable than wireless systems; however, they are more difficult to install, because wires must be passed inside walls or under floors.

▶ Alarm system needs reliable sensors.

Sensors are the eyes and ears of a security system. They are usually installed on outside doors and windows for perimeter protection. They are also placed inside the home to defend interior spaces and valuable objects. Most alarm professionals recommend placing sensors on all ground-floor windows and doors, and on any upper-floor openings that an intruder could reach.

The most common type of window and door sensor, the magnetic switch, comes in two parts; set one part into a door or window frame, attach the other to the door or the window sash. If a burglar opens the window or door, contact is broken and the alarm goes off. If you enjoy sleeping with windows open, mount a second contact in the frame several inches above the first. Wait to arm the system until the window is in the open position; the alarm will sound if the window moves. For extra protection install security screens; these look like regular insect screens, but will activate an alarm if cut or removed. Another type of sensor is the plunger switch, used for perimeter protection; when

Tip *For an easy-to-use, reliable alarm system, look for these features:*
(1) Built-in, rechargeable batteries in the control panel provide emergency power.
(2) Bypass switches allow you to activate sensors in one part of the house while leaving sensors in another area off so you don't trip them.
(3) Remote access allows you to set the alarm using a push-button phone.
(4) Two-way communication allows staff at the monitoring station to listen to what is happening at your house after an alarm goes off, and if necessary to talk back to give warnings or ask questions. Often, combination speaker/microphone units are mounted near keypads.

(continued on page 238)

a door or window is opened, a button pops out and the alarm sounds.

To thwart an intruder who decides to smash a windowpane, install sensors that detect breaking glass. One type is metal-foil ribbon that is placed around the window edge; when the foil rips, the alarm sounds. Another type of sensor detects vibrations. Yet another type, the audio sensor, picks up the frequency of shattering glass. Often a single audio sensor mounted on a wall can protect a roomful of windows.

Install at least one sensor inside the house to catch intruders who slip by perimeter detectors. Interior sensors use a variety of technologies. Passive infrared (PIR) sensors measure slight changes in room temperature; an intruder's body heat will trigger the alarm. Ultrasonic sensors emit inaudible sound waves; when the waves bounce off an intruder, the alarm sounds. Microwave sensors operate in a similar fashion, except they send out high-frequency radio waves. Active infrared sensors (electronic eyes) will trigger the alarm when someone interrupts a beam emitted from the detector. Many manufacturers now combine two technologies in one detector in order to minimize false alarms. (See right.)

Pressure-activated pads can be put under carpeting in doorways and on stairs. Use exterior sensors to scan driveways and yards. Smoke detectors can also be added to most systems.

If you are installing your own system, measure the spaces you want protected before you buy the sensors, so you can purchase ones with appropriate ranges. Read available literature and discuss your options with security professionals to determine what types of sensors would work best in different locations. Follow manufacturer's instructions carefully when you install the components.

▶ Security system trips frequently.

The most common cause of false alarms is human error—someone forgets to turn off the system after walking in the front door, or leaves a ceiling fan running, which then triggers a motion detector. If you trip the alarm frequently, get a control panel that emits a loud warning tone. You'll have a few seconds to reset the system before the actual alarm sounds.

Pets are also common culprits. If your cat or dog trips the sensors, install a detector with a "pet-alley lens" that blacks out the bottom half of the room where the pets are most likely to walk around. Of course, these lenses won't help if your cat jumps onto a table or a savvy intruder crawls instead of walks.

Passive infrared sensors, which detect heat, can be activated by sunlight. To minimize this problem, make sure your infrared sensors include white-light filters (these also reduce false alarms triggered by car headlights).

If you cannot identify the source of persistent false alarms, which is sometimes the case, replace your sensors with dual-technology sensors. The most common type combines microwave and passive infrared detectors, both of which must be triggered in order to sound the alarm; the two technologies double-check each other. For example, a passive infrared sensor by itself might respond to sunlight; however, a microwave sensor does not measure heat, so a dual-tech sensor would not sound the alarm.

Some newer sensors on the market contain microprocessors that constantly monitor the environment and adapt to any changes. An adaptive-technology sensor can distinguish between a pet or a person entering the room, for instance, and temporarily make the sensor slightly less sensitive, so the alarm will not be triggered. When the pet leaves, the sensor returns to its original sensitivity.

▶ Apartment needs security system.

Self-contained, portable alarms can protect spaces in situations where installing an entire system is not feasible. A portable alarm, often shaped like a VCR, contains a siren, a sensor, and controls to set the alarm. Position the unit on a shelf, plug it into an electrical receptacle or slip in the batteries, and turn it on. Most models use passive infrared technology and can scan anywhere from 500 to 9,000 square feet. Look for a delay feature, which gives you time to leave without tripping the alarm and time to shut it off when you return. If you think you may expand your system later, choose an alarm that has terminals where you can wire on additional components, such as door and window sensors.

Other self-contained alarms have special applications. Hang a doorknob alarm on an interior knob; it will sound its siren when someone touches the outside handle. A wedge-shaped door stop alarm slips under an in-swinging door and goes off when someone pushes from the outside. Sliding glass doors and windows can be protected with an electronic bar that lies in the bottom track of the sliding door or window; it will sound a piercing whistle at the slightest pressure. You can place similar bars in single- or double-hung windows between the top frame and the lower sash.

Tip *Features to look for in an alarm system (continued):*
(5) Backup communication for monitored alarms ensures that the alarm will be transmitted even if an intruder cuts phone wires. Most alarm systems use the house phone line to communicate with the security company's monitoring center. If this line is cut, the system is worthless. For backup, install a second phone line, a cellular phone connection, or a radio transmitter. Or, relocate the incoming phone line so it cannot be reached by an intruder.
(6) Supervised wireless alarms (alarms with a built-in self-monitoring feature) check the system regularly to make sure everything is working. Sensors in wireless systems often run on batteries; if a battery runs down, the sensor won't function. A supervised system will emit a beep or display a warning if something is amiss.

From heating systems to major appliances, most homes contain complex mechanical systems with dozens of moving parts, electrical circuits, and electronic components. Manufacturer's manuals are the most complete source of repair information, but this chapter will help you diagnose and solve more than 200 of the most common problems associated with these systems.

▶ *Furnace needs inspection and maintenance.*

A furnace should be inspected and serviced by a professional annually, especially if it is more than 15 years old. An older furnace can develop potentially deadly carbon monoxide leaks. However, if your furnace is newer and you maintain it yourself, you can reduce professional inspections to once every three or four years.

Before attempting to work on your furnace, read the owner's manual. If you don't have a manual, contact the manufacturer to see if you can obtain one. Otherwise, have a professional inspect the furnace when you can be present. Ask the technician to tell you what the parts of the furnace are and how they work, and to show you how to light the pilot, reach and service the fan, and change the filters.

For annual maintenance, clean the furnace every autumn before turning it on. When the furnace is turned off and cool, open the furnace door (you may have to remove screws). Vacuum the fan compartment gently but thoroughly. Clean out the firebox or burner compartment, and use a vacuum brush attachment to gently remove soot from the walls of the chamber. If the furnace blower is not prelubricated, put a few drops of oil into each port (using a flex-nozzle oil can if needed). Inspect the fan and remove any obstructions or debris caught in it. Check the fan belt tension (it should "give" ½ to ¾ inch when pushed with a finger); the owner's manual should show you how to adjust the belt. Lubricate the fan and the motor bearings according to the instructions in the manual. Inspect the warm-air plenum (the sheet-metal box on top of the furnace) and repair any holes with duct tape. Put in a fresh filter. If the furnace includes a humidifier, clean the humidifier according to manufacturer's directions, and scrape away any mineral buildup from the unit.

For monthly maintenance, clean or replace the filters. Turn off the furnace and locate the panel that covers the filter near the blower (it will usually be in front of the return-air duct, a large pipe leading to the blower compartment). Slide out the filter and see if it's dirty. Dirty fiberglass filters must be replaced, but plastic-foam or metal ones are washable; use warm water and a mild laundry detergent. Let the filter dry thoroughly (use a hair dryer to speed up the process) before reinstalling it. Slide the cleaned or new filter into place, positioning it according to the airflow direction marked on it.

▶ *Fan motor hums but fan doesn't spin.*

Turn off power to the furnace, open the panel to the fan, and manually rotate the fan to make sure it's not frozen or obstructed. If it's frozen or very hard to move, lubricate it according to the owner's manual; usually a few drops of lubricant in the oil cup will be sufficient. Continue operating it by hand, and see if it begins to move more easily.

Now check the tension on the fan belt. When you press the belt with a finger, it should "give" about

Locating system components

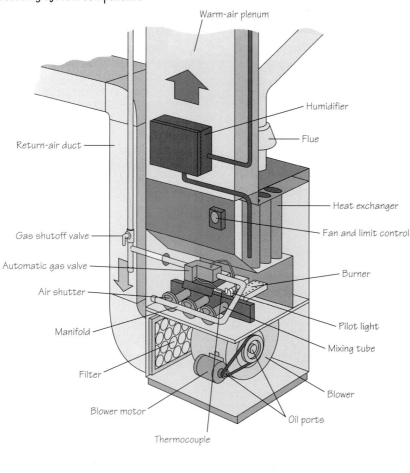

- Warm-air plenum
- Humidifier
- Flue
- Return-air duct
- Heat exchanger
- Fan and limit control
- Gas shutoff valve
- Automatic gas valve
- Burner
- Air shutter
- Manifold
- Pilot light
- Mixing tube
- Filter
- Blower
- Blower motor
- Oil ports
- Thermocouple

Tip *Most large appliance companies have toll-free "800-numbers" to provide customer service, including technical help in diagnosing and solving problems. All 800-numbers nationwide are listed with the "800" telephone information line: 1-800-555-1212.*

½ to ¾ inch. If the belt tension is incorrect, tighten or loosen the belt accordingly, following instructions in the owner's manual. If the belt is torn, remove it and replace it with a new one of the same size. Also check to see if the bearings are frozen; if so, oil them with the lubricant the manufacturer recommends, and use pliers to loosen them. Finally, check the mounting bolts for the bearings; tighten any that are loose.

If when you turn the furnace on again the fan still fails to work, the problem may be the blower control switch. Use a volt-ohmmeter to test whether the switch is receiving electric power. If it isn't, replace the switch or call for repairs. If the furnace is a new, solid-state model with electronic ignition, you won't be able to check or repair any function of the control module; it will have to be replaced.

Loosening motor tension

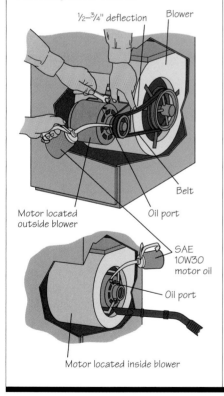

½–¾" deflection

Blower

Belt

Motor located outside blower

Oil port

SAE 10W30 motor oil

Oil port

Motor located inside blower

▶ *Gas furnace won't start.*

First make sure the furnace is turned on and receiving electricity. If your thermostat has a *Fan Only* switch, flip it to see if the fan comes on; if so, the furnace has power and the problem lies elsewhere. Otherwise, make sure all furnace power switches are on; many furnaces have one switch on or near the furnace, plus an emergency switch near the basement stairs. Check for a blown or loosened fuse or tripped circuit breaker. If the fuse blows or the circuit trips whenever you try to start the furnace, call a professional. If power checks out, press the red reset button on the furnace and see if the furnace starts. If this doesn't work, try holding down the reset button for about a minute.

If the furnace still doesn't start, check that there's gas. First make sure the manual gas valve is turned on; usually, in the *On* position the handle is aligned with the pipe. If it is, try another gas appliance (such as the stove) to see if there's gas to your building; if there isn't, call the gas company. Then check that the pilot is lit. Most furnaces have an inspection panel on the side or end; you can remove it to see the pilot. If the pilot is off, relight it, carefully following the instructions printed on the metal plate attached to the furnace (or as noted in the manual). If the pilot won't stay lit, see page 142.

Next look to the thermostat. (If the furnace is not controlled by a thermostat, check the manual to discover what type of controller it has. A modern, electronic set-back controller may merely have a dead battery or may be improperly programmed. If replacing the battery or reprogramming the thermostat doesn't revive it, have it repaired professionally.) To check a thermostat, see page 252.

If the thermostat works properly, the next step is to check the safety valve, which prevents gas from flowing to the furnace if the pilot goes out. To light a cold furnace, you can override the safety by pressing a spring-loaded red button, which allows gas to flow to the pilot only. Hold down the button for a minute or so; when it is released, the pilot should stay lit and the gas should flow as needed. (If the pilot goes out immediately, see page 142.) If the pilot stays lit but the burner still doesn't come on, either the millivolt generator or the transformer (depending on the type of furnace) is the next area to test. Use a volt-ohmmeter according to manufacturer's directions to see if there's electricity in the generator or transformer.

If the cause of the failure isn't any of the above, look at the limit switch, a temperature-activated electric safety switch. High temperatures above the safe limit cause the contacts to open, which shuts down the burner. If the contacts get stuck in the open position, there'll be no electrical flow and the furnace won't start. With the power off use a continuity tester or volt-ohmmeter to determine if the contacts are stuck open. If this is the problem, replace the switch. If the furnace still won't start, call a repair technician.

▶ *Pilot is lit but burner won't go on.*

A dirty or malfunctioning thermocouple is usually the problem. With the furnace turned off, clean the thermocouple (see page 142). If this fails to work, remove the thermocouple, buy an identical one, and install it. Make sure the sensor lines up in the path of the pilot flame.

Tip *How large should a furnace be? It used to be that homebuilders installed the largest size of furnace available because energy was cheap. Rising energy costs make it worthwhile to size a furnace more accurately, taking into account the size of the home, the local climate measured in degree days (how cold it gets and how often), the amount of insulation and window glass, and the amount of air infiltration into the home. If you have a new furnace installed, a heating contractor should make this calculation; in many areas local energy codes require it.*

▶ *Pilot won't light, relight, or stay lit.*

Before working on the pilot, make sure it has been out for at least five minutes and that the thermostat is turned to its lowest temperature setting. If the furnace is in a gusty area, the wind may be blowing out the pilot. Partially enclose the furnace to protect it from gusts. If this isn't the problem, try to locate the pilot adjusting screw (not all models have one); it is a cock-type device (rotates but does not tighten) that can get dirty or clogged. To clean it, rotate it completely a few times with a screwdriver. Now try to relight the pilot (you may have to try with the adjusting screw in different positions). If the pilot lights but won't stay lit, turn the adjusting screw so the flame burns strongly enough to stay lit. If the flame doesn't respond or the pilot didn't light in the first place, the pilot orifice may be clogged. Carefully clean out the orifice with a toothpick or toothbrush; blow or brush away any loose debris.

If the pilot still won't light, the furnace may not be receiving any gas. Make sure the manual shutoff valve is open. If it is, turn on another gas appliance (such as the stove) to see whether your household has a gas supply. If it does, test whether gas is reaching the furnace itself: First make very sure there are no open flames (such as a lighted cigarette) nearby. With furnace turned off, and using great care, loosen the connection of the gas pipe to the furnace only slightly. If you don't hear a hiss and can't smell gas after a few seconds, gas isn't reaching the furnace. Tighten the connection and contact the local gas company. If you can smell gas, *immediately* tighten the gas connection again; gas supply is not the problem.

Next check the thermocouple, which consists of a slim rod-shaped sensor in the pilot flame and a flexible connector that transfers heat from the pilot flame to a safety valve inside the control valve unit. If the pilot flame goes out, the thermocouple signals the safety valve not to release gas to the furnace. To test the thermocouple, press the spring-loaded red button, which allows gas to flow to the pilot only, and light the pilot. Hold down the button long enough to let the pilot heat the thermocouple (about 60 seconds). When you release the button, the pilot should stay lit and the gas should flow as needed. If the pilot won't stay lit except when you hold down the button, the thermocouple is the problem. Try cleaning the sensor tip with a wire brush and scraping it as necessary with a blunt knife. (Use no liquid.) If it is bent so that it is out of the pilot flame, bend it slightly back into place. If neither of these measures works, replace the thermocouple. Loosen the nut that connects one end to the combination control valve; at the other end loosen the nut that holds the sensor to the bracket, and slide the sensor out of the bracket hole. Connect the new thermocouple in the same way. If this doesn't work, replace the safety valve or call a repair person.

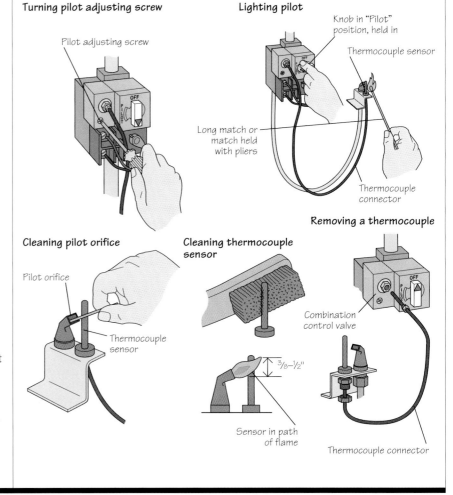

Turning pilot adjusting screw

Pilot adjusting screw

Lighting pilot

Knob in "Pilot" position, held in

Thermocouple sensor

Long match or match held with pliers

Thermocouple connector

Removing a thermocouple

Cleaning pilot orifice

Pilot orifice

Thermocouple sensor

Cleaning thermocouple sensor

³⁄₈–½"

Sensor in path of flame

Combination control valve

Thermocouple connector

Tip *A gas-burning appliance located in a closet or other enclosed space must have a source of combustion air. In the past a grille in the door was sufficient for providing the air; however, it meant that warmed air from the house was being drawn out through the furnace. Now it is common to provide outside combustion air directly to the furnace through a separate duct. The most sophisticated systems have an air-to-air heat exchanger as part of the house ventilation system. It prewarms air coming into the home by drawing it through an exchanger warmed by outgoing flue gases from the furnace (the two streams of air pass through separate tubes and don't mix).*

▶ Burner won't shut off.

Either the thermostat is defective or the safety valve is stuck open. Disconnect one wire of the thermostat and see if the burner goes off. If it does, replace the thermostat. If it doesn't, the safety valve is defective and should be replaced. Turn the manual shutoff valve to *Off* and call a furnace repair person.

▶ Furnace area has gas odor.

If the odor is strong, evacuate the house immediately, leaving doors open behind you; shut off the main gas valve and call the gas company or 9-1-1. For mild, nuisance odors, locate the source of the gas leak with soapy water: Mix liquid dishwashing soap and water in a spray bottle and spray all connections around the furnace until they drip; look for large bubbles, which indicate leaking gas. Tighten the leaking connection with two wrenches; check again with soapy water. Leaks from any other source, such as a cracked pipe or valve, should be repaired by a professional.

▶ Furnace air isn't warm enough.

First make sure that warmed air isn't escaping before it gets circulated through the ducts. With the furnace turned on, inspect the plenum for leaks at one or more of its corners. If you feel heat escaping, turn off the furnace, let it cool, and seal the leaks with metallic duct tape. Next check the blower. Turn off the furnace and examine the blower to see if it turns freely. Check that the belt is intact and has proper tension and alignment. Inspect the filter and, if it hasn't been replaced recently, install a new one.

If the air is initially cold and then warms up, or is chilly only at the end of the blower cycle, the fan control needs adjusting. It is located in a control box mounted on the furnace. Remove the cover; there should be two pointers, marked *Fan Off* and *Fan On,* clipped to the outside edge of a round wheel. (If there's a third pointer, labeled *Limit,* it should *not* be moved.) If the problem is cold air being circulated before it warms up, move the *Fan On* pointer a few degrees higher. If the problem is cold air being circulated after the warm cycle, move the *Fan Off* pointer a few degrees higher. (These adjustments may also decrease fuel efficiency, so you may have to settle for a trade-off.)

If none of these measures solves the problem, inspect the burners; look at the height, shape, and color of the flame from each burner. The flames should be similar to those on a gas stove: Most of the flame should be blue with yellow-orange only at the tip. Flames should be tapered—rounded at the bottom and narrowing to a point at the tip. If the color of the flame on one or more burners is wrong (too orange, for example), the burner is getting the wrong gas/air mixture. Protecting your hands with thick oven mitts, turn the adjustable shutter until the flame is the correct color, or call a technician. If the flame on one or more burners is short and flat looking, the orifice of the burner is probably clogged. Turn off the furnace, let the burners cool, and clean them. Using no liquids or cleaners, scour the burners with a stiff wire brush; use a dull knife to scrape off stubborn crusts, and finish by reaming out each orifice with pipe cleaners. Brush or vacuum away debris.

If the blower and burners are operating efficiently and air coming out of the registers still isn't warm enough, heat is being lost through leaking or poorly insulated ducts. Joints should be sealed tightly with metallic duct tape, and all ducts and joints should be insulated with at least 1 inch of blanket insulation or equivalent. See page 242.

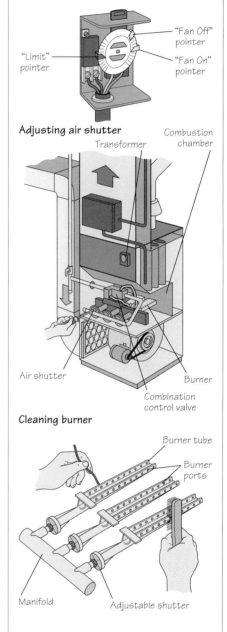

Adjusting fan limit control

"Limit" pointer

"Fan Off" pointer

"Fan On" pointer

Adjusting air shutter

Transformer

Combustion chamber

Air shutter

Burner

Combination control valve

Cleaning burner

Burner tube

Burner ports

Manifold

Adjustable shutter

Tip   *When sealing ducts with tape, use metallic duct tape rather than the more common fabric duct tape. The metallic tape is fireproof and forms a tighter seal.*

SOLVING MECHANICAL PROBLEMS

▶ Burners have sooty deposits.

Carbon deposits accumulate when the flame is not burning cleanly because of an incorrect mixture of air and fuel. With the furnace off and cooled, clean the burners as described on opposite page.

▶ Ducts have asbestos covering over them.

Ducts in many older homes are covered with asbestos insulation, which looks like whitish gray plaster. If it is disturbed it releases tiny fibers into the air that may cause health problems over time. It's better to encapsulate or insulate asbestos than to try to remove it. Call a heating and cooling company or an asbestos abatement firm to have it done.

▶ Ducts aren't properly insulated.

You can increase heating comfort and energy savings significantly by making sure all of the ducts are sealed and insulated. Unless the ducts have asbestos insulation (a gray, plasterlike coating; see above), this is a job most homeowners can do if they are willing to put up with some mess and can work in tight, dark spaces (it's nice to have a helper for company). Buy a roll of metallic duct tape and several rolls of R-11 fiberglass duct insulation (buy extra, making arrangements to return what you don't use). Wear long pants, a long-sleeved shirt, a dust mask, and gloves. Make sure the furnace is turned off and cooled. Work outward from the furnace along each branch duct, whether in the attic or basement. Expose each joint, make sure it is secured with at least 3 sheet-metal screws, and seal it with metallic duct tape. Then wrap duct insulation around the duct, joints,

dampers, and other components so all exposed metal is covered. When you finish wrapping a section, secure the end of the insulation by wrapping wire around the duct or pinning the end of the insulation to itself with 16d nails, much like pinning two pieces of cloth together with straight pins; don't rely on tape. If the duct is in an area where it is exposed to contact, such as a basement or large attic, wrap plastic sheeting or bubble wrap around the insulation and tape it with duct tape.

Sealing and insulating ducts

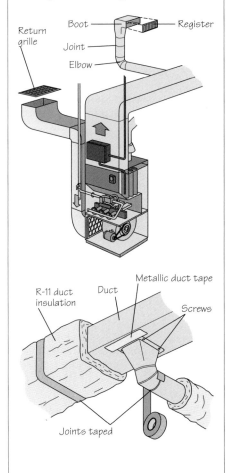

Return grille
Boot
Joint
Elbow
Register

Metallic duct tape
R-11 duct insulation
Duct
Screws
Joints taped

▶ Filter hasn't been replaced for six months.

The filter should be replaced (or at least cleaned) at the start of the heating season and (depending on how much dust normally gets into the furnace area) about once every month or two for as long as the furnace is regularly turned on. For cleaning techniques, see page 240.

▶ Air is circulating too much dust, even with new filter.

Was the furnace cleaned and vacuumed before it was turned on? If so, look for leaks around the filter and in the duct work. You can also minimize circulating dust by creating cheesecloth filters for the registers throughout the house. Spread the cheesecloth and fold it over once or twice to form pads the size of the register grilles. Secure the pads to the backs of the grilles with rubber bands. Check the pads every month or so (when you change the furnace filters). Whenever they are dirty, wash them by hand and return them to the grilles when dry. Also consider upgrading to a more efficient filter, such as a HEPA or an electrostatic filter. You can also improve the air circulating in your home with a portable air cleaner.

▶ Whole house smells musty and unpleasant during winter.

Dirt and dust in the furnace may be causing the smell. Before turning the furnace on for the first time each autumn, vacuum it inside and out, or have a professional do this. Check the furnace air filters for dust and grime, and clean or replace them if necessary. Have the

Tip *The average life expectancy of a gas-fired or oil-fired furnace is 18 years, according to the National Association of Home Builders.*

furnace professionally cleaned if it hasn't been done recently (three or more years).

Merely heating a house may intensify normal, ambient odors (such as smelly pets, dirty rugs, and dusty drapes, blinds, and upholstery) that are not apparent when windows are open and rooms are cool. A thorough house cleaning solves this problem. Also consider obtaining an air purifier or portable air filter. (See discussion of ventilation, pages 260 and 261.

▶ Air comes out too slowly or too fast.

There are three ways to adjust the flow of air from a warm-air duct system. One is at the registers, each of which should have a control for opening and closing the register baffles. If opening them doesn't increase airflow enough, or closing them yields loud whistling sounds, look for damper controls along the duct leading to the register and adjust them (see opposite). The third way to control airflow is to adjust the fan speed, which will affect flow throughout the entire system.

Most fans are driven by a belt connecting the fan to a pulley on the motor shaft. Some pulleys have a rotating adjustment to vary the belt speed. Loosen the setscrew and rotate the outer wheel of the pulley clockwise to increase speed, counterclockwise to reduce speed; then tighten the setscrew. If the pulley is not adjustable, replace it with one that is slightly smaller (for faster fan speed) or slightly larger (for slower fan speed). To remove a pulley, shut off power to the fan motor, loosen the motor mount adjusting bolt to release belt tension, and slip the belt off the pulley. Loosen the

setscrew on the pulley wheel and slide the wheel off the motor shaft. Reverse the process to install a new pulley. The pulley shaft should have a slotted keyway with a small key (shim) in it that aligns with a slot in the pulley. Be sure to save the key when you remove the old pulley and insert it into the keyway when you install the new one. It keeps the pulley from slipping on the shaft.

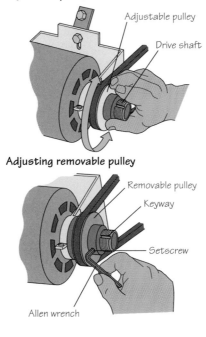

Adjusting fan speed with adjustable pulley

Adjustable pulley

Drive shaft

Adjusting removable pulley

Removable pulley

Keyway

Setscrew

Allen wrench

▶ Some rooms are too hot and others are too cool.

Opening and closing wall air registers isn't sufficient to even out the heat in a house. (Closing a register only wastes heat.) Instead adjust the duct dampers to balance heated airflow evenly through all rooms. (A damper is a disk inside the duct that rotates on a pivot, controlled manually by a straight lever or butterfly lever on the side of the duct.) Look for damper controls along ducts in

the attic or basement. Most dampers have lever handles on the side; older types may simply have locking nuts. If the ducts are covered by insulation, look for telltale lumps. Depending on the type, you can loosen the nuts by hand or with a slotted screwdriver; adjust the dampers by hand and tighten the nuts firmly again.

To achieve the best results, adjust the angle of the dampers to between 45 and 90 degrees. Provide a slight flow (45-degree angle) through the ducts to rooms you rarely use, to rooms that are closest to the furnace, and to any rooms that are consistently too warm for other reasons. Fully open dampers (90 degrees, with handle parallel to the duct) on ducts that go to cool areas, especially those that are far from the furnace. If there are no dampers, consider installing them where two sections of duct are joined. The best locations are at the branches of a Y or T fitting, so you can adjust two dampers at the same spot.

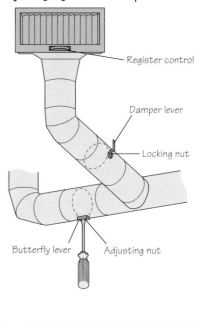

Adjusting register and dampers

Register control

Damper lever

Locking nut

Butterfly lever   Adjusting nut

Tip *If your forced-air heating/cooling system includes return-air registers at both ceiling and floor levels and you want to increase furnace efficiency, obtain or make magnetic sheets (made from the same material as flexible refrigerator magnets) to cover the metal grilles. (Look for lightweight magnetic sheeting at building-supply or crafts-supply stores). Because hot air rises, cover the ceiling-level return duct in winter so that only the cooler air near the floor is returned to the furnace. In summer, cover the floor-level return register so that only the warm air near the ceiling is returned.*

SOLVING MECHANICAL PROBLEMS

▶ Heat goes on and off at night.

If you don't want to turn off the heat at night or set the thermostat to a low temperature, you can adjust the thermostat so it doesn't respond so quickly to dipping temperatures. Inside the thermostat is a control called the anticipation-adjustment lever; it determines the actual temperature at which the furnace goes on and off. This temperature will be slightly different from the thermostat setting. For instance, if you set the thermostat for 65° F, you can set your anticipation adjustment to have the furnace come on when room temperature drops to 60° F, or 62° F, or 64° F. If the adjustment is set for a very narrow range (say, two or three degrees), the furnace will turn on and off frequently. If it is set for a wider range (five to seven degrees), the furnace will turn on and off less frequently.

To change the adjustment, turn off the power to the thermostat (if there is no thermostat switch near the furnace, trip the circuit breaker). Open the thermostat. The anticipation adjustment (also called a heat anticipator) is an arrow or dial, labeled either *More* or *Less*. Set the anticipation adjustment to a slightly wider range (*More*). See also page 254.

If you have a type of thermostat that allows different settings for night and day, try setting the night temperature considerably lower (for instance, 55° to 60° F). The furnace will go on and off less frequently, and you'll save fuel costs as well. Set the timer to switch to the daytime temperature about an hour before you usually get up, so the house will be warm when you arise.

▶ Burner or combustion chamber is cracked.

Have it replaced immediately. A crack in the combustion chamber can be dangerous.

▶ Fan squeaks, or blower makes unusual noises.

Remove the cover to the blower compartment and inspect the fan to see if any obstacles are caught in it. On older fans, lubricate moving parts (following instructions in the manual). If the fan has a belt, check the belt tension and adjust it if necessary. (See page 240.) Check the bearings for side play and, if excessive, adjust or replace them. On modern models with direct drive (rather than a belt and bearings), the fan will probably have to be replaced.

▶ Small objects fall down registers into ducts.

The register grilles can be easily removed by unscrewing or in some cases merely lifting them. If you want the objects back, use a vacuum cleaner (with a long tube attachment but no nozzle) to retrieve objects from the ducts; when you're done, rummage inside the vacuum bag. To prevent future losses, obtain pieces of screening from the hardware store and use wire cutters to cut them slightly larger than the registers. Place the register on top of the screening and fold the edges of the screening so that it tightly hugs the register frame. Secure, if necessary, with string or thin wire, and replace the registers on the ducts.

▶ Steam heaters don't heat.

Make sure the thermostat (if you have one) is turned on and the setting is above room temperature. Check radiator valves; turn them to make sure they are open and not shut or stuck barely open. See if the boiler is turned on. Check the boiler gauge. If the level of the water is low, the boiler won't operate. Turn off the boiler and let it cool completely before refilling it. (Adding cold water to a hot boiler is likely to crack it.) When you've refilled and restarted the boiler, the heat may come on; however, call for a professional inspection to find out why the boiler went dry.

If none of these measures is successful, call a technician. Most steam radiator repairs require professional expertise because of the danger of scalds from the steam and the potential for boiler explosions. (If you are a renter, contact your building superintendent or landlord; landlords are required by law to provide heat.)

▶ Some steam radiators have heat and others don't.

If only some of the radiators are cold, the valves of those radiators may not be working. Check that the inlet valve (also called the shut-off valve) near the floor is open all the way. If your floor is slanted, the slant of the radiator may be causing the malfunction. Shim up the radiator legs (with pieces of wood or the equivalent) until the radiator is level. If the pipe doesn't move slightly as well, do not force it; you may loosen connections.

A radiator also may not work if the steam vent (also called an air vent) is clogged with mineral deposits. Turn off the inlet valve to

---

Tip *All heating systems have certain advantages and disadvantages. The advantages of a warm-air system (sometimes called forced-air, or heated-air) are: (1) circulating air can be filtered, humidified, or dehumidified; (2)the same duct work can be used for central air conditioning; (3) heat exchangers can be integrated with the duct system to bring fresh air into the home; (4) the furnace can be upgraded to a higher efficiency; and (5) air can be heated quickly. Disadvantages are: (1) the ducts are awkward and hard to conceal; (2) the system can be noisy and drafty; (3) the ducts transmit sound between rooms; and (4) the system warms the air but not the objects and surfaces of a room.*

the radiator (to make sure no steam comes in and scalds you). Unscrew the steam vent by hand (or with large pliers), inspect it, and attempt to wash it clean. If it is still clogged, buy a new vent (available at plumbing or heating outlets). Many models of vents offer adjustable air openings, so you can easily regulate the steam pressure in the radiator to adjust it to the room temperature. Coat the threads of the new vent with joint compound specified for steam radiators, screw the vent into place, and turn the intake valve back on.

Checking a cold radiator

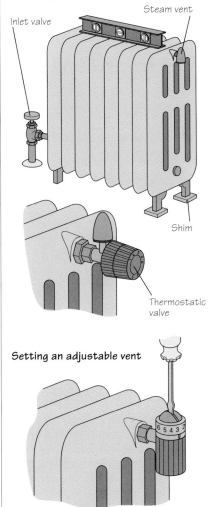

Setting an adjustable vent

▶ *Radiator valve leaks.*

Using pliers, tighten the bonnet on the stem of the valve. If this fails to stop the leak, replace the valve. First shut off the system and let it cool. Loosen the steam vent at the top of the radiator and open the main drain for the system long enough for any water in the radiator to drain down past the valve. Loosen the valve connections, using two wrenches at each joint, and remove the valve. Coat the threads of the new valve or pipe connections with joint compound specified for steam radiators, then install it. Tighten all connections with two wrenches, making sure the bonnet on the valve is tight. Turn on the boiler, wait for steam to come out of the steam vent, then close it and inspect the new valve for leaks.

Removing a valve

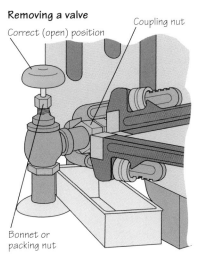

▶ *Pipes knock.*

The pipes may be knocking because the radiator is on a slant or the inlet valve is ajar. Try shimming the radiator (see left), and readjusting the valve so that it's fully open or fully shut. If neither step works, the problem is probably with the

steam-trap bellows, which is part of the steam-trap cap on valves of radiators connected to two pipes. A failed bellows allows steam and cold water to escape from the radiator together, producing the knocking sound. Turn off the inlet valve and let the radiator cool. Using a pipe wrench, take off the steam-trap cap. Inside the cap there's a flexible bellows. Use pliers or a small wrench to unthread the bellows from the cap, then take the bellows to a heating-supply store to help the dealer select a compatible new one. Coat the threads of the cap and of the new bellows with joint compound specified for steam radiators, thread the new bellows into the cap, and tightly fasten the cap to the radiator again.

Removing steam-trap cap

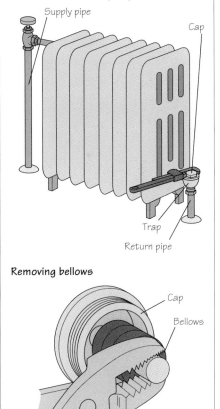

Removing bellows

SOLVING MECHANICAL PROBLEMS

▶ Steam-heated rooms are unevenly heated.

You can adjust the heat for an individual room by adjusting the inlet valve in its radiators to increase or decrease the steam. Remove any obstructions (such as drapes) that prevent warm air from reaching the center of the room. Consider replacing old steam vents with adjustable vents (see page 246) that will allow you greater control over the output of each radiator. To increase the general efficiency of a radiator, consider painting all metal parts with nonreflective, dark-colored paint to reduce heat loss. In a room that is chronically cold, place a sheet of heavy-duty aluminum foil between the radiator and the wall to reflect heat back into the room.

▶ Boiler pilot light stays on during summer.

Turning it off will decrease your energy bill. However, when the pilot is off in cool, moist weather, condensation can damage the unit's heat exchanger if it isn't corrosion resistant. Check with the dealer or manufacturer to find out if the unit is corrosion resistant.

▶ Radiator smells horrible and causes sneezing or coughing when first turned on.

The smell (and sneeze-production factor) is burning dust. Before turning on a radiator for the first time of the season, place some newspapers or rags under and around it to protect the floor. Thoroughly dust the top, the pipes, and (if possible) the back and then use a spray bottle filled with warm water to thoroughly rinse every part you can reach.

▶ Hot-water heating system heats unevenly.

In hydronic systems (which use hot water instead of steam), adjustable valves function the way dampers function in hot-air system ducts. Try tuning the valve adjustment for each room, opening or closing various valves slightly to see what changes; it will take several days to do this. If there are no valves, consider having a technician install some. If the system currently has a single thermostat controlling all heating to the house, consider having separate room thermostats or zone temperature controls installed. This installation will probably be costly, but may ultimately repay its costs in fuel savings as well as comfort.

▶ Hot-water heat doesn't come on.

Check to see if the boiler is turned on, that the gauge shows that hot water is flowing through the system, and that the valve on the radiator or convector (if there is a valve) is open. If none of these is the problem, call for professional service.

▶ Inlet valve leaks.

If the inlet valve for a convector leaks, tighten the bonnet to the valve with pliers or a small wrench. If this doesn't work, the valve needs replacing. Call a professional.

▶ Hot-water convectors in some rooms are cold.

Air is probably trapped in the chambers of those convectors (or radiators), preventing water from flowing into them. To "bleed" the air, look for the bleeder valves at the end of each radiator or baseboard convector. Place a thick layer of newspapers under the bleeder valve and have a cup or small

saucepan ready. Wearing oven mitts, use a hex-head key, allen wrench, or screwdriver to loosen the brass screw of the bleeder valve until it starts hissing; the hissing is the escaping air. Immediately place the cup under the valve. Once the hissing stops and a steady stream of hot water starts to pour into the cup, tighten the valve screw.

Opening a bleeder valve

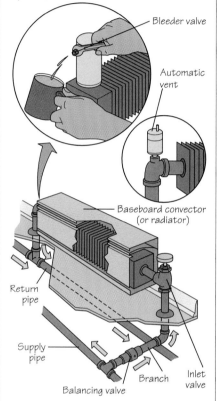

Bleeder valve

Automatic vent

Baseboard convector (or radiator)

Return pipe

Supply pipe

Balancing valve

Branch

Inlet valve

▶ Hot-water pump makes noises.

The bearings are probably dry and worn. Because modern pumps have sealed bearings, the entire pump must be replaced or rebuilt. Even a pump with accessible bearings should be rebuilt by a qualified technician; the seals are delicate membranes that must be installed and lubricated correctly to withstand constant water pressure.

Tip   *To maximize the heating potential of convectors or radiators: (1) remove obstructions to airflow through the convector, such as draperies or furniture; (2) attach aluminum foil to the wall behind the radiator; and (3) paint a radiator (not convector, which has thin fins) flat black.*

▶ Convector fins are bent.

Bent convector fins interfere with airflow. You can straighten them using broad-nosed pliers or a tool called a fin comb that you may find in plumbing-supply stores.

Straightening convector fins

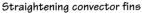

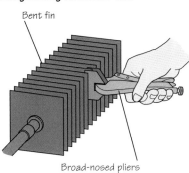

Bent fin

Broad-nosed pliers

▶ Pipes leak.

If you can see water under exposed piping, see if it is from a leaky valve, which you might be able to repair by tightening the bonnet. If the leak is from a loose joint or cracked pipe, and you don't have extensive experience in working with pipe and fittings, have it repaired by a plumber. Simply tightening a connection may loosen other connections, and replacing a cracked pipe will involve cutting and threading pipe or soldering copper tubing.

▶ Relief valve on expansion tank leaks.

An expansion tank has an air chamber to absorb changes in water pressure as the water heats and cools. In some the air and water are in the same compartment; in others a diaphragm separates them. If the expansion tank is a diaphragm type (or you're not sure), have a professional service it. For other types of

tanks, replace the valve. First turn off the system, let it cool, and shut the valve between the boiler and tank. Drain the tank by attaching a garden hose to the combination relief valve and opening both parts of it. When the tank is empty, unscrew the old valve and take it with you when you buy a new one, to make sure the new one will be compatible. Screw on the new valve, close it, refill the system according to manufacturer's or installer's instructions, and restart the system.

Replacing expansion tank relief valve

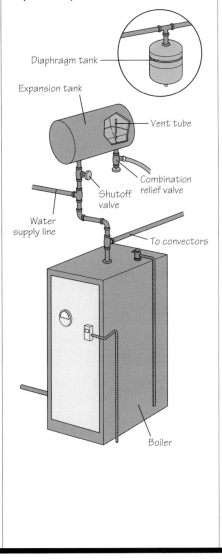

Diaphragm tank

Expansion tank

Vent tube

Combination relief valve

Shutoff valve

Water supply line

To convectors

Boiler

▶ Pipes in concrete slab are broken or corroded.

This ranks as one of the most difficult problems in this book, first because it is almost impossible to pinpoint exactly where the problem is and, second, because the solution is a choice between destroying the floor and having a completely new heating system installed. Get help.

▶ Concrete slab may have pipes where you want to drill or nail.

Assume there's a pipe right where you want to drill or nail and abandon the idea. However, if you have no choice and are willing to take some risks, there are two methods for guessing where pipes may be. One is to remove all floor covering—carpet, pad, wood flooring, resilient sheet, whatever—to expose the bare concrete. Then turn the radiant heating system to the highest setting. Moisten the floor and watch while the floor heats up. Areas that dry out first are most likely where the heating pipes are. Mark the pattern on the floor with chalk. Another way to locate hidden pipes is with a magnet—so long as you know the pipes are iron or steel (many are copper or plastic). When you do find pipe locations, you still won't know how far below the surface they are; they can be as little as ½ inch to more than 2 inches below the surface.

Tip *The advantages of a hot-water, or hydronic, heating system are: (1) quiet operation, (2) even heat, (3) efficient energy conversion, (4) ease of adjusting heat levels through zoning, and (5) ease of concealing pipes. Disadvantages are: (1) the system can't be used to filter or humidify the air, (2) it can't be integrated with central air conditioning, and (3) it requires a long start-up time.*

▶ *Oil burner stopped working and won't go back on.*

First make sure that the burner is getting electricity: it's plugged in, turned on, and the fuse isn't blown nor the circuit breaker tripped. Make sure, too, that there's enough oil in the storage tank. If these conditions check out, it's likely that the limit switch (near the heat exchanger) turned the burner off to prevent a fire because the fan wasn't working. Unplug the oil burner, open the panel, and inspect the fan. Remove any obstructions, lubricate the fan (according to manufacturer's instructions), check that the fan belt is intact, and check belt tension (see page 240). If the fan hasn't been cleaned recently, vacuum it gently; then plug in the burner again and see if it works.

If not, the furnace igniters may be defective, causing the safety switch attached to the stack control to turn off the pump to prevent the pump from spraying unlighted oil into the combustion chamber and possibly causing a fire. On the face of the stack (the large pipe leading into the chimney or flue), there's a reset button. Push the button firmly to get the stack control to recycle. It will remove any unburned oil from the firebox so that the unit can start again. The burner should go through its starting cycle once more, and should light this time. (If the

problem occurs again, the igniter will have to be replaced.)

If the burner still doesn't start, use a volt-ohmmeter to see whether the contacts on the limit switch are stuck open. (If that's the case, the meter will show there is no electricity in the switch.) Replace the switch if it is defective. If none of these measures gets the burner working, call for professional repairs.

▶ *Oil tank is filled but oil isn't reaching the burner.*

Trace the fuel path from tank to burner and make sure valves are open. If so, check the fuel filter. Turn off the electric circuit to the furnace, shut the fuel valve, and place a pan under the filter canister. Remove the canister by loosening the nut at the top; remove the filter cartridge, empty the canister, and wipe it clean. Check for blocked fuel lines at the canister top. Replace the filter and gasket and reassemble the filter unit. If there is no oil filter, look for a pump strainer on the end of the motor shaft; remove the cover and clean out the strainer with kerosene and a toothbrush. Next check the nozzle and nozzle filter (if it has one) inside the air tube. To remove the firing assembly (nozzle and igniters), mark its position in the air tube and disconnect the fuel line. Pull out the assembly and check for clogs in the fuel line and nozzle tip; carefully clear the tip with a piece of fine wire. If it won't clear, remove the nozzle tip and buy a replacement. If the problem still isn't solved, you may have to drain the oil tank to remove moisture. Also see left.

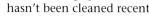

Locating oil-burner components

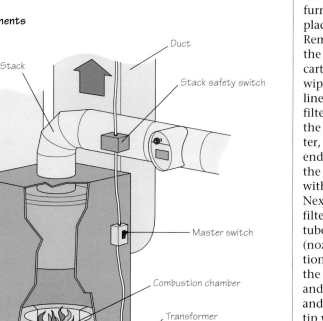

Air intake

Stack

Duct

Stack safety switch

Master switch

Combustion chamber

Transformer

Motor reset button

Oil-burner motor

Fan

Igniter

Air tube

Oil filter

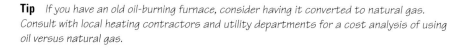

Tip *If you have an old oil-burning furnace, consider having it converted to natural gas. Consult with local heating contractors and utility departments for a cost analysis of using oil versus natural gas.*

▶ Oil burner stops working just when it's coldest.

If the oil storage tank is located outdoors, at subzero temperatures the oil will thicken into a slow-moving sludge that won't flow through the transfer lines into the burner. If moisture gets into the lines, it may turn to ice and block the line entirely. Consider relocating the tank indoors (for instance, in the basement). For safety's sake, though, make sure the tank's new location is at least 7 feet away from the burner.

▶ Oil burner sounds like a backfiring car.

If the ignition is delayed, when the oil is ignited a small explosion occurs that sounds like a car back-firing. Soot or oil in the furnace room are other telltale signs of delayed ignition. To prevent it, check and clean all filters. Use a volt-ohmmeter to check that the voltages from the transformer (low voltage) and in the line (house voltage) are correct; if incorrect, call for repairs. If these steps don't work, you may have to drain the bottom of the fuel storage tank to reduce moisture, or you may have to replace or reset the electrodes, following instructions in the owner's manual. (Or you may prefer to have a technician complete these tasks.)

▶ Oil burner shoots out soot or oil spray.

The ignition is delayed. See above.

▶ Flame does not burn cleanly.

Heavy soot indicates a poor flame. First, with the burner and its power circuit both turned off, check the stack for heavy soot deposits and remove them with an old vacuum cleaner (or replace the stack pipe). Then make sure that the air intake is fully open; adjust by loosening the nut. Next remove the burner nozzle, screen, and igniters, clean them, then inspect them carefully; a visibly damaged burner nozzle or ignition assembly will require replacement. When you return the igniter assembly to the burner (whether it's new or the old one), set the gaps according to manufacturer's recommendations (or have an electrician do so). If these steps don't work, you'll need professional service.

Locating burner components

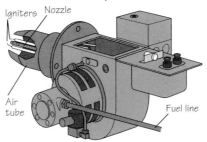

Igniters Nozzle

Air tube

Fuel line

Removing nozzle and igniters

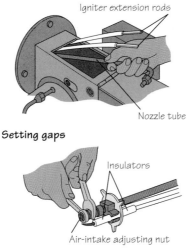

Igniter extension rods

Nozzle tube

Setting gaps

Insulators

Air-intake adjusting nut

▶ Electric baseboard heater won't go on.

Make sure the heater is turned on, that the thermostat is set higher than room temperature, and that the heater is receiving electricity. Electric heaters are more likely to trip circuit breakers and blow fuses than nearly any other appliance. (If fuses or breakers are difficult to reach, plug a lamp or small appliance into the wall receptacle for the heater to see if it works.) To decrease the frequency of electrical shutoffs, avoid using the heater at the same time as any other "electricity eater" (iron, toaster, electric stove or cookware, large numbers of electric lights), especially those connected to the same breaker or fuse. If this is impractical, consider having an electrician wire each element of the heater to a separate breaker in the household breaker box so that the electrical draw of the heater will be spread evenly throughout the house. If all of these factors check out, call for professional repairs. "Doing it yourself" on electric heaters and their thermostats isn't recommended, because these appliances typically operate on a 240-volt circuit, a voltage at which a shock can be fatal.

▶ Heat pump takes too long to heat or doesn't get house warm enough.

If you know that the heat-pump system is large and powerful enough to heat the whole house (because it's been sufficient in the past and the weather is normal), look for dirty filters. Turn off the pump and clean or replace the filters if necessary (usually this should be done about four times a

Tip *Increase the efficiency of electric baseboards by giving them a thorough cleaning at least once every heating season. Although they don't have fans, they depend on a free flow of air over the heating fins to warm the room. Disconnect or turn off power to the unit and remove the cover panel (usually attached with screws). Clean off the fins carefully with a dry paint brush (wear gloves); then, using a brush attachment, vacuum away the dust and debris.*

SOLVING MECHANICAL PROBLEMS

year). Clean condenser coils if they are dirty. If the fins are clogged with dirt, brush them with a stiff-bristled brush; do not use a wire brush or knife, however, because this can puncture the coil and allow the refrigerant to leak out (which is illegal, in addition to damaging the heat pump). Keep foliage well away from the outdoor coil. Check the fans for debris and clear any obstructions. Check fan belt tension, and lubricate the motor housing if bearings aren't sealed. Finally, check the level of refrigerant. The pump may need recharging; have this done professionally. If all these steps fail to work, call for professional repairs.

Heat pumps work best in mild-winter areas because their heat source (ground heat), although steady, cannot attain high temperatures. In an exceptionally cold winter, you may need to add portable space heaters. For the longer term consider having the system permanently linked to an auxiliary heat source. If you have a gas water heater, you may be able to extend hot-water pipes into a baseboard heating unit for convenient and efficient heating. Electrical heating can be hooked into the system quickly, but is usually expensive to operate. Probably the most economical auxiliary in the long term is a solar hot-water system.

You can also improve the performance of a heat-pump system by sealing air leaks throughout the house (windowsills and sashes, cracks, and the like) and improving insulation to the whole house.

▶ Heat pump goes on and off constantly or runs constantly.

Usually, this happens when the pump has no outdoor thermostats, or the outdoor thermostats aren't set correctly and are overreacting to changes in weather. You can install as many outdoor thermostats as your heat pump has strip heaters, but usually three or four are sufficient. Their cost will swiftly be repaid in energy cost savings. Consult a heat-pump dealer or technician about setting the trigger temperatures and anticipation adjustment on the outdoor thermostats; each one will require a slightly different setting to obtain the best results, and the settings will vary according to the climate in your area.

▶ Thermostat does not activate furnace.

See that the thermostat setting is higher than room temperature. If it includes a system switch, make sure it's set to *Heat*. If the thermostat area is dusty, remove the thermostat cover and blow strongly on the controls inside to remove any dust that may be preventing the contact points from closing. Further action depends on the type of thermostat you have.

One common type of thermostat uses a heat-sensitive bimetallic strip to open and close an electrical contact; if it does not close the contact, the furnace won't turn on. You can easily check it by taking off the cover and short-circuiting the two wire terminals inside the thermostat (they are low voltage—there's no danger of shock). Make sure the furnace switch is on so the burner will ignite. Then touch a screwdriver blade across the screw terminals for a minute or two. If the burner goes on, the problem is a broken thermostat. (You may need a helper to

watch the burner. Otherwise hold the screwdriver in place for several minutes until the blower comes on; you should be able to hear it.) If the burner or blower doesn't go on, the problem is a broken thermostat wire or defective furnace. You can check for a broken wire at the furnace: Short the screw terminals that are connected to the thermostat wire. If the burner goes on, the wire is broken and should be replaced; if it doesn't, see page 241.

An older type of thermostat uses a glass bulb partly filled with mercury, similar to a fever thermometer. This type won't function properly if it's mounted unevenly. Remove the cover and first check that the red and white wires are properly fastened to their terminals. (If not, turn off the power to the furnace, preferably at the breaker; remove the thermostat, refasten the wires, and reinstall it.) If the wires are correctly fastened, change the temperature setting to the coldest position, and watch to see if the mercury slowly flows to one end of the bulb. Now change the temperature setting to the warmest position. The mercury should move to the other end of the bulb. If it does not, try leveling the thermostat by remounting it. Check the screws on the wall plate; if they've pulled loose, that's probably why the thermostat isn't operating. Re-anchor them solidly; you may have to screw new holes a few inches from the old ones to do this. If the screws are intact, loosen them, and use a small carpenter's level to remount the thermostat evenly. Check again to see if the mercury flows back and forth when you change the setting. If not, replace the thermostat. If the mercury does flow correctly, reinstall the cover, set the thermostat for a warm temperature, and see if

Tip *A thermostat is an electric switch that is activated by changes in temperature. The moving part that makes and breaks contact to open and close the electric circuit is usually a strip of two different metals, bonded together, that react differently to temperature changes. For instance, as the temperature rises, the metal on one side of the strip expands while the other metal remains stable, causing the strip to bend. As it bends, the movable end separates from an electrical contact point, breaking electrical contact. As the temperature drops, the side of the strip that had expanded contracts, allowing the strip to return to its normal position and restore electrical contact.*

the furnace will turn on. If not, check for a broken thermostat wire by shorting the screw terminals at the furnace, as described.

Testing a thermostat by bypassing it

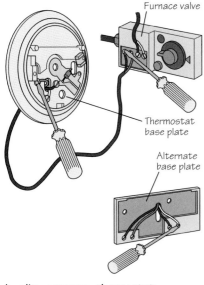

Furnace valve

Thermostat base plate

Alternate base plate

Leveling a mercury thermostat

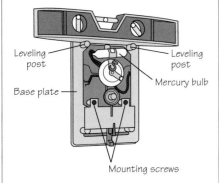

Leveling post

Leveling post

Mercury bulb

Base plate

Mounting screws

▶ Room temperature doesn't match thermostat setting.

You can expect a minor discrepancy between the thermostat reading and the setting you choose for it, but if the reading is significantly different from room temperature (5° F or more) the thermometer may be defective, or the unit may be located in an area that's warmer or cooler than the rest of the house (for instance, a south wall is often warmer, and a drafty area will be cooler). First check to see if it is an older mercury thermostat that needs to be leveled (see opposite page). Then consider relocating the thermostat. It should be placed on an interior wall at least 5 feet above the floor, away from any drafts or direct heat (including sunlight), and away from corners or dead spots behind doors. It should not be placed on a wall that has a duct or pipe inside. To relocate it, you will have to reroute the wires through the attic or basement into the wall of the new location (see page 205). It may be easier to run new wire from the thermostat to the furnace; thermostat wire is light gauge and relatively inexpensive.

If these minor adjustments don't solve the problem, the thermostat may have to be recalibrated. Read the instructions in the owner's manual, call a technician, or replace the thermostat.

▶ Thermostat lags in turning heat on or off.

Theoretically, a thermostat could activate the heating or cooling system every time the temperature varied only 1° F from your chosen set temperature. However, this would be annoying (and inefficient) because the system would be constantly cycling on and off. Therefore, thermostats have a range of a few degrees of change before they signal the heating or cooling system to go on or off. With most thermostats you can adjust this range yourself, to increase or decrease the time it takes for the thermostat to react to a temperature reading—except for electric resistance heaters (such as electric baseboards). In this case the thermostat is probably a high-voltage type, which could cause fatal shocks; have it serviced professionally.

To adjust a thermostat, turn off the power to the furnace. (You may find a switch near the furnace; if not, trip the circuit breaker.) Remove the thermostat cover and look for the anticipation-adjustment dial or arrow (some thermostats may not have one). Set the adjustment to *Less* if you want to decrease the reaction time; *More* if you want to increase it.

If the house takes too long to warm up after the thermostat activates the furnace, it's probably the fault of the heating system, not the thermostat. The furnace may be too small to heat the house adequately, or the furnace may not be functioning properly. (See page 241.)

Adjusting anticipation control

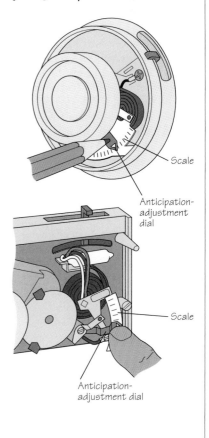

Scale

Anticipation-adjustment dial

Scale

Anticipation-adjustment dial

Tip   *Where should the thermostat be located? Most experts recommend that it be mounted on a wall where it won't be in the path of a draft, and in a room where the desired temperature will be average for the whole house (or the rooms being heated by the system it controls). It should also be on a wall that is convenient to reach, near the main traffic path. Avoid placing a thermostat near a fireplace or on a wall that receives direct sunlight.*

▶ Furnace cycles on and off too rapidly.

Adjust the anticipation adjustment slightly in the direction of *More*. (See page 253.)

▶ Thermostat needs testing.

If you suspect that your thermostat is broken (see page 252) but want to pinpoint the exact problem, you can test it with a volt-ohmmeter according to the owner's manual for the thermostat.

Start by turning off the power to the thermostat and the appliance it governs. Hold the tester probes on the thermostat terminals. If the tester shows no continuity (circuit is not completed through the thermostat), the thermostat contacts are stuck open and it will have to be replaced. If the tester shows continuity, it indicates that the thermostat contacts are closed. To find out if they open properly, you will have to test the thermostat under live conditions by heating it to a temperature at which its contacts should open.

The easiest and safest way to do this is to heat it in a clean skillet. An electric skillet is easiest to use because you can determine its exact temperature. However, an experienced cook may be able to perform the test using a cast-iron skillet heated to approximately the right temperature. (This is particularly easy when testing a furnace thermostat, which should open its contacts at a very moderate temperature.) To test, turn off the power, disconnect the wires from the thermostat, and remove it from the wall bracket. Place it facedown (terminals up) in the skillet (unless it has a mercury capsule that should remain level, in which case prop it upright in the pan). Turn on heat to the skillet and let it reach the required temperature (the temperature noted in the owner's manual or, for a furnace, a temperature that's warm to the touch). Put on oven mitts and hold the probes of the tester across the thermostat terminals. The tester should show no power, indicating that the contacts have opened and the thermostat is good. If not, the thermostat should be replaced.

Testing thermostat for open contacts

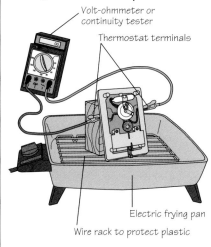

Volt-ohmmeter or continuity tester

Thermostat terminals

Electric frying pan

Wire rack to protect plastic

▶ New thermostat doesn't work as well as the old one.

You may need to experiment with the anticipation-adjustment control so the thermostat has the same lag period as the old one before turning the furnace on or off (see page 253). Also make sure that you have followed all installation instructions, including placing it in a proper location. If it still performs erratically, the new model may be defective. Thermostats are highly sensitive instruments and can fall out of adjustment. Immediately exchange it at the store where you bought it, trying a different model or brand.

▶ New programmable thermostat needs installing.

To remove the old thermostat, turn off the power to the furnace (and thermostat). Remove the thermostat cover to expose the wire connections and the mounting screws for the bracket. Remove the mounting screws to expose the wires. Before disconnecting the wires from the thermostat, mark each wire so you will know which terminal screw it should be attached to. To keep the wires from falling back inside the wall and to prevent accidental shorting, tape each one *separately* to the wall as you disconnect it. Install the new thermostat, following the instructions that came with the unit. Use hollow-wall fasteners to mount the bracket on the wall so the screws will not come loose. Carefully connect wires to the proper terminals; if you aren't sure, check on the furnace itself to see which wires are connected to which terminals. Use a continuity tester to trace wires if they aren't color-coded. After installing the thermostat, program it according to manufacturer's instructions.

Removing old thermostat

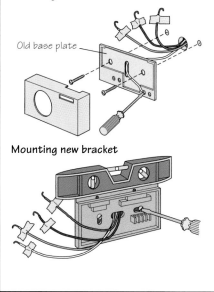

Old base plate

Mounting new bracket

Tip *A programmable thermostat saves on heating costs and increases comfort. You can program it to keep the house at a cool temperature at night and while you're at work, and to raise the temperature to a comfortable level before you get up or get home.*

▶ *Humidifier unit leaks or overflows.*

First use a carpenter's level to check that the humidifier is level both horizontally and vertically. If not, adjust the mounting. Then check the float valve; see whether its adjustment is set for the right water level and inspect its condition. If the valve is stuck open (usually because mineral deposits have made it too heavy to float), try cleaning it: Scrape off mineral deposits from the float and from the needle and seat on the inlet valve. If the float valve itself is leaking, or if the small rubber button that seals the outlet looks worn, replace the float valve. If this doesn't stop the overflows, the unit may be incorrectly installed or the media pads may need to be replaced or repositioned. Call for professional service.

Checking humidifier components

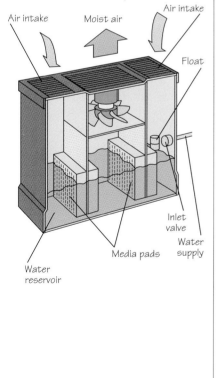

Air intake

Moist air

Air intake

Float

Inlet valve

Water supply

Media pads

Water reservoir

▶ *Humidifier has corrosion or calcium buildup.*

You can clean out buildup of calcium and lime by spraying a mild acid, such as vinegar, inside the humidifier. Start with a solution of 1 part vinegar to 3 parts water; strengthen as necessary. At least once a year, turn off the water, remove the humidifier element, and scrape off mineral buildup. Corrosion, however, will require professional repairs.

▶ *Humidifier unit makes strange noises.*

An occasional gurgle is probably normal. Check that water is running and inspect the float valve to make sure it's not stuck open or closed. Make sure that the duct edges to the unit are not bent; if so, straighten them. Otherwise, call for repairs.

▶ *Portable humidifier won't run.*

First check that the unit is plugged in and the receptacle is live. (Try another small appliance or lamp in the receptacle.) Make sure the cord is intact. If the air is already more humid than the setting of the humidistat (the humidity-sensing device), the unit won't work until the air is drier. (If the humidifier is new, it may take a few hours to adjust and start running.)

The machine may be jammed because of mineral buildup on the belt, rollers, drum, or (in newer ultrasonic models) the nebulizers. Start by unplugging the humidifier and emptying the reservoir. Lift out the belt and rollers (if applicable) or the drum. Change the evaporator belt at least once a year, and more often in desert conditions. Remove the pad from the drum. Scrub these parts with a solution of ¼ cup detergent in 1 quart hot

water, and return them to the humidifier. Add fresh water to the reservoir. In an ultrasonic model, once a week gently wipe the nebulizer with white vinegar, using a soft cloth, and rinse off. Check the air filter; if dirty, remove it and clean it with cool water. In hard-water areas, consider using bottled distilled water in place of tap water in any type of humidifier. If cleaning the unit doesn't start it, check for a broken or misaligned drive belt (see below). If this too fails to start it, take it in for service.

Checking components of a warm-mist humidifier

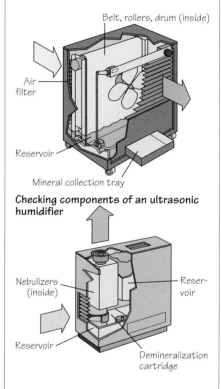

Belt, rollers, drum (inside)

Air filter

Reservoir

Mineral collection tray

Checking components of an ultrasonic humidifier

Nebulizers (inside)

Reservoir

Reservoir

Demineralization cartridge

▶ *Portable humidifier's fan squeaks.*

Manually rotate the fan blades to make sure the fan isn't frozen or obstructed. If it is frozen or very hard to move, lubricate it according to the owner's manual; usually, a

Tip *Adding humidity to the air makes people comfortable at lower temperatures. If the air is dry, most people are comfortable with an air temperature between 75° and 80° F. If the air has more than 50 percent relative humidity, the same people will be comfortable at a temperature as low as 70° F.*

SOLVING MECHANICAL PROBLEMS

few drops of lubricant in the oil cup will be sufficient. Continue operating it by hand, and see if it begins to move more easily. Lubricate the fan motor once a year (according to the owner's manual), more often if using the unit the year around. Check the tension and condition of the fan belt; it should give about ½ inch. Check the bearings; if they're frozen, oil them with the lubricant recommended by the manufacturer and use pliers to loosen them.

▶ Portable humidifier emits odors.

To kill odor-producing bacteria breeding in the reservoir, clean the reservoir at least once a week, using a solution of 1 tablespoon chlorine bleach per pint of water. Rinse with plain water. If odor persists, clean the evaporator belt with the same chlorine solution, and use water treatment tablets in the reservoir. (For special occasions or to purge the chlorine smell, you can add a few drops of rose water, orange-flower water, or a light cologne or aftershave to the reservoir water.)

▶ Portable humidifier won't stop running.

If the unit is new and the home is extremely dry, it may be necessary for the humidifier to run for a long time before the proper humidity is reached. Check for open windows or an open fireplace damper that may be pulling out the humidified air. Otherwise, it's likely that either the on-off switch or the humidistat (the humidity sensor) is broken. Disconnect the power cord, locate the humidistat, and test it with a volt-ohmmeter; then test the switch. Be sure you are testing in low-humidity conditions. If the meter registers an electric current (continuity) in either case, the electrical contacts of that part are

stuck in a closed position, keeping the machine running. Replace the broken part. If this doesn't work, have the machine repaired professionally. If you feel the machine isn't worth repairing, just unplug the humidifier whenever you want to turn it off and plug it back in when the air feels dry.

Testing humidistat

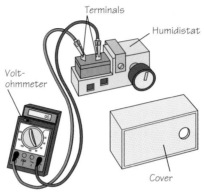

▶ Dehumidifier unit doesn't start or won't stay on.

Check that the unit is plugged into a live receptacle; if using it consistently blows the fuse or trips the breaker, try a different receptacle to avoid overloading a circuit. If the problem recurs, have the unit repaired professionally.

If room temperature is below 65° F, the unit may be blocked with ice; few models function well below 70° F. Try the unit again when the room is warm. If you've been repeatedly turning it on and off, turn it on and wait about two minutes to see if it starts again.

Check to see if the collector bin is full of water. If so, empty it and try it again. If the unit still doesn't start, unplug it and disconnect one lead to the humidistat. Simultaneously rotate the knob and test the humidistat with a volt-ohmmeter. If there's no current, the humidistat has to be replaced.

▶ Dehumidifier motor or fan squeaks.

Check the owner's manual to find out where the lubrication points are and what type of lubricant to use. (Most dehumidifiers have an oil cup for inserting lubricant.) Lubricate according to the manual. If the sound is more like a rattle than a squeak, tighten the screws on the fan hub. If this doesn't stop it, check the fan motor for worn bearings. Unscrew the mounting nuts and then unscrew the fan from the shaft. If you can move the shaft in any direction, a bearing is worn out, and the motor will need to be replaced. Consult the manual for specific instructions.

Tightening fan-hub screws

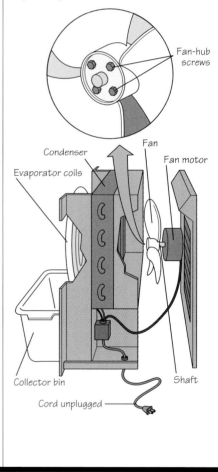

Tip *A dehumidifier should be cleaned periodically. With the power turned off, unscrew the panel(s) and vacuum the inside, including the fan and coils. Scrub mineral deposits from the coils with a stiff wire brush.*

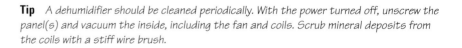

► Dehumidifier has water under it.

Usually this means the collector bin is overflowing. Empty the collector. If the unit has a drain trough under the coils, remove any obstruction in the drain hole. If water continues to collect, check the owner's manual to see if the unit has an overflow-prevention switch. If so, disconnect it and test it with a volt-ohmmeter; if the meter shows no current (continuity), the contacts are stuck open and the switch will need to be replaced. If the problem recurs, corrosion may have eaten a hole in some part of the mechanism. Call for professional repairs.

► Dehumidifier evaporator coils collect frost.

Many models frost up when operated at a room temperature under 65° F. If it's warm, the problem may be dirty coils or too little airflow. Clean the coils by unplugging the unit, removing the outer cabinet, and letting moisture evaporate; then wipe the coils gently with a soft-bristled brush (such as a refrigerator-coil brush) and/or vacuum the coils. If the dehumidifier is right next to a wall, move it an inch or two away from the wall to allow better airflow.

If ice-ups continue, turn up the speed of the dehumidifier (if it has a speed switch). If the dehumidifier has a deicer control (a bimetallic thermostatic device attached to the suction line), it may be faulty. Obtain a replacement and clamp it over the suction line in the same place, according to manufacturer's instructions, or have a repair person do so.

► Window air conditioner needs routine maintenance.

Once a year when the weather is warming up, clean the unit or have it cleaned and inspected professionally. (In areas with high air pollution, a professional should clean the unit.) To clean it yourself, unplug the unit and, with a helper, remove it from the window. Set it outdoors on an improvised work table (such as on sawhorses); if that is impractical, set it on an up-ended heavy-duty plastic laundry basket (or equivalent) in the bathtub. Wrap all electrical components in heavy plastic bags secured with duct tape. Vacuum the evaporator fins clean, and then wash both the evaporator and condenser coils with a garden hose or handheld shower sprayer until clear water percolates through. Let drain.

Next pull out the filter; it is usually a thin sheet of foam rubber located behind the face grille. Check its condition and wash it with a mild detergent if it's dirty (and washable), or replace it if it's worn or isn't washable. Oil the fan motor according to the owner's manual. Remove the plastic bags and return the unit to the window. Don't try to add refrigerant yourself; call a professional. You risk not only ruining the system, but illegally releasing CFCs (chlorofluorocarbons) into the atmosphere.

The filter should be cleaned or changed at least once a month, more often in smoggy or dusty weather. In most areas the coils need a thorough cleaning just once a year, but if there's heavy air pollution, clean them about once a month.

Cleaning filter and coils

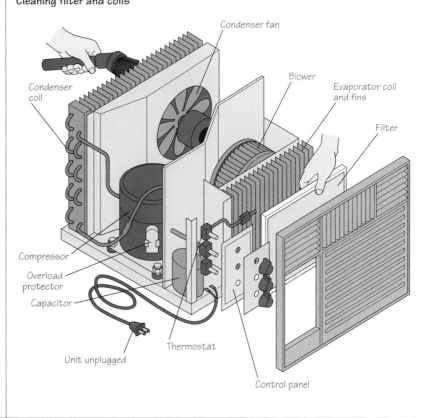

Condenser fan

Condenser coil

Blower

Evaporator coil and fins

Filter

Compressor

Overload protector

Capacitor

Thermostat

Unit unplugged

Control panel

Tip *Whenever you take the cover off an air conditioner, beware of touching the capacitor, as it stores an electric charge. You can discharge it and render it safe (so long as the unit is unplugged) by touching a screwdriver blade across the two terminals and holding it there for a few seconds; be sure the screwdriver handle is insulated. Don't touch the blade and don't let the blade touch anything else. Some capacitors discharge automatically, but assume it doesn't and perform this maneuver anyway.*

▶ Room air conditioner doesn't turn on.

If the fuse hasn't blown nor the circuit breaker tripped, check to see if the cord or plug is damaged; if so, replace it. If not, unplug the unit and check the switch with a continuity tester or volt-ohmmeter to see if the switch is stuck in the *Off* position (the tester will indicate no continuity). If the switch is faulty, replace it. If turning on the unit consistently blows the fuse or trips the breaker, try a receptacle in a different room; if the problem continues, call for professional repairs.

▶ Room air conditioner doesn't cool room.

First check to see if anything is blocking the front of the unit. Then close the door to the room and turn the thermostat to the coldest position and see if that works better. If not, check the filter; if it is dirty or ripped, clean it or replace it. Open the unit and see if the coils are dirty; if so, remove the unit from the window and clean the coils (see page 257), or have the unit professionally cleaned. If the unit is connected to the receptacle with a long extension cord, it may not be getting enough power to operate at full capacity; change the cord to a larger gauge (at least No. 14). Also check to see that the thermostat is working (see pages 252 and 253). The refrigerant level may be low; if so, call a professional to replenish it.

▶ Room air conditioner cycles on and off too rapidly.

Follow the procedures outlined above. In addition, the thermostat may be adjusted to go on and off in too narrow a temperature range (see page 254).

▶ Room air conditioner may be too small.

Before you buy a larger unit, for long-term savings consider reducing air infiltration and increasing shade. Caulking air leaks, adding window coverings, replacing single-glazed windows with double-glazed units, planting shade trees and installing trellises, and screening the porch are some of the steps you can take to cool your house while reducing energy use. Installing a ceiling fan or, even better, a whole-house fan can also diminish reliance on air-conditioning.

▶ Window air conditioner is subject to winter exposure.

Weather-induced corrosion of the case is usually a minor problem that can be repaired with touch-up paint, but if winters are severe or rain is highly acidic, you can protect the unit by covering the outside portion with a heavy-duty garbage bag or similar sturdy plastic sheeting secured with duct tape. If frequent hailstorms are damaging the case, make a double or triple layer of plastic foam or bubble wrap (available at office-supply stores), poke many small holes in it for ventilation, and tape it to the top of the unit.

If the main problem is the draft that comes through the vents, remove the inside front cover and place a piece of plastic between the unit and the front cover for the winter, or obtain a quilted air conditioner cover. Be sure to remove the plastic inside the unit before starting it up again.

▶ Central air conditioner doesn't turn on.

First make sure that the unit is plugged in, switched on, and receiving electricity (the fuse isn't blown or the circuit breaker isn't tripped). If the fuse blows or circuit breaker trips whenever you turn on the unit, call for repairs. After a power outage, do not use the air conditioner for at least six hours or you may damage the compressor.

Check the thermostat to make sure that the setting is below room temperature and set to *Cool* or *Auto*, and that the fan switch is set to *Auto* or *On*. Check the coil outside to see if the fan is running; if not, check the condition of the blades and belt (see below). Make sure that the filters aren't clogged with dirt. If none of this is the problem, check that the thermostat is working (see page 252). Otherwise, the problem is probably a jammed or frozen compressor unit. Call for professional service.

▶ Central air conditioner needs routine maintenance.

At the start of warm weather, give the air conditioner an annual checkup and cleaning, or have it done professionally. First trim away any shrubbery that's growing close enough to restrict airflow to the outside condenser unit. Before starting work on the air conditioner itself, turn off the main power switch and thermostat; during the work, don't touch the capacitor, its terminals, or the wires leading from it, because the capacitor stores a heavy electric charge (see Tip, page 257).

Tip   A coating of frost on air conditioner coils usually indicates overuse. There are several simple ways to reduce the air-conditioning load and decrease operating costs: (1) turn off the air conditioner when no one is home; (2) consider opening windows and using an electric fan when temperatures are semibearable; (3) have a whole-house fan installed to remove hot air from the house; and (4) seal or weather-strip all gaps around the air conditioner to keep the cooled air inside.

Remove the cowl from the condenser. Cover the compressor and other electrical parts with large plastic bags secured with duct tape, and wash the fins and coils with a garden hose until clean water percolates through. If fins are bent, straighten them with broad-nosed pliers or a fin comb (available at plumbing or heating outlets); wear heavy gloves (such as oven mitts or garden gloves). Carefully inspect the coils with a flashlight; if they're still very dirty, call a technician to clean the unit (watch the operation closely, so you will be able to do it yourself next year). Lubricate the condenser motor and fan motor according to the owner's manual. Check the fan for dirt and check the fan belt tension (see page 240). Oil the fan and fan bearings, following the instructions in the owner's manual. If the cupped portion of the fan blade is heavily coated with dirt (more than $\frac{1}{16}$ inch thick), call a professional to clean it. Replace the fan compartment cover tightly, and replace the cowl.

Indoors, clean the evaporator fins with a soft brush and, if necessary, straighten them with a fin comb. Change the air-intake filter. Rinse the drain pan with a solution of ¼ cup chlorine bleach in 1 pint water to keep algae and bacteria from breeding. Every month check the air-intake filter and replace it (or wash it, if it's washable) when dirty, and rinse or spray the drain pan with a bleach-and-water solution.

If the level of refrigerant is low, only a professional can recharge it legally and safely. In regions with severe air pollution, have a professional perform the annual cleaning.

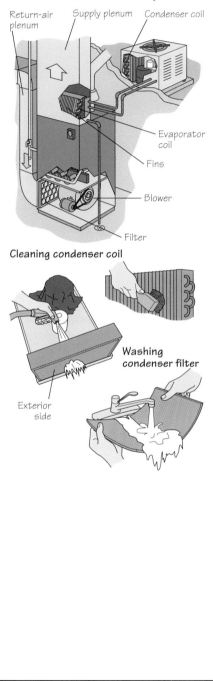

Cleaning air-conditioning components

Return-air plenum · Supply plenum · Condenser coil · Evaporator coil · Fins · Blower · Filter

Cleaning condenser coil

Exterior side

Washing condenser filter

▶ *Central air conditioner doesn't cool house enough.*

Make sure the thermostat and fan are set correctly, and check that the fan is running. Make sure nothing is restricting airflow. Check for unnecessary cool-air loss, such as open windows or doors. Close drapes, blinds, or shades in any room that doesn't require outside light. See opposite page for additional cooling strategies. Check the filters and condenser for dirt, and make sure nothing is obstructing the fan. If the compressor isn't turning easily, or if none of the above measures helps, call for professional repairs.

▶ *Outdoor compressor is exposed to weather.*

Clean and wax the cabinet with auto-body polish to protect the finish. Consider making or buying a ventilated protective shed or a tarp of breathable, water-repellent fabric (such as house wrap used in new construction) that you can use in winter and remove in summer. (Be sure there is ventilation to allow moisture to evaporate, or the compressor is liable to rust.) During air-conditioning season the compressor can't be enclosed because free airflow is vital to its functioning.

If severe summer hailstorms are denting the compressor, obtain a "breathable foam" mattress pad of the appropriate size; cut it to the exact size of the top of the compressor, and attach it by any means possible (such as crisscrossing duct tape or electrical wire). Monitor the pad to see how quickly it dries after a storm; if it remains wet after a day of sunshine, remove it, let it dry, and then poke many small holes in it with a barbecue fork or similar instrument before returning it to the compressor top. Continue monitoring, and be prepared to remove

Tip *For guidelines to size an air conditioner, you can obtain a "Cooling Load Estimate Form" from: Publications Department, Association of Home Appliance Manufacturers, 20 North Wacker Drive, Suite 15, Chicago, IL 60606; 312-984-5800. There is a nominal fee for the guidelines.*

SOLVING MECHANICAL PROBLEMS

the pad to dry it out after storms. For more permanent hailproofing, consider building a box-shaped shed, a few inches taller and wider than the compressor, from sheets of windowscreening stitched together with thin wire; attach the mattress pad to the top to keep hailstones from breaking the screen.

▶ Air conditioner doesn't work properly following power outage.

Keep an air conditioner turned off for six hours after a power outage. Before then the compressor can't operate correctly and may be damaged if turned on. If you suspect that power outages occurred while you were asleep, don't use the air conditioner until the power supply has stabilized.

If your thermostat is electronic (setback) with no backup battery, a power outage may have erased the programming (along with that on your VCR and microwave clocks). Reprogram the thermostat.

▶ Air conditioner filter hasn't been cleaned for a month.

Clean it or change it. Filters should be cleaned every 30 days, unless your area has pure mountain air.

▶ Condenser unit makes strange sounds.

If the unit is new, be aware that it is normal for the condenser to make a few odd noises. However, if an older unit starts making strange noises, especially if it also stops cooling properly, call for repairs.

▶ Evaporative air conditioner doesn't cool enough.

Evaporative air conditioners are nicknamed "swamp coolers," but it would be more accurate to call them "desert coolers" because they work best in low humidity. The higher the humidity, the less efficiently they work, and in rain or heavy fog, they're useless.

If the humidity is low and the cooler still doesn't cool enough, check to see if the fan is working (see page 240). If the coils are dirty, clean them (see page 258). Make sure there's an adequate supply and flow of water. If the unit is clogged with deposits, clean it with white vinegar and rinse with water. If it shows signs of corrosion, you may have to have it patched or even replaced.

▶ Evaporative air conditioner emits foul odor.

To kill odor-producing bacteria in the water, mix ¼ cup chlorine bleach with 1 pint water in a spray bottle. Spray the solution onto the cooler, coils, and drain pan. Rinse by spraying them again with plain water. Repeat once a week.

▶ Evaporative air conditioner has squeaking or strange sound.

If the condenser is outside, look in the box to make sure no varmints (such as reptiles or small rodents) are living in it. (Proceed cautiously in rattlesnake country!) If it's infested, evict the squatters and their nests. Look on top; if birds are nesting there, you'll have to either evict them or put up with chirps until they fly south. Next check the alignment and tension of the pulleys; call for professional service if necessary. Lubricate the bearings, following the owner's manual instructions. Clear the fan of any obstructions, and lubricate the fan motor according to the manual. If the unit still makes noises, call for professional repairs.

▶ House has mold, mildew, or musty odors.

Musty, mildewy odors and visible mold are caused by water condensing inside the home. To address the immediate odor problem, scrub visible mildew and mold from walls and shades with mildew-killing or fungicidal cleanser (available at hardware stores) or a mixture of 4 tablespoons chlorine bleach in 1 quart water. Follow all label directions. If drapes smell mildewed, wash or dry-clean them. Be sure all clothing is clean and dry before storing it in closets. Weather and safety permitting, open some windows at night; if you obtain good cross-ventilation by opening windows on opposite sides of the house, the breeze will draw out much moisture. To minimize the problem in the future, install ventilating fans in the kitchen, laundry, and bathrooms (even those with windows); attach them to ducts to discharge moisture to the exterior. Make sure the clothes dryer is ducted to the outdoors. Whenever you paint interior rooms, have a mildewcide additive mixed into the paint by the paint dealer. Arrange furnishings and window coverings to allow maximum sunlight and cross-ventilation.

▶ ... especially in summer.

Moldy smells are especially common during humid summers in "tight" homes that have been caulked, weather-stripped, and/or insulated against heat loss. Improving air circulation should do much to solve the problem. If windows are "sweaty" and water puddles on the sill, open window coverings on bright days to let the sun dry the sills and frames. Thin the foliage of dense tree and shrub growth outside the windows if you don't need it for shade. In warm weather, if

Tip *Unlike auto air conditioners, household air conditioners should never be run when the temperature is below 60° F, as this may seriously damage the compressor.*

Tip *Freezing? Try turning the thermostat to a lower (warmer) setting and/or turn it off and substitute a fan at night.*

you have a forced-air furnace in the basement, open or remove the basement door and run the blower continuously for as long as necessary to dry out excess moisture. Also consider installing extra foundation and attic vents to dry out the crawl space and roof.

If your ceiling is at least 10 feet high, consider installing a paddle-style decorative ceiling fan; when run in reverse (counterclockwise), it will force warm air down from the ceiling to dry out the windows and walls. (Also consider, as a larger installation, a whole-house fan, which will drastically cut cooling bills and reduce some heating needs as well.)

To stop humidity in the crawl space from rising into the flooring, lay plastic sheeting (6 mil polyethylene) directly over the dirt. Overlap the sheets by about 6 inches, securing the seams with fabric duct tape. The soil surrounding the home should be graded away from the foundation. Water foundation plantings before 10 a.m. so soil can dry by nightfall, and consider drip irrigation or spot watering rather than wholesale sprinkling. The downspouts from the roof should, optimally, discharge into subsurface drainage pipes; a less costly alternative is a pipe extender (usually a flexible self-coiling tube) that can dump the water several feet away from the house.

▶ … especially in winter.

In some climates, especially if the house is uninsulated and/or leaky, mildew and musty smells are worst in the winter when there are chilly fogs and winter rains. Dehumidifying crystals (calcium chloride, available at hardware stores and home centers) can absorb some excess moisture in bedrooms, living areas, closets, and storage rooms.

Half-fill open or ventilated containers (such as lidless plastic food containers or large powdered-sugar shakers) with the crystals; use at least 36 ounces of crystals for large rooms, 12 to 24 ounces in closets, and 8 to 12 ounces in mildew-prone drawers and trunks. Monitor the containers weekly to dump water and replace dissolved crystals. Also consider installing louvered doors on closets to minimize clothing mildew. Consider obtaining one or more portable dehumidifiers; inexpensive, low-wattage models that can not only function at cool room temperatures (around 65° F) but also provide a little warmth are most commonly found at boating-supply and RV-supply stores. Air-to-air heat exchangers can also help dehumidify in cold weather, but they are very costly and rather unreliable.

▶ House may have carbon monoxide buildup.

Virtually all combustion-based appliances (furnace, stove, fireplace, vehicles running in garage) vent carbon monoxide. An old furnace is liable to develop a dangerous leak in the heat exchanger, and a well-caulked, weather-stripped, and insulated house is more likely to have a buildup than one that is well ventilated (or simply leaky). Carbon monoxide is not detectable to the senses, but some possible indications are persistently stale or stuffy air, very high indoor humidity and "sweating" windows, accumulations of soot around the fireplace or furnace, and no draft or a hot draft in the chimney. Health symptoms are similar to those of a persistent severe flu.

To minimize gas buildup, have the chimney cleaned and cleared of any blockage every fall; check all indoor flue pipes for obvious cracks

and leaks. Make sure the water heater is properly vented and not leaking. Don't use kerosene heaters, unvented gas heaters, or the kitchen stove for space heating. Replace worn out or loose tailpipes and mufflers on vehicles that park in the garage, and never run a car inside the garage for longer than it takes to start it and move it to the driveway. Have the furnace professionally inspected in late summer every year (especially if it is old), and make sure the furnace has access to enough outside air (consult the owner's manual for recommended ventilating area). Replace furnace filters monthly, and check the color of burner flames on the furnace and gas stove.

You can also buy a carbon monoxide detector. Models are available for prices ranging from a few dollars to $100 and up. The least expensive ones don't have an alarm and must be monitored by observation; more expensive models sound alarms and may combine smoke, carbon monoxide, and gas detection, or may even shut off a malfunctioning furnace.

▶ Kitchen or bathroom lacks exhaust fan.

When buying a fan consider capacity and sound level. Fans are rated by their capacity to exchange air, shown in cubic feet per minute (CFM), and by their noise levels (sones). One formula used by some heating contractors to determine the minimum-sized fan is to multiply the square feet of the room (its length times its breadth) times 2 for the kitchen, and times 1.07 for the bathroom. If ceilings are high—or if you love long showers, have a big household, or cook a lot (or in large quantities)—choose a considerably larger-capacity fan than indicated by the CFM rating.

Tip *Health experts recommend that a home have enough ventilation for one complete air exchange every two hours. Older homes with leaks and drafts accomplish this fairly easily, but newer homes that are tightly insulated and weather-stripped should have a ventilating system to ensure a continuous supply of fresh air.*

SOLVING MECHANICAL PROBLEMS

A sone is equivalent to the sound level of a quiet refrigerator. Fans range from 1 sone (fairly quiet) up to 4 sones. The lower-sone-rated fans will cost more but will be more pleasant to use and may last longer. Lower-priced units usually have a propeller blade motor. Higher-priced fans usually have a centrifugal (squirrel-cage) motor, which is quieter and more efficient.

The size of the duct work venting the fan is just as important as the size of the fan. Never downsize ducts below the minimum recommended by the fan manufacturer. If in doubt, have a professional size the ducts. Also, in some areas a duct through an unheated attic or wall cavity will have to be insulated.

Ventilating a kitchen

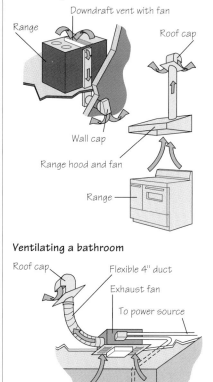

Range
Downdraft vent with fan
Roof cap
Wall cap
Range hood and fan
Range

Ventilating a bathroom

Roof cap
Flexible 4" duct
Exhaust fan
To power source
Wire to switch

▶ *Kitchen fan won't go on.*

If the problem isn't a tripped circuit breaker or blown fuse, see if the fan is getting power. First turn off the circuit breaker that controls the fan. Then find where the fan switch is connected to the house wiring (either at terminals on the switch itself or at connectors inside the fan junction box). If wires are joined by connectors in a junction box, carefully disconnect them and leave the house wires exposed so they are not touching anything. (Don't do anything to house wires if they're connected directly to the switch; you can test for power by touching probes directly to the screw terminals.) Restore power and, with a volt-ohmmeter or neon voltage tester, check the house wires for live voltage by touching one probe to the ground wire, the other to each house wire (or switch terminal), in turn. If no combination of wires indicates live voltage,

the problem is in the house wiring. Call an electrician.

If the wires do have power, the problem is in the switch or fan motor. Turn off the power and test the switch for continuity, either with the volt-ohmmeter or a continuity tester. Touch a probe to each switch terminal. (If there are more than two, make sure one probe touches the "line" terminal, where the house wire is connected.) If the switch shows no continuity in any setting, it is faulty and should be replaced. If it shows continuity, the problem is the fan motor. First make sure that the fan blades turn freely; if not, see if they are hung up on the housing or some other obstacle, or if they have frozen bearings. If not, remove the fan motor. Take it to a small-appliance parts dealer for a replacement. Install the new motor according to manufacturer's directions.

Testing for power
Note: Power on for this test.

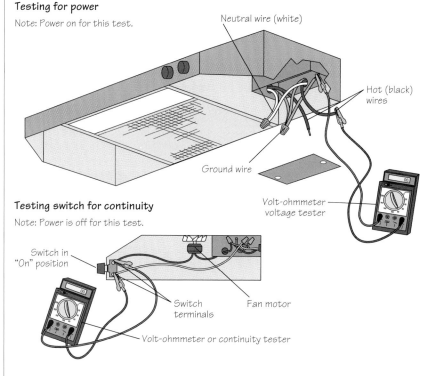

Neutral wire (white)
Hot (black) wires
Ground wire
Volt-ohmmeter voltage tester

Testing switch for continuity
Note: Power is off for this test.

Switch in "On" position
Switch terminals
Fan motor
Volt-ohmmeter or continuity tester

Tip *When choosing a kitchen fan, look for a model that's easy to clean. It should have a removable, washable filter.*

► Kitchen vent fan clears air too slowly or not at all.

Check (if you don't know for sure) that the fan is actually connected to a duct for venting; if not, it is just moving the grease and smoke around the room. Then check to see if the fan blade or cage may be loose from the motor shaft, causing it to spin less rapidly than the motor and to lag at the beginning and end of its run. Next check to see whether the exterior vent opening is obstructed. Also check for blockage in the duct by turning on the fan and holding a piece of lightweight paper over the vent opening; if the paper doesn't blow freely, the damper may be shut or there may be an obstruction in the duct.

To inspect the damper, which is usually installed between the fan unit and the first duct fitting, you may have to remove the fan itself to gain access. If so, turn off the circuit breaker for the fan and remove the cover. Remove the filter and wash it in hot soapy water and set it aside to dry out thoroughly. Disconnect the electrical connection: Some models have a plug you can pull; others have connections inside a junction box located next to the fan motor. Then unscrew the mounting bolts and remove the fan unit. The damper flap(s) should move freely with no resistance. If not, look for a bent flap that needs straightening, or stuck pivots that you should clean, straighten, or lubricate.

The fan may be operating below capacity if it's gummed up with grease. Clean every part that you can reach inside the duct, using a grease-dissolving household cleaner. If all this fails, you may need a more powerful unit and possibly a new duct.

► Kitchen hood light goes off.

If the bulb is burned out, replace it with an oven bulb to keep it from burning out so frequently. If it still goes out, or won't light, check the switch and all wiring connections. First turn off the circuit breaker that controls the hood. To make sure it's the right one, run the fan before turning off the breaker; it will stop running when you switch off the correct breaker. With power off, inspect the bulb socket, wire leads, wire connectors, and light switch terminals for loose or broken connections; you may have to loosen screws to remove cover plates. If no likely culprits emerge, check the switch for continuity with a volt-ohmmeter or continuity tester (with the power off). Touch one probe to the switch terminal with the house wire connected to it, the other probe to the terminal with a wire leading to the light(s). The tester should indicate continuity when the switch is in the *On* position. If not, replace the switch.

► Kitchen hood filter hasn't been cleaned for two months.

Check the filter (and fan blades, if possible) at least once a month (more often if you are a frequent fryer) and clean as needed with a grease-dissolving cleanser or hot sudsy dishwater. If the filter is missing, write down the make and model of the hood or measure the opening to the fan housing and buy a replacement filter at a hardware store, kitchen appliance dealer, or small-appliance parts dealer.

► Kitchen hood admits cold draft.

All ducts for kitchen and bathroom fans should be fitted with a damper that shuts automatically when the fan is not running. The easiest type to install when the hood and duct are already in place is at the exterior vent opening. Measure the interior dimensions of the duct where it terminates outside the house (either on the roof or exterior wall) and obtain a vent cap with a back-flow preventer of the same size; some are plastic, others metal. Install it on the exterior according to manufacturer's instructions. Make sure nothing interferes with the automatic operation of the damper, such as a bent duct or loose piece of siding.

► Kitchen fan is too noisy.

Make sure all screws and bolts are tight, and oil the fan motor according to manufacturer's directions. Make sure the fan is connected to a duct to the outside (if not, it will be extranoisy as well as useless). If the noise is a whistling sound, the duct may be too long and twisty and may have to be redone. Otherwise, consider upgrading to a fan with a lower sone rating. Also consider changing to the type of powerful fan (such as a restaurant-type fan) that is mounted at the exterior end of the duct, so that most of the noise occurs outdoors.

► Kitchen fan has only one speed.

If the kitchen has cross-ventilation or if the fan is sufficiently powerful at that speed, you may be able to get by with only one speed. Otherwise, contact the manufacturer to see if a multispeed switch is available to replace the one-speed switch for the model you have.

Tip *A kitchen fan is essential for removing household pollutants from the home. Normal cooking activities produce not only odors and steam, but in a year's time they can release into the air more than a gallon of vaporized grease.*

▶ Kitchen hood controls are hard to reach.

You can obtain an inexpensive remote-controlled device from a housewares or building-supply store, or from many housewares mail-order catalogs. These devices consist of a receiver unit that you install between the fan and power source, and a remote-controlled sending unit that you place wherever it is convenient to use. To connect, simply unplug the fan from its receptacle, plug the receiver unit into the receptacle instead, and plug the fan into the receiver unit. Turn the fan settings to those you use most often, and use the remote-controlled device to turn the system on and off.

▶ Kitchen hood gets in the way of cooking.

Unfortunately, you'll probably have to remove the hood and raise it, or replace it with one that is more functional. Otherwise, if the hood is built into the wall behind the stove and can't be moved, consider moving the stove out an inch or so. If it won't move because it is attached to rigid gas pipes, have the pipes replaced with a flexible connector and shutoff valve; it's safer as well as more convenient.

▶ Bathroom walls and ceiling have moisture.

Hot, moist air does considerable damage to bathrooms; it accelerates the deterioration of wallcoverings, wallboard, ceiling, insulation, and framing, and fosters the growth of mildew. The best solution to the problem is a ventilating fan, even if the bathroom has an openable window. An easier but less effective remedy for severe moisture is a dehumidifier. Small, low-priced, low-wattage dehumidifiers (including

standing or hanging models) suitable for bathrooms may be found at boating-supply and RV-supply stores and in some housewares mail-order catalogs. Other partial remedies include bathing with the door or window open, wiping down the walls after each shower, switching to shower curtains made of a breathable fabric (such as a house-wrap used in home construction), using a small stand-alone fan, and using a small electric heater recommended for bathrooms.

If you already have an exhaust fan, it may not be drawing properly. If the fan has a flapper valve that opens when the fan is on, check to see whether the valve indeed opens. Check that the duct is free of obstructions. If the fan is operating properly, it may not be powerful enough to draw the air out of the room; consider upgrading. Alternately, let the existing fan run for 10 minutes or so after you have left the bathroom, with the door open so that dry air can enter the room. (You can install a timer switch to turn it off automatically.)

▶ Bathroom fan is vented to attic and not to outside.

A bathroom fan duct that terminates in the attic does considerable harm; it sends moisture into the attic, which can produce wet insulation and rot the ceiling and rafters. Attic venting also diminishes the ability of the fan to draw in fresh air and rid the bathroom of moisture. The fan should preferably be vented through the roof. Cut a 4-inch-diameter hole through the roof sheathing and roofing and install a roof cap (with a back-flow preventer) over it. Tuck the cap flange under the shingles above it

(you may have to remove nails) and lap it over the shingles below it. Connect the fan duct to the bottom of the cap. If the duct is too short, buy a length of the same diameter (3- or 4-inch) flexible aluminum duct and join it to the old duct by slipping the ends of both ducts over a short length of rigid aluminum duct tubing of the same diameter. Secure each end with a hose clamp. If a roof termination is impossible, install a wall cap (with a back-flow preventer) on an exterior wall (except for one on a property line) and connect the duct to it.

Installing a roof cap

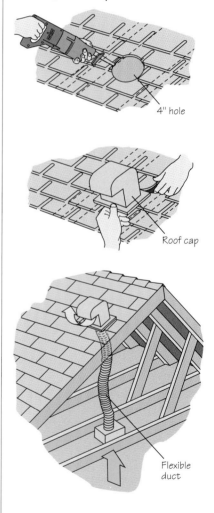

4" hole

Roof cap

Flexible duct

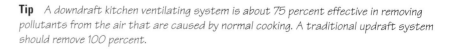

Tip *A downdraft kitchen ventilating system is about 75 percent effective in removing pollutants from the air that are caused by normal cooking. A traditional updraft system should remove 100 percent.*

▶ Bathroom fan duct admits cold air into room.

First look for gaps between the fan housing and the ceiling cutout. Caulk with a bead of silicone sealant along the edge of the opening. Buy a roof- or wall-mounted duct cap with a back-flow preventer and install it where the duct terminates outside. If you live where winters are very cold, consider switching to a type of ventilating fan with an insulated, motorized exhaust hood that opens only when the fan is on. Various models are available, some with the fan blower installed in the hood for quieter operation.

Installing an insulated ventilating hood

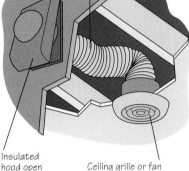

Flexible duct

Insulated hood open

Ceiling grille or fan

▶ Bathroom ceiling has mildew even though fan is always used.

Scrub the existing mildew with a mildewcide liquid or spray cleaner, or with a solution of 4 tablespoons chlorine bleach in 1 quart water. Follow all label precautions. If the infestation is severe, strip the paint before washing, and repaint with a mildew-retarding oil-based paint. To prevent future growth, see opposite page. The problem may

be especially acute if the bathtub or shower is in a corner; you may need a stronger fan to draw all the air out of the room, or you may have to leave the fan on longer, open the door during showers, or add a small dehumidifier to the room.

▶ Attic or roof fan doesn't come on.

These fans are controlled by automatic switches that activate the fan when the attic temperature reaches a certain point, or by timers for automatic operation. There should also be a manual switch—either in the attic or downstairs in the house somewhere—that controls power to the fan unit.

First check that the fuse or circuit breaker for the fan has not blown or tripped, then make sure the manual switch is on. Next be certain that the conditions activating the fan are met (right time or temperature). If the fan still does not come on, turn off the circuit breaker for the fan and look for obstructions or a broken belt.

Next test the wiring for power to the fan; expose the terminals or wires where the house wiring is connected to the fan unit, make sure that any wires you disconnect are not touching anything else, and restore power. With a voltage tester or volt-ohmmeter, carefully touch one probe to a ground wire and the other to the hot (black) wire of the house wiring (be sure the manual switch is on). If the tester shows no power for this wire or any other, the problem is in the wiring; call an electrician. If the tester shows power, the problem is in the switch or the

fan motor. The fan will have either a timer switch or a temperature switch. Test either switch by turning off power and using a continuity tester or a volt-ohmmeter (set for 4x1 ohms resistance). For a timer, adjust the clock so it shows time within the set limits and touch the tester probes to both power terminals. For testing the temperature switch, the temperature should be above the lower limit of the switch (usually around 90° F; choose a hot day or remove the switch and heat it up in a frying pan to make sure; see page 254). If either switch does not show continuity, replace it. If it does show continuity, the problem may be the fan safety switch or fan motor. Test the safety switch for continuity to see if the contacts are stuck open. It it's not faulty (needing replacement) the problem is probably the fan motor. Remove it and buy an exact replacement motor at a small-appliance parts dealer or fan specialty store.

▶ Attic fan hasn't been cleaned for six months.

Attics are often dusty; accumulated dust on the fan could impair its operation. Turn off the power to the fan and wash it with a sponge and warm water, cleaning every part that you can reach.

▶ Attic fan has no safety switch.

Should a fire break out, an attic fan that has no switch to cut off power at high temperatures (200° F) can feed the flames with air. Add-on safety switches are inexpensive. To install one, place a junction box along the power wires near the fan to house the switch connections. Splice the switch into the hot (black) wire between the fan thermostat and the power source.

Tip *The cost of electricity for running an attic fan is about one-tenth the cost of running a central air conditioner. A fan doesn't replace the need for air-conditioning—at least for the hottest days—but it reduces the cooling load for an air conditioner significantly.*

SOLVING MECHANICAL PROBLEMS

▶ *Whole-house fan hasn't been inspected for a year.*

A whole-house fan is a powerful machine that should be inspected and serviced at least once a year. If you do it yourself, clean the fan blades and louvers, check the fan belt tension, tighten loose screws and bolts, and lubricate the bearings, motor housing, and fan as directed by the manufacturer. While you're at it, clean all the vent screens in the attic to increase potential airflow.

Servicing a whole-house fan

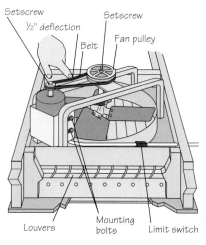

▶ *Ceiling fan doesn't circulate air properly.*

Check the condition of the paddle blades; repair any obvious damage. Some fans have blades with adjustable pitch; follow manufacturer's directions to slant them properly. If the fan is a model with a reverse switch, change the rotation of the blades with the change of seasons. The fan should direct air downward in summer to create a breeze and upward in winter to move the warm air from the ceiling.

▶ *Ceiling paddle fan wobbles or is working loose from ceiling box.*

Correct the immediate problem by turning off the circuit breaker for the fan and tightening all screws and bolts that connect the fan to the ceiling box. Check to see that the box itself is not loose and that it is heavy enough to meet the fan manufacturer's recommendations; if not, replace it with a stronger box. Then inspect the fan blades and observe operation at a slow speed to see if they wobble due to loose screws, missing hardware, or unevenly balanced paddles. Make necessary corrections (for example, replace a nicked paddle with a new one). If the fan still wobbles, the problem may be a bent shaft or worn shaft bearing in the motor. Have it professionally repaired.

▶ *Ceiling box for paddle fan is working loose from ceiling.*

Electrical boxes for paddle fans have stricter requirements for reinforcement than other ceiling electrical boxes. If the box is loose, remove it entirely and replace it with a reinforced box approved for ceiling fans. First turn off the circuit breaker for the fan and disconnect it from the box (you will need a helper to support the fan while you disconnect the wires). Then test all wires in the box with a voltage tester to be sure the power is off. If you have access to the box from the attic, proceed from there. Otherwise, to remove wires from the box and the box itself you will have to

cut away some of the ceiling. If so, cut it back to the centers of the joists on either side of the box so you will have framing for attaching a wallboard patch. Secure the bracket for the new box to each joist with two 1¼-inch wallboard screws (nailing may disturb the ceiling); slide the box into position, and secure it in place by tightening the screw clamp. Patch the ceiling opening (if applicable) and install the fan. Secure the holding strap to the box with two screws and the central lug provided with the box; then connect the wires and screw the fan canopy to the holding strap.

Installing a new ceiling box

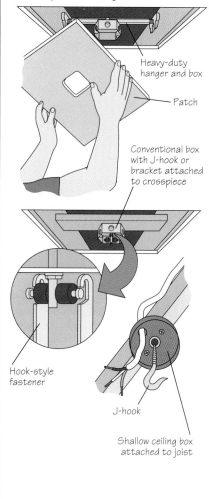

▶ Range or cooktop controls are within child's reach.

Until the child is old enough to learn not to touch the controls, you can disable the range when you're not actually using it: For any type of range, pop the control knobs off and keep them in a handy yet childproof place; for a gas range with electronic ignition, unplug the range; for a 240-volt electric range, turn off the circuit breaker. Also consider installing a childproof shield (usually heatproof plastic, and available at some range dealers, children's furnishings stores, and housewares mail-order catalogs) at the front of the cooktop to keep the toddler from being able to touch pots or flames on the range.

▶ Range controls are hard to turn.

Grease may be gumming up the knobs and valves. Pop off the knobs by tugging them outward. (You may need to slip a dish cloth behind the knob to help you pull it off.) Soak knobs in warm water with a strong, grease-cutting detergent; then ream them out with wet, soapy pipe cleaners and rinse well. While knobs are off, spray the parts of the valves that are reachable with spray-on no-rinse cleanser and rub them clean with paper towels or a small, sturdy brush. Return the knobs to the rods. If this isn't sufficient, clean the valves themselves. Turn off the gas and unplug the range (the knobs may have electronic-ignition controls). Take the valves apart with two wrenches and clean them with steel wool and paint thinner. Lubricate them with a high-quality long-term lubricant, and then reassemble.

If controls are hard to turn because they're hard to grip, replace them. Find new knobs at an appliance parts dealer or large building-supply store. Bring an old knob with you to make sure the new knobs will fit.

▶ Gas burners with electronic ignition don't light.

If you have a modern range with electronic ignition (no pilot light; just a clicking sound before the burner lights), check that the stove is plugged securely into the electrical receptacle and that the circuit breaker isn't tripped or the fuse blown. Try turning on a burner and holding a lighted kitchen match to it. If it doesn't light, the stove is probably not receiving gas. Check the gas shutoff valve to make sure it's on. (The valve may be located under the cooktop, at the bottom of the cabinet, or behind the stove. When the handle is in line with the pipe, the valve is open; at right angles, it's closed.) You can verify the lack of gas by *carefully* loosening the gas connection to the stove only slightly, first making sure there are no open flames nearby (such as a cigarette or pilot light). If you hear no hiss and smell no gas, there's no gas supply. Retighten the connection and call the gas company. If you do smell gas, *immediately* tighten the connection. The problem is most likely in the range. Call for professional service.

If the burner will light with a match, check that the igniter is working: Remove the range top (after taking off the grates), turn off the lights, and turn on a burner. If you don't hear clicking and don't see sparks, the igniter is faulty and needs to be replaced. If the igniter sparks, the pilot light electrode may be dirty. To clean it, unplug the range and remove the metal bridge

or cover from above the pilot electrode (a small pointed metal rod between the tubes that lead to the burners). Clean the electrode with a soft cloth or small brush. If this doesn't work, call for professional service.

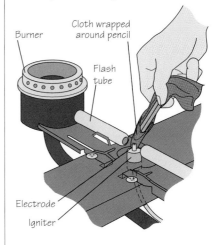

Cleaning electronic-ignition electrode

Burner

Cloth wrapped around pencil

Flash tube

Electrode

Igniter

▶ Gas burners with pilot don't light.

First check to see if the pilot light is on. It may be hidden under the range top; remove the grates and lift it up like a car hood. Some cooktops have one central pilot light for all burners, others have a pilot for each burner. If the pilot light is out and won't relight when you hold a match to it, look for the pilot adjusting screw along the tube that feeds gas to the pilot, near the gas manifold, and rotate it with a screwdriver while holding a match to the pilot. If the pilot still won't light, the cooktop may not be receiving gas (see opposite page). If there is gas, the pilot orifice may be clogged. Clean the pilot and its

Tip *Electronic, or "pilotless," ignitions have replaced standing pilot lights in new ranges and cooktops. Because they don't require a continuously burning pilot flame, they save energy. Electronic ignitions also provide a safety factor: They reignite a burner if the flame is blown out accidentally. In addition, they reduce heat buildup in the appliance, which is a welcome relief on hot days.*

SOLVING MECHANICAL PROBLEMS

cover, using a small copper wire or a pipe cleaner for the pilot; clear the pilot orifice with a straight pin or sewing needle (the actual orifice may be at the end of a feeder tube, not where the flame occurs). If the pilot still won't light, call for professional repairs.

If the pilot is lit and burners won't light, check the flash tubes radiating from it to each burner, making sure each tube is aligned in the slots or tabs that hold it in place (be careful—they may be hot). If the burner still won't light, you may need to increase the flame on the pilot; turn the pilot adjusting screw until the flame is robust. If you are successful, readjust the pilot to the lowest flame required for lighting the burners. If the burners won't light, try turning on one burner and lighting it with a match. If it lights, check the flash tube between it and the pilot again for misalignment or obstructions. If that's not the problem, call a repair technician.

Adjusting pilot

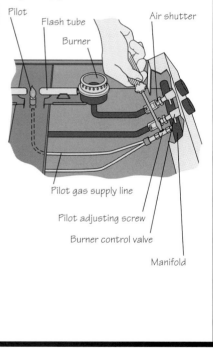

Pilot

Flash tube

Burner

Air shutter

Pilot gas supply line

Pilot adjusting screw

Burner control valve

Manifold

▶ One burner on gas range won't light.

Remove the range top. Check the flash tube (the tube leading from the pilot light to the burner). It may be knocked askew, so that gas can't reach the burner; jiggle it into place so slots, tabs, or other "feet" are aligned (be careful—it may be hot). Check it for obstructions, clear out any blockage with a pencil or pipe cleaner (depending on the diameter of the tube), and scrub the tube with a strong grease-cutting detergent. If it's too hard to remove from the stove, try reaming it out in place with a cleanser-soaked pipe cleaner or paper towel wrapped tightly around a pencil. If the burner still won't light, it may not be receiving gas due to clogged orifices or a faulty control valve. Clean out any clogs (see right). If that doesn't help, call a technician.

▶ Gas pilot light keeps going out.

The pilot flame is probably too low. Trace the gas supply tube running from the pilot light to the gas manifold (pipe with branches to burners); there should be an adjusting screw along the supply tube. Use a screwdriver to adjust the height of the pilot flame; the adjusting device is a cock (rotates without unscrewing) so you can turn it either way. Also check for drafts that may be blowing out the pilot: open windows, an open entryway without a curtain, frequently slammed doors, or a kitchen fan without a backdraft preventer.

▶ Gas burner has weak or uneven flame.

The burner is probably clogged with spilled food or grease. Remove the range top. If the burner has a removable cap, wash the cap in hot water and a grease-cutting detergent; rinse well, dry, and replace. If not, use pipe cleaners dipped in a no-rinse grease-cutting cleanser to ream out all the flame holes in the burner. If this does not clean out the grease sufficiently, lift out the burner assembly (removing any retaining screws from the support, if necessary) and wash it in hot sudsy water. Rinse well, immediately wipe dry, and use a hair dryer to dry the holes. If it still burns weakly, the control valve may be defective. Call a technician.

▶ Gas burners aren't hot enough.

Assuming the burners have been cleaned (see above), look at the flames themselves. They should be steady, tapered, and mainly blue with a little orange at the tip. If the flames are short and flat, too orange or yellow, or all-blue and roaring, the mixture of air to gas is incorrect. To adjust the gas/air mixture, look for an air shutter below each burner. Loosen the shutter retainer screw and open or close the shutter until the flame is steady, shapely, and blue with orange at the tip. Wear an oven mitt and be prepared to turn off gas to the burner should it go out suddenly while you are

Tip *The maximum output of individual burners for gas ranges and cooktops, measured in BTUs, varies from around 5,000 for small burners to 15,000 for burners on commercial-style ranges for residential use. Most older cooktops and range tops have two burners rated at 6,000 or 7,000 BTUs, and two burners rated around 9,000 BTUs. Now, it is more common for cooktops to have two burners rated at 8,000 or 9,000 BTUs and two at 11,000 or 12,000 BTUs.*

adjusting it. On some cooktops you can also adjust gas flow to each burner. If the gas flow is not already at maximum, increase flow by turning the adjusting nut located where the gas supply line for the burner branches off from the manifold.

If the burner flames grow weak only when the oven or broiler is on (or is set to a high temperature), the gas pipes in the house may not be sized correctly. Have a qualified plumber or heating specialist check them. If the pipes are not the problem, the range does not have a high enough BTU (heating capacity) rating to support both the stovetop and the oven at once. The only solutions are to replace the range with one that has a higher BTU rating, or to use an auxiliary appliance (such as a microwave oven or other electric cooker) in place of the oven, broiler, or a burner. Also consider obtaining a heat-powered oven convection fan to increase the efficiency of the oven so you can bake or roast more quickly or at a lower temperature.

▶ *Electric burner heats up only halfway or not at all.*

First see if the burner element is defective. Turn off power to the range. Slightly raise the edge of the burner element; pull it straight out. Switch it with another element of the same size that works, restore power, and turn on the burner. If there isn't another burner to switch it with, test it with a continuity tester or volt-ohmmeter (set at 4×1 ohms resistance). First touch the probes to the terminals to make sure current flows through the coil. Then touch the probes to each terminal and the outer shell of its coil, in turn; current should *not* flow.

If the suspect element does not test or work properly, buy a new one to replace it. If it does, the problem may be a faulty receptacle in the original burner cavity. Turn off power to the range, remove the drip pan from the defective burner, and locate the receptacle. Remove the bracket screw and pull the receptacle out (the wires will still be attached). If it's caked with crud, clean it off; use an emery board or sandpaper to clear the slots. If the receptacle is broken or the wires charred, replace it; disconnect the wires from the terminal screws in the back of the receptacle and take the old one to an appliance parts dealer for an exact replacement (bring the burner element too). If the wires are burned or the burner still doesn't work, call a technician.

Adjusting the burner air shutter

Removing a burner element

Testing receptacle

Cleaning a receptacle

Testing continuity of element

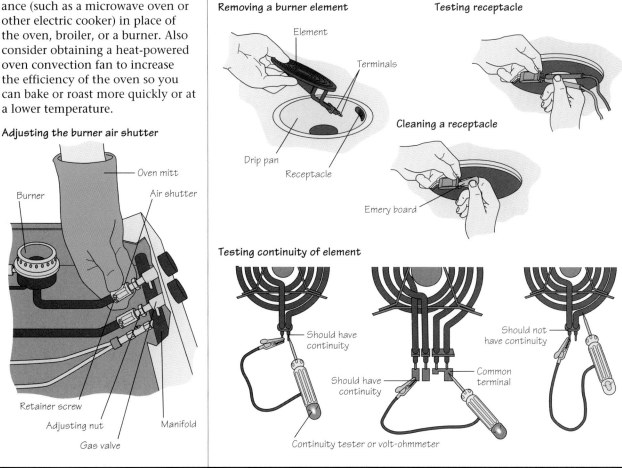

Tip   *When using a volt-ohmmeter (sometimes called a multitester) always recalibrate the zero setting before testing continuity. Set the selector dial for 4×1 ohms resistance, and touch the probes together. The electricity should flow effortlessly through the probes, with no resistance, yielding a 0 reading on the ohms scale. If the needle doesn't rest at the 0 mark, turn the ohms adjusting knob until it does. Now the tester is ready to use.*

SOLVING MECHANICAL PROBLEMS

▶ *Electric range is dead; nothing works.*

Check that there's electric power: Is the range plugged in? Have the circuit breakers been tripped or the fuses blown? Electric ranges are 240-volt and receive service from a pair of fuses or circuit breakers (which have their handles linked together). With some electrical installations the circuit breaker or fuse block for the range may be located with the main electrical disconnecting device, not in the circuit-breaker panel. If the range has a pull-out fuse block with cartridge fuses in it, the only way to check if they have blown is to test them. Pull out the fuse block, remove the cartridge fuses, and touch the probes of a continuity tester (or volt-ohmmeter set for R×1 ohms resistance) to each end of the fuse. If the stove is receiving power but won't work, call for service. At 240 volts, a shock can be fatal.

▶ *Electric burner has only one temperature—hot!*

The switch that controls the electricity to the burner is probably stuck in the full-heat position and should be replaced by a technician.

▶ *Electric self-venting range doesn't have hookup for duct.*

No duct hookup or connection is required. The hood and blower on the ceiling (or wall) should take care of the oven as well as the cooktop exhaust. A down-draft range, on the other hand, which has a vent and blower mounted on the cooktop, must be connected to a duct. Such ranges are usually ducted through the floor or out the lower part of the wall behind the range.

▶ *Gas oven burner won't light.*

First make sure that the unit is receiving gas: Light a burner on the cooktop; if it won't go on, check the gas shutoff valve. (See page 267.) If no gas is reaching the range, call the gas company.

If the oven has electronic ignition, make sure it's plugged in and receiving power. (Try a burner on the cooktop, or a small appliance plugged into the same receptacle as the range.) Local fluctuations in electric power can briefly disable electronic ignitions; try again in a few minutes. If you don't hear any clicking when you turn on the oven, or if there's a lot of clicking followed by silence (and still no burner ignition), the igniter is broken and needs to be replaced. Some oven igniters are sparkless and don't make a clicking sound; you can tell if they are working because they glow red-hot.

If the oven has a gas pilot light, the pilot has probably gone out. The oven pilot is often at the bottom rear; you'll have to pull out the broiler "drawer" to reach it. Look for a red reset button; it should be near the front, but if it's back near the pilot light, you'll need a long pole, such as a broom handle, to reach it. Have some long fireplace or barbecue matches and a set of tongs or long-handled pliers handy. Kneeling by the open oven door, light the match (and keep it lit) and grasp it in the tongs or pliers. Keeping your head out of the oven to protect hair and eyelashes, press the red button with one hand (or with the broom handle) while with the other you apply the lighted match to the oven pilot until it lights. This may take several tries; persist. Once the pilot is on, the burner should light. If the pilot light goes out frequently, it may be set too low. Look for a pilot adjusting screw for the oven pilot under the range top (not all ranges have one). With a screwdriver, set the screw for a higher flame.

If the pilot works but the burner still won't go on, call a technician.

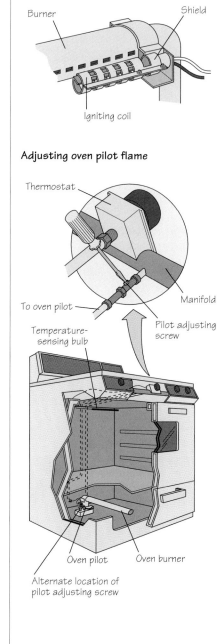

Checking sparkless igniter

Burner — Shield

Igniting coil

Adjusting oven pilot flame

Thermostat

To oven pilot

Temperature-sensing bulb

Manifold

Pilot adjusting screw

Oven pilot — Oven burner

Alternate location of pilot adjusting screw

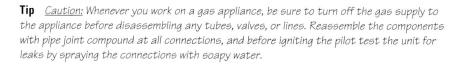

▶ Gas broiler won't light.

The thermocouple (a sensor device attached to the pilot light, that prevents gas flow unless the pilot is on) may be dirty, out of place, or broken. If you can reach it, you may be able to clean it and reposition it. (See page 242.) Otherwise, have a technician repair or replace it.

▶ Gas broiler flame is too weak.

If the broiler heats unevenly or poorly, grease spatters may have clogged many of the burner ports. Turn off gas to the appliance to extinguish the pilot and let it cool. If possible, remove the burner unit to clean it: Unscrew the brackets that hold it in place and gently place it on a work surface covered with newspapers. Ream out all the burner ports with pipe cleaners and clean the surface. If necessary, scrub it with a no-rinse household cleaner and dry it immediately; dry out the portholes with a hair dryer. If you can't remove the burner, clear the holes with pipe cleaners.

▶ Gas oven light doesn't work.

Make sure the stove is receiving electricity. Replace the bulb with an oven-rated type designed to withstand high temperatures (available in most supermarkets). Turn off power to the oven at the fuse or circuit-breaker panel, and let the bulb and its housing cool before beginning to work. If the bulb has a cover, remove it carefully; replace the bulb and restore the cover. Restore power and try turning on the bulb again. If this fails, the door switch is defective. Turn off power, open the oven door, and remove the switch by gently prying it out from the door frame (use a screwdriver on each side). Disconnect the wires and test the switch by touching each probe of a continuity

tester or volt-ohmmeter to the switch terminals. It should have continuity when you push in the switch button. If it does not, replace the switch. If the light still doesn't work, call a technician.

Removing an oven light switch

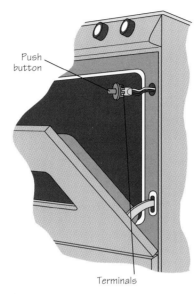

Push button

Terminals

▶ Gas oven vents directly into the room.

Old-fashioned woodburner and trashburner ovens had flue pipes, but modern gas and electric ovens don't need them. Many of them vent to the cooktop, which in turn is vented by the hood and blower unit. In urban areas many residences (especially older multifamily rental properties) have no stove hoods, vent fans, or duct work, and hence only vent into the kitchen; in this situation, a window fan set to exhaust (and cleaned frequently) can do much to clear the air.

▶ Gas oven doesn't hold its set temperature.

If the oven cools down (even when the door has not been opened), inspect the door gasket. If the gasket is worn, torn, or cracked, replace it. In some models you can just pull it off and attach a new one. In others you'll need a repair person to loosen the oven liner or remove the door.

If the oven overheats consistently, check if it has an exhaust vent at the back of the cooktop or under one of the cooktop burners. Clear any obstructions from the vent, and make sure that the hole in the stovetop reflector pan is aligned with the hole of the vent.

The thermostat may need to be recalibrated, the temperature sensor may need replacing, or the oven may have lost insulation (due to rodents tearing it out for their nests). In such events, call for professional repairs.

▶ Gas oven thermostat does not maintain set temperature.

The control knob that governs the oven thermostat may have drifted slightly into a setting that's too high or too low. You can adjust the control knob, although it may take several tries over several days to get it precisely right.

First obtain a high-quality oven thermometer (or better yet, a precise temperature tester, available at appliance parts stores), place it in the middle of the center oven rack, and record what temperature the oven reaches after 20 minutes at each of several temperature settings. (You'll probably have to let the oven cool and start over again to get a full and accurate range of readings.) The temperature regulator is a complicated spring-loaded device located behind the oven

---

Tip *For energy efficiency choose a convection oven, which uses a fan to blow heat over the food. Such ovens use about one-third less energy than conventional ovens.*

control knob. Remove the knob but do *not* remove the control (it's difficult to reassemble once the spring has sprung). In some ovens there will be a pointer and notches on the back of the knob; by moving the pointer a notch, you'll change the oven temperature 10° F. (You may have to loosen screws on the back of the knob, or use a screwdriver to lift the pointer slightly, before you can move the pointer.) On other ovens there'll be nothing on the back of the knob, but you'll see an adjusting screw at the front of the control; use a screwdriver to move it just a hair. Now turn on the oven again and see what temperature it reaches after 20 minutes at a moderate setting (350° F). Try it again at higher and lower settings. Be prepared to make several trial-and-error attempts before the oven performs precisely as desired.

If altering the temperature regulator fails, the oven thermostat may have to be replaced or recalibrated professionally.

Adjusting oven temperature regulator

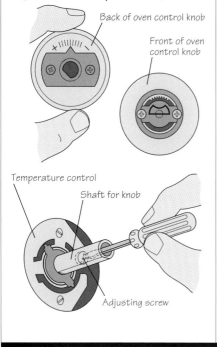

Back of oven control knob

Front of oven control knob

Temperature control

Shaft for knob

Adjusting screw

▶ Gas oven sweats.

Check for a worn-out gasket and replace it (see page 271).

▶ Baked food is often burned or soggy.

If food is often burned, the oven is probably running hot; if soggy, it's running cool. Obtain a high-quality oven thermometer, place it in the middle of the center rack, and compare the temperature to that of the setting to verify. Adjust the control knob (see page 271) and/or replace or recalibrate the thermostat (or call a technician to do so). Until the oven is repaired, if it is running cool, bake food at the back and well to the side on a high rack; if oven is too hot, use a low rack and place food in the center front area. Consider obtaining a heat-activated convection fan to keep the air circulating evenly in the oven and eliminate hot and cool spots.

▶ Baked food tastes awful.

Assuming neither the cook nor the recipe is at fault, it's probably residue from a caustic oven cleaner turning to vapor and settling on the food. With oven turned off, fill a spray bottle with hot water and spray all over the oven (including broiler); wipe with clean rags or paper towels. Heat the oven to 400° to 450° F and then open the door. If an unpleasant smell persists, let the oven cool, wash it with hot water again. Refill the spray bottle with bottled unsweetened lemon juice (or vinegar) and spray and wipe once more. Consider switching to a lye-free oven-cleaning product in which the active element is baking soda, vinegar, or citrus oil.

▶ Electric oven bakes food unevenly.

There may not be sufficient air circulation inside the oven. Consider installing a heat-activated portable convection fan or a permanent convection fan unit.

▶ Electric oven consistently overbakes or underbakes food.

The temperature regulator is no longer accurate. Turn off power at the circuit breaker and detach the oven control knob. You may be able to adjust the temperature regulator (see page 271). If not, the temperature regulator will have to be replaced; call a technician.

▶ Electric oven light doesn't work.

Assuming that the oven is getting power, the bulb may be loose or burned out. Obtain an oven-safe appliance bulb (available at supermarkets). Turn off power to the oven at the fuse or circuit-breaker panel, and let the bulb and its housing cool before beginning work. If the bulb has a cover, remove it carefully. Replace the bulb and return the cover. Restore power and try turning on the bulb again. If this fails, the problem may be the switch (see page 271).

▶ Automatic oven-cleaning feature doesn't work.

It's likely that either the temperature regulator is broken or the oven door latch is broken (see opposite page). Both should be professionally repaired, especially the latter: Don't try to overcome the door-lock mechanism to force the oven to clean itself, because the influx of air into the oven when the temperature is at flash point (550° F) can

Tip *The power for an electric oven is controlled by a separate circuit breaker. Because the oven is a 240-volt appliance, it has a double breaker consisting of two 120-volt breakers connected together.*

cause a flaming explosion of vaporized grease.

If you decide to ignore the self-cleaning feature for the present, when you clean the oven by hand make sure to rinse off all traces of oven cleaner, because chemical residues will damage the porcelain if you later decide to have the self-cleaning feature repaired. Choose a noncaustic, kitchen-safe type of cleaner (for example, one based on citrus oils, vinegar, or baking soda rather than lye) to minimize the danger of chemical residue.

▶ Electric oven door latch is broken.

Check the manufacturer's directions for the oven to see if you can correct the problem. If not, call for professional repairs; along with the lock itself, the fault could lie in the front door-lock switch or lock solenoid.

▶ Electric oven or broiler doesn't work.

First make sure power is on for the oven (see page 270). Next check the burner element for the oven or (if different) the broiler. To test the element, turn off power to the oven at the circuit-breaker or fuse panel, and then carefully remove the element according to manufacturer's directions. Test the element for continuity by removing the wires and, with a volt-ohmmeter (set for 4×1 ohms resistance) or a continuity tester, holding a probe to each terminal of the element. If there is no continuity, it is defective. If there *is* continuity between one terminal and the outer covering of the element, the element has a short circuit and should be replaced. Inspect the wires; if they're burned, call for

professional repairs. If the element and wires are in good condition, the thermostat control is defective and will have to be repaired or replaced.

Removing an oven heating element

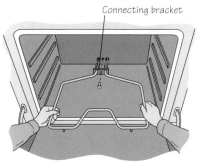

Connecting bracket

Note: Power must be off.

Testing an oven heating element

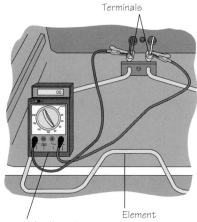

Terminals

Element

Volt-ohmmeter

▶ Microwave oven has lingering odor from burned food.

Pour a cup of water into an oven-proof bowl and add 1 tablespoon of lemon juice. Place in the microwave and bring to a boil at the highest setting. Lower the temperature to "simmer" (or equivalent) and lightly boil for three minutes. Remove the cup and wipe dry the inside and door of the microwave. If this doesn't remove the odor, repeat the process.

▶ Microwave oven heats intermittently.

The air vents may be blocked, causing the oven to overheat and turn off. Check the owner's manual for locations of the air vents, and (with the unit unplugged) inspect them and clean them if clogged. Let the oven cool one hour, then try again. If this doesn't work, the thermal cutout switch may be defective. Have it professionally repaired, assuming that the estimated repair cost is markedly less than that of a new machine.

▶ Microwave oven takes longer to cook than cookbook says.

Various models of microwaves have different wattages. The less expensive models usually have a lower wattage than higher-priced ones. This means that foods cook more slowly or require a higher setting. Aside from defrosting or keeping hot foods warm, routinely use the highest setting for cooking.

If the microwave is operating on the same circuit with any other appliance, cooking time will increase when the other appliance is also in use. If you are remodeling your kitchen, provide a dedicated circuit for the microwave oven (not because it draws so much power, but to avoid having other appliances interfere with its operation). Fluctuations in local voltage will also prolong cooking time.

Tip   *Just how does a microwave work? A transformer steps up 120-volt house current into high-voltage current, which enters a magnetron (electronic tube) that converts it to electromagnetic waves. These waves are guided into the oven compartment, where a fanlike stirrer at the top spins and bounces them around. Another fan keeps the magnetron cool. The waves agitate molecules in the food, causing friction that produces heat.*

▶ Microwave oven needs installing over a range.

A combination microwave oven and exhaust hood will let you exhaust kitchen odors while having all your cooking appliances in a single area. These combinations, which cost considerably more than standard microwaves, can either vent back into the kitchen or connect to the existing duct work. The steps you will need to take to install them are: removing the existing range exhaust hood; installing a ventilating duct, if required; running a new 20-amp electrical line that places the microwave on its own circuit (or having an electrician do this); and installing the new unit.

Disconnect the power and remove the old range hood before buying the new unit so you can measure the distance from the wall to the center of the exhaust hood and choose a model with similar dimensions.

▶ Microwave oven may be leaking radiation.

There are several inexpensive microwave radiation detectors on the market (including one with magnetic backing that you can leave attached to the side of the unit). To use a detector, turn on the oven and move the probe over the vents, the door, and the door cracks. If radiation is leaking, the probe will glow bright red. Have a leaking unit repaired professionally or replace it.

▶ Microwave oven emits sparks.

See whether grease has collected on the heads of the screws that hold a shelf. If so, wash the screws with warm soapy water, using a sponge or dishcloth. Metal (or metal-trimmed) containers or utensils, including dishware trimmed with gold, silver, platinum, or cobalt blue, shouldn't be used in the microwave; nor should plastic-coated metal bag ties. A temperature probe will cause sparks if it's plugged into the microwave but not inserted into food. And if the unit has a metal cooking rack, it will cause sparks if it's not firmly hooked into place or if it's left on the oven floor while the unit is operating.

If none of these possibilities is causing the problem, have the machine serviced professionally; however, get an estimate for repair costs first, as a new microwave may cost little more.

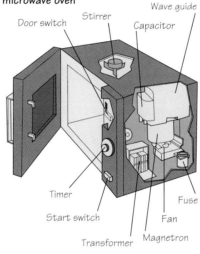

Identifying components of a microwave oven

Door switch · Stirrer · Wave guide · Capacitor · Timer · Start switch · Fan · Transformer · Magnetron · Fuse

▶ Dishes don't get dry.

Make sure the *Power Dry* (or *Hot Dry*) button is fully depressed and is not popping out again. If machine is very heavily loaded or is loaded incorrectly, some items may not dry. (Check the owner's manual for proper loading.) Open door immediately after drying cycle is complete, to vent any remaining water vapor before it settles onto the dishes again. If all this fails, call for service.

▶ Dishwasher is spewing suds.

When suds erupt from all orifices, immediately turn off the dishwasher, leaving its door shut. You can now take as much time as you need to clean the foam from the floor and sink cabinet before proceeding further. Dishwashers can cope only with the nonsudsing dishwasher detergents designed for them. Eruptions occur whenever even a small amount of a foaming cleaner (such as regular dishwashing liquid, laundry detergent, or even many types of general-purpose household cleaners) gets into a dishwasher. This is one of the most common reasons for service calls; fortunately, the repair is easy.

Turn off the water supply to the dishwasher; then turn the unit on again (still without opening the door), and immediately set it to the *Drain* or *Exhaust* portion of the cycle. (If there's no specific *Drain* button, rotate the timer dial until you can hear draining noises or, in a portable model, can see the exhaust; normally, this occurs during the last minute or so before the drying cycle begins). Let the unit drain completely, turn it off, and remove the dishes. The bottom of the machine will be filled with suds. Remove the bottom basket and scoop out and discard as much foam as possible. To purge the remainder, start the dishwasher again (still without water), immediately setting it to *Drain*. Once draining is complete, fast-forward to *Off*, and then to *Drain* again. Repeat six or seven times or until all foam is purged from the bottom of the dishwasher.

To prevent a recurrence, use only dishwasher detergent. If dishes have been soaking in the sink (or have been filled with household cleaners), rinse thoroughly before loading them in the dishwasher.

Tip *Microwave ovens have fairly complex components that should be repaired professionally. However, if you are comfortable with analyzing circuits and working on electronic equipment, you may be able to diagnose and replace faulty switches, a broken door latch, or defective fan on your own. Consult the owner's manual if you wish to attempt repairs yourself.*

▶ Dishwasher needs routine maintenance.

Dishwashers clean dishes but not themselves. Grease-wads, glass shards, pottery chips, and suicidal measuring spoons will eventually affect a dishwasher's functioning. Every month, on a regular schedule, remove all baskets. If they are grimy, clean them in the sink or bathtub. Repair any nicks in the basket coatings or on walls with dishwasher-epoxy coating (from a hardware store). Remove any rust spots with rust-removing compound. With a screwdriver, wrench, or fingers, loosen the nut attaching the spray arms. Shake arms vigorously under very warm running water and/or use pipe cleaners to remove all foreign matter (broken glass, food bits) from the holes.

Clean the tub of debris and then clean the pump screen (it's in the depression in the bottom of the dishwasher, usually under the lower spray arm). With many models, you'll have to feel around carefully to find and pick out the broken glass and small utensils that may be lodged in the pump area. If it's necessary to use a cleaner on any dishwasher part, rinse very well. Wash the door of the dishwasher with hot water and use a slightly abrasive soapless scouring sheet dipped in hot water to clean under the door-crack and along the unit's lower front wall (the areas you can't actually see, where a sticky grease-and-soap sludge collects). Scrape out any dried soap from the soap dispenser cups, and if the cover doesn't move freely, rinse off any dried soap that's impeding it. If the machine has an air gap, remove its cover and clean any grime collecting there. Return everything to its place, and refill the rinsing agent dispenser (if applicable).

▶ Dishwasher won't start.

First check to make sure electric power is getting through. Make sure that the unit is turned on, that the circuit breaker hasn't tripped or the fuse blown, and that the door is latched properly. On some portable models the machine won't start unless the faucet is turned on. If the dishwasher is plugged into a receptacle under the sink shared by the garbage disposer, make sure the plugs aren't reversed; the disposer outlet may be controlled by a switch that is off. If none of these is the problem, verify that the dishwasher receptacle is receiving power by plugging in a lamp or small appliance. If there's no power, see page 208. If the dishwasher is wired directly to a junction box, with no plug, turn off power to the circuit, remove the junction box cover, carefully disconnect the wires, turn the circuit back on, and test the circuit wires for power. If there's no power, call an electrician.

If power is getting through and the unit still won't start, the door latch, the door switch, or the motor may be the problem. If the latch doesn't engage completely, it may not be tripping the door switch. Have the latch replaced. If the latch works, test the door switch. Turn off power at the circuit breaker and remove the control panel: Open the door, remove the screws that hold the inside door panel, take off the panel, and remove the exposed screws at the top of the door that hold the control panel to the front of the door. Steady the control panel with one hand and close the door, then lower the panel carefully to expose the door switch. Disconnect

Locating dishwasher components

Cleaning the spray arms and pump screen

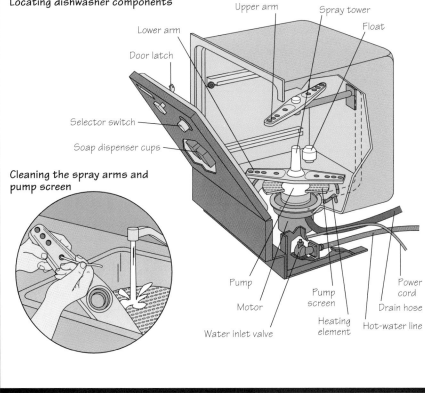

Upper arm
Spray tower
Lower arm
Float
Door latch
Selector switch
Soap dispenser cups
Pump
Motor
Pump screen
Power cord
Drain hose
Heating element
Hot-water line
Water inlet valve

Tip *The average dishwasher lasts about 11 years, according to the Association of Home Appliance Manufacturers, but many models can last as long as 20 years with proper use and care.*

the two wires from the switch and latch the door shut. With a continuity tester or volt-ohmmeter (set for 4×1 ohms resistance), touch the two probes to the two terminals. If there is no continuity, replace the door switch. If there is, call for repairs to the motor.

Removing control panel

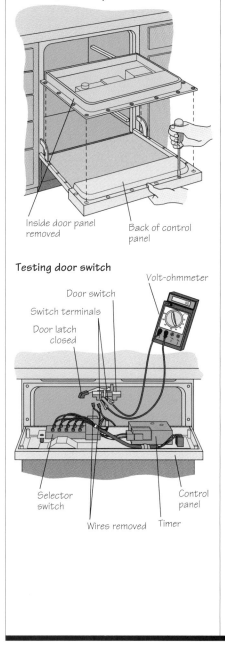

Inside door panel removed

Back of control panel

Testing door switch

Volt-ohmmeter

Door switch

Switch terminals

Door latch closed

Selector switch

Wires removed   Timer

Control panel

▶ *Dishwasher won't stop filling.*

Immediately turn off the water and leave the dishwasher door shut. Allow the machine to complete its cycle. After dishwashing is complete, check the float switch; the float should move up and down freely. If jiggling it doesn't make it function, shut off all power to the dishwasher, disconnect the wires from the switch, unscrew the float switch, and replace it with a new one.

If the float switch works, the problem may be in the timer or in the inlet valve. Remove as much water from the bottom as possible. Lift the pump filter and clean it; pumps often collect broken glass, lightweight utensils, long-lost earrings, and the like, which can interfere with functioning. Replace the filter, shut the door, and turn the water on again. Start the washer and turn it off after a few seconds. If the water doesn't stop, the inlet and/or drain valve is the problem and should be replaced; call for repairs. If the water does stop, continue running the dishwasher through its full cycle. If it overfills again, complete the cycle, turn off the water, and check the timer (see right), or call for repairs.

Removing float switch

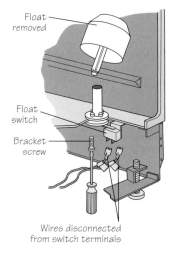

Float removed

Float switch

Bracket screw

Wires disconnected from switch terminals

▶ *Dishwasher leaks.*

If the machine isn't overfilling (see left), and if the leak is clear, not foamy, check to see that the machine is level by opening the door and setting a carpenter's level on the ledge (or hold the level against the edge of the door opening). To level the machine, open the bottom access panel and use a wrench to turn the adjusting screw on one or more legs (you may have to loosen locknuts first; retighten them when the machine is level).

If the leak persists, check the float valve; the float should move up and down freely. If there are trickles around the door, the door may not be tight. Loosen the screws in the lock strike, then readjust the strike so that it will be firmly aligned with the door latch. If there is a gasket around the door, check that it is in place and not cracked, broken, or caked with debris; if it is faulty, replace it. Also check the water supply tube and drain hose; tighten the clamps, if applicable. If the leak persists, call for service.

▶ *Dishwasher won't fill or continue cycle.*

Make sure that the water is turned on and that the water valve is open. (The water valve may be located under the sink, under the floor in the basement, or in a closet or garage behind the wall.) Also look to see whether the dishwasher float valve is stuck; the float should move up and down freely. If not, it will need replacement or servicing.

Water pressure should be between 20 and 120 psi; if it's too low, the machine can't fill sufficiently to run. To test, with no other water running in the house, place a ½-gallon container under the hot-water faucet nearest the dishwasher. Turn on the faucet; the container should fill in 14

Tip   *A normal dishwasher cycle has two washes and three rinses. An energy-saving cycle, which is intended for lightly soiled dishes, has one wash and two rinses. A heavy-duty cycle usually consists of three washes and four rinses.*

seconds or less. If pressure is too low, contact the local water company to learn if this is an areawide problem or if your house pipes need to be replaced. You may be able to operate the dishwasher in a low-pressure area by avoiding use of the dishwasher when any other water in the house (including toilet) is in use. If the house pressure is adequate, the water line to the dishwasher may be blocked. To check, close the shutoff valve, remove the front access panel, disconnect the water line from the dishwasher, place a bucket or pan under it, and open the shut-off valve slowly to see if water sprays out in full force, then close it. If pressure is weak, disconnect the line from the valve and either clear the line or replace it.

Finally, a faulty timer may be closing the inlet valve too early, or the automatic shutoff valve may be faulty. Read the owner's manual to learn whether you can readily reach these parts or will need a service call. Checking the timer involves turning off power, removing the panel from the inside of the door, loosening the control panel screws, closing the door, and pulling the control panel out from the door front (with the wires attached). The timer consists of a motor that runs a clock that trips a series of switches, in sequence. Disconnect the motor wires from the wires leading to the power source and test the motor by touching the probes of a continuity tester to the two motor leads; if there is no continuity, the motor is faulty and the timer must be replaced. Next check the switch terminals for continuity. Unplug the block of wires from the switch to expose several pairs of terminals. With a continuity tester or a volt-ohmmeter (set for 4×1 ohms resistance), test each pair for continuity, turning the timer knob to the dishwashing cycle that those terminals control. (Consult the owner's manual or wiring diagram on the door to identify which terminals control what cycle.) If any pair fails the continuity test, replace the timer.

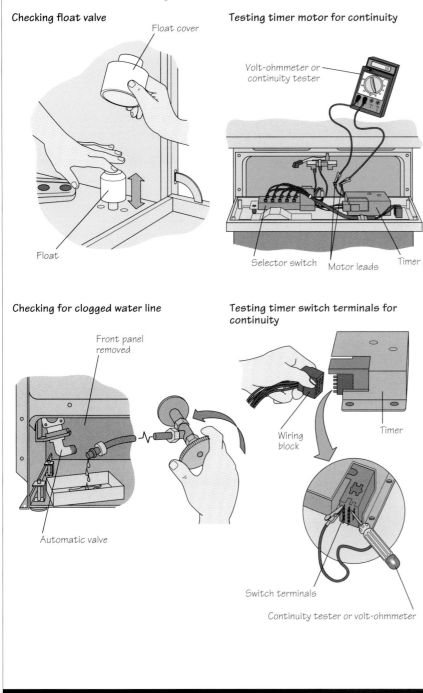

Checking float valve

Float cover

Float

Checking for clogged water line

Front panel removed

Automatic valve

Testing timer motor for continuity

Volt-ohmmeter or continuity tester

Selector switch

Motor leads

Timer

Testing timer switch terminals for continuity

Wiring block

Timer

Switch terminals

Continuity tester or volt-ohmmeter

Tip *Many dishwashers have an internal mechanism for grinding up food scraps, just like a garbage disposer, and ejecting the remains with the drain water. It is located in the center of the tub floor, over the pump, and has a screen guard that prevents dishes (but not silverware) from getting snagged by the disposer blades.*

▶ Dishwasher won't drain and leaves standing water in bottom.

A small amount of water must always remain at the bottom of the dishwasher. If a lot of water is left, check and clean the pump filter or screen. Also check for a kink or clog in the drain hose; you may be able to work the clog free by pushing it through to the end. If not, turn off power to the machine, remove the front access panel, detach the hose from the drain valve by loosening the hose clamp (be ready for an outflow), detach the other end from the air gap (or sink drain, if there is no air gap), and poke a long wire through it to clear it; or call for service. If the hose isn't blocked, the air gap (usually located on the countertop or sink deck) may be clogged with debris. Remove the debris with tweezers, a brush, or a wire. Also check for blockage in the sink P-trap or drainpipe. If these steps don't solve the problem, call for service.

Disconnecting drain hose and cleaning air gap

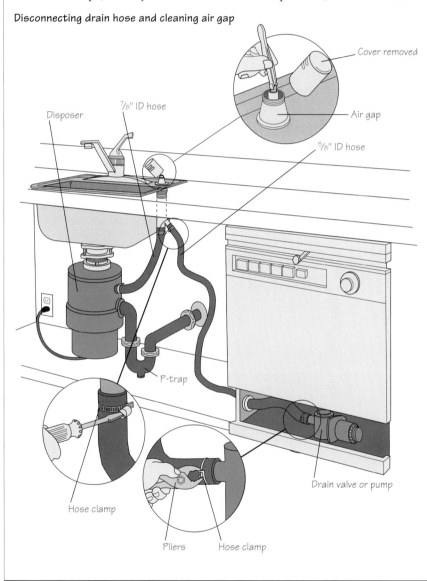

▶ Dishwasher air gap leaks.

Make sure that the hoses are properly connected. The hose from the outlet side of the dishwasher pump goes to the inlet tube (smaller diameter) of the air valve. The hose from the outlet side of the air gap (larger diameter) goes to the sink drain or disposer. Check the hose to the sink drain to make sure there is no kink or debris in it, and clear it or replace it if necessary; also check the sink P-trap and drain to make sure they aren't blocked. If none of these is the problem, the air gap may be defective. To replace it, disconnect the hoses from the bottom of the gap; remove the cover and tightening nut from the top of the gap and slip it down through the sink or countertop opening.

▶ Dishes don't get clean.

Poor performance may be caused by food particles and other matter clogging the spray arms and pump. Perform the maintenance routine (see page 275), cleaning arms, pump screen, door area, and soap cup. Add rinsing agent if cup is empty (the rinsing agent reduces spotting on glassware). When you load the unit, make sure that dishes aren't tightly nested and that no tall dishes interfere with the action of the spray arms. (Rotate each arm before you start the machine to be sure it's not impeded.) Make sure no silverware is sticking out of the bottom of the silverware basket. Fill soap cups less than completely full, and don't wet the detergent before starting the machine.

Water that isn't hot enough can cause poor performance. See that your water-heater thermostat is set to the temperature recommended in the owner's manual. If dishes are washed just after someone has filled a bathtub or taken a long shower,

Tip *If the dishwasher drain hose is not connected to an air gap above the sink counter, make sure the hose is secured in such a way that it loops as high as possible under the counter close to its connection with the drainpipe. Secure the top of the loop to the bottom of the countertop with a hose bracket.*

the hot-water supply may be used up; run the dishwasher only when there's plenty of hot water.

If the problem persists, the heating element may be faulty. Use an immersible thermometer (such as a confection or deep-fry thermometer) to check how hot the tap water is after it has been running for about a minute. If it is considerably below the water-heater thermostat setting, the problem is with the water heater. If not, measure the temperature of the water inside the dishwasher when it is partly full. If it is below 150° F, call for service.

▶ Dishwasher is too noisy or makes unusual noises.

Unusual noises are caused by spray arms whacking dishes or utensils, dishes or utensils whacking each other, and fallen utensils getting whacked or ground up by the pump; utensils may also be poking out the bottom of the silverware basket. Check the owner's manual for proper loading of the machine. Load tall items at the edges of the baskets, where they can't interfere with the rotation of the spray arms. Load other items carefully to minimize their chances of escaping from their slots or racks and colliding with each other. Lightweight items (such as shallow aluminum mixing bowls, shot glasses, and plastic measuring cups) often float up and interfere with the spray arms or else plunge down into the pump area. You can obtain enameled wire-mesh minibaskets (at hardware and housewares stores) to lock up small items; a lightweight bowl can be anchored by placing a large wire-mesh colander or sieve firmly over it. Some

items (such as tiny plastic measuring spoons) may simply have to be washed in the sink.

As soon as you hear strange noises (thuds, crunches, grinding) unlatch the dishwasher door and wait a few seconds for the machine to stop completely. Open the door and check for loose utensils. Wearing rubber gloves to protect against hot water, correct the loading. If something has broken, turn off power and temporarily remove the bottom basket so you can fish out all the shards from the pump area and the baskets; broken glass or ceramic is liable to damage the pump. Turn on power and lock the door again to resume dishwashing.

If the dishwasher makes a sound like a distant tambourine, spray arms may be full of food bits or broken glass. Remove arms and clean them (see page 275). For grinding noises check and clear the pump area. If grinding sounds persist, there may not be enough water in the machine (at least 1 inch above the sump) when the dishwasher is running. If this is the problem, call for service.

▶ Silverware gets tarnished.

Real silver, silver plate, and any other precious metal (including fine china edged with gold, silver, platinum, or cobalt blue) shouldn't be washed in a dishwasher, precisely because the process does produce tarnish. However, if you must, wash them separately from other dishes on a short cycle and immediately dry each piece by hand with a soft dish towel.

If the silverware is actually stainless steel and you're getting black streaks, it's not tarnish. Aluminum cookware often creates black streaks on other utensils in

the dishwasher; it should be washed separately, or kept well away from other utensils. Throwaway aluminum baking pans are prone to melt in hot water and should not be dishwasher-cleaned at all.

▶ Soap dispenser won't open.

See whether a buildup of dried soap is caked in the cup; if so, clean it out. If someone packed in and tamped down too much soap, the soap may have formed a hard lump when it got wet, sealing the dispenser shut. If you can't jiggle the cup open again, wash dishes using the short cycle for a few weeks, or use the long cycle by adding soap manually at the end of the fill cycle. After a dozen or so loads, the soap lump will have dissolved and the problem should correct itself. Otherwise, replace the dispenser.

▶ Dishwasher basket has lost plastic coating.

You can dip the worn spots into the rubberized plastic dip used to coat tool handles, and/or cover worn spots with hot-melt glue or dishwasher epoxy. Alternatively, buy clear flexible tubing (¼-inch OD, ⅛-inch ID) at the hardware store. Cut ¼-inch pieces and slide them over the exposed tips of the racks.

▶ Dishwasher emits odor resembling melting wax.

Some plastic item (such as a container lid) may have fallen into the bottom of the unit and gotten wedged up against the heating element. Unplug the dishwasher. When it's cooled, inspect the area around the element, feeling around for the unseen object.

Tip   *To diminish routine noisiness, consider sliding a layer or two of rubber-backed carpet (for instance, low-priced samples or scraps from a carpet store) or a rubber doormat or thick bath mat under the machine.*

▶ Light doesn't come on when door is opened.

Make sure the switch next to the light unit (if it has a master switch) is set to *On* and that the refrigerator is actually plugged in and running. Unplug the unit and replace the bulb with an appliance bulb of the same wattage specified for refrigerators. If this doesn't work, the door switch or the light circuit may be defective and need replacing. To check the door switch, unplug the refrigerator and carefully pry out the switch with a putty knife. Disconnect the wires and touch the probes of a continuity tester or volt-ohmmeter (set for 4×1 ohms resistance) to the terminals of the switch. It should show continuity when the plunger is out. If there are four terminals, test one pair at a time with the plunger in both positions. One pair should test for continuity with the switch on, the other pair with the switch off. If the switch doesn't test accordingly, replace it. If the light still doesn't work, call for repairs.

Testing the door switch

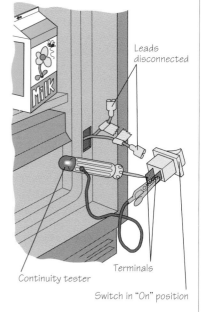

Leads disconnected

Continuity tester

Terminals

Switch in "On" position

▶ Motor doesn't run.

Assuming the unit isn't in its defrost cycle, check that it is plugged in and receiving power. (If the interior light doesn't come on when you open the door, see if another small appliance will work when plugged into the refrigerator receptacle. If not, check the circuit breaker or fuse.) Check that the temperature control is turned on; turn it off and on several times to see if the compressor starts. If it doesn't, call for service. If it starts but then turns off again, remove all other appliances from the circuit and see if it starts again. If so (or if the plug feels hot) the problem may be voltage drops on the circuit or house electrical system. Turn off power to the circuit and call an electrician.

▶ Refrigerator doesn't keep food cold enough.

If the refrigerator is located next to a range, a heating vent, or in direct sunlight, consider relocating it. Check that the thermostat control is set to a temperature between 34° and 40° F. If not, adjust it one notch or number and allow the temperature to stabilize for 24 hours before changing it again. Make sure there is nothing (such as a food package or partly opened or crooked bin or compartment) that's preventing the door from closing solidly. Make sure the base grille is not blocked, and check whether the condenser coil behind the grille is clogged with dust. (In a very old refrigerator, the coil may be in the back.) At least once a year, vacuum the coil gently with a crevice-cleaning tool or dust carefully with a refrigerator-coil brush. Also make sure the compartment fan is running.

Heat may also be coming from the refrigerator light if it is not turning off when the door is shut. Push each switch button (the one at the light and the one near the door). If one of the switches does not turn the light off, it is faulty. With power off, remove the switch and test it for continuity with a volt-ohmmeter or continuity tester (see left).

Cleaning condenser coils

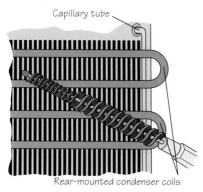

Capillary tube

Rear-mounted condenser coils

Condenser coils

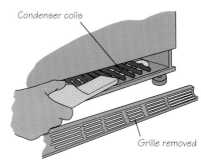

Grille removed

▶ Refrigerator or freezer is running too cold.

Check that the thermostat is set for the correct temperature (38° to 40° F). If not, change it one number or notch and let it stabilize for 24 hours before adjusting it again. Otherwise, the thermostat may be faulty or the temperature-sensing bulb may be defective or improperly positioned. Call for service to have both replaced at the same time.

Tip *The coolant used in most refrigerators is freon or a similar chlorofluorocarbon (CFC). Because of environmental concerns about CFCs, refrigerator manufacturers now offer optional coolants.*

▶ Refrigerator runs constantly.

If the thermostat control is adjusted for a very cold temperature (34° F or under), try keeping the refrigerator at 40° F instead. Also check the condenser coils for dust and dirt and clean if necessary. If large amounts of hot food are placed in the unit, it may cause the motor to run, as could hot weather. Locating the unit with insufficient clearance behind or above it (minimum 2 inches), next to a range or hot-air vent, or in direct sunlight could also be a cause. Leaving the door open too long or opening it too often makes the refrigerator run; make sure nothing is keeping the door from shutting solidly. Finally, carefully inspect the door gasket; if cracked, broken, or loose, replace it. (Another sign of a problem gasket is water collecting in the lower bins.) To test, close the door on a piece of paper. When you pull the paper out, you should feel tension. If you don't, replace the gasket (see right).

▶ Water drips onto floor.

First see whether the drain from the freezer is clogged. To clear the drain, remove ice from the floor of the freezer; mix 1 teaspoon baking soda in 2 cups hot water, and pour it down the drain using a bulb baster.

If the refrigerator is located in a cool area (garage, utility room), condensation from the heat given off by the freezer motor can build up and drip onto the floor. To check, place a small room heater near the unit and keep it turned on for a day or two. If this stops the dripping, move the refrigerator to a warmer spot. Also note that when a self-defrosting refrigerator/freezer

is kept in an area that's near freezing, the freezer portion may turn off, and food inside will spoil. If the room with the refrigerator is merely chilly at night (in the 60° F range), turn the freezer temperature up one notch.

Also examine the tubes leading to and from the motor. If they are coated with frost (which in turn melts and leaks), try insulating the suction line (near the compressor) with foam tubing insulation or wraparound plumbing insulation (from a plumbing-supply store).

Check the drain pan under the refrigerator for cracks and replace if necessary.

▶ Ice builds up too quickly in bottom of freezer.

First make sure that nothing is keeping the freezer door from shutting completely. Warm air entering the freezer causes massive condensation, which freezes into ice (which in turn pushes the door even more ajar, causing more ice to form). Defrost the freezer and some of the food in it and rearrange the remaining food. Also clear the drain (see left).

In certain refrigerator/freezer models, if the insulation around the drain hole in the freezer gets wet, it never dries. The frozen moisture then clogs the defrost hole, so defrost water settles on the freezer deck and turns to ice. A factory-authorized technician may be able to install a low-wattage heater that will keep moisture from icing up the drain hole.

▶ Frost forms too quickly in standard refrigerator.

The door is not sealing properly or is being opened too often. First make sure that the refrigerator is level and tilted slightly backward, so the door shuts automatically. (See page 282.) Examine the gasket; if it is cracked, torn, or loose, replace it. (See below.)

▶ Refrigerator door gasket needs replacing.

Unplug the refrigerator and roll the gasket back to see how it's attached to the door. It may be attached by retainer strips, by screws along with retainer strips, or by screws only. If it's secured by retainers only, pull the gasket out of the grooves and take it to the appliance store to be sure you get a comparable replacement. If the new gasket is wrinkled, soak it in hot water for 15 minutes before installing it. Start at a top corner and work toward the other, pushing the narrowest edge of the gasket into the groove. Then work down the sides, one at a time, and finally press the bottom into place.

If the gasket has screws as well as a retainer, use a screwdriver (or nut driver if applicable) to loosen the screws. Slip out the gasket and take it with you when you buy a new one. Slide the edge of the new gasket under the retainer at the top corners of the door. Tighten the center screw just enough to hold the gasket. Work down one side, then the other, and then across the bottom, tightening the center screw of each side just enough to hold the gasket. Now gently tighten the screws at the corners, and then the remaining screws.

If the gasket is held by screws only, use a nut driver or screwdriver to remove all the screws. Pull the

---

Tip *Most refrigerators need clearance behind them for air to circulate through the condenser coils. Built-in refrigerators, which fit flush with the cabinetwork around them, have the compressor and condenser coils mounted on the top of the unit, with air circulated through a front grille.*

gasket off the door and take it with you when you buy a replacement. Install the new gasket, starting in a top corner and working toward the opposite corner, putting the screws back in as you go. Work down each side in turn and then across the bottom. Do not overtighten the screws.

Removing an old door gasket

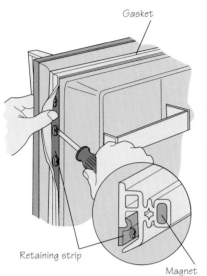

Gasket

Retaining strip

Magnet

Installing a new gasket

Retaining strip

Gasket

▶ Refrigerator makes strange noises.

If the noise is a rattling or vibration, it may indicate the refrigerator is not resting solidly on the floor, because either the floor or the legs are uneven. Place a carpenter's level on top and see if the horizontal line is straight. If not, adjust the roller screws or front leveling legs by turning them clockwise with a wrench to raise the appliance or counterclockwise to lower it. If the drain pan is rattling, move it so that it's clear of the compressor. If you have some strong-backed helpers, you can put a layer or two of rubber-backed carpeting (such as thick bath mats, large rubber doormats, or inexpensive carpet scraps from a carpet store) under the refrigerator to diminish noise.

If the unit is aging, note that older refrigerators develop strange noises. Usually, it's one of the fan motors imitating a jet taking off or a panicky jungle bird. Listen to the condenser fan motor and the evaporator fan motor, and if you have an ice maker, listen to that motor as well. Replace whichever one is making the noise. If the unit is very old, consider replacing the refrigerator.

▶ Refrigerator door wanders when open.

The refrigerator should be level but tilted slightly back so the door closes by itself. To adjust it, remove the front access panel near the floor. Place shims under the front legs or, if they have adjusting screws, turn the screws to extend the feet slightly (you may have to loosen a locknut first). To make adjustment easier, have a helper use a crowbar to lift the front of the refrigerator slightly near the leg you are adjusting; place some padding and a scrap of plywood under the

crowbar to protect the floor. Be very careful—don't put your fingers under the unit while it is raised.

▶ Refrigerator emits strong, caustic odor.

If the refrigerator is very old it may be leaking a sulphur dioxide refrigerant. Open windows, evacuate the room, and call for service. With more modern refrigerators the refrigerant is odorless and not likely to be causing the odor. Try the strategies for eliminating food odors (see below), or call for service.

▶ Refrigerator has unpleasant odors inside and in drip pan.

Prepare a solution of 1 gallon hot water, ½ cup baking soda, and 3 squirts dishwashing detergent. Turn off the unit and remove all food. Wash the whole interior (including bins, door trays, and shelves) with the cleaning solution. Pull out bins and wash the refrigerator floor.

If you have seen evidence of spilled liquid, also check the drip pan under the refrigerator; remove it and, if it is dirty, wash it with the solution. Return it to position and search for a drain trap on the bottom shelf. Pour more of the solution down the trap; then rinse the drip pan again. (If it is moldy, see next paragraph.) Inspect the former contents of the refrigerator and discard red-haired butter, black spinach, orange sour cream, green cheddar, and the like. Return bins and food to the unit and turn it back on.

If the drip pan has smelly mold, scrub with a solution of hot water and mildew-killing cleaner or chlorine bleach, using a scouring cloth or pad. If possible, let dry in hot

Tip *Washing the gasket frequently with soapy water prevents mold. If it's already moldy, you might try washing it several times with a liquid detergent, a mildew-killing cleaner (check label before buying, in case cleaner can't be used on rubber), or a mixture of 4 tablespoons chlorine bleach in 1 quart hot water.*

sun (or wipe dry). Check and clean the drip pan frequently (about every two weeks at first, then every three or four months if mold does not return). If refrigerator is leaking heavily into the drip pan, encouraging mold, check the door gasket for looseness or cracks; excess condensation due to a loose seal may be causing the leakage.

▶ Refrigerator cord won't reach wall receptacle.

If you can't move the refrigerator closer to the receptacle, use a heavy-duty extension cord (no smaller than No. 14 wire) and set the controls slightly colder. Alternatively, replace the cord or install a new receptacle.

▶ Refrigerator finish is chipped or color is undesirable.

Touch up small chips with appliance-repair paint (available at hardware stores in several standard colors). To change colors entirely, use automotive spray paint or have the unit painted by an auto-body shop.

▶ Inside of door has crack.

For tiny cracks, clean the crack with cleanser and dry thoroughly. Spread a thin bead of silicone sealer (available in tubes at hardware stores) along the crack. (Most caulks specify a minimum temperature before applying. Check the label; you may need to shut off the refrigerator, empty it, and let it warm up before applying the caulk.) With a wet putty knife, press sealer into the crack. Then scrape off excess sealer. For large cracks, have the liner replaced by a trained technician. If it's not done correctly, the liner may pull away from the door completely when the door shelves are filled with food.

▶ Refrigerator damages flooring when moved.

The best way to move a refrigerator is with an appliance dolly, which any rental agency should have. Otherwise, protect the floor with clean pieces of plywood or other paneling ($5/16$-inch flooring underlayment works well). Tip the refrigerator back and slide the first piece under it. Spray the bottoms of the feet or casters with furniture polish to make them slick, and slide or roll the refrigerator over the plywood. Have at least one helper.

▶ Ice maker doesn't work.

Check that the stop arm is in the *On* (down) position and that the water supply is connected and turned on. Check water pressure in the house (see page 276) and the unit. Ice cubes piled in the bin will cause the ice maker to shut off. Finally, the freezer may be too warm to make ice. Use a refrigerator/freezer thermometer to check the temperature, or see whether ice cream in the unit is melting. If so, set controls a notch colder.

Checking ice-maker stop arm

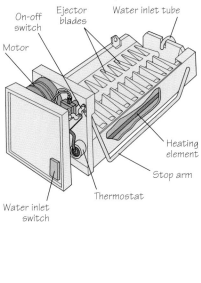

On-off switch · Ejector blades · Water inlet tube · Motor · Heating element · Stop arm · Thermostat · Water inlet switch

▶ Motor of standard standup freezer groans.

Before calling for service, see if the freezer is overfilled and/or ice encrusted, or if a package is keeping the door from closing all the way. Defrost the unit and remove some of the food.

▶ Warm air flows out from under refrigerator.

The compressor under the refrigerator normally emits warm air. Clean the compressor coils if they are dirty and hence overheating, and return the bottom grille so that it is firmly in place. If the bottom grille has vanished, obtain a replacement to minimize dust accumulation.

▶ Automatic defrost doesn't function.

The automatic defrost system has a number of components, any one of which could be causing the problem. Obtain a repair manual for the brand and model of your refrigerator if you wish to diagnose and repair it yourself. Otherwise, call for service.

▶ Washing machine won't start.

Make sure that the machine is plugged in and that the circuit breaker hasn't tripped or the fuse blown. Check to see whether a small appliance will work plugged into the same receptacle. If absence of power is not the problem, see that the lid is closed and check the lid switch (see page 284). Try turning the dial to a different cycle or a different stage of the cycle. If this starts the machine, the timer is probably faulty and will need replacing. If it doesn't start the machine, the motor is defective and may need to be replaced. Call for repairs.

Tip *To reduce odors in a refrigerator, place an open or vented container of baking soda or activated charcoal in a corner. Check it every few months and replace it when it starts to smell bad.*

Tip *To prevent door cracks, avoid overcrowding the door shelves or placing sharp-edged items on them.*

▶ Tub fills but motor won't start or makes noises.

Make sure the lid is firmly latched. If the motor makes no noise, test the lid switch, with the lid down, by inserting a pencil or wood chopstick under the indentation on the lid and pushing the switch. If this starts the motor, the lid-latching mechanism needs to be replaced. If it doesn't, the switch itself may be defective. To remove it for testing, unplug the machine, open the lid, and lift up the top panel. Remove the two screws that hold the switch in place and disconnect the wires from the switch (mark or label them). Touch the probes of a continuity tester or a volt-ohmmeter (set for R × 1 ohms resistance) to the two terminals. It should show continuity when you depress the switch button; if not, replace the switch. If the lid safety switch is not the problem (or the motor is making noises), call for service.

Removing lid safety switch

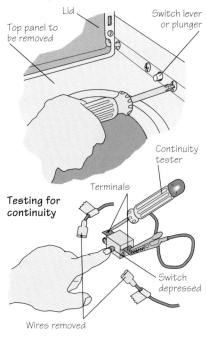

Top panel to be removed

Lid

Switch lever or plunger

Continuity tester

Terminals

Testing for continuity

Switch depressed

Wires removed

▶ Tub doesn't fill.

Make sure that the hose bibbs are turned on all the way, and that the water valve is turned on. Check to see that the control button for the desired water level is fully depressed. Check for clogs in the hose filters and clean them. (See right.) Also look for (and straighten) kinks in the inlet hoses. Next see if the timer is the problem by moving it up a notch or two and pressing the start button. If the machine starts filling, the timer is faulty; replace it.

If these steps don't solve the problem, check the solenoid of the inlet valve with a volt-ohmmeter or continuity tester. First unplug the machine, shut off the hose bibbs, and disconnect the hoses. If the inlet valve is accessible through the back panel of the machine, release the valve by removing the screws that hold it to the bracket, and pull it out from the bracket with wires attached. Otherwise, gain access by removing the top panel and the splash guard that surrounds the tub rim. With the valve in view, note which wires are connected to the four terminals; disconnect them. Test continuity between the terminals of each pair (if you use a volt-ohmmeter, set it for R × 100 ohms resistance). If there is no continuity, the solenoids don't draw current and are unable to open the valves; replace the valve.

If the inlet valve works and shows continuity (around 800 ohms on each test), check the water temperature switch. Look for it inside the control panel behind the temperature button. Note how the wires are connected to the four terminals and detach them. Check each pair of terminals with the switch on *Cold*. If neither pair shows continuity, replace the switch. If one pair shows continuity, verify that it is the correct pair

by studying the wiring diagram in the owner's manual or on the back of the control panel; the probes should be touching the terminals designated for cold water. If the water temperature switch is not the problem, call for service.

Checking continuity of inlet valve

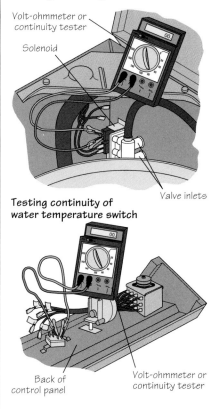

Volt-ohmmeter or continuity tester

Solenoid

Valve inlets

Testing continuity of water temperature switch

Back of control panel

Volt-ohmmeter or continuity tester

▶ Tub fills very slowly.

Check whether both the hot- and cold-water bibbs are fully open. If so, the hose filters (or the pipes) may be plugged up. At the back of the machine are hose connections marked *Hot* and *Cold*. Close the bibbs and unscrew the hoses from the washer. (If necessary, carefully use pliers to loosen them;

Tip *If you need to move a washing machine or other heavy appliance to gain access to the back, always get help. To keep from damaging the floor, tilt the machine back and place pads of carpet or heavy cardboard under each front leg. Do the same for the rear legs as soon as you have access; then slide the machine on the pads. If you need to check the bottom of the machine, tilt it against a wall or other barrier and prop it up firmly. Be sure to unplug the machine, disconnect water lines, and empty all water before moving or tilting it.*

don't squeeze the hose end out of shape.) There may be filter screens just inside; clean them with a cotton swab or a small dishwashing brush dipped in hot water (if they are very dirty, use some dishwashing detergent as well). Replace them if they are bent or crushed. If the fitting has dome-shaped removable filter screens, clean them or replace them. Also disconnect the hoses from the bibbs to see if they have filters that need cleaning or replacement. While they are off, hold a bucket under each faucet and turn it on. If water doesn't come out full force, the problem is probably poor water pressure. (See page 159.) If the water comes out with normal force but the tub still fills very slowly, the problem could be a defective inlet valve or water temperature switch (see page 284.)

▶ Tub won't spin.

If the washer stops when it's full of water, lift the lid, redistribute the laundry, and close the lid; if it starts again, the load was merely unbalanced. If the machine starts again only after several minutes' wait, it may not be receiving enough voltage to work well. Check voltage with a volt-ohmmeter, following directions in the meter manual, or call for service. If the tub stops spinning entirely but the motor runs, the problem is probably a loose or broken drive belt or faulty transmission. You can probably replace a belt yourself (see right). In older machines with direct drive, the friction material that locks the brakes, clutch, and spin wheel together may have dried out, making the transmission slip. Get an estimate before repairing it; the cost of reconditioning the unit will probably be close to that of replacing it with a new one.

▶ Motor hums but nothing happens.

Consult the owner's manual to find out whether your model has a drive belt or a transmission. If the machine has a drive belt, it may be broken. To repair it yourself, if the owner's manual does not include a diagram of the drive belt, see if you can obtain a repair manual (through the appliance dealer or the customer service department of the manufacturer). Pull the unit away from the wall and disconnect it. If the belt is accessible from the rear, unscrew the rear access panel. If it is accessible only from the bottom, with a helper lay the machine on its side on carpet or other padding (water may drain out).

Check the belt tension by pressing the belt. The correct tension varies in different models and makes; check the manual for its recommendation. If the belt is loose, tighten it according to manufacturer's directions. For most models this involves using a socket wrench to loosen the mounting nuts, then pulling the motor back against the belt and retightening the nuts. Also check the pulleys by taking hold of each of them in turn and trying to shake them from side to side. If a pulley is loose, tighten its setscrew. If the belt or pulley is worn or torn, replace it. In many models this may require major disassembly; call for service and get an estimate before authorizing the repair—it may approach the price of a new unit.

If your unit has direct drive, the transmission may have failed. Transmission repairs are extremely expensive; get an estimate and compare it to the cost of replacing the unit.

Adjusting belt tension . . .

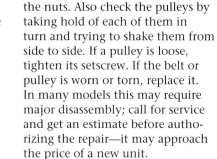

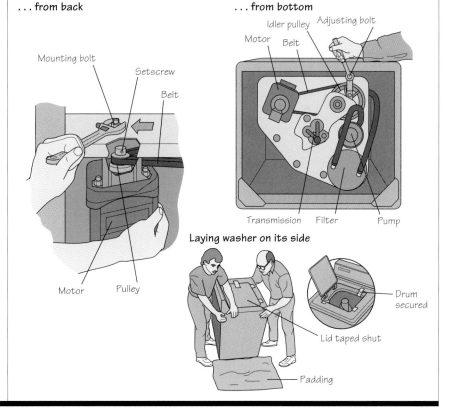

Tip *Whenever you buy a new washing machine, replace the old rubber supply hoses with new ones. For maximum protection, buy polymer hoses with an outer wrapping of stainless steel mesh—they are virtually burstproof.*

▶ *Clothes come out wet or tub won't drain.*

For weak spin, first check to see if the machine is overloaded or if the load has become unbalanced. If clothes come out wet or machine fails to drain, unplug the washer and check the drain hose for clogs or kinks and remove them. Bail out most of the water, plug in the unit, turn it on again, and set the control to *Spin*. If the machine still doesn't spin or drain properly, look to the drive belt and pulleys (see page 285). If agitation is slow as well, the unit may have a faulty transmission or brake, requiring professional repair.

An uncommon but possible cause of failure to spin is binding, caused by dried detergent or grease coating the gasket around the tub or by clothing trapped between the basket and the tub; check for and correct these conditions. Other possibilities include motor carriage needing lubrication, a broken motor carriage roller, a damaged water pump, or a defective tub bearing. Get an estimate for repairs.

▶ *Agitator doesn't work properly.*

Check to see if the unit will agitate on other cycles or other stages of the cycle. If not, the drive belt or transmission may be faulty (see page 285), or the timer may be defective. To test the timer, unplug the machine and remove the back plate from the control panel (you may need to unscrew the control panel first). Locate the mechanism behind the timer knob and disconnect the wires leading to the motor from the wiring plug. With a continuity tester or volt-ohmmeter (set for R × 1 ohms resistance), test the continuity of the timer motor by touching the probes to the two wire leads that you disconnected. If the tester shows no continuity, the timer motor is defective; replace

the complete timer unit. If the motor shows continuity, check the switch terminals of the timer. Mark and disconnect the wires (or pull out the block with all wires attached) to expose several pairs of terminals. Test each pair for continuity, turning the timer knob to the cycle that those terminals control. (Consult the owner's manual or wiring diagram on the door to identify which terminals control what cycle.) If any pair fails the continuity test, replace the timer.

If, when you tested the agitator on another cycle, it started up, the problem may be a faulty water-level switch. To test it, unplug the machine and locate the switch inside the control panel behind the selector knob. Detach the plastic air tube (the air pressure in this

tube changes as the water level in the tub changes). Mark and disconnect the wires from the switch terminals. With a volt-ohmmeter (at R × 1) or a continuity tester, check all the terminals in pairs (three combinations in all). If no pair, or more than one pair, has continuity, replace the switch. If one pair has continuity, note it and proceed to testing the other pairs with different air pressures. To do this, blow lightly into the hole you disconnected the tubing from (or attach tubing of the same diameter and blow into it) until you hear a click. Test the terminals at this setting; a different pair should show continuity. Repeat the process; the third pair should now show continuity. If not, replace the switch. If the problem persists, call for service.

Performing initial test of water-level switch

Air hose

Water-level switch

Testing timer motor and switch terminals

Motor leads

Timer motor

Timer

Switch terminals

Changing pressure in water-level switch

Tip *Although washing-machine hoses are designed for heavy use, there's always a chance an old one will weaken and burst. To avoid this, you can shut off the hose bibbs when you're not using the machine, to take pressure off them and eliminate the chance of leaks or bursting while nobody is home.*

▶ Water is too cold or too hot.

Check the hose bibbs to be sure both are fully open; if the hoses are connected to a sink faucet, be sure the shutoff valves under the sink are fully open. Check the water hoses to see if they are reversed; disconnect both hoses from the bibbs, switch them, and test. If water is too cool, check the setting on your water heater; if it's under 120° F, raise it slightly. Note that if you run the washing machine right after someone has filled the bath, taken a long shower, or done dishes, there may not be enough hot water left to service the washer.

Clean the filters in the hoses and replace them if they are bent or crushed. If there is still a problem, test the hose bibbs or faucet by disconnecting the hose, holding a bucket underneath, and turning on the water. If little or none comes out, the pipe itself is probably clogged and needs to be replaced. The final possibility is that the temperature selection switch is faulty and needs to be replaced.

▶ Water doesn't shut off automatically.

First turn off the machine and un-plug it. If water continues to run into the machine, the inlet valve is faulty and should be replaced. Turn off the bibbs, empty the tub (bailing it out by hand, if necessary), and replace the valve. Consult the owner's manual to learn whether the valve is accessed by removing the cabinet top or the rear service panel. Leaving the machine unplugged, disconnect the inlet hoses and remove the screws holding the valve in place; lift out the valve assembly. Loosen the clamp connecting the nozzle hose with the

valve outlet and remove the hose. Mark and disconnect the wires from the valve solenoid terminals. Install a new valve by reversing the procedure.

If the water stops flowing when you pull the plug, the timer may be faulty. Plug the machine back in and advance the timer knob. If the water stops, replace the timer (or have it done by a repair person). If water doesn't stop, the water-level switch is probably faulty. Test it (see opposite page) or call for service.

Removing the inlet valve

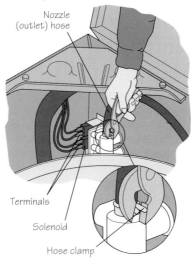

Nozzle (outlet) hose

Terminals

Solenoid

Hose clamp

▶ Drainpipe overflows.

The tub could be overfilling (see right), the branch drain that the washing machine is on may have a sudden discharge from some other plumbing fixture (such as the dishwasher or a draining bathtub), or the standpipe may be clogged or improperly sized or plumbed. To check for clogs, work a drain auger down the standpipe. Also look for a cleanout plug under the floor or behind the wall where the standpipe is located; open it carefully and have buckets handy. Use the auger to clear obstructions down-

stream from the cleanout. If you don't encounter anything but the standpipe still overflows, it is probably plumbed incorrectly. It should be 2 inches in diameter, terminate at least 34 inches above the floor, have a P-trap below it between 6 and 18 inches above the floor, and have a vent pipe connected to the drain line within 3 or 4 feet of the trap, depending on local code requirements. If it shares a branch drain with the kitchen, the drain should be 3-inch-diameter pipe. All horizontal drainpipes should be sloped ¼ inch per foot. If you find substandard plumbing conditions or aren't sure, call a plumber.

▶ Washing machine leaks.

First try to figure out when and where it leaks. If the leak occurs behind the washer, check the inlet hoses for cracks, and if necessary replace the hoses. Check the hose bibbs; if the leaking comes from there, tighten the packing nuts and hose connections with a wrench. Inside the machine check the nozzle hose (connected to the inlet valve) and replace it if it is cracked.

If the machine leaks when it's full, check the pump hoses for loose connections or cracks. For access, unplug the machine, turn off hose bibbs, remove supply hoses, and remove the rear service panel. If the hoses and connections are all intact, the pump may be leaky and need replacement, or else the water-level switch (which turns off water intake when the machine is full enough) may be faulty, allowing excess water to leak out through the overflow tube. To stop the leak, have the

Tip *The drain hose of a washing machine, also called a purge hose, usually discharges into a vertical pipe located behind the machine. This standpipe should be at least 36 inches above the floor to provide enough capacity to serve as a small catch basin for discharged drain water. It also holds the discharge end of the drain hose high enough so water gets trapped in the bottom of the hose between washings, ensuring that the rubber seals in the drain valve do not dry out and crack. To keep the drain hose from popping out of the discharge pipe or splashing water onto the floor, connect it to the pipe with a rubber friction cap made for this purpose: Simply slide it onto the top of the pipe, tighten the hose clamp provided with it, and force the end of the drain hose through a hole in the top of the cap.*

pump or switch replaced by a technician. (However, if the leak is slight, repairs may not be worth the cost. If the leak is from the overflow tube, just place a small container under it to catch the drips.)

Checking for leaks

Valve inlets
Nozzle tube
Drain hose
Hose bibbs
Vent to roof

Drain standpipe
P-trap
Drainpipe

▶ Suds end up on roof.

The drain is partially clogged downstream from the vent pipe, allowing water to drain away but causing suds to back up through the plumbing vent until they spill out onto the roof. Clear the drain with a drain auger, working down through the standpipe, the roof vent, or any cleanouts located along the drain line and branch drain that serve the washing machine. Or call a plumber.

▶ Machine is excessively noisy.

A quick way to diminish washing-machine noise is to slide a layer or two of rubber-backed carpeting under the machine or the drip pan. (Check at a carpet store for low-priced samples and scraps.) Make sure the machine is level (see below) in case vibration is contributing to the noise.

Also check to see if a bobby pin, small nail, or similar object has gotten stuck through one of the bottom holes in the basket; it could be hitting the antiswirl device on the pump hose and causing a clattering sound.

▶ Machine shakes and vibrates.

First level the machine: Screw the adjustable legs as far down as possible so the machine is close to the floor. Using a carpenter's level and open-ended or adjustable wrench, adjust the legs so the machine is level back-to-front and side-to-side. After leveling, tighten the locknuts on each leg. If leveling the machine doesn't correct vibration problems, check to see whether the installers left the retaining bolts (for shipping) on both sides of the service panel. If so, the bolts are compressing the springs, so they can't absorb vibration; remove them.

The bolts that hold the gear case to the support braces may be loose. Check the owner's manual or a repair manual for exact procedure. For most models the procedure is to unplug the machine, disconnect the hoses, move the machine away from the wall, and remove the rear service panel. Tighten all the nuts holding the gear case to the support braces (the gear case is under the tub, attached to a large mounting plate). Reattach the service panel and hoses and restore power.

If this doesn't work, replace the snubber and spring rod. The snubber is a piece of plastic that holds the spring rod, which (in turn) reduces vibration. Unplug the washer, lift the top, and find the snubber and spring rod (usually in a rear corner). Pull up the spring rod to release it from the snubber, then unscrew the snubber. Remove the nut and bolt attaching the spring rod to the frame. Press the bolt down to release it; the rounded end of the spring rod will also come free. Slip the hook end of the rod out of the holes. Install the new snubber and spring rod (by reversing the whole process).

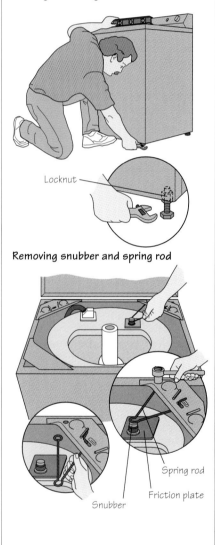

Leveling a washing machine

Locknut

Removing snubber and spring rod

Spring rod
Friction plate
Snubber

Tip *For a washing machine located in the house, especially in bedroom areas or upstairs areas directly over living space, have a sheet-metal shop fabricate a 2-inch-deep drip pan to place under the washer, just slightly larger than the outside dimensions of the machine. For maximum overflow protection, install a drain fitting in the side of the pan and run 3/4-inch pipe from it to a safe discharge point (such as a floor drain or outdoors).*

▶ Water pipes bang when washer shuts off.

A washing-machine inlet valve snaps shut quickly, causing water rushing through the pipes to stop suddenly and create a hammering sound. To suppress the noise, install water-hammer shock absorbers (available at home centers or plumbing-supply stores). Get the kind that can be installed on the hose bibbs (as opposed to those installed on the water pipes, usually inside the wall). Shut off the hose bibbs, unscrew the hoses carefully, and screw the shock absorbers onto the bibbs. (Make sure the washers from the hoses and the shock absorbers are still in place.) Reconnect the hoses.

Installing water-hammer shock absorbers

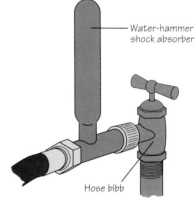

Water-hammer shock absorber

Hose bibb

▶ Washer screeches as spin cycle ends.

The brake seals are probably dry. To service the brake, unplug the machine, shut off the hose bibbs, and disconnect the hoses. Open the lid and secure the tub with fabric duct tape fastened from the top panel into the inside of the tub at several points. Close the lid and tape it shut. Place a rug, blanket, or beach towels over the floor and

(with a helper) tip the washer and lay it gently on its side. Using a squirt-gun oil can, lubricate the brake with the lubricant recommended in the owner's manual. (There should be an opening in the transmission pulley that lets you reach the brake.) Turn the pulley clockwise for two turns to distribute the lubricant. Now return the machine to operating position and operating condition.

▶ Machine spins when it's not in the spin cycle.

The main bearing may be damaged or the solenoid may be faulty. In either case you'll probably need professional repairs. Especially if the machine is aging, get an estimate before committing; repair costs may be close to those of buying a new machine.

Lubricating brake seals

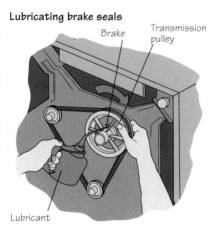

Brake

Transmission pulley

Lubricant

▶ Washer screeches as spin cycle starts.

This is usually caused by a drive belt glazed to a shiny hardness by a pulley spinning against it while it's stuck in place. To replace, see page 285. Some belts are much harder to replace than others, so you may need to call for repairs. Get an estimate first.

▶ Clothes dryer won't start.

Make sure the door is shut firmly, the switch is turned on, and the unit is plugged in. Check for a blown fuse or tripped circuit breaker. Electric dryers draw 240 volts and have a pair of fuses or circuit breakers; both must be functioning for the unit to run effectively. If you reset the breaker or replace the fuse but it blows again as soon as you start the dryer, call an electrician or appliance repair person.

The most common reason a dryer won't start is that lint is plugging up the exhaust hose and air vent. Go outside and see if there's lint all the way to the end of the duct; if so, just pull out as much of it as you can. If there is a damper, turn it parallel to the duct and clean it of lint with a straightened-out wire coat hanger. (If the duct is long, use rubber bands to attach securely a two-tined cooking fork to a long stick or broom handle, and use the tines to "comb" out lint from well back in the duct. If duct is very long (20 feet or so) you may need professional service to clean it all the way; also look into renting an industrial vacuum cleaner. Return to the dryer, remove the exhaust hose, and shake out lint. Also clean the lint from the lint filter. If exhaust vents are severely clogged, disassemble the vent pipes, run a rag through each piece, and wrap joints with fabric duct tape when reassembling. Now try the dryer again.

If it still won't run, try poking the door safety switch with a chopstick or pencil while the door is closed. If the dryer starts up, the switch plunger is faulty; replace

Tip *Most washers and dryers have self-adjusting rear legs for leveling the machine front-to-back. Simply tilt the machine forward to raise the legs off the floor, then let it down slowly. If the machine is still not level, raise or lower the front legs with a wrench and repeat the process. When the machine is level, press down on opposite corners for a final check. It shouldn't rock.*

SOLVING MECHANICAL PROBLEMS

the switch. If the dryer doesn't turn on, test the switch to make sure it's not the problem. First turn off the power, then remove the top panel to gain access to the switch. Remove the wire leads and test for continuity by touching the probes of a continuity tester or volt-ohmmeter (set for 4×1 ohms resistance) to both terminals and pushing in the switch button. If there is no continuity, replace the switch. If the switch has continuity, reconnect the wires and test the start switch in the same way (with power off). If none of this works, call for repairs. The timer may have failed or the motor may have burned out.

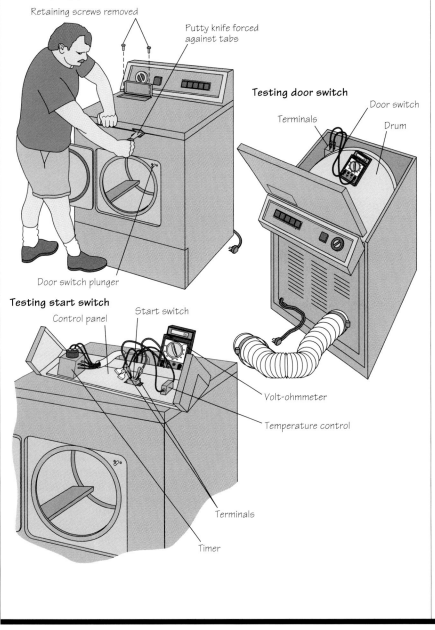

Removing top panel

Retaining screws removed

Putty knife forced against tabs

Door switch plunger

Testing door switch

Terminals

Door switch

Drum

Testing start switch

Control panel

Start switch

Volt-ohmmeter

Temperature control

Terminals

Timer

▶ Clothes dryer attracts mice.

Attracted by warmth and lured by lint, the creatures are coming in through the duct and the exhaust vent. If you have a draft preventer (flapper) on the vent pipe indoors, check to see whether it is staying open when dryer is off; if so, replace it. Also consider installing an automatic vent flapper designed for the outdoor end of the duct (this will make the duct harder to clean, however).

▶ Electric dryer won't heat enough or at all.

Electric dryers normally run on two fuses or circuit breakers. If one of the two is blown or tripped, often the dryer will run but won't heat. If a breaker or fuse continues to trip, call an electrician or appliance repair technician. If the breakers or fuses are sound, the problem may be a faulty thermostat (see opposite page) or broken heating element (call for repairs and get an estimate).

▶ Dryer takes too long to dry clothes.

If the machine is overloaded, the clothing doesn't toss well and does not dry. If the washing machine is ultralarge and the dryer is compact or normal, one washer-load will make two or three dryer-loads. If a few items (rugs or large towels) are large, heavy, and/or very wet, they should be dried separately on a longer or hotter cycle (following label directions for the fabric).

If loads are normal and still take a long time to dry, check that the flapper on the vent duct hood is wide open when the dryer is on; if it isn't, loosen or replace the flapper. Also check for lint clogging the filter, exhaust vents, and duct, and clear them out as needed.

Tip   *If the bulb in your clothes dryer keeps burning out, make sure it matches the specifications for your model (check the owner's manual). The bulb should be an appliance bulb, not a regular light bulb. Other possibilities: If the cover over the bulb has vanished, if the door to the dryer is left open, or if the dryer isn't level, the bulb is liable to burn out quickly. If other bulbs in the house also burn out quickly, check with the electric company to see if there have been power surges in your area.*

▶ *Clothes dryer motor needs replacing.*

If the dryer does not run and the switches are not at fault, the problem is most likely a defective motor. Installing a new dryer motor is not a difficult repair. Unplug the dryer (or shut off the circuit breakers) and move it away from the wall. Remove the screws that hold the lint screen in place. With a screwdriver tip protected by a rag, pry up the top (see opposite). Then remove the front panel and (if applicable) the toe panel. Remove the drive belt by pushing the idler pulley toward the motor. Lift the drum out of the dryer. You can now reach the motor. You'll need two open-end wrenches. Place one of them on the hub of the blower wheel (fan) at the rear of the motor. Place the other on the motor shaft holding the pulley. Holding the blower wheel hub steady, turn the belt pulley wrench clockwise to disconnect the blower wheel from the motor. Now check the floor of the dryer; in some models the motor is secured to the floor by two clamps. Unscrew these clamps. Then disconnect the wires attached to the motor; you can now remove the old motor. Install the new motor in reverse order. However, if the new motor doesn't have a belt pulley included, remove the pulley from the old motor (either unscrew it or pull it off with a wheel puller), and attach it to the new motor.

▶ *Dryer won't turn off when door is opened.*

The door safety switch is defective. It is usually behind the cabinet front, near the door hinge. To repair it, first unplug the dryer or shut off the circuit breakers. If the dryer is gas powered, shut off the gas valve for the dryer (by turning the handle 90 degrees) and proceed very carefully when moving the dryer, to avoid causing a dangerous gas leak.

Assuming the switch is located behind the cabinet front, remove the screws at the rear of the appliance and take off the cabinet front. Inspect the switch area. If a wire has fallen out of the switch, reattach it, turn on the electricity, and see if dryer works now. If wires are intact, disconnect them from the switch, remove the screws holding the switch in place, and install a new switch (from an authorized dealer or repair facility). Turn the power and gas back on and relight the pilot.

▶ *Gas dryer won't heat although drum turns.*

Avoid moving the dryer during diagnosis and repair, to avoid causing a gas leak. First check to see if the pilot light is out. Look for the pilot behind the lower access panel (if it does not open easily, look for a release spring). Read the directions printed on the inside of the panel. Usually, you can relight a pilot by holding down the reset button for about 30 seconds while holding a long fireplace match to the pilot. The pilot should remain lit. If it goes out, repeat the process. If it still won't stay on, replace the thermocouple (see page 242).

If the pilot is not out, check for lint blocking the exhaust vent and duct and clean it out.

The dryer may not be heating enough because the burner has

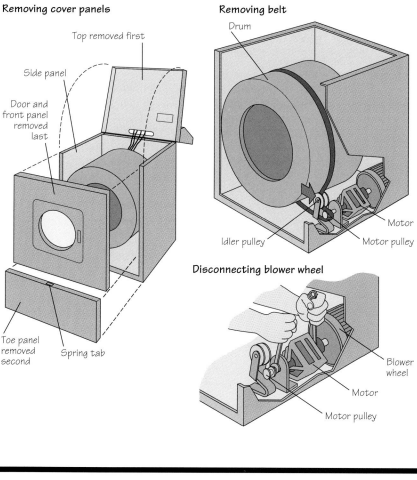

Removing cover panels

Top removed first
Side panel
Door and front panel removed last
Toe panel removed second
Spring tab

Removing belt

Drum
Idler pulley
Motor
Motor pulley

Disconnecting blower wheel

Blower wheel
Motor
Motor pulley

Tip Dryer lint, which is highly combustible, poses a fire hazard if it is not cleared out of the lint trap and exhaust duct periodically. Clean the trap before each use. Disconnect the vent duct from the back of the machine and check for lint buildup at least twice a year—more often if the duct vents upward.

SOLVING MECHANICAL PROBLEMS

an improper gas/air mixture. If the flame has a yellow tip or a lot of orange, there's too much air in the mixture; if it's all pale blue and roaring, there's not enough air. To adjust, turn off the dryer and let the burner cool. Loosen the small screw on the air vent, then, wearing an oven mitt, turn on the dryer and adjust the air vent to create a steady, quiet, tapered blue flame.

Finally, one of the thermostats may be faulty. Clothes dryers use several thermostats. High-limit (safety) thermostats open the circuit to shut off the heat whenever the temperature reaches a preset point, to prevent overheating. If the contacts of such a thermostat are stuck open, the heat won't go on. Turn off electric power to the unit, and look for high-limit thermostats in the heating element or burner. To test one of them, disconnect the two wires attached to it, and join them to one another with a jumper wire (short length of wire with alligator clips attached to each end). Restore power and start the dryer; if the dryer starts to heat up, the thermostat is bad. Turn off the dryer immediately and install a new thermostat. If there is more than one high-limit thermostat, test the other in the same way. *Do not run the dryer with jumper wires except as a test.*

Cool-down thermostats work by closing their contacts while dryer heat is on, and opening them when drying is completed, so the heat turns off while the dryer is still on (providing a cool-down period). If this thermostat fails, the dryer will not warm up. Test this thermostat in the same way as for the high-limit thermostat.

Temperature-control thermostats close and open to maintain a correct drying temperature. They are usually connected between the timer and the heating unit. Turn off power to the unit, remove the thermostats, and test them with a volt-ohmmeter and an electric skillet (see page 254).

Adjusting gas-air mixture

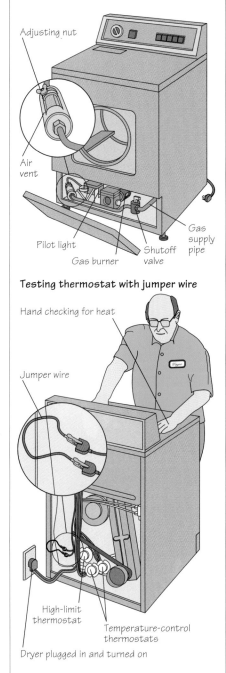

Adjusting nut

Air vent

Pilot light

Gas burner

Shutoff valve

Gas supply pipe

Testing thermostat with jumper wire

Hand checking for heat

Jumper wire

High-limit thermostat

Temperature-control thermostats

Dryer plugged in and turned on

▶ *Drum doesn't turn.*

The drive belt is probably broken. To quickly tell, rotate the drum by hand and listen for the loose belt thwacking against the side. The location of the belt and the method for replacing it depend on the make and model of the dryer; it's best to consult the owner's manual and, if possible, a repair guide for the model (see also page 291). Some models (those that have a single long belt that wraps around the drum and runs to the motor pulley) require that the whole cabinet be disassembled to replace the belt; these are better repaired by a professional. After learning from the manual how to reach the belt, also check to see if the problem might be a loose pulley instead of a defective belt. Tighten the setscrew of any loose pulley, and see if the dryer works now.

If the belt needs replacing and it's feasible for you to do it, note the model number of the dryer so you can buy an exact duplicate. Follow manufacturer's directions for replacing the belt. The process usually involves releasing a tension spring and threading the new belt onto the pulley.

▶ *Drum is rusty and stains clothes.*

Some manufacturers make custom touch-up paint (available from authorized appliance repair shops) that differs from regular appliance touch-up paint because it can withstand high heat. To repair the rust, first pull the plug or turn off the electric current. Remove all rust with fine-grade sandpaper. Vacuum the dust from the inside of the drum and wipe the sanded spots with a rag moistened with vinegar. Let dry. Then spray on the paint, covering all the rust spots, and let dry for 48 hours. Run the dryer

Tip *If the dryer makes excessive noise, check for coins, buttons, and other objects inside the drum. For thudding sounds, check for sneakers in the dryer (they are harmless, just noisy). If the noise is due to the machine vibrating or rocking back and forth, level it by adjusting the feet. Also consider placing rubber-backed carpet scraps or a rubber doormat under the legs to reduce noise.*

empty on high heat for 30 minutes; then soak a large, clean white rag in water, wring it out, place in dryer, and dry on high heat for 30 minutes. Inspect the rag for paint. If any paint appears, let the drum dry another 48 hours and test again. When no paint comes off on the rag, you can use the dryer.

▶ Dryer stops before clothes are dry.

If the dryer has an electronic system that senses when clothes are dry and shuts off the unit, try adjusting the load. Remove items that can be hung to finish drying, and shake out large items like sheets. Restart the machine. If it still will not continue until clothes are dry, the sensing system should be checked. Call for service.

For a dryer with conventional timing, assuming you have set the timer for a long-enough drying period, see page 290.

If the dryer has a defective timer, it will stop early only once, then stop completely. To check a timer, unplug the dryer and remove the back plate from the control panel (you may have to remove the front of the panel instead; look for screws on the bottom front corners). First check the timer motor for continuity; mark and remove the wires connected to the motor terminals and touch the probes of a volt-ohmmeter (set for R × 1 ohms resistance) or a continuity tester to the terminals. If there is no continuity, replace the timer unit. If there is continuity, mark and remove the wires attached to the switch terminals. Set the timer control to *Off* and test all pairs of terminals; if any tests for continuity, the timer is defective and should be replaced. Then switch the control

knob through all the cycles; a different pair of terminals should show continuity for each setting (except *Off*). If not, replace the timer.

Testing timer motor

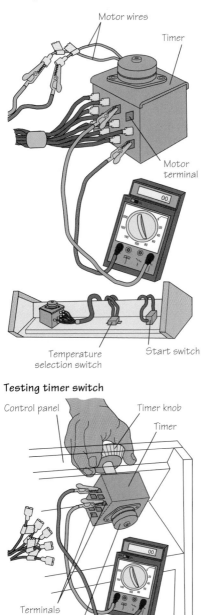

Motor wires

Timer

Motor terminal

Temperature selection switch

Start switch

Testing timer switch

Control panel

Timer knob

Timer

Terminals

Timer motor

▶ Dryer is unvented and leaves air too humid.

If the dryer is close to an exterior wall, buy a dryer vent cap to install in the wall and a length of 4-inch-diameter flexible dryer duct to connect it to the exhaust duct behind the dryer. Before cutting the wall, make a small hole and explore with a piece of wire to make sure there are no obstructions. Mark a cut line on the interior wall by tracing around the duct, and cut out the opening with a wallboard saw. Remove insulation, if necessary, to expose the back of the exterior wall sheathing. Drive a nail through the wall sheathing at the center of the hole; use it as a reference for marking the hole on the outside of the wall and cutting through the siding. After cutting the hole, caulk around it, insert the vent cap, and secure it to the siding with HDG screws. On the inside, caulk around the duct where it extends through the interior wall, slide the decorative collar over it, and attach the flexible dryer duct to it with a hose clamp. Attach the other end of the duct to the dryer exhaust vent. Push the dryer into place.

If you can't vent it to the exterior, obtain a vent bucket (from an appliance store or repair shop) and attach it to the exhaust outlet at the back of the dryer.

Installing a dryer vent

Siding

Vent cap (with damper)

Flexible duct

Tip *Vinyl ducts are not ideal for a clothes dryer because if they are long, they can accumulate enough lint to become a fire hazard. If you are using vinyl, keep the duct short. If you have a choice, use aluminum.*

APPENDIX

▶ *Building Your Tool Kit*

	Basic Kit	Intermediate Kit	Advanced Kit
All-purpose Hand Tools			
Storage	Tool box (19") Tool apron	Bigger tool box (32") Tool belt	Very big tool box Portable workbench
Layout	Tape measure (25') Combination square Torpedo level Pencils	Steel framing square 24" or 30" level Plumb bob Chalk line and chalk Bevel gauge Awl	100' steel tape measure 6'6" level Compass dividers (6") Water level Stair layout buttons
Cutting	Utility knife and blades Compact crosscut saw Hacksaw and blades	Wallboard saw Coping saw Mini hacksaw Miter box	Doweling jig Side cutters
Shaping	Rasping plane Wood chisels (½", 1", 1½")	Block plane Whetstone and oil Aviation snips	Jack plane Hatchet Cold chisels Brick chisel
Hammering & Prying	Hammer, curved claw (16 oz) Nail sets (½₂", ₃⁄₃₂") Flat pry bar	Framing hammer (20 oz) Nail puller (cat's paw) Crowbar 3-lb maul	10-lb sledgehammer Chipping hammer Rubber mallet
Fastening	Screwdrivers, standard Screwdrivers, Phillips Needle nose pliers (6") Channel lock pliers (1½" jaw) Adjustable wrenches (5", 8") Allen wrench set Adjustable clamps (2)	Socket wrench set Locking pliers (5", 10") Staple gun Nut drivers (³⁄₁₆"–½") Center punch	Wrenches, open-end/box Deep sockets for socket wrench Staple hammer Pipe clamps Butt marker Self-centering screw punch or Vix bit
Smoothing & Sealing	Sandpaper (assorted) Four-in-hand file Putty knife (1¼") Taping knife (5" or 6") Caulking gun	Files (flat, round, triangular) Wire brushes (steel, brass) Taping knives (12", 24")	Pole sander Cement trowels Brick trowel

Power Tools	⅜" drill
	  and twist drill set
	  and spade bits (¼"–1½")
	  and countersink pilot bits
	 Jigsaw and blades
	 Extension cord (50' of
	  No. 14 wire)
		Circular saw and 3 blades:
		  20-tooth carbide tip
		  40-tooth carbide tip
		  metal-cutting
		 Cordless drill
		  and screwdriver bits
		 Pad sander
		 Belt sander
		 3-pronged plug adapter
		 Extension cord (50' of
		  No. 12 wire)
			Router
			 10" table saw
			 Reciprocating saw
			 Power miter box
			 Power screw gun
			 Orbital sander
			 ½" drill
			 ¾" hammer drill
			 Bench grinder
			 Shop vacuum

Safety Gear	Eye protection Dust mask Latex gloves Flashlight Voltage tester (neon)	Respirator mask Knee pads Ear protection Hard hat Work gloves	First-aid kit (separate from home kit) Portable lights

	Basic Kit	Intermediate Kit	Advanced Kit

Basic Supplies & Fasteners	White PVA glue
	Electrical tape
	Masking tape
	Spackling compound
	Nails, finishing (3d, 4d, 6d, 8d)
	Nails, common (8d, 16d)
	Nails, HDG box (4d, 6d)
	Brads (assorted)
	Screws, wallboard (1¼", 2", 3")
	Screws, sheet-metal (⅜–1")
	Screws, wood (1" × #6, 1¼" × #8,
	    1¼" × #12)
		Carpenter's wood glue
		Duct tape
		Steel wool
		Graphite powder
		Silicone lubricant
		Wire, steel (2–3 sizes)
			Nails (roofing, wallboard,
			    duplex, concrete)
			Screws (full assortment)
			Hollow-wall fasteners
			Stove bolts (assorted)
			Lag screws (assorted)
			Machine bolts (assorted)

Painting Tools	2" cut-in brush 3" brush Roller and covers Roller tray Extension handle Drop cloths	1½" sash brush Brush spinner Pull scraper	HVLP (high-volume, low- pressure) sprayer
Plumbing Tools	Plunger Drain auger Pipe joint tape Pipe joint compound Plumber's putty Pipe wrenches (12", 14") Pipe solvent cement	Closet auger Basin wrench Tubing cutter Propane or MAPP gas torch Lead-free solder Flux and brush Sand cloth (emery cloth)	Tubing bender Seat wrench Seat dressing tool Spud wrench Bonnet wrench Strainer wrench
Electrical Tools	Voltage tester, neon (2) Multipurpose tool Continuity tester	Circuit analyzer Wire stripper Cable stripper Volt-ohmmeter Very small screwdriver Electrician's pliers	Fish tape Conduit bender Soldering gun
Tile Tools	Notched adhesive trowel Rod saw Rubber float	Tile nippers Snap cutter Rubbing stone	Wet saw

▶ Tips for Buying Tools

- Except for a few basic tools, don't buy a tool until you need it.

- Assume that you'll have to buy a tool each time you do a project (if you don't need to, it will seem like a bonus).

- Buy the highest quality tool you can afford.

- Consider used tools and garage sales—many older tools are of high quality.

- Keep a tools "wish list" in your wallet or purse (and give copies to close friends).

- Keep tools sharp. Have saws, blades, and chisels sharpened regularly.

- Obtain extra tools for helpers, especially a tape measure, utility knife, hammer, pry bar, putty knife, screwdrivers, and nail sets.

▶ Nominal Lumber Sizes and Their Actual Equivalents (in inches)

Nominal	Actual	Nominal	Actual	Nominal	Actual
1 × 2	¾ × 1½	1 × 10	¾ × 9¼	2 × 6	1½ × 5½
1 × 3	¾ × 2½	1 × 12	¾ × 11¼	2 × 8	1½ × 7¼
1 × 4	¾ × 3½	2 × 2	1½ × 1½	2 × 10	1½ × 9¼
1 × 6	¾ × 5½	2 × 3	1½ × 2½	2 × 12	1½ × 11¼
1 × 8	¾ × 7¼	2 × 4	1½ × 3½	4 × 4	3½ × 3½

▶ Lumber Shrinkage

The following lumber sizes (in inches) are established by the American Lumber Standards Committee.

Nominal	Dry	Green
1	¾	2⁵⁄₃₂
2	1½	1⁹⁄₁₆
4	3½	3⁹⁄₁₆
6	5½	5⅝
8	7¼	7½
10	9¼	9½

▶ Header Sizes

Most codes do not have tables for sizing headers over doors and windows, but have only formulas for calculating beam sizes. However, the following sizes are generally accepted rules of thumb for headers in various situations.

Location	Size of Header (4 × or built-up 2 ×)	Maximum Span
Single Story or Top Story	4 × 4	4'
	4 × 6	6'
	4 × 8	8'
	4 × 10	10'
	4 × 12	12'
Lower Floor, With Floor Above	4 × 4	3'
	4 × 6	4'
	4 × 8	7'
	4 × 10	8'
	4 × 12	9'

Note: Increase sizes where accumulated loads concentrate on a header.

▶ Plywood Veneer Grades

The following grades are used in descending order of quality:

N. Smooth surface, suitable for natural finishes. Made of select grade wood. Free of open defects.

A. Smooth surface. Natural finish can be used if you are not too demanding.

B. Solid surface with circular repair plugs, shims, and tight knots. Some minor splits are permitted.

C Plugged. Splits cannot be more than ⅛ inch. Some repair and broken grain permitted.

C. Tight knots up to 1½ inches are allowed. Repairs, discoloration, limited splits, sanding defects, and stitching (piecing) are permissible if they do not impair the strength.

D. Knots and knotholes up to 3 inches wide are allowed. Splits and stitching are permitted.

▶ Insulation Thicknesses

To achieve the listed R-value for a particular type of insulation material, use the thickness specified.

Insulation	R-11	R-19	R-22	R-30	R-38
Fiberglass batts/blankets	3½"	6"	6½"	10"	12½"
Rock wool batts/blankets	3"	5½"	6"	9"	10½"
Fiberglass loose fill	5"	8½"	10"	13½"	17½"
Rock wool loose fill	4"	6½"	7½"	10½"	13½"
Cellulose loose fill	3"	5"	6"	8"	10½"

▶ Types of Insulation

Form	R-Value per Inch	Materials	Principal Use	Installation Method	Comments
Blankets or Batts	3.7	Rock wool	Walls	Fitted between wood-frame studs, joists, and beams	Most common form do-it-yourselfers use; suited for standard stud and joist spacing without obstructions; batts easier to handle than blankets
	3.3	Glass fiber	Floors		
			Ceilings		
			Attics		
			Roofs		
Loose or Blown Fill	2.9	Rock wool	Floors	Poured between joists or blown into place	Easy to use in irregularly shaped areas; blown fill, the only option for finished areas, should be installed by a professional
	2.2	Glass fiber	Walls		
	3.6	Cellulose fiber	Hard-to-reach places		
	2.4	Vermiculite	Finished areas		
	2.7	Perlite			
Rigid Panels	4.0	Molded polystyrene	Unfinished walls	Cut to fit and secured in place; must be covered with finish material for fire safety	High insulating value for relatively little thickness; all but fiberglass are highly flammable
	5.0	Extruded polystyrene	Basement masonry walls		
	7.4	Isocyanurate board	Exterior surfaces		
	4.5	Fiberglass board			

▶ Recommended Exposures of Wood Roof Shingles

Shingle Size	3 in 12 Roof	4 in 12 or Steeper Roofs
16"	3¼"	5"
18"	4½"	5½"
24"	5¾"	7½"

▶ Maximum Weather Exposure for Wood Singles and Shakes on Walls

Shingle Length	Single Course	Double Course
16"	7½"	12"
18"	8½"	14"
24"	11½"	16"

▶ Recommended Exposure of Roof Shakes

Shake Length	Roof Slope Less Than 6 in 12	6 in 12 or More
18"	5½"	7½"
24"	7½"	10"

▶ Proportions for 1 Cubic Yard of Concrete (in pounds)

Type of Project	Maximum Size of Aggregate	Cement	Sand	Gravel	Total Aggregate	Water	Air Entrainment
Foundations	⅜"	565	1,630	1,190	2,820	285	–
and Footings	¾"	520	1,310	1,730	3,040	260	–
	1"	490	1,260	1,870	3,130	245	–
Slabs, Patios,	⅜"	580	1,570	1,190	2,760	290	7%
and Foundations	¾"	580	1,250	1,730	2,980	290	6%
in Cold Climates	1"	535	1,170	1,870	3,040	270	6%

Note: 1 sack of cement equals 94 pounds. Water weighs 8 pounds per gallon.

▶ Mixing Your Own Concrete

If you need only a small quantity of concrete—1 yard or less—mix it by hand or in a small cement mixer. To make a 1-cubic-foot batch, divide each of the figures in the proportions chart by 27 (there are 27 cubic feet in 1 cubic yard). For instance, to make 1 cubic foot, the first row of ingredients would become: 22 pounds of cement, 105 pounds of aggregate, and 11 pounds of water. If you need more than 1 cubic foot, weigh the first batch of ingredients in buckets on a bathroom scale. Use a separate container for each ingredient, marking on the side of the container how high it needs to be filled to reach the desired weight. Fill the buckets to the same marks for the remaining batches.

Mix the dry ingredients together first, then add the water. If you are using a machine, have it mix the entire batch for at least three minutes. When you are through with the mixer, clean it out by throwing one or two shovelfuls of gravel and some water in it. Let them scour the inside of the mixer for a while, and then dump them.

▶ Ordering Ready-Mixed Concrete

If you need more than 1 yard, or you want air entrainment in the mix, have the concrete delivered by a ready-mix company. Specify the following when ordering:

Cement Content. Use the proportions chart to calculate the number of sacks of cement you will need in each cubic yard.

Aggregate Size. For most jobs ¾-inch aggregate is suitable, but if you are having the concrete pumped by a small pumper truck that has only a 3-inch hose, you will need to specify ⅜-inch aggregate.

Water/Cement Ratio. Specify .5 or ask for the supplier's recommendation.

Slump. This term is used to describe the consistency of fresh concrete. It refers to the number of inches a 12-inch-high tower of concrete slumps when it is fresh. A 1-inch slump is a very stiff mix, a 10-inch slump very soupy. For residential projects 4 inches is average.

Air Entrainment. Air entrainment is an additive that enhances the durability of concrete in cold climates. Consult the proportions chart for the percentage to be added.

Strength. You may be asked to specify the strength or load-bearing capacity of your concrete. Most residential needs vary from a minimum strength of 2,000 psi to more than 4,000 psi. Be aware that the proper handling and curing of the concrete, not just the correct proportions, are needed to attain the specified strength.

In addition to the per-yard delivery charge, be aware of other fees you may have to pay. A short-load charge is an additional fee for small orders (generally less than 4 yards). A stand-by charge is also customary; this is for any additional time the truck must remain at your site after the allotted per-yard time limit expires (usually about five minutes per yard). The amount can skyrocket if you are not prepared when the truck arrives.

If the truck cannot get close to your forms (for instance, a patio in a backyard), arrange for a pumper truck to arrive shortly before the concrete. You can rent one from the ready-mix supplier or an independent pumping company. Even if you think the concrete truck might reach your forms by backing into the driveway, it is better to have the concrete pumped than to take a chance on having to pay for a broken sidewalk.

► Nail Lengths

Size	Length
2d	1"
3d	1¼"
4d	1½"
6d	2"
8d	2½"
10d	3"
12d	3¼"
16d	3½"
20d	3¾"
30d	4½"
40d	5"
60d	6"

► Nail Finishes

Aluminum. Aluminum throughout.
Blued. Steel, heated to high temperature for light rustproofing.
Bright. Plain steel; rusts.
CC. Cement-coated steel, for light rustproofing.
EG (electrogalvanized). Steel, coated with zinc by electrolysis.
HDG (hot-dipped galvanized). Steel, coated with zinc by dipping.
Stainless Steel. Rustproof steel.
VC. Vinyl-coated steel; vinyl reduces friction and provides adhesion; rusts.

► Nail Uses

Box. Siding; exterior trim; fencing; wood shingles.
Brad. Molding; paneling.
Casing. Molding, where head is not countersunk.
Common. Framing; general construction.
Concrete. Concrete; brick; stucco.
Duplex. Temporary forms and bracing.
Finishing. Trim; cabinetwork.
Paneling. ¼" sheet paneling.
Ringed Shank. Flooring; subflooring.
Roofing. Composition shingles; building paper.
Sinker. Framing; general construction.
Spiral Shank, Aluminum. Redwood and cedar siding.
Spiral Shank, HDG. Decks; fences.
Wallboard. Wallboard.

► Nailing Schedule for Residential Construction

Codes specify the size, number, and placement of nails for framing connections. This table cites specifications typical of most codes. However, check with local officials to be sure these figures are in compliance with applicable codes.

Connection	Number and Size of Common Nails	How Nailed
Joist to sill or girder	3 8d	Toenailed
Built-up girders and beams of 3 members	20d 32" OC at top and bottom, staggered	Facenailed
Bridging to joist, each end	2 8d	Toenailed
Ledger strip (ribbon) at each joist	3 16d	Facenailed
1 × 6 subfloor, to each joist	2 8d	Facenailed
Wider than 1 × 6 subfloor	3 8d	Facenailed
2" subfloor to joist or girder	2 16d	Facenailed
Soleplate to joist or blocking	16d at 16" OC	Facenailed
Soleplate to stud	2 16d	End nailed
	4 8d	Toenailed
Top plate to stud	2 16d	End nailed
Doubled studs	16d at 16" OC	Facenailed
Built-up corner studs	16d at 24" OC	Facenailed
Doubled top plates	16d at 16" OC	Facenailed
Top plates, laps, and intersections	2 16d	Facenailed
Continuous header, 2 pieces	16d at 16" OC along each edge	Facenailed
Continuous header to stud	4 8d	Toenailed
Ceiling joists to plate	3 8d	Toenailed
Ceiling joists, laps over partitions	3 16d	Facenailed
Ceiling joists to parallel rafters	3 16d	Facenailed
Rafter to plate	3 8d	Toenailed
1" brace to each stud and plate	2 8d	Facenailed
1 × 8 sheathing or less, each bearing	2 8d	Facenailed
Wider than 1 × 8 sheathing, each bearing	3 8d	Facenailed

► Nailing Schedule for Wood Flooring

This chart shows the nail sizes and spacing for various wood-flooring materials. For planking wider than 4 inches, #9 or #12 screws should be used for additional fastening.

Flooring	Fastener	Spacing
Tongue-and-Groove Flooring Blind-Nailed (minimum ⅝" subfloor)		
½" × 1½"	1½" machine-driven fastener; 5d screw, cut steel, or wire casing nail	10" apart
⅜" × 1½"	1¼" machine-driven fastener; 4d bright wire casing nail	8" apart
¾"	2" machine-driven fastener; 7d or 8d screw or cut nail	10"–12" apart
¾" × 2¼"	2" machine-driven fastener; 7d or 8d screw or cut nail	10"–12" apart
¾" × 3¼"	2" machine-driven fastener; 7d or 8d screw or cut nail	10"–12" apart
¾" × 3" to 8" plank	2" machine-driven fastener; 7d or 8d screw or cut nail	7"–8" apart into and between joists
Square-Edge Flooring Facenailed		
⁵⁄₁₆" × 1½"	1" 15-g fully barbed flooring brad	2 nails every 7"
⁵⁄₁₆" × 2"	1" 15-g fully barbed flooring brad	2 nails every 7"

Source: National Oak Flooring Manufacturers Association.

▶ Wall Fasteners (for hanging or attaching objects to a wall)

Where Fastening	Type of Wall Finish	Light Load	Medium Load	Heavy Load
Into Studs		Picture hanger	Wood screw	Lag screw, or 1 × 2 strip attached at each stud with lag screw
Between Studs	Wallboard	Picture hanger Sheet-metal screw	Expansion bolt Plastic anchor Drive-point hollow-wall fastener Plastic screw-in anchor Toggle bolt	
	Plaster with wood lath	Picture hanger Brad Sheet-metal screw	Sheet-metal screw Expansion bolt Toggle bolt	
Masonry	Brick	Concrete nail Adhesive-backed hanger (for masonry)	Concrete nail Plastic anchor with screw/nail Fluted plastic anchor with screw	Lead shield and lag screw
	Concrete	Concrete nail Adhesive-backed hanger (for masonry)	Concrete nail Plastic anchor with screw/nail Fluted plastic anchor with screw	Lead shield and lag screw Self-anchoring expansion bolt Epoxy bolt system

▶ Wallboard Fasteners

This table shows the spacing required from center to center for each kind of fastener when applying wallboard to walls or ceilings. The table also gives an estimate of the quantity of fasteners needed per 1,000 square feet of wallboard.

Fastener	Spacing: Ceilings	Spacing: Walls	Quantity Needed per 1,000 Square Feet
¼" or 1⅜" annular-ring nail	7"	8"	5¼ lb, 325 nails/lb
6d (1⅞" cement-coated wallboard nail)	7"	8"	6¼ lb, 375 nails/lb
5d (1⅝" cement-coated wallboard nail)	6"	7"	5¼ lb, 365 nails/lb
1¼" Type W wallboard screw	12"	16"	Approx. 1,000 screws
1" Type S wallboard screw	12"	12"	Approx. 875 screws
1⅝" Type S wallboard screw	16"	16"	Approx. 565 screws

▶ Common Wood Screw Options

Length	⅜" to 6"
Gauge	#2 to #16*
Head	Round, flat, bevel
Slot	Standard, Phillips, square-head
Material	Zinc-plated steel, brass-plated steel, solid brass, some stainless steel and chrome-plated steel

*Higher gauge = larger diameter.

Common Lag Screw Options

Length	1" to 12"
Diameter	¼", 5/16", ⅜", ½"
Head	Square, hex

▶ Size of Screwdriver to Use

Screw Gauge	Standard Driver	Phillips Driver
#1	⅛"	No. 0
2, 3	⅛"	No. 1
4	5/32"	No. 1
5, 6	3/16"	No. 2
7	7/32"	No. 2
8, 9	¼"	No. 2
10	5/16"	No. 3
12, 14, 16	⅜"	No. 3
18 & up	½"	No. 4

▶ Bolt Types & Common Sizes

Type	Length	Diameter
Machine	1"–12"	¼"–¾"
Carriage	1"–12"	¼"–¾"
Stove	½"–4"	⅛"–5/32"

Nuts and usually washers are used with bolts.

▶ Nails per Pound

(common nails)

Nail Size	Quantity	Nail Size	Quantity
2d	845	12d	60
3d	540	16d	45
4d	290	20d	30
6d	165	30d	20
8d	100	40d	17
10d	65	60d	10

▶ *Adhesives & Mortars*

Type	Description	Uses
Polyvinyl acetate (PVA)	Water-based white glue; inexpensive; sets quickly, dries clear; is not waterproof	Multipurpose; for interior use only
Aliphatic adhesive	Carpenter's wood glue; stronger and slower setting than PVA white glue	Multipurpose; for woodworking
Hide glue	Comes in granules, which must be dissolved in warm water; must be kept warm while using	Woodworking joints and veneers
Powdered casein	Mix 15 minutes before using; somewhat water-resistant	Oily woods such as teak and yew
Resorcinol	Catalyst (two-component) glue	High-moisture situations such as kitchen and bath cabinets; outdoor projects
Epoxy	Catalyst glue	Adhering wood to other materials
Contact cement	Water-resistant glue; solvent-based type is flammable	Bonding veneers and laminates
Construction adhesive	Caulklike adhesive available in cartridges	For reinforcing structural connections: subfloors, sheathing, paneling, decking; interior and exterior types available

For Tile Setting

Type	Description	Uses
Type I mastic	Solvent-based organic tile adhesive; ready to use; flammable	Setting tile in damp areas
Type II mastic	Latex-based organic tile adhesive; easy to clean; nonflammable	Setting tile in dry areas
Dry-set mortar	Portland cement mixed with sand, additives, and water	Setting tile over mortar bed, backer board, or concrete
Latex–portland cement mortar	Portland cement mixed with sand, liquid latex (sometimes diluted with water); water-resistant; high workability	Setting tile in damp areas over mortar or concrete
Epoxy adhesive	Epoxy resin mixed with hardener; works best between 70° and 85° F; expensive	Setting tile over plywood or old resilient floor
Epoxy mortar	Epoxy resin mixed with hardener, sand, and portland cement	Setting tile over uneven surface

▶ *Comparison of Caulking Materials*

Caulking Material	Life	Application	Remarks
Oil-based	1–2 years	All household surfaces	Least expensive, least durable of all caulks. Oil tends to seep out and may stain unprimed surfaces while drying out caulk itself, leading to shrinking, cracking, and the need for replacement.
Latex-based	3–10 years	Indoors; outside only if painted and not where seal moves or is subject to moisture; only for narrow joints (less than ¼")	Because it is water soluble, should not be used where it will become damp. Insufficiently flexible to withstand frequent expansion and contraction; shouldn't be used on movable joints. May disintegrate on concrete or cement.
Acrylic-based	10 years	All applications, indoors and out; for joints up to ½" × ½"	Durable, fast-curing (about 1 hour), does not stain. Should not be painted.
Butyl rubber	3–10 years	Outdoors, especially on metal and stone; good in places where water may collect, such as eaves and downspouts, since it is water-resistant; only for narrow or moderately narrow joints (less than ½")	Needs no paint. Make take more than a week to cure. Will shrink over time.
Elastomeric (synthetic base: silicone, poly-sulfide, or polyurethane)	20 years +	All applications, but does not adhere to paint; polysulfide doesn't adhere to porous materials	Highly flexible, long-lasting caulk. May be used on large joints. Some types require surface priming before application, and some cannot be painted.
Polyurethane or urea formaldehyde foam	Varies with exposure	Not a true caulking material but excellent for filling large cracks	Available in aerosol cans. Expands tremendously. Must not be exposed to direct sunlight. Excellent as a filler before caulking.

▶ Selecting Exterior Primers

Material	Primer
Painted wood	Oil-based exterior primer
Bare wood (nonstaining)	Latex exterior primer
Bare redwood or cedar	Oil-based exterior primer
Stucco	Latex stucco primer
Vinyl	Latex house paint or oil-based primer
Galvanized steel	Zinc chromate primer
Bright steel	Latex metal primer
Rusted steel	Oil-based rusty-metal primer

▶ Selecting Interior Primers & Sealers

Surface	Product
New wallboard	Latex primer or PVA sealer
New plaster	Latex or alkyd primer
Painted wallboard	Spot-prime stains and repaired patches with white-pigmented shellac; prime old, worn painted surface with latex or alkyd primer
Painted plaster	Same as painted wallboard
Bare wood to be painted	Alkyd enamel sealer or undercoat
Painted wood to be painted	Spot-prime repairs with white-pigmented shellac
Bare wood to be clear-finished	Sanding sealer
Masonry	Alkyd or latex penetrating sealer
Metal	Alkyd enamel sealer or undercoat, with rust inhibitors if needed

▶ Professional Painting Tips

• Use a beveled paint roller to spread paint in corners without buildup.

• Paint heating-system registers and grilles with aerosol paint.

• Avoid overbrushing enamel paint. Working quickly, apply a generous finish coat and brush lightly. Do not try to touch up areas you've already painted. If you have problems, let the paint dry, degloss, and repaint.

• Wipe paint off your paint shield after each use.

• Reduce paint odor by stirring a few drops of vanilla extract into the paint. There are also commercial paint fragrances. Both override normal paint odor.

• Use painting tape to mark borders and other areas where you don't want paint to bleed under the tape edge. This tape has a unique microbarrier edge that prevents such seepage. It also won't leave a sticky residue or remove the undersurface when pulled up.

▶ Which Paint (Sheen) Should You Use?

Area	Best Choice	Acceptable Choice
Ceiling	Flat	Eggshell
Living room	Flat	Eggshell
Hallway	Flat	Eggshell
Bedroom	Flat	Eggshell
Child's room	Eggshell	Semigloss
Bathroom	Semigloss or Gloss	Eggshell
Kitchen	Semigloss or Gloss	Eggshell
Kitchen cabinets	Semigloss or Gloss	Eggshell
Woodwork, windows	Semigloss or Gloss	Eggshell

▶ Sandpaper Selection Guide

40-grit (extra coarse)	For stripping and extraheavy sanding of painted surfaces
60-grit (coarse)	For stripping and heavy sanding of painted surfaces
100-grit (medium)	For first sanding of wallboard and plaster walls, painted walls, and wood surfaces
120-grit (medium fine)	For first and final sanding of wallboard and plaster walls, painted and varnished walls, and wood surfaces
150-grit (fine)	For final sanding of painted and varnished walls and wood surfaces
Medium wallboard	For first sanding of wallboard and plaster walls, and bare or painted screen
Fine wallboard screen	For final sanding of wallboard and plaster walls, painted or bare

▶ Roller Naps

Finish Texture	Surface to Be Painted	Nap Size
Smooth	Walls, floors, finish work, cabinets	3/16", 1/4"
Medium smooth	Walls	3/8", 1/2"
Rough	Textured walls, light stucco walls, masonry floors	3/4", 1"
Extrarough	Brick, concrete block, masonry, stucco	1 1/4"

▶ Copper Wire: Sizes, Ampacity & Use

For aluminum wire, use two sizes larger.

Wire Gauge Number	Ampacity Type T, TW wire (cable assemblies)	Ampacity Type THW wire (individual connectors)	Use
18	7		Cords, low-voltage, bells
16	10		
14	15		General circuit wiring for lights and receptacles
12	20		
10	30		Individual appliances: heaters, ranges, dryers, water heaters, ovens; branch-circuit feeders
8	40		
6	55		
4	70	85	
2	95	115	Main service conductors and branch-circuit feeders
1	110	130	
0 (1/0)	125	150	
00 (2/0)	145	175	
000 (3/0	165	200	

Note: Receptacles and switches have ampere ratings that are to be matched to the type of wire being used. Most of them are stamped *15 amp,* which means they should be used with No. 14 wire. However, the NEC permits the use of No. 12 wire, which has an ampacity of 20 amperes, for use with 15-amp receptacles and switches.

▶ Color Coding of Wires & Terminal Screws

Function	Wire Color	Terminal Screw Color
Grounding	Bare copper Green Green and yellow	Green
Neutral (grounded)	White	Silver
Hot	Black Red Blue White made black*	Brass Bronze (common terminal of 3-way switch)

*Occasionally, when wiring is done with cable, the white wire must function as a hot wire (for example, a switch loop between a light fixture and 2-way switch, or the traveler wires between two 3-way switches). Common practice is to mark both ends of such a wire with black paint or electrical tape.

▶ Wire Talk: What Labels Mean

AC	Armored cable, which is flexible metallic sheathing
ACT	Armored cable that has wires with thermoplastic insulation
AWG	American Wire Gauge; a system of wire sizes
BX	Old trade name for flexible armored cable
NM	Nonmetallic cable for dry locations only
NMC	Nonmetallic cable for dry or damp (aboveground) locations
R	Rubber insulation
SE	Service-entrance wire; has plastic sheathing over neoprene insulation
T	Thermoplastic insulation
THW	Thermoplastic, heat- and water-resistant insulation
TW	Thermoplastic, water-resistant insulation
UF	Underground feeder cable with thermoplastic sheathing for direct burial
USE	Underground service-entrance wire with rubber and neoprene sheathing
w/G	With ground; designates cable with ground wire

Note: Wire refers to single- or multi-strand conductors. *Cable* refers to two or more conductors, insulated from each other, wrapped in sheathing.

Number of Conductors* Permitted in an Electrical Box

Box Size (Metal)†		Maximum Number of Conductors		
Inside Dimensions	Cu. In.	No. 14	No. 12	No. 10
Round or Octagonal				
4 × 1¼	12.5	6	5	5
4 × 1½	15.5	7	6	6
4 × 2⅛	21.5	15	13	12
Square				
4⅝ × 1¼	25.5	12	11	10
4⅝ × 1½	29.5	14	13	11
4⅝ × 2⅛	42	21	18	16
Device Box				
3 × 2 × 1½	7.5	3	3	3
3 × 2 × 2	10	5	4	4
3 × 2 × 2¼	10.5	5	4	4
3 × 2 × 2½	12.5	6	5	5
3 × 2 × 2¾	14	7	6	5
3 × 2 × 3½	18	9	8	7
Junction Box				
4 × 2⅛ × 1½	10.3	5	4	4
4 × 2⅛ × 1⅞	13	6	5	5
4 × 2⅛ × 2⅛	14.5	7	6	5

*When Counting Conductors:

Each hot wire	=	1 conductor
Each neutral wire	=	1 conductor
Total of all ground wires	=	1 conductor
Each switch or receptacle	=	1 conductor
Each cable clamp or fixture stud	=	1 conductor

†For plastic boxes refer to capacity, in cubic inches, stamped inside box.

Recommended Locations of Electrical Boxes

Type of Box	Location of Center of Box
Switch	48" above floor
Receptacle	12" above floor; 44" above floor if over a countertop
Baseboard heater	Usually 6" above floor; varies
Ceiling fixture	Center of ceiling (find by measuring diagonals)
Junction box	Wherever accessible; cannot be concealed

Minimum Requirements for Electrical Fixtures

The following specifications will help you to place light fixtures, switches, receptacles (outlets), and appliances. Consult National Electrical Code (NEC) or your local building department for additional restrictions. Code requirements are minimum; when going to the trouble and expense of installing new wiring, it is good practice to increase the number of fixtures and receptacles in anticipation of future needs.

Lights. Every room, hallway, stairway, outdoor entrance, and attached garage must have at least one permanent light fixture controlled by a wall switch located at each entrance. The light can be mounted on the ceiling or any wall, and you may use as many individual fixtures as you wish. The following list includes some exceptions to this rule:

- A wall receptacle controlled by a wall switch at the entrance to a room may be substituted for a permanent light fixture in any room except the kitchen or a bathroom.
- Light fixtures for utility rooms, crawl spaces, and attics without stairs can be controlled by pull chains instead of wall switches.
- Lighting for hallways, stairways, and outdoor entrances can be activated by specialized switches. These include remote, central, or automatic switches.
- Additional recommendations. Lighting fixtures should also be installed to illuminate the front of a furnace, laundry equipment in a basement or garage, bathroom mirrors, and clothes closets. Fixtures in clothes closets must be located on the ceiling or on the wall above the door. Pendant fixtures are not allowed—most codes assume that fixtures of this type could cause an overstuffed closet to become a fire hazard.

Switches. The switch for the main light fixture of a room should be located at the entrance to the room—at each entrance, if there is more than one. The switch must be on the latch side of a hinged door so the door does not interfere with the access to the switch. Do not locate switches in bathrooms where it is possible to reach them while using the shower or bathtub. Attic stairs must be illuminated by a light that is controlled by a switch at the foot of the stairs. Lights for basement stairs must have a switch at the head of the stairs as well as one at any other entrance.

Receptacles. Receptacles, also called convenience outlets, must be located in every room no more than 12 feet apart. (The NEC actually requires that no point along the floor line of any wall be more than 6 feet from an outlet.) On a wall with more than one door opening (including closets), there should be at least one outlet between the doors unless that section of wall is less than 2 feet wide.

Place receptacles for a kitchen counter no more than 4 feet apart. Standard practice is to install at least one outlet for each foot of counter.

Laundry rooms must have at least one receptacle positioned within 6 feet of any appliance.

Bathrooms should have at least one receptacle adjacent to the washbasin. All bathroom outlets must be protected by GFCI devices.

There must be at least one receptacle outdoors, as well as one in the garage and one in the basement. They must all be GFCI protected.

Appliances. Any 240-volt appliance or permanent 120-volt appliance should have its own receptacle or junction box.

▶ Drain, Waste & Vent Pipe Sizes

Codes specify the exact size of all drain-pipes; the sizes are not minimums. The size of fixture outlet, trap (outlet and trap must be the same size), and vent depends on the amount of water flowing through the fixture. Codes measure the flow in *fixture units*. The chart summarizes typical code requirements. Remember that codes specify pipe sizes in fixture units, not by fixture type.

Typical Code Requirements

Fixture	Fixture Units	Trap Size (in inches)	Vent Size (in inches)
Toilet	4	3	2
Washing machine	3	2	1½
Shower	2	2	1½
Bathtub	2	1½	1¼
Kitchen sink	2	1½	1¼
Washbasin	1	1¼	1¼
Kitchen or laundry	varies	2	1½
Bathroom	varies	3	2
Whole house	varies	3 or 4	total = drain size

▶ Which Supply Stop (Shutoff Valve) to Use

Inlet Options	For Connecting to . . .
½" compression fitting	Copper tubing
½" IPS (coarse) female threads	Threaded galvanized pipe or threaded adapter on copper tubing
IPS male thread (or ⅜" "coarse-threaded nut")	½" threaded pipe fitting (IPS female threads)

Outlet Options	For Connecting to . . .
¼", ⅜", or ½" compression fitting	Smooth end of ¼", ⅜", or ½" OD supply tube Flexible tubing with fine-thread compression nut on one end
⅜" or ½" slip-joint fitting with rubber cone washer	Smooth end of ⅜" or ½" OD supply tube (smooth end of tube should be flared)

Optional Configurations	For . . .
Angle stop	Changing direction of piping
Straight stop	Keeping piping in straight line
Double outlet/triple outlet	Controlling 2 or 3 fixtures

▶ Recommended Minimum Fixture Clearances

(Verify against local codes)

Toilet
From centerline to side wall	15"
From tank to basin on side	4"
From back wall to obstruction in front of toilet	48"

Washbasin
From side to side wall	4"
From side to toilet tank	4"
From side to bathtub	6"
Clearance in front	24"

Shower
Clearance inside, between walls	32"
Clearance in front for door swing	28"

▶ Rough-In Dimensions for Bathroom Fixtures

	Toilet	Basin	Bathtub	Shower
Distance of below-floor drainpipe from back wall	Varies; 12"	—	6"–10" —	Center of stall
Height of drain stub above floor	—	15"–17"	—	—
Height of supply shutoff above floor	5"–10"	19"–21"	—	—
Distance of shutoff from centerline of fixture	6"	8"	—	—
Height of faucet above finish floor	—	—	26"	46"
Height of tub spout above finish floor	—	—	20"	—
Height of showerhead above finish floor	—	—	65"–76"	65"–76"

DWV (Drain-Waste-Vent) Fittings: Which Fitting to Use?

	Drain & Waste Pipes	Vent Pipes
Joining Pipes at a Change of Direction		
Horizontal to vertical	Short- or long-sweep ¼ bend Two ⅛ bends Sanitary tee Double tee, or elbow with side inlet (where 2 horizontal pipes join at a vertical pipe)	¼ bend or 90° vent ell Sanitary tee (inverted), wye (inverted)
Vertical to horizontal	Long-sweep ¼ bend Two ⅛ offset bends Wye and ⅛ bend (combo wye) Closet bend (for toilet connections only)	¼ bend or 90° vent ell Two ⅛ bends (offset)
Horizontal to horizontal	Long-sweep ¼ bend ⅛, ¹⁄₁₆, or ⅙ bend Wye or combo wye	¼ bend or 90° vent ell ⅛, ¹⁄₁₆, or ⅙ bend
Joining Pipes, No Change of Direction		
Same type of pipe, identical size	Coupling or no-hub coupling	Coupling or no-hub coupling
Same type of pipe, different sizes	Reducing coupling	Reducing coupling
Different types of pipe	Adapter (glued plastic fitting to threaded fitting, plastic to copper, and such), or no-hub connector	Same as drain
Miscellaneous Joints		
Joining pipe to fitting of larger size	Reducing bushing	Reducing bushing
Joining fitting to fitting	Street fitting to street fitting; or hub fitting to hub fitting, with close nipple	Same as drain
Offset bends	Various combinations of bends	Same as drain
P-trap (rough in)	Adjustable P-trap: solid joints Adjustable P-trap: slip joints (where allowed)	
Cleanout: vertical pipe	Wye and cleanout fitting Sanitary tee and cleanout Test tee	
Cleanout: horizontal pipe	Cleanout fitting (end of run) Wye and cleanout fitting Cleanout tee	

ABS (acrylonitrile-butadiene-styrene) Black plastic pipe used for drain-waste-vent pipes in plumbing systems; pipe is joined to fittings with solvent.

Acoustical spray Popcornlike texture sprayed onto ceilings for sound-deadening and decorative purposes.

Acoustic tile Ceiling tile made of fibrous material to absorb sound; usually 12 inches square.

Adhesive Any type of glue, but usually refers to high-strength glues used for installing subflooring, wallboard, paneling, carpet, tile, or mirrors.

Aggregate The rock, gravel, and sand used in making concrete.

Air gap A device through which a pump-drained appliance (dishwasher, washing machine) must discharge its waste water before that water enters the drain system; prevents waste water from siphoning back into the appliance.

Aliphatic adhesive A glue (usually yellow but sometimes white) derived from vinyl acetate compounds that are modified with aliphatic polymers; takes longer to dry but is stronger than ordinary white (PVA) glue; generally referred to as carpenter's wood glue.

Allen wrench Hexagonal, rod-shaped tool for turning allen screws, which have hexagon-shaped depressions in the head.

Amp, ampere A unit of measurement of electric current, used in quantifying the rate at which electrons flow past a given point in a wire or other conductor.

Ampacity The capacity of a conductor for carrying electricity, measured in amperes.

Anchor bolt A device used to secure a wood mudsill to a concrete or masonry foundation wall or slab.

Angle stop A shutoff valve, or stop, for sinks and other plumbing fixtures; "angle" refers to the fact that the inlet and outlet sides of the valve are at right angles to each other and thus change the direction of piping.

Annular-ring nail Nail with ribs or rings around the shank for better holding.

Antiscald valve (faucet) A tub and/or shower valve that automatically balances the hot and cold water to maintain an even temperature.

Astragal A molding for double doors that attaches to the edge of one of the doors to cover the gap between the two doors when they are closed.

Backbrushing Blending fresh paint into a previously painted area so there is no obvious line.

Ballast A magnetic coil that provides the starting voltage or stabilizes the current in a circuit (as of a fluorescent lamp).

Baluster A vertical member of a railing, on a staircase, for instance.

Balustrade A railing made up of a top rail, balusters, and often a bottom rail.

Band joist A joist nailed across the ends of floor or ceiling joists; also called a rim joist.

Barge rafter The rafter at the outside edge of a roof overhang; also called verge rafter.

Baseboard A trim board placed at the base of a wall next to the floor.

Base molding A strip of wood used to trim the upper edge of a baseboard.

Base shoe A strip of wood used to trim the bottom edge of the baseboard next to the floor. Also called a carpet strip.

Basin wrench Tool for removing or installing nuts or bolts in hard-to-reach places, usually under sinks.

Batt A precut length of fiberglass insulation.

Battens Narrow pieces of wood used over the joints of wider pieces, especially on board-and-batten siding.

Beam A structural member, usually steel or heavy timber, used to support floor or ceiling joists or rafters; also called girder.

Bearings Movable rings placed over the ends of a motor shaft or other arbor (shaft) to eliminate friction as the shaft rotates in its mount.

Bearing wall A wall that supports floor loads or roof loads, with a girder or foundation support underneath it.

Bevel A surface cut at an angle other than 90 degrees across the edge, end, or face of a piece of wood or other material.

Bevel gauge A measuring tool with two arms that can be adjusted and set at any angle, then used for duplicating that angle.

Bibb A faucet with male threads that allow a hose to be attached; also called hose bibb or sillcock.

Blanket insulation Fiberglass, mineral wool, or other insulation in the form of mats or blankets that can be rolled out between joists or studs.

Blocking Short pieces of wood nailed between joists or studs for reinforcement; with joists, similar to bridging.

Bob A weight suspended on a string for testing true vertical alignment.

Bonding agent A liquid adhesive used for enhancing the bond between old concrete and fresh concrete.

Bonnet The packing nut of a bibb or faucet that holds the valve stem in place.

Bridging Narrow wood or metal members placed on the diagonal between joists to stiffen the joists and spread the weight load; similar to blocking; also called cross-bracing.

BTU (British thermal unit) A measurement of heat; specifically, the amount needed to raise the temperature of 1 pound of water 1° F, starting at 39° F.

Bull nosing A tile or board with a blunt, rounded edge, used for finishing exposed edges or corners.

Bus bar A rigid conductor at the main power source to which three or more circuits are connected.

Bushing A sleeve inserted into a hole or fitting to protect it from contact with the cable, shaft, or other device set in the hole.

Butt hinge A door hinge attached to the edge of a door and the face of the jamb, so only the knuckles of the hinge show when the door is shut.

Butt joint The junction of two pieces of wood where the end of one meets the side of another at a right angle.

BX Electrical cable sheathed in a flexible metallic covering.

-by Indicates the second dimension in lumber sizes—for example, 2x4; when the second dimension is omitted, as in 2-by, it refers to any board that is that thick.

Capacitor An electronic component that stores and intensifies electrical current for an instantaneous discharge.

Carpenter's wood glue Also called aliphatic adhesive, it is used for woodworking projects.

Carriage _See_ stringer.

Carriage bolt A bolt with a smooth rounded head.

Cartridge   The replaceable unit in some washerless faucets; controls the flow of water.

Casement window   A window with hinges attached to the side of the sash, so it can be opened outward like a door.

Casing   Molding used to trim door and window openings between the jambs and walls, like a picture frame.

Cast polymer   A synthetic material used for sinks, countertops, and shower bases. Also called cultured marble.

Caulk   Viscous material used to seal joints and make them water- and airtight.

Cement   A strong adhesive material; or, one of the components of concrete.

Centerset faucet   Faucet design in which spout and controls are built into a single unit.

Chair rail   A type of molding installed horizontally along a wall, just above the wainscoting at the same height as a chair back.

Chamfer   A small bevel cut along the edge of a piece of wood.

Channel lock pliers   Large pliers with adjustable parallel jaws.

Chase   An enclosed space, such as inside a finished wall, for running duct work or vent pipes between floors.

Chimney cap   The mortar or concrete top of a chimney that surrounds the flue pipe.

Chimney hood   A metal or concrete cap for keeping rain and snow out of a chimney flue; also called weather cap.

Circuit   The complete path of an electric current, leading from a source (generator or battery) through components (for example, electric lights), and back to the source.

Circuit breaker   A safety device used to interrupt the flow of power when the electricity exceeds a predetermined amount. Unlike a fuse, a circuit breaker can be reset.

Circuit breaker panel   In an electrical system, the main service panel where electricity is distributed to branch circuits through a series of circuit breakers.

Circular saw   A power saw with a circular blade.

Clapboard   An archaic term for horizontal beveled siding with overlapping boards.

Cleanout   Easy-to-reach opening in the drain system; used in removing obstructions.

Cleat   A strip of wood fastened to a surface and used as a support or to provide a foothold or handhold.

Closet auger   A drain auger for cleaning obstructions out of a toilet drain.

Closet flange   A plumbing fitting that connects a toilet to its waste pipe and the floor.

Code   A set of regulations that specifies how buildings must be constructed or the electrical, plumbing, and mechanical components installed; local codes are usually based on model codes widely adopted throughout the region or across the country.

Cold chisel   A solid-steel chisel intended to be struck with a hammer, used for chipping or breaking metal.

Collar tie   A horizontal board nailed between two rafters to keep them from spreading apart; also called a collar beam or tie beam.

Combination square   An adjustable measuring tool that reads both right angles and 45-degree angles.

Common nail   A standard nail, available in a variety of lengths, used for general construction.

Compressor   A machine that compresses air for use with air tools; or the part of a refrigerator or air conditioner that compresses fluid as part of a cycle to create temperature changes in that fluid.

Concrete   A mixture of cement, aggregate, and water that hardens through a chemical process called hydration.

Concrete block   Hollow blocks made of concrete, joined with mortar for constructing walls and foundations.

Construction adhesive   Strong adhesive, usually packaged in tubes for a caulking gun, used for gluing subfloor panels, insulation, paneling, and other building components together.

Continuity   An uninterrupted electrical path.

Continuity tester   A tool for testing whether electric current can flow through a wire or electrical device; used to test the wire or device when power is turned off.

Convector   A heating device, consisting of water pipes encased in multiple metal fins, that uses hot water to heat the surrounding air, which then rises and circulates through the room in natural air currents.

Coped joint   A junction in which one end of a piece of molding is cut to fit the shaped face of another. Unlike a miter joint, it doesn't develop a gap between the boards if they shrink.

Coping saw   Handsaw with a very thin blade for cutting tight curves; used to follow molding profiles in making coped joints.

Corbel   A recessed area in the surface of a ceiling.

Corner bead   A strip of formed sheet metal that protects the corner of a stucco or plaster wall.

Cornice   The overhang of a roof at the eaves, usually consisting of a fascia board, soffit, and decorative molding. Or, any decorative member placed at or near the top of a wall.

Counterboring   Deepening the hole for a screw or bolt so the head can be covered and concealed with a plug.

Countersinking   Boring the end of a hole for a screw or bolt so the head can be brought flush with or below the surface. Also, sinking or setting a nail or screw so the head is flush with or slightly below the surface.

Courses   Layers or rows of material, such as shakes or shingles on a roof or bricks in a wall.

CPVC (chlorinated polyvinyl chloride)   Plastic used to form rigid gray- or pastel-colored pipe from which hot-water supply lines are made.

Crawl space   The area under a house, usually with a dirt floor and not enough headroom for a basement.

Cripple wall   A low wall between the foundation and first floor; also called pony wall.

Crowbar   A 2- to 3-foot steel bar with a curved hook at one end and a flattened chisel shape at the other end, used for prying up boards and pulling nails.

Crown molding   A convex molding used horizontally wherever an interior angle is to be covered (usually at the top of a wall, next to the ceiling).

Curb   A frame for holding a skylight above the roof.

Cushion-back carpet   Carpet with foam backing attached, which allows it to be glued directly to a floor without a separate pad.

d Represents penny, after "denarius," a Roman coin of low value. Used to designate nail size—for example, 8d nail = eight-penny nail.

Dado A rectangular channel cut across the grain of a piece of lumber.

Damper A movable flap that closes a chimney flue or ventilating duct to prevent outside air from entering the house.

Dead bolt A door lock with a metal bar that slides into a recessed cavity in the door jamb.

Decking screw A hot-dipped galvanized screw, similar to a wallboard screw but usually in longer lengths, that can be driven without drilling a pilot hole; often used for attaching 2-by decking lumber.

Diverter Valve for changing the flow of water from one outlet to another.

Dolly varden siding Bevel siding with a rabbet in the bottom edge to accept the top edge of the piece below it.

Doorjamb The case that surrounds a door; consists of two upright side pieces called side jambs and a top horizontal piece called a head jamb.

Dormer An extension of attic space jutting out from the main roof.

Double-glazed, -ing Describes a double thickness of glass; two panes separated by a sealed space filled with air, an inert gas such as argon, or a solid transparent gel.

Double-hung window A window with an upper sash and lower sash that slide up and down.

Dovetail joint An interlocking joint created by cutting evenly spaced tapered slots into the end of one board, which creates a row of tooth-like projections that slide into corresponding slots cut into the end of the other board. If the teeth are straight and not tapered, the joint is called a finger joint.

Dowel joint A joint created by inserting dowels into the edges of two boards.

Downspout Vertical pipe, metal or plastic, for carrying water down from roof gutters.

Drain auger A coiled wire device, with a crank and hooked end, for unclogging drains; also called a plumber's snake.

Drip cap A wood molding or metal piece placed above a door or window frame. Causes water to fall beyond the outside edge of the frame.

Drip edge A piece of angled metal placed along the edge of a roof. Prevents water from running down the fascia or cornice.

Drywall *See* Wallboard.

Dry well A hole for collecting water and dispersing it into the ground.

Ducts Pipes that carry air from a furnace or air conditioner to the living areas of a structure, or that carry exhaust air from a fan or ventilator.

Durable species Trees with wood that is naturally resistant to rot, such as redwood, cedar, and cypress. Does not need to be pressure treated for exterior use.

DWV (drain-waste-vent) All or part of the plumbing system that carries waste water to the sewer and gases to the roof.

Eave Lowest overhanging part of a sloping roof, or the area under it.

Efflorescence A white powdery substance that forms on concrete or masonry walls, left by water seeping through the wall and leaching out certain salts.

Electrical box A metal or plastic box used to contain wire terminations where they connect to other wires, switches, or receptacles.

Electrical conduit Tubing used to enclose electrical conductors; the most common types are EMT (electrical metallic tubing, or "thin-wall"), rigid (thick-walled, like steel water pipe), and plastic.

Electrical connector A device with a threaded metal sleeve inside an insulating cap, that screws onto the ends of two or more electrical conductors to make a firm connection; commonly referred to as wire connector or solderless connector.

Epoxy A type of adhesive that is extremely strong and durable, made by mixing a catalyst with a hardener at the time of use.

Escutcheon Ornamental plate for covering a wall opening where pipe penetrates, or the part of a faucet that covers the stem.

Expansion bolt A bolt with a tapered end or other device that spreads and grips the sides of a hole as the bolt is tightened; usually used in concrete or masonry; also a hollow-wall fastener consisting of a screw inside a sleeve that expands behind the wall as the screw is tightened.

Face frame The frame that forms the front of a cabinet and shows between the doors and drawers.

Face nailing Driving nails perpendicular to the surface of a board or joint of two pieces of wood. Also called direct nailing.

Fascia board A flat board, typically parallel to the ground, that forms the face of the cornice or eave of a roof; the member to which most gutters are attached.

Feather To smooth patching compound or other mastic material so the thickness tapers to nothing at the outside edges of the filled area.

Fiberglass insulation Insulating material made from glass fibers; may be loosely textured blankets, matted boards, or lightweight beads.

Fiberglass-mesh tape Self-sticking fabric of loosely woven fiberglass.

Field nailing Nailing in the interior portions (not edges) of plywood or other panels.

Finishing nail A thin nail with a small, compact head, available in various lengths; leaves very small impression in the wood surface.

Fire stop A solid, tight-fitting piece of wood or other material placed between studs, joists, or stair stringers to prevent the spread of fire and smoke. In a frame wall, usually a piece of 2x4 cross-blocking between studs.

Fish To feed wires through tight spaces, such as wall cavities.

Fish tape Flat steel spring or nylon wire with hooked ends; used to pull wires through conduits or walls.

Flange A rim that allows one object to be attached to another object.

Flashing Sheet metal, roofing felt, or other material used at the junction of two surfaces on a roof to prevent the entry of water.

Float To evenly spread a material such as plaster, mortar, or concrete.

Float valve A valve, regulated by a hollow float, that shuts on and off automatically when water reaches certain levels, used in toilets, sump pumps, dishwashers, and other fixtures with variable water levels; also called ballcock valve.

Flue In a chimney or vent, the opening through which smoke and other gases pass.

Fluorescent bulb A bulb in which a coating on the inside of a glass tube is made to glow by an electric current.

Flush A term of relationship in which the surfaces of two or more objects form a smooth plane.

Flux An acid-bearing substance spread on a metal surface so solder will bond to the metal.

Foam backer rod Filler material for building up gaps prior to caulking.

Forced-air heating *See* Warm-air heating.

Forms The temporary structure, usually of wood, that shapes poured concrete.

Foundation seal Insulation or similar material placed between the top of a foundation wall and the wood sill for sealing out drafts, dust, and air infiltration.

Foundation sill A 2-by board bolted to the top of a foundation wall for supporting the floor joists or a low cripple wall; also called sill plate or mudsill.

Framing The skeletal structure of a building; usually wood.

Frass Fine sawdust produced by wood-boring insects.

Frost line The lowest depth at which the ground can be expected to freeze in a given region. It determines the required minimum depth for foundation footings and basement wall insulation.

Fur To build out a wall or ceiling by attaching 1-by strips (furring) to the framing members.

Furring Narrow strips of wood, usually 1-by strips, attached to walls or ceilings; forms a true surface on which to fasten surface materials; also called strapping.

Gable The triangular part of an exterior wall formed by the slopes of the roof.

Gas cock The type of valve used for gas lines; has a lever or lug handle that, when parallel with the pipe, indicates that the valve is open and, when perpendicular to the pipe, indicates that the valve is closed.

GFCI (ground fault circuit interrupter) An electrical safety device that monitors a receptacle or circuit for minute leakages of current and that deadens the receptacle or circuit whenever there is a potential for electrical shock.

Girder *See* Beam.

Glazing Material, usually glass, used for windowpanes.

Glazing compound Putty used for sealing the gap between a windowpane and the frame.

Grade The surface of the ground around a building; the process of scraping and filling the ground to slope or level the surface.

Ground A conducting connection between an electrical system and the earth that usually does not carry current unless a short circuit occurs.

Ground wire The safety wire (green or bare) in a circuit intended to provide a safe path for voltage surges or disconnected hot wires. Its purpose is to allow the voltage to discharge rapidly enough to open the circuit breaker or other overcurrent device.

Grout Cement-based material, sometimes with sand added, for filling joints between tiles; thin concrete mix used to fill hollow cavities of concrete-block wall.

Hardboard A synthetic wood panel made by chemically converting wood chips to fibers and then forming the panels under heat and pressure.

Hard-wire To wire a fixture or appliance directly into the electric circuit rather than attach it with a removable plug.

Hardwood The wood of broad-leafed, often deciduous, trees such as oak or maple; not a reference to the actual hardness of the wood.

Hawk A board with a handle on the bottom, used for carrying mortar or plaster; also called a mortarboard or a hod.

HDG (hot-dipped galvanized) Process for coating metal hardware, such as nails and screws, with zinc to protect them from corrosion.

Header A horizontal member over a door, window, or other opening that supports the framing members above it (also called a lintel); also, a beam used to support the ends of joists.

Heat-bond tape Glue-impregnated tape used for seaming carpet.

HEPA (high efficiency particulate air) filter Used for vacuum cleaners or respirators to remove dust with microscopic fibers.

Hinge knuckle The part of a hinge where the leaves intertwine; the linked knuckles hold the hinge pin.

Hip The convex angle formed by the meeting of two roof slopes, usually at a 90-degree angle to each other.

Hollow-wall fastener A device for hanging objects on a wall; fastens to the wall surface between studs.

Hot-melt glue Adhesive that is ready for bonding when heated.

Hot wire(s) The wires of a house circuit that are not connected to a ground and that carry power to receptacles and appliances; usually identified with black, blue, or red insulation.

HVAC (heating, ventilation, and air-conditioning) Mechanical systems that are often grouped together and installed by the same tradespeople.

ID Inside diameter of a pipe.

Incandescent bulb A bulb that produces light when electricity heats a metal filament to incandescence; a standard household lamp emitting a yellow-white light.

IPS (iron pipe size) Uniform sizing of threaded pipe fittings.

Jack post A steel column with a screw jack attached to its top for raising and shoring beams.

Jalousie A type of window with a number of narrow horizontal panes that pivot together.

Jamb The frame surrounding a door or window, consisting of two vertical pieces called side jambs and a top horizontal piece called a head jamb.

Jigsaw A portable power saw with a narrow reciprocating blade, usually used for cutting curves; also called saber saw.

Joist One of a series of parallel members, usually 2-by lumber, that support a floor or ceiling.

Jumper wire A short length of wire used temporarily while testing for electrical continuity.

King stud In wall framing, a full-length stud on either side of a door or window that, together with the trimmer stud, frames the opening.

Lag screw A screw, usually large, with a square or hexagonal head, designed to be driven with a wrench.

Lally column A steel post filled with concrete, used in basements to support heavy house loads.

Laminate A thin veneer, often plastic, used as a surfacing material and intended to be bonded to a solid substrate; to build up a board or panel by gluing or fastening several members together.

Laminated glass Safety glass consisting of two panes adhered to an intermediate layer of tough plastic material.

Lap joint A woodworking joint in which both pieces lap over each other, usually at right angles, and one or both pieces are notched to accept the mating piece.

Lath   A building material of metal, gypsum, wood, or other material that is used as a base for plaster or stucco; thin strips of wood.

Leach field   The drain field for a septic system, where perforated pipes are buried in the ground to disperse the water.

Ledger   A board or strip of wood fastened to the side of a framing member such as a wall, on which other framing members (usually joists) rest or to which they are attached.

Level   Parallel to the surface of a body of still water. Also, a device used to determine when surfaces are level or plumb.

Lintel   *See* Header.

Louver   One of a series of parallel slats in a window or door arranged to permit ventilation and to limit or exclude light, vision, or weather. Louvers can be stationary or movable.

Low-E (low-emissivity) glass   Used for energy conservation; has a coating on one side, or a film suspended between two panes, of a microscopically thin layer of metal oxides that admits visible light but reflects heat waves.

Low-voltage lighting   Lighting that operates on 12-volt current rather than on the standard 120 volts (a few systems use 24 volts). Power is supplied by a transformer, which is connected to 120-volt current.

LP (liquid propane)   Bottled gas used for heating and cooking.

Main disconnect   The electrical device for disconnecting a home electrical system from the main conductors connected to the utility company's wires.

Manifold   A chamber that distributes a fluid or gas from a single pipe to several other pipes, tubes, or conduits.

Masonry   Any construction made of stone, bricks, concrete blocks, poured concrete, and similar materials. Also, the technique of building this kind of construction.

Mast   Electrical conduit that encloses the main conductors of a home electrical system.

Masthead   *See* Weatherhead.

Mastic   A viscous material used as an adhesive for setting tile or resilient flooring.

Media pad   An evaporation pad in a humidifier that wicks moisture from the reservoir and releases it into the air.

Mineral spirits   A petroleum distillate used as a solvent and thinner, primarily with oil-based paints and varnishes.

Miter   Usually a 45-degree cut, but can be a cut at any angle that is matched by a cut of the same angle.

Miter joint   A joint between two boards with matching miter cuts at the ends, used to conceal the end grain of both boards.

Molding   A strip of wood with a decorative profile cut along the edges or face of the wood, used to cover exposed joints or edges, or as a decoration.

Molly bolt   *See* Expansion bolt.

Mortar   A mixture of sand and portland cement; used for bonding bricks, blocks, tiles, or stones.

Mortise and tenon joint   A woodworking joint made by cutting a mortise, or hole, in one piece and, on the other piece, a tenon, or projection, to fit into the mortise.

Mortise dead bolt   A dead bolt that fits into a mortise bored into the doorjamb, rather than into a surface-mounted metal pocket.

MSHA-NIOSH (Mine Safety and Health Administration–National Institute for Occupational Safety and Health)   A regulatory agency responsible for setting safety standards for certain occupational practices and equipment.

Mudsill   *See* Foundation sill.

Mullion   The vertical divider between the windows in a unit that is made up of two or more windows.

Muntin   A strip of wood that divides a window sash into separate panes.

NEC (National Electrical Code®)   A set of rules sponsored by the National Fire Protection Association, under the auspices of the American National Standards Institute, to protect persons, buildings, and their contents from dangers due to the use of electricity.

Needle nose pliers   Pliers with a long, very slim nose.

Neutral wire   In a circuit, any wire that is kept at zero voltage. The neutral wire completes the circuit from source, to fixture or appliance, to ground. The covering of neutral wires is always white.

Newel   The main post at the foot of a stairway. Also, the central support of a winding or spiral flight of stairs.

Nipple   Short length of pipe, externally threaded at both ends.

NMC (nonmetallic-sheathed cable)   Electrical cable consisting of two or more insulated wires, sheathed in plastic or nonmetallic material; used indoors; often referred to by the trade name Romex®.

Nominal size   The dimensions used to describe a piece of lumber, even if the actual dimensions are less due to planing.

Nosing   The part of a stair tread that projects over the riser. Also, the rounded edge on any board.

OC (on center)   Indication that the distance between repetitive structural members, such as studs or joists, is measured from centers, rather than edges, of the members. (The measurement from the edge of one member to the closest edge of the next member is referred to as span.)

OD   Outside diameter of a pipe.

Ohm   A unit of measurement used in electrical wiring to indicate resistance to electrical current in a circuit or electrical device; equal to the resistance in a conductor in which 1 volt of potential difference produces a current of 1 ampere.

Orbital sander   An electric sander that vibrates in a tight oscillating pattern (as opposed to the wider circular pattern of a disk sander).

O-ring   A rubber ring used as a gasket and having a circular cross section.

Packing string   String impregnated with flexible watertight material; used for wrapping around valve stems to provide a leakproof seal.

Particleboard   A form of composite board or panel made of wood chips bonded with adhesive.

Penny   *See* d.

Phillips head   Describes a screwdriver with an X-shaped tip or a screw with an X-shaped slot.

Pigtail   In an electrical installation, a short length of wire used to connect a device to an electrical box or the circuit wiring.

Pilaster   A vertical structure that protrudes from the face of a wall for structural or decorative purposes; often resembles a column embedded into the facade.

Pilot   In a gas appliance, a continuously burning flame that ignites the burner.

Pilot hole   A hole drilled to guide a screw or nail; minimizes splitting and provides the optimum gripping surface for screw threads.

Plate A horizontal framing member at the bottom or top of a stud wall. The soleplate is at the bottom; the top plate is above the studs; and a cap plate is above the top plate.

Plenum A large chamber in warm-air heating systems where ducts converge at the furnace.

Plumb Truly vertical; exactly perpendicular to a level surface.

Plumber's putty Putty used when installing plumbing fixtures for sealing drain fittings, gaps around faucets, and similar watertight joints.

Plywood A wood product made up of thin layers, or veneers, of wood bonded together with adhesive, usually at right angles to each other.

Pointing Filling and finishing the mortar joints of brickwork.

Polarity Alignment of electrical conductors or terminals to ensure the safe and continuous flow of electricity; maintained by the use of color-coded wires and terminals: white wire and silver-colored terminals for neutral conductors; black, red, or blue wire and brass-colored terminals for hot conductors; and green or bare wire for ground wires.

Polycarbonate A tough, transparent plastic that, in sheet form, can be used as a shatterproof windowpane.

Post A vertical support member, usually made up of only one piece of lumber or a metal pipe or I beam.

Pressure-balancing valve An anti-scald tub-and-shower valve that senses the water pressure of the hot- and cold-water inlets and keeps them balanced should the pressure in either one suddenly change.

Pressure-treated lumber Lumber that is rot-resistant due to preservatives injected into it under pressure; used in applications—such as outdoor structures or foundation sills—where the wood may be in contact with the ground, the weather, concrete, or masonry.

Primer Paint formulated for coating a surface so it is properly sealed and will provide maximum adhesion for the finish coat, or topcoat, of paint; when applied, it is referred to as the undercoat.

Programmable thermostat A thermostat with a microprocessor that can be programmed to switch on the cooling or heating system at set times.

Pry bar A short, flat, curved bar that is used for prying up boards and pulling nails.

Psi (pounds per square inch) A measurement of water or air pressure.

P-trap A curved plumbing fitting, resembling a broken letter "P" and usually consisting of two pieces, that connects a fixture tailpiece to the drain system; designed to trap enough water to prevent sewer gas from entering the house through the drain line.

PVA (polyvinyl acetate) Used in primers designed to cover bare plaster or wallboard, and in white glue.

PVC (polyvinyl chloride) A rigid, white or beige plastic used for plumbing pipe for supply and DWV systems.

Rabbet A square-edged channel cut along the edge of a board, similar to a dado or groove.

Radiant heating Heating system that utilizes electrically heated panels or hot-water pipes in the floor or ceiling that radiate heat to warm the room surfaces.

Rafters The main framing members that support the roof.

Rebar Reinforcing bars or rods for concrete and concrete-block work.

Receptacle A device, commonly called an outlet, through which an electrical plug can make contact with an electric circuit; most devices are duplex, with two receptacles.

Reciprocating sander A finish sander in which the pad vibrates back and forth.

Reciprocating saw A heavy-duty handheld power saw with a long slender blade that vibrates back and forth; used for demolition and rough framing.

Resilient flooring Thin floorcovering material, such as vinyl or linoleum, installed as tiles or in large sheets.

Ridge The horizontal line where two roof slopes meet. Usually the highest place on the roof.

Ridge beam A large board, running the length of a roof, that provides support to the upper ends of the rafters when they have no collar ties or ceiling joists to keep them from spreading apart.

Ridge board A 1-by or 2-by board running the length of a roof, against which pairs of rafters abut.

Rim joist A joist nailed across the ends of the floor or ceiling joists; also called band joist.

Rip cut A cut made by a saw along the same direction as the grain.

Rip saw A saw for cutting boards in the same direction as the grain.

Rise In a stairway, the vertical measurement from one tread to the next. In a roof, the vertical measurement from the top of the wall plates to the tip of the ridge.

Riser In plumbing, the supply tube that connects a faucet to its shut-off valve; in stair construction, each of the vertical boards between the treads of a stairway.

Rough lumber Lumber as it comes from the saw, before it is surfaced.

Rout To cut grooves, mortises, or rabbets into a board, or to shape the edges, usually with a router.

Router A power tool that uses a variety of interchangeable bits to rout grooves of various sizes and shapes or to cut various shapes into the edges of boards.

Saber saw See Jigsaw.

Safety glass Glass, such as tempered or laminated glass, that won't break into sharp shards when shattered.

Sash The frame that holds the glass panes in a window; either movable or fixed.

Screw terminal A means of connecting wiring to electrical devices using a threaded screw.

Scuttle A hatch for access into an attic.

Seat The part of a faucet or valve that the movable member presses against to form a seal when the valve is shut.

Septic tank An underground tank that receives water and waste from a house sewer, in which the solids settle and are transformed into a rich sludge through the activity of anaerobic bacteria.

Service entrance The place where the electrical system of a building is connected to wires from a utility company; components include the mast, conductors, meter, main disconnect, and service-entrance panel (circuit-breaker or fuse panel).

Set-back thermostat A thermostat that can be adjusted to switch on a heating system at set times by means of moving stops on a clock wheel.

Setscrew A screw that is tightened against a blade, bit, shaft, rod, or other component to hold it in place.

Shake   A thick wood shingle, usually edge-grained.

Sheathing   Boards or panels, such as plywood or structural hardboard, fastened to the roof framing or wall framing, to which the roofing or siding is applied; often serves a structural function for earthquake or wind resistance.

Sheet-metal screw   A screw with a sharp point and deep threads that extend from tip to head, used for attaching pieces of sheet metal.

Shim   A thin piece of wood or metal, often wedge-shaped, inserted between parts of a structure to bring them into alignment.

Shiplap siding   Horizontal board siding with V joints and rabbeted bottom edges that allow the boards to lie flush against the sheathing or framing.

Shock absorber   In plumbing systems, a vertical length of capped pipe extending from the supply pipe where it enters the fixture; supplies an air cushion to prevent water hammer.

Shoring   Temporary support of a floor, ceiling, or roof.

Shutoff valve   Fitting for shutting off water flow to a pipe or fixture.

Sill   The bearing member in the structural framing that rests on the foundation wall. Also, the member forming the lowest side of an opening, such as a doorsill or windowsill.

Sill plate   *See* Foundation sill.

Single-pole switch   An electrical switch in which the internal mechanism either breaks the flow of electricity or directs it to one pole, or terminal; commonly called a two-way switch.

Sister   To reinforce a joist or other framing member by nailing a board of the same size to it.

Sizing   A liquid coating traditionally used to prepare wall surfaces for wallcoverings; usually not necessary when a primer undercoat is used.

Slab   A concrete floor, usually 4 inches thick and reinforced with heavy wire mesh.

Sleepers   Boards, usually pressure-treated 2x4s, that are attached to a concrete slab for supporting a wood subfloor.

Soffit   An overhead, boxlike enclosure. On the exterior of the house, it encloses the area beneath an overhanging roof eave. In interior spaces, it is a dropped section of ceiling that may conceal obstructions.

Softwood   The wood of conifers such as Douglas fir, pine, and redwood; the term has no reference to the actual hardness of the wood.

Solenoid   An electromagnet that moves a rod into and out of a position in which it engages some other mechanism.

Soleplate   In a stud wall, the bottom horizontal member, which is nailed to the subfloor; also called a bottom plate.

Solid-surface material   A type of synthetic countertop material that has the same color and texture all the way through, rather than a finish coat applied over a core of a different material.

Spackling compound   Puttylike patching material for plaster walls.

Spade bit   A drill bit for boring wood that has a flat cutting blade with a pointed end, rather than a twisted or drum shape.

Spalling   The spontaneous flaking or popping off of small chips from a concrete surface due to freezing.

Spark arrester   A metal screen for chimney tops that prevents embers from escaping with the smoke.

Splice   A connection made by joining two or more wires.

Square   A term used to describe an angle of exactly 90 degrees. Also, a device used to measure such an angle. Also, a unit of measure equaling 100 square feet used in describing amounts of roofing or siding material.

Square-drive screw   A screw with a square indentation on the head for driving with a square-shanked driver; similar to a hex-head or Phillips-head screw; also called Robertson screw.

Stack   A 4-inch vertical pipe that serves as the main plumbing vent and drain for a bathroom.

Standing pilot   A pilot flame for a gas appliance.

Standpipe   A vertical drainpipe for washing machines.

Starter   A device used with many fluorescent fixtures to strike an arc between the electrodes when the fixture is turned on.

Stile   A vertical framing member in a panel door, wainscoting, or a paneled wall.

Stock   Wood or other material that is cut and shaped for joining.

Stool   The horizontal shelf on the interior of the bottom of a window.

Stove bolt   A bolt with a screw head and a threaded shank to which a nut can be attached.

Stringer   In a stairway, the supporting member to which the treads and risers are fastened. Also called a carriage.

Stud   In wood-frame construction, the vertical 2x4 boards in a wall, usually spaced 16 inches apart.

Subfloor   Boards, plywood, or other panels attached to the joists, which provide a base for the finish floor.

Substrate   Backing material used under a tile or laminate countertop installation.

Sump   A pit in the lowest area of a basement floor for collecting water from the surface of the floor.

Sump pump   A pump for removing water from a sump.

Surfaced lumber   Lumber planed smooth, usually on all four sides.

Taping knife/blade   *See* Wallboard knife.

Temperature-balancing valve   An antiscald tub or shower valve that senses the temperature of the incoming hot and cold water and makes adjustments to keep them balanced.

Terminal   A screw or other structure for connecting wires to an electrical device.

Thermocouple   A device for gas burners that monitors the pilot light and deactivates the main gas valve if the pilot light goes out.

Thermostat   A switch activated by temperature changes.

Thin-set adhesive   Cement-, latex-, or epoxy-based tile-setting adhesive that must be mixed with a liquid; stronger and more heat- and water-resistant than organic adhesives.

Three-way switch   An electrical switch in which the internal mechanism directs the flow of electricity to one of two poles; used in pairs to control a single fixture.

Thumb latch   A type of safety window lock.

Toenailing   Driving nails obliquely through the end of one board into another, when the end of the first board abuts the face of the second.

Toggle bolt   A hollow-wall fastener with a device on the end that, when inserted through a small hole in the wall, spreads out like two wings and prevents the bolt from being pulled back through the hole.

Tongue-and-groove boards Interlocking siding or flooring boards with a narrow projection milled along one edge that fits into a matching groove cut along the edge of the next board.

TPRV (temperature-pressure relief valve) A safety valve for water heaters that prevents steam from building up in the tank should the heater malfunction.

Transformer A device that converts current of one voltage into current of another voltage; used with doorbells and low-voltage lighting systems.

Trap In plumbing, a U-shaped fitting that allows water and sewage to flow through it while blocking the flow of air and gas from the other direction.

Traveler wires Pairs of wires, used in the wiring connections for three- or four-way switching systems, that connect the switches together but don't connect to the light fixture or the electrical source.

Tread In a stairway, the horizontal surface on which a person steps.

Trimhead screw A wallboard screw with a very small head.

Trimmer stud A stud that supports a header for an opening in a wall.

Truss An assembly of wood or metal members that serves as a relatively lightweight but strong framework to take the place of rafters and joists in the support of a roof or floor.

Try square A small square used to scribe cut lines on boards or to test right angles.

TSP (trisodium phosphate) A powerful cleaning compound that is mixed with water and used for scrubbing walls and ceilings in preparation for painting.

Twist drill A conventional screw-like drill bit, intended for boring metal but often used on wood.

Two-way switch See Single-pole switch.

Ufer ground An electrical ground consisting of a 20-foot length of rebar embedded in the foundation footing.

UL label A label applied to manufactured devices that have been tested for safety by Underwriters' Laboratories, Inc., and approved for placement on the market. These laboratories establish safety standards and are supported by insurance companies, manufacturers, and other parties interested in electrical safety.

Undercoater A primer specified for preparing wall surfaces for wallcoverings.

Underlayment The material placed under the finish coverings of roofs or floors to provide waterproofing as well as a smooth, even surface on which to apply finish material.

Underliner Canvaslike fabric for smoothing walls prior to applying wallcoverings.

Underwriter's knot A knot used to tie two insulated conductors at the terminals inside an electrical plug or fixture; used to relieve strain on the terminal connection.

Urethane A chemical compound that adds durability to floor finishes, paints, and other coatings.

Utility knife A knife with replaceable blades that resemble single-edged razor blades.

Valley A roof depression formed where two roof slopes converge.

Valve grease Lubricant for the internal parts of a faucet or valve.

Vapor barrier Plastic sheeting or similar material used to block moisture; applied to framing before wallboard is installed or over bare ground in the crawl space. When applied under wallboard, it prevents moist air in the living space from penetrating into the wall or ceiling cavity where it may condense and be trapped in cold weather.

Veneer A thin layer of wood or other material, usually one that has beauty or value, that is applied for economy or appearance on top of an inferior surface.

Vent In plumbing, a pipe that goes through the attic to the roof to allow sewer gases to escape and air to enter the plumbing system to prevent the siphoning of the fixture traps; any opening for air circulation, usually into an attic or crawl space.

Vent stack In plumbing, the largest vent pipe; branch vents may be connected to it; also called the main vent.

Volt A unit that measures electrical pressure; comparable to pounds of pressure in a water system.

Volt-ohmmeter An electrical testing device that measures the live voltage of connected circuits (alternating current or direct current) or the impedance (in ohms) of disconnected wires or devices.

Wainscoting Decorative paneling that covers only the lower portion of a wall.

Wallboard Panels used for finishing interior walls and ceilings, consisting of a core of gypsum plaster covered on both sides by layers of paper. Also called gypsum wallboard, gypboard, drywall, and Sheetrock®, a trade name.

Wallboard knife A broad, flat putty knife for applying and smoothing wallboard compound; also called taping knife.

Wallboard screw A type of screw intended to be driven with an electric screwdriver or drill, with a sharp point and deep, sharp threads that extend from point to head; used for many applications.

Wallboard tape Nonadhesive, perforated paper tape for covering wallboard joints.

Warm-air heating Heating system consisting of a furnace and a network of ducts and registers to distribute heated air; also called forced-air heating.

Washing soda A cleaning product for walls and other surfaces, sold as a powder; known by the trade name Spic and Span®.

Watt A unit that measures electric power; the unit by which utility companies meter electrical consumption. Volts × amperes = watts of electric energy used.

WD-40® Trade name for an all-purpose lubricant.

Weatherhead A weathertight fitting at the top of a mast where the main conductors are connected to the overhead wires from a power pole; also called masthead.

Weather stripping Strips of metal, plastic foam, or other materials placed around doors and windows to keep out air, moisture, or dust.

Weep holes Small holes at the bottom of a concrete or masonry retaining wall that allow moisture trapped behind the wall to escape.

Wicking The process of water being transferred through a porous material by capillary action.

Wire connector See Electrical connector.

Wood screw A screw for fastening wood pieces. It has tapered threads and a section of unthreaded shank between the threads and head. The head can be rounded, beveled, or flat.

Wrecking bar A long steel bar with a point at one end and a flattened chisel shape at the other, for demolition work.

U.S./Metric Measure Conversion Chart

	Symbol	**Formulas for Exact Measures**			**Rounded Measures for Quick Reference**		
		When you know:	Multiply by:	To find:			
Mass	oz	ounces	28.35	grams	1 oz		= 30 g
(weight)	lb	pounds	0.45	kilograms	4 oz		= 115 g
	g	grams	0.035	ounces	8 oz		= 225 g
	kg	kilograms	2.2	pounds	16 oz	= 1 lb	= 450 g
					32 oz	= 2 lb	= 900 g
					36 oz	= 2¼ lb	= 1000 g (1 kg)
Volume	pt	pints	0.47	liters	1 c	= 8 oz	= 250 ml
	qt	quarts	0.95	liters	2 c (1 pt)	= 16 oz	= 500 ml
	gal	gallons	3.785	liters	4 c (1 qt)	= 32 oz	= 1 liter
	ml	milliliters	0.034	fluid ounces	4 qt (1 gal)	= 128 oz	= 3¾ liter
Length	in.	inches	2.54	centimeters	⅜ in.		= 1.0 cm
	ft	feet	30.48	centimeters	1 in.		= 2.5 cm
	yd	yards	0.9144	meters	2 in.		= 5.0 cm
	mi	miles	1.609	kilometers	2½ in.		= 6.5 cm
	km	kilometers	0.621	miles	12 in. (1 ft)		= 30.0 cm
	m	meters	1.094	yards	1 yd		= 90.0 cm
	cm	centimeters	0.39	inches	100 ft		= 30.0 m
					1 mi		= 1.6 km
Temperature	°F	Fahrenheit	⅝ (after subtracting 32)	Celsius	32° F		= 0° C
					68° F		= 20° C
	°C	Celsius	⅞ (then add 32)	Fahrenheit	212° F		= 100° C
Area	in.^{2}	square inches	6.452	square centimeters	1 in.^{2}		= 6.5 cm^2
	ft^2	square feet	929.0	square centimeters	1 ft^2		= 930 cm^2
	yd^2	square yards	8361.0	square centimeters	1 yd^2		= 8360 cm^2
	a.	acres	0.4047	hectares	1 a.		= 4050 m^2